THE ULTIMATE
ROSE
BOOK

Abrams, New York

THE ULTIMATE ROSE BOOK

STIRLING MACOBOY

TOMMY CAIRNS, EDITOR, NEW EDITION

features

12/26/09 - Gift (Peter)

contents

'Jilly Jewel'

He who would have beautiful Roses in his garden,

must have beautiful Roses in his heart

THE REVEREND S. REYNOLDS HOLE (1819–1904)

foreword

Dr Tommy Cairns's well-known love of roses has catapulted him around the world repeatedly in a most wondrous journey, during which he has experienced the rose in all her lavish beauty, both in parochial settings and as the focus of sophisticated events. His credentials as a rosarian are legendary: he has judged international rose trials, lectured at world rose conventions, and served as president of both the American Rose Society and the World Federation of Rose Societies – and in 2005 he was awarded the Dean Hole Medal by the Royal National Rose Society of Great Britain.

With this major revision and updating, Tommy Cairns has successfully brought this highly regarded book into the twenty-first century, adding some 300 new entries while tastefully interlacing a number of new feature essays on diverse subjects, including the 'Peace' rose, the power of red roses, and David Austin's 'English Roses', to mention just a few. Tommy has shared with you, the reader, his most intimate knowledge of the rose, delivered with the mastery of a fine composer but carefully blended to entertain as well as to educate.

All rose entries have been extensively revised to include a significant amount of additional information, while retaining the individuality and charm of Stirling Macoboy's style. Personally, I am delighted that Tommy has chosen to devote an entire section to Miniature Roses and Mini-Flora, reflecting the explosion in this category during the last 20 years, as well as to give the Old Garden Roses their own showcase. As in the original edition, the entries don't just provide practical advice, they are a veritable treasure trove of anecdotal stories and interesting historical facts – enough to please the most discriminating reader.

The book is Herculean in its coverage: a reference work to please the thirsty scholar, a vital source of information for the casual gardener, a treatise by passionate rose-lovers for equally passionate rose-devotees, a bible of rose knowledge, an oracle to be consulted – and, perhaps most of all, a fitting tribute to the 'Queen of Flowers'.

FRANK BENARDELLA
PAST PRESIDENT, AMERICAN ROSE SOCIETY
MILLSTONE TOWNSHIP, NEW JERSEY, USA

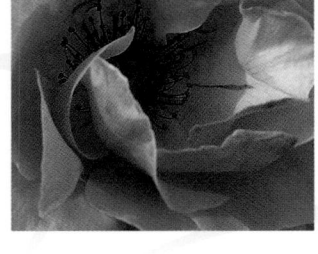

introduction

When Stirling Macoboy decided to write this book – a project he himself said had been on his writing schedule for more than 40 years – he little knew what a treasure trove of information and photographs he would bequeath to the world of rose-lovers. Some 15 years have now passed since he prepared the last edition, and with the rose-loving public's desire for reliable information growing in tandem with the many exciting new developments that are taking place in the world of rose-breeding, the time seems right to publish a new, updated edition of this unique book.

When I was commissioned to undertake this work, I felt both daunted and exhilarated by the task that lay ahead. Inspired by my long-standing passion for roses, I set out to review the entries and features and to plan a revised and expanded edition, paying particular attention to the development of both new classifications and new varieties since 1993. It quickly became clear that the rose entries would be best divided into four sections based on the major classifications: Wild Roses, Old Garden Roses, Modern Roses, and Miniatures and Mini-Flora. This makes it easier for readers to locate the types of roses they have a particular interest in and to compare different varieties in terms of their color, form and habit. But the nucleus of the revision is the introduction of approximately 300 new roses into this compilation of some 1500 roses – all of which have been selected not just for their historical and botanical importance but also, importantly, for their beauty and their popularity with home gardeners. In particular, the growing popularity of Miniatures and Mini-Flora has been recognized.

In writing the new entries and updating the existing entries, great care has been taken to preserve Stirling Macoboy's individual style and his anecdotal stories about the names, origin and history of different varieties. These were integral and much-loved features of the original edition. All entries have been revised to incorporate new information, including details of fragrance, time of flowering, habit, size, parentage and breeder. There are approximately 400 new photographs, and as in the

'Cherry Parfait'

previous edition every rose is illustrated. Several new feature essays have been introduced, and existing essays have been thoroughly revised and updated with new images and illustrations.

As I completed the work, I was left with two enduring thoughts. First and foremost, I was filled with admiration for Stirling Macoboy's passion for roses and his dedication to fulfilling the dual role of writer-photographer. Second, and more personal, was an awareness of the strength of my commitment to extending the life of this book. It often happens that projects become obligations rather than something we do for pleasure. But not so here. I derived great satisfaction from the process of revising and, I hope, augmenting this immensely practical and valuable book. Inevitably, I learned a good many new facts and refreshed my knowledge of many old ones along the way, continuing the tradition of always learning more as you journey through the world of roses.

There is an old Scottish song popularized by Sir Harry Lauder in the early 1900s that urges us to 'keep right on to the end of the road'. The journey through the wonderful world of roses has many curves and bends and no ending. Each year that passes adds to our store of knowledge about roses – but the discoveries and accomplishments that await coming generations are limitless. In all their wonderful variations of color, fragrance and form, roses through the years have brought enormous joy and pleasure to people all around the world. Long may their – and Stirling Macoboy's – magnificent legacy endure.

TOMMY CAIRNS, KM, DHM   2007
STUDIO CITY, CALIFORNIA, USA

The Classification of Roses

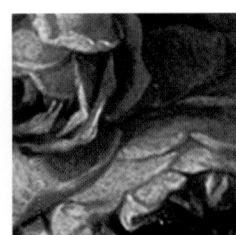

The rose may rank with the lily as the oldest of cultivated flowers. Unlike the chaste lily, however, which has only recently consented to the gardener's desire that her species intermarry, the rose is a wanton, only too happy to accept another's pollen and bring forth new forms and colors to tease and delight her admirers. No wonder the ancients dedicated the rose to Venus!

This profligacy has two consequences for those who would get to know the rose. First, the wild species are very variable indeed, and the status of those in our gardens is apt to be uncertain from the all too common hybrids masquerading as species. Second, the rose has become the flower most hybridized and 'improved' by gardeners, so that the number of garden varieties on the nursery lists runs into the thousands, and more are being added all the time. This is no exaggeration. One American digest of available roses lists more than 10 000 names in 2007.

Rose-fanciers had tried since the beginning of the nineteenth century to bring order to the bewildering multitude by enlisting each garden rose under the banner of the species to which it seemed to have the most affinity. As the ever more complex hybrids grew less and less like any Wild Rose, rosarians then started to place them with some regard for their ancestry, in classes with names like Hybrid Tea, Bourbon, Climbing Floribunda and the like. There were over 30 of these classes.

Confusing as this system was to the uninitiated, the rose world clung to it until 1979, when the World Federation of Rose Societies finally adopted a simplified classification, into which a rose is fitted not by its supposed ancestors, but by the characters that it displays as a garden plant. The system was revised in 2000 but remains unchanged in essence.

According to this system, the thousands of named roses are divided into three broad groups:

1. Wild Roses (also called Species Roses), which include both the truly wild species and those garden forms that are inseparably associated with them.

2. Old Garden Roses, which are those groups of horticultural origin that were already established prior to the year 1867, when 'La France' was seen to be the first of what, with hindsight, we now see as the Modern Roses.

3. Modern Roses, the predominant roses of today and still, unlike the Old Garden Roses, in active development by hybridists.

If ever a picture were worth a thousand words, it is here. The diagram on the facing page shows how the three broad groups are themselves subdivided.

RIGHT *Rosa laevigata*, the 'Cherokee Rose', a vigorous climbing Wild Rose

BELOW An Old Garden Rose, the Gallica 'Belle Isis'

'Golden Celebration', a much-admired Modern Rose

GENUS ROSA

Wild Roses   (150–200 varieties)

Old Garden Roses

Alba
Ayrshire
Bourbon and Climbing Bourbon
Boursalt
Centifolia
China
Damask
Hybrid Bracteata and Climbing Hybrid Bracteata
Hybrid China and Climbing Hybrid China
Hybrid Eglanteria and Climbing Hybrid Eglanteria
Hybrid Foetida and Climbing Hybrid Foetida
Hybrid Gallica
Hybrid Multiflora
Hybrid Perpetual and Climbing Hybrid Perpetual
Hybrid Sempervirens
Hybrid Setigera
Hybrid Spinosissima
Miscellaneous OGRs
Moss and Climbing Moss
Noisette
Portland
Tea and Climbing Tea

Modern Roses

Floribunda and Climbing Floribunda (cluster-flowered)
Grandiflora and Climbing Grandiflora (large-flowered)
Hybrid Gigantea
Hybrid Tea and Climbing Hybrid Tea (large-flowered)
Hybrid Kordesii (classic shrub)
Hybrid Moyesii (classic shrub)
Hybrid Musk (classic shrub)
Hybrid Rugosa (classic shrub)
Hybrid Wichurana (rambler)
Large Flowered Climber
Miniature and Climbing Miniature (dwarf clustered-flowered)
Mini-Flora and Climbing Mini-Flora (patio)
Polyantha and Climbing Polyantha
Shrub (modern shrub)

The evolution of the rose

The classification diagram on the previous page was not devised for the benefit of botanists, rather for that of gardeners, and it is easy for us to overlook one important fact about it.

The fundamental division in the genus *Rosa* is not between the various types of garden roses, but between the Wild Roses and the domesticated breeds of roses that gardeners have developed in the course of the 6000 years or so that people have been growing plants in gardens. It is certainly true that the Wild Roses are ancestral to garden roses, and that they can be cultivated in gardens; but the Wild Roses and the garden roses inhabit very different worlds.

Wild Roses

A species is defined as a group (or 'population') of naturally occurring plants (or animals or fungi) that are all sufficiently alike to be regarded as closely related and that pass their likeness on to their offspring down the generations – they 'breed true', as we say.

But not in gardens. Bring a wild rose into the garden, and it will accept the pollen of any other rose in the neighborhood. Even if the original plant were grown from seed collected in the wild, its garden-raised seedlings will be hybrids and the strain will be adulterated. To keep it true, the gardener must now propagate them asexually – that is, from cuttings or by grafting. The resulting plants are still members of their species, but can we call them Wild Roses any more? They are garden plants now, and many rosarians prefer to call them 'Species Roses'.

Yet a tiger in a zoo remains a tiger still, and a wild rose in captivity still breathes the fragrance of its ancestral home. Never mind that the ones we have chosen for our gardens are often not truly representative of their species as we would encounter it in the wild: that we have chosen the plants with the biggest flowers or the brightest colors, the ones with the neatest habit of growth – even those rare freaks, those with double flowers, whose lowered fertility dooms them to extinction in the wild. Our 'Wild Roses' may have one foot in the garden, but our classification was devised for the guidance of gardeners, not the edification of botanists!

A single, glorious bloom of *R. centifolia* adorns this painting of 1667, *Woman Taking Fruit*, by the Flemish artist Abraham Brueghel (1631–1697).

Garden Roses

The Wild Roses have evolved without human assistance – although in our increasingly polluted and degraded environment they may need our help to survive – but people have controlled and guided the evolution of the garden rose ever since the day they first brought representatives of ancestral species into their gardens.

A rose in a garden does not have to perpetuate itself from seed as one in the wild does; as long as the gardener takes cuttings and makes grafts, it can be perpetuated for as long as we want to keep it – and it does not matter whether it is pure-bred, either. Hybrids are welcome.

It took rose-lovers a while to realize the possibilities. The conventional wisdom for centuries was that it simply was not worth growing roses from seed. It could be done, but as the seedlings were almost always inferior to their parents, why bother?

The answer is to create new varieties, and it is said that it was the Dutch who first realized that if they raised seedlings in large numbers, it did not matter if only one in 1000, or one in 10 000, was worth keeping and propagating asexually. The others could just be discarded. That is what rose-breeders still do, and it is said that between 1600 and the mid-1720s Dutch gardeners produced and named nearly 200 new roses, including their masterpiece, *R. centifolia*, which despite its Latin name is no species but the quintessential garden rose, completely sterile and unable to survive without human assistance.

Then, toward the end of the eighteenth century, flower gardening experienced a surge of popularity. The demand for new roses grew, especially in France under the influence of the rose-loving Empress Joséphine; and specialist rose-growers and breeders arose to meet it.

The roses they created in the early years of the nineteenth century are the Old Garden Roses we cherish today. Many have vanished, but the best, with their sumptuous, full-bosomed flowers and sweet scent, remain to delight us.

'Soleil d'Or', the first brilliantly colored Modern Rose

As we have noted, 1867 is the watershed date that marks the division between the Old Garden Roses and the Modern Roses. The Hybrid Teas not only combined the greater continuity of bloom of the Chinese roses with the hardiness of the European types, they brought the elegant, high-centred flower they had inherited from the Teas into fashion. They remain the leading class today, and they had a hand in the creation of all the new classes of the twentieth century – including the Floribundas, the Shrub Roses, the repeat-blooming climbers and the ground cover roses.

And what of our new century? The roses of our gardens carry the blood of only about 20 of the 200 or so species of Wild Roses. What riches remain for the rose-breeders of the future to discover?

ABOVE 'Monte Carlo', a shapely Hybrid Tea

LEFT *R. macrantha*, a Wild Rose, but not a true species: it is thought to be an ancient hybrid of *R. gallica*.

Guide to the Entries

The approximately 1500 roses described in this book are divided into four main categories, and within each category they are listed alphabetically.

Wild Roses (naturally occurring species)

This section contains a representative selection of Wild Roses (also known as Species Roses) that are botanically important and horticulturally desirable. The list is by no means comprehensive; some 150–200 native species are found in the northern hemisphere: in Asia – notably in China and Japan – in the Middle East, in Europe and in North America. Stirling Macoboy's original selections have been retained, and a number of additional species of botanical or genetic importance have been added.

Old Garden Roses

Old Garden Roses are defined as roses belonging to any of the classes that were in existence before 1867, when the first Hybrid Tea, 'La France', was introduced. Some breeders continue to produce varieties that belong to these classes, and these are still classified as Old Garden Roses by virtue of their parentage and characteristics.

Modern Roses

This section is by far the largest of the four. It still represents the somewhat eclectic mixture compiled by Stirling Macoboy in 1993, but some of the original entries have been deleted to make way for some 300 newer roses, which have been selected as representing innovative trends in rose-breeding during the latter part of the twentieth century and the beginning of the twenty-first century.

Miniatures and Mini-Flora

Since 1990 the category of Miniature Roses has seen phenomenal growth and is now rivalling its sister category, Floribundas, in popularity. (Stirling Macoboy recognized this trend in 1993 when he devoted a separate section to Miniatures.) This growing popularity has given rise to a new classification called Mini-Flora for those cultivars too big to be a Miniature but too small to be a Floribunda. Accordingly, this section has been considerably expanded to reflect the many new varieties that have exploded onto the scene in recent years.

Arrangement of entries

Entries include the following information (as appropriate):

Botanical name (in italics) or **cultivar name** (in single quotes). In most cases, the cultivar name is the name registered with the American Rose Society's International Registration Authority. Occasionally, preference has been given to the name the raiser gave the rose, mainly where a rose is especially popular under its original name in a particular country. If you are seeking a favorite rose and cannot find it, be sure to check the index.

Classification, as recognized by the International Registrar for Roses (IRAR), an international program administered by the American Rose Society (ARS).

Color class, as designated by the ARS. The color class is a category and is not intended to describe the huge range of shades roses exhibit; the flower color is described within each entry. In addition, the color of a rose varies with climate, growing conditions and age (many blooms fade with age), and it can also appear slightly different in a photograph than it does in nature because of such things as lighting conditions on the day it was photographed. Where a photograph does not exactly match the text description, it may be for any of these reasons.

Synonyms (alternative names used at different times or in different countries). These are listed in alphabetical order.

Description and history (as appropriate). The entry for each rose gives a description of the flower and the foliage and, if known, the history of the rose. If the rose varies from the norm for its class in habit, cultivation requirements or disease proneness or resistance, this is mentioned.

Codename (if applicable). This is a unique name made up of three capitalized letters – usually the first three letters of the breeder's or introducer's name (for example, KOR for Kordes) – followed by lower case letters. The codename provides the public, and those who administer Plant Patent and Plant Variety copyright laws, with a sure means of identifying a rose.

Breeder details (if known), including name, country and date of registration. In the case of most Modern Roses, the year of registration is given. If the date of introduction differs significantly from this, this is usually noted in the text. If the variety is not registered, the date given is the year of introduction. The date given for Wild Roses is usually the year the variety was introduced to the Western world.

Parentage (if known or recorded). This is given in the standard form (seed parent × pollen parent). In more complex genealogies, a series of brackets indicates the parents used.

Time of flowering – spring, summer or repeat flowering. The terms 'spring flowering' and 'summer flowering' generally refer to the fact that there is only one bloom cycle followed immediately by fruit or hip production. 'Repeat flowering' indicates that the cultivar is remontant (meaning it rises again) – that is, it will give flowers all year long from spring to the fall/autumn, in cycles, usually 6–8 weeks apart.

Fragrance The fragrance is noted on a scale from none to very intense, and in some cases it is described.

Growth habit Whether the plant is a bush, climber, rambler or ground cover is noted, and its average height and width are given.

Hardiness zones are given as a range (see pages 450–451 for more information).

Major awards the rose has received are listed at the end of the entry.

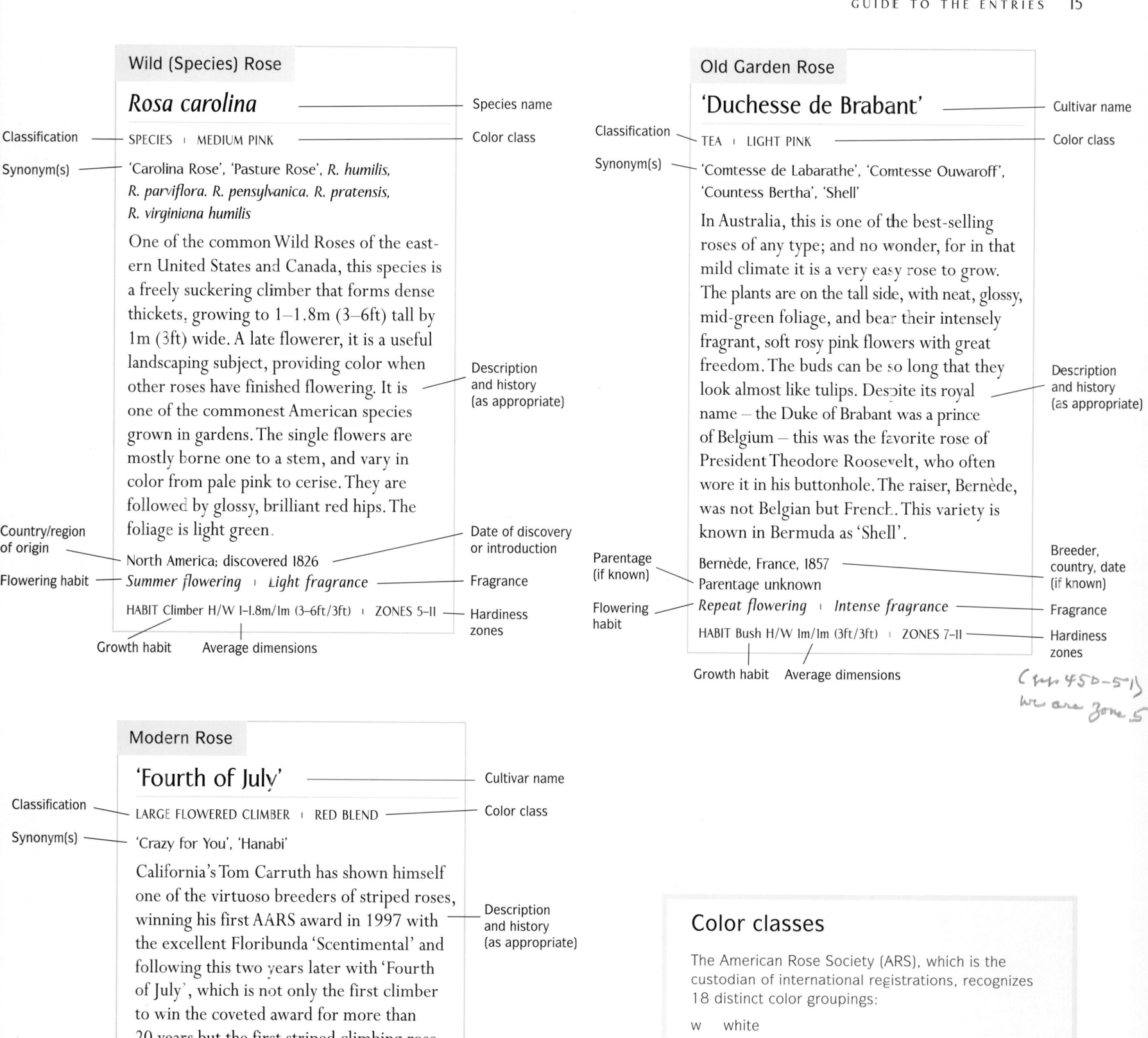

Wild (Species) Rose

Rosa carolina — Species name

Classification — SPECIES | MEDIUM PINK — Color class

Synonym(s) — 'Carolina Rose', 'Pasture Rose', *R. humilis, R. parviflora. R. pensylvanica. R. pratensis, R. virginiana humilis*

One of the common Wild Roses of the eastern United States and Canada, this species is a freely suckering climber that forms dense thickets, growing to 1–1.8m (3–6ft) tall by 1m (3ft) wide. A late flowerer, it is a useful landscaping subject, providing color when other roses have finished flowering. It is one of the commonest American species grown in gardens. The single flowers are mostly borne one to a stem, and vary in color from pale pink to cerise. They are followed by glossy, brilliant red hips. The foliage is light green. — Description and history (as appropriate)

Country/region of origin — North America; discovered 1826 — Date of discovery or introduction

Flowering habit — *Summer flowering | Light fragrance* — Fragrance

HABIT Climber H/W 1–1.8m/1m (3–6ft/3ft) | ZONES 5–11 — Hardiness zones

Growth habit   Average dimensions

Old Garden Rose

'Duchesse de Brabant' — Cultivar name

Classification — TEA | LIGHT PINK — Color class

Synonym(s) — 'Comtesse de Labarathe', 'Comtesse Ouwaroff', 'Countess Bertha', 'Shell'

In Australia, this is one of the best-selling roses of any type; and no wonder, for in that mild climate it is a very easy rose to grow. The plants are on the tall side, with neat, glossy, mid-green foliage, and bear their intensely fragrant, soft rosy pink flowers with great freedom. The buds can be so long that they look almost like tulips. Despite its royal name – the Duke of Brabant was a prince of Belgium – this was the favorite rose of President Theodore Roosevelt, who often wore it in his buttonhole. The raiser, Bernède, was not Belgian but French. This variety is known in Bermuda as 'Shell'. — Description and history (as appropriate)

Parentage (if known) — Bernède, France, 1857 — Breeder, country, date (if known)
Parentage unknown

Flowering habit — *Repeat flowering | Intense fragrance* — Fragrance

HABIT Bush H/W 1m/1m (3ft/3ft) | ZONES 7–11 — Hardiness zones

Growth habit   Average dimensions

(pp 450–51) we are zone 5

Modern Rose

'Fourth of July' — Cultivar name

Classification — LARGE FLOWERED CLIMBER | RED BLEND — Color class

Synonym(s) — 'Crazy for You', 'Hanabi'

California's Tom Carruth has shown himself one of the virtuoso breeders of striped roses, winning his first AARS award in 1997 with the excellent Floribunda 'Scentimental' and following this two years later with 'Fourth of July', which is not only the first climber to win the coveted award for more than 20 years but the first striped climbing rose of the modern era. It is a typical modern climber, not overly vigorous and bearing its clusters of Floribunda-style flowers in profusion throughout the season. They are only barely semi-double, the better to show off their white stripes and splashes, which are laid over a bright red ground. Every flower is different; and backed by dark, disease-resistant leaves, they bring to mind fireworks bursting in the night sky. — Description and history (as appropriate)

Codename — WEKroalt | Carruth, USA, 1999 — Breeder, country, date (date of registration; if not registered, date of introduction)

Parentage — 'Roller Coaster' × 'Altissimo'

Flowering habit — *Repeat flowering | Apple fragrance* — Fragrance

HABIT Climber H/W 3m/2.5m (10ft/8ft) | ZONES 5–11 — Hardiness zones

Growth habit

Awards — All-America Rose Selection 1999 — Average dimensions

---

Color classes

The American Rose Society (ARS), which is the custodian of international registrations, recognizes 18 distinct color groupings:

w	white
ly	light yellow
my	medium yellow
dy	deep yellow
yb	yellow blend
ab	apricot and apricot blend
ob	orange and orange blend
op	orange-pink and orange-pink blend
or	orange-red and orange-red blend
lp	light pink
mp	medium pink
dp	deep pink
pb	pink blend
mr	medium red
dr	dark red
rb	red blend
m	mauve and mauve blend
r	russet

wild roses

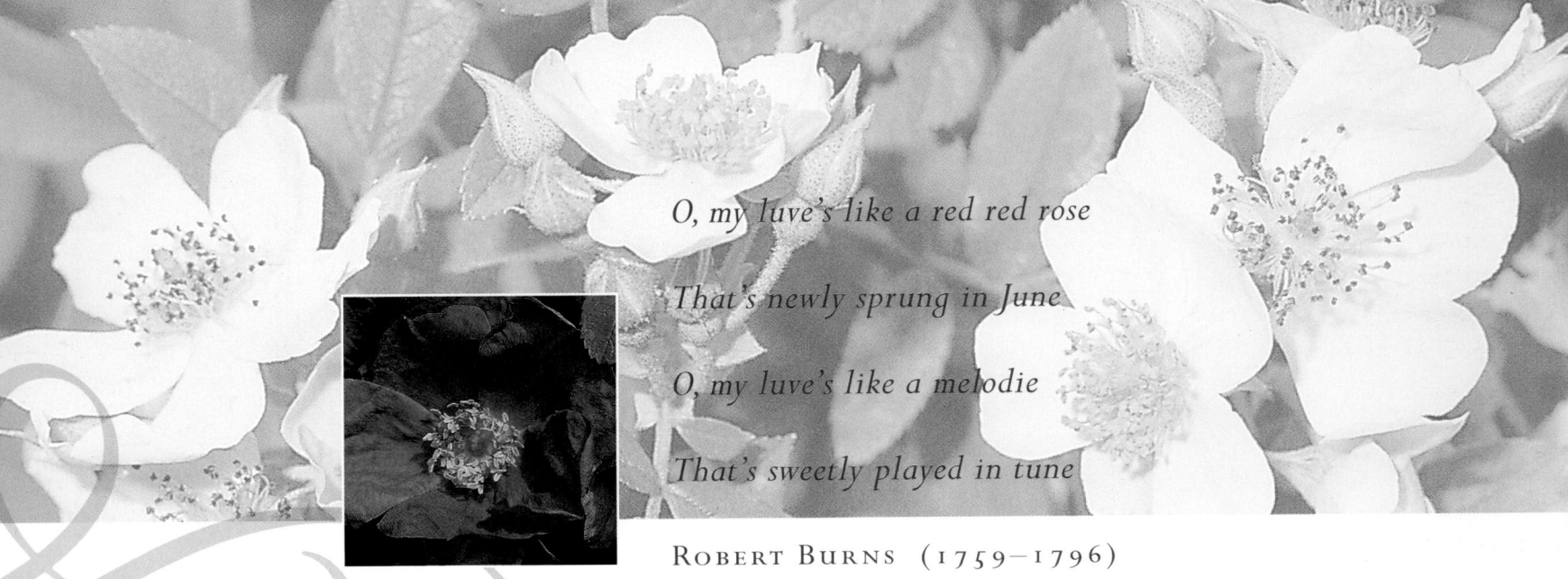

wild roses

When the Scottish poet penned these now-famous lines, published in 1794, a rose to him and to his audience would have been a wild rose growing by the side of a country lane – perhaps the lovely double rose we now know as *R. pimpinellifolia andrewsii*. It would be another 25 years before roses were cultivated and established in European gardens. This rose is one of the group of naturally occurring roses known as Wild Roses, or Species Roses – the ancestral species from which the rose has evolved into the diverse forms we know today.

Toward a definition of Wild Roses

Numbering between 150 and 200, Wild Roses originated in the northern hemisphere, but are now found in most countries of the world. It is notoriously difficult to define and classify them. One major criterion is that they generally have five petals, five being a natural number in the wild, but there are exceptions. One Wild Rose, *R. omeiensis pteracantha*, has only four petals, and many other roses classified as Species Roses are semi-doubles and doubles, with 8–24 petals. Other distinguishing features of Wild Roses include the ability to reproduce inherent characteristics into successive generations, and the ability to propagate themselves faithfully from fertilized seed (usually by self-pollination). Most Wild Roses carry 14 chromosomes (two sets of seven) and are described as diploid (meaning double: in this case, two similar complements of chromosomes). Beyond these simple criteria, the comprehensive definition of a Wild Rose has yet to be determined.

The matter is further complicated by the propensity of roses in their natural habitat to double their petal count and to produce color mutations and natural hybrids, thus making it even more difficult to differentiate between the true original species and the hybrid offspring. This has resulted in a legacy of a large number of both natural and garden hybrids designated as true species, with latinized names given them by eighteenth- and nineteenth-century botanists. The majority of these have been embraced as deserving of the title Wild Rose, and most are attractive.

Classifying Wild Roses

In an attempt to classify Wild Roses, taxonomists such as the American botanist Alfred Rehder originally divided the Genus Rosa into four subgenera: three of them very small – namely, Hulthemia, named after the Dutch Botanist Van Hulthem; Hesperrhodos, from the Greek meaning 'Western roses'; and Platyrhodon, from the Greek meaning 'flaky rose' – and one major, Eurosa, which contains the roses we commonly recognize today as Wild Roses. The Hulthemia subgenus was subsequently disqualified from belonging to the rose family, because this group has solitary leaves attached to the stem instead of compound leaf-sets, like all other roses. Both the Hesperrhodos and Platyrhodon subgenera are distinguished by having prickly hips, with Hesperrhodos further distinguished by retaining the hips on the plant for a long time, whereas in the case of Platyrhodon the hips drop off the plants early.

Eurosa, distinguished by having smooth hips, is divided into 10 sections, based on the physical characteristics of the roses and the chromosome count in the cell nucleus – 14 (Diploid), 28 (Tetraploid), 42 (Hexaploid) or 56 (Octaploid). The chart shows these 10 sections and the major species within each. The most important of these sections are the Carolinae, all members of which are American; the Chineses, which originated in China and are of great importance, as it is from *R. chinensis* and *R. gigantea* that practically all of our Modern Roses descend; the Cinnamomeae, from Europe, Asia and North Africa, comprising more than 50 species of great genetic diversity, including the noteworthy *R. rugosa* and *R. moyesii*; the Gallicanae, from central and southern Europe into Asia, whose chief representative is *R. gallica*, father of the Gallicas, Damasks and Centifolias; the Pimpinellifoliae, from Asia, spreading to Europe, and encompassing the Burnet Rose (*R. pimpinellifolia*) and most of the yellow-flowered Wild Roses; and the Synstylae, from China, which include a large number of white-flowered diploid climbers and wichuranas.

The selection of Wild Roses you will find in this book reflects the difficulties inherent in defining and classifying these elusive roses. I have included *H. persica*, the one important species from the rose's sister genus, Hulthemia, for its intrinsic interest; *R. foetida* also appears, although, as Stirling Macoboy pointed out in his introduction in the previous edition, some may argue that it is, in fact, an ancient garden rose that has 'gone wild'. All of Stirling Macoboy's original selections remain, with updated text as necessary and in some cases new photographs, and I have included eight additional Wild Roses. I believe that this section well represents these fascinating ancient roses and provides an attractive showcase for their diversity, their historical significance, and their beauty both in the wild and in the garden.

Rosa acicularis nipponensis

GENUS ROSA	Platyrhodon	R. roxburghii
		R. roxburghii normalis
	Hesperrhodos	R. stellata
		R. stellata mirifica
	Eurosa	
	Banksianae	R. banksiae
		R. banksiae alba-plena
		R. banksiae lutea
		R. banksiae normalis
		R. cymosa
	Bracteatae	R. bracteata
	Caninae	R. canina
		R. eglanteria
		R. glauca
		R. pomifera
		R. tomentosa
	Carolinae	R. carolina
		R. foliolosa
		R. nitida
		R. palustris
		R. virginiana
	Chineses (Indicae)	R. chinensis
		R. gigantea
	Cinnamomeae	R. acicularis
		R. blanda
		R. cinnamomea plena
		R. davidii
		R. macrophylla
		R. nutkana
		R. rugosa
		R. woodsii
	Gallicanae	R. gallica
		R. gallica officinalis
		R. gallica veriscolor
	Laevigatae	R. laevigata
	Pimpinellifoliae	R. ecae
		R. foetida
		R. hugonis
		R. omeiensis pteracantha
		R. pimpinellifolia
		R. primula
		R. xanthina
	Synstylae	R. arvenis
		R. filipes
		R. moschata
		R. multiflora
		R. sempervirens
		R. setigera
		R. soulieana
		R. wichurana
GENUS HULTHEMIA	Hulthemia	H. persica
	× Hulthemosa	× H. hardii

Hulthemia persica

SPECIES | YELLOW BLEND

'Barberry Rose', *H. berberifolia*, *Lowea berberifolia*, *R. berberifolia*, *R. persica*, *R. simplicifolia*

Distinct from all other roses in lacking stipules (the leafy bits at the bases of leaves) and having simple (undivided) leaves and prickly hips, *H. persica* is usually given a genus of its own, although it is closely allied to the genus *Rosa*. Its flowers are unique, too – single, solitary, and bright yellow, with red blotches at the base of the petals. It makes a small shrub only 1m (3ft) tall, but it may extend its root system far beyond this distance. It is difficult to propagate and establish, and you are far more likely to see its hybrid by an unknown rose, × *Hulthemosa hardii*, than *H. persica* itself. Indeed, it is × *Hulthemosa hardii* that is shown in the photograph. To accommodate hybrids between *Hulthemia* and roses, a hybrid genus was created in 1941 under the name × *Hulthemosa*. The small shrubs that make up this hybrid group are all xerophytes (plants adapted to living in dry conditions), having veinless leaves and a long root system. They look more like roses than *Hulthemia*, with pinnate (feathered) rose foliage and leaflets arranged in pairs along the leaf stalk and a single leaflet at the end.

Afghanistan, Iran and Russia; discovered 1790
Summer flowering | *No fragrance*

HABIT Bush H/W 1m/60cm (3ft/2ft) | ZONES 5–11

× *Hulthemosa hardii*

Rosa acicularis

SPECIES | DEEP PINK

'Arctic Rose', 'Circumpolar Rose', 'O-Takane-bara', 'Prickly Rose'

This rose is unique among Wild Roses in occurring right around the northern hemisphere,

Rosa arvensis

Rosa acicularis

being found in Asia, the far north of Europe and North America. No other species hops the continents like this. *Acicularis* means 'needled' and refers to the thin, sharp spines that cover the stems. A low, dense shrub that grows to 1m (3ft) tall, it is garden-worthy for its single, pink flowers, which appear very early in the spring, and for its extreme hardiness. There is also a double form, pictured here. The foliage is mid-green.

Asia, Europe and North America; discovered 1805
Spring flowering | *Moderate fragrance*

HABIT Bush H/W 1m/1m (3ft/3ft) | ZONES 3–10

Rosa arvensis

SPECIES | WHITE

'Field Rose', *R. repens*, *R. serpens*, *R. silvestris*

Native to western and southern Europe and the British Isles, this rambler is one of the few roses in that region that does not belong to the *R. canina* group. A summer-flowering plant that can easily cover hedges and embankments, even in light shade, it bears sweetly scented, single, pure white flowers on long, trailing stems that extend up to 3m (10ft). The leaves are dark green. This species is

believed to be the 'Musk Rose' referred to by Shakespeare, Milton and Keats, since it was the only Wild Rose growing in Britain in earlier times that could have been mistaken for the true 'Musk Rose', *R. moschata*. The two species are, however, closely related.

Europe and Britain; discovered 1750
Summer flowering | *Light fragrance*

HABIT Rambler H/W 3m/3m (10ft/10ft) | ZONES 4–10

Rosa banksiae banksiae

SPECIES | WHITE

'Banksiae Alba', 'Haku mokko', 'White Banksia', 'White Lady Banks's Rose', *R. banksiae alba*, *R. banksiae alba-plena*

This species is one of the four forms of *R. banksiae* still in cultivation, all of which possess similar, charming traits. These huge, wide-spreading ramblers grow to 9–15m (30–50ft) tall and produce masses of small, single or semi-double to fully double rosette flowers in cascading clusters. The wild species is a single, white form that grows in central China and is recognized as *R. banksiae normalis*. Although discovered in 1796, it was not introduced to the West until 1877, where it usually died as a result of frost. *Rosa banksiae banksiae* is the popular fragrant, double, white form. It is a hybrid that was taken from Canton to London's Kew Gardens by William Kerr in 1807 and named in honor of Sir Joseph Banks's wife, Dorothea. Banks achieved fame as the leader of the team of naturalists who accompanied Captain James Cook on his round-the-world voyage in the *Endeavour* in 1768–71, which subsequently led to the British colonization of Australia, in 1788. He was president of the Royal Society in London for more than 40 years, and played a major role in developing Kew Gardens.

Rosa banksiae banksiae

Rosa banksiae lutea

A vigorous, thornless plant with double, white flowers complemented by light green foliage, it is the most rampant of the R. banksiae group, spreading up to 9m (30ft) wide. The hips tend to be on the small side. Like its two sisters, the very popular R. banksiae lutea (see entry) and R. banksiae lutescens (a less popular, single, yellow variety introduced some 50 years later), and the single wild form (R. banksiae normalis), it is a little tender in frosty climates and produces its best display in warmer, sheltered climates.

China; introduced 1807
Spring flowering ı *Sweet fragrance*
HABIT Rambler H/W 9–15m/9m (30–50ft/30ft) ı ZONES 7–11

Rosa banksiae lutea

SPECIES ı LIGHT YELLOW

'Kimokko Bara', 'Lady Banks's Rose', 'Yellow Lady Banks's Rose', R. banksiae luteaplena

With double, soft primrose yellow blooms and a growth habit very similar to that of R. banksiae banksiae but slightly less rampant, this is the form of the 'Lady Banks's Rose' that is best known in gardens. Like all the R. banksiae species, it puts on its best display in a warm, sunny climate, making a curtain of blossom in spring. The foliage is small, dark and evergreen.

China; discovered 1824
Spring flowering ı *Moderate fragrance*
HABIT Rambler H/W 9–15m/9m (30–50ft/30ft) ı ZONES 7–11
❁ Royal Horticultural Society Award of Garden Merit

Rosa banksiae normalis

Rosa beggeriana

SPECIES ı WHITE

R. cinnamomea sewerzowii, R. lehmanniana, R. regelii, R. silverhjelmii

Not well known among gardeners, R. beggeriana is native over a large area of central Asia, from Iran and Afghanistan to some of the old Soviet Republics and western China. It makes a large, wide-spreading shrub that grows to 2.5m (8ft) tall. The foliage is slightly greyish. The small, single, pure white flowers are carried over a long season and followed soon after by deep red or purple hips scarcely bigger than peas.

Iran; discovered 1868
Summer flowering ı *Light fragrance*
HABIT Bush H/W 2.5m/2.5m (8ft/8ft) ı ZONES 4–11

Rosa beggeriana

Rosa blanda

SPECIES ı MEDIUM PINK

'Hudson's Bay Rose', 'Labrador Rose', *R. fraxinifolia, R. gratiosa, R solandri, R. subblanda, R. virginiana blanda*

The English gardener–botanist William Aiton, who helped George III and Sir Joseph Banks to develop Kew Gardens in London, named this species in 1773. It was then newly brought from North America, where it grows wild in the cold north-eastern regions. The name he chose is Latin for 'charming', 'gentle' or 'alluring'. A shrub that grows up to 1.5m (5ft) tall, it is notable for its hardiness, lack of thorns and very early flowering in spring. The single, pink flowers are usually borne several to a stem. The foliage is mid-green.

North America; introduced 1773
Spring flowering ı *Light fragrance*
HABIT Bush H/W 1.5m/1m (5ft/3ft) ı ZONES 4–11

Rosa blanda

Rosa bracteata

Rosa brunonii

Rosa bracteata

SPECIES | WHITE

'Chickasaw Rose', 'Macartney Rose', *R. lucida*,
R. macartnea

Quite unlike other roses, the 'Macartney Rose'
is distinguished by its dense, deep green mass
of evergreen foliage, its fierce thorns and its
large, single, pure white flowers. Best suited
to warm climates, it is a shrubby, vigorous
climber that can reach a height of 3m (10ft),
making a good cover when grown up against
a wall or draped over a fence. Said to be
the only rose quite immune to black spot,
R. bracteata owes its English name to Lord
Macartney, the English ambassador to its
native China in 1793, and its Latin one to
the leafy bracts surrounding the flowers.

China; discovered 1793
Repeat flowering | Light fragrance

HABIT Climber H/W 3m/3m (10ft/10ft) | ZONES 4–11

Rosa brunonii

SPECIES | WHITE

'Himalayan Musk Rose', *R. brownii*,
R. moschata nepalensis

Often confused with the true 'Musk Rose'
(*R. moschata*), this rambler did not make its

way to Europe and the United States from its
native Himalayas until 1823. By the turn of
the century the nickname was firmly established, and to distinguish it from the true
'Musk Rose', it was generally referred to
as the 'Himalayan Musk Rose'. It is distinct,
however, in its much greater vigor – it can
reach a height of 12m (40ft) – its grey-green
foliage and the fact that it flowers in summer
(whereas *R. moschata* flowers in late summer
or the fall/autumn), when it covers its large
frame with masses of richly scented, single,
white flowers.

Himalayas; introduced 1823
Summer flowering | Light fragrance

HABIT Rambler H/W 12m/9m (40ft/30ft) | ZONES 3–10

Rosa californica

SPECIES | LIGHT PINK

'California Wild Rose', *R. gratissima*

The 'California Wild Rose' is claimed by
Washington and Oregon as well, and also
reaches over the Canadian border into British Columbia. Although the double form,
R. californica plena, is most commonly seen
in gardens, the simple, five-petalled wild
form is also garden-worthy. A neat bush that
grows to 2.5m (8ft) tall, it has mid-green
foliage and sprays of lilac-pink flowers in
summer, with a few odd ones to follow
later in the season.

North America; discovered c. 1878
Summer flowering | Light fragrance

HABIT Bush H/W 2.5m/1.5m (8ft/5ft) | ZONES 3–10

Rosa canina

SPECIES | LIGHT PINK

'Brier Bush', 'Dog Rose', *R. leucantha, R. pseudos-
cabrata, R. sirculosa, R. sphaerica*

This species and its close relatives – which
include 'Abbotswood', 'Andersonii', 'Kiese'
and *R.× hibernica* – are the Wild Roses of
western Europe. Often used as a rootstock,
it has gone wild in some of the countries to
which it has been introduced, and is commonly seen growing alongside lanes and
pathways, especially in Britain. A large,
prickly shrub that grows to 3m (10ft) tall,
it produces single, pale pink flowers in
spring, followed by red hips. It is thought
to be one of the ancestors of the Alba rose.
The form shown here is one often seen in
Australia and known as the Adelaide form.

Europe; discovered pre-1730
Spring flowering | Light fragrance

HABIT Bush H/W 3m/1.8m (10ft/6ft) | ZONES 3–10

Rosa carolina

SPECIES | MEDIUM PINK

'Carolina Rose', 'Pasture Rose', *R. humilis,
R. parviflora. R. pensylvanica. R. pratensis,
R. virginiana humilis*

One of the common Wild Roses of the eastern United States and Canada, this species is
a freely suckering climber that forms dense
thickets, growing to 1–1.8m (3–6ft) tall by
1m (3ft) wide. A late flowerer, it is a useful
landscaping subject, providing color when

Rosa californica

Rosa californica plena

Rosa canina

Rosa carolina

Rosa chinensis spontanea

other roses have finished flowering. It is one of the commonest American species grown in gardens. The single flowers are mostly borne one to a stem, and vary in color from pale pink to cerise. They are followed by glossy, brilliant red hips. The foliage is light green.

North America; discovered 1826
Summer flowering ı Light fragrance
HABIT Climber H/W 1–1.8m/1m (3–6ft/3ft) ı ZONES 5–11

Rosa chinensis spontanea

SPECIES ı DARK RED

'Bengal Rose', 'China Rose', *R. chinensis indica*, *R. indica*, *R. indica vulgaris*, *R. nankinensis*, *R. sinica*

Not many Westerners have seen the rare *R. chinensis spontanea,* which grows in the remote mountains of western China, but it is the most important of all Wild Roses. All our repeat-blooming Modern Roses are

descendant hybrids of this species. The Chinese garden form is shown here, an ever-blooming climber with double, deep pink flowers that grows to 1.5m (5ft) tall. It will just have to stand in for the wild form. The wild species has single, red flowers and a more erratic habit, and grows to almost 1.8m (6ft) tall. Plant explorer Roy Lancaster finally introduced it to Britain from China around 1980. The flowers of both forms turn a deeper red as they age against their highly complementary backdrop of glossy foliage.

China; discovered 1759
Repeat flowering ı Light fragrance
HABIT Climber H/W 1.8m/1m (6ft/3ft) ı ZONES 6–11

Rosa cinnamomea plena

SPECIES ı MAUVE

'Cinnamon Rose', 'Double Cinnamon', 'Rose du Saint Sacrament', 'Rose of May', 'Stevens Rose', 'Whitsuntide Rose', *R. cinnamomea*, *R. foecundissima*, *R. majalis*

The old herbalists smelled cinnamon in the bark of this shrub, although no one else ever has. Regardless, *R. cinnamomea plena* has replaced the earlier name *R. majalis*, which, as has often happened, was originally given to the double-flowered garden forms of the species. It is, however, a species of more interest to botanists than to gardeners. Growing to 1.8m (6ft) tall, it produces single, five-petalled, deep lilac flowers with a pungent scent very early in spring. The foliage is a dull green.

Asia and Europe; discovered c. 1600
Spring flowering ı Light fragrance
HABIT Bush H/W 1.8m/1.2m (6ft/4ft) ı ZONES 4–11

Rosa cinnamomea plena

Rosa davidii

SPECIES ı LIGHT PINK

'Father David's Rose'

Discovered in 1869 in the mountains of western China by the French missionary and naturalist for whom it is named, *R. davidii* was not introduced to the West until the famous plant collector E. H. Wilson sent seed to Europe in 1903. Elegant sprays of single, bright pink flowers appear in summer, and the large, scarlet hips that follow make for one of the finest displays of hips to be seen on any rose. It forms an open shrub that grows to 3m (10ft) tall, with light green leaves.

China, near the border with eastern Tibet; discovered 1869
Summer flowering ı Light fragrance
HABIT Bush H/W 3m/1.5m (10ft/5ft) ı ZONES 4–10

Rosa davidii

Rosa ecae

Rosa ecae

SPECIES ı DEEP YELLOW

Widespread in central Asia, this species needs a dry climate. A dainty shrub that grows to 1.2m (4ft) tall, it is adorned in spring with multitudes of small, single flowers of a dazzling deep yellow. The equally dainty, fern-like foliage is purple-tinted when young. The curious scientific name honors Eleanor Carmichael Aitchison (ECA), the wife of the British soldier–botanist who discovered it in 1880. 'Helen Knight' and 'Golden Chersonese' are probably the best-known hybrids of this very pretty Wild Rose. 'Golden Chersonese' prefers a cool climate.

East of Caspian Sea into Afghanistan; discovered 1880
Spring flowering ı *Light fragrance*
HABIT Bush H/W 1.2m/1m (4ft/3ft) ı ZONES 4–11

Rosa eglanteria

SPECIES ı LIGHT PINK

'Eglantine Rose', 'Sweet Brier Rose', 'Sweetbriar', *R. rubiginosa, R. suavifolia, R. walpoleana*

This species is rather similar to its close relative the 'Dog Rose' (*R. canina*) and, like it, something of a pest with its shrubby growth and numerous sharp, annoying prickles. The 'Sweet Brier Rose' can be immediately distinguished, however, by the delicious, apple-like fragrance of its greyish green leaves. It makes a lanky, rather unattractive plant 1.8–3m (6–10ft) tall, with single, pink flowers in spring and oval, whiskery red hips in the fall/autumn. Like the 'Dog Rose', it is native over most of Europe. There are several hybrids, 'Lord Penzance' being the best known. Other,

Rosa eglanteria

Rosa × engelmannii

equally attractive, hybrids include 'Fritz Nobis', 'Janet's Pride' and 'Magnifica'.

Europe; ancient
Spring flowering ı *Moderate fragrance*
HABIT Bush H/W 1.8–3m/1.5m (6–10ft/5ft) ı ZONES 5–11
🏆 Royal Horticultural Society Award of Garden Merit

Rosa × engelmannii

SPECIES ı DEEP PINK

R. acicularis engelmannii, R. bakerii, R. engelmannii, R. melina, R. oreophilia

There is a great deal of confusion among botanists over *R. × engelmannii*. The shrub known by this name that was collected last century by Dr Engelmann in Colorado is a form of the widespread *R. acicularis*, and *R. arkansana* has sometimes impersonated it in British gardens. Be that as it may, the pretty, single-petalled, pink rose with mid-green leaves shown in the photograph bore the label *R. engelmannii* in the Royal Botanic Gardens, Kew, and is included as a minor contribution to the ongoing debate.

North America; discovered 1891
Summer flowering
HABIT Bush H/W 1m/1m (3ft/3ft) ı ZONES 4–10

Rosa farreri persetosa

SPECIES ı MEDIUM PINK

'Threepenny Bit Rose', *R. elegantula* 'Persetosa'

One of the most unusual of roses on account of the contrast between the size of the shrub, which grows to 1.5m (5ft) tall and wide, and the daintiness of the minute foliage and the soft, star-like, single, pink flowers, only 9mm (⅜in) in diameter, *R. farreri persetosa* was discovered in 1914 by the great plant collector Reginald Farrer. It likes a cool, moist spot. The very small, pale green, ferny leaves color nicely in the fall/autumn, and the tiny hips, only 6 mm (¼in) long, are orange. The name *persetosa* refers to the innumerable bristles on the stems. The British nickname 'Threepenny Bit Rose' refers to Britain's pre-metric currency, the flowers being the size of the threepenny bit, at that time the smallest British coin.

China; discovered 1914
Summer flowering ı *Fragrant*
HABIT Bush H/W 1.5m/1.5m (5ft/5ft) ı ZONES 6–11

Rosa farreri persetosa

Rosa filipes

SPECIES ı WHITE

'Kiftsgate'

'Kiftsgate' is the most usually encountered form of this giant-growing rambler from western China. Its Latin name comes from *filipendula*, which means hanging by a thread, alluding to the way the flowers hang from weak stems. It was named after Kiftsgate

Rosa foetida persiana ('Persian Yellow')

Rosa foetida

Rosa filipes ('Kiftsgate')

Rosa foetida bicolor ('Austrian Copper')

Court in Gloucestershire, where it was first cultivated in Britain at an uncertain date but probably around 1954 – which is remarkable, given that this species was discovered in 1908. It takes time to establish, and will then grow to 4.5m (15ft) tall and spread far and wide, adorning itself with a multitude of intoxicatingly scented, single, white flowers in spring and carrying glistening, scarlet hips far into winter. It is not a plant for the average garden; one specimen in England has spread to a width of some 45m (148ft). The foliage is dark green. It prefers cool climates, and needs very little pruning other than the removal of unsightly dead branches.

China; discovered 1908; introduced by Murrell, England, UK, (?)1954
Spring flowering ı *Moderate fragrance*

HABIT Rambler H/W 4.5m/4.5m (15ft/15ft) ı ZONES 4–11

Rosa foetida

SPECIES ı MEDIUM YELLOW

'Austrian Briar', 'Austrian Yellow', *R. chlorophylla, R. lutea*

Despite the name, the 'Austrian Briar' comes not from Austria but from the Middle East. It acquired the name Austrian when Flemish doctor and pioneer botanist Charles de l'Ecluse introduced it to Holland from Vienna in the 1560s. It is an upright shrub that grows to 3m (10ft) tall, and when it is in flower, no plant is more dazzling. The dull green leaves are, however, rather susceptible to black spot. There are two popular descendants, the single-petalled 'Austrian Copper' (*R. foetida bicolor*) and the double-petalled 'Persian Yellow' (*R. foetida persiana*). In full bloom

and viewed from a distance, 'Austrian Copper' resembles a vivid setting sun with its mass of orange-red flowers with bright yellow centres. It occasionally reverts back to its parent, usually by producing a branch of completely yellow flowers. 'Persian Yellow', a double, bright yellow variety introduced to Europe from Persia (modern-day Iran) in 1837, was the pollen parent of the early Hybrid Tea Roses through the work of the great rose breeder Joseph Pernet-Ducher of Lyon, thereby injecting into some Modern Roses the yellows and oranges we know today.

Iran, Iraq and Turkey; discovered before 1542
Summer flowering ı *Moderate to sickly sweet fragrance*

HABIT Bush H/W 3m/1.8m (10ft/6ft) ı ZONES 4–11

Rosa foliolosa

SPECIES ı MEDIUM PINK

This strange and very graceful species from Oklahoma and Arkansas grows to only 45cm (18in) tall. In addition to its diminutive size, it is characterized by its narrow leaflets, luxuriant growth, compact habit and almost complete lack of thorns. The name *foliolosa*, given by the distinguished American naturalist Thomas Nuttall, means 'leafy' or covered with leaflets. The flowers are single, mostly

Rosa foliolosa ('Ann Endt')

solitary, and medium pink. The variety shown here is a cultivated hybrid called 'Ann Endt'. It has large, single, carmine flowers that appear in summer and then continue, a few at a time, until the fall/autumn, when they form round, deep rose-red hips. With a similar growth habit to its parent, it has lush, bright green foliage that colors brightly in the fall/autumn.

USA; discovered 1880
Summer flowering ı *Fragrant*

HABIT Bush H/W 45cm/40cm (18in/15in) ı ZONES 4–10

Rosa forrestiana

SPECIES ı DEEP PINK

Scottish plant collector George Forrest (better known for his rhododendrons) introduced this beautiful species from western China to Europe around 1920. A shrub that grows to 1.8m (6ft) tall, it wreathes its arching branches with clusters of single, pale pink to deep pink flowers in spring. Each bunch wears a distinctive collar of bright green bracts, which persist to set off the bright red, flask-shaped hips. The foliage is mid-green.

China; introduced c. 1920
Spring flowering ı *Light fragrance*

HABIT Bush H/W 1.8m/1.2m (6ft/4ft) ı ZONES 4–10

Rosa forrestiana

Rosa gallica

SPECIES ı DEEP PINK

'French Rose', 'Provins Rose', *R. austriaca, R. grandiflora, R. olympica, R. rubra, R. sylvatica*

Rosa gallica, the 'French Rose', is the progenitor of the garden Gallicas we know today and their numerous descendants. The Latin name refers to Gaul, the ancient name for a region of western Europe that included present-day France. In recognition of its importance, botanists have assigned this species a section of its own within the genus *Rosa*, namely Gallicanae. Although no longer found growing wild, it was not confined to France but was fairly ubiquitous across central and southern Europe, extending into Asia. It is a neat,

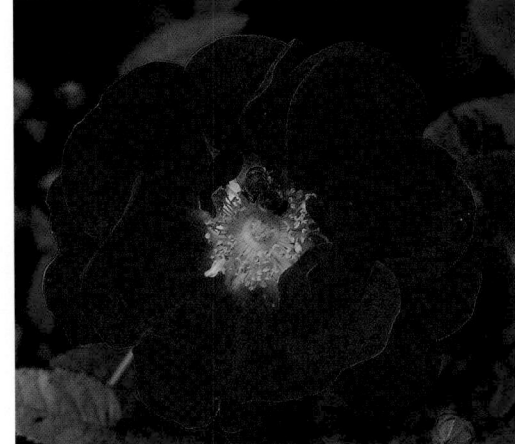

Rosa gallica officinalis

almost thornless shrub that suckers freely, growing to 1–1.2m (3–4ft) tall. The leaves are mid-green and soft to the touch. The single-petalled, solitary flowers bloom in summer, and have a slight fragrance. They are usually pink, but there are sufficient natural variations for deeper pink and light crimson specimens to occur. Two other important Species Roses derived from *R. gallica* are in cultivation today, *R. gallica officinalis* and *R. gallica versicolor* (see entries).

Central and southern Europe and the Middle East; ancient
Summer flowering ı *Light fragrance*

HABIT Bush H/W 1–1.2m/1m (3–4ft/3ft) ı ZONES 5–11

Rosa gallica officinalis

SPECIES ı DEEP PINK

'Apothecary's Rose', '(The) Apothecary's Rose of Provins', 'Double French Rose', 'Officinalis', 'Red Rose of Lancaster', 'Rose of Provins', *R. gallica maxima, R. gallica plena, R. officinalis, R. provincialis, R. × centifolia provincialis*

An early cultivated form that dates to c. 1400, this is one of two important Species Roses that derive from the Wild Rose *R. gallica*. It blooms in summer, bearing clusters of large, semi-double, bright pink to crimson flowers with golden stamens. While it has the same growth habit as its parent, it is a more garden-worthy plant, with dense, firm-textured, grey-green foliage that forms an attractive hedge. In the fifteenth century this rose was most widely known as the 'Apothecary's Rose', owing to a remarkable characteristic that is not evident at first sight. Its flowers, not especially fragrant on the bush, become intensely so when they are dried. Thus it was and remains the pre-eminent choice for the various medicinal and culinary uses to which the rose is put. If you find an antique recipe that calls simply

Rosa gallica

Rosa gallica versicolor

for 'red Rofes', this is the rose that is meant. It is also thought to be the 'Red Rose of Lancaster', the rose chosen as one of the emblems of the House of Lancaster during England's War of the Roses (1455–1485), when the opposing House of York took the white Alba rose as one of its emblems. One legend has it that the fighting continued until a bush appeared in the English countryside bearing roses that were pure red, pure white and a mixture of red and white, inspiring the two families to come together to resolve their differences. *Rosa gallica versicolor* (see entry) is sometimes said to be the striped rose.

Central and southern Europe and the Middle East; introduced c. 1400
Summer flowering ı *Strong fragrance*

HABIT Bush H/W 1–1.2m/1m (3–4ft/3ft) ı ZONES 5–11

Rosa gallica versicolor

SPECIES ı PINK BLEND

'Rosa Mundi', *R. gallica rosa mundi, R. gallica variegata, R. mundi*

The second of two important Species Roses that derive from the Wild Rose *R. gallica* and are still in cultivation today, *R. gallica versicolor* is virtually identical to *R. gallica officinalis* in growth habit, foliage, and the shape and form of its blooms. Its blooms are, however, of a strikingly different color, their deep pink to crimson petals being irregularly striped with white. One legend associates this striped form with England's War of the Roses (see *R. gallica officinalis*). Yet another connects it to Fair Rosamund, the mistress of Henry II – hence the common name 'Rosa Mundi'. As this legend has it, a crimson-and-white-striped rose sprouted outside the royal castle after her death, but Henry died in 1177 and there is nothing in the historical record to support this association. It has also been said that the medieval Crusaders brought 'Rosa Mundi' back to England from the Near East, but the first recorded mention of this species is that it was grown around 1596 by pioneering English gardener John Gerard. It then disappears from the record until 1659, when it was mentioned in *The Garden Book of Sir Thomas Hanmer*. Its origins must remain a mystery – a mystery steeped in two legends!

Central and southern Europe and the Middle East; introduced c. 1596
Summer flowering **·** *Moderate fragrance*

HABIT Bush H/W 1–1.2m/1m (3–4ft/3ft) **·** ZONES 5–11

Rosa gigantea

Rosa gigantea

SPECIES **·** WHITE

R. macrocarpa, R. × odorata gigantea, R. xanthocarpa

Everything about this vigorous climber, which can reach a height of 15m (50ft), justifies the name – the long, arching branches; the great, drooping, mid-green, semi-glossy leaves; the large, single flowers, 14cm (5 ½in) in diameter, with their silky, reflexed petals in white, palest yellow or pale pink; and the 2.5cm (1in) long, yellowy-orange, pear-shaped hips. It has passed these qualities on to its descendants,

the Tea Roses, which are thought to have been bred by long-ago Chinese gardeners from this species and *R. chinensis* (although the hips of Tea Roses vary widely in size, shape and color). A native of the jungles of Burma and southern China, it is shy of the slightest frost.

Burma and China; discovered 1889
Spring flowering **·** *Light fragrance*

HABIT Climber H/W 15m/9m (50ft/30ft) **·** ZONES 4–11

Rosa giraldii

SPECIES **·** PINK BLEND

The mountains of western and central China are the heartland of the rose, but were one of the last regions of the world to be explored by Western botanists. It was not until the late nineteenth century that species such as *R. giraldii* were introduced to British and European gardens. Not, perhaps, outstanding, it is still a pretty shrub, growing to 1.8m (6ft) tall and weeping in habit, with fine, mid-green foliage and single, pink flowers in spring.

China; discovered 1897
Spring flowering **·** *Light fragrance*

HABIT Bush H/W 1.8m/1.2m (6ft/4ft) **·** ZONES 4–10

Rosa glauca

SPECIES **·** MEDIUM PINK

R. ferruginea, R. giraldii, R. ilseana, R. lurida, R. rubrifolia

This enchanting species from central Europe is one of the most popular of Wild Roses among gardeners, mainly owing to the color and grace of its leaves, which are purple in youth and grey, touched with plum, at maturity. The single, pink flowers and dark red hips play a distinctly secondary role. A thornless shrub, it grows to 1.8m (6ft) tall.

Central Europe; discovered 1814
Summer flowering **·** *Light fragrance*

HABIT Bush H/W 1.8m/1.8m (6ft/6ft) **·** ZONES 4–10
Royal Horticultural Society Award of Garden Merit

Rosa glauca

Rosa giraldii

Rosa helenae

Rosa helenae

SPECIES **·** WHITE

R. floribunda, R. moschata helenae, R. moschata micrantha

The great plant collector Ernest Wilson, better known as E. H. Wilson, named this beautiful species, which he discovered in central China, in honor of his wife. Tragically, both he and his wife were killed in a car accident in 1930, shortly after his return to America. One of the most garden-worthy of the 'Himalayan Musk Roses', this tall-growing rambler bears great bunches of deliciously scented, single, creamy white blooms in summer, followed by the finest display of red hips of any of the group. The foliage is dark green and semi-glossy. Reaching a height of up to 4.5m (15ft), it can easily be grown up a tree or against the side of a house.

China; discovered 1907
Summer flowering **·** *Intense fragrance*

HABIT Rambler H/W 4.5m/4.5m (15ft/15ft) **·** ZONES 4–11

Rosa hemisphaerica

Rosa hemisphaerica

SPECIES | MEDIUM YELLOW

'Sulphur Rose', *R. glaucophylla*, *R. rapinii*,
R. sulphurea

For many years this was the only double
yellow rose available, so European gardeners put up with its cantankerousness in the
hope that it might consent to open a bloom
or two. It really is only a success in warm,
dry climates like that of its native Armenia,
Iran and Turkey. A slender and almost thornless shrub, with distinctly grey leaves, it
grows to 1.5m (5ft) tall. As has often been
the case, it was discovered and named long
before the wild, single-petalled form, which
was only discovered in 1933 and is identified
as *R. hemisphaerica rapinii*.

Armenia, Iran and Turkey; discovered 1623
Summer flowering | Light fragrance
HABIT Bush H/W 1.5m/1.2m (5ft/4ft) | ZONES 4–11

BELOW *Rosa hugonis*
RIGHT INSET *Rosa laevigata*
FAR RIGHT INSET *Rosa laevigata rosea*

Rosa hugonis

SPECIES | MEDIUM YELLOW

'Father Hugo Rose', 'Father Hugo's Rose',
'Golden Rose of China'

This beautiful yellow rose caused quite a stir
in 1899 when missionary Father Hugh Scallon
sent it to Britain from central China. The single,
yellow flowers, borne in spring along arching
branches, and the ferny, pale green foliage
are very pretty. A shrub that grows to 1.8m
(6ft) tall, it is not an easy rose to grow, and
you are more likely these days to see one
of its hybrids, such as 'Cantabrigiensis'
or 'Headleyensis'.

China; discovered 1899
Spring flowering | Light fragrance
HABIT Bush H/W 1.8m/1.2m (6ft/4ft) | ZONES 4–10
Royal Horticultural Society Award of Garden Merit

Rosa laevigata

SPECIES | WHITE

'Cherokee Rose', *R. camellia*, *R. cherokeensis*,
R. hystrix, *R. nivea*, *R. sinica*, *R. ternata*, *R. triphylla*

The State Flower of Georgia, USA, is one
of the very earliest roses to bloom in spring,
its large, single, white flowers shining against
the glossy, dark green, evergreen foliage.
Unusually, this Wild Rose has leaf sets that
are made up of only 3 leaves, while most

other species generally have leaf sets of 5 or
7 leaves. It is native to China, but botanists
have debated whether it is also American ever
since 1803, when French botanist André
Michaux found it growing apparently wild in
the southern states of America, in the lands of
the Cherokee Indian tribes. This beautiful, if
thorny, climber is suited to mild climates only
and will grow to 5m (16ft) tall. *Rosa laevigata
rosea*, the 'Pink Cherokee', is not as rampant,
growing to 1–1.8m (3–6ft) tall, but is otherwise similar in habit.

China; discovered 1759
Spring flowering | Light fragrance
HABIT Climber H/W 5m/3.5m (16ft/12ft) | ZONES 4–10

Rosa longicuspis

SPECIES | WHITE

R. charbonneaui, *R. irridens*, *R. lucens*,
R. willmottiana

Introduced to cultivation early in the twentieth
century, this rambler is the most manageable
of the 'Himalayan Musk Roses' in gardens.
Growing to 6m (20ft) tall, it has almost evergreen foliage with shiny, dark green leaflets
that are almost 10cm (4in) long. The young
shoots are an attractive reddish color, but it
is the scent of the flowers that leaves the most
lasting impression – fruity, like ripe bananas!
The single, white flowers appear in summer.

China; discovered 1915
Summer flowering | Moderate fragrance
HABIT Rambler H/W 6m/4.5m (20ft/15ft) | ZONES 4–11

Rosa longicuspis

Rosa macrantha

Rosa macrantha

SPECIES ι LIGHT PINK

Often questioned as a true Wild Rose, this species bears a strong resemblance to *R. gallica*. It is a vigorously spreading and arching rambler, growing to 1.8m (6ft) tall and 1.2m (4ft) wide. The single flowers are of a clear pink, fading quickly to near white, and have a good, strong fragrance. The foliage is prone to mildew. While the exact origins of this Wild Rose are still the subject of debate, a close relative, *R.* × *macrantha*, was found in France in 1823. It shows the same resemblance to Gallicas, with large, wide, single flowers and distinctive stamens often described as little toadstools.

Origin unknown
Spring flowering ι *Strong fragrance*
HABIT Climber H/W 1.8m/1.2m (6ft/4ft) ι ZONES 4–11

Rosa macrophylla

SPECIES ι DEEP PINK

R. hoffmeisteri, R. hookeriana

There are some rose species characterized by much larger leaves, but they were unknown when *R. macrophylla* was discovered in

China in 1818. A large, open-growing shrub that grows to 2.5m (8ft) tall and 1.2m (4ft) wide, it is almost thornless and has matt, mid-green foliage and dark, mahogany-colored wood. Elegant, single, deep pink flowers bloom in early summer, and are followed by red hips rather like those of its relative *R. moyesii* but even larger, although less elongated. It is a true Himalayan, growing at altitudes of 4000m (13 000ft). Not a plant for the small garden or – especially during pruning season – the weak at heart!

China; discovered 1818
Summer flowering ι *Light fragrance*
HABIT Bush H/W 2.5m/1.2m (8ft/4ft) ι ZONES 4–11

Rosa macrophylla

Rosa moschata

Rosa moschata

SPECIES ι WHITE

'Musk Rose', *R. ruscinonensis*

The rose the nineteenth-century botanists dubbed the 'Musk Rose' is a short climber, notable mainly for its musky fragrance and its habit of producing its clusters of single,

white flowers after all other roses have bloomed. It grows to only 2.5m (8ft). Thomas Cromwell, the Earl of Essex, brought it to England from Italy, which puts the date before he lost his head in 1540. It was always said to have come from Persia (modern-day Iran), although it is now known to be native to Madeira, North Africa and Spain as well. About 100 years ago its name began to be attached to a usurper, *R. brunonii*, the 'Himalayan Musk Rose'. Indeed, it almost vanished until British rosarian Graham Stuart Thomas rediscovered it in a garden north of London in the early 1960s. It is an important ancestor of Modern Roses.

Iran, Madeira, North Africa and Spain; discovered c. 1540
Summer flowering ι *Strong, musk fragrance*
HABIT Climber H/W 2.5m/1.8m (8ft/6ft) ι ZONES 4–10

Rosa moyesii

SPECIES ι MEDIUM RED

R. fargesii, R. macrophylla rubrostaminea

This mountain rose was named in honor of the Reverend J. Moyes of the China Inland Mission, a friend of plant collector E. H. Wilson, who discovered it around 1890 in the southwestern part of China, near the Tibetan border. It is one of the most desirable of Wild Roses by virtue of the unique color of its single flowers – a lustrous, crimson red – and its truly magnificent hips – orange-red, flagon-shaped and an impressive 7cm (2 ½in) long. It is, however, a gaunt and ungainly shrub, growing to 3m (10ft) tall, and many people prefer such selected garden forms as 'Geranium' to the wild plant. The foliage is greyish green. Pink-flowered versions are sometimes called *R. holodonta*.

China, near Tibetan border; discovered c. 1890
Summer flowering ι *Light fragrance*
HABIT Bush H/W 3m/2.5m (10ft/8ft) ι ZONES 4–10

Rosa moyesii

TOP *Rosa multibracteata*
ABOVE *Rosa multiflora*

Rosa nipponensis

Rosa nitida

Rosa multibracteata

SPECIES ｜ LIGHT PINK

R. reducta

This Wild Rose from Sichuan is noteworthy for the airy gracefulness of its growth. A shrub that grows to 1.8m (6ft) tall, it has finely cut, pale green leaves and clusters of single, clear pink flowers that are nicely set off by the pale green bracts that give the species its name. *Rosa multibracteata* has played an important role, often not fully recognized, in the breeding of Modern Roses, being an ancestor of 'Tropicana' (also known as 'Super Star') and 'Floradora', and a parent of 'Queen Elizabeth'.

China; discovered 1910
Repeat flowering ｜ *Light fragrance*

HABIT Bush H/W 1.8m/1.2m (6ft/4ft) ｜ ZONES 4–11

Rosa multiflora

SPECIES ｜ WHITE

R. dawsoniana, R. franchetii paniculigera,
R. intermedia, R. linkii, R. microcarpa,
R. multiflora thunbergiana, R. polyantha,
R. thunbergii, R. thyrsiflora, R. wichurae

Garden forms of this rambler with double and colored flowers had been arriving in Europe from China and Japan since about 1810, and it was not until 1862 that the wild species was introduced from Japan. Growing to 4.5m (15ft) tall by 3m (10ft) wide, this Wild Rose is a most important parent, not only to a host of ramblers, including 'Carnea' and 'Platyphylla', but also to the dwarf Poly-anthas and through them the Floribundas. It would hardly be seen in gardens today except for its popularity as a rootstock.

The small, single flowers are creamy white and borne in large clusters against a back-drop of pale, lime-green leaves.

China, Japan and Korea; discovered c. 1810
Summer flowering ｜ *Light fragrance*

HABIT Rambler H/W 4.5m/3m (15ft/10ft) ｜ ZONES 4–11

Rosa nipponensis

SPECIES ｜ DEEP PINK

'High Mountain Rose', 'O-Takane-bara',
R. acicularis nipponensis

Endemic to the high mountains in the central areas of Honshu and Shikou, Japan, this species is usually found growing on the edges of forests. It resembles *R. acicularis* in many respects, but is smaller, with a fruity fragrance and different foliage. Both species have leaf sets

containing 7 to 9 leaflets, but the leaflets of
R. nipponensis have fine-toothed margins,
whereas those of *R. acicularis* have scalloped
margins. The two species have very similar
flowers, single and medium to deep pink.
Both form small, dense shrubs that grow
to 1m (3ft) tall.

Japan; discovered 1894
Spring flowering · *Fruity fragrance*
HABIT Climber H/W 1m/1m (3ft/3ft) · ZONES 4–10

Rosa nitida

SPECIES · MEDIUM PINK

'Shining Rose', *R. blanda*, *R. redutea rubescens*,
R. rubrispina

This neat, low-growing shrub from North
America earns its name from its highly
polished leaves, *nitida* meaning 'shining'.
Gardeners also admire its delicately scented,
single, rose-pink flowers and the red hips
that gleam among its bronze foliage in the
fall/autumn. Only 45cm (18in) tall, it grows
naturally in the swamps of eastern Canada
and New England, and is one of the few
roses that will endure poor drainage.

North America; discovered c. 1807
Summer flowering · *Light fragrance*
HABIT Bush H/W 45cm/30cm (18in/12in) · ZONES 4–11

Rosa nutkana

SPECIES · MEDIUM PINK

'Nutka Rose', *R. manca*, *R. muriculata*, *R. spaldingii*

Native to North America, this Wild Rose has
beautiful single, soft lilac-pink flowers with
highly contrasting bright yellow stamens. A shrub
that grows to 3m (10ft) tall, it blooms from
May to June. The hips are scarlet and rich in
vitamin C, and often used to make teas, jams
and jellies.

Canada and North America; discovered c. 1876
Spring flowering · *Heavy, rose fragrance*
HABIT Bush H/W 3m/1.8m (10ft/6ft) · ZONES 4–11

Rosa omeiensis pteracantha

Rosa omeiensis pteracantha

SPECIES · WHITE

'Maltese Cross Rose', 'Wingthorn Rose',
R. serica pteracantha

The single, white flowers of this large, ferny-
leafed Wild Rose from China are unique in
having only four petals, while all others have
five-plus. Lovely as they are, the flowers
are rather fleeting. The most extraordinary
feature of this shrub is its thorns – bright
scarlet, translucent and with a pronounced
wedge shape, they dominate the stems and
are a sight to behold in the early morning
sun! Prune the branches well to encourage
many new growths, as on old branches the
thorns go grey and ordinary. This plant makes
a substantial bush, growing to 3m (10ft) high
and 1.8m (6ft) wide.

China; discovered 1890
Spring flowering · *Light fragrance*
HABIT Bush H/W 3m/1.8m (10ft/6ft) · ZONES 4–10

Rosa palustris

SPECIES · MEDIUM PINK

'Marsh Rose', 'Swamp Rose', *R. carolina*,
R. caroliniana, *R. corymbosa*, *R. elongata*,
R. fragrans, *R. hudsoniana*, *R. pensylvanica*,
R. salicifolia, *R. virginiana*

Palustris is Latin for 'swamp-loving', and this
pretty shrub from eastern North America
lives up to its name, preferring moist, boggy
ground. It is garden-worthy for its delicate,
single, deep bright pink flowers and its subtle
fall/autumn color. It grows to 1.8m (6ft) tall
by 1m (3ft) wide, suckering freely to form a
compact and pleasing thicket when plants are
spaced about 1m (3ft) apart.

North America; discovered 1726
Summer flowering · *Light fragrance*
HABIT Bush H/W 1.8m/1m (6ft/3ft) · ZONES 3–10

Rosa nutkana

Rosa palustris

Rosa pendulina

SPECIES | DEEP PINK

'Alpine Rose', *R. alpina*, *R. cinnamomea*,
R. franxinifolia, *R. glandulosa*

Native to central and southern Europe, the
'Alpine Rose' is not very often seen in gardens.
It should be, for it is a pretty, thornless shrub
that adorns its trailing branches in spring with
single, plum-red flowers. The young leaves
are reddish, too, maturing to dark green.
Plants normally grow to 1.8m (6ft) tall and
1.2m (4ft) wide. It is thought by many to
be the progenitor of the thornless Boursalt
Roses, although some botanists give the
credit for this to *R. blanda*.

Europe; discovered 1794
Summer flowering | *Light fragrance*
HABIT Bush H/W 1.8m/1.2m (6ft/4ft) | ZONES 4–10

Rosa pisocarpa

Rosa pimpinellifolia

SPECIES | WHITE

'Burnet Rose', 'Scotch Rose', *R. spinosissima*

The 'Scotch Rose' is now correctly called the
'burnet-leafed rose' (*pimpinellifolia*), but many
botanists still call it *spinosissima*, the 'thorni-
est rose'. It deserves that name, for the neat
little bushes, which grow to 1m (3ft) tall and
wide, are completely covered, down to the
smallest twigs, in sharp spines. The small,
scented, single flowers appear in spring
and may be yellow, white or pink. There
are several double-flowered garden forms
also known as 'Scotch Roses', and in recent
years the species has been much used by
hybridists to create lusty Shrub Roses.
The foliage is ferny and greyish green.

United Kingdom; discovered c. 1800
Spring flowering | *Light fragrance*
HABIT Bush H/W 1m/1m (3ft/3ft) | ZONES 3–11

Rosa pisocarpa

SPECIES | MEDIUM PINK

The botanical name means the 'pea-fruited
rose', which would be a good English name

for it, too, as it describes the size of the little
red hips exactly. Native to western North
America, ranging from California into British
Columbia, it is a relatively prickle-free shrub
that grows to 1.8m (6ft) tall. The single, pink
flowers come in clusters of up to five. The
foliage is dark green and gives an attractive
fall/autumn display.

North America; discovered c. 1882
Summer flowering | *Light fragrance*
HABIT Bush H/W 1.8m/1.2m (6ft/4ft) | ZONES 4–10

Rosa pomifera

SPECIES | MEDIUM PINK

'Apple Rose', *R. hispida*, *R. villosa*

This Wild Rose gets its nickname from
the remarkable hips it produces in the fall/
autumn – large, orange, apple-shaped and
covered with bristles. It is a dense, wide-
spreading shrub, growing to 1.2m (4ft) tall
and 1.8m (6ft) wide. The flowers are single
and a clear pink. The clean-cut, light green
leaves age greyish and downy.

Asia and Europe; discovered 1771
Spring flowering | *Light fragrance*
HABIT Climber H/W 1.2m/1.8m (4ft/6ft) | ZONES 4–11

ABOVE *Rosa pendulina*
BELOW *Rosa pimpinellifolia*

Rosa pomifera

Rosa primula

SPECIES ׀ LIGHT YELLOW

'Incense Rose', *R. sweginzowii*

Somewhat like *R. hugonis* at first sight, although with rather paler yellow flowers, *R. primula* scores over its rather temperamental rival with the intense aroma of its fern-like, mid-green leaves, which have the strongest scent of any rose foliage. It is easier to grow, too, although, like most roses from central Asia, it is happiest in a warm, dry climate. A short to medium-sized shrub with single flowers, it grows to 1m (3ft) tall and spreads to about the same width. The name, that of the primrose, is obvious enough from the color of the blooms, but is a piece of botanical naughtiness.

Turkestan to northern China; discovered 1910
Spring flowering ׀ Strong fragrance

HABIT Bush H/W 1m/1m (3ft/3ft) ׀ ZONES 4–11

❀ Royal Horticultural Society Award of Garden Merit

Rosa primula

BELOW LEFT *Rosa roxburghii normalis*
BELOW RIGHT *Rosa roxburghii plena*
BOTTOM *Rosa roxburghii hirtula*

Rosa roxburghii normalis

SPECIES ׀ LIGHT PINK

'Burr Rose', 'Single Chestnut Rose'

The wild, single 'Chestnut Rose', with its soft pink flowers, was introduced to the West in 1908, more than 80 years after the double, deep lilac form known as *R. roxburghii* (and also as *R. roxburghii plena*). Both have characteristically flaking bark and prickly, chestnut-like hips, and both bloom early in spring, with the odd flower to follow. The double form is more favored in gardens. It was first grown in the West in 1824, having previously been introduced to the Calcutta Botanic Garden by Dr William Roxburgh, who imported it from Canton. Both forms make attractive shrubs to 1.8m (6ft) tall, with ferny, greyish green leaves. There is also a single-petalled Japanese version, *R. roxburghii hirtula*, which is a deeper pink.

China and Japan; introduced 1908
Spring flowering ׀ Light fragrance

HABIT Climber H/W 1.8m/1.5m (6ft/5ft) ׀ ZONES 4–11

Rosa rugosa alba

Rosa rugosa rubra

Rosa rugosa

Hips of *Rosa rugosa alba*

Rosa rugosa

SPECIES ı MAUVE

'Hedgehog Rose', 'Japanese Rose', 'Kiska Rose', 'Ramanas Rose', 'Rugosa Rose', 'Tomato Rose', *R. ferox, R. regeliana*

The name *R. rugosa* refers to a group of wild species found in Japan, Korea and China. The original, single-petalled wild species is recognized as *R. rugosa typica* or *R. rugosa rugosa*, but there are many forms and hybrids of *R. rugosa* among garden roses, known by such common names as 'Rugosa Rose', 'Japanese Rose' and 'Ramanas Rose', since the seedlings of all Species Roses quite readily produce a variety of progeny of many different colors and forms. In their native Asia, the roses in this group grow by the seashore, spreading widely from suckers to make dense, hedge-like shrubs up to 3m (10ft) wide. Among their many different colors are a lovely pure white variety named *R. rugosa alba* and a stunning mauve-red variety named *R. rugosa rubra*. In winter they produce very ornamental, orange-red, tomato-shaped hips that are rich in vitamin C and provide a food source for birds, mice and squirrels. The foliage is bright green and quilted. Well-known hybrids include 'Blanc Double de Coubert', 'F. J. Grootendorst', 'Frau Dagmar Hartopp', 'Hansa', 'Roseraie de l'Haÿ' and 'Schneezwerg' (see Modern Roses section).

China, Japan and Korea; discovered 1845
Repeat flowering ı *Strong fragrance*
HABIT Bush H/W 3.5m/3m (12ft/10ft) ı ZONES 3–10

Rosa sempervirens

SPECIES ı WHITE

R. alba Allioni, R. atrovirens, R. balearica

The Victorians nicknamed the hybrids of this plant 'evergreen roses', as they partially retained their glossy, dark green foliage throughout the winter. The flowers are single, pure white and fragrant, and borne in small clusters on a semi-vigorous climber that grows to 6m (20ft) tall and can spread the same distance. Modern rose-breeders have made good use of this plant's ability to ramble and scramble. The hips, usually small and orange-red, are produced in the late fall/autumn. Popular hybrids include 'Adélaide d'Orléans' and 'Félicité Perpetue' (see Old Garden Roses section).

Mediterranean and Northern Africa; discovered 1629
Spring flowering ı *Moderate fragrance*
HABIT Rambler H/W 6m/6m (20ft/20ft) ı ZONES 4–11

Rosa sempervirens

Rosa setigera

SPECIES ı DEEP PINK

'Prairie Rose', *R. fenestrata, R. trifoliate*

The 'Prairie Rose' is commonly found in the east and Midwest of the United States.

Its Latin name means 'bristly'. It is the only member of the Synstylae class (see introduction) that is native to America and that has pink flowers instead of the normal sun-bleached white. A shrubby sort of climber with bright green leaves, it grows to 1.8m (6ft) tall and produces long, arching canes that often layer like blackberries when they touch ground. Large, single flowers are borne in large bunches and carried until quite late in the season. Interestingly, each plant is likely to have flowers fertile in the stamens or the stigmas, but not in both. Two hybrids, now rarely seen, were raised in the United States in the 1840s, 'Baltimore Belle' and 'Long John Silver'.

North America; discovered 1810
Summer flowering ı *Slight fragrance*
HABIT Climber H/W 1.8m/1.8m (6ft/6ft) ı ZONES 4–11

Rosa setipoda

SPECIES ı LIGHT PINK

R. macrophylla crasseaculeata

With its arching growth, its ferny, pleasantly scented, mid-green leaves, its perfectly symmetrical, single, pink flowers and its bunches

Rosa setigera

of flagon-shaped hips, *R. setipoda* is much more elegant than the 'Sweet Brier Rose' *(R. eglanteria)*. It resembles the 'Sweet Brier Rose' in the scent of its leaves, although its leaves have a more pine-like fragrance. A native of China's Hobei province, this shrub was introduced to Europe by plant collector E. H. Wilson in 1901. It grows to 4m (13ft) tall and 3m (10ft) wide.

China; discovered 1895
Summer flowering ⏐ *Light fragrance*
HABIT Bush H/W 4m/3m (13ft/10ft) ⏐ ZONES 4–10

Rosa setipoda

Rosa sinowilsonii

SPECIES ⏐ WHITE

The name honors the great plant collector E. H. Wilson, nicknamed 'Chinese' Wilson, who found this rose on sacred Mount Omei in the Chinese province of Sichuan. It is notable for its splendid leaves, which are huge, dark green and glossy, their undersides often tinted with red. The single, white flowers, produced in great big bunches, are scented like orange blossom. It is very tender, however, and needs a mild climate for successful

Rosa sinowilsonii

Rosa soulieana

cultivation. A climber of exceptional size, it will grow as tall as 6m (20ft) and spread about the same distance.

China; discovered 1904
Summer flowering ⏐ *Orange blossom fragrance*
HABIT Climber H/W 6m/6m (20ft/20ft) ⏐ ZONES 7–11

Rosa soulieana

SPECIES ⏐ WHITE

This tall-growing shrub has grey-green leaves and an elegant, dense-mounding habit that gives it a pleasingly mountain-like appearance. It can reach a height of 5m (16ft), easily covering a small structure or climbing into a tree. The small, single, white flowers are borne in clusters in summer, and the display of orange-red hips in the fall/autumn is truly a sight to behold. A striking characteristic of this rose is that the stamens in the centre of the flowers often look as though they have been carved from ivory.

Western China; discovered 1896
Summer flowering ⏐ *Light fragrance*
HABIT Bush H/W 5m/3m (16ft/10ft) ⏐ ZONES 5–10

Rosa stellata mirifica

Rosa stellata mirifica

SPECIES ⏐ MAUVE

'Sacramento Rose', 'The Gooseberry Rose', *R. mirifica*

The rare, strange and beautiful *R. stellata mirifica* resembles a gooseberry bush but is more prickly. It is often mistakenly identified as *R. stellata*, since these two Wild Roses are very similar. Both are native to the mountains of New Mexico and California, but *R. stellata* is temperamental in gardens and you are more likely to see the more vigorous *R. stellata mirifica*. Among other places, it grows around the rim of the Grand Canyon in Arizona. It makes a low shrub of about 1m (3ft) tall and wide, with bright green foliage and single, glossy-petalled flowers in bright mauve-pink. Spiky red hips usually follow in the fall/autumn.

California and New Mexico; discovered 1916
Summer flowering ⏐ *Light fragrance*
HABIT Bush H/W 1m/1m (3ft/3ft) ⏐ ZONES 4–10

Rosa sweginzowii

Rosa virginiana

Rosa webbiana

Rosa tomentosa

Rosa sweginzowii

SPECIES ı MEDIUM PINK

Sometimes called the 'pink *moyesii*', R. *sweginzowii* tends to suffer by comparison with its flamboyant, red-flowered relative, although with its greater height and pleasing shape it is, in fact, a better garden plant. Its single, clear pink flowers are very lovely; its flagon-shaped hips, which often ripen before the fall/autumn, equally fine. The foliage is mid-green. It makes a tall shrub 1.8–3m (6–10ft) high. That it was E. H. Wilson who introduced it from western China should be sufficient guarantee of its beauty. Do not overlook it.

China; discovered 1909
Summer flowering ı *Light fragrance*

HABIT Bush H/W 1.8–3m/2.5m (6–10ft/8ft) ı ZONES 3–10

Rosa tomentosa

SPECIES ı LIGHT PINK

R. *cuspidata*, R. *dimorpha*

Do not confuse this Wild Rose with its close relative R. *pomifera*, which you may know by the older name of R. *villosa*, one of its synonyms. The names *tomentosa* and *villosa* both mean 'downy' or 'fuzzy'. *Rosa tomentosa* grows the larger of the two, its foliage is less grey, and its single flowers are a brasher pink. Whereas R. *pomifera* makes a tall, bushy shrub, to 3m (10ft) tall, R. *tomentosa* is smaller, growing to 1.8–2.5m (6–8ft), and hardier. Sometimes it is difficult to distinguish it from R. *canina*. The downiness of the leaves that gives it its name is not always very obvious.

Asia Minor and Europe; discovered 1820
Summer flowering ı *Light fragrance*

HABIT Bush H/W 1.8–2.5m/1.8m (6–8ft/6ft) ı ZONES 4–10

Rosa virginiana

SPECIES ı MEDIUM PINK

'Virginia Rose', R. *humilis lucida*, R. *lucida*, R. *lucida alba*, R. *pennsylvanica*

This native of the eastern United States is one of the most beautiful of all flowering Wild Roses. A tall shrub that can reach a height of 1.8m (6ft), it is compact rather than spreading in habit and will form a thicket hedge if you grow it from cuttings on its own roots. The single, bright pink flowers appear late over a long season; the foliage turns a stunning rich, tawny gold in the fall/autumn; and the orange-red hips are first-rate. The young leaves are dark green and very glossy.

North America; discovered 1807
Summer flowering ı *Light fragrance*

HABIT Bush H/W 1.8m/1.2m (6ft/4ft) ı ZONES 3–11
🏵 Royal Horticultural Society Award of Garden Merit

Rosa webbiana

SPECIES ı MEDIUM PINK

'Tibetan Rose', R. *unguicularis*

The closely related R. *sertata*, also from the Himalayas, often impersonates the 'Tibetan Rose' in gardens, for these two shrubs are similar in beauty and grace. Both flower in spring, adorning arching, purplish green branches with sprays of single, pale pink flowers, and follow them up with decorative hips. Both grow to 1.8m (6ft) tall by 1.5m (5ft) wide. British rose breeder and writer Jack Harkness once described R. *webbiana* as 'the Fairy Queen of the wild roses for its sweetness and grace'. Elegant is the word for both species.

Himalayas and Turkey; discovered 1879
Spring flowering ı *Light fragrance*

HABIT Bush H/W 1.8m/1.5m (6ft/5ft) ı ZONES 4–11

Rosa wichurana and hips

Rosa wichurana

SPECIES ı WHITE

'Memorial Rose', 'Teriha-noibara' ('Shiny-leafed Field Briar'), *R. bracteata, R. luciae, R. luciae wichurana, R. luciaetaquetiana, R. mokanensis, R. taquetii*

This important species was discovered in Asia around 1860 by a German botanist, Dr Wichura. However, its potential to bequeath its rambling habit to its progeny went untapped for almost 40 years. A vigorous rambler that produces foliage in massive abundance, it can reach a height of 4.5–6m (15–20ft), making it ideal for climbing up a tree or a wall, or covering an archway. Small, single, white blooms are borne in clusters in spring, followed in the fall/autumn by small, dark red hips. The name 'Memorial Rose' comes from the fact that this rambler has often been planted in cemeteries, white being the color of remembrance. It has been much used in breeding programs to produce modern Miniatures that can grow on their own roots instead of on a budded plant. It has also been responsible for the development of a large number of modern climbers and ramblers (often called wichuran ramblers).

Asia; discovered c. 1860
Spring flowering ı *Moderate fragrance*
HABIT Rambler H/W 4.5–6m/6m (15–20ft/20ft) ı ZONES 3–11

Rosa willmottiae

SPECIES ı MAUVE

Ellen Willmott of Warley Place in Essex was the author of *The Genus Rosa,* published in 1914, and a legendary Edwardian English gardener. It is appropriate that the Chinese Wild Rose dedicated to her should be of a delicate, feminine beauty. This shrub grows considerably wider than tall, to 1.5m (5ft) high by 2.5m (8ft) wide, and has small, greyish green leaves. The thin stems bear clusters of single, lilac-pink flowers in summer, and there are small, pear-shaped hips in the fall/autumn.

China; discovered 1904
Summer flowering ı *Light fragrance*
HABIT Climber H/W 1.5m/2.5m (5ft/8ft) ı ZONES 3–11

Rosa willmottiae

Rosa woodsii

SPECIES ı MEDIUM PINK

'Mountain Rose', *R. deserta, R. fimbriatula, R. macounii, R. maximilianii, R. mohavensis, R. pyrifera, R. sandbergii, R. woodsii mohavensis*

Rosa woodsii, the matriarch of this clan, grows in the west of the United States but is not at all common in gardens, its offspring *R. woodsii fendleri* being more vigorous and garden-worthy. The latter was introduced from North America in 1888. A good plant for hedges, it makes a very bushy shrub that grows to 1.8m (6ft) tall, well clad with soft, greyish green leaves that show off the single, lilac-pink flowers crowded in clusters on short twigs in summer. The flowers of both species have a lilac scent. Both species also have bright red hips that are small but abundant enough to be decorative in the fall/autumn.

North America; discovered 1820
Summer flowering ı *Lilac fragrance*
HABIT Bush H/W 1.8m/1.2m (6ft/4ft) ı ZONES 3–11

Rosa woodsii fendleri

Rosa xanthina

SPECIES ı MEDIUM YELLOW

'Manchu Rose', *R. xanthinoides*

The true wild species *R. xanthina* (also identified as *R. xanthina spontanea)* is the single-petalled form shown in the photograph. It comes from China, and, as has often happened with imported Chinese plants, the name was mistakenly given to a double-flowered garden clone. One such clone, called 'Canary Bird' when it was introduced to Europe in 1907, was thought at the time to be the original wild form, but it now appears that it was a seedling of European garden origin. *Rosa xanthina* is a tallish shrub with mid-green leaves that can reach a height of 1.8m (6ft) and spread the same distance. In spring it is covered with scented, single, bright yellow flowers.

China and Korea; discovered 1906
Spring flowering ı *Light fragrance*
HABIT Climber H/W 1.8m/1.8m (6ft/6ft) ı ZONES 3–11

Rosa xanthina

old garden roses

old garden roses

Heritage

While the wealthy Greeks and Romans of the ancient world admired roses for their beauty and perfume, they made no attempt to hybridize new varieties. Apparently they were well satisfied with the serendipitous, and highly prized, results of natural pollination. It was not until the sixteenth and seventeenth centuries that breeders began to take a serious interest in roses. The Dutch in particular performed some outstanding pioneer work with *R. centifolia*, as evidenced by the frequent appearance of its many progeny in Dutch still-life flower paintings of that era. Such deliberate breeding, combined with natural pollination, produced over centuries the roses we know today as Old Garden Roses or (perhaps a better term) Heritage Roses. Their charm and beauty are at their peak when the blooms open wide, like 'a saucer or a goblet filled with petals', as Stirling Macoboy described them in the first edition of this book. They are further characterized by their intense fragrance and their harvest of red hips in the fall/ autumn and winter, providing a magnificent tapestry of color at a time when – particularly in northern hemisphere gardens – other flowers have finished.

Old Garden Roses are officially defined by the American Rose Society as those classes of roses that existed prior to 1867, the year the first Hybrid Tea, 'La France', was introduced. It should be understood that not every variety in these classes has to date prior to 1867 – the class itself must have existed before that pivotal date. Roses with the appropriate characteristics hybridized after 1867 still qualify as Old Garden Roses.

The Royal National Rose Society groups the Old Garden Roses according to whether they are climbing or non-climbing, although it must be said that the distinction is not always straightforward. Another interesting question is whether they are once flowering or repeat flowering. The leading group of summer-flowering Old Garden Roses are all cousins of the central European *R. gallica*, and might informally be called the Old French Roses; they include the Hybrid Gallica, Damask, Centifolia, Moss and Alba Roses. Most of the surviving cultivars of *R. gallica* were raised in France and are the roses particularly associated with the rather tragic Joséphine de Beauharnais, Napoleon's first empress. They are mostly twiggy shrubs with small, sharp prickles and matt, suede-textured leaves, and produce flowers similar in size to (and rarely larger than) the Floribunda Roses in threes and fives in summer. Alas, mildew often follows, but it does not seem to impair their vigor very much. Planting them in the company of later-flowering perennials will help mask any late-season dowdiness. The generally recognized groups are as follows.

Hybrid Gallica Roses

Once simply known as the French Roses, these are the neatest and most compact growers, their almost thornless branches rarely rising more than 1m (3ft) or so and displaying their abundant flowers well above the leaves. The colors are usually in rich tones from pink through to purple, with many cultivars going in for such bizarre stripes and blends that this group was nicknamed the 'Mad Gallicas' in the old days. Their fragrance is rarely less than intense. Winter-hardy and easy to grow, these roses can often be seen dominating the hedges along the byways and country lanes of Europe. The most famous member of this class is *R. gallica officinalis*, also known as the 'Apothecary's Rose', which was greatly valued for its medicinal properties and its rose oil.

Damask Roses

The Damask Roses are thought to have been brought to Europe from Damascus by the Crusaders in the twelfth and thirteenth centuries. They are very thorny, growing to about 1.5m (5ft) or so, and very lax in their habit. They come in soft tones of pink and white, and their fragrance is invariably strong and sweet. The legendary attar of roses is made from a Damask Rose grown in Bulgaria. A small sub-group, the Autumn Damasks, are sparingly repeat flowering.

Centifolia Roses

Centifolias are about the same size as the Damasks but are 'lax' to the point of floppiness. (A strategically placed stake or two will be useful.) These 'hundred-petalled' roses bear nodding blooms in soft colors and have a wonderfully rich scent. Called 'Cabbage Roses' for their globular form, the flowers are not very large, 10cm (4in) or so in diameter, and the smaller varieties would be more fittingly compared to a brussels sprout. The drooping leaves are rounded and a soft, pale green. They are also known as Provence Roses. Recent studies of their chromosomes indicate that they have a complex heritage involving *R. gallica*, *R. phoenicia*, *R. moschata*, *R. canina* and *R. damascena*. 'Crested Moss' and 'Fantin-Latour' are good examples of this group.

Moss and Climbing Moss Roses

These varieties originally arose as variants of the Centifolias, and the older varieties differ from them only in the resinous, perfumed 'moss' that grows on the outside of their buds. As an added bonus, pine-scented oleoresins are released when the moss is rubbed between the fingers. Later Mosses are derived from the Damasks as well, and some of them are sparingly repeat flowering. These

'Madame Hardy'

pp 44 -113

OLD GARDEN ROSES

Non-climbing
- *Alba* —
- *Bourbon*
- *Centifolia* —
- *China* —
- *Damask* —
- *Hybrid Bracteata*
- *Hybrid China*
- *Hybrid Eglanteria*
- *Hybrid Foetida*
- *Hybrid Gallica* —
- *Hybrid Perpetual*
- *Hybrid Setigera*
- *Miscellaneous Old Garden Roses*
- *Moss*
- *Portland*
- *Tea* —

Climbing
- *Ayrshire*
- *Bourbon*
- *Boursault*
- *Climbing Moss* —
- *Climbing Tea*
- *Hybrid Bracteata*
- *Hybrid China*
- *Hybrid Eglanteria*
- *Hybrid Foetida*
- *Hybrid Multiflora*
- *Hybrid Perpetual*
- *Hybrid Sempervirens*
- *Hybrid Setigera*
- *Hybrid Spinosissima*
- *Noisette*

plants are winter-hardy, usually growing to 1–1.8m (3–6ft) tall. The Victorians adored them, and they feature on many pieces of embroidery, in valentines, on teacups and the like. Mossy Miniature Roses have been raised, but in most of their characteristics they conform more closely to Miniatures than to the old Moss Roses. Climbing varieties include 'Cumberland Belle', 'Climbing Red Moss' and 'Wichmoss'.

Alba Roses

Not all Alba Roses are white, as their name implies; they also come in delicate shades of pink. Supporting the widely held belief that this group descends directly from *R. canina*, the stems and foliage are very similar to those of *R. canina* but more refined. The other partner in this marriage is believed to be either *R. damascena* or *R. gallica*. Whatever their exact origins, the dozen or so members of this class are all noted for their vigor and sweet fragrance. The tallest of the Old Garden Roses, they make densely twiggy bushes up to 2.5m (8ft) tall and need only light pruning, as the old wood will continue to flower for years. Their foliage is usually distinctly greyish in tone, and the leaflets are single-toothed, whereas those of most roses are double-toothed. Many regard them as the most refined and elegant of the Old Garden Roses. Typical members of this class are 'A Feuilles de Chanvre' and 'Königin von Dänemark'.

In both Old Garden Roses and Modern Roses, the habit of repeat flowering is a gift from the China and Tea Roses. These were Chinese garden roses of some antiquity that were introduced at the end of the eighteenth century to European gardens, where further cultivars were created from the original imports. Both are descended from the elusive *R. chinensis*, so it is not surprising that they are as alike as sisters.

China Roses

China Roses are natural hybrids of *R. chinensis*. There are a number of forms, both single and double, pink and red, that were derived naturally from the original, single-petalled *R. chinensis* when the wild species was cultivated in home gardens as well as casually along the roadside in China. Two members of this class that have been of pivotal importance in breeding Modern Roses are 'Slater's Crimson China' and 'Old Blush'.

Hybrid China Roses

This group of roses is derived from *R. chinensis* and a red form of *R. chinensis* once named *R. semperflorens* and better known as 'Slater's Crimson China'. The pink form of *R. chinensis* known as 'Old Blush', which was introduced to gardens in both the Netherlands and England in 1781, is credited with passing on the habit of repeat flowering possessed by most of our Modern Roses today. The plants are petite, 60cm–1m (2–3ft) tall, with stems that are often too weak to support the clusters of blooms. 'Hermosa' is an example. A few, such as 'Gruss an Teplitz', grow as tall as 1.5m (5ft). They are not hardy and need protection to survive winter climates. Repeat blooming and a spicy fragrance are their hallmark – and their legacy to Modern Roses.

Tea and Climbing Tea Roses

The Tea Roses are larger, more heavily wooded bushes, with broader, smooth leaves and large flowers, 12cm (4in) or more in diameter, that nod on weak flower stalks. While the exact origin of this class is steeped in botanical confusion, the forerunner was probably a cross between *R. gigantea* and *R. chinensis* with the highly regarded habit of repeat flowering. In 1810 the Fa Tee Nurseries of Canton, in China, sent such a cross, *R. indica odorata*, to Sir Abraham Hume in England – the variety was later given the name 'Hume's Blush Tea-scented China'. The second Tea Rose to arrive in Europe, *R. odorata ochroleuca*, was collected during an 1824 expedition to China by the Royal Horticultural Society.

Tea Roses are shapely in the modern style, the buds long and the petals reflexing, and are deliciously fragrant. Early sailors must have thought they smelled like tea, but any resemblance to the scent of tea escapes most people. They are said to show their *R. gigantea* ancestry in their long petals, generally in pale shades of pink, salmon and yellow or a blend of these colors. Unlike the Chinas, which usually darken as they age, the Teas fade in the sun. They are even more tender than the Chinas, growing best in the subtropical climates in which most Modern Roses sulk. In Britain and much of the United States they are greenhouse plants,

cosseted by the heirs of those Victorian rosarians who thought them the most beautiful and elegant roses in the world. The Climbing Teas are mostly sports from bush rose varieties, but a few are climbers from birth. They share the beauty and tenderness of their bush fellows, and most repeat their bloom very well. All Teas should be pruned very lightly.

Bourbon Roses

The Bourbon Roses are so named because the first plant was a seedling found in 1817 on the Île de Bourbon, in the Indian Ocean. Their fragrant blooms have the quartered form (the centre petals folded and packed into four distinct quarters) typical of European varieties and come in the same range of colors (no yellow). They are borne on bushes like tallish Chinas or shrubby Teas, the leaves smooth and the flowers sometimes nodding like Teas. The plants are generally thornless, ranging in size from 60cm–4.5m (2–15ft), and are repeat bloomers. In the bush rose category, 'Adam Messerich' and 'Boule de Neige' are typical examples. Of the climbing varieties, 'Blairii No. 2' and 'Zéphirine Drouhin' are well known today.

Portland Roses

These roses are descendants of a variety transported from France to England in the eighteenth century – as legend has it, by the Duchess of Portland. Much loved for its repeat-flowering habit, it was regarded as an important stud rose by French breeders and became the matriarch of a lineage of roses with similar properties. The plants grow to only 1.2m (4ft) tall, and in appearance are like repeat-flowering Gallicas, with smoother leaves that usually sit up close beneath the large, fragrant flowers, like ruffs.

Hybrid Perpetual Roses

This class blends all the various strains to make large bushes with large flowers, sometimes huge and cabbage-like and usually splendidly fragrant. These roses are further characterized by their repeat-blooming habit and their height, growing to 1.8m (6ft) tall. The name 'Perpetual' is a little optimistic, as many are very shy-flowering indeed in the fall/autumn. The French 'Hybrides Remontants' would meet modern truth-in-advertising laws better. Hybrid Perpetuals need more water and fertilizer than modern bush roses do, and come in a more limited color range: white, pink and crimson. The class was recognized around 1820, and the ancestry of this group is primarily based on Bourbons crossed with almost any other partner. Climbing varieties include 'Australian Beauty', 'Climbing Jules Margottin', 'Climbing Baronne Prévost', 'Climbing Frau Karl Druschki' and 'Paul's Lemon Pillar'.

Hybrid Spinosissima Roses

These climbers are more commonly referred to as Austrian Briars, Scotch Roses or Burnet Roses. They flower in late spring or early summer, and were popular in Scotland in the early years of the nineteenth century. Descendants of *R. pimpinellifolia*, they have a mostly upright growth habit – growing anywhere from 1–3.5m (3–12ft) tall – and more than their quota of thorns! The leaves

'Blairii No. 2'

and plum- and russet-toned foliage in the fall/autumn. The most popular members of this class are 'Golden Chersonese' and the medium yellow 'Helen Knight'.

Hybrid Eglanteria Roses

Often referred to as Sweet Briar (or Brier) Roses, these summer-flowering hybrids are similar to *R. canina* and are characterized by their perfumed foliage. Their spreading growth habit in the wild can be groomed to turn them into impenetrable hedges. Examples of this class are 'Lord Penzance' and 'Hebe's Lip', both of which form medium-sized bushes.

Noisette Roses

The Noisettes were first bred by John Champneys, a rice-grower from South Carolina, who crossed 'Old Blush' (a gift from a French friend and neighbor, Philippe Noisette) with the 'Musk Rose', *R. moschata*. In return, he gave some seeds to Philippe Noisette, who sent both seeds and plants to his brother Louis in Paris, who eventually named the class Noisette for his family. These summer-flowering climbers are often large and sprawling, growing to 6m (20ft) tall, with large clusters of pink or cream flowers appearing somewhat later in the spring than most Old Garden Roses do. Examples are 'Crépuscule' and 'Lamarque'.

Boursault Roses

These roses were originally raised in the early nineteenth century under the auspices of the celebrated French rosarian whose name they bear. They are supposed to be crosses of *R. pendulina* with the garden roses of the day, but some experts think it was *R. blanda*

that gave them their most important characteristics, their early bloom and their lack of thorns. Their scent is only mild, and none is repeat flowering. Few are grown today.

Ayrshire Roses

Ayrshire Roses are easily recognized by their habit of climbing tall and cascading elegantly over whatever thicket they choose to call home. These roses are reported to prefer a cold climate, but they have adapted well even to Californian climates. The founding member of the class was discovered in the backyard garden of a Mr Dalrymple by Mr J. Smith of Monksgrove Nurseries in Etcher, Scotland. As a boy growing up in the Scottish countryside, I can well remember its ubiquitous presence along the lanes to school. Two members of this class of summer-flowering ramblers are 'Bennett's Seedling' and 'Dundee Rambler'.

Hybrid Bracteata Roses

This class is derived from the Wild Rose *R. bracteata* (better known as the 'Macartney Rose'). These hybrids have a climbing habit or a tendency to sprawl in an angular fashion, and come complete with vicious thorns guaranteed to inflict multiple scratches upon – and indeed to draw blood from – the casual gardener. They tend to be tender and are prone to setbacks, but they will recover. The most notable member of the class is 'Mermaid'.

Hybrid Foetida Roses

Generally this group is dominated by medium-sized climbers, such as *R. foetida bicolor* (also called 'Austrian Copper'), and vigorous shrubs, such as 'Harison's Yellow' and 'Stanwell Perpetual'. Significantly, they possess the genetic trait that provides yellow pigmentation to Modern Roses.

Hybrid Multiflora Roses

This small group consists of vigorous climbers that spread anywhere from 1.8–9m (6–30ft), bearing flowers in distinctive corymbs or clusters. They are more upright than their close cousins, the Hybrid Wichuranas. An example is 'Seven Sisters'.

Hybrid Sempervirens Roses

Commonly known in Victorian times as 'evergreen roses' owing to their retention of green foliage even in winter, these hybrids are dense ramblers and scramblers, providing ideal decoration for an archway, a pergola or a wall. An example is 'Adélaide d'Orléans'.

Hybrid Setigera Roses

This group of hybrids is derived from the North American Wild Rose *R. setigera* ('Prairie Rose'). They are ramblers that can withstand severe winter climates. Two varieties popular in earlier times that have inherited their parent's characteristically healthy foliage are 'Baltimore Belle' and 'Long John Silver'.

'A Feuilles de Chanvre'

'A Feuilles de Chanvre'

ALBA ı LIGHT PINK

'Hemp-leaved Rose', *R. cannabina*

A very old Alba that at one time was thought to be extinct, the 'Hemp-leaved Rose' is fortunately still with us. It is a charming rose, with sprays of medium-sized, double, scented, white flowers and long, narrow, greyish leaves reminiscent of those of the marijuana plant. The plant is small for an Alba; a metre (3ft) or so is as tall as you will see it.

Braun, Germany, 1800
Parentage unknown
Summer flowering ı *Slight fragrance*
HABIT Bush H/W 1m/1m (3ft/3ft) ı ZONES 5–10

'Adélaïde d'Orléans'

'Agatha'

'Adam Messerich'

'Adam Messerich'

BOURBON ı MEDIUM RED

'Adam Messerich' is a late addition to the Bourbon group and could pass for a vigorous Floribunda with its upright, almost thornless branches and its clusters of medium-sized, semi-double, raspberry-pink flowers. The blooms are not over-stuffed with petals, and are richly fragrant. Some extra manure and water after the first flowering will be needed to ensure a generous follow-up, as this rose does not have quite as many repeat-flowering genes as do subsequent modern hybrids. The foliage is a glossy, leaden green. The parentage is something of a cocktail, mixed by Peter Lambert of Trier, in Germany.

Lambert, Germany, 1920
'Frau Oberhofgärtner Singer' × ('Louise Odier' seedling × 'Louis Phillipe')
Repeat flowering ı *Moderate fragrance*
HABIT Bush H/W 1.5m/1.2m (5ft/4ft) ı ZONES 5–11

'Adélaïde d'Orléans'

HYBRID SEMPERVIRENS ı WHITE

The flowers are very pretty, initially palest pink with deeper touches, turning to pure white after a few days, and they are scented. The clusters of semi-double blooms tend to nod from the branches, making this very dainty and rather restrained rambler a good choice for a pergola. The foliage is matt

'Agathe Incarnata'

'Alain Blanchard'

green and mildew-resistant, and persists virtually all year in a mild climate. The rose was raised in 1826 by M. Jacques, who named it in homage to Adélaïde, the daughter of his employer, the Duke of Orléans, who went on to become King Louis Phillipe of France.

Jacques, France, 1826
Probably *R. sempervirens* × unknown garden rose
Summer flowering ı *Moderate fragrance*

HABIT Rambler H/W 4.5m/3m (15ft/10ft) ı ZONES 5–11

🌼 Royal Horticultural Society Award of Garden Merit 1993

'Agatha'

HYBRID GALLICA ı LICHT PINK

'Agatha Francofurtana', *R. gallica agatha*

While formally classified as *R. gallica agatha,* this variety is better known worldwide as 'Agatha'. Rather taller than the Gallica norm, it has arching branches and somewhat greyish leaves. The double flowers are on the small side and not especially shapely, but they are an attractive pink with washes and tones of mauve and violet, and sweetly fragrant. Not much is known about this rose, which is thought,

like 'Empress Joséphine', to be related to *R. cinnamomea plena.*

Europe and Southwest Asia; introduced c. 1800
Parentage unknown
Summer flowering ı *Sweet fragrance*

HABIT Bush H/W 1.5m/1.2m (5ft/4ft) ı ZONES 5–11

'Agathe Incarnata'

HYBRID GALLICA ı MEDIUM PINK

The soft pink color is unusually clear and even in tone for a Gallica. The flowers, usually borne in small clusters, are beautifully quartered and richly perfumed. The bush is more or less of average Gallica height, 1.5m (5ft) or so, with downy foliage. The branches are very thorny, which leads some admirers of 'Agathe Incarnata' to see the influence of the Damask Rose in her breeding.

Europe; introduced 1800
Parentage unknown
Summer flowering ı *Moderate fragrance*

HABIT Bush H/W 1.5m/1.2m (5ft/4ft) ı ZONES 5–11

'Alain Blanchard'

HYBRID GALLICA ı MAUVE

Striped roses are not particularly uncommon, especially among the 'Mad Gallicas' (a nickname that some of the more bizarrely striped Gallica cultivars earned in the old days). Here is one that is *spotted*, in two shades of crimson! The whole combination takes on a purple cast as the semi-double flowers age, and is well set off by golden stamens. The effect is much more attractive and subtle than it sounds. The plant is compact and upright, with rather dull green foliage that is sometimes subject to mildew. It is said to have been raised by Jean-Pierre Vibert of Angers and introduced in 1839, but some suspect it may be older.

Vibert, France, 1839
Parentage unknown
Summer flowering ı *Moderate fragrance*

HABIT Bush H/W 1.2m/1.2m (4ft/4ft) ı ZONES 5–11

'Alika'

HYBRID GALLICA ı MEDIUM RED

'Gallica Grandiflora', 'Rose Pavot', *R. gallica
grandiflora*

For a Gallica, 'Alika' does have large flowers,
although at only 10cm (4in) or so they are
hardly enormous by modern standards. They
are, however, a clear, light crimson without
any purple, semi-double and softly scented.
The leaves are rough-textured and dull green.
This rose is notable for its extreme resistance
to cold, which is not surprising given that it
is thought to have originated in St Petersburg
(just when is not known). It has also been known
as 'Gallica Grandiflora', and appeared under
this name in the 1881 catalogue of Regal and
Kesselring of Finland. 'Alika' was brought to
the United States by Professor N. E. Hansen
of North Dakota in 1906 and introduced into
commerce there in 1930. Hansen used it in
his breeding program for hardy roses. Wilhelm Kordes has used it as a parent, giving

'American Beauty'

'Alika'

us, among other things, the remarkable
Shrub Rose 'Scarlet Fire'.

Russia, before 1881; introduced by Hansen, USA,
1906; introduced into commerce 1930
Parentage unknown
Summer flowering ı *Moderate fragrance*

HABIT Bush H/W 1.8m/1.5m (6ft/5ft) ı ZONES 3–10

'Alister Stella Gray'

NOISETTE ı LIGHT YELLOW

'Golden Rambler'

The double flowers are of Floribunda size and
open from perfect buds to old-style quarterings. They are a rich yellow, with a touch of
apricot in the centre and paler at the edges,
and deliciously fragrant. The plant is quite
shrubby, with distinctive zigzag shoots, but
is best trained as a climber. It usually takes
some time to get going, and does best in a
mild climate. The flowers come throughout
the season, in small clusters at first and then
in much larger ones, on the strong, late summer growth. Alister Stella Gray was presumably a relative of the raiser, Alexander Hill
Gray, of Bath.

Gray, England, UK, 1894
Parentage unknown
Repeat flowering ı *Moderate fragrance*

HABIT Bush H/W 4.5m/3m (15ft/10ft) ı ZONES 7–11

🏅 Royal Horticultural Society Award of Garden
Merit 1997

'Alister Stella Gray'

'Anna Olivier'

'Archduke Charles'

'Arethusa'

'American Beauty'

HYBRID PERPETUAL I DEEP PINK

'Madame Ferdinand Jamin'

In fact, 'Madame Ferdinand Jamin' is the original name, bestowed on this rose by Henri Lédéchaux in 1885. It was not until 10 years later that it was introduced to the United States as 'American Beauty'. It dominated the flower shops of the United States for half a century, and it has become the official flower of the District of Columbia. The flowers are large, double, fragrant and very full, with 50 petals, and deep pink to almost red in color. The foliage is dull green and susceptible to mildew. It is an awkward rose in the garden, being gawky in growth and not very free-blooming in the fall/autumn, unless conditions are ideal. Grow it for history's sake.

Lédéchaux, France, 1885
Parentage unknown
Repeat flowering I *Intense fragrance*
HABIT Bush H/W 1.2m/1.2m (4ft/4ft) I ZONES 5–10

'Anna Olivier'

TEA   PINK BLEND

From its introduction in 1872, by Claude Ducher of Lyon, until the advent of the more brilliantly toned salmon and yellow Tea Roses of the 1920s, 'Anna Olivier' was one of the most popular of garden roses. It is still as beautiful as ever, its large, double flowers delicately blending cream, buff and pale pink, its fragrance still pleasing, the plant still free-blooming and reliable. The leaves are olive-green. Of course, it has the usual Tea Rose inability to cope with severe cold, but it is one of the hardier Teas and is well worth a favored spot in the garden.

Ducher, France, 1872
Parentage unknown
Repeat flowering I *Light fragrance*
HABIT Bush H/W 1.2m/1.2m (4ft/4ft) I ZONES 7–11

'Archduke Charles'

CHINA I RED BLEND

This rose should have been photographed in a great bunch to show it properly, for no two flowers are quite alike. Basically, the flowers are pale pink, but this becomes overlaid with deeper pink and even crimson in the sun, the color intensifying as they age. They are of Floribunda size, sweetly fragrant, and

borne all season long on a compact, twiggy bush. The foliage is small and dark green. The Archduke Charles was the father of Emperor Franz Joseph, who ruled the Austro-Hungarian Empire for 68 years – the third-longest ruler in recorded European history.

Laffay, France, before 1837
Parentage unknown
Repeat flowering I *Sweet fragrance*
HABIT Bush H/W 1.2m/1m (4ft/3ft) I ZONES 6–11

'Arethusa'

HYBRID CHINA I YELLOW BLEND

The bush is on the large side for a China Rose, but with its slender stems and dark, shiny foliage, 'Arethusa' still retains much of the China Rose daintiness. Like most of its class, it is in flower throughout the season. The color of the flowers varies with the time of year; sometimes it is more sulphur-yellow, at others more apricot or pale pink (as in the photograph). The flowers are moderately full and are arranged in small sprays. The foliage is small and dark green. 'Arethusa' is a relatively new Hybrid China, having been introduced only in 1903. Arethusa was the goddess of fountains to the ancient Greeks, and as such, no doubt, a regular visitor to gardens.

Paul, England, UK, 1903
Parentage unknown
Repeat flowering I *Light fragrance*
HABIT Bush H/W 1m/1m (3ft/3ft) I ZONES 6–11

'Arrillaga'

HYBRID PERPETUAL I LIGHT PINK

The double, 50-petalled flowers are enormous, but they are saved from blowsy vulgarity by their perfect form and the tenderness of their soft pink color. And they are fragrant, too. The foliage is matt green. The plant is in scale with the blooms, growing tall and wide,

'Arrillaga'

so plant it at the back of the bed. It is a reliable fall/autumn performer, as good as most Hybrid Teas in this respect, but it is happiest in a mild climate. 'Arrillaga' is a rather late Hybrid Perpetual, having been introduced only in 1929.

Schoener, USA, 1929
(*R. centifolia* × 'Mrs John Laing') ×
'Frau Karl Druschki'
Repeat flowering ı *Moderate fragrance*

HABIT Bush H/W 1.5m/1.2m (5ft/4ft) ı ZONES 5–10

'Arthur de Sansal'

PORTLAND ı MAUVE

It is just the coincidence of alphabetical order, but 'Arthur de Sansal' does make a good introduction to the Portland Roses. It is like a Gallica in its double, quartered flowers, in its rich red and purple tonings, and in its fragrance, but it has the China Rose's ability to flower repeatedly throughout the season. It also displays the short stems characteristic of Chinas, so that the flowers seem to sit among the leaves, like camellias. Like most Portlands,

'Baron de Bonstetten'

'Arthur de Sansal'

the plant is bushy and compact, a desirable trait for modern gardens. The foliage is matt green and can be susceptible to mildew. If its claimed parentage is partially correct, 'Arthur de Sansal' should perhaps be classified as a Hybrid Perpetual. M. Cochet, who introduced it in 1855, claimed it as a hybrid of 'Géant des Batailles' ('Giant of Battles'), a Hybrid Perpetual.

Cochet, France, 1855
Possibly 'Géant des Batailles' × unknown
Repeat flowering ı *Moderate fragrance*

HABIT Bush H/W 1m/60cm (3ft/2ft) ı ZONES 6–11

'Baron de Bonstetten'

HYBRID PERPETUAL ı DARK RED

This rose is considered to be a classic and elegant representative of the Hybrid Perpetuals, bearing double, flat, velvety maroon blooms on strong stems. The stems are well equipped with thorns, which turn a very dark purple on ageing. The petal count is somewhere around 80, giving this variety substantial staying power as a cut flower. It cannot, however, survive hot climates, which will turn the petals to potpourri on the bush! It was named for a wealthy Swiss estate owner with a passion for roses.

Liabaud, France, 1871
'Général Jacqueminot' × 'Géant des Batailles'
Repeat flowering ı *Moderate fragrance*

HABIT Bush H/W 1.2m/1m (4ft/3ft) ı ZONES 5–10

'Baron de Wassenaer'

MOSS ı DEEP PINK

The buds are not conspicuously mossy, and the light crimson flowers, borne in clusters, are not very distinctive, but they are scented, and the plant is one of the strongest and most reliable of the Mosses. For this reason it is

popular with nurseries, appearing in most selections of Old Garden Roses, and it can make a pleasing display in the garden. The foliage is matt and mid-green. Eugène Verdier named the rose for the musician Baron de Wassenaer in 1854.

Verdier, France, 1854
Parentage unknown
Summer flowering ı *Light fragrance*

HABIT Bush H/W 2m/1.2m (7ft/4ft) ı ZONES 5–10

'Baron de Wassenaer'

'Baron Girod de l'Ain'

'Baronne Henriette de Snoy'

'Baron Girod de l'Ain'

HYBRID PERPETUAL | RED BLEND

'Royal Mondain'

'Baron Girod de l'Ain' is a most distinctive rose. Its medium-sized flowers are dark red with a fine piping of white around the petal edges, and strongly fragrant. It is a sport of the plain crimson 'Eugène Fürst' (also well worth a look) and was introduced by a French gentleman named Reverchon in 1897. The bush is tall and a little leggy (peg it down), and needs good soil to give as good a show of flowers in the fall/autumn as in summer. The foliage is dull green. The only rose that could be confused with it is 'Roger Lambelin', which is even more strikingly patterned but apt to be a sickly grower.

Reverchon, France, 1897
'Eugène Fürst' sport
Repeat flowering | *Strong fragrance*
HABIT Bush H/W 1.2m/1m (4ft/3ft) | ZONES 5–10

'Baronne Henriette de Snoy'

TEA | PINK BLEND

'Baroness Henrietta Snoy', 'Baroness Henriette Snoy'

It is surprising that this aristocratic beauty is not better known, for it is one of the most cold-tolerant of the Teas, and its sumptuous flowers, large and double, are strongly fragrant. They are usually a blend of pale pink and cream, but sometimes the 'Baroness' touches up her peaches-and-cream complexion with carmine, as though she were in a party mood. The plant is tall and inclined to be leggy, but that is a fault that gentle pruning will do much to correct. The foliage is glossy green.

Bernaix, France, 1897
'Gloire de Dijon' × 'Madame Lombard'
Repeat flowering | *Strong fragrance*
HABIT Bush H/W 1.5m/1m (5ft/3ft) | ZONES 7–11

'Baronne Prévost'

HYBRID PERPETUAL | MEDIUM PINK

Raised in 1842, 'Baronne Prévost' is one of the earliest Hybrid Perpetuals and remains one of the most popular, flowering freely all season. The double blooms have the perfect Old Garden Rose quartered form, and are rose-pink with shadings of lilac. They are of good size, too, and powerfully fragrant. The foliage is matt green. It is a great survivor; plants over a century old have been reported in South Africa, where it was much used for hedging in former times. (It is rather thorny.) Like all roses, it rewards the gardener's care. It was raised by M. Desprez of Yèbles, in France. It is unlikely that the Baronne Prévost here honored was connected with the rather disreputable eighteenth-century novelist the Abbé Prévost.

Desprez, France, 1842
Parentage unknown
Repeat flowering | *Strong fragrance*
HABIT Bush H/W 1.5m/1.2m (5ft/4ft) | ZONES 5–10
Royal Horticultural Society Award of Garden Merit 1993

'Baronne Prévost'

TOP LEFT 'Beauté Inconstante'
TOP RIGHT 'Belle Isis'
INSET 'Belle de Crécy'

'Beauté Inconstante'

TEA I ORANGE BLEND

'Beauté de Lyon'

It used to be a rosarian's *bon mot* not so very many years ago that this was one of the most beautiful of roses, provided you were not too fussy about advance knowledge of the color. Indeed, no two flowers are ever the same, although the flowers usually fall within the salmon-pink to cerise range. It can be pale and blushing or almost scarlet, but it is always fragrant. It makes an average Tea Rose bush, with glossy, dark green leaves and wiry stems. 'Beauté Inconstante' (and there's a subtly evocative French name for you!) was introduced by Joseph Pernet-Ducher in 1892.

Pernet-Ducher, France, 1892
Parentage unknown
Repeat flowering I *Moderate fragrance*

HABIT Bush H/W 1.5m/1m (5ft/3ft) I ZONES 5–10

'Belle de Crécy'

HYBRID GALLICA I MAUVE

The legend that this rose, which British writer Beverley Nichols once called 'the most feminine flower in the world', was named for Madame de Pompadour has, alas, been shown to be untrue; but that scarcely spoils the beauty of these blooms. Double and perfectly formed in the Old French style, they are sweetly fragrant and come in the most beautiful blends of pink, mauve and violet. 'Belle de Crécy' looks best in the garden if two or three bushes are planted in a tight clump, and needs the best of treatment. The rather small, rough leaves are dark green.

Hardy, France, before 1829
Parentage unknown
Summer flowering I *Moderate fragrance*

HABIT Bush H/W 1.2m/1m (4ft/3ft) I ZONES 4–11
🌹 Royal Horticultural Society Award of Garden Merit 1993

'Belle Isis'

HYBRID GALLICA I LIGHT PINK

In the early nineteenth century, there was a craze for all things Egyptian. One of the minor manifestations of this was the naming of this charming rose for the Egyptian goddess of love, wisdom and beauty. Some modern enthusiasts speculate that 'Belle Isis' is descended from *R. arvensis*, albeit very distantly. They cite the foliage, unusually bright green for a Gallica; the scent of the flowers, said to resemble myrrh; and especially the color of the flowers. This is pale salmon-pink, a shade unique among the Old French Roses. This is all rather academic; for most of us, 'Belle Isis' is a typical Gallica, its growth compact, its double flowers scented and shapely. It is an excellent garden rose. As seed parent to 'Constance Spry', introduced by David Austin in 1961, it was the progenitor of 'English Roses' in the late twentieth century, injecting its bloom form and repeat-flowering habit into their genealogy.

Parmentier, France, 1845
Parentage undisclosed
Summer flowering I *Strong fragrance*

HABIT Bush H/W 1.2m/1m (4ft/3ft) I ZONES 4–11

'Bengale Centfeuilles'

CHINA ı PINK BLEND

The name translates as the 'Hundred-petalled China', not to be confused with *R. centifolia* (the 'Hundred-petalled Rose')! The French name 'Bengale' for the China Roses comes from the fact that the first specimens to reach European gardens travelled via the Botanic Gardens in Calcutta. They are, in fact, of Chinese stock. This is one of the oldest of them, the reference books giving 1804 as the date of introduction, and it could well be a Chinese cultivar. It is a very pretty rose, its many-petalled blooms a blend of soft pinks, deeper in hot weather, paler in cool. It is dainty in growth and flowers for months. The foliage is a glossy green, plum-tinted when young.

Noisette, France, 1804
Parentage unknown
Repeat flowering ı *Moderate fragrance*

HABIT Bush H/W 2.5m/1.2m (8ft/4ft) ı ZONES 5–10

INSET 'Bengale Centfeuilles'
BELOW 'Bennett's Seedling'

'Bengale Cerise'

HYBRID CHINA ı MEDIUM RED

This rose is paler than most of the Crimson China Roses. The small flowers are cherry-red rather than crimson ('cerise' is French for 'cherry'), but otherwise it conforms to the class. The foliage is dark green, with plum tints when young. Like most Chinas, it does not like the cold. It was introduced in the mid-nineteenth century. It would be a nice choice to tuck in among larger-growing Old French Roses, providing flowers when the others have finished flowering.

Fellemberg, France, 1857
Parentage unknown
Repeat flowering ı *Light fragrance*

HABIT Bush H/W 1.2m/1m (4ft/3ft) ı ZONES 6–11

'Bennett's Seedling'

AYRSHIRE ı WHITE

'Thoresbyana'

Loosely double and sweetly musk-scented, the flowers are clear white and borne in small and large clusters in summer. The foliage is dark, and the rampant stems often show the purple tone that characterizes the Ayrshire Rambler Roses. No one knows how they got that name. It is thought that they may be derived from *R. arvensis* and that the first

'Bengale Cerise'

varieties may have originated in Ayrshire, Scotland. They have the characteristic of flowering well in shade and in cold climates. 'Bennett's Seedling' was raised in England in 1840 by a Mr Bennett, the gardener to Lord Manners at Thoresby, in Nottinghamshire.

Bennett, England, UK, 1840
Seedling of *R. arvensis*
Summer flowering ı *Light fragrance*

HABIT Rambler H/W 6m/3m (20ft/10ft) ı ZONES 4–10

'Blairii No. 2'

'Black Prince'

fragrant, and lovely in their blending of blush with richer pink. Its only fault is that it flowers very sparingly after its lavish first crop. Mr Blair did not reveal the parentage. By the way, 'No. 1' is still around. Most people do not think it as good as 'No. 2'.

Blair, England, UK, 1845
Possibly 'Parkes's Yellow' × unknown
Summer flowering ı *Strong fragrance*
HABIT Climber H/W 3.5m/1.8m (12ft/6ft) ı ZONES 5–11
🏵 Royal Horticultural Society Award of Garden Merit 1993

'Blanc de Vibert'

PORTLAND ı WHITE

'Blanche de Vibert'

The lemon-yellow blooms fade quickly to a milky white in strong sunlight, and are strongly fragrant. The flower form is cupped and double, the blooms borne on the strong stems characteristic of Hybrid Perpetuals. The light green foliage is disease-resistant, and suggestive of Gallica heritage. Although it is a smallish plant, it produces a substantial quantity of blooms through the year. However, wet weather can cause the flowers to ball and rot before opening, and the plant also dislikes poor soil. 'Blanc de Vibert' is an ideal variety for a small garden or to grow in a container on the patio or deck.

Vibert, France, 1847
Parentage unknown
Repeat flowering ı *Strong fragrance*
HABIT Bush H/W 1.2m/1m (4ft/3ft) ı ZONES 5–10

'Blairii No. 2'

HYBRID CHINA ı LIGHT PINK

Mr Blair's second seedling, which along with 'No. 1' came out in 1845, is being recognized as a most desirable climbing rose for an arch or a wall, its flowers being of good size,

'Blanc de Vibert'

'Black Prince'

HYBRID PERPETUAL ı DARK RED

The name refers to the color, a blackish crimson with a sheen like black velvet. In hot weather it is apt to be just crimson. 'Black Prince' grows well enough, although it is somewhat prone to mildew. Grow it for the sake of its gorgeous individual flowers (fragrant, of course) rather than its contribution to the garden. The foliage is dull green. Edward, known as the Black Prince, was the eldest son of Edward III and the much-admired victor at the Battle of Poitiers in 1356 (one of England's three great victories over France during the Hundred Years' War).

Paul, England, UK, 1866
Parentage unknown
Repeat flowering ı *Light fragrance*
HABIT Bush H/W 1.5m/1m (5ft/3ft) ı ZONES 5–10

'Blue Boy'

'Blush Damask'

'Blue Boy'

MOSS ı MAUVE

In 1958, Wilhelm Kordes announced two modern shrub roses, 'Black Boy' and 'Blue Boy'. 'Black Boy' seems to have dropped out (do not confuse it with the popular Alister Clark climber of the same name), but 'Blue Boy' is worth a second look, despite the fact that it flowers only in summer. It is a small shrub, but the flowers can be very striking and are fragrant. Double and fairly large, and shapely in the modern style, they blend rich crimsons and violets, which look very well against the greyish leaves.

Kordes, Germany, 1958
'Louis Grimmard' × 'Independence'
Summer flowering ı *Intense fragrance*
HABIT Bush H/W 1m/1m (3ft/3ft) ı ZONES 5–10

'Blush Boursault'

BOURSAULT ı PINK BLEND

'Calypso', 'Rose de l'Isle'

The now almost forgotten Boursault Roses take their name from an influential rosarian of Napoleon's time. It was said that his approval of a new variety guaranteed its popularity,

'Blush Boursault'

and he particularly liked this small group of thornless climbing roses. M. Boursault's original rose was red. The illustrated 'Blush Boursault' is a pale pink version. The very large, very double flowers are prettily blowsy, although not very fragrant, and they do not like wet weather, tending to ball, but they come very early in the season (one flowering only) and the plant later performs the unusual trick for a rose of giving a display of leaves in the fall/autumn. For the rest of the time, the foliage is dark green, and the plant is practically evergreen.

Probably France, 1848
Parentage unknown
Summer flowering ı *Slight fragrance*
HABIT Climber H/W 4.5m/3m (15ft/10ft) ı ZONES 5–11

'Blush Damask'

DAMASK ı LIGHT PINK

'Blush Damask' is the Old Garden Rose that is most likely to be encountered in forgotten gardens and old cemeteries in Australia and South Africa. Of ancient origin, it is a great survivor. Few roses are easier to grow, and in season the bushy plant is well covered with small clusters of small, double, rose-pink blooms. The color is a bit deep in tone to earn the name 'Blush' today, but it is much the same color as the China Rose called 'Old Blush', another great survivor. Sweetly fragrant, 'Blush Damask' has two faults: its blooming season is rather short (there is no repeat) and the spent flowers tend to cling to the bushes. Deadheading is called for.

Ancient origin
Parentage unknown
Summer flowering ı *Sweet fragrance*
HABIT Bush H/W 1.2m/1m (4ft/3ft) ı ZONES 5–10

'Blush Noisette'

'Blush Noisette'

NOISETTE ı WHITE

'Rosier de Phillipe Noisette', *R. × noisettiana*

Grow this rose for its history, certainly, but be prepared to be charmed by the pinkish white flowers, borne freely for most of the season on an almost thornless plant, and by the intensity of its fragrance. The foliage is mid-green and leathery. Raised at some time around 1817 in Charleston, South Carolina, by Phillipe Noisette, a French nurseryman resident there, 'Blush Noisette' is a seedling of 'Champneys' Pink Cluster', a rose that grew in the garden of John Champneys, a wealthy local rice grower. It attracted admiration as the first frost-hardy repeat-flowering climber, and has proved to be an important parent of other roses.

Noisette, USA, before 1817
Seedling of 'Champneys's Pink Cluster'
Repeat flowering ı *Intense fragrance*
HABIT Climber H/W 2m/1.2m (7ft/4ft) ı ZONES 5–11

'Blush Rambler'

the color a clear, deep pink, well set off by rather glossy foliage. Its lack of hardiness probably accounts for its lack of popularity. Those who garden in mild climates will not find this a drawback. Created by M. Eugene Hardy at the Luxembourg Gardens in Paris, it was introduced at some time before 1837.

Hardy, France, before 1837
Parentage unknown
Repeat flowering ı *Strong fragrance*

HABIT Bush H/W 1.2m/1m (4ft/3ft) ı ZONES 7–11

'Boule de Neige'

BOURBON ı WHITE

There are some lovers of Old Garden Roses who consider 'Boule de Neige' to be the most perfect white rose ever raised. Each of the double blooms is as regular and symmetrical as a camellia, its heart warmed with a hint of ivory; then the flowers reflex into perfect, snow-white globes, just like a snowball (which is what 'Boule de Neige' means). No snowball, however, ever smelt like this rose; it is very fragrant. The dark green foliage sets the flowers off perfectly, but you may need to watch out for black spot. Good cultivation will ensure a fine fall/autumn display.

Lacharme, France, 1867
'Blanche Lafitte' × 'Sappho'
Repeat flowering ı *Strong fragrance*

HABIT Bush H/W 1.2m/1m (4ft/3ft) ı ZONES 5–11

'Boule de Neige'

'Bon Silène'

'Bullata'

CENTIFOLIA ı MEDIUM PINK

'Lettuce-leafed Rose', 'Rose à Feuilles de Laitue', *R. × centifolia bullata*

Back in the days of the Empress Joséphine, gardeners treasured several forms of *R. centifolia* that are distinguished by their unusual leaves: the 'celery-leafed', the 'peach-leafed' and others. This one, the 'lettuce-leafed', is apparently the only survivor today. Its leaves really are quite splendid: very large, all

thornless. Vigorous in growth, this is a pretty cottage garden rose.

Cant, England, UK, 1903
'Crimson Rambler' × 'The Garland'
Summer flowering ı *Lemon fragrance*

HABIT Bush H/W 3.5m/3m (12ft/10ft) ı ZONES 5–11

'Blush Rambler'

HYBRID MULTIFLORA ı LIGHT PINK

The semi-double, pale pink flowers open wide to show their stamens, and come in large sprays. The flowers themselves are not large, but have a refreshing lemon fragrance. The foliage is light green and only faintly glossy, and the flexible branches are almost

'Bon Silène'

TEA ı DEEP PINK

Not one of the more famous Tea Roses, 'Bon Silène' is still desirable. If the double flowers are a little 'thin' when open, the buds are long and elegant, the fragrance strong, and

'Bullata'

puckered and quilted ('bullata' in botanese), and richly tinted with pink, like a Manoa (Mignonette) lettuce. They give the bush a luxuriant air that makes it more decorative in the garden than *R. centifolia*. The very double flowers come singly or in clusters, and with their full-petalled form, sweet pink color and delicious fragrance they are almost exactly the same as those of *R. centifolia*.

Cultivated in the 1500s
R. centifolia sport
Summer flowering ı *Intense fragrance*
HABIT Bush H/W 1.5m/1.2m (5ft/4ft) ı ZONES 4–10

'Cabbage Rose'

CENTIFOLIA ı MEDIUM PINK

'Provence Rose', 'Rose des Peintres', *R. centifolia*, *R. gallica centifolia*

This, the original of the Centifolia group, is the very double, full, soft pink rose with overlapping petals that features in so many antique flower paintings (hence the French

'Cabbage Rose'

name, which means 'Painters' Rose') and on old china and chintz. The artists do not exaggerate its beauty, but they could hardly convey the wonderful sweetness of its perfume! Indeed, it has for many years been grown in the south of France to supply the perfume industry there with attar of roses. In the garden, it makes a tallish, rather floppy bush that is all the better for a discreet stake or two, so that it does not collapse under the weight of its luxuriant flowers, which can come singly or in clusters. The broad leaves are a velvety mid-green. It flourishes best in good, rich soil.

Europe, before 1600
Parentage unknown
Summer flowering ı *Moderate fragrance*
HABIT Bush H/W 1.8m/1.5m (6ft/5ft) ı ZONES 5–11

'Camaieux'

HYBRID GALLICA ı MAUVE

This is one of the few Gallicas that needs cosseting, for it is a rather small, weak bush except in the best of conditions. It is worth a bit of trouble for the sake of its extraordinary flowers. Loosely double and very frgrant, they are striped in a constantly changing blend of tones – now pink and white, now violet and blush-pink, now almost pink and grey. The foliage is dull green and rough to the touch. The name, which most English speakers find unpronounceable, refers to a decorative technique known as 'camaieu'. The meaning varies somewhat between the different decorative arts, but a painting or decoration done in varying shades of the same color is described as 'en camaieu'. 'Camaieux' was introduced in 1830, and is thought to have come from Jean-Pierre Vibert.

Vibert(?) France, 1830
Parentage unknown
Spring flowering ı *Intense fragrance*
HABIT Bush H/W 1m/1m (3ft/3ft) ı ZONES 5–11

'Cardinal de Richelieu'

HYBRID GALLICA ı MAUVE

'Cardinal Richelieu', 'Rose Van Sian'

When the buds first show color, 'Cardinal de Richelieu' looks as though it will be pink, but as the fluffy pompons open, they take on the most wonderful shades of violet and grape-purple. The flowers are beautifully fragrant. The bush is tall for a Gallica (about head-high), with smooth, mid-green leaves that possibly betray non-Gallica blood. The name honors the great seventeenth-century French statesman, but the rose dates from some 200 years after his death; it was raised at some time before 1847.

Laffay, France, before 1847
Parentage unknown
Summer flowering ı *Light fragrance*
HABIT Bush H/W 1.2m/1m (4ft/3ft) ı ZONES 4–11
Royal Horticultural Society Award of Garden Merit 1993

'Catherine Mermet'

TEA ı LIGHT PINK

The perfect form, delicate color and sweet fragrance of 'Catherine Mermet' made it the darling of nineteenth-century florists, who grew it by the thousands in their greenhouses, although it was much less often seen

'Camaieux'

'Cardinal de Richelieu'

'Catherine Mermet'

in gardens. This rose is an exception to the nurseryman's rule that a good greenhouse rose will not do well in the garden, for 'Catherine Mermet' is, in fact, a first-rate garden rose, at least in sunny climates where rain does not spoil the blooms. The large, double blooms are a most beautiful shade of warm, light pink, fading as they age. The foliage is dark green. There is a sport, 'Bridesmaid', which is said to hold its color better. There is also a white sport, called 'The Bride'. It is the original, however, raised by Jean-Baptiste Guillot in 1869, that has remained the most popular.

Guillot, France, 1869
Parentage unknown
Repeat flowering ı *Moderate fragrance*
HABIT Bush H/W 1.5m/1.2m (5ft/4ft) ı ZONES 7–11
Royal Horticultural Society Award of Garden Merit 1993

'Celestial'

ALBA | LIGHT PINK

'Céleste'

'Bleu céleste' is the Sèvres factory's name for a turquoise glaze used on some of its porcelain. The rose 'Celestial' is neither turquoise nor blue, however! Celestial or 'heavenly', certainly, and if you decide that this is the most beautiful pink rose there is, you will find yourself in very good company. The flowers are not very double, but they are exquisitely formed at all stages of their life; and they are an especially delicate, clear shade of pink. Naturally, being an Alba Rose, they are sweetly fragrant, and the finely cut, greyish foliage sets them off to perfection. The bush is bushy and upright, usually about head-high.

Ancient origin
Parentage unknown
Summer flowering | *Moderate fragrance*
HABIT Bush H/W 1.8m/1.2m (6ft/4ft) | ZONES 5–10
🏵 City of Monza Prize for the Best Landscape Rose 1984

LEFT INSET 'Celestial'
RIGHT INSET 'Céline Forestier'
BELOW 'Céline'

'Céline'

BOURBON | MEDIUM PINK

This rose was photographed at the Roseraie de l'Haÿ. The blooms are large, double, full of petals and fragrant, and borne in large clusters; the color is a delightful soft, medium pink; and the smooth leaves are broad and handsome. Some American experts, however, are convinced that 'Céline' is, in fact, 'Fantin-Latour', having been popularized in the 1860s as an understock – hence its survival, unlabelled, in old gardens. Look at the pictures of both. What do you think?

Laffay, France, 1824
Parentage unknown
Summer flowering | *Light fragrance*
HABIT Bush H/W 1.5m/1.2m (5ft/4ft) | ZONES 5–11

'Céline Forestier'

NOISETTE | LIGHT YELLOW

Like most roses that derive their yellow color from the yellow Tea Roses, 'Céline Forestier' is happiest in climates with mild winters. In cold climates, it needs a sheltered

'Cels Multiflora'

wall. In any case, it is likely to be slow to get started. The double flowers are very fine – large, quartered in the old style, pale Tea Rose yellow with notes of peach, and intensely fragrant. They are borne in clusters right through the season on a plant that is happiest with minimal pruning. The foliage is mid-green.

Trouillard, France, 1842
Parentage unknown
Repeat flowering | *Intense fragrance*
HABIT Bush H/W 2.5m/1.2m (8ft/4ft) | ZONES 7–11
🏵 Royal Horticultural Society Award of Garden Merit 1993

'Cels Multiflora'

HYBRID MULTIFLORA | LIGHT PINK

You may not find this rose except in specialist collections, but it is worthy of note. The smallish flowers are a delicate blend of pale pink and apricot, and softly scented. It is a little taller and heavier in the leaf than most

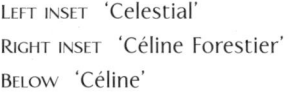

Chinas; for this reason, some authorities suspect that it has Tea Rose blood. Like most of the Teas, it is a little on the tender side. The foliage is a glossy green. Of unknown parentage, it was introduced in 1836 by M. F. Cels, a leading Paris nurseryman in Napoleon's time, and the well-known French breeder Hardy. The name 'Multiflora' refers to the characteristic of bearing many flowers on the same stem, a trait this rose inherited from the Species Rose *R. multiflora*.

Hardy/Cels, France, 1836
Parentage unknown
Repeat flowering | Light fragrance

HABIT Bush H/W 1.5m/1m (5ft/3ft) | ZONES 4–11

'Charles Lefèbvre'

'Celsiana'

'Champion of the World'

'Charles de Mills'

'Celsiana'

DAMASK | LIGHT PINK

If you are lucky enough to own a Georgian house, 'Celsiana' would be a lovely rose to adorn it, its crinkly, semi-double, loosely silky flowers being supremely elegant and intensely fragrant. Borne in clusters of 3–4, they open soft pink, quickly paling almost to white. The plant is a typical Damask, being on the tall side and having arching branches and smooth, soft, greyish green leaves. The leaves have a slight fragrance.

France, before 1732
Parentage unknown
Summer flowering | Intense fragrance

HABIT Bush H/W 1.5m/1.2m (5ft/4ft) | ZONES 5–10

'Champion of the World'

HYBRID PERPETUAL | MEDIUM PINK

'Mrs de Graw', 'Mrs DeGraw'

This is a pretty rose, with large, double, refined flowers in a pleasing shade of rose-pink suffused with lilac. It was raised in 1894 by a Mr Woodhouse, who was evidently quite proud of it. The blooms are fragrant, and are borne on and off through the rose season on a sprawling, vigorous bush that grows to the size of a Hybrid Tea, reaching a height of 1.8m (6ft) in moderate climates. The foliage is mid-green.

Woodhouse, England, UK, 1894
'Hermosa' × 'Magna Charta'
Repeat flowering | Moderate fragrance

HABIT Bush H/W 1.8m/1.2m (6ft/4ft) | ZONES 5–10

'Charles de Mills'

HYBRID GALLICA | MAUVE

'Bizarre Triomphante'

Instantly recognizable by its flat, symmetrical form (not quartered, but more like a carnation) and its gorgeous crimson, maroon and purple colors, this is one of the best garden roses among the old-timers. The foliage is parsley green. The almost thornless bush virtually smothers itself with many-petalled flowers every year, and does not need cosseting to make it do so. Its only fault is a lack of fragrance, although some refined souls find 'Charles de Mills' a bit vulgar in his exuberance. No one knows who the gentleman was, or even if this is the original name for the rose.

Hardy, France, before 1746
Parentage unknown
Summer flowering | No fragrance

HABIT Bush H/W 1.2m/1.2m (4ft/4ft) | ZONES 4–11

Royal Horticultural Society Award of Garden Merit 1993

'Charles Lefèbvre'

HYBRID PERPETUAL | DARK RED

'Marguerite Bressac', 'Paul Jamain'

At their best, the flowers of 'Charles Lefèbvre' can be magnificent. A rich, reddish crimson shaded purple, they are huge and shapely, with 70 petals, and fragrant, too. Hot weather is inclined to rob them of their depth of color. This rose was one of the most popular Hybrid Perpetuals for very many years, and is still worth a second look. The bush is upright, vigorous and relatively thornless, and usually gives a good fall/autumn display. The rather light green foliage may need to be protected from both mildew and rust.

Lacharme, France, 1861
'Général Jacqueminot' × 'Victor Verdier'
Repeat flowering ı *Moderate fragrance*

HABIT Bush H/W 1.2m/1m (4ft/3ft) ı ZONES 5–10

'Chevy Chase'

HYBRID MULTIFLORA ı DARK RED

Although this rose is classified as a Hybrid Multiflora, its seed parent was the Chinese *R. souliena,* known for its grey leaves. These, however, are not much in evidence in 'Chevy Chase', its leaves being a more conventional green. The dark crimson flowers are double, with 65 petals, and are borne in clusters of 10–20. The foliage is soft, light green and wrinkled, with good resistance to mildew. Although not repeat flowering, this is an outstanding rambler and deserves to be better known. It was introduced in 1939, rather late in the period when ramblers were fashionable, and well before the American actor Chevy Chase rose to prominence. He and the rose both take their name from a small town in Michigan.

Hansen, USA, 1939
R. soulieana × 'Eblouissant'
Summer flowering ı *Moderate fragrance*

HABIT Rambler H/W 4.5m/3m (15ft/10ft) ı ZONES 4–11

'Chevy Chase'

'Claire Jacquier'

'Claire Jacquier'

NOISETTE ı LIGHT YELLOW

'Mlle Claire Jacquier'

One of the most vigorous of repeat-flowering climbers, 'Claire Jacquier' is quite capable of smothering the facade of a two-storey house with its dark green leaves, which it will spangle with clusters of flowers in the spring and intermittently afterward. The peachy yellow of the buds has faded almost to cream by the time the blooms are fully open, so the effect is subtle rather than dazzling. The fragrance is lovely.

Bernaix, France, 1888
Possibly *R. multiflora* × Tea Rose
Repeat flowering ı *Moderate fragrance*

HABIT Climber H/W 4.5m/2.5m (15ft/8ft) ı ZONES 7–11

'Communis'

MOSS ı MEDIUM PINK

'Common Moss', 'Mousseux Ancien', 'Old Pink Moss', 'Pink Moss', *R. centifolia muscosa*

'Common' because it was once found in almost every cottage garden, the 'Common Moss' is a rose of uncommon beauty. Indeed, many people hold it to be the most beautiful of the Moss Roses. It is thought to be a sport of *R. centifolia* and is almost exactly like it in its habit and foliage, adding to the large, double, luminous pink flowers the charm of 'mossy' sepals, whose resinous scent adds a note of contrast to the sweet fragrance of the petals. If you stroke the buds gently, the 'moss' will leave its scent on your fingers. The foliage is a soft green.

France, before 1700
Probably *R. centifolia* sport
Summer flowering ı *Sweet fragrance*

HABIT Bush H/W 1.5m/1.5m (5ft/5ft) ı ZONES 5–10

'Communis'

'Complicata'

'Complicata'

HYBRID GALLICA ı PINK BLEND

'Ariana d'Algier'

One of the loveliest of single roses, 'Complicata' is hardly a typical Gallica, being a great, rambling bush that is quite capable of clambering 3m (10ft) into other shrubs and cascading over them with its large, shining pink flowers set amidst clear green leaves. It is rather deficient in scent, and rather too straggly to grow

'Comte de Chambord'

on its own. The best way to grow it is to plant it in a mixed shrubbery where it can grow as it pleases, with only mild discipline at pruning time. Pruning time in this case means after flowering, as the hips are nothing special. The name does not mean 'complex' but 'folded together' – there is a distinct pleat in each petal.

Parentage unknown
Summer flowering ⏐ *Very slight fragrance*
HABIT Bush H/W 3m/1.8m (10ft/6ft) ⏐ ZONES 5–11

'Comte de Chambord'

PORTLAND ⏐ PINK BLEND

Gracefully scrolled buds open to very double, 10cm (4in) wide flowers in the old French style – flat, sometimes quartered, and filled with petals. The blooms are rose-pink, usually tinged with lilac, and strongly, sweetly fragrant. The bush is about as tall as a modern bedding rose, with lettuce-green leaves, and flowers on and off throughout the season. 'Comte de Chambord' is the most popular of the Portland Roses, younger brothers to the Hybrid Perpetuals, and as charming an Old Garden Rose as any. Its name honors the sad and romantic grandson of Charles X, who refused the crown of France and died in exile.

Robert et Moreau, France, 1863
Parentage unknown
Repeat flowering ⏐ *Intense fragrance*
HABIT Bush H/W 1.2m/1m (4ft/3ft) ⏐ ZONES 5–11
❀ Royal Horticultural Society Award of Garden Merit 1993

'Comte de Nanteuil'

HYBRID GALLICA ⏐ MAUVE

'Boule de Nanteuil', 'Comte Boula de Nanteuil'

In its heyday, 'Comte de Nanteuil' was one of the most popular of roses. Just about every writer in the early days of Queen Victoria's reign recommended it enthusiastically. Then it fell into an obscurity from which it has only relatively recently been rescued. Rose-lovers can once again admire its large, double, perfectly quartered blooms, its rich yet soft colors – the flowers mauve-pink to crimson purple, their centre sometimes fiery crimson, set against olive-green, suede-textured leaves – and its sweet fragrance. The plant is compact and robust.

Roeser, France, c. 1834
Parentage unknown
Summer flowering ⏐ *Sweet fragrance*
HABIT Bush H/W 1.2m/1m (4ft/3ft) ⏐ ZONES 4–11

'Comtesse de Murinais'

MOSS ⏐ WHITE

Reaching a height of 1.8m (6ft), 'Comtesse de Murinais' is one of the tallest of the Moss Roses, with light green leaves and beautiful big, double flowers. Tinted with blush in the

'Comte de Nanteuil'

bud, they open soft pink, and pale to creamy white (as in the photograph). They are strongly perfumed. The 'moss' is lush and hard to the touch. This probably indicates that this rose has 'Quatre Saisons Blanc Mousseux' in its breeding, although it flowers only in the summer. It was raised by Jean-Pierre Vibert and introduced in 1843 – triumphantly, as it was the first white Moss Rose to be raised from seed, and thus completely new.

Vibert, France, 1843
Parentage unknown
Summer flowering ⏐ *Strong fragrance*
HABIT Bush H/W 1.8m/1.2m (6ft/4ft) ⏐ ZONES 5–10

'Comtesse du Cayla'

'Comtesse du Cayla'

HYBRID CHINA ⏐ ORANGE BLEND

The long buds open to loosely formed, semi-double, nodding flowers of flame shot with yellow, fading rapidly to shrimp-pink. They have a pleasing tea fragrance. The glossy foliage is intensely purpled when young, the dark tone lasting long enough to set off the flowers. The bush is the size of a small Floribunda. It is one of the hardiest of the Chinas, despite its evident Tea blood.

Guillot, France, 1902
Parentage unknown
Repeat flowering ⏐ *Moderate fragrance*
HABIT Bush H/W 1m/1m (3ft/3ft) ⏐ ZONES 6–11

'Coupe d'Hébé'

BOURBON ⏐ DEEP PINK

This is one of those lax roses that can be trained as a pillar, and most of its admirers find that it performs best that way. It can also be pegged down in the Victorian manner. Either way, the flowers will be sumptuous – large, very double and with a waxy texture, they are full

'Comtesse de Murinais'

'Crested Moss'

CENTIFOLIA ı MEDIUM PINK

'Chapeau de Napoléon', 'Crested Provence Rose', 'Cristata', *R. centifolia cristata, R. centifolia muscosa cristata*

Legend has it that the 'Crested Moss' was found growing in a crack in a convent wall in Switzerland in 1820 (a little after Napoleon's heyday), and the resemblance between the cockaded, mossy buds and the Emperor's tricorne hat is undeniable. Although this variety is clearly a Centifolia, the name reflects its somewhat mossy appearance, the moss being confined to the sepal edges. The globular, warm pink flowers are almost exactly like those of 'Communis' (also known as *R. centifolia muscosa* and 'Common Moss'), and just as fragrant. Similarly, the growth is rather floppy, and the broad, coarsely toothed foliage is a flat green. It is the unique and beautiful buds that give this rose its irresistible charm.

Vibert, France, 1826
Parentage unknown
Summer flowering ı *Strong fragrance*
HABIT Bush H/W 1.5m/1.2m (5ft/4ft) ı ZONES 5–11
✿ Royal Horticultural Society Award of Garden Merit 1993

'Coupe d'Hébé'

'Crépuscule'

NOISETTE ı APRICOT BLEND

Aptly named for the twilight, the flowers are a blend of burnished gold and salmon, the amount of pink varying with the time of year. Informal in shape, they are deliciously scented, and they are produced right through the season, particularly in a mild climate. The glossy, dark-leafed plant is virtually thornless, and can either be allowed to grow as a large, sprawling shrub or be trained as a moderately vigorous climber. 'Crépuscule' is probably more widely admired now than it was when introduced in 1904, when it would have seemed a little tame beside the new-fangled roses coming from M. Pernet-Ducher, such as 'Soleil d'Or' and 'Madame Eduard Herriot'.

Dubreuil, France, 1904
Parentage undisclosed
Repeat flowering ı *Light fragrance*
HABIT Climber H/W 3.5m/1.5m (12ft/5ft) ı ZONES 7–11

'Crépuscule'

of soft pink petals and fragrance. Alas, there is only one crop per year, with a very occasional flower in the fall/autumn. The foliage is glossy green. Hebe, the Greek goddess of youth, was the cupbearer to the gods.

Laffay, France, 1840
Bourbon hybrid × China hybrid
Summer flowering ı *Intense fragrance*
HABIT Pillar H/W 2m/1.5m (7ft/5ft) ı ZONES 5–11

'Crested Moss'

'D'Aguesseau'

HYBRID GALLICA ı MEDIUM RED

While this rose can be the most vivid red, occasionally shaded with purple, it is often just as it is here: a deep pink shaded with deeper tones in the centre. Either way it is an attractive variety, the double flowers large, shapely and fairly scented, the matt green foliage luxuriant, the habit erect and compact. Henri d'Aguesseau, Chancellor of France from 1717 to 1750, is best remembered for his reforms of French law in the early eighteenth century, but it is more likely that this rose was named for his grandson, the Marquis d'Aguesseau, who died in 1826, three years after the rose was introduced to gardeners, probably by Jean-Pierre Vibert.

Vibert(?), France, 1823
Parentage unknown
Summer flowering ׀ *Light fragrance*

HABIT Bush H/W 1.2m/1m (4ft/3ft) ׀ ZONES 4–11

'Deuil de Paul Fontaine'

MOSS ׀ MAUVE

'Paul de Fontaine'

This rose was described as 'very vigorous' when it was introduced in 1873. This is no longer true. It needs the best of care to do well, and never makes a big bush. But the flowers are extraordinary: large for an Old Garden Rose and cupped, they blend dark tones of crimson, purple and maroon, all overlaid with a blackish sheen. The buds are somewhat mossy. It forms a very prickly bush, and if you can make it happy, it will flower repeatedly. The name is well suited to the sombre colors, meaning 'Mourning for Paul Fontaine'.

Fontaine, France, 1873
Parentage unknown
Repeat flowering ׀ *Moderate fragrance*

HABIT Bush H/W 1.2m/1m (4ft/3ft) ׀ ZONES 5–10

'Devoniensis'

TEA ׀ WHITE

'Magnolia Rose'

This famous Old Garden Rose has a popular climbing counterpart. The original bush form is not overly vigorous, is well furnished with light green leaves (but few thorns), and comes into bloom early in the season. It is rarely without at least a few of its softly fragrant

'Deuil de Paul Fontaine'

blossoms, which blend cream and palest peach-pink. They are open-quartered in the old style, from long buds, and their scent is reminiscent of *Magnolia virginiana*. 'Devoniensis' is one of the first notable roses to have been raised by a man named Foster from Devon, who introduced it in 1838. The climbing sport, discovered in England by a Mr Pavitt, came out in 1858.

Foster, England, UK, 1838
Parentage uncertain, perhaps 'Elinthii' × yellow China
Repeat flowering ׀ *Moderate fragrance*

HABIT Bush H/W 1m/60cm (3ft/2ft) ׀ ZONES 7–11

'Duc de Guiche'

HYBRID GALLICA ׀ MAUVE

'Senat Romair'

Crimson verging on magenta and veined with purple, the large, double, intensely fragrant flowers of 'Duc de Guiche' are models of perfection in the Old Garden Rose style, their petals most beautifully reflexed and their centres quartered around a green heart. The foliage is dark green and rough. The plant is inclined to sprawl; careful pruning

'Devoniensis'

'Duc de Guiche'

and perhaps the assistance of a dahlia stake are needed. Nothing is known about the Duc de Guiche, but there is still a Duc de Guise, a scion of the royal house of Lorraine. Perhaps M. Prévost's catalogue suffered a misprint back in the early 1800s.

Prévost, France, 1835
Parentage unknown
Summer flowering ׀ *Intense fragrance*

HABIT Bush H/W 1.2m/1.2m (4ft/4ft) ׀ ZONES 5–11

'D'Aguesseau'

ABOVE LEFT 'Duchess of Portland'
ABOVE RIGHT 'Duchesse de Montebello'

'Duchesse d'Angoulême'

'Duchesse de Brabant'

Duchesse d'Angoulême, was the daughter of Louis XVI and Marie Antoinette. Having survived the Revolution, she remained a leading royalist during the Empire, dying a widow in exile in 1851. Jean-Pierre Vibert christened his rose in her honor in 1821.

Vibert, France, 1821
Probably Gallica × Centifolia hybrid
Summer flowering ı *Sweet fragrance*

HABIT Bush H/W 1.2m/1m (4ft/3ft) ı ZONES 5–11

'Duchesse de Brabant'

TEA ı LIGHT PINK

'Comtesse de Labarathe', 'Comtesse Ouwaroff', 'Countess Bertha', 'Shell'

In Australia, this is one of the best-selling roses of any type; and no wonder, for in that mild climate it is a very easy rose to grow. The plants are on the tall side, with neat, glossy, mid-green foliage, and bear their intensely fragrant, soft rosy pink flowers with great freedom. The buds can be so long that they look almost like tulips. Despite its royal name – the Duke of Brabant was a prince of Belgium – this was the favorite rose of President Theodore Roosevelt, who often wore it in his buttonhole. The raiser, Bernède, was not Belgian but French. This variety is known in Bermuda as 'Shell'.

Bernède, France, 1857
Parentage unknown
Repeat flowering ı *Intense fragrance*

HABIT Bush H/W 1m/1m (3ft/3ft) ı ZONES 7–11

'Duchess of Portland'

PORTLAND ı MEDIUM RED

'Duchesse de Portland', 'Portland Rose', 'Rosier de Portland', 'Scarlet Four Seasons', 'The Portland Rose', *R. paestana*

'Scarlet' is an exaggeration. The abundant flowers are bright carmine-red, opening to show golden stamens. They are fragrant, but not especially so. The neat, Gallica-like bush has bright green foliage and will, if treated generously, flower a second time in the fall/ autumn. This is a rose of great historic importance, being the prototype of Portland Roses, which resulted from the marriage of the Old French Roses and the China Rose. Of Italian origin, how it came to be associated with the Duchess of Portland, one of the eighteenth

century's great amateur botanists, remains a mystery.

Italy, c. 1790
'Autumn Damask' × 'Slater's Crimson China'
Repeat flowering ı *Light fragrance*

HABIT Bush H/W 1m/60cm (3ft/2ft) ı ZONES 6–11

'Duchesse d'Angoulême'

HYBRID GALLICA ı LIGHT PINK

'Agathe Marie Louise', 'Agathe Précieuse', 'Duc de Angoulême', 'Reine de Prusse', 'Wax Rose'

With its somewhat lax growth, smooth foliage and sprays of nodding flowers, this cannot be described as a typical Gallica. It is a very desirable one, though, with its blush-pink petals, so fine that they are almost transparent, and its delightful fragrance. It was a favorite for growing as a standard in the old days. For all its laxity, the plant is even in its growth, and it is only very lightly armed with thorns. Marie-Thérèse Charlotte,

'Duchesse de Montebello'

HYBRID GALLICA I LIGHT PINK

'Duchesse de Montebello' is a lovely member of the Gallica family, and displays the family characteristics of matt, greyish foliage and a summer-only flowering season. One of the taller Gallicas, it makes arching sprays of delightful, shapely, double blooms in a shade of pale pink that has a softness and clarity unusual among this group. A delightfully feminine rose, with a soft, feminine perfume.

Laffay, France, 1829
Parentage unknown
Summer flowering I *Moderate fragrance*

HABIT Bush H/W 1.2m/1m (4ft/3ft) I ZONES 5–11

'Dundee Rambler'

'Duke of Edinburgh'

'Duke of Edinburgh'

HYBRID PERPETUAL I DARK RED

This rose is a fairly typical red Hybrid Perpetual. The large, double flowers are dark and velvety at their best, but the plant needs the best of care to make them so. The flowers are scented, the bush erect but compact. The foliage is matt green and rather prone to mildew. Raised by William Paul and introduced in 1868, 'Duke of Edinburgh' was named for Alfred, Duke of Edinburgh, the son of Queen Victoria and the father of Queen Marie of Romania.

Paul, England, UK, 1868
'Général Jacqueminot' × seedling
Repeat flowering I *Moderate fragrance*

HABIT Bush H/W 1m/60cm (3ft/2ft) I ZONES 5–10

'Dundee Rambler'

AYRSHIRE I WHITE

This rose is not unlike 'Bennett's Seedling', but the compact, double, white flowers that come in large clusters have more petals, the plant habit is generally a little bushier, and it has a less intense fragrance. The foliage is

'Dupontii'

matt and mid-green. 'Dundee Rambler' was raised by a Mr Martin, who lived in a house called 'Rose Angle' in Dundee, Scotland, where he raised seedling roses. He named it for his home town.

Martin, Scotland, UK, c. 1850
Thought to be *R. arvensis* × Noisette
Spring flowering I *Light fragrance*

HABIT Rambler H/W 6m/3m (20ft/10ft) I ZONES 4–10

'Dupontii'

MISCELLANEOUS OGR I WHITE

R. freudiana, R. × *dupontii*

Believed to be a cross between *R. gallica* and *R. moschata*, 'Dupontii' is named for André Dupont, an early director of the Luxembourg Gardens in Paris, so it is a safe guess that it was raised there; exactly when is not known, but before 1817. It makes a head-high bush well filled with greyish leaves and – in summer only – covered with large, single flowers in palest, palest pink. When covered in its virginal blossoms 'Dupontii' is an enchanting sight, but the oldest wood needs regular thinning out or the bush will be all twigs and few flowers.

Europe, before 1817
Possibly *R. gallica* × *R. moschata*
Summer flowering I *Sweet fragrance*

HABIT Bush H/W 1.8m/1.2m (6ft/4ft) I ZONES 5–11

'Echo'

HYBRID MULTIFLORA I PINK BLEND

'Baby Tausendschön'

This small shrub bears medium-sized, semi-double blooms in blends of pink tones, from dark pink to almost white. The flowers are fragrant and are borne in large trusses on strong stems, but they need deadheading to stimulate the next bloom cycle. The plant is compact, with glossy, green leaves. 'Echo' would look handsome in a mass planting as a border, and also makes an attractive container specimen.

Lambert, Germany, 1914
'Tausendschön' sport
Repeat flowering I *Moderate fragrance*

HABIT Bush H/W 1.2m/1m (4ft/3ft) I ZONES 4–11

'Echo'

The Rose in China

THE NURSERY TRADE IS
NOT KNOWN FOR CREATING
MILLIONAIRES. NURSERYMEN MUST
MEASURE THEIR SATISFACTION MORE
IN TERMS OF THE DELIGHT THEIR PLANTS BRING, BOTH
TO THEM AND OTHERS, THAN IN TERMS OF THE PROFITS
TO BE MADE FROM THEM. CONSIDERED THUS, THE
LATE EIGHTEENTH-CENTURY PROPRIETORS OF
THE FA TEE NURSERIES IN CANTON (KWANGDON) MUST
RANK AS THE MOST SUCCESSFUL NURSERYMEN EVER, FOR
THEIR PLANTS NOT ONLY GAVE DELIGHT, THEY CREATED
A REVOLUTION IN GARDENING HALF A WORLD AWAY.

ABOVE The roses of the Fa Tee had two great disadvantages in the eyes of Western gardeners – only mild fragrance and intolerance of the cold. So it is not surprising that they soon fell from popularity in the face of their 'improved' descendants, surviving (in the West) only in the gardens of enthusiasts. This is Redouté's portrait of 'Slater's Crimson China', long thought lost but rediscovered in Bermuda in the 1950s.

BELOW In 1797, Lord Macartney headed a British diplomatic mission to the Chinese court. The Chinese disliked his manners, and Macartney returned to London not having won any of the trade concessions for which the British had hoped. He did not return empty-handed, however, as in his baggage were plants of R. bracteata, known ever since as the 'Macartney Rose'.

LEFT Rosa moyesii

European gardeners at this time were greatly captivated by the prodigious floral richness of China, which they had glimpsed in the decorations on Chinese screens, porcelains and furniture. There can scarcely have been a captain of a European ship landing in China – whether his prime objective was tea, silk or porcelain – who did not bring orders for new and exciting plants. The Qing government, however, restricted 'foreign devils' to the port of Canton, and that meant that their plant-hunting had to be confined to the local nursery.

The local nursery was the Fa Tee, or 'Flowery Land'. It must have been quite an establishment, for from it came chrysanthemums, deciduous magnolias, *Camellia reticulata*, tree peonies, Indian azaleas, the tiger lily and yet other plants without which we cannot imagine our gardens today.

Their selection of roses does not appear to have been very large: the yellow and white Banksian Roses; possibly some of the early pale garden forms of *R. multiflora*; the red and pink China Roses 'Slater's Crimson China' and 'Old Blush'; and the Tea-scented Roses 'Hume's Blush Tea-scented China' and 'Parks's Yellow'. These last four are perhaps the most important ancestral roses of all, for they bequeathed to our modern roses the true dark crimson color, relatively smooth and prickle-free stems, the long-budded flower shape we love so much today, and, above all, the priceless gift of repeat flowering.

The cradle of the rose

The modern rose is the descendant of the roses from the Fa Tee Nursery. Where the Fa Tee got its roses from, we do not know. It is certain that the China Roses are of high antiquity, for we see roses very like our 'Old Blush' painted on Chinese screens and porcelain many hundreds of years old. The English geneticist C. C. Hurst speculated that they were originally bred from *R. gigantea*, a great climber from the south of China, and the rare and elusive Wild Rose *R. chinensis*, only recently run to ground in China's remoter far western provinces. All we can say for certain is that they were the creation of unknown Chinese gardeners at some unknown time. When, after the Opium Wars, travel in the Chinese empire became easier, other garden roses found their way to the West. Late in the nineteenth century, such a wealth of rose species was discovered in the mountain provinces of western China that many botanists regard the area as the homeland and cradle of the rose. These include such beauties as *R. moyesii*, *R. hugonis*, *R. setipoda* and the Himalayan Musks.

The Chinese are much more relaxed about gardening than the Japanese, and flowers feature more prominently in their gardens than they do in the austere, religion-centred gardens of Japan, but even so, the rose has never played the leading role in China that it

ABOVE Fine porcelain is so identified with the Chinese that the English-speaking world called it simply 'china'. This is a rare and little-known type, a covered cup from a service made exclusively for the Qing dynasty Empress Dowager Ci Xi – and, it is said, designed by her.

LEFT This Chinese moon flask decorated in Famille rose colors with birds and flowers dates from the Yuan dynasty, c. 1280–1368.

ABOVE Chinese painters divide their subject matter into three broad categories: people, landscape, and flowers and birds. Workers in the decorative arts follow their lead. Pieces decorated with people and landscapes may look merely quaint to Western eyes (and, indeed, Chinese connoisseurs are apt to dismiss them as vulgar), but who can resist the charm of flowers and birds in a piece like this carved panel in gilded wood?

has in the West. Perhaps the superstition that its thorns might bring prickly discord into the house where roses are brought has played a part; perhaps their delicate beauty has seemed tame beside the 'king of flowers', the gorgeous tree peony, and the chrysanthemum; or was it that the China Roses possessed only relatively mild scent? European poets universally praise the rose as much for its fragrance as for its beauty and see it as an emblem of womanhood. Chinese painter-poets (male chauvinists to a man!) focused on plants like the pine and bamboo, seen as embodying masculine virtues.

Not that that stopped gardeners from cultivating and developing their roses. There is a book written during the Sung Dynasty that describes some 40 different roses. Europe at that time, during the twelfth and thirteenth centuries, could with difficulty have gathered only half a dozen.

In modern times, Chinese culture reflects a love of all flowers. The old Chinese roses are still grown, and works of art and decoration featuring them are still being made as beautifully as ever. *Rosa rugosa*, native to China as well as Japan, is still grown in fields to supply flowers to distil into wine (as intoxicating as it is delicious, it is said) and to flavor cakes and tea – rose-flavored China tea can sometimes be found in gourmet shops. And it seems the Chinese were well ahead of the West in discovering the benefits of giving children rose-hip syrup.

The gardeners of the Fa Tee would be amazed at the modern Western roses they would now see growing in the grounds of the Temple of Heaven in Beijing, yet how proud they would be to know that they were the offspring of their own roses, sent to foreign lands all those years ago and now returning to the land of their ancestors.

ABOVE The tradition of decorating furniture with flowers delicately rendered in lacquer has a 2000-year history. This cabinet is brand new, and the roses look like modern Hybrid Tea Roses, not ancient China Roses. At its feet, another of the Empress Dowager's pieces, this time a flowerpot.

'Edna Walling'

HYBRID MULTIFLORA | WHITE

Edna Walling was a leading designer of gardens and writer of gardening books in Australia during the 1940s and 1950s. It brings great prestige to own an Edna Walling garden today, and her many admirers will no doubt rush to plant the rose named in her honor. Originally available as a weeping standard (which would not have pleased Edna Walling), it is really a very pretty rambler; it is lavish with its clusters of white, and sometimes rose-pink (as in the photograph), blooms in spring but more sparing thereafter. The foliage is glossy and dark green.

Clark, Australia, 1940
Parentage unknown
Repeat flowering | *Light fragrance*

HABIT Rambler H/W 3m/1.8m (10ft/6ft) | ZONES 4–11

'Empress Joséphine'

'Empress Joséphine'

HYBRID GALLICA | MEDIUM PINK

'Francofurtana', 'Frankfurt Rose', 'Impératrice Josephine', 'Souvenir de l'Impératrice Joséphine', *R. turbinata, R. × francofurtana*

The flowers are large for an Old Garden Rose and loosely shaped, with wavy, papery petals that blend light and deep pink and have shadings and veinings of mauve and violet. There is not much fragrance, however. The bush is short and compact, and practically thornless, and has smooth, greyish leaves, all of which indicate hybrid ancestry. It is thought that the parents might have been *R. gallica* and *R. pendulina,* but no one knows who created

it or just when in the early nineteenth century it was given its name in honor of the most famous rosarian in history.

Early 1800s
Thought to be *R. gallica* × *R. pendulina*
Summer flowering | *Light fragrance*

HABIT Bush H/W 1.5m/1.2m (5ft/4ft) | ZONES 5–11

🏵 Royal Horticultural Society Award of Garden Merit 1993

'Enfant de France'

HYBRID PERPETUAL | LIGHT PINK

Although not well known, this a good rose, deserving of attention. The fully double flowers are large and usually quartered in form, and of a soft, silvery pink. They have a lovely silky, velvety texture and are heavily perfumed to boot. The foliage is generous, forming a highly complementary canopy of a greyish dark green. The plant is compact, with an upright growth habit reminiscent of the Portlands, and looks well growing alongside a variety of Portlands. It can tolerate poor soil conditions.

Lartay, France, 1860
Parentage unknown
Repeat flowering | *Intense fragrance*

HABIT Bush H/W 1m/60cm (3ft/2ft) | ZONES 5–11

'Eugénie Guinoisseau'

MOSS | MEDIUM RED

'Eugénie de Guinoisseau'

There is not much moss on the buds, but the flowers of this rose are very attractive – of good size for an Old Garden Rose, double, cupped in form, and a pleasant blend of mallow-pink fading to mauve. They are borne throughout the season on a tall, almost thornless bush. The foliage is dark and rather glossy. This is evidently a rose with much China Rose

'Eugénie Guinoisseau'

'Everest'

'Fantin-Latour'

blood. The scent is very good. Another repeat-flowering Moss Rose in mauve-pink, called 'Impératrice Eugénie', was introduced by Guillot in 1856. It should not be confused with this variety.

Guinoisseau, France, 1864
Parentage unknown
Repeat flowering | *Light fragrance*

HABIT Bush H/W 1.8m/1.2m (6ft/4ft) | ZONES 5–10

'Everest'

HYBRID PERPETUAL | WHITE

'Everest' is one of the last Hybrid Perpetuals, having been raised in 1927 by the great English amateur raiser Walter Easlea. It deserves more attention than it gets, for the flowers are large, high-centred, shapely and fragrant, although they are not really snowy but tinted with lemon toward the centre. The foliage is light green and the bush is compact, more like a Hybrid Tea than a typical sprawling Hybrid Perpetual. Indeed, this rose's only fault is its dislike of wet weather.

Easlea, England, UK, 1927
'Candeur Lyonnaise' × 'Madame Caristie Martel'
Repeat flowering ⏐ *Light fragrance*

HABIT Bush H/W 1m/1m (3ft/3ft) ⏐ ZONES 5–10

'Fantin-Latour'

CENTIFOLIA ⏐ LIGHT PINK

This is one of the all-time great roses! The flat, double blooms are perfectly formed in the Old Garden Rose fashion, have an intense fragrance and are a delightful shade of soft pink. With good soil it will make a head-high bush, whose branches will arch under the weight of the abundant blooms it bears over a long summer season. The foliage is broad, smooth and dark green. Little is known about its history. It was discovered in a garden, labelled simply 'Best Garden Rose', by the English rosarian Graham Stuart Thomas, who points out that it is not a pure-bred Centifolia, despite its official classification. He named it for Henri Fantin-Latour, the great nineteenth-century French painter of flowers.

Parentage unknown
Summer flowering ⏐ *Intense fragrance*

HABIT Bush H/W 1.5m/1.2m (5ft/4ft) ⏐ ZONES 4–10

ABOVE 'Enfant de France'
RIGHT 'Edna Walling'

'Félicité Perpétue'

HYBRID SEMPERVIRENS · WHITE

Do not be confused by the name: 'Félicité Perpétue' is not perpetual flowering. It seems that the raiser, M. Jacques, gardener to the Duke of Orléans, wanted to honor the Virgin Martyrs Felicity and Perpetua. They may consider themselves honored indeed, for this rose, thought to be a descendant of *R. sempervirens,* has been regarded as one of the best of all ramblers ever since it was introduced, in 1827. It is practically evergreen, although its dark leaves, plum-colored in youth, quite vanish under the clusters of perfect rosettes borne late in the rose season. The very double flowers are quite large and flat, and softly fragrant. In 1879 this variety produced a sport, 'Little White Pet', a small Floribunda bush that is indeed perpetually in bloom.

Jacques, France, 1827
Thought to be *R. sempervirens* × Noisette
Summer flowering · *Light fragrance*
HABIT Rambler H/W 4.5m/3m (15ft/10ft) · ZONES 5–11
❀ Royal Horticultural Society Award of Garden Merit 1993

'Félicité Parmentier'

ALBA · LIGHT PINK

Its compact habit, its handsome, grey-green foliage, and the shapeliness of its double, sweetly scented flowers, their petals exquisitely

'Félicité Perpétue'

layered and folded, make 'Félicité Parmentier' one of the most desirable of the Old Garden Roses. It is usually described as pale pink, but in a hot climate the blooms fade to blush-white almost as soon as they open. The bush grows to no more than 1m (3ft) tall. The Parmentiers were a family prominent in French horticulture at the time this rose was introduced, but the details of its raiser and parents are forgotten.

Before 1828
Parentage unknown
Summer flowering · *Sweet fragrance*
HABIT Bush H/W 1.2m/1m (4ft/3ft) · ZONES 5–10
❀ Royal Horticultural Society Award of Garden Merit 1993

'Ferdinand Pichard'

HYBRID PERPETUAL · RED BLEND

It is a matter of opinion whether this exuberantly striped rose belongs with the Hybrid Perpetuals (the official classification) or with the Bourbons. This is not a typical sprawling, cabbage-like Hybrid Perpetual, but a daintier, compact bush with light green leaves and cupped and fragrant double blooms in pale pink with yellow stamens, their petals boldly striped with crimson and purple. It flowers repeatedly throughout the season. It was raised in 1921 by a French gentleman called Tanne, who perhaps felt that at that late date a Bourbon would be too old-fashioned to sell. Do not overlook it.

Tanne, France, 1921
Parentage unknown
Repeat flowering · *Moderate fragrance*
HABIT Bush H/W 1.5m/1.2m (5ft/4ft) · ZONES 5–10
❀ Royal Horticultural Society Award of Garden Merit 1993

'Fornarina'

MOSS · MEDIUM PINK

Individually, the flowers of 'Fornarina' are not particularly exciting, just two-tone pink and fragrant, but they are borne very freely on a compact bush with dark green leaves,

'Fornarina'

so this variety can make quite a show during the growing season. In 1862, when it was raised, European art was more influenced by the style of Raphael than ever before (or since), so it was timely to name a rose after Raphael's mistress, the celebrated beauty nicknamed 'La Fornarina', 'The Baker's Daughter'.

Moreau et Robert, France, 1862
Parentage unknown
Repeat flowering · *Moderate fragrance*
HABIT Bush H/W 1.2m/1m (4ft/3ft) · ZONES 5–11

'Francis E. Lester'

HYBRID MUSK · WHITE

This is an outstanding rose, capable of making a wide, lax shrub or clambering to some 4.5m (15ft) over a support, which it will smother in midsummer with its richly perfumed flowers. These are single, shapely and white flushed with pale pink. The young foliage is maroon, maturing to a glossy, dark green.

Lester Rose Gardens, USA, 1946
'Kathleen' × unnamed variety
Summer flowering · *Moderate fragrance*
HABIT Rambler H/W 4.5m/3m (15ft/10ft) · ZONES 4–9

'Frau Karl Druschki'

HYBRID PERPETUAL · WHITE

'F. K. Druschkii', 'Reine des Neiges', 'Schneekönigin', 'Snow Queen', 'White American Beauty'

On its introduction by Peter Lambert in 1901, 'Frau Karl Druschki' was hailed as the finest white rose yet. In cooler climates, the centre of the large, double, 35-petalled blooms can exhibit an attractive blush-pink tone. More than 100 years later, many people would still award it this title, citing the statuesque beauty of the huge, high-centred blooms and the freedom with which they are borne on a dark-foliaged, easy-to-grow bush. They forgive its lack of

BOTTOM LEFT 'Félicité Parmentier'
BOTTOM RIGHT 'Ferdinand Pichard'

'Francis E. Lester'

'Frau Karl Druschki'

scent. Frau Karl Druschki was the wife of the President of the German Rose Society at that time.

Lambert, Germany, 1901
'Merveille de Lyon' × 'Madame Caroline Testout'
Repeat flowering ı *No fragrance*

HABIT Bush H/W 1.5m/1m (5ft/3ft) ı ZONES 5–10

'Frühlingsgold'

HYBRID SPINOSISSIMA ı MEDIUM YELLOW

'Spring Gold'

The almost single, soft yellow flowers of 'Frühlingsgold' are seen everywhere in Germany – in gardens, in parks and even in those odd little patches of earth that turn up in city centres. This is a tribute to the beauty of this 1937 Kordes creation; few late spring shrubs are more beautiful or fragrant. It is also a tribute to its toughness and ability to flourish with minimal care. It forms an arching shrub about 2m (7ft) tall that is elegant despite the spininess of its branches. After the spring flowering, there will be further blooms if the season is kind. The light green foliage is large, soft and wrinkled.

Kordes, Germany, 1937
'Joanna Hill' × R. spinosissima hispida
Spring flowering ı *Intense fragrance*

HABIT Bush H/W 2m/1.5m (7ft/5ft) ı ZONES 5–11

Royal Horticultural Society Award of Garden Merit 1993

'Frühlingsgold'

'Frühlingsmorgen'

HYBRID SPINOSISSIMA ı PINK BLEND

'Spring Morning'

The elegant habit of 'Frühlingsgold' is attenuated into gawkiness in 'Frühlingsmorgen'; you really need to plant a few together in a clump. Then the branches will interlace and will bear, among their dark, bluish green foliage, clusters of some of the loveliest single roses of all, their pink melting to primrose around the maroon stamens. They have an odd, medicine-chest kind of scent. Although this 1942 Kordes creation is usually credited with being repeat flowering, do not expect more than a very few fall/autumn flowers. There will be large, red hips, though.

Kordes, Germany, 1942
('E. G. Hill' × 'Cathrine Kordes') ×
R. spinosissima altaica
Spring flowering ı *Moderate fragrance*

HABIT Bush H/W 1.8m/1.2m (6ft/4ft) ı ZONES 5–11

'Frühlingsmorgen'

'Frühlingszauber'

HYBRID SPINOSISSIMA ı MEDIUM PINK

'Spring Magic'

This 1942 Kordes creation comes from the same cross as 'Frühlingsmorgen' but has never achieved the popularity of its sister. It is not as good a plant, being very spindly and leggy, and the semi-double flowers lack the elegance of the single flowers of 'Frühlingsmorgen'. Nonetheless, they are bright and cheerful in cerise-pink and yellow, and make a splash of color in spring, with a few dark red hips to follow later. The foliage is dark green.

Kordes, Germany, 1942
('E. G. Hill' × 'Cathrine Korces') ×
R. spinosissima altaica
Spring flowering ı *Light fragrance*

HABIT Bush H/W 2m/1.5m (7ft/5ft) ı ZONES 5–11

'Général Jacqueminot'

HYBRID PERPETUAL ı RED BLEND

'Gén. Jacqueminot', 'General Jack', 'Jack Rose', 'La Brillante', 'Mrs Cleveland', 'Richard Smith', 'The Jack Rose', 'Triomphe d'Amiens'

'Général Jacqueminot' is one of the all-time great studs of the rose world: just about every red rose we have, and many of the other red blends, can be traced back to it. It would be interesting to know if M. Jacqueminot himself,

'Frühlingszauber'

a veteran of Napoleon's wars and an old man by the time his rose came out in 1853, had so large a progeny. 'General Jack' is still worth growing. It makes a tall, slightly leggy bush, flowering freely in spring and repeating well if it is fed and watered, but watch out for mildew. Opening from scarlet-crimson buds, the double, 27-petalled flowers are dark red with a whitish reverse, and borne on long, strong stems. The foliage is a rich, glossy mid-green.

Roussel, France, 1853
Probably a seedling of 'Gloire des Rosomanes'
Repeat flowering | *Intense fragrance*

HABIT Bush H/W 1.5m/1.2m (5ft/4ft) | ZONES 5–10

'Général Jacqueminot'

'Georg Arends'

'Général Schablikine'

TEA | ORANGE PINK

'Général Schablikine' has always enjoyed a reputation for being a reliable Tea for cool climates. It is certainly a vigorous, free-flowering rose, but even in its heyday (it came out in 1878) it was looked down on by the flower-show fanatics for its quartered form, which disqualifies it from the show bench. The coral-red blooms are borne in abundance on stronger stems than are usual among the Teas. It is not very fragrant. The foliage is a glossy, dark green. The somewhat mysterious General Schablikine was presumably a hero of the Crimean War and had achieved elder statesman status by the time Gilbert Nabonnand named his rose.

Nabonnand, France, 1878
Parentage unknown
Repeat flowering | *Slight fragrance*

HABIT Bush H/W 1m/60cm (3ft/2ft) | ZONES 7–11

'Georg Arends'

HYBRID PERPETUAL | MEDIUM PINK

'Fortuné Besson'

A leading catalogue once suggested that if you bought this rose you should rename it after the prettiest lady of your acquaintance. One must protest: firstly, there is enough confusion from renaming already, and secondly, why not name a rose for a man? Especially one of the leading German nurserymen of his day. 'Georg Arends' is one of the loveliest of pink roses, blending the qualities of two famous parents. The bush is tall and sturdy, the double, 25-petalled flowers large, shapely, delicately colored and fragrant. The foliage is leathery and mid-green.

Hinner, Germany, 1910
'Frau Karl Druschki' × 'La France'
Repeat flowering | *Intense fragrance*

HABIT Bush H/W 1.5m/1.2m (5ft/4ft) | ZONES 5–10

'Georges Vibert'

HYBRID GALLICA | RED BLEND

The ruffled flowers are of purplish red and very prettily striped or streaked in white. The double blooms are large and flat, and fragrant, too. The bush is compact and upright, with the typical Gallica leaves but perhaps more thorns than is usual for the group. Georges Vibert was presumably a member of the family of Jean-Pierre Vibert, the famous

'Général Schablikine'

rose-breeder of Angers. It was very gracious of M. Robert, as a rival, to dedicate this rose to him – but perhaps the two families were connected by marriage. The year was 1853.

Robert, France, 1853
Parentage unknown
Spring flowering | *Moderate fragrance*

HABIT Bush H/W 1m/1m (3ft/3ft) | ZONES 5–11

'Georgetown Noisette'

'Georgetown Noisette'

NOISETTE | WHITE

Now in the collection of the Huntington Botanical Garden in San Marino, California, this rose was apparently found in Georgetown, in the District of Columbia, and can be characterized as a 'found Noisette' awaiting proper identification some day. The ruffled flowers are fragrant and very pretty, sometimes peachy-toned but more often big, blowsy blooms of pure white. The foliage is a glossy green. Like most of its class, it is a climber, although rather a modest one. Whatever its original name may be, why not adopt 'Georgetown Noisette' officially?

Parentage unknown
Repeat flowering | *Moderate fragrance*

HABIT Climber H/W 4.5m/3m (15ft/10ft) | ZONES 7–11

'Ghislaine de Féligonde'

HYBRID MULTIFLORA | LIGHT YELLOW

Pronounce the lady's name as 'Elaine de Féligonde' and you have got over the main obstacle to the revival of this rose – its awkward Flemish name. It is rarely seen these days, but it is one of the most charming of ramblers, bearing clusters of 10–20 flowers, with the added bonus that it sometimes bears a second crop. The fat little buds are quite a strong yellow, but they open to blooms of the palest cream with pink tints. The foliage is a glossy green and resistant to mildew. It was raised by the

French firm of E. Turbat et Cie and introduced in 1916. 'Ghislaine de Féligonde' is of fairly restrained vigor.

Turbat, France, 1916
'Goldfinch' × unknown
Repeat flowering ׀ *Slight fragrance*

HABIT Rambler H/W 2.5m/2.5m (8ft/8ft) ׀ ZONES 4–11

'Gloire de Dijon'

CLIMBING TEA ׀ ORANGE PINK

'Old Glory'

In its Victorian heyday, 'Gloire de Dijon' was regarded as the very best of all climbing roses, growing with abandon even in light shade. Alas, its vigor has declined, and it can sometimes be difficult to establish now. Give it the very best of everything, for the large, double flowers are marvellous – great quartered cabbages in rich buff-pink shaded orange toward the centre, and richly fragrant. They are borne throughout the season, and with their strong stems make good cut flowers. The foliage is broad, semi-glossy and mid-green. This rose was made famous by the writings of the Reverend Dean Reynolds Hole, the first President of the (now Royal) National Rose Society, who nominated it as his all-time favorite rose.

Jacotot, France, 1853
Thought to be unknown Tea Rose ×
'Souvenir de la Malmaison'
Repeat flowering ׀ *Moderate fragrance*

HABIT Climber H/W 3.5m/2.5m (12ft/8ft) ׀ ZONES 5–11

🏵 World Federation of Rose Societies Old Rose Hall of Fame 1988, Royal Horticultural Society Award of Garden Merit 1993

'Gloire de Guilan'

DAMASK ׀ LIGHT PINK

The formal date of introduction is 1949, but this is, in fact, an ancient rose, brought from what was then Persia (present-day Iran) by English garden writer Nancy Lindsay, who tells us that it was used in Persia to make attar of roses. There is no reason to doubt this, for its flat, very double, quartered, clear pink flowers are richly fragrant. They are borne in profusion amidst foliage that Lindsay aptly describes as 'mint-green'. 'Gloire de Guilan' is rather sprawling in habit.

Persia, ancient origin; introduced by Lindsay, England, UK, 1949
Parentage unknown
Summer flowering ׀ *Intense fragrance*

HABIT Bush H/W 1.8m/1.2m (6ft/4ft) ׀ ZONES 5–10

TOP 'Georges Vibert'
LEFT INSET 'Gloire de Guilan'
MIDDLE INSET 'Ghislaine de Féligonde'
RIGHT INSET 'Gloire de Dijon'

'Gloire des Mousseux'

MOSS | MEDIUM PINK

'Madame Alboni'

The 'Glory of the Mosses' in truth! 'Gloire
des Mousseux' has the largest flowers among
the mosses – as large as those of many of the
Hybrid Teas. Borne in clusters, they open
from beautifully mossed buds to double,
clear pink flowers, fading a little but holding
their rich fragrance. The bush is erect, tallish
and well clad with pale green leaves.

Robert, France, 1852
Parentage unknown
Summer flowering | *Intense fragrance*

HABIT Bush H/W 1.2m/1m (4ft/3ft) | ZONES 5–10

'Gloire des Rosomanes'

HYBRID CHINA | MEDIUM RED

'Ragged Robin', 'Red Robin'

Credited to Jean-Pierre Vibert, the official
date being 1825, 'Gloire des Rosomanes'
lurks unsuspected in many American gardens,
where it has often been used as an understock. It is sometimes recommended as a
good rose for hedging, a job it does well in
warm climates like California, although the
tall plants are perhaps not quite bushy enough.
The large, semi-double flowers are borne in
large clusters, making a bright show of crimson for most of the rose season, and there is
some fragrance. 'Rosomane' is one of those
French words that does not quite translate into
English – it means someone crazy about roses.

Vibert, France, 1825
Parentage unknown
Repeat flowering | *Moderate fragrance*

HABIT Bush H/W 1.2m/1.2m (4ft/4ft) | ZONES 6–11

TOP 'Gloire des Rosomanes'
LEFT 'Goldfinch'
ABOVE 'Glory of Edzell'

'Glory of Edzell'

HYBRID SPINOSISSIMA | LIGHT PINK

'Glory of Edsell'

This variety is usually classed as a Scotch Rose
(*R. spinosissima*), but whereas most of the Scotch
Roses make compact, even dwarf, bushes, this
one will happily grow more than head-high.
It wreathes its spiny branches in spring with
single, clear pink flowers; a few dark hips
follow in the fall/autumn. The foliage is ferny
and matt green. Its vigor suggests that it might
be a hybrid, but with what no one knows.
Indeed, none of the authorities admits to
knowing much about this pretty rose.

Parentage unknown
Spring flowering | *Light fragrance*

HABIT Bush H/W 1.5m/1.2m (5ft/4ft) | ZONES 5–11

'Goldfinch'

HYBRID MULTIFLORA | LIGHT YELLOW

This was an attempt by William Paul to raise
a yellow rambler. The fat little buds are a
rich, deep, golden yellow, and open to small,

semi-double flowers with golden brown
anthers. The rich yellow of the petals holds
quite well indoors, but in the sunshine the
petals take on a primrose color that rapidly
fades first to cream and then to white. The
effect is still pleasing, and 'Goldfinch' can
be a good choice for a position where a flat
white would be too stark. The flowers are
borne in clusters and are sweetly scented,
but there is only the one annual burst. The
plant is almost thornless, with small, glossy,
wrinkled foliage.

Paul, England, UK, 1907
'Hélène' × unknown
Summer flowering | *Slight fragrance*

HABIT Climber H/W 2.5m/1.5m (8ft/5ft) | ZONES 4–11

'Grace Darling'

TEA | WHITE

The heroine of many an English schoolboy
in times past was the 15-year-old lighthouse-
keeper's daughter Grace Darling, who rescued
the passengers from a shipwreck on the English coast. That was in 1838. In 1885, one of
those schoolboys, the now grown-up Henry

'Gloire des Mousseux'

'Grace Darling'

Bennett, paid homage to her with this exquisite rose, large, double and globular in form. It opens creamy white edged in pink, quickly ageing to a medium pink. It was one of the earlier Teas to win popularity. It still retains it to a remarkable degree – it is seen from Sydney to Vancouver to the Isle of Guernsey (itself the scene of several notable shipwrecks). The medium-sized bush blooms very freely and continuously, and the flowers are well scented. The foliage is bright green.

Bennett, England, UK, 1885
Parentage unknown
Repeat flowering ı *Moderate fragrance*
HABIT Bush H/W 1m/60cm (3ft/2ft) ı ZONES 7–11

'Great Maiden's Blush'

ALBA ı WHITE

'Cuisse de Nymphe', 'Grande Cuisse de Nymphe', 'Incarnata', 'La Royale', 'La Séduisante', 'La Virginale', 'Maiden's Blush', *R. alba incarnata*, *R. alba rubicanda*, *R. alba rubicanda plena*, *R. carnea*, *R. incarnata*, *R. rubicans*

With fine, blue-grey foliage and exquisite blooms, this ancient classic variety combines

'Great Maiden's Blush'

all the most desirable attributes of the Albas. The rosette-shaped flowers are very double, ruffled and usually pure white – but sometimes blush-pink (as in the photograph), depending on the growing conditions – and have a lovely, refined perfume. In Victorian England this rose went by the name of 'Maiden's Blush', and in France by the more seductive name of 'Cuisse de Nymphe' ('Nymph's Thigh'). It is a highly desirable rose for connoisseurs of old roses. Be warned, however, that it dislikes wet weather, and that in a warm climate thrips can be a serious problem, ruining the buds before they open.

Europe, c. 1400 or earlier
R. alba × *R. centifolia*
Summer flowering ı *Intense fragrance*
HABIT Bush H/W 1.8m/1.5m (6ft/5ft) ı ZONES 5–11

'Green Rose'

CHINA ı WHITE

'Green Rose', 'Monstrosa', 'Viridiflora', *R. chinensis viridiflora, R. viridiflora*

No one seems to know the origin of the 'Green Rose', but it has been around since at least the 1850s and looks as though it will find its way into catalogues for years to come. Not because it is any great beauty, but because it is such a curiosity. The double flowers can easily be mistaken for foliage. They are green, often touched with bronze, with narrow, leaf-like petals. In bud it is quite a pretty plant, but when the flowers open, the 6cm (2½ in) pompons are apt to be spoiled by maroon blotches. Naturally, there is no scent, but the flowers are very long-lasting and are quite often used in arrangements. The bush grows to about 1m (3ft) tall and wide and flowers all season. The foliage is dark green and glossy.

Bambridge and Harrison, cultivated before 1856
Parentage unknown
Repeat flowering ı *No fragrance*
HABIT Bush H/W 1m/1m (3ft/3ft) ı ZONES 7–9

'Gros Choux d'Hollande'

CENTIFOLIA ı LIGHT PINK

'Big Cabbage of Holland'

The name is very unromantic, translating literally as 'Big Cabbage of Holland'. Little is known about this rose. It is sometimes classed as a Bourbon and sometimes as a Centifolia. It is, however, a very handsome rose, with lush, green leaves and big, double,

'Green Rose'

'Gros Choux d'Hollande'

rose-pink blooms with symmetrically arranged petals. It is also full of fragrance. The bush is fairly compact and upright, with little of the Centifolia floppiness. Some authorities claim it as repeat flowering, but do not count on it. Usually the lavish summer display is all there is.

Parentage unknown
Summer flowering ı *Intense fragrance*
HABIT Bush H/W 2m/1.5m (7ft/5ft) ı ZONES 5–10

'Grüss an Teplitz'

HYBRID CHINA ı MEDIUM RED

'Virginia R. Coxe'

This is one of those roses that some people adore, while others cannot quite understand the fuss. Of wildly mixed ancestry, it makes

'Grüss an Teplitz'

a tall, rather rangy bush, which you can train to a pillar or prune back to about 1.5m (5ft), or even use as a hedge. The blooms are double and deep crimson, with 33 petals, and borne in nodding clusters of half a dozen or so. They are richly fragrant. This rose is happiest in a warm climate, when it is constantly in bloom, but watch out for mildew! The foliage is a dark, leaden green, tinted bronze-red when young.

Geschwind, Germany, 1897
(['Sir Joseph Paxton' × 'Fellenberg'] × 'Papa Gontier') × 'Gloire des Rosomanes'
Repeat flowering ∙ *Intense, spicy fragrance*

HABIT Bush H/W 1.5m/1.2m (5ft/4ft) ∙ ZONES 6–11

World Federation of Rose Societies Old Rose Hall of Fame 2003

'Harison's Yellow'

HYBRID FOETIDA ∙ DEEP YELLOW

'Harisonii', 'Yellow Rose of Texas', *R. foetida harisonii, R. lutea hoggii, R. × harisonii*

You would be hard put to find a rosebush growing on the Lower West Side of Manhattan these days, but that is where 'Harison's Yellow' originated around 1830, on what was then Mr Harison's suburban estate. You see it all over America, lingering in pioneer gardens long after the pioneers, and even their houses, have vanished. It is very pretty: a neat, tallish bush with dainty, mid-green foliage, covered in spring with semi-double, cupped, soft yellow blooms with golden stamens. You can distinguish 'Harison's Yellow' at once from its British sibling, 'Williams's

Double Yellow', by the fact that the latter has green carpels instead of stamens.

Harison, USA, c. 1830
Probably 'Persian Yellow' × *R. spinosissima*
Spring flowering ∙ *Moderate fragrance*

HABIT Bush H/W 1.2m/1m (4ft/3ft) ∙ ZONES 4–11

Royal Horticultural Society Award of Garden Merit 1993

'Harison's Yellow'

'Hebe's Lip'

'Hebe's Lip'

HYBRID EGLANTERIA ∙ WHITE

'Margined Lip', 'Reine Blanche', 'Rubrotincta', *R. damascena rubrotincta*

A compact bush for a Damask, bearing some of the most charming blooms among the Old Garden Roses: almost single (with a petal count in between single and double), and creamy white with a crimson margin to the petals, as though a goddess had been putting on her

lipstick. The foliage is a fresh green. The plant follows up its rather short summer season with pretty hips. A proliferation of names is often a sign of a long history, and 'Hebe's Lip' is of very ancient origin, despite its late date of introduction into commerce.

Ancient origin; introduced by Paul, England, UK, 1912
Probably *R. damascena* × *R. eglanteria*
Summer flowering ∙ *Moderate fragrance*

HABIT Bush H/W 1.2m/1.2m (4ft/4ft) ∙ ZONES 5–11

'Heinrich Münch'

HYBRID PERPETUAL ∙ MEDIUM PINK

'Heinrich Münch' suffers from the fault that costs so many of the Hybrid Perpetuals popularity nowadays: it is not at all perpetual. Indeed, it is decidedly shy with its fall/autumn blooms unless it is generously encouraged with watering and fertilizer. Do not begrudge it, for the flowers are gorgeous: immense, scented cabbages with 50 petals in a beautifully clear and luminous shade of pink, set against large, semi-glossy, green foliage. A good one would cause quite an upset among the modern Hybrid Teas on an exhibition bench. It was named for the German amateur who raised it, and was introduced in 1911 by Wilhelm Hinner, who at that time had a nursery at Lohausen (now a suburb of Düsseldorf).

Hinner, Germany, 1911
'Frau Karl Druschki' × ('Madame Caroline Testout' × 'Mrs W. J. Grant')
Repeat flowering ∙ *Moderate fragrance*

HABIT Bush H/W 1.8m/1.2m (6ft/4ft) ∙ ZONES 5–10

'Heinrich Schultheis'

HYBRID PERPETUAL ∙ LIGHT PINK

Why that doyen of English rose-breeders Henry Bennett should have named this 1882 creation for Herr Schultheis is hard to say –

'Heinrich Schultheis'

'Heinrich Münch'

'Henry Nevard'

'Henri Martin'

The records of its raiser and parentage are lost. The alternative (but now unused) French name means 'Majestic Rosette'.

France, early 1900s
Parentage unknown
Summer flowering ⦁ *Moderate fragrance*

HABIT Bush H/W 1.2m/1.2m (4ft/4ft) ⦁ ZONES 5–11

'Henri Foucquier'

mein Herr certainly seems foreign among such company as 'Grace Darling', 'Her Majesty' and 'Lady Mary Fitzwilliam'. But the name seems apt, for this is very much a man's rose, brilliant pink in tone, double, well filled with petals, and enormous. It must have been the pride of many a Victorian exhibitor. It is very pleasing to record that the blooms are intensely fragrant; the bush is strong, with large, semi-glossy, green foliage; and the flowers come early and late.

Bennett, England, UK, 1882
'Mabel Morrison' × 'E. Y. Teas'
Repeat flowering ⦁ *Intense fragrance*

HABIT Bush H/W 1.2m/1m (4ft/3ft) ⦁ ZONES 5–10

'Henri Foucquier'

HYBRID GALLICA ⦁ MEDIUM PINK

'Cocard Majesteuse', 'Henri Fouquier'

The bush is a bit lax for a Gallica but almost thornless, and the double flowers are handsome, with evenly arranged, rich pink petals that fade to mauve-pink. It is a good garden rose, responding well to a little bit of extra attention. The foliage is mid-green and smooth.

'Henri Martin'

MOSS ⦁ MEDIUM RED

'Red Moss'

This is not, despite its alternative name, a dark red rose, but rather of that color that is so common among roses and that might be called red or deepest pink at the beholder's whim. It is a lovely, fragrant rose, semi-double and borne in clusters of 3–8. It has an elegant habit and neat, dark green foliage, although it is true that there is not a great deal of moss on the buds. Raised by Laffay and introduced in 1862, it was named for the popular historian Henri Martin, one of the circle that promoted the gift of the Statue of Liberty from France to America.

Laffay, France, 1862
Parentage unknown
Summer flowering ⦁ *Moderate fragrance*

HABIT Bush H/W 1.5m/1.2m (5ft/4ft) ⦁ ZONES 5–10

Royal Horticultural Society Award of Garden Merit 1993

'Henri Foucquier'

'Henry Nevard'

HYBRID PERPETUAL ⦁ DARK RED

Although the color of 'Henry Nevard' is usually described as dark red, it is more accurate to call it bright crimson. The double, cupped blooms are large – sometimes very large – and nicely formed. They hold both their bright color and sweet fragrance very well in hot weather. The bush is vigorous and more compact than is usual for a Hybrid Perpetual, and the leathery, dark green foliage is resistant to black spot. It is English-bred, by Frank Cant in 1924, a late date for a new Hybrid Perpetual to be introduced.

Cant, England, UK, 1924
Parentage unknown
Repeat flowering ⦁ *Intense fragrance*

HABIT Bush H/W 1.2m/1m (4ft/3ft) ⦁ ZONES 5–10

'Hermosa'

HYBRID CHINA ı LIGHT PINK

'Armosa', 'Madame Neumann', 'Melanie Lemaire'

'Hermosa' is attributed to the obscure French breeder Marcheseau, the date being some time before 1837, but several breeders claimed it, giving it names of their choice. It is thought to be a seedling of 'Old Blush', which it rather resembles, except that it is not so tall (rarely more than knee height), has more petals (they number 35), and has more lilac in its pink. It is free with its flowers from early to late summer, and in the nineteenth century it was considered the best rose for a low hedge. However, there is not a lot of scent to speak of. The foliage is a dark bluish green and semi-glossy.

Marcheseau, France, before 1837
Possibly a seedling of 'Old Blush'
Repeat flowering ı *Light fragrance*

HABIT Bush H/W 1m/60cm (3ft/2ft) ı ZONES 7–11

'Hippolyte'

'Hermosa'

'Hiawatha'

HYBRID MULTIFLORA ı RED BLEND

Raised by an American breeder in 1904, 'Hiawatha' makes a big show late in the season with its large, single, carmine flowers with white centres and golden anthers. The plant is vigorous, and the foliage is leathery and rich green. For many years it was one of the most popular of ramblers, but it is less seen nowadays; its lack of scent is against it. In 1905 'Hiawatha' gained the obvious companion, 'Minehaha', from the same breeder.

Walsh, USA, 1904
'Crimson Rambler' × 'Paul's Carmine Pillar'
Summer flowering ı *No fragrance*

HABIT Rambler H/W 4.5m/3.5m (15ft/12ft) ı ZONES 4–11

'Homèr

'Hippolyte'

HYBRID GALLICA ı MAUVE

'Hippolyte' is tall for a Gallica, sometimes growing head-high, and the leaves, dark green and smooth, indicate some foreign blood. The flowers, in soft shades of magenta-purple, are among the most perfectly formed of roses, and fragrant. They are not at all large, but they come in graceful sprays on thornless stems that often arch equally gracefully. This is another old beauty whose pedigree has been lost. Do not confuse her with a very ordinary carmine Hybrid Perpetual called 'Hippolyte Jamain', which is occasionally met with.

Europe, early 1800s
Parentage unknown
Summer flowering ı *Moderate fragrance*

HABIT Bush H/W 1.2m/1.2m (4ft/4ft) ı ZONES 5–11

'Homère'

TEA ı PINK BLEND

'Duchess of Kent', 'The Cape Buttonhole Rose'

Like his poems, the rose Robert et Moreau named after Homer in 1858 seems everlasting. Some of the oldest rosebushes in the world

'Hiawatha'

'Honorine de Brabant'

'Indica Alba'

'Ipsilanté'

are 'Homère'. Even in Britain's cool climate it endures, for it is the hardiest of the Teas. It is a real beauty: a double bloom, variable in color, as many Teas are, but always a delight with its blends of cream and rose-pink, its ruffled petals and its fine fragrance. The bush is strong and not over-tall at 1.2m (4ft) or so, and has glossy, dark green foliage and few (but stout) thorns. Expect 'Homère' to bloom heavily all season.

Robert et Moreau, France, 1858
Parentage unknown
Repeat flowering | *Moderate fragrance*

HABIT Bush H/W 1.2m/60cm (4ft/2ft) | ZONES 7–11

'Honorine de Brabant'

BOURBON | PINK BLEND

Many of the Bourbons are refined to the point of daintiness, but this one is on the bold side, with large, broad, light green leaves and good-sized, double blooms that open wide to show stripes and pencillings of violet and mauve over pale pink. It is a tall grower, and can be either used as a large shrub or trained as a pillar rose. It flowers lavishly in spring and quite well thereafter. It has good fragrance and few thorns. Who Honorine de Brabant was is now a mystery; nor does anyone know the raiser's name or the exact date of this excellent rose, possibly from around the 1840s.

Possibly c. 1840s
Parentage unknown
Repeat flowering | *Moderate fragrance*

HABIT Bush H/W 1.8m/1.5m (6ft/5ft) | ZONES 5–11

'Indica Alba'

HYBRID CHINA | LIGHT PINK

R. indica alba

In their day, the China Roses tended to be red or pink, and it seems that white varieties were always very rare. They are even rarer now, so it is worth recording this one, which was photographed in the garden of the tomb of I'timad-ud-Daula at Agra, its label reading *'Rosa indica alba'*. Not much is known about this variety, but it grows into a compact bush bearing white flowers. The mid-green foliage seems a bit coarse for a China Rose. What a disappointment if it is actually an imposter!

'Old Blush' sport
Repeat flowering | *Moderate fragrance*

HABIT Bush H/W 1m/1m (3ft/3ft) | ZONES 6–11

'Ipsilanté'

HYBRID GALLICA | MAUVE

The stems are more prickly than those of most Gallicas, and the dark green foliage not as finely cut as is usual, but the flowers are quite superb: very large, double, beautifully quartered, sweetly fragrant and of softest lilac-pink. This rose was highly regarded in its day and deserves to be better known today.

Vibert, France, 1821
Parentage unknown
Summer flowering | *Sweet fragrance*

HABIT Bush H/W 1.2m/1m (4ft/3ft) | ZONES 5–11

'Irene Watts'

CHINA | WHITE

This is a superb rose that produces silken blooms of soft apricot ageing to buff-white. Although it is classified as a China Rose, its blooms are much larger than those of the typical China. They are fully double, with large petals and a unique button 'eye' in the centre. When placed in a vase or floated in a bowl of water, this rose will quickly fill the entire room with its lovely, sweet fragrance.

'Irene Watts'

The plant is low-growing but quite vigorous, with lush, dark green, disease-resistant foliage. A profuse bloomer, 'Irene Watts' is an excellent choice for containers or borders or even a low hedge.

Guillot, France, 1896
Seedling of 'Madame Laurette Messimy'
Repeat flowering | *Sweet fragrance*

HABIT Bush H/W 45cm/45cm (18in/18 in) | ZONES 5–11

'Jacques Cartier'

PORTLAND ⏐ LIGHT PINK

Who would have thought that the great French explorer could ever be caught up in a case of mistaken identity! The American Rose Society has decided that the rose many of us have long admired under his name is not the real 'Jacques Cartier', a Portland introduced by Moreau et Robert in 1868, but a light pink Hybrid Perpetual called 'Marchesa Boccella', which was introduced by Desprez in 1842. The confusion goes back to the 1970s, when 'Marchesa Boccella' was mistakenly identified as 'Jacques Cartier' and went on to be sold as such in the United States for some 25 years. The real 'Jacques Cartier' has very double, pretty pink blooms with darker centres, their 50 petals ruffled and fluted (but not serrated) like a carnation. The bush is compact and vigorous, with abundant green foliage. The scent is only moderate, but the fall/autumn blooms are especially abundant.

Moreau et Robert, France, 1868
'Baronne Prévost' × 'Portland Rose'
Repeat flowering ⏐ *Intense, sweet fragrance*
HABIT Bush H/W 1m/60cm (3ft/2ft) ⏐ ZONES 5–11

LEFT 'Jacques Cartier'
BELOW 'Ispahan'

'Ispahan'

DAMASK ⏐ MEDIUM PINK

'Isfahan', 'Pompon des Princes', 'Rose d'Isfahan'

'Ispahan' is one of the most garden-worthy of the Old French Roses, both for its long flowering season – just about the longest of any once-blooming rose – and the clarity and softness of its color, which at first sight might be dismissed as just plain pink. Loosely shapely buds open to double flowers that are richly scented and borne in almost Floribunda clusters on a bushy, upright bush about 1.5m (5ft) tall. The foliage is small, glossy and mid-green. Ispahan is the former capital of Persia (present-day Iran), a country known for the beauty of its architecture, its carpets and its roses, although whether this was one of them no one is sure.

Parentage unknown
Summer flowering ⏐ *Intense fragrance*
HABIT Bush H/W 1.5m/1m (5ft/3ft) ⏐ ZONES 4–10
🌹 Royal Horticultural Society Award of Garden Merit 1993

ABOVE 'James Mason'
RIGHT 'Jaune Desprez'

ABOVE 'Jean Ducher'
BELOW 'James Mitchell'

'James Mason'

HYBRID GALLICA · MEDIUM RED

A lot of people do not know this, but the well-known British star of such movie classics as *The Man in Grey* was a keen admirer of roses. It was a delight when Peter Beales introduced the brilliant blood-red rose he named 'James Mason' in the year of the great actor's death, 1982. Its interesting parentage makes it three parts Gallica. The flowers are more than single (with a petal count in between single and double), and fragrant. The foliage is mid-green and luxuriant, sometimes so much so that the flowers are almost hidden amongst it.

Beales, England, UK, 1982

'Scarlet Fire' × 'Tuscany Superb'
Summer flowering · Sweet fragrance

HABIT Bush H/W 1.5m/1.2m (5ft/4ft) · ZONES 5–11

'James Mitchell'

MOSS · DEEP PINK

No one remembers who James Mitchell was, but his rose was raised by Eugène Verdier in 1861. It is an odd choice to bear a man's name, the small, double, powder-pink flowers flushed with lilac being on the dainty side, and prettily shaped. The buds are nicely mossy, and the flowers fragrant. The arching bush can smother itself with flowers in its late spring season. It has neat, dark green foliage, and is usually the first of the Moss Roses in bloom.

Verdier, France, 1861
Parentage unknown
Summer flowering · Moderate fragrance

HABIT Bush H/W 1.5m/1.2m (5ft/4ft) · ZONES 5–10

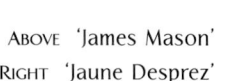

'Jaune Desprez'

NOISETTE · YELLOW BLEND

'Desprez à Fleur Jaunes', 'Noisette Desprez'

In contrast to the brilliant Modern Roses bred from *R. foetida persiana* ('Persian Yellow'), the flowers of this rose are closer to cream. The yellow is very pale, although often shot with suggestions of peach and apricot. The double blooms, borne on slender footstalks, are of Tea Rose shape and have a warm fragrance. The foliage is pale green. In its day, this rose was regarded as one of the most powerfully scented of all. This is a large and vigorous climber that is lavish with its flowers from the beginning to the end of the season.

Desprez, France, 1830
'Blush Noisette' × 'Parks's Yellow Tea-scented China'
Repeat flowering · Moderate fragrance
HABIT Climber H/W 6m/3m (20ft/10ft) · ZONES 7–11

'Jean Ducher'

TEA · ORANGE PINK

Compared with Modern Roses in the same peach-pink to apricot color range, their tones intensified by descent from *R. foetida persiana* ('Persian Yellow'), the nodding blooms of 'Jean Ducher' may seem pallid. This rose is, however, a good example of the refinement and delicacy that Victorian rose-lovers so admired. Not that there is anything languishing about the plant, which is one of the hardiest of the Teas, bearing its globular, scented flowers in great abundance for most of the year. The foliage is narrow and bronze-green, tinted plum when young. The name commemorates a member of the Ducher family, rose-breeders for more than a century.

Ducher, France, 1873
Parentage unknown
Repeat flowering · Moderate fragrance
HABIT Bush H/W 1.2m/1m (4ft/3ft) · ZONES 7–11

'Jenny Duval'

HYBRID CHINA · DEEP PINK

Old Garden Rose fanciers still argue about the identity of this rose. Since 'Jenny Duval' is not mentioned in the old rose books, some historians have declared that it is the same as 'Président de Seze'; others take the view that it is quite different. It is worth the fuss, for it is one of the most remarkably colored roses

'Jenny Duval'

in existence. It usually opens pale lilac, but as the flowers expand and age, the petals are apt to take on every shade of purple, magenta, pink and violet that you can think of, all in the same flower – the outer petals, being the oldest, taking on the deepest colors – and without stripes or blotches. It is scented, and it has been known to make a show of fall/ autumn foliage. It probably dates from some time in the early nineteenth century.

Probably early 1800s
Parentage unknown
Summer flowering ᛁ *Moderate fragrance*
HABIT Bush H/W 1m/1m (3ft/3ft) ᛁ ZONES 6–11

'Kathleen Harrop'

BOURBON ᛁ LIGHT PINK

A 1919 introduction from Alexander Dickson & Sons of Northern Ireland, 'Kathleen Harrop' is a sport from 'Zéphirine Drouhin'. Like its parent, it is a climber, thornless, repeat flowering and fragrant. It differs from its parent in being slightly less vigorous and in its much softer color, which is mid-pink with slightly deeper tones on the reverse. The foliage is matt green and susceptible to mildew. 'Kathleen Harrop' has always been overshadowed by its celebrated parent, but it is a most lovely rose. Try planting mother and daughter together; their colors are wonderfully harmonious.

Dickson, Northern Ireland, UK, 1919
'Zéphirine Drouhin' sport
Repeat flowering ᛁ *Moderate fragrance*
HABIT Climber H/W 3m/1.8m (10ft/6ft) ᛁ ZONES 5–11

'Kazanlik'

DAMASK ᛁ DEEP PINK

'Trigintipetala', *R. damascena trigintipetala*
Originating long ago in the rose fields of Bulgaria, this variety was used extensively to

'Kazanlik'

make attar of roses. The warm-pink blooms are shaggy and semi-double, with 30 petals, and are borne on weak stems. They are very fragrant. The petals of this rose are ideal for making potpourri.

Middle East, ancient origin
Parentage unknown
Summer flowering ᛁ *Strong fragrance*
HABIT Bush H/W 1.5m/1.2m (5ft/4ft) ᛁ ZONES 5–10

'Königin von Dänemark'

ALBA ᛁ MEDIUM PINK

'Belle Courtisanne', 'Naissance de Venus', 'Queen of Denmark', 'Reine de Denmarck', 'Reine du Dänemark'

'Königin von Dänemark' is the most richly colored of the Alba Roses, with blooms that initially open a brilliant pink but have paled by the time they are fully open. The flowers are very double and most perfectly quartered. In its day, it was a leading exhibition rose. The fragrance is superb, but the plant is inclined to be tall and leggy. The bluish green foliage sets off the flowers nicely. 'Königin von Dänemark' was raised by James

'Kathleen Harrop'

'Königin von Dänemark'

Booth and introduced in 1816. The Booth nursery was in Schleswig-Holstein, then part of Denmark but now in Germany.

Booth, Denmark, 1816
Probably *R. alba* × Damask hybrid
Summer flowering ᛁ *Moderate fragrance*
HABIT Bush H/W 1.5m/1.2m (5ft/4ft) ᛁ ZONES 5–10
🌹 Royal Horticultural Society Award of Garden Merit 1993

'La Reine'

HYBRID PERPETUAL ᛁ MEDIUM PINK

'Reine des Français', 'Rose de la Reine'

Pointed buds open to large, double, globular flowers with 78 petals. The flowers are full of fragrance, and their color is best described simply as rose-pink. The bush is upright, with mid-green foliage, and grows to about 1m (3ft) tall. It repeats its flowering without

'La Reine'

needing as much encouragement as some Hybrid Perpetuals do. Raised by Laffay in 1842, it was one of the first of its class, and for many years one of the most popular of all roses. It has also been a most famous parent. Few indeed are the later roses that cannot trace their pedigrees to it.

Laffay, France, 1842
Parentage unknown
Repeat flowering ⁞ *Moderate fragrance*

HABIT Bush H/W 1m/60cm (3ft/2ft) ⁞ ZONES 5–10

'La Ville de Bruxelles'

DAMASK ⁞ DEEP PINK

'Ville de Bruxelles'

If you want to see what a perfect flower in the Old French style looks like, this rose can be relied on to produce many of them – double, immaculately quartered, deliciously fragrant and a rich, unshaded pink. They are large, too, for a Damask, often reaching 13cm (5in) in diameter. Alas, the slender branches often bow under the weight of the blooms. The foliage is light green, glossy and plentiful. This variety, although of French origin, was named by Jean-Pierre Vibert to honor the capital city of Belgium.

Vibert, France, 1849
Parentage unknown
Repeat flowering ⁞ *Moderate fragrance*

HABIT Bush H/W 1.5m/1m (5ft/3ft) ⁞ ZONES 5–10

🌺 Royal Horticultural Society Award of Garden Merit 1993

'Lady Hillingdon'

TEA ⁞ YELLOW BLEND

Elegant is the word for this rose, the most popular of the Teas for its hardiness, its delicious tea fragrance, and the way in which the plum-colored young leaves set off the slim and shapely, semi-double, yellow flowers to perfection. The leaves mature to a dark, purplish green. Good as the bush is, it is as a climber that 'Lady Hillingdon' is most often seen – and with good reason, because it is the most continuously flowering climbing rose there is. Give it a sheltered wall in cold climates, for it is not all that hardy. The bush came out in 1910, from the English firm of Lowe & Shawyer. The climbing sport was introduced by an English breeder named Hicks in 1917.

Lowe & Shawyer, England, UK, 1910
'Papa Gontier' × 'Madame Hoste'
Repeat flowering ⁞ *Moderate fragrance*

HABIT Bush H/W 1m/60cm (3ft/2ft) ⁞ ZONES 7–11

'La Ville de Bruxelles'

'Lady Hillingdon'

'Lamarque'

'Léda'

'Lamarque'

NOISETTE ı WHITE

'General Lamarque', 'The Marshal'

The flowers of this charming Old Garden Rose are almost pure white and easily recognizable by their lemon-yellow centres. They are large and double, but loose in their petals and form. They are borne quite plentifully throughout the season, mostly in clusters, especially after the plant has become fully established. 'Lamarque' is a very hardy grower, sending out long, trailing shoots that make it an ideal choice for a trellis or a large archway. It was named in honor of Jean Maximilien Lamarque (1770–1832), a French commander during the Napoleonic Wars, who later became a member of the French parliament. A Bonapartist and a republican, he was known for his active suppression of Royalist and Legitimist activities. His death was the catalyst for the uprising in Paris in June of 1832 that formed the basis of Victor Hugo's novel *Les Misérables*.

Maréchal, France, 1830
'Blush Noisette' × 'Parks's Yellow Tea-scented China'
Repeat flowering ı *Intense fragrance*
HABIT Climber H/W 4.5m/2.5m (15ft/8ft) ı ZONES 6–11

'Léda'

DAMASK ı WHITE

'Painted Damask'

There are two forms of this early nineteenth-century rose; they are just about identical, except for their color. The English prefer the white form, with its carmine-stained petal tips – hence the name 'Painted Damask'. The French prefer the pink, on whose petals the carmine stains are less conspicuous. Most books illustrate the English form. So, just to be different, this book shows you the French. Both are luxuriant growers, given good treatment, with lush, dark green leaves. Naturally, they are splendidly fragrant. In Greek legend, Leda was the maiden seduced by Zeus (disguised as a swan, of all things). One of the children of the union was the beautiful and ill-fated Helen of Troy.

Probably early 1800s
Parentage unknown
Summer flowering ı *Moderate fragrance*
HABIT Bush H/W 1m/1m (3ft/3ft) ı ZONES 5–10

'Lord Penzance'

HYBRID EGLANTERIA ı YELLOW BLEND

Attracted by the fragrant leaves of *R. eglanteria*, the 'Sweet Brier Rose', Lord Penzance crossed it with garden roses in a big way in his gardens at Godalming in Surrey, in the south of England. Between 1894 and 1895, he brought out no fewer than 14 Sweet Briers with brighter-colored flowers than are usual for the group. Like their parent, they are mostly large, scrambling shrubs suitable only for the most informal of gardens. Most were raised from various Hybrid Perpetuals and given the names of heroines from Walter Scott novels; but two were raised from yellow roses, and

'Lord Penzance'

these the noble lord named for himself and his lady. They are more modest in habit; their foliage is small, dark and fragrant; and the single flowers, borne in clusters, are salmon-pink and gold for his lordship, pale yellow for 'Lady Penzance'.

Penzance, England, UK, 1894
R. eglanteria × 'Harison's Yellow'
Summer flowering ı *Moderate fragrance*
HABIT Bush H/W 2m/1.8m (7ft/6ft) ı ZONES 5–11

'Lorraine Lee'

HYBRID GIGANTEA ı PINK BLEND

Probably the best-known Australian-raised rose, 'Lorraine Lee' was released by Alister Clark in 1924. He used a second-generation *R. gigantea* seedling, 'Jessie Clark', as seed parent, and named the rose for a distant cousin visiting from England. Alas, the lady could have had no joy from her rose at home: it needs a hot summer to bear its shapely, long-budded flowers. The blooms are quite large and double, and a lovely shade of coral with a glow of gold at their heart. They are softly fragrant. The foliage is leathery and a rich green. Although it is not hardy for northern climates, 'Lorraine Lee' thrives exceptionally well in Australia.

Clark, Australia, 1924
'Jessie Clark' × 'Capitaine Millet'
Repeat flowering ı *Moderate fragrance*
HABIT Bush H/W 3m/1.8m (10ft/6ft) ı ZONES 7–11

'Louis Philippe'

HYBRID CHINA ı MAUVE

'Louis Philippe d'Angers'

The variety commonly known today as 'Louis Philippe' was raised by Modeste Guérin in

'Louis Philippe'

ABOVE 'Lorraine Lee'
LEFT 'Louise Odier'

1834. Take care not to confuse it with a variety of the same name raised by Eugène Hardy 10 years earlier, in 1824. It makes a rather sparsely leafed bush similar to a small-growing Floribunda, and bears clusters of double, loosely formed, 8cm (3in) flowers in deep pink to crimson all season, sometimes with a purple overcast but almost always markedly paler at the petal edges, as though someone had bleached them. The foliage is a glossy mid-green. This is a rose that needs extra care in cultivation to show its true colors.

Guérin, France, 1834
Parentage unknown
Repeat flowering ı *Moderate fragrance*

HABIT Bush H/W 60cm/60cm (2ft/2ft) ı ZONES 6–11

'Louise Odier'

BOURBON ı DEEP PINK

One of the most elegant of pink roses, 'Louise Odier' bears full, double blooms so perfect in their symmetry that they have often been compared to camellias. They are a lovely shade of warm pink suffused with lilac, and exhale a beautiful perfume. The bush is sturdy and on the tall side, with healthy, bright green leaves, and flowers as continually as a modern bush rose. It would make a good hedging plant, and is also tolerant of shady situations. It came from the French raiser Margottin, few of whose roses are grown today, in 1851.

Margottin, France, 1851
Parentage unknown
Repeat flowering ı *Intense fragrance*

HABIT Bush H/W 1.5m/1.2m (5ft/4ft) ı ZONES 5–11

'Madame Alfred Carrière'

NOISETTE ı WHITE

For all that it came out in 1879, 'Madame Alfred Carrière' can still claim to be the first choice among white climbing roses. True, the large, double, globular blooms are not perfectly white but tinted with blush at their heart, yet they look white in the mass, and there are masses of them all season. The plant

'Madame Alfred Carrière'

'Madame Berkeley'

'Madame Hardy'

'Madame Ernest Calvat'

'Madame de Watteville'

is vigorous but manageable, the foliage is light green and usually disease-free, and there is plenty of fragrance. What more could one want? It does not like hot, dry winds, which can bring thrips.

Schwartz, France, 1879
Parentage unknown
Repeat flowering ı *Intense fragrance*
HABIT Climber H/W 4.5m/3m (15ft/10ft) ı ZONES 7–11
🌹 Royal Horticultural Society Award of Garden Merit 1993

'Madame Berkeley'

TEA ı PINK BLEND

Like so many of the Teas, 'Madame Berkeley' changes the color of her dress with the seasons, sometimes preferring a blend of pinks, at others adding touches of gold. One of the most freely blooming of the Teas, it is a fine garden plant in a warm climate, although the individual blooms are not especially shapely and only moderately fragrant. The glossy, green foliage is red-tinted when young.

Bernaix, France, 1898
Parentage unknown
Repeat flowering ı *Moderate fragrance*
HABIT Bush H/W 1m/60cm (3ft/2ft) ı ZONES 7–11

'Madame de Watteville'

TEA ı YELLOW BLEND

'Madame de Watteville' is officially described as lemon-yellow with pink on the petal

edges, but like most of the Teas it varies very much with the season. The flower illustrated here is showing quite a lot of pink. The blooms are large, double and shapely, and sweetly fragrant. The bush is moderate-sized and slim-wooded, with glossy, dark green leaves. Like many Teas, it will flower all year long in a mild climate. It makes a good container plant.

Guillot et Fils, France, 1883
Parentage unknown
Repeat flowering ı *Moderate fragrance*
HABIT Bush H/W 1m/1m (3ft/3ft) ı ZONES 7–11

'Madame Ernest Calvat'

BOURBON ı MEDIUM PINK

'Madame Ernst Calvat', 'Pink Bourbon'

Introduced by the widow of Lyon rose-breeder Joseph Schwartz in 1888, 'Madame Ernest Calvat' is a sport of 'Madame Isaac Pereire', and like its parent can be trained to a pillar or grown as a large shrub. Also like its parent, it is richly fragrant, but it differs in its color, being flesh-pink with deeper shadings. The wonderful plum tonings of the young growth, which mature to bright green, provide a perfect setting for the great, blowsy

flowers. It needs good soil to be seen at its best, when it is one of the great Victorian roses.

Schwartz, France, 1888
'Madame Isaac Pereire' sport
Repeat flowering ı *Moderate fragrance*
HABIT Bush H/W 1.5m/1.2m (5ft/4ft) ı ZONES 5–11

'Madame Hardy' p 41

DAMASK ı WHITE

It is the dream of every rose-breeder to dedicate a beautiful rose to the woman he loves. It was the privilege of Eugène Hardy, back in 1832, to honor his wife with one of the most beautiful roses of all. With its perfect whiteness, occasionally tinged flesh-pink, and soft, sweet fragrance, 'Madame Hardy' is irresistible. The large, double flowers are cupped, and borne in clusters. The bush is vigorous but inclined to flop; discreet staking is usually in order. This laxity of habit, the coarsely toothed, dark green leaves, and the feathery, pine-scented sepals all suggest that it is not a pure-bred Damask. *Rosa centifolia* may have contributed to its beauty.

Hardy, France, 1832
Parentage unknown
Summer flowering ı *Light fragrance*

HABIT Bush H/W 1.5m/1.5m (5ft/5ft) ı ZONES 5–10

🏵 Royal Horticultural Society Award of Garden Merit 1993, World Federation of Rose Societies Old Rose Hall of Fame 2006

'Madame Isaac Pereire'

'Madame Pierre Oger'

'Madame Joseph Schwartz'

'Madame Isaac Pereire'

BOURBON ı DEEP PINK

'Madame Isaac Pereire' is claimed to be the most powerfully fragrant of all roses, and the scent of the great, multi-petalled blooms is certainly delicious. Their color does not always appeal to modern tastes, however. It is shocking pink, heavily overlaid with magenta, which means that this rose needs careful placement

in the garden. The bush is strong enough to train as a pillar, and it flowers repeatedly. The foliage is bright green. 'Madame Isaac Pereire' needs the best of everything if it is to perform well. The lady honored by M. Garçon of Rouen in 1881 was the wife of a Parisian banker.

Garçon, France, 1881
Parentage unknown
Repeat flowering ı *Heavy fragrance*

HABIT Bush H/W 2m/1.5m (7ft/5ft) ı ZONES 5–11

🏵 Royal Horticultural Society Award of Garden Merit 1993

'Madame Joseph Schwartz'

TEA ı WHITE

'White Duchesse de Brabant'

A popular variety that makes an exceptionally good cut flower for the home, 'Madame Schwartz' has double, cupped blooms of virginal white with just a hint of pink. Like most Teas, it prefers a cool, sunny spot in the garden. The bush grows to a height of only 1–1.2m (3–4ft) in most climates. It is prone to black spot, and it dislikes wet weather, which will spoil the delicate blooms.

Schwartz, France, 1880
Probably a 'Duchesse de Brabant' sport
Repeat flowering ı *Moderate fragrance*

HABIT Bush H/W 1–1.2m/1m (3–4ft/3ft) ı ZONES 6–11

'Madame Pierre Oger'

BOURBON ı PINK BLEND

It does not often happen with roses that a sport becomes more popular than its parent, but here is one instance. Lovely as the rose-pink of 'Reine Victoria' is, it looks ordinary beside 'Madame Pierre Oger', which is the most exquisite of palest rose-pinks, blushing deeper where the sun strikes the flowers, giving them a translucent delicacy. In all other respects the plant quite resembles its parent; the two look well growing together. Madame Pierre Oger was the mother of M. A. Oger of Caen, in Normandy, who discovered the sport. Eugène Verdier introduced the rose in 1878.

Oger, France, 1878
'Reine Victoria' sport
Repeat flowering ı *Sweet fragrance*

HABIT Bush H/W 1.2m/1.2m (4ft/4ft) ı ZONES 5–11

'Madame Plantier'

ALBA ı WHITE

This rose is really best thought of as an unusually long-limbed and rather lax-growing Alba with some characteristics inherited from the Damasks. English writer and gardener Vita

'Madame Plantier'

Sackville-West put the long branches to good use in her world-famous gardens at Sissinghurst Castle in Kent by training them into the lower branches of her apple trees, creating an effect that she described as crinolines of white flowers. Individually, the very double blooms are well filled with petals and shapely, their whiteness warmed in a cool season with hints of creamy pink. The fragrance is first-rate, but the clusters of blooms come only in summer. The foliage is a light greyish green.

Plantier, France, 1835
Thought to be *R. alba* × *R. moschata*
Summer flowering ı *Moderate fragrance*

HABIT Climber H/W 3.5m/2.5m (12ft/8ft) ı ZONES 5–11

'Madame Zöetmans'

DAMASK ı WHITE

'Madame Zöetmans' is rather like 'Madame Hardy' and came out two years earlier. In its day, its admirers thought it superior, but in the years since it has been rather eclipsed by its rival. Do not overlook it, though. It is still a beauty, with double, perfectly formed, scented flowers, their whiteness warmed with hints of pink; and the plant is strong and free with its blooms. The foliage is mid-green and rough.

Marest, France, 1830
Parentage unknown
Summer flowering ı *Moderate fragrance*

HABIT Bush H/W 1.2m/1m (4ft/3ft) ı ZONES 5–10

RIGHT 'Madame Zöetmans'
LEFT INSET 'Mademoiselle de Sombreuil'
RIGHT INSET 'Marbrée'

'Mademoiselle de Sombreuil'

TEA | WHITE

'La Biche'

Mlle de Sombreuil was a heroine of the French Revolution who by an act of bravery saved her father from the guillotine. The rose named in her memory did not come out until 1850, having been raised by a M. Robert (not to be confused with M. Robert of Moreau et Robert). It is a splendid flower, large, double and bursting with petals in delicate tones of cream and white, occasionally with just a hint of pink. The scent is superb. It dislikes cold climates, and even in a mild climate it appreciates loving care. The foliage is medium green and semi-glossy.

Robert, France, 1850
Seedling of 'Gigantesque'
Repeat flowering | Moderate fragrance
HABIT Bush H/W 1.5m/1m (5ft/3ft) | ZONES 5–11

'Marbrée'

PORTLAND | RED BLEND

'Marbrée', which means 'marbled', seems a bit unimaginative as a name for a rose. It is not all that appropriate, either, as the flowers are not marbled but delicately spotted with palest pink on a deeper pink background. This is a most unusual pattern, and the loosely semi-double flowers, with their golden stamens, show it off nicely. There is little fragrance, unfortunately, but the bush, taller than most of the Portlands, is a reliable repeat bloomer. The foliage is smooth, pointed and olive-green. The raisers, Robert et Moreau, must have been at a loss for words in 1858.

Robert et Moreau, France, 1858
Parentage unknown
Repeat flowering | Slight fragrance
HABIT Bush H/W 1.2m/1m (4ft/3ft) | ZONES 5–11

'Marchesa Boccella'

HYBRID PERPETUAL | LIGHT PINK

'Marquise Boccella', 'Marquise Bocella'

In the 1970s, 'Marchesa Boccella' was mistakenly identified as the Portland Rose 'Jacques Cartier' and went on to be sold as such in the United States for some 25 years. She has since reclaimed her independence and her true identity as a Hybrid Perpetual. One of the first things one notices about 'Marchesa Boccella' is the feathery sepals that surround the buds, which open gracefully into large, quartered,

'Marchesa Boccella'

rosette-shaped flowers of a delicate, clear pink. The petals are smaller than usual for a Hybrid Perpetual, and the flower stems are strong and straight, and covered with small thorns. The plant is upright in habit but dwarf-sized for its type, growing to only 1–1.2m (3–4ft) tall.

Desprez, France, 1842
Parentage unknown
Repeat flowering | Moderate fragrance
HABIT Bush H/W 1–1.2m/60cm (3–4ft/2ft) | ZONES 5–11

'Marchioness of Londonderry'

HYBRID PERPETUAL | LIGHT PINK

'Sachsengruss'

We are listing this rose under the name by which it is usually sold in the United States, but it is almost certain that it is not Alex Dickson's white 1893 Hybrid Perpetual. It is actually a German-raised one called 'Sachsengruss', aka 'Tendresse'. Under either name, this is a magnificent rose. It a huge flower, but is saved from vulgarity by the delicacy of its palest pink tones. It is very long-lasting in the vase, holding its perfect, high-centred form until the petals drop. The bush is lanky enough to

'Marchioness of Londonderry'

train as a climber. There are few prickles, but beware of mildew on the matt green leaves.

Neubert, Germany, 1912
'Frau Karl Druschki' × 'Mme Jules Gravereaux'
Repeat flowering | Light fragrance
HABIT Bush or climber H/W 1.8m/1.2m (6ft/4ft) | ZONES 6–10

'Maréchal Davoust'

MOSS | MEDIUM PINK

In life, Davoust was one of Napoleon's senior officers. His rose befits his rank, being a large, bold flower in shades of strong pink with suffusions of lilac, and nicely scented. The moss is dark green, and the bush is compact and free with its flowers, although only in the summer season. The foliage is smooth and mid-green.

Robert, France, 1853
Parentage unknown
Summer flowering | Moderate fragrance
HABIT Bush H/W 1.2m/1m (4ft/3ft) | ZONES 6–11

'Maréchal Davoust'

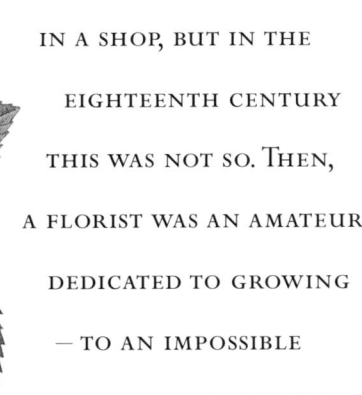

The Empress Joséphine

NOWADAYS A FLORIST IS A PERSON WHO MAKES A LIVING SELLING FLOWERS IN A SHOP, BUT IN THE EIGHTEENTH CENTURY THIS WAS NOT SO. THEN, A FLORIST WAS AN AMATEUR DEDICATED TO GROWING — TO AN IMPOSSIBLE STANDARD OF PERFEC-TION — ONE OF A VERY SMALL NUMBER OF 'FLORIST'S FLOWERS'. THESE INCLUDED THE TULIP, THE CARNATION, THE AURICULA AND THE RANUNCULUS — BUT NOT THE ROSE, WHICH WAS A FLOWER FOR THE GARDENER AND THE POET RATHER THAN THE HOBBYIST. THE ROSE'S PRE-EMINENCE TODAY IS DUE, MORE THAN TO ANYONE ELSE, TO THE EMPRESS JOSÉPHINE.

Child of destiny

Joséphine was born Marie-Joséphe Rose Tacher de la Pagerie in 1753. Legend has it that while she was a child living on the West Indian island of Martinique, an elderly West Indian seer predicted that both she and a playmate would become queens. This must have seemed a remote prospect to Joséphine when at the age of 16 she was married off to the Vicomte de Beauharnais. Her friend Aimé de Rivery did indeed, after a string of adventures that read like the plot of some grand opera, become the Sultana of Turkey.

In the meantime, Joséphine's loveless marriage produced two children, Eugène and Hortense. Then, the Vicomte de Beauharnais became embroiled in the politics of the French Revolution and ended up on the guillotine in 1794, a fate the Vicomtesse was lucky to escape. Despite the revenues of the Beauharnais estates, Joséphine was reduced, so the malicious gossip of the day had it, to living by her charms.

Though no great beauty, she was one of those women who fascinate every man they meet. Among her admirers was the young Napoleon Bonaparte, still a mere artillery expert but already destined for greatness. He fell passionately in love with her, and, perhaps more for security than for love, she consented to marry him in 1796.

In 1798, they bought the undistinguished Château de la Malmaison near Paris for their country residence. While her husband's military and political career carried him to ever greater glory, culminating in his coronation as Emperor of the French in 1804, Joséphine redecorated Malmaison from top to bottom in exquisite, and extravagant, taste and made its gardens the envy of Europe.

A centre of botanical research

She was no Louis XIV, interested only in terraces and fountains as a backdrop for imperial pomp, but a genuine and knowledgeable lover of plants. Malmaison became a leading centre of botanical research, and Empress Joséphine financed expeditions to places far beyond her husband's empire to bring back rarities for her collections.

It is said that she introduced more than 200 new plants to France, among them the dahlia, the Chilean bellflower, named in her honor *Lapageria rosea*, and the still rare *Brunsvigia josephinae* from South Africa, as charming (and as temperamental) as the lady herself. The leading botanists of the day studied and classified the new arrivals, and on hand to record them all for science was the greatest flower painter of them all, Pierre Joseph Redouté.

TOP Redouté's painting of *R. frankofurtana*, the rose now always known as 'Empress Joséphine'. It is a beautiful rose, well worthy of the proud name.

LEFT Joséphine de Beauharnais (1763–1814), Empress of France, consort of Napoleon Bonaparte, at Malmaison, France, 1800. The painting is by François Gerard (1770–1837).

and her Roses

ABOVE Napoleon presiding over his wife's garden.

LEFT Château de Malmaison seen from its park, painted by French artist Pierre Joseph Petit n the late eighteenth century.

Joséphine's great love, however, was the flower whose name she bore, the rose. She set out to grow every variety in existence. Her gardeners, led by a Scot named Hewartson, created new varieties, and eventually the rose garden at Malmaison could boast more than 250 varieties. Quite an achievement, when one remembers that only 50 years before even the great Linnaeus could muster only 20. They were grown, if Redouté's magnificent portraits are anything to go by, to a hitherto unknown standard of perfection What exciting days they must have been for lovers of the rose, as the ancient roses of China began to arrive and to transform the roses of the West beyond recognition. It was to Malmaison that they came. Despite the bitter war raging between England and France for the domination of Europe, ships carrying Joséphine's roses were allowed through the Royal Navy's stern blockade of the French ports — by order, it is said, of the Prince Regent himself. Truly, the beauty of the rose transcends politics.

A dignified retirement

Alas, politics intruded on Joséphine's marriage. Unable to bear Napoleon a son, she was divorced for reasons of state in 1809. Theirs had been a stormy marriage. There is no doubt, however, that Napoleon loved and respected her to the last, through the bitter days of the empire's collapse. She lived out her life in dignified retirement among her beloved flowers, and died at Malmaison in 1814.

Redouté's great book *Les Roses* finally came out in 1817, dedicated not, as history might wish, to Joséphine's memory but to a lady of the newly restored Bourbon monarchy. Such are the realities of politics and patronage. The world remembers the roses as hers, however. It was she who first revealed to gardeners their infinite variety and established the rose as a universal favorite — a position it has never lost.

Joséphine's daughter Hortense, by then the Queen of the Belgians, inherited Malmaison. After several changes of ownership, it passed to the French state. The château survives, open to the public and filled with treasures, a monument to both Joséphine and Napoleon. The estate has been much curtailed, however, and lovely as the gardens still are, their full glory is but a memory.

The rose lives on, of course, and all lovers of beauty owe a debt of gratitude to the girl from Martinique. Many of her favorites are grown still — there is a collection of them at the Roseraie de l'Haÿ — and those who would can drink deep of their beauty and perhaps muse upon the fate of empires.

'Souvenir de la Malmaison' is not one of Joséphine's, but a creation of 1843. Legend has it that the Grand Duke Michael of Russia, disappointed that there were no roses remaining at Malmaison, named it in her memory.

'Maréchal Niel'

'Marie d'Orléans'

'Marie Louise'

'Maréchal Niel'

NOISETTE ꞁ MEDIUM YELLOW

This rose was raised in 1864 by Joseph Pradel of Lyon and named in honor of Adolphe Niel, who had a distinguished career in the French military and earned his Marshal's baton at the Battle of Solferino, in Italy. No yellow rose quite so fine had been seen before, and it remains one of the loveliest: soft and pure in color, perfect in form and deliciously fragrant. It made M. Pradel a rich man. It is very tender, and a large, heated greenhouse is needed to grow it in cold climates. In earlier times, a bunch of 'Maréchal Niel' from the florist was the epitome of luxury. In a frost-free climate, it will adorn a wall with its pale green foliage and great, nodding, double blooms the color of butter for most of the year.

Pradel, France, 1864
Seedling of 'Cloth of Gold'
Repeat flowering ꞁ *Intense fragrance*

HABIT Climber H/W 4.5m/2.5m (15ft/8ft) ꞁ ZONES 7–11

'Marie d'Orléans'

TEA ꞁ MEDIUM PINK

An 1884 introduction from Gilbert Nabonnand, and named for a lady of the House of Orléans, a cadet branch of the royal House of Bourbon (which ruled France for some 200 years), 'Marie d'Orléans' appears to be living in the dignified retirement of historic rose collections these days. She should go back out into the wider society of rose gardens, where her large, double, prettily quartered blooms in shades of salmon-pink and coral, and her fragrance, would find her many new admirers. The foliage is bronze-green.

Nabonnand, France, 1884
Parentage unknown
Repeat flowering ꞁ *Moderate fragrance*

HABIT Bush H/W 1.2m/1m (4ft/3ft) ꞁ ZONES 7–11

'Marie Louise'

DAMASK ꞁ MEDIUM PINK

It seems rather tactless of the gardeners at Malmaison, the Empress Joséphine's house, to have dedicated a rose to Napoleon's second wife in 1813, when Joséphine, his divorced first wife, was still in charge of the garden! Clear pink and fragrant, 'Marie Louise' bears some of the largest blooms to be found among the Old French Roses. The very double flowers are, indeed, so large and full of petals that without the assistance of a supporting stake the slender Damask branches usually fail to hold them up and the flowers end up spattered with mud. Perhaps it was Joséphine herself who suggested the name, in barbed courtesy. The foliage is matt and light green.

France, 1813
Parentage unknown
Summer flowering ꞁ *Intense fragrance*

HABIT Bush H/W 1.2m/1m (4ft/3ft) ꞁ ZONES 5–10

'Marie van Houtte'

'Mary Queen of Scots'

'Marie van Houtte'

TEA ı PINK BLEND

'Mademoiselle Marie van Houtte'

Louis van Houtte was a distinguished Belgian horticulturalist who by 1870 owned Belgium's most successful nursery. Presumably Mlle Marie was his daughter. The rose dedicated to her was introduced by Claude Ducher in 1871 and is still regarded as one of the best of all the Teas – for its hardiness, its vigorous growth, its perfect form and the sweet scent of its blooms. There appear to be two strains about: one in yellow and pink, in the manner of 'Peace'; the other, the one in the photograph, much paler, in lemon-white and blush Both are lovely. The foliage is leathery and rich green, with plum tints when young.

Ducher, France, 1871
'Madame de Tartas' × 'Madame Falcot'
Repeat flowering ı Moderate fragrance

HABIT Bush H/W 1m/60cm (3ft/2ft) ı ZONES 7–11

'Mary Queen of Scots'

HYBRID SPINOSISSIMA ı MEDIUM PINK

Legend has it that this very pretty rose was brought from France to Scotland by the beautiful and tragic lady whose name it bears. Experts pour cold water on that romantic story, saying 'probably late nineteenth century'. Grow it for sentiment or just for the beauty of its little scented flowers in parma violet and lilac, borne in springtime profusion on a neat, dwarfish bush. Like most of the Scotch Roses, its mid-green leaves turn plum and russet in the fall/autumn and it prefers a cool climate. It is popular in Ireland.

Probably late 1800s
Parentage unknown
Spring flowering ı Moderate fragrance

HABIT Bush H/W 1m/1m (3ft/3ft) ı ZONES 4–10

'Master Hugh'

MISCELLANEOUS OGR ı DEEP PINK

Strictly speaking, 'Master Hugh' ought to be listed among the Species Roses, as it is raised from seed of *R. macrophylla* collected in the wild in China. However, it is so much more splendid than most forms of the Wild Rose that it has been propagated as a cultivar. Maurice Mason introduced it in 1970. The bush is big, to nearly 4.5m (15ft) tall and 2.5m (8ft) wide, and has mid-green foliage. The flowers, borne in clusters, are large, single and elegant, with five large, soft pink petals. They are preceded by young shoots covered with a greyish bloom like hoar frost and followed by the most splendid hips – large, orange-red and flagon-shaped. Indeed, rose connoisseurs rate this variety as one of the 10 roses worth growing for the value of their ornamental hips.

Mason, England, UK, 1970
Seedling of *R. macrophylla*
Spring flowering ı Slight fragrance

HABIT Climber H/W 4.5m/2.5m (15ft/8ft) ı ZONES 4–11

'Mélanie Soupert'

TEA ı WHITE

The lady in real life was a member of the great Luxembourg nursery family that founded the firm Soupert et Notting. Lyon rose-breeder Joseph Pernet-Ducher honored her some years later, in 1905, with his 'Madame Mélanie Soupert', one of his sensational golden roses. This one is a Tea, and far from sensational with its delicate shades of pale pink with the occasional suggestion of apricot, but is a very pretty rose nonetheless. The foliage is dark green. It was introduced in 1882 and does not seem to be generally available any more. This is one for the specialist grower.

Nabonnand, France, 1882
Seedling of 'Gloire de Dijon'
Repeat flowering ı Moderate fragrance

HABIT Bush H/W 1.2m/1m (4ft/3ft) ı ZONES 7–11

'Mélanie Soupert'

'Master Hugh'

'Mermaid'

'Milkmaid'

'Monsieur Tillier'

'Mermaid'

HYBRID BRACTEATA ı LIGHT YELLOW

Like the mermaids of legend, 'Mermaid' is indeed an alluring beauty, but, also like them, is not easy to live with. The problem lies in this plant's prodigious vigor; the brittle, viciously thorny branches are difficult to train. If you have the room to give it its head, there is no climbing plant more beautiful.

The shining foliage is more or less evergreen, and the huge, perfect, five-petalled flowers, 7–10cm (3–4in) in diameter, are single, softly scented and of palest yellow, and crowned with great bosses of amber stamens that still look beautiful after the petals have fallen.

Paul, England, UK, 1918
R. bracteata × double yellow Tea Rose
Repeat flowering ı *Moderate fragrance*
HABIT Climber H/W 9m/6m (30ft/20ft) ı ZONES 3–10

'Milkmaid'

NOISETTE ı WHITE

For many years, this vigorous climber adorned the trellis around the rose garden at the Botanic Gardens in Adelaide, South Australia, with its rich green leaves and fragrant blooms. It is an Australian rose, bred by Alister Clark in 1925. The small, semi-double flowers, borne in clusters, are a lovely soft egg-yolk-yellow, rapidly paling to milk-white. It is not quite as continuously flowering as its parent, although it does offer plenty of sprays of flowers after its spring crop.

Clark, Australia, 1925
'Crépuscule' × unnamed variety
Repeat flowering ı *Moderate fragrance*
HABIT Climber H/W 3.5m/3m (12ft/10ft) ı ZONES 7–11

'Monsieur Tillier'

TEA ı ORANGE PINK

'Archiduc Joseph'

There is some doubt about the identity of this rose, credited to Pierre Bernaix in 1891,

'Mousseux du Japon'

some claiming that it is actually Nabonnand's 'Archiduc Joseph'. Under either name it is an outstanding and easily grown rose for a warm climate. The double blooms are abundant and quite large, opening quartered and fragrant from plump buds. They are a blend of warm colors, but the overall impression is of coral-pink softly touched with magenta, an unusual and attractive combination. The olive-green foliage sets the flowers off very well, and the bush is upright and compact.

Bernaix, France, 1891
Parentage unknown
Repeat flowering ı *Moderate fragrance*
HABIT Bush H/W 1.2m/1m (4ft/3ft) ı ZONES 7–11

'Mousseux du Japon'

MOSS ı MAUVE

'Japonica', 'Moussu du Japon'

The books all say that this is the mossiest of all Moss Roses, the moss not growing simply on the buds but also on the stems and even on the leaves. Perhaps so, but it seems to need the very best of cultivation and a cool climate for this to happen. It is often no more mossy than most other Mosses. There are more attractive flowers in the group than this one's rather small, semi-double flowers of magenta-pink.

Japan, before 1900
Parentage unknown
Summer flowering ı *Moderate fragrance*
HABIT Bush H/W 1.2m/1m (4ft/3ft) ı ZONES 6–11

'Mrs B. R. Cant'

TEA ı MEDIUM PINK

'Mrs Benjamin R. Cant'

The seed parent is thought to be 'Red Safrano', a sport from the early 1839 Tea Rose 'Safrano', whose exact parentage is recorded as 'Parks's Yellow' × 'Mrs Desprez'. The double, cupped blooms are a soft, silvery rose-pink with a deeper rose-pink reverse, and open to fully blown masterpieces that last for days on the bush. They are strongly fragrant. Like other Tea Roses, the plant is on the small side, rarely exceeding 1.2–1.5m (4–5ft) in height. It is highly rated by members of the American Rose Society (scoring 8.9 out of 10 points).

Cant, England, UK, 1901
Parentage unknown
Repeat flowering ı *Strong rose fragrance*
HABIT Bush H/W 1.2–1.5m/1m (4–5ft/3ft) ı ZONES 5–11

'Mrs B. R. Cant'

'Mrs Dudley Cross'

'Mrs Dudley Cross'

TEA ı YELLOW BLEND

'Dudley Cross'

This was a leading exhibition rose in its day. Sometimes the 'Mrs' is dropped from the name. The double flowers are enormous and full-petalled, in straw-yellow with shadings of apricot and pink, the pink being more

'Mrs John Laing'

obvious in the fall/autumn. They are not
borne all that freely, and the plant is not very
tolerant of cold. The foliage is glossy green,
and the stems are thornless. Presumably its
English raiser, William Paul, grew it in a greenhouse. If you garden in a warm climate and
relish the idea of occasional sensational flowers, you might like to try 'Mrs Dudley Cross'.
It is not very fragrant, however.

Paul, England, UK, 1908
Parentage unknown
Repeat flowering ı *Slight fragrance*
HABIT Bush H/W 1.2m/1m (4ft/3ft) ı ZONES 7–11

'Mrs John Laing'

HYBRID PERPETUAL ı MEDIUM PINK

Ever since Henry Bennett brought out this
rose in 1887, rosarians have been singing its
praises, led by the Reverend Samuel Reynolds Hole, Dean of Rochester from 1887
to 1904 and one of the founders of the (now
Royal) National Rose Society: 'Not only in
vigour, constancy, and abundance, but in form
and features – Beauty's Queen!' All one can
add to *that* is that after more than 100 years
the bush remains vigorous and free with its
flowers, which are as enchanting as ever –
large and double, with 45 petals, yet not in the
least blowsy; cool pink with just a hint of lilac;
and sweetly fragrant. The foliage is light green.

'Mrs Paul'

'Mrs John Laing' features in the breeding of
some quite recent roses.

Bennett, England, UK, 1887
'François Michelon' × unknown
Repeat flowering ı *Moderate fragrance*
HABIT Bush H/W 1.5m/1.2m (5ft/4ft) ı ZONES 5–10

'Mrs Paul'

BOURBON ı LIGHT PINK

In 1863, the great English rosarian William
Paul dedicated a crimson rose, 'Mrs William
Paul', to his wife. It is rarely encountered
now. When his turn came in 1891, William's
son, George, was less formal: his wife's
rose is simply 'Mrs Paul'. It is a seedling of
'Madame Isaac Pereire', resembling its parent in its tall, almost climbing branches, its
bright green leaves, and its large, sweetly
scented, rather blowsy flowers. They are of
palest blush-pink, in contrast to the brash,
deep shade of 'Madame Isaac Pereire' or the
rosy pink of her sport 'Madame Ernest Calvat'.
The three look splendid together, but do not
expect the blooms of 'Mrs Paul' to be quite

'Mrs Reynolds Hole'

up to the standard of the other two, except
in the fall/autumn.

Paul, England, UK, 1891
'Madame Isaac Pereire' × unknown
Repeat flowering ı *Moderate fragrance*
HABIT Bush H/W 1.5m/1.2m (5ft/3ft) ı ZONES 5–11

'Mrs Reynolds Hole'

TEA ı PINK BLEND

The Reverend Samuel Reynolds Hole, Dean
of Rochester from 1887 until his death in 1904,
was one of the great nineteenth-century evangelists of the rose and the first president of
the (now Royal) National Rose Society, still
the world's largest and most influential rose
society. Alexander Dickson dedicated a double,
silvery carmine Hybrid Tea to him in 1904,
named 'Dean Hole'. It took the French
gallantry of the Nabonnand brothers to
commemorate the Dean's wife, which they
did three years later, in 1907. 'Mrs Reynolds
Hole' is carmine shaded purple, and is a large,
double bloom as buxom as a Victorian matron.
The bush is sturdy; the dark green foliage is
glossy and abundant.

Nabonnand, France, 1900
Parentage unknown
Repeat flowering ı *Moderate fragrance*
HABIT Bush H/W 1.2m/1m (4ft/3ft) ı ZONES 7–11

'Mutabilis'

CHINA ı YELLOW BLEND

'Tipo Ideale', *R. chinensis mutabilis*, *R. mutabilis*,
R. turkistanica

The origins of this wonderful rose are something of a mystery. It was introduced by Swiss

'Mutabilis'

botanist Henri Correvon in 1932, having been presented to him by Prince Borromeo of Italy 40 years before. Whether it originated in the prince's great gardens at Isola Bella, on Italy's Lake Maggiore, or in China, no one knows. Its slim stems build up to a densely leafy bush – 3m (10ft) tall and wide if left unpruned, a third of those dimensions if pruned firmly – that covers itself with sprays of single blooms like butterflies. They open Tea Rose yellow but pass to pink, carmine and crimson, creating a tapestry of different colors. There is no other rose quite like it. The finely cut, dark green foliage is plum-colored when young.

Parentage unknown
Repeat flowering ı *No fragrance*

HABIT Bush H/W 3m/3m (10ft/10ft) ı ZONES 6–11
Royal Horticultural Society Award of Garden Merit 1993

'Niphetos'

TEA ı WHITE

The name is mock classical Greek for 'snowy', and indeed 'Niphetos' reigned as the purest of white roses from its introduction by Bougère in 1843 until 'Frau Karl Druschki' came along in 1901. It was a great favorite with nineteenth-century florists, who grew it in glasshouses (it dislikes both cold and wet) and wired its weak stems to hold the flowers up.

To modern eyes, the large, globular blooms are floppy when open, but the buds are as long and elegant as anyone could desire. The foliage is pale green. There is also a rampant climbing sport, which came from the English firm of Keynes, Williams & Co. in 1889.

Bougère, France, 1843
Parentage unknown
Repeat flowering ı *Intense fragrance*

HABIT Bush H/W 3m/1.8m (10ft/6ft) ı ZONES 7–11

'Oeillet Flamand'

HYBRID GALLICA ı PINK BLEND

The French name means 'Flemish carnation', and the very double flowers are indeed like carnations in their ruffled fullness. They are striped with pink, purple and white, the exact proportion of the three colors varying from year to year. Sometimes the overall effect is quite dark, as in the photograph, with the striping a subtle, two-tone effect. At other times the effect is more one of dark stripes on a pale ground. The growth is typical Gallica: compact but not too thorny. The foliage is mid-green and rough.

Vibert, France, 1845
Parentage unknown
Summer flowering ı *Intense fragrance*

HABIT Bush H/W 1.2m/1m (4ft/3ft) ı ZONES 5–11

'Niphetos'

'Oeillet Flamand'

'Oeillet Panachée'

striped with deep pink, and have small, flat, quilled petals. They are not especially large, but they are fragrant. The bush is a dainty affair, growing to 1m (3ft) or so tall. The foliage is mid-green and smooth.

Verdier, France, 1888
Parentage unknown
Summer flowering ∣ *Moderate fragrance*
HABIT Bush H/W 1m/60cm (3ft/2ft) ∣ ZONES 5–10

'Omar Khayyám'

'Oeillet Panachée'

MOSS ∣ PINK BLEND

'Striped Moss'

This rose, which came from Charles Verdier in 1888, its parents unrecorded, is not seen very often. There are probably better striped roses, but this one does add the charm of brownish moss. The blooms are pale pink

'Old Blush'

CHINA ∣ MEDIUM PINK

'Common Blush China', 'Common Monthly', 'Last Rose of Summer', 'Monthly Rose', 'Old Pink Daily', 'Old Pink Monthly', 'Parsons' Pink China'

'Blush' usually suggests a very pale pink rose, but 'Old Blush' is a mid-pink. Like many of the Old China Roses, however, it does blush

deeper with age. The semi-double flowers are not overlarge, 8cm (3in) or so in diameter, but they are borne in loose sprays in great abundance from spring to the fall/autumn. They are softly fragrant. The bush is tallish and slender, with narrow, pointed, mid-green leaves. Introduced to Europe from China in 1789, it is one of the most important of all roses historically. All the repeat-flowering Modern Garden Roses probably descended from 'Old Blush'. Yet far from being a superannuated dowager, it is still one of the most desirable of roses; no cottage garden is complete without it.

China, discovered by Parsons 1752; introduced to Europe 1789
Parentage unknown
Repeat flowering ∣ *Slight fragrance*
HABIT Bush H/W 1.8m/1.2m (6ft/4ft) ∣ ZONES 6–11
World Federation of Rose Societies Old Rose Hall of Fame 1988

'Omar Khayyám'

DAMASK ∣ LIGHT PINK

'My grave', wrote Omar Khayyám, 'shall be in a place where the breeze shall scatter rose petals upon it.' It was so; a rose grows on the poet's grave at Naishapur in Iran (formerly Persia) to this day. In 1893, seeds of this rose were planted at the grave of Edward FitzGerald, the translator of *The Rubaiyat*, in Suffolk, England. It is this rose from FitzGerald's grave that has been propagated and introduced as 'Omar Khayyám'. A typical Damask, it has downy, soft green leaves and bears abundant

'Old Blush'

'Pearl'

the modern Floribundas, it is hardly one of the more gorgeous rose species. If you fancy trying this rambler, you would be best to choose a form selected for its appearance. 'Pearl' is as good as any. Its single-petalled, white blooms and its hips are larger than usual, and quite attractive in their season. The foliage is light green.

Turner, England, UK, 1915
Selected form of *R. multiflora*
Summer flowering | *Slight fragrance*
HABIT Rambler H/W 3m/2.5m (10ft/8ft) | ZONES 4–11

'Pergolèse'

PORTLAND | MAUVE

A most attractive Old Garden Rose, 'Pergolèse' is compact in habit and as free with its shapely, strongly perfumed blooms in the fall/autumn as in spring. The small to medium-sized flowers are borne in small clusters and are fully double, starting off a rich purple-crimson and quickly fading with age to a soft lilac-mauve. The foliage is lush and dark green.

Moreau et Robert, France, 1860
Parentage unknown
Repeat flowering | *Strong fragrance*
HABIT Bush H/W 1m/1m (3ft/3ft) | ZONES 5–11

'Paul Neyron'

small, very double, quartered flowers in clear pink in summer. Not a first-rate bloom, perhaps, but one full of history, sentiment and fragrance. The flowers are followed by orange-red hips.

Iran; introduced 1893
Parentage unknown
Summer flowering | *Moderate fragrance*
HABIT Bush H/W 1m/1m (3ft/3ft) | ZONES 5–10

'Paul Neyron'

HYBRID PERPETUAL | MEDIUM PINK

Until 'Peace' came along, 'Paul Neyron' held, unchallenged, the heavyweight title – the 'Largest Rose in the World'. When aided by good soil and lavish manuring, it can still be a knockout, the fat buds opening to extremely

large, double flowers that have 50-plus petals and are often 20cm (8in) or more in diameter. Their rich pink color is so distinctive that the color 'neyron rose' has become part of the gardener's vocabulary. The bush is tall, with large, rich green foliage, and flowers freely and repeatedly. 'Paul Neyron' was raised by Antoine Levet in 1869. If you remember gigantic roses like pink cabbages in your grandmother's garden, they were almost certainly this variety.

Levet, France, 1869
'Victor Verdier' × 'Anna de Diesbach'
Repeat flowering | *Moderate fragrance*
HABIT Bush H/W 1.2m/60cm (4ft/2ft) | ZONES 5–10

'Pearl'

HYBRID MULTIFLORA | WHITE

Some years ago, *R. multiflora* enjoyed quite a vogue in the United States as a 'living crash barrier' – it was planted along highways to form a thicket dense enough to catch cars that ran off the road – and as a 'living fence' or clipped hedge in gardens. For all its importance as an understock and as an ancestor of

'Pergolèse'

'Petite de Hollande'

'Petite de Hollande'

CENTIFOLIA ⎪ MEDIUM PINK

'Petite Junon de Holland', 'Pompon des Dames', *R. centifolia minor*

The name translates as 'Little One from Holland', and while not a Miniature, this rose is a smaller version of the 'Cabbage Rose'. The small, double, clear pink flowers, only 4 cm (1½ in) in diameter, are of the same exquisite form; the coarsely toothed foliage is a similar soft green; the bush is shorter and bushier, but similarly very free with its flowers, which are borne in clusters. The only thing about it that is not reduced is the perfume. English rosarian Graham Stuart Thomas, a lover of Old Garden Roses, describes it as one of the very best Centifolias to grow where space is limited.

c. 1800
Parentage unknown
Summer flowering ⎪ *Strong fragrance*
HABIT Bush H/W 1.2m/1m (4ft/3ft) ⎪ ZONES 4–10

'Petite Lisette'

CENTIFOLIA ⎪ DEEP PINK

A Vibert introduction of 1817, 'Petite Lisette' is almost a Miniature Rose. The bush is only about 1m (3ft) tall, and the leaves and flowers

'Petite Lisette'

are about half the normal size. The flowers, 2.5cm (1in) pompons, are cool pink and beautifully fragrant. The foliage is small, deeply serrated and greyish green. The whole plant is of diminutive charm. It is a fine rose for the front of a border of Old Garden Roses or to include in a mixed planting.

Vibert, France, 1817
Parentage unknown
Summer flowering ⎪ *Strong fragrance*
HABIT Bush H/W 1m/1m (3ft/3ft) ⎪ ZONES 4–10

'Prince Camille de Rohan'

HYBRID PERPETUAL ⎪ DARK RED

'La Rosière', 'Souvenir d'Auguste Rivoire'

The flowers of this 1861 introduction from Eugène Verdier are cupped and very double, but not very large. Their stalks tend to be weak,

'Prince Camille de Rohan'

and unless the plant is given the best of soil and cultivation, it is inclined to be weak and afflicted with rust. Why, then, has 'Prince Camille de Rohan' survived? For the sake of its fragrance and its ravishing color: a deep, deep velvety red shaded with maroon. In this respect there are few roses to equal it, and rosarians continue to pamper it. When it is happy, it flowers abundantly in both summer and the fall/autumn. The foliage is dull green.

Verdier, France, 1861
'Général Jacqueminot' × 'Géant des Batailles'
Repeat flowering ⎪ *Intense fragrance*
HABIT Bush H/W 1.2m/3m (4ft/3ft) ⎪ ZONES 6–10

'Quatre Saisons Blanc Mousseux'

MOSS ⎪ WHITE

'Perpetual White Moss', 'Quatre Saisons Blanche', 'Rosier de Thionville'

If you cannot cope with the cumbersome French name, by all means use the English, remembering that both are gross exaggerations. Like 'Quatre Saisons' (better known as 'Autumn Damask'), from which it sported, gaining moss and changing color on the way, the 'Perpetual White Moss' only gives a skimpy display to follow its summer crop. A cluster of blooms can, however, be very pretty, the silky whiteness of the double flowers set off by the brownish, rough-textured moss. Its growth habit and its greyish green, downy foliage are just like those of its parent, and its fragrance is just as good.

Laffay, France, before 1837
'Autumn Damask' sport
Repeat flowering ⎪ *Strong fragrance*
HABIT Bush H/W 1.2m/1m (4ft/3ft) ⎪ ZONES 5–10

golden stamens. The plant is vigorous and healthy-looking, and flowers abundantly throughout the season. As an added bonus, there is a good display of small hips at the end of the season.

c. 1830
Parentage unknown
Repeat flowering ı *Musk fragrance*

HABIT Rambler H/W 6–9m/6–9m (20–30ft/20–30ft) ı
ZONES 5–10

🌹 Royal Horticultural Society Award of Garden Merit 1993

'Quatre Saisons Blanc Mousseux'

'Queen of Bourbons'

BOURBON ı PINK BLEND

'Bourbon Queen', 'Reine des Iles Bourbon', 'Souvenir de la Princesse de Lamballe'

Introduced in 1834 by M. Mauget of Orléans, this rose was named for the ill-fated confidante of Queen Marie Antoinette, Marie Thérèse Louise de Savoie-Carignan, Princesse de Lamballe (1749–1792). An Italian–French courtier and an aristocrat of the House of Savoy, the princess is one of the best-known victims of the French Revolution, having been torn to pieces by the mob for refusing to take an oath repudiating the monarchy. It is a lovely rose, medium-sized, mallow-pink and scented, with crinkled petals. Do not expect many blooms after the first flowering, although there will be some. The bush is on the tall side, its branches lax enough to allow it to be trained either as a shrub or as a short climber. The foliage is dull green.

Mauget, France, 1834
Parentage unknown
Summer flowering ı *Moderate fragrance*

HABIT Bush H/W 1.8m/1.2m (6ft/4ft) ı ZONES 5–11

'Rambling Rector'

HYBRID MULTIFLORA ı WHITE

The evocatively named 'Rambling Rector' is an old cultivar of unknown origin that was discovered growing around ancient structures

and on old garden estates in England. Given the chance, it is capable of rambling 6–9m (20–30 ft) in all directions, and can easily smother a hedgerow, ramble extensively through trees, or cover an eyesore (such as a garden shed). The small, semi-double, white flowers come in large clusters and are most attractive when fully open and displaying their rich

'Rambling Rector'

'Queen of Bourbons'

'Reine des Mousseuses'

MOSS   LIGHT PINK

This rose is not often seen, but it is deserving
of a wider audience. The flowers are full and
well scented, their pink petals beautifully
arranged, and the buds are mossy. The plant
is perhaps bushier than some Mosses, with
dark green foliage.

Moreau et Robert, France, 1860
Parentage unknown
Summer flowering   Strong fragrance

HABIT Bush H/W 1.2m/1m (4ft/3ft)   ZONES 5–10

'Reine des Violettes'

HYBRID PERPETUAL   MAUVE

'Queen of the Violets'

Officially classed as a Hybrid Perpetual since
its introduction by Millet–Malet in 1860,
'Reine des Violettes' would be better placed
among the Bourbons, both for its slender,
thornless branches and for its delightful flat,
quartered blooms, which are moderately
sized and very double. The flowers come
in wonderful blends of mauve and purple,
sometimes soft and delicate, at others
startling, and always beautifully set off by
the smooth, grey-green leaves. It is also
intensely fragrant. Give it the best of
everything; it needs and deserves it.

Millet–Malet, France, 1860
'Pius IX' × seedling
Repeat flowering   Intense fragrance

HABIT Bush H/W 1.5m/1m (5ft/3ft)   ZONES 5–10

'Reine des Mousseuses'

'Reine des Violettes'

'Reine Victoria'

BOURBON   MEDIUM PINK

'La Reine Victoria', 'Reine'

It is intriguing that the rose named for Queen
Victoria should not only be French-raised (by
Joseph Schwartz of Lyon, in 1872) but should
also be a member of a class named for the
French royal family. 'Reine Victoria' suggests
the lady in her youth rather than her plump
middle age, for the double, soft rose-pink
blooms with their shell-shaped petals have a
dainty perfection, like a rose on a Victorian
teacup. 'Reine Victoria' has a beautiful fragrance and blooms throughout the season,
but it must have the best of cultivation to
show its full beauty. The foliage is light green
and smooth.

Schwartz, France, 1872
Parentage unknown
Repeat flowering   Strong fragrance

HABIT Bush H/W 1.2m/1m (4ft/3ft)   ZONES 5–11

'Rêve d'Or'

'Robert le Diable'

'Rêve d'Or'

NOISETTE   MEDIUM YELLOW

'Golden Chain'

'Rêve d'Or' means 'Golden Dream'. The
rose, however, is a soft, buttery yellow with
tints of peach. It is a very lovely rose, climbing strongly enough to adorn the front of a
house with its glossy, dark green leaves, tinted
with copper in their youth, and its generous
sprays of richly scented, frilly blooms, which
open from pointed buds to flowers some
10cm (4in) in diameter. It likes warmth, and
needs a sheltered spot in cool climates. The
flowers come all season. Madame Ducher
introduced it in 1869. Nine years later, in
1878, it produced a sport, 'William Allen
Richardson', which starts out life a much
deeper color, almost orange, before fading
out completely to a bleached-out apricot.
'Rêve d'Or' is much the nicer rose all round.

Ducher, France, 1869
Seedling of 'Madame Schultz'
Repeat flowering   Moderate fragrance

HABIT Climber H/W 3.5m/2.5m (12ft/8ft)   ZONES 7–11

'Rose de Meaux'

'Reine Victoria'

'Robert le Diable'

HYBRID GALLICA · MAUVE

'Robert le Diable' may not be one of the better Old Garden Roses for the garden, as the bush is both lax and spindly. Its flowers are extraordinary, however. Formed in the Old Garden Rose style, they display an astonishing range of quite sombre colors as they age – crimson, purple, dove-grey and violet. The flower centre is often green. The scent is good but not overpowering, and the foliage is matt and soft green. The raiser and date of origin are unknown, but it would seem a safe guess that it came out around 1831, when Giacomo Meyerbeer's opera *Robert le Diable* was the sensation of Paris.

Probably c. 1831
Parentage unknown
Summer flowering · Moderate fragrance
HABIT Bush H/W 1m/1m (3ft/3ft) ZONES 5–11

'Roger Lambelin'

HYBRID PERPETUAL · RED BLEND

This is one of those roses that you either love – finding its very double, dark crimson flowers, deckle-edged in white, quite unusual and beautiful – or hate – thinking it bizarre and unhealthy-looking. Perhaps people in the latter camp have never seen a good specimen, for it is not an easy rose to grow, needing good, rich soil and protection from any diseases that may be about. The foliage is mid-green and dull. If it likes you, it flowers repeatedly and fairly freely.

Schwartz, France, 1890
'Fisher Holmes' sport
Repeat flowering · Light fragrance
HABIT Bush H/W 1.2m/1m (4ft/3ft) · ZONES 5–10

'Rose de Meaux'

CENTIFOLIA · MEDIUM PINK

'De Meaux', 'Pompon Rose', *R. centifolia pomponia, R. dijoniensis, R. pomponia, R. pulchella*

Rose historians have been arguing for more than 200 years over the origin of this little charmer, which is in effect a miniature version of *R. centifolia*. It has sometimes been said that it was found growing in the garden of a gentleman called Dominique Séguier, who was bishop of Meaux, in France, from 1637 to 1659. Others suggest that the name is probably linked to Saint Fiacre of Ireland, patron saint of gardeners, who settled in France in the year 628 on land granted to him by Saint Faro of Meaux, who was bishop at the time. Whatever its origin, this variety was introduced in England by a man named Sweet at some time before 1789. 'Rose de Meaux' bears its scented pink pompons, set off by soft, pale green leaves, in late spring, on a twiggy plant 1m (3ft) or so tall. There is also a white version with pink at the hearts of the flowers.

Introduced by Sweet, England, UK, before 1789
Parentage unknown
Summer flowering · Moderate fragrance
HABIT Bush H/W 60cm/60m (2ft/2ft) · ZONES 4–10

'Roger Lambelin'

'Rose du Roi'

'Rose de Rescht'

PORTLAND ı DEEP PINK

Despite its fairly recent date of discovery and reintroduction, by well-known English gardening writer Nancy Lindsay, nothing is known about the origin of this rose. The only trait betraying its ancestors, the Damasks, is the short flower stems. It makes a compact bush with dense, bright green foliage, and blooms in several bursts through the season. The very double flowers, in the form of rosettes, are cerise becoming flushed and shaded with magenta. They are sweetly scented. It is one of the best Old Garden Roses for the modern garden, almost as prolific and continuous as a Floribunda, at least while it is young. Old bushes need severe discipline at pruning time or they get lazy.

Discovered and reintroduced by Lindsay, England, UK, 1950
Parentage unknown
Repeat flowering ı *Intense, damask fragrance*
HABIT Bush H/W 1m/60cm (3ft/2ft) ı ZONES 5–11
Royal Horticultural Society Award of Garden Merit 1993

'Rose du Roi'

PORTLAND ı MEDIUM RED

'Crimson Perpetual', 'Lee's Crimson Perpetual'
Historically, this is one of the most important of roses, being one of the progenitors of the Hybrid Perpetuals and thus of their descendants, the Hybrid Teas. It is evidently suffering from old age, as it needs good cultivation in order to grow well and to bear, throughout the season, its large crimson

blooms, semi-double and fragrant. The bush is on the short side, and the foliage is small and dark green. It was raised in the gardens of the Palace of Saint-Cloud, Paris, and legend has it that the director of the gardens, Le Comte Lelieur, resigned when the raiser, Ecoffay, in a display of loyalty to the newly restored king, Louis XVIII, dedicated the rose to the king rather than to him. It was introduced in 1815.

Ecoffay, France, 1815
Parentage unknown
Repeat flowering ı *Intense fragrance*
HABIT Bush H/W 1m/1m (3ft/3ft) ı ZONES 5–11

'Rose-Marie Viaud'

HYBRID MULTIFLORA ı MAUVE

'Rosemary Viaud'
Introduced by an otherwise unknown French rosarian named Igoult in 1924, this vigorous rambler is a seedling of 'Veilchenblau' and resembles its parent in its lack of thorns and its glossy, light green leaves. Many people consider it superior to 'Veilchenblau', for its little flowers are more double and richer in color. Borne in small clusters, they open a rich purple and fade through every pretty shade of lilac and mauve. It is a good idea to grow both roses, as 'Rose-Marie Viaud' does

not start blooming until 'Veilchenblau' has nearly finished. Do not confuse this variety with 'Rose Marie', a pink Hybrid Tea from the 1920s.

Igoult, France, 1924
Seedling of 'Veilchenblau'
Summer flowering ı *Moderate fragrance*
HABIT Rambler H/W 4.5m/1.8m (15ft/6ft) ı ZONES 4–11

'Rubens'

TEA ı WHITE

The great painter has always been known for the glowing brilliance of his reds and for the plump voluptuousness of his naked ladies. The rose Moreau et Robert chose to name in his honor in 1859 was of a color described in those days as 'flesh color'. The blending of pale pinks with ivory and cream is exceptionally lovely. The large, double flowers have a bronzy yellow centre, and are shapely and endowed with the true tea fragrance. Owing to its lack of hardiness, 'Rubens' is one of the lesser-known Teas these days, but gardeners in mild climates should not overlook it. The foliage is bright green and smooth.

Robert et Moreau, France, 1859
Parentage unknown
Repeat flowering ı *Moderate, tea fragrance*
HABIT Bush H/W 1m/1m (3ft/3ft) ı ZONES 7–11

RIGHT 'Rose-Marie
INSET 'Ru

'Rose de Rescht'

'Russelliana'

HYBRID MULTIFLORA | MAUVE

'Old Spanish Rose', 'Russell's Cottage Rose', 'Scarlet Grevillea', 'Souvenir de la Bataille de Marengo'

The Grevilleas are a group of shrubs, native to Australia, to which no rose bears the slightest resemblance. It is thought that the name 'Scarlet Grevillea' may indicate that this rose was introduced from the Far East around 1840 by Sir Charles Greville. If he was indeed responsible, he was guilty of false advertising, for 'Russelliana' is hardly scarlet but rather a deep magenta-pink, fading to a much softer, dusty mauve as the flowers age. The blooms are double, flat and scented, and borne in clusters. The plant is one of the strongest of ramblers, with coarse, mid-green foliage. Some say that it derives from a cross between *R. multiflora* and *R. setigera*. It has proved itself to be a great survivor in difficult conditions, its long canes withstanding severe winters and the accompanying wind chill factors.

Probably Spain; introduced c. 1840
Probably *R. multiflora* × *R. setigera*
Summer flowering | *Moderate fragrance*

HABIT Rambler H/W 3m/3m (10ft/10ft) | ZONES 4–11

'Salet'

'Russelliana'

'Sanguinea'

The plant is generous with its flowers, and produces an ample canopy of mid-green foliage to complement them. In Victorian times, this rose was popular as a boutonniere for gentlemen.

Beauregard, France, 1839
'Parks's Yellow' × 'Madame Desprez'
Repeat flowering | *Moderate fragrance*

HABIT Bush H/W 1m/60cm (3ft/2ft) | ZONES 7–9

'Salet'

MOSS | MEDIUM PINK

Most authorities who write about the Old Garden Roses are inclined to be disparaging about 'Salet', and it is true that there are classier roses available. In its favor, however, the buds are well mossed, and the clear bright pink blooms, very large, double, ruffled and fragrant, have considerable charm and are

'Safrano'

TEA | APRICOT BLEND

The name is an obvious reference to the beautiful color of the large, fully double blooms, a saffron-tinted apricot-yellow with a sulphur-yellow base. The flowers hold their color best if kept out of full sun, and are able to withstand wet weather without losing their beauty.

'Safrano'

borne in great abundance throughout the season. This is by far the most reliably repeat flowering of the Moss Roses. The bush is of Floribunda size, with few thorns and pale green leaves. An 1854 creation of François Lacharme of Lyon, it has more recently been used in the breeding of modern Moss Roses.

Lacharme, France, 1854
Parentage unknown
Repeat flowering ı *Moderate fragrance*

HABIT Bush H/W 1.2m/1m (4ft/3ft) ı ZONES 5–10

'Sanguinea'

CHINA ı DARK RED

'Bengal Cramoisi Double', 'Bengal Rose', 'Blood-red China Rose', 'La Sanguine', *R. indica cruenta*

'Sanguinea' is a temperamental variety but holds an historically important position, being thought to be a sport from 'Slater's Crimson China'. The blooms are large and single-petalled, not very fragrant, and of a darker crimson than those of its famous (presumed) parent. They appear as small clusters of flowers from spring to first frost, although like most China Roses 'Sanguinea' will bloom all year in a frost-free climate. The foliage is pale green, red-tinted in youth. The plant habit is awkwardly angular and sparse.

Probably China; discovered 1887
Thought to be 'Slater's Crimson China' sport
Repeat flowering ı *Moderate fragrance*

HABIT Bush H/W 1m/60cm (3ft/2ft) ı ZONES 6–11

'Serratipetala'

CHINA ı PINK BLEND

'Rose Oeillet de Saint Arquey', *R. chinensis serratipetala*

The French name suggests that the flowers look like carnations, and indeed they do with their serrated petals. The color is interesting: the inner petals are candy-pink, the outer ones are dark crimson. These unique blooms are borne in small clusters throughout the season, but never very freely, and the bush is inclined to be scrawny. There is little scent. The leaves are glossy and dark green. It is definitely a rose for the specialist.

Vilfray, France, 1912
Parentage unknown
Repeat flowering ı *Slight fragrance*

HABIT Bush H/W 1m/60cm (3ft/2ft) ı ZONES 6–11

'Seven Sisters'

HYBRID MULTIFLORA ı PINK BLEND

'Seven Sisters Rose', *R. cathayensis platyphylla, R. multiflora grevillei, R. multiflora playtphylla, R. platyphylla, R. thoryi*

This is an old Oriental rose, thought to have been brought to Europe from China in 1816. The name is probably a translation from the Chinese. There are usually many more than seven blooms in each of its clusters, and each bloom is different in color. They open almost purple, then fade through pink to white before the petals drop. At the time it was introduced to the West, there were few richly colored climbing roses, and even now, when we have so many, a plant of 'Seven Sisters' smothered in softly scented blooms in varied colors is a charming sight indeed. The foliage is broad and a lush, bright green. Give it a sheltered spot, as it is rather sensitive to cold.

China, 1816
Parentage unknown
Summer flowering ı *Moderate fragrance*

HABIT Climber H/W 3.5m/3m (12ft/10ft) ı ZONES 4–11

'Slater's Crimson China'

CHINA ı MEDIUM RED

'Chinese Monthly Rose', 'Crimson China Rose', 'Old Crimson China', 'Semperflorens', *R. bengalensis, R. chinensis semperflorens, R. diversifolia, R. indica semperflorens, R. semperflorens*

It is never easy to be certain of the correct identification of the various Crimson China Roses, all rather alike, that survive in various botanic gardens. The rose pictured is almost certainly 'Slater's Crimson China', long believed to be extinct but rediscovered in Bermuda in the mid-twentieth century. The height of the bush, the dark green leaves, plum-toned in youth, and the small clusters of brilliant crimson flowers do match the descriptions in the reference books as well as old pictures of this variety, such as the well-known drawing by Redouté. 'Slater's Crimson China' is a rose of commanding importance, for until it arrived in England from China's Fa Tee Nurseries in the 1790s, there were no true dark red roses in the West, only purple

'Slater's Crimson China'
TOP INSET 'Seven Sisters'
BOTTOM INSET 'Serratipetala'

'Soleil d'Or'

Pernet-Ducher's 20 years of breeding with the mulish 'Persian Yellow' (*R. foetida persiana*), it was not quite the longed-for yellow bush rose. It is rather a blend of yellow and coral-pink. It was, however, the start of something new. All the modern yellow roses, and a great many roses of other colors, descend from 'Soleil d'Or'. These days, however, it is best left to the collections of botanic gardens. The large, double flowers may be pretty, but the bush is weak and the glossy, rich green foliage is very susceptible to black spot.

Pernet-Ducher, France, 1900
'Antoine Ducher' × *R. foetida persiana*
Repeat flowering ı *Moderate fragrance*
HABIT Bush H/W 1m/1m (3ft/3ft) ı ZONES 5–10

'Sophie's Perpetual'

CHINA ı PINK BLEND

This is yet another Old Garden Rose that has been brought back into popularity after being almost forgotten. How it came to be neglected is hard to explain, for it is a willing grower and bears blooms of great charm, cupped in form and of palest pink heavily shaded and flushed deeper, sometimes so deep as to be almost red. The flowers are fragrant, the growth tall enough for this rose to be trained as a pillar. The foliage is dark green, and the bush has few prickles. Its original name has been forgotten, and it is now named for Countess Sophie Benckendorff, who planted it in the 1920s in her garden at (what is now known as) Lime Kiln House, in Suffolk. Humphrey

Brooke and his wife (Countess Sophie's grand-daughter) later acquired the property and restored the garden. Brooke rediscovered the rose and reintroduced it as 'Sophie's Perpetual' in 1960.

Paul, England, UK, before 1905; rediscovered by Brooke, 1960
Parentage unknown
Repeat flowering ı *Moderate fragrance*
HABIT Bush H/W 2.5m/1.2m (8ft/4ft) ı ZONES 6–11

'Souvenir de la Malmaison'

BOURBON ı LIGHT PINK

'Queen of Beauty and Fragrance'

Forget the romance of the name and look at this famous rose objectively. The wide, double flowers, as large as a Hybrid Tea, are blush-pink, quartered and fragrant, and so beautiful that they are a fitting tribute indeed to the Empress Joséphine, the first wife of Napoleon Bonaparte. The bush is strong and healthy, with glossy, mid-green foliage, and can be counted on to repeat its flowering. The English name is no exaggeration. In warm climates, which this rose prefers, it is one of the first roses to bloom and the last to finish. It was raised by Jean Béluze of Lyon in 1843.

Béluze, France, 1843
'Madame Desprez' × Tea Rose
Repeat flowering ı *Intense, spicy fragrance*
HABIT Bush H/W 1.8m/1.8m (6ft/6ft) ı ZONES 5–11
🌹 World Federation of Rose Societies Old Rose Hall of Fame 1988

'Sophie's Perpetual'

Gallicas. All our true red roses derive their gorgeous color from 'Slater's Crimson China'.

China; introduced by Slater 1792
Parentage unknown
Repeat flowering ı *Moderate fragrance*
HABIT Bush H/W 1m/1m (3ft/3ft) ı ZONES 6–11

'Soleil d'Or'

HYBRID FOETIDA ı YELLOW BLEND

No rose ever created a greater sensation than 'Soleil d'Or' did on its first showing in Paris in 1900. The first fruit of Joseph

'Souvenir de la Malmaison'

'Souvenir de Madame Breuil'

'Souvenir de Madame Léonie Viennot'

CLIMBING TEA | YELLOW BLEND

Refer to her affectionately as 'Madame Léonie', but do not overlook this rose if you need a beautiful and uncommon climbing rose. In cold climates, give her the warmest wall. Prune her only lightly, if at all, for the finest flowers come from the old wood. The large, very double flowers, in shining blends of salmon and cream, are exquisitely long-budded and shapely. They are richly fragrant, too, and borne in profusion all season. The foliage is a glossy bronze-green.

Bernaix, France, 1897
Parentage unknown
Repeat flowering | Heavy fragrance

HABIT Climber H/W 3.5m/2.5m (12ft/8ft) | ZONES 5–11

'Souvenir de Madame Léonie Viennot'

'Souvenir de Madame Breuil'

BOURBON | DEEP PINK

This rose is quite a charmer, with heavily mossed buds and cup-shaped flowers in deep carmine laced with purple, fading to magenta-pink. The bright green foliage is broad, with a hint of gloss, suggesting Bourbon ancestry, and the plant is vigorous and bushy. Not much is known about its origin. It probably dates from the 1850s or thereabouts.

Probably c. 1850s
Parentage unknown
Repeat flowering | Light fragrance

HABIT Bush H/W 1.5m/1.2m (5ft/4ft) | ZONES 5–11

'Souvenir de Pierre Vibert'

MOSS | RED BLEND

Jean-Pierre Vibert of Angers is one of the most renowned of the early rose-breeders. His famous 'Baronne Prévost', along with other roses of his, can be found in this book. He flourished in the 1840s and 1850s, and the date of 'Souvenir de Pierre Vibert', 1867, is probably about right for his colleagues Moreau et Robert to have dedicated this rose to his memory. It is the sort of rose he would have been happy to have raised himself, its large, double flowers richly colored and shapely, in shades of crimson to pink and violet, the buds nicely mossed. The bush is of only moderate vigor, but it often gives a few fall/autumn blooms. The foliage is matt and lush green.

Moreau et Robert, France, 1867
Parentage unknown
Repeat flowering | Moderate fragrance

HABIT Bush H/W 1.2m/1m (4ft/3ft) | ZONES 5–10

'Souvenir de Pierre Vibert'

'Souvenir du Docteur Jamain'

HYBRID PERPETUAL · DARK RED

This rose is much admired by English lovers of Old Garden Roses, but it does not like hot climates, which will scorch the flowers. Try giving it a little shade in the afternoon, and then you can look forward to large, fragrant flowers, not so double that the golden stamens cannot light up the port-wine colors of the petals. It is inclined toward legginess, and needs the best of cultivation to be seen in its full beauty. The foliage is mid-green and smooth.

Lacharme, France, 1865
Seedling of 'Charles Lefèbvre'
Repeat flowering · Moderate fragrance

HABIT Bush H/W 3m/2m (10ft/7ft) · ZONES 6–10

'Stanwell Perpetual'

HYBRID SPINOSISSIMA · WHITE

This rose was discovered as a seedling in the garden of a man called Lee, who lived in Stanwell, Middlesex. He subsequently introduced the variety, in 1838. The sprawling, grey-leafed bush is heavily prickled but rarely without at least a few flowers. Delightful they are, too: blush-pink, double, full of petals and softly scented. No rose could be a more charming introduction to the beauty of the Old Garden Roses. Leave the bush unpruned and allow it to establish itself at its natural height and width of around 1.5m (5ft).

Lee, England, UK, 1838
R. damascena bifera × *R. spinosissima*
Repeat flowering · Slight fragrance

HABIT Bush H/W 1.5m/1.5m (5ft/5ft) · ZONES 4–10

TOP 'Souvenir de Thérèse Levet'
LEFT 'Souvenir d'Elise Vardon'
INSET 'Souvenir du Docteur Jamain'

'Souvenir de Thérèse Levet'

TEA · DARK RED

Regarded in its day as one of the very best of the red Tea Roses, 'Souvenir de Thérèse Levet' is not often seen these days. It was raised by Antoine Levet and introduced in 1886, and obviously named for a member of his family. It is not among the hardier of the Teas, and when compared with our many rich and brilliant red roses, its muted crimson might seem a trifle dull. It is a good rose, however, shapely and scented, and it flowers quite well all season. In hot weather the color is apt to be a paler red, almost cherry-red. The foliage is glossy and dull green.

Levet, France, 1886
'Adam' × unknown
Repeat flowering · Moderate fragrance

HABIT Bush H/W 1m/60cm (3ft/2ft) · ZONES 7–11

'Souvenir d'Elise Vardon'

TEA · WHITE

Victorian rose-lovers poured extravagant praise on the beauty of this rose, and abuse on its reluctance to produce flowers in any quantity. Perhaps it was just the English climate, for in warmer climates it seems to give a perfectly good account of itself. The flowers are lovely in their soft shades of cream, apricot and pink and in their perfect form. Raised by Marest of Paris in 1855, 'Souvenir d'Elise Vardon' was the first rose to display the high-centred, spiral form, with no hint of quartering, that we now accept as the ideal. The foliage is semi-glossy.

Marest, France, 1855
Parentage unknown
Repeat flowering · Moderate fragrance

HABIT Bush H/W 1m/60cm (3ft/2ft) · ZONES 7–11

'Stanwell Perpetual'

'Tea Rambler'

HYBRID MULTIFLORA | ORANGE PINK

Raised by William Paul in 1904, 'Tea Rambler' was rather overshadowed at the time by the instant popularity accorded 'Dorothy Perkins'. Now it has many admirers, who appreciate its soft color – pink with just a hint of salmon – neat shape and delicate fragrance. The double flowers are smallish but are carried in good-sized clusters, and look well against the slim branches and disease-resistant, mid-green leaves. The name is appropriate, for the rose does combine the rambler style with something of the elegance of the Tea Roses – although not, unfortunately, with their ability to flower repeatedly.

Paul, England, UK, 1904
'Crimson Rambler' × Tea Rose
Summer flowering | *Moderate fragrance*

HABIT Rambler H/W 4.5m/2.5m (15ft/8ft) | ZONES 4–11

'Thalia'

HYBRID MULTIFLORA | WHITE

'White Rambler'

For many years one of the most popular white ramblers, 'Thalia' is something of a back number now, when there are so many to choose from. A large old plant of 'Thalia', however, in full, late spring bloom, its great trusses of small, double, creamy flowers set against dark green leaves and exhaling their sweet fragrance, can still cause Oohs and Aahs of delight. It is not repeat flowering, though, and a heavy shower of rain will ruin the display.

Schmitt, France, 1895; introduced by Lambert, Germany, 1895
R. multiflora × 'Paquerette'
Spring flowering | *Sweet fragrance*

HABIT Rambler H/W 3.5m/2.5m (12ft/8ft) | ZONES 4–11

LEFT 'Tea Rambler'
BELOW 'Thalia'

'Trier'

'Tricolore de Flandre'

HYBRID GALLICA ꞏ PINK BLEND

Finely striped in purple and blush, 'Tricolore de Flandre' is much in the mould of 'Camaieux'. It is a little less subtle in its tonings, perhaps, but it makes up for that by being easier to grow. Its small, double flowers have a few more petals, too, but this is no great advantage in displaying the stripes. It is sweetly scented, and the plant is compact and rather bushy, with rough-textured, mid-green foliage. The name is a patriotic gesture by the raiser, Louis van Houtte, who by 1870 owned Belgium's most successful nursery.

Van Houtte, Belgium, 1846
Parentage unknown
Summer flowering ꞏ *Moderate fragrance*

HABIT Bush H/W 1m/60cm (3ft/2ft) ꞏ ZONES 5–11

'Trier'

HYBRID MULTIFLORA ꞏ WHITE

Introduced by Peter Lambert in 1904, 'Trier' was, in its day, admired as the most perpetually flowering of climbing roses. Nowadays we have many repeat-flowering climbers, and 'Trier' is remembered chiefly as the progenitor of Joseph Pemberton's Hybrid Musks. Its scented, semi-double, off-white flowers come in bunches throughout the season, and

'Tricolore de Flandre''

look attractive against the pale green leaves. It is decidedly shrubby in growth and needs much encouragement to climb to its potential height of 2.5m (8ft). It is believed to be a self-pollinated seedling of the now almost extinct rambler 'Aglaia'. Trier, founded by the Romans, is the town in Germany where Lambert had his nursery.

Lambert, Germany, 1904
'Aglaia' × unknown
Repeat flowering ꞏ *Moderate fragrance*

HABIT Climber H/W 2.5m/1.8m (8ft/6ft) ꞏ ZONES 4–11

'Tuscany'

HYBRID GALLICA ꞏ MAUVE

'The Old Velvet Rose'

Often claimed to be of high antiquity, and to be the 'Velvet Rose' described by pioneering English gardener John Gerard in the sixteenth century, 'Tuscany' is one of the very best of all the almost-black roses, its wine-dark blooms set off by golden stamens. The flowers are large

'Variegata di Bologna'

and semi-double, and the bush is compact and floriferous, with leaden green foliage. Some think that this rose is of Italian origin and owes its dark color to *R. pendulina*; most think that it looks to be pure-bred *R. gallica*. Many prefer its sport, 'Tuscany Superb', which dates from some time before 1837, to the original. The flowers are larger, the scent sweeter and the foliage more luxuriant.

Parentage unknown
Summer flowering ꞏ *Moderate fragrance*

HABIT Bush H/W 1m/1m (3ft/3ft) ꞏ ZONES 4–11

'Variegata di Bologna'

BOURBON ꞏ RED BLEND

This is a latecomer for a Bourbon, having been introduced by an otherwise obscure Italian rosarian named Bonfiglio in 1909. In some ways it is the most striking of all striped roses, its pinkish, off-white flowers being lavishly striped with violet. The blooms are large, double and well scented, and borne in clusters of 3–5. The bush is tall and arching, with leaden green foliage, and flowers lavishly in spring but sparingly thereafter. It needs rich soil. Starved, it is susceptible to black spot.

Bonfiglio, Italy, 1909
Parentage unknown
Repeat flowering ∣ *Moderate fragrance*
HABIT Bush H/W 1.8m/1.5m (6ft/5ft) ∣ ZONES 5–11

'Veilchenblau'

HYBRID MULTIFLORA ∣ MAUVE

'Blue Rambler', 'Blue Rosalie', 'Blue Veil', 'Rosalie', 'Violet Blue'

'Veilchenblau' was introduced in 1909 with loud claims that here at last was the blue rose. Blue it is not: rather, the little semi-double, cupped flowers, borne in generous clusters, open purple and pass to delicate shades of lilac and mauve. Hot sun bleaches them to dowdiness, so this is one of the few roses that are best grown in light shade. The foliage is large, glossy and light green. Its proud raiser, Herr Schmidt of Erfurt, could not have foreseen that, thornless and easily raised from cuttings, his rambler would be widely used as an understock.

Schmidt, Germany, 1909
'Crimson Rambler' × 'Erinnerung an Brod'
Summer flowering ∣ *Moderate fragrance*
HABIT Rambler H/W 4.5m/3.5m (15ft/12ft) ∣ ZONES 4–11

'Veilchenblau'

'Tuscany'

'Vick's Caprice'

HYBRID PERPETUAL ∣ PINK BLEND

'Wick's Caprice'

Vick was the gentleman in whose Rochester, New York, garden this rose appeared in 1891 as a sport from 'Archiduchesse Elisabeth

d'Autriche'. It is an upright, not overly tall bush, with large, mid-green leaves. The large, double, cupped flowers of lilac-pink are pleasantly fragrant but memorable mainly for their bizarre stripings of white and carmine. Each bloom is different, and the plant flowers repeatedly. Its fault is its intolerance of wet weather, which makes the flowers 'ball' and refuse to open.

Vick, USA, 1891
'Archiduchesse Elisabeth d'Autriche' sport
Repeat flowering ∣ *Moderate fragrance*
HABIT Bush H/W 1.2m/1m (4ft/3ft) ∣ ZONES 5–10

'White Maman Cochet'

TEA ∣ WHITE

'Maman Cochet' was introduced by S. Cochet in 1893. It is one of the most commonly encountered Tea Roses in America. It is not included in this book, however, despite its indestructible vigor and perfect form, as there are many other pink Old Garden Roses that

outclass it. The white sport, introduced by John Cook of Baltimore in 1896, is a different matter. Its creamy blooms, blushed with palest pink in the sun, are lovely. Do not expect it to endure much rain or cold, though, and prune it only very lightly. The foliage is semi-glossy and dark green, with plum tints.

Cook, USA, 1896
'Maman Cochet' sport
Repeat flowering ∣ *Moderate fragrance*
HABIT Bush H/W 1m/60cm (3ft/2ft) ∣ ZONES 7–11

'White Maman Cochet'

'Vick's Caprice'

'William III'

'Williams's Double Yellow'

'William III'

HYBRID SPINOSISSIMA | MAUVE

William III, the Dutchman also known as William of Orange, ascended the throne of England, Scotland and Ireland in 1689, and it would be delightful to record that his rose dates from that time, but history is not so kind. Although its precise date is unknown, it is generally attributed to the early nineteenth century, when Scotch Roses were fashionable.

'William Lobb'

It is one of the most distinctive of them, a compact, prickly bush that covers itself in spring with small, semi-double flowers, pale on the underside of the petals, a wonderful purple on top. Black hips follow, and the fall/autumn usually sees burnished tones in the tiny, dark foliage as it dies off.

Probably early 1800s
Parentage unknown
Spring flowering | *Moderate, spicy fragrance*
HABIT Bush H/W 1m/1m (3ft/3ft) | ZONES 5–11

'William Lobb'

MOSS | MAUVE

'Duchesse d'Istrie', 'Old Velvet Moss'

This is one of the grand Victorian roses, tall (it is best trained to a pillar) and bearing gorgeous-colored blooms. The semi-double flowers open wide and informally to display just about every shade of soft purple, fading to dove-grey and lilac. The foliage is matt and soft green, and the bush is very prickly. There is not much moss, but there is a good deal of fragrance. Appropriately, this rose honors one of the great Victorian gardeners. William Lobb was responsible for seeking out and introducing all kinds of plants, not just roses, to English gardens. His rose is French-bred, and came from Laffay in 1855.

Laffay, France, 1855
Parentage unknown
Summer flowering | *Strong fragrance*
HABIT Bush H/W 2.5m/1.5m (8ft/5ft) | ZONES 5–10

'Williams's Double Yellow'

HYBRID SPINOSISSIMA | MEDIUM YELLOW

'Double Yellow Scots Rose', 'Lutea Plena', 'Old Yellow Scotch', 'Prince Charlie's Rose'

Raised in 1828 by John Williams of Pitmaston, Worcestershire, 'Williams's Double Yellow' makes a compact bush 1.2m (4ft) tall, with dark leaves, the usual Scotch Rose profusion of thorns, and masses of smallish, semi-double, golden flowers. The flowers hold their color without fading, but one might wish that the petals dropped more cleanly. Still, that is only a minor defect in this very

'Yolande d'Aragon'

'Zéphirine Drouhin'

'York and Lancaster'

hardy, easily grown rose. It is sometimes confused with 'Harison's Yellow', a semi-double, yellow Hybrid Foetida originally discovered growing in New York, but a quick glance at the heart of the flowers will allow you to tell them apart, for instead of the golden yellow stamens of 'Harison's Yellow', 'Williams's Double Yellow' has green carpels. The raiser was the distinguished English pomologist who, although he did not discover it, introduced and gave his name to the famous 'Williams's Bon Chretien' pear, known as the 'Bartlett' in America.

Williams, England, UK, 1828
Spring flowering ı Intense, sweet fragrance
HABIT Bush H/W 1.2m/1m (4ft/3ft) ı ZONES 5–11

'Yolande d'Aragon'

PORTLAND ı MAUVE

This rose is one of the earlier Portlands, raised by Jean-Pierre Vibert in 1843. As one might expect, the large, very double flowers are flat and quartered in the Old French manner. Nicely scented, they vary in their precise tone of pink, being sometimes quite clear rose and at other times decidedly washed

with mauve. The bush is upright and not too tall, and repeats its flowering reliably. The foliage is matt and mid-green.

Vibert, France, 1843
Parentage unknown
Repeat flowering ı Rich fragrance
HABIT Bush H/W 1.2m/1m (4ft/3ft) ı ZONES 5–11

'York and Lancaster'

DAMASK ı PINK BLEND

'York et Lancastre', *R. damascena variegata*, *R. damascena versicolor*

During the War of the Roses (1455–1485), the English Houses of York and Lancaster had, respectively, a white and a red rose among their emblems. 'York and Lancaster' is not white and red, however, but white flecked with pale pink. The double blooms are sometimes all one color (as in the photograph) or even half and half, but never striped. They are of informal shape, borne in sprays, and fragrant. The foliage is downy and light grey-green. The origin of this rose is unknown, but it is thought to be very old. It is sometimes said to be the rose Shakespeare described as 'nor red nor white' in his Ninety-Ninth Sonnet. Do not

confuse it with 'Rosa Mundi' (*R. gallica versicolor*), which is a very different rose indeed.

Parentage unknown
Repeat flowering ı Moderate fragrance
HABIT Bush H/W 1.5m/1.2m (5ft/4ft) ı ZONES 5–10

'Zéphirine Drouhin'

BOURBON ı MEDIUM PINK

You will find the odd prickle, but 'Zéphirine Drouhin' is mostly thornless, which makes it the ideal climbing rose to hang over a picket fence, as it will not harm passers-by. Paint the fence white, and it will show up the brilliant cerise of the smallish, double, clustered blooms that appear on and off all season and are delightfully fragrant. Do not plant it against a wall; unless it is out in the fresh air, it will most likely get mildew. The foliage is light green and smooth. 'Zéphirine Drouhin' is the only recorded creation of the French raiser Bizot, and came out in 1868.

Bizot, France, 1868
Parentage unknown
Repeat flowering ı Moderate, damask fragrance
HABIT Climber H/W 3m/1.8m (10ft/6ft) ı ZONES 5–11

modern roses

modern roses

pp 120 — 419

Modern Roses are the group of rose classes that were introduced on or after 1867, the year Guillot's 'La France', regarded as the first Hybrid Tea, was introduced. This medium pink variety represented a giant step forward in the history of rose-breeding. Unique among roses of the time, it possessed the general habit of a Hybrid Perpetual and the elegantly shaped buds and free-flowing character of a Tea Rose – characteristics inherited from its parents, 'Madame Victor Verdier' and 'Madame Bravy'. Recognition of 'La France' as the first of a new group of roses was slow in coming. Its significance was hotly debated in the *Gardener's Chronicle*, the popular horticultural magazine of the era, and it would be almost 20 years before serious breeding of new Hybrid Teas began.

Modern Roses account for most of the roses grown in gardens today, in terms of both the number of plants sold and the number of cultivars available, and can be divided into three main categories: bush, shrub, and climbers and ramblers.

BUSH ROSES

The bush roses are perhaps the most important. They are the roses most people choose when they want to add a few roses to the garden, and they provide a sufficiently diverse range of colors to please even the most discerning gardener. Their great virtue is their habit of repeat flowering: with reasonable care a bush rose can be expected to keep on flowering from the end of spring until the late fall/autumn. Their growth habit is awkward, and the stiffly upright, thorny bushes are not enhanced by the pruning and trim-

ming needed to ensure a plentiful supply of flowers. Out of bloom they have no visual appeal beyond a canopy of mostly attractive green foliage, and the base of the plant is often bare. Planting lower-growing plants in front for camouflage can help. In cold climates, where they grow waist-high and you look down on the flowers, they are acceptable, but in a warmer climate, where they often grow head-high or taller, one is only too aware of the thorny stems and the fact that the blooms are largely out of view, particularly if you are of small stature! The most popular of all roses today are found within this group.

Hybrid Tea and Grandiflora Roses

The Hybrid Tea and Grandiflora Roses are large-flowered roses grown for the beauty of the individual flowers, which are borne singly or at most in threes or fours. Whether they have only 5 or as many as 70 petals (30 is about the norm), they are expected to display the classical form, the petals slowly unfurling from a high, conical centre. They are at their best when about two-thirds open, the full-blown flowers often not quite fulfilling the promise of the sculptured buds. American hybridists tend to favor more refined flowers, the British and Europeans those of more buxom build. Most cultivars have flowers in the range of 11–15cm (4½–6in), but there are occasional giants that can touch 18cm (7in). These tend to be shy with their blooms. Their height varies with soil, climate and pruning, but in most places 'average' implies a bush of 1–1.5m (3–5ft) tall, and they offer a range of fragrances, from none to overwhelming.

120 - 419

More than 10,000 varieties of Hybrid Teas have been introduced since 'La France' made its appearance, offering a great diversity of colors, including many blends and even stripes. In 1941, Californian breeder Walter Lammerts introduced a deep pink variety named 'Charlotte Armstrong', which became an All-America Rose Selections (AARS) winner. It had more elegance, form and charm than either of its parents, 'Soeur Thérèse' (a product of several generations by Kordes of Germany) and 'Crimson Glory' (the end result of a long line of breeding by Pernet-Ducher of France). The next breakthrough followed soon after. When Meilland's 'Peace' appeared in 1945, displaying perfect form and color, it was launched into immediate stardom (see pages 230–1).

Thanks to the gene pool provided by these two outstanding Hybrid Teas, the development of the modern Hybrid Tea quickly accelerated, and Hybrid Teas grew in popularity during the years that followed. California's Herbert Swim produced such favorites as 'Sutter's Gold' (1950), 'First Love' (1951), 'Mojave' (1954) and 'Pink Parfait' (1960), and other breeders produced dozens of other varieties.

While the history of Hybrid Teas goes back more than 100 years, the classification known as Grandiflora is of twentieth-century origin. In 1954, Walter Lammerts introduced 'Queen Elizabeth', a medium pink variety derived by crossing the Hybrid Tea 'Charlotte Armstrong' with the Floribunda 'Floradora'. This new variety not only displayed the characteristics of its seed parent 'Charlotte Armstrong', but also bore clusters, or trusses, of flowers and grew to a height of 1.8–2.5m (6–8ft). It was named the world's best rose in 1980 by the World Federation of Rose Societies, but it cannot claim to be the first registered Grandiflora. That honor goes to 'Buccaneer', registered by Herbert Swim in 1952.

'Marilyn Monroe' (Hybrid Tea)

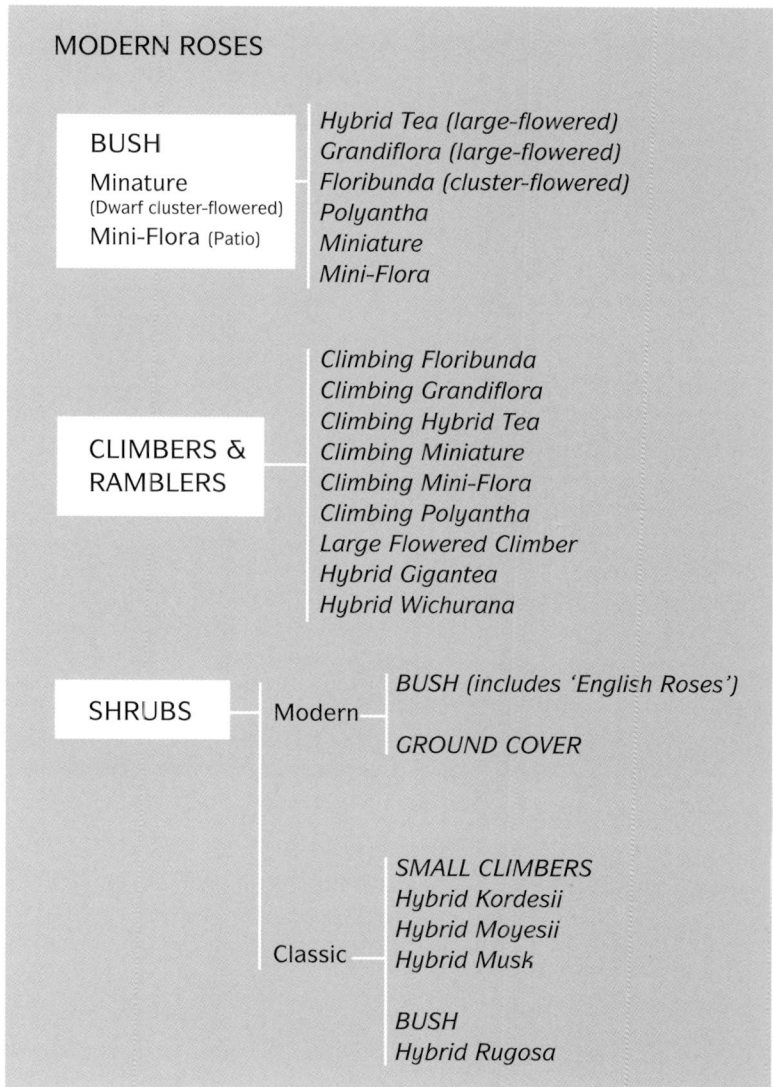

MODERN ROSES

BUSH Minature (Dwarf cluster-flowered) Mini-Flora (Patio)	*Hybrid Tea (large-flowered)* *Grandiflora (large-flowered)* *Floribunda (cluster-flowered)* *Polyantha* *Miniature* *Mini-Flora*
CLIMBERS & RAMBLERS	*Climbing Floribunda* *Climbing Grandiflora* *Climbing Hybrid Tea* *Climbing Miniature* *Climbing Mini-Flora* *Climbing Polyantha* *Large Flowered Climber* *Hybrid Gigantea* *Hybrid Wichurana*

SHRUBS

Modern
- *BUSH (includes 'English Roses')*
- *GROUND COVER*

Classic
- *SMALL CLIMBERS*
  Hybrid Kordesii
  Hybrid Moyesii
  Hybrid Musk
- *BUSH*
  Hybrid Rugosa

Floribunda Roses

Svend Poulsen from Denmark realized his lifelong dream in 1924 when he produced 'Else Poulsen', derived by crossing a Polyantha called 'Orléan's Rose' with the Hybrid Tea 'Red Star'. This founding member of a group later called Floribunda (cluster-flowered) Roses produced large clusters of 10-petalled, bright rose-pink blooms on long stems, providing a massive color display in a garden landscape. It was not until 1952 that the term Floribunda came into use to describe this class of rose, replacing the previous term, Hybrid Polyantha. In the ensuing years, the popularity of these roses has grown to rival that of the Hybrid Teas.

Floribunda Roses are grown for the massed effect of their clusters of blooms, each cluster bearing from 5 or so to as many as 30 flowers, with solitary flowers only on the weaker shoots. The individual blooms range from about 6cm (2½in) to as large as 14cm (5½in). As a general rule, the larger the flower, the smaller the cluster. The shape of each bloom is less important than that the cluster as a whole be nicely arranged, with the flowers not bunched up tight but given sufficient room to expand unhampered. Some of the newer cluster-flowered roses approach the large-flowered rose ideal, while others are just open and flat; and still others are quartered and ruffled, in the Old Garden Rose style. The range of colors is perhaps the widest of any group, but most Floribundas are deficient in scent.

'Brass Band' (Floribunda)

You can expect a Floribunda Rose to be a little shorter and bushier in growth than a Hybrid Tea or a Grandiflora – and often healthier – although both very tall and dwarf cultivars exist. Floribunda Roses come into bloom a week or so later than the large-flowered roses. There is no reason not to mix large-flowered and cluster-flowered roses in the same bed, as long as you take the heights of your chosen cultivars into account.

Around 1980, Bill Warriner of Jackson & Perkins stimulated a renewal of interest in Floribundas in America with the introduction of varieties that included 'Cherish', 'French Lace', 'Sun Flare', 'Impatient', 'Intrigue' and 'Summer Fashion'. These creations, mostly AARS winners, displayed the symmetry and wide color range of Hybrid Teas but had smaller flowers. Toward the end of the twentieth century, yet another development in Floribundas began to take shape. Ralph Moore's successful experiments with striped Miniature Roses had encouraged some rose-breeders to try to produce Floribundas with striped flowers. Tom Carruth captured the attention of the rose world in 1997 when he introduced the vividly red-and-white-striped Floribunda 'Scentimental', which won coveted AARS status. Success had come from a skilful cross of the popular single-petalled, orange Floribunda 'Playboy', from Alec Cocker in Scotland, with the Floribunda 'Peppermint Twist', from California's Jack Christensen; the latter's seed parent was the striped Moore Miniature 'Pinstripe'.

Polyantha Roses

The Polyantha Roses are bush roses also, but are distinguished by their dwarf growth and tiny flowers – a bloom of 5cm (2in) is very large for the group – which are carried in clusters of up to 100 blooms. Popular in the 1920s, they are not much loved today. They derive their cluster-flowering habit from *R. multiflora*, and

when crossed with large-flowered roses gave rise to the earliest cluster-flowered roses, which were at first called Hybrid Polyanthas and later Floribundas.

Miniatures and Mini-Flora

Miniature and Mini-Flora Roses have their own section in this book, mainly to avoid confusing the reader with their scale.

SHRUBS

Although a dictionary will tell you that 'bush' and 'shrub' mean the same thing, Shrub Roses are a distinct group, usually growing larger and having a spreading habit. As such, some of them are less suitable for growing in beds in a formal rose garden. Again, they are a mixed bag; some, like 'Scarlet Fire' or 'Frühlingsgold', are spring flowering only; but the majority are repeat flowering. Some are just overgrown Floribunda Roses. You will find many of the Shrub Roses described as 'Park Roses', 'Landscape Roses', 'Romanticas', 'Amenity Roses' or some such, according to the whims of the raisers' marketing people. These are not, however, official or recognized groups. Shrub Roses can deliver the whole range of colors and scents. David Austin's 'English Roses' are the largest group within this subdivision. Many Shrub Roses are exceptionally tough, resistant to extreme cold, and easy to grow.

Modern Shrubs

'English Roses'

This group, mostly from British hybridizer David Austin, seeks to unite the perfume, full-petalled flowers and elegance of growth of the Old Garden Roses with modern colors and the habit of repeat flowering. Called 'English Roses', they have become the height of fashion and have enjoyed a long run of popularity since they were introduced in the 1980s. Other European breeders, such as Meilland, have introduced their own versions of 'English Roses' under such names as 'Romantica' or 'Renaissance' Roses. More detailed information about 'English Roses' will be found on pages 162–3.

Ground Cover Roses

The Ground Cover Roses that are coming from various raisers are of mixed breeding, some being bred from the Japanese-raised Climbing Miniature 'Nozomi', others from various ramblers. Their performance seems to fall short of their marketing promise; so far, not many are sufficiently dense or evergreen to really suppress weeds, one of the first duties one asks of a good ground-cover plant.

Classic Shrubs

To distinguish those Shrubs bred as direct hybrids of Wild (Species) Roses, the American Rose Society has grouped them together and classified them as Classic Shrubs as follows.

Hybrid Kordesii, mostly raised by Wilhelm Kordes and named for German cities, are a distinct group of pillar roses noted for their continuity of bloom and extreme resistance to disease and cold, which they inherit from the Wild Roses *R. wichurana* and *R. rugosa*.

The *Hybrid Musks* are a small group raised in England in the 1920s. They are arching in growth and can be trained as small pillars or pruned harder to grow more like cluster-flowered roses.

Hybrid Moyesii, bred from the Wild Rose *R. moyesii* from China, are noted for their ability to give a good crop of flowers in the summer and then a heavy, colorful display of hips in the fall/autumn. They are mostly small climbers.

The *Hybrid Rugosas*, a large group, are splendid, large shrubs of solid, bushy growth, well clad with wrinkled, light green leaves and quite disease-proof. They vary in growth, but are mostly about 1.8m (6ft) high and as much wide, their fiercely armed branches making a thicket of growth that makes all other roses look flimsy. Pruning is easy: a rough trim and the removal of obviously dead wood are sufficient.

CLIMBERS AND RAMBLERS

Climbing roses are something of an assortment. First there are the climbing sports from the bush roses, both large-flowered and cluster-flowered, whose blooms are usually identical to the bush cultivars from which they sprang, and whose names, prefixed by the word 'Climbing', they still bear. Examples include 'Climbing Iceberg' and 'Climbing Double Delight'. They are not always reliably repeat flowering, however, and you should check this point when buying them. They are apt to be rather stiff in growth. Distinct from this first group are what are called the natural climbers, specifically bred to climb. Some, like 'Albertine' and 'Alberic Barbier', are only spring flowering, although most of the newer cultivars repeat to a greater or lesser extent. They tend to be less vigorous than the climbing sports mentioned above, and many of the more restrained are excellent pillar roses for training on verandah posts or the like to create pillars of bloom. The flowers may be either large-flowered or cluster-flowered in style, and fragrant or not. Just about the full range of colors is available.

The third and last group is much better described as ramblers derived from planned breeding (mostly by Alec Barbier in France and Water Manda in America) using *R. wichurana* and *R. gigantea*. As the term rambler implies, these plants grow exceptionally large, extending as much as 12m (40ft) in every direction – far enough to cover a small house!

'Climbing Iceberg'

'About Face'

'Abbaye de Cluny'

'Abraham Darby'

'Abbaye de Cluny'

HYBRID TEA ǀ APRICOT BLEND

'Romantic Seranade'

This lovely rose has won numerous awards in the European Rose Trials and yet, curiously,

is not as widely grown as it deserves to be. The flowers are in the style of Old Garden Roses, large, double and cupped, with 26–40 petals, but come in modern apricot tones. They are long-lasting, and seem to hold their form well. They are freely borne throughout the season, usually one to a stem, on a vigorous, upright plant of medium height and bushy habit. The foliage is semi-glossy and medium green.

MEIbrinpay ǀ Meilland, France, 1996
'Just Joey' × ('Louis de Funes' × 'MEInan')
Repeat flowering ǀ *Moderate, spicy citrus fragrance*
HABIT Bush H/W 1.5m/1.2m (5ft/4ft) ǀ ZONES 4–10
🏵 Monza Gold Medal 1993, Lyon Gold Medal 1994, Belfast Gold Medal and Prize of the City of Belfast 1995

'About Face'

GRANDIFLORA ǀ ORANGE BLEND

The 35-petalled flowers are light orange, with a distinctly darker, bronzy-red reverse, and arguably at their most beautiful when fully open. They are borne mostly singly, but sometimes in small clusters. This very tall and upright plant performs best in cooler weather, in terms of both bloom size and

color. It is vigorous, free-flowering and easy to maintain, with good disease resistance.

WEKosupalz ǀ Carruth, USA, 2004
(['O Sole Mio' × seedling] × 'Midas Touch')
× 'Hot Cocoa'
Repeat flowering ǀ *Apple fragrance*
HABIT Bush H/W 1.8m/1.2m (6ft/4ft) ǀ ZONES 4–10
🏵 All-America Rose Selection 2005

'Abraham Darby'

SHRUB ǀ ORANGE PINK

'Abraham Darby' grows into a large, arching shrub or, with encouragement, a modest climber. The peach-pink and yellow blooms are large, cupped and very double, with a rich, fruity fragrance. The colors, however, tend to be very pale in warm climates. It has mid-green foliage and the stems are quite thorny. It is named for one of the great pioneers of the Industrial Revolution, whose ironworks stood not far from where David Austin's nursery is located.

AUScot ǀ Austin, England, UK, 1990
'Aloha' × 'Yellow Cushion'
Repeat flowering ǀ *Rich, fruity fragrance*
HABIT Bush/climber H/W 1.5m/1.5m (5ft/5ft) ǀ ZONES 5–11

'Adolf Horstmann'

HYBRID TEA | YELLOW BLEND

Deep amber-yellow, with some red and orange flushes in warm weather, the double, elegantly formed flowers of 'Adolf Horstmann' are large and long-lasting, but only slightly scented. The foliage is copper-tinted when young, maturing to a pleasing glossy green. The bush is upright and of average height. 'Adolf Horst-mann' has become popular with florists because of its long stems and lovely color, but it is a good garden rose, too. The name honors a friend and colleague of Reimer Kordes.

Kordes, Germany, 1971
'Colour Wonder' × 'Dr A. J. Verhage'
Repeat flowering | *Slight fragrance*

HABIT Bush H/W 1.8m/1.2m (6ft/4ft) | ZONES 5–11

'Agnes'

'Adolf Horstmann'

'Agnes'

HYBRID RUGOSA | MEDIUM YELLOW

Introduced in 1922, 'Agnes' is the result of a search for a yellow rose hardy enough for Canadian winters. It is certainly able to take the cold. Gardeners in much milder climates will also admire its big, ruffled, double blooms, which blend shades of yellow and amber and exhale a rich fragrance. It is sparing with its repeat flowering. The plant is less bushy and solid than is usual with Rugosas, but is still attractive with its arching branches and bright green leaves. It is occasionally subject to black spot. There is a huge display of flowers in spring, with scattered blossoms thereafter.

Saunders, Canada, 1900
R. rugosa × R. foetida persiana
Repeat flowering | *Moderate fragrance*

HABIT Bush H/W 1.8m/1.5m (6ft/5ft) | ZONES 5–11

'Alain'

FLORIBUNDA | MEDIUM RED

The smallish, bright red, semi-double flowers show golden stamens and come in large clusters. They are only slightly fragrant, but long-lasting in water. The bush is compact, with glossy, dark green foliage. For many years regarded as one of the very best red Floribundas, 'Alain' is still a sound, easy-to-grow variety. Its only fault is a tendency to be a little slow with its repeat bloom. It is quite uncommon today. Raised by Francis Meilland, it was named for his young son, who also grew up to be a successful rose breeder.

Meilland, France, 1948
('Guinée' × 'Sykrocket') × 'Orange Triumph'
Repeat flowering | *Slight fragrance*

HABIT Bush H/W 1.2m/3m (4ft/3ft) | ZONES 5–11

🏵 Lyon Gold Medal 1946, Geneva Gold Medal 1948

'Alain'

'Albéric Barbier'

HYBRID WICHURANA | WHITE

When this rose came out in 1900, the cata-logues were fond of describing it as 'yellow, fading to cream', but this was wishful think-ing. In fact, the flowers are cream, fading rapidly to white. 'Albéric Barbier' is as pretty a white rose as any to clad a house or a long fence. The double flowers are of Floribunda size and fragrant; they come in clusters and are borne in great profusion. The foliage is glossy and dark green. It is a very hardy rose for a rough spot. It is also mildew-resistant, and very good for city gardens.

Barbier, France, 1900
R. wichurana × 'Shirley Hibberd'
Repeat flowering | *Moderate fragrance*

HABIT Rambler H/W 4.5m/3m (15ft/10ft) | ZONES 6–11

🏵 Royal Horticultural Society Award of Garden Merit 1993

'Albéric Barbier'

'Albertine'

LARGE FLOWERED CLIMBER ı ORANGE PINK

One of the most popular of all the climbing roses, 'Albertine' bears masses of double, salmon-pink blooms, richly scented, informal in shape, and paling as they age. The foliage is glossy, red-tinted when young, and the vigorous branches are plentifully endowed with hooked prickles. There is only one flowering, over several weeks, but with luck you might see a fall/autumn flower or two. Mildew will probably strike, but not hard enough to impair the plant's strength. This rose was very popular in the 1920s and 1930s.

Barbier, France, 1921
R. wichurana × 'Mrs A. R. Waddell'
Summer flowering ı *Strong fragrance*

HABIT Climber H/W 4.5m/3m (15ft/10ft) ı ZONES 6–11

Royal Horticultural Society Award of Garden Merit 1993

'Alchymist'

'Alec's Red'

'Alchymist'

SHRUB ı APRICOT BLEND

'Alchemist', 'Alchymiste'

If the old alchemists made gold as beautiful as this, they would have been happy indeed! Full and quartered in the old style, the very double flowers are deep yellow, overlaid with buff and peach, and quite strongly scented. The foliage is glossy and mid-green, red-tinted when young. The wood is thorny; and the plant is of medium vigor. It is a good rose for a trellis or a tall pillar, and is tolerant of cold weather.

Kordes, Germany, 1956
'Golden Glow' × *R. eglanteria* hybrid
Summer flowering ı *Moderate fragrance*

HABIT Bush H/W 3.5m/2.5m (12ft/8ft) ı ZONES 4–10

'Alec's Red'

HYBRID TEA ı MEDIUM RED

The plump buds give promise of a much deeper color than the full-petalled flowers of 'Alec's Red' deliver. They are rarely stronger than cherry red. They do, however, hold their color well, without fading or 'blueing', and they are quite strongly fragrant. The bush is of average height, with mid-green foliage. 'Alec's Red' is at its best in a cool climate. It was introduced in 1970 after winning the RNRS President's International Trophy.

COred ı Cocker, Scotland, UK, 1973
'Fragrant Cloud' × 'Dame de Coeur'
Repeat flowering ı *Moderate fragrance*

HABIT Bush H/W 1.8m/1.2m (6ft/4ft) ı ZONES 5–11

Royal National Rose Society President's International Trophy 1970, Belfast Fragrance (R. J. Frizzell Memorial) Award 1972

'Alexander'

HYBRID TEA ı ORANGE RED

'Alexandra'

Outshining even its parent 'Super Star' in color, 'Alexander' is also notable for the vigor of its growth. Indeed, the bushes are so much larger than average it is sometimes classed as a Shrub Rose. The double, 25-petalled flowers are of bright vermilion-red and open to a good size from elegantly turned buds. The petal edges are often scalloped. They do not have much scent. In cool climates, this is a fine rose for the back of the border. It was named in honor of Earl Alexander of Tunis.

HARlex ı Harkness, England, UK, 1972
'Super Star' × ('Ann Elizabeth' × 'Allgold')
Repeat flowering ı *Slight fragrance*

HABIT Bush H/W 2m/1.5m (7ft/5ft) ı ZONES 5–11

Belfast Gold Medal and Prize of the City of Belfast 1974, Royal Horticultural Society Award of Garden Merit 1993

'Alexandra'

HYBRID TEA ı YELLOW BLEND

'Alexandra' has beautifully formed flowers of deep yellow shaded with amber and pink. They are exquisite against the glossy foliage. The rose shown here was photographed at the famous Portland Rose Gardens in Portland, Oregon, where the climate seems ideal for it. Alas, 'Alexandra' seems only to appear in German catalogues. Do not confuse it with 'Alexander', which has 'Alexandra' as

'Albertine'

'Alexander'

'Alexandra'

a synonym, or with the pale yellow Tea Rose 'Alexandra', introduced in 1900.

KORbaxand ı Kordes, Germany, 1973
Parentage undisclosed
Repeat flowering ı *Slight fragrance*

HABIT Bush H/W 1.4m/1m (4ft 6in/3ft) ı ZONES 5–11

'Alexandre Girault'

LARGE FLOWERED CLIMBER ı PINK BLEND

One of the most admired, and most often photographed, features in any of the world's beautiful rose gardens is the great trellis that forms the centrepiece of the Roseraie de l'Haÿ near Paris. It is completely covered with 80 plants of this rose. On seeing its performance there, you would think the rose-lovers of the world would be clamoring to have these double, vivid carmine flowers, lightened with a touch of gold at the petal bases, in their own gardens. Yet for many years, this glossy-leafed, easily grown rose disappeared from the catalogues. Now it is available again.

Barbier, France, 1909
R. wichurana × 'Papa Gontier'
Summer flowering ı *Moderate fragrance*

HABIT Rambler H/W 3.5m/3.5m (12ft/12ft) ı ZONES 6–11

'Alexandre Girault'

'Alleluia'

HYBRID TEA ı RED BLEND

'Chandon Rosier', 'Hallelujah'

The large, 30-petalled blooms are of deep velvety red, with a white reverse. With exceptional form and strong, straight stems, they last well when cut, but they are only slightly scented. The foliage is glossy and deep green. Introduced in 1980, this is a good rose for warm, dry climates.

DELatur ı Delbard, France, 1982
(['Impeccable' × 'Papa Meilland'] × ['Glory of Rome' × 'Impeccable']) × 'Corrida'
Repeat flowering ı *Slight fragrance*

HABIT Bush H/W 1.8m/1.2m (6ft/4ft) ı ZONES 5–11

'Allgold'

FLORIBUNDA ı MEDIUM YELLOW

'All Gold'

Introduced in 1955, 'Allgold' is a major landmark in rose-breeding. Never before had there been a yellow Floribunda of such rich, unfading color, nor one anywhere near as reliable and generous in its performance. Nowadays, its semi-double flowers, borne singly and in large trusses, might seem a trifle ordinary against some of the larger and more double newcomers, but it remains one of the best of its class. The glossy, dark green foliage is

unusually resistant to black spot. Prune one or two branches hard each year to keep the plants bushy.

LeGrice, England, UK, 1958
'Goldilocks' × 'Ellinor LeGrice'
Repeat flowering ı *Slight fragrance*

HABIT Bush H/W 1.2m/1m (4ft/3ft) ı ZONES 4–11

'Allgold'

'Alleluia'

'Allspice'

HYBRID TEA ι MEDIUM YELLOW

'Allspice' is not extremely fragrant, but still pleasantly so. The books say it smells of honey and tea, but this does not seem obvious. The long buds open to wide, ruffled, double flowers of medium yellow. The bush is tall, and the foliage is mid-green.

AROall ι Armstrong, USA, 1977
'Buccaneer' × 'Peace'
Repeat flowering ι *Moderate fragrance*
HABIT Bush H/W 1.8m/1.2m (6ft/4ft) ι ZONES 5–11

TOP LEFT 'Allspice'
TOP RIGHT 'Alnwick Castle'
BOTTOM 'Aloha'

'Alnwick Castle'

SHRUB ι PINK BLEND

'The Alnwick Rose'

The most desirable attributes of Old Garden Roses have been captured in this Modern Rose. The pretty, rich pink blooms are deeply cupped when fully open and age pleasingly to a softer pink at the outer edges. With its rounded growth habit, the bush is attractive at all times of the year – whether in bud, covered in newly opened blooms or resplendent with fully opened, aged masterpieces. It is named for the wonderful rose garden constructed at Alnwick Castle in England.

AUSgrab ι Austin, England, 2002
Parentage unknown
Repeat flowering ι *Old rose fragrance with just a hint of raspberry*
HABIT Bush H/W 1.2m/75cm (4ft/30in) ι ZONES 5–10

'Aloha'

CLIMBING HYBRID TEA ι MEDIUM PINK

This very popular variety flowers almost continuously, bearing medium-sized blooms of two-tone pink flushed with salmon. The double flowers are well furnished with petals and are pleasantly fragrant. The foliage is dark and leathery. The growth is hardly rampant, so grow it on a pillar or prune it a little harder to make a large shrub. Several other varieties introduced later in the twentieth century have been given the same name and should not be confused with this classic.

Boerner, USA, 1949
'Mercédes Gallart' × 'New Dawn'
Repeat flowering ι *Moderate fragrance*
HABIT Bush H/W 3m/1.8m (10ft/6ft) ι ZONES 4–11

'Alpine Sunset'

HYBRID TEA ι APRICOT BLEND

Richly tinted with sunset colors of peach-yellow, pink and apricot when young, the very large and shapely flowers pass to more delicate tints with maturity. They are double and strongly scented, and come in reasonable profusion on a shorter than average, bushy plant with mid-green foliage and very thorny

'Ambassador'

'Amber Queen'

'Amanda'

'Altissimo'

'Alpine Sunset'

branches. It is a fine rose for the show bench, and British gardeners admire the flowers' resistance to wet weather.

Cant, England, UK, 1974
'Dr A. J. Verhage' × 'Grandpa Dickson'
Repeat flowering ı *Moderate fragrance*

HABIT Bush H/W 1.5m/1.2m (5ft/4ft) ı ZONES 5–11

'Altissimo'

LARGE FLOWERED CLIMBER ı MEDIUM RED

'Altus'

The name is optimistic. 'Altissimo' means 'highest', but this very popular rose is only a moderately vigorous climber. The large, single-petalled flowers are much admired for their brilliant scarlet color, which holds without turning magenta, and look particularly fine when dusted with golden yellow pollen. They are borne throughout the season, but are only slightly fragrant. The foliage is dark and leathery. It is customary to describe this rose as a red 'Mermaid', but there is not much resemblance. Keep 'Altissimo' right away from red-brick walls; the colors clash.

DELmur ı Delbard–Chabert, France, 1966
'Ténor' × unknown
Repeat flowering ı *Slight fragrance*

HABIT Climber H/W 3m/1.8m (10ft/6ft) ı ZONES 5–11
🌹 Royal Horticultural Society Award of Garden Merit 1993

'Amanda'

FLORIBUNDA ı MEDIUM YELLOW

Fat buds open to medium-sized, double flowers of clear yellow, borne in large, well-spaced clusters. There is a slight fragrance. The bush is compact, a little on the short side perhaps, with pale green leaves. It grows well in England. It is not to be confused with the Miniature Rose 'Red Ace' (AmRUda), which is also called 'Amanda' in some catalogues.

BEEsian ı Bees, England, UK, 1979
'Arthur Bell' × 'Zambra'
Repeat flowering ı *Slight fragrance*

HABIT Bush H/W 1.2m/1m (4ft/3ft) ı ZONES 5–11

'Ambassador'

HYBRID TEA ı ORANGE BLEND

The beautifully formed double flowers are pale orange shot with yellow in their youth, fading to apricot with age, and are well up to exhibition size. They are borne on long stems on a taller than average bush with dark leaves. Do not confuse this rose with the 1930

American Hybrid Tea of the same name. That had smaller flowers in a blend of apricot and coral-pink, and, unlike Meilland's 'Ambassador', was very fragrant

MEInutzan ı Meilland, France, 1979
Seedling × 'Whisky Mac'
Repeat flowering   *Slight fragrance*

HABIT Bush H/W 2m/1.2m (7ft/4ft) ı ZONES 4–11

'Amber Queen'

FLORIBUNDA ı APRICOT BLEND

'Prinz Eugen von Savoyen'

With blooms of a clear amber-yellow, 'Amber Queen' has the reputation of being one of the most generous with its flowers of all Modern Roses. The double flowers are medium-sized, shapely and scented, and borne in clusters of 3–7. Their warm color is complemented by the dark, maroon-tinted foliage. The bush is low-growing, and the raiser says that it is ideal as a standard. It was introduced in England in 1984 and in the United States in 1988.

HARroony ı Harkness, England, UK, 1983
'Southhampton' × 'Typhoon'
Repeat flowering ı *Slight fragrance*

HABIT Bush H/W 1m/60cm (3ft/2ft) ı ZONES 5–11
🌹 Belfast Dari Award 1986, All-America Rose Selection 1988, Gold Star of the South Pacific, Hamilton (New Zealand) 1988

TOP LEFT 'Ambridge Rose'
LEFT 'America'
RIGHT 'American Heritage'

'Ambridge Rose'

LARGE FLOWERED CLIMBER ⋅ APRICOT BLEND

This is a very desirable rose, made even more so by its strong, myrrh scent. The very double, pure apricot blooms start off as cupped and open to a loose rosette formation, the color paling gently toward the petal edges. They are borne in small clusters on a medium-sized bush with semi-glossy, medium green foliage. This stunning rose was named as a tribute to the long-running British TV series *The Archers,* set in the fictitious English village of Ambridge.

AUSwonder ⋅ Austin, England, 1994
'Charles Austin' × seedling
Repeat flowering ⋅ *Strong, myrrh fragrance*

HABIT Bush H/W 110cm/60cm (3ft 6in/2ft) ⋅ ZONES 4–11

'America'

LARGE FLOWERED CLIMBER ⋅ ORANGE PINK

The shapely, very double flowers are of glowing salmon with a slightly paler reverse. With disbudding they can be large enough for the show bench, and they are strongly fragrant. They are borne sometimes singly but mainly in small clusters; the foliage is large and medium green. Hard pruning will keep 'America' as a shrub, at least in cool climates, but it is not a rose for hot, humid summers. Introduced in 1976, the year of the American Bicentennial, it is in fact the third rose to bear the name. The previous two were a pale pink Hybrid Tea of 1912 and a pink rambler of 1915.

JACclam ⋅ Warriner, USA, 1976
'Fragrant Cloud' × 'Tradition'
Repeat flowering ⋅ *Strong fragrance*

HABIT Climber H/W 3m/1.8m (10ft/6ft) ⋅ ZONES 6–11
All-America Rose Selection 1976

'American Heritage'

HYBRID TEA ⋅ YELLOW BLEND

The pale salmon-pink that suffuses the cream and ivory of the long buds gradually takes over completely as the large, double, high-centred flowers of 'American Heritage' mature. They are charming at all stages, although there is little scent. The foliage is large and dark green, and the bush tall, although not as tall (or quite so easily grown) as its parent 'Queen Elizabeth'.

LAMlam ⋅ Lammerts, USA, 1965
'Queen Elizabeth' × 'Yellow Perfection'
Repeat flowering ⋅ *Slight to no fragrance*

HABIT Bush H/W 1.8m/1.2m (6ft/4ft) ⋅ ZONES 5–11
All-America Rose Selection 1966

'American Pillar'

HYBRID WICHURANA ⋅ PINK BLEND

The short flowering season of 'American Pillar' and its susceptibility to mildew are leading gardeners to reject it in favor of newer repeat-flowering climbers. In its season, it makes a

'American Pillar'

'American Pride'

almost complete lack of scent, it is in fact a rather good red rose. The color is dark yet lively, and the double flowers are well formed, with the central petals ruffled in the open bloom. The plant is a little taller than average, with matt, dark green foliage, and it flowers very freely.

JACared · Warriner, USA, 1978
Parentage undisclosed
Repeat flowering · *Slight to no fragrance*

HABIT Bush H/W 1.5m/1.2m (5ft/4ft) · ZONES 5–11

'Ami des Jardins'

FLORIBUNDA · ORANGE PINK

'Finale'

This is a pleasing garden rose, of a clear orange-red color that does not turn magenta with age. It has little scent, unfortunately. Despite its French name, and the fact that it seems nowadays to be grown only in France, it is a German rose, bred by Kordes.

KORami · Kordes, Germany, 1964
'Nordlicht' × 'Meteor'
Repeat flowering · *Very slight fragrance*

HABIT Bush H/W 1m/60cm (3ft/2ft) · ZONES 5–11

'Amiga Mia'

SHRUB · MEDIUM PINK

'Amiga Mia' is an unusually vigorous bush rose, and pruned like one will stand about 1m (3ft) tall. The double flowers are large and graceful, and borne singly or in clusters of half a dozen. They are a delicate shell-pink and quite fragrant. The leaves are leathery and dark green. One of Dr Buck's cold-resistant and disease-resistant, but still lovely, roses, it was introduced in 1979 and named in affectionate tribute to the late Dorothy Stemler, the great Californian rose-grower.

Buck, USA, 1978
'Queen Elizabeth' × 'Prairie Princess'
Repeat flowering · *Moderate fragrance*

HABIT Bush H/W 1m/60cm (3ft/2ft) · ZONES 4–9

'Ami des Jardins'

colorful display with its big clusters of small, single flowers, carmine with white centres. Although more or less scentless, they last well when cut. The foliage is leathery and glossy. The plant is really a bit too vigorous for a pillar; plant it against the house or over a pergola. It is best in cold climates, and flowers in late summer only. It has native American blood.

Van Fleet, USA, 1902
(*R. wichurana* × *R. setigera*) × red Hybrid Perpetual
Summer flowering · *Slight fragrance*

HABIT Climber H/W 6m/3m (20ft/10ft) · ZONES 6–11

'American Pride'

HYBRID TEA · DEEP RED

A lack of scent always seems a more serious fault in red roses than in roses of other colors, but if 'American Pride' can be forgiven its

'Amiga Mia'

'Amsterdam'

FLORIBUNDA · ORANGE RED

The foliage of 'Amsterdam' is dark mahogany when young and retains its dusky tone even in maturity, making the orange-red of the semi-double flowers seem even more fiery. For this reason it stands out among the many other Floribundas of this color. It is a good, healthy rose for the garden and for cutting.

'HAVam' · Verschuren, The Netherlands, 1972
'Europeana' × 'Parkdirektor Riggers'
Repeat flowering · *No fragrance*

HABIT Bush H/W 110cm/60cm (3ft 6in/2ft) · ZONES 5–11

'Angel Face'

FLORIBUNDA · MAUVE

This is a pretty rose, with double, 8cm (3in) flowers ruffled and flounced in shades of mauve and rose. It is much less ethereal than most modern mauve roses, and is well scented, too. The flowers are borne in large clusters, and the foliage is dark green. It is, however, one of those roses that need the best of care if they are to be an asset to the

'Amsterdam'

'Angel Face'

'Ann Elizabeth'

'Anne Letts'

'Anne Marie Trechslin'

'Anne Cocker'

garden. Give it fertile soil, keep it well watered, and have a spray gun handy, as it is susceptible to black spot.

Swim and Weeks, USA, 1968
('Circus' × 'Lavender Pinocchio') × 'Sterling Silver'
Repeat flowering ı *Strong, citrus fragrance*

HABIT Bush H/W 1m/60cm (3ft/2ft) ı ZONES 5–11

All-America Rose Selection 1969, American Rose Society James Alexander Gamble Fragrance Medal 2001

'Ann Elizabeth'

FLORIBUNDA ı MEDIUM PINK

A tall grower that with light pruning could almost be a Shrub Rose, 'Ann Elizabeth' bears its open, semi-double flowers in grace-ful sprays. They are a gentle color, rose-pink with just a hint of coral, and are set off by

dark green foliage that is bronze-tinted when young. It was named for the raiser's grand-daughter.

Norman, England, UK, 1962
Parentage undisclosed
Repeat flowering ı *Slight fragrance*

HABIT Bush H/W 1m/60cm (3ft/2ft) ı ZONES 5–11

'Anne Cocker'

FLORIBUNDA ı ORANGE PINK

This eye-catching variety produces double flowers of luminous vermilion. They are medium in size, with some 36 petals, and very long-lasting, making them popular among flower arrangers. They are freely produced throughout the season, sometimes singly but mostly in wide clusters, each bloom displaying perfect form and symmetry. The plant is vigorous, upright and bushy, with glossy, light to medium green foliage. It was named for the hybridizer's wife, herself an accomplished hybridizer.

Cocker, Scotland, UK, 1971
'Highlight' × 'Colour Wonder'
Repeat flowering ı *Slight fragrance*

HABIT Bush H/W 1m/60cm (3ft/2ft) ı ZONES 4–11

'Anne Harkness'

FLORIBUNDA ı APRICOT BLEND

Regarded as the standard for the Floribunda class, 'Anne Harkness' produces spectacular sprays of 10–20 blooms on one strong, straight stem, providing a ready-made bouquet. The double, saffron-orange blooms shade to gold at the petal edges, which are most attractively ruffled; the color fades with age, particularly in strong sunlight. The rose was

named to celebrate the 21st birthday of the raiser's daughter.

HARkaramel ı Harkness, England, UK, 1980
'Bobby Dazzler' × (['Manx Queen' × 'Prima Ballerina'] × ['Chanelle' × 'Piccadilly'])
Repeat flowering ı *Slight fragrance*

HABIT Bush H/W 1m/60cm (3ft/2ft) ı ZONES 5–11

'Anne Letts'

HYBRID TEA ı PINK BLEND

Clear pale pink, but paler still on the petal reverse, the flowers are large, double and perfectly formed, and also pleasantly fragrant. The foliage is glossy and medium green, and the rather spiny bushes are a little shorter than average. Needing both good cultivation and fine weather to give of its best, this is not a rose for the ordinary gardener, but the enthusiast will find its flowers unbeatable on the show bench. It was named for the hybridizer's mother.

Letts, England, UK, 1954
'Peace' × 'Charles Gregory'
Repeat flowering ı *Moderate fragrance*

HABIT Bush H/W 1.5m/1m (5ft/3ft) ı ZONES 5–11

'Anne Marie Trechslin'

HYBRID TEA ı DEEP PINK

'Anne Marie'

'Deep pink' does not do justice to the color of 'Anne Marie Trechslin', which is actually a blend of pink and apricot, heavily overlaid with copper-red. The flowers are large, double and shapely, and very fragrant, although the bush is sometimes a little shy of flowering. The foliage is leathery and dark green. This is the sort of rose that appeals to artists, and indeed Mlle Trechslin is one of the foremost

'Anne Harkness'

'Antique Silk'

'Apricot Nectar'

painters of rose portraits, having illustrated several books and been commissioned to paint watercolors of most roses elected to the Word Federation of Rose Societies Rose Hall of Fame.

MEIfour ı Meilland, France, 1968
'Sutter's Gold' × ('Demain' × 'Peace')
Repeat flowering ı *Strong fragrance*

HABIT Bush H/W 1.5m/1.2m (5ft/4ft) ı ZONES 4–11

Monza Fragrance Award 1968

'Antique Silk'

FLORIBUNDA ı WHITE

'Champagner', 'Champagne'

Florists are likely to call this delightful, very long-stemmed rose 'Champagne', although the International Registration Authority prefers 'Antique Silk' to avoid confusion with Bob Lindquist's Hybrid Tea 'Champagne', which came out in 1960. Either name suits the delicate off-white of the double flowers perfectly. They are not large, but they are most perfectly shaped and, unusually for a greenhouse rose, scented. The flowers are exceptionally long-lasting, making them good for cutting. The leaves are medium green. It does quite well in the garden, too. Reimer Kordes scored a real hit with it in 1982.

KORampa ı Kordes, Germany, 1985
'Annabel' × seedling
Repeat flowering ı *Slight fragrance*

HABIT Bush H/W 106cm/60cm (3ft 6in/2ft) ı ZONES 5–11

'Apricot Nectar'

FLORIBUNDA ı APRICOT BLEND

It is surprising that 'Apricot Nectar' was not classed as a Grandiflora in the United States, where it was bred. It is a tall-growing plant, and the double flowers are very large for a Floribunda – too large for the rather tight clusters, in fact. Some thinning of the buds is usually called for, so that the remaining flowers can each expand in freedom. That is this variety's only fault. The cupped flowers are very attractive in their peach and apricot tonings, their elegant form and their fruity fragrance. The bush is quite disease-resistant, with glossy, dark green foliage.

Boerner, USA, 1965
Seedling × 'Spartan'
Repeat flowering ı *Strong, fruity fragrance*

HABIT Bush H/W 1m/60cm (3ft/2ft) ı ZONES 5–11

All-America Rose Selection 1966

'Apricot Queen'

HYBRID TEA ı APRICOT BLEND

Blending salmon-pink with apricot, the large, double flowers of 'Apricot Queen' are full and ruffled, with 45 petals, although not quite of show-bench form. They are moderately scented of tea, and are borne abundantly on a sturdy bush with dull green foliage. Despite its age, this variety remains an excellent garden rose, particularly in climates with humid summers.

Howard, USA, 1940
'Mrs J. D. Eisele' × 'Los Angeles'
Repeat flowering ı *Moderate fragrance*

HABIT Bush H/W 1.8m/1.2m (6ft/4ft) ı ZONES 5–11

All-America Rose Selection 1941

'Apricot Queen'

The Rose in Poetry

EVER SINCE THE DAYS OF THE ANCIENT GREEKS, POETS HAVE SUNG THE BEAUTY OF THE ROSE. IT HAS BECOME THE STANDARD AGAINST WHICH ALL OTHER FORMS OF BEAUTY ARE COMPARED.

As Edmund Waller put it in the early years of the seventeenth century:

Go, lovely Rose!
  Tell her that wastes her time and me,
That now she knows,
  When I resemble her to thee,
How sweet and fair she seems to be.

The rose is a fleeting blossom, its moment of perfection brief. Scarcely have its petals opened in the morning sun to reveal the flower in all its fullness than they begin to fade; and before long they are falling. So poet after poet has seized upon the rose when he wishes to sing of the transience of youth and beauty – indeed, of love and of life itself. Everyone knows the lines of Waller's contemporary Robert Herrick:

Gather ye rosebuds while ye may,
Old time is still a-flying:
And this same flower that blooms today
Tomorrow may be dying . . .

but how many know that the poem is called 'Advice to Virgins'? Or know its concluding quatrain?

Then be not coy, but use your time,
And while ye may, go marry:
For having lost but once your prime,
You may forever tarry.

Pierre de Ronsard was an ardent lover of the rose. Time and again it blossoms in his love poems, which are among the jewels of the French language and which have won him the accolade of the Prince of Poets:

Prends cette rose aimable comme toi,
Qui sers de rose aux roses les plus belles . . .

(Take this rose, lovely as thyself, who art of all roses the most beautiful . . .)

Not that Dorothy Parker would have been impressed:

Why is it no one ever sent me yet
One perfect limousine, do you suppose?
Ah no, it's always just my luck to get
One perfect rose.

But she was a world-weary city girl and no gardener. Shakespeare, a country man at heart, loved flowers and refers to the rose more than 60 times in his works. It blossoms at the very beginning of his sonnets:

From fairest creatures we desire increase,
That thereby beauty's rose might never die . . .

In his Thirty-fifth Sonnet, he forgives his friend some injury:

Roses have thorns, and silver fountains mud,
Clouds and eclipses stain both sun and moon;
And loathsome canker lives in the sweetest bud.
All men make faults . . .

TOP 'Poetry', a Hybrid Tea from Kordes, is one of the few strongly scented flower-shop roses.

LEFT The French poet Pierre de Ronsard (painting based on the funerary bust on his tomb at St Cosme priory, near Tours, France) with the rose named after him to mark the 400th anniversary of his death in 1585.

ABOVE 'Tuscany', the 'old velvet rose'.
LEFT The Hybrid Musk 'Penelope', still quite new when Vita celebrated it in verse.
BELOW 'Gloire de Dijon', D. H. Lawrence's favorite rose.

And in the final tragic scene of *Othello*, when the Moor, maddened by jealousy, kisses the sleeping wife whom he adores but who he has sworn must die:

> . . . *When I have pluck'd thy rose,*
> *I cannot give it vital growth again,*
> *It must needs wither: I'll smell it on the tree.*

There can hardly be a dry eye in the house. But enough of high tragedy; let us go out into the garden. Names come and go in the rose catalogues, and it is a rare poet who will risk the immortality of his or verse by naming specific roses. One who dared was Vita Sackville-West, the doyenne of Old Rose lovers, who lists some of her favorites in a long poem celebrating the beauty of her garden in Kent:

> . . . *th' embroidered Tuscany,*
> *The scented Cabbage, and the damascene;*
> *Sweet briar, lovelier named the Eglantine;*
> *But above all the Musk*
> *With classic names, Thisbe, Penelope,*
> *Whose nectarous load grows heavier than the dusk . . .*

Keats, on the other hand, was more concerned to capture the impression of a moment on a summer morning walk in the country:

> *I saw the sweetest flower wild nature yields,*
> *A fresh-blown musk-rose; 'twas the first that threw*
> *Its sweets upon the summer . . .*
> *And as I feasted on its fragrancy,*
> *I thought the garden rose it far excelled.*

D. H. Lawrence also celebrates the fleeting moment, as he watches his wife showering in the morning sunlight:

> . . . *Golden shadows glow as*
> *She stoops to the sponge, and her swung breasts*
> *Sway like full-blown yellow*
> *Gloire de Dijon roses.*

After that breathless moment we may feel grateful for Gertrude Stein's gentle reminder that, after all is said and done, a rose is just a flower:

> *A rose is a rose is a rose.*

'April Hamer'

HYBRID TEA ı PINK BLEND

The large, fully double flowers are shell-pink with bright pink petal edges, and popular with Australian exhibitors. They are pleasantly fragrant. The bush is robust and quite vigorous, with plenty of dark green, disease-resistant foliage, and blooms prolifically throughout the season.

Bell, Australia, 1983
'Mount Shasta' × 'Prima Ballerina'
Repeat flowering ı *Moderate fragrance*
HABIT Bush H/W 1.5m/1.2m (5ft/4ft) ı ZONES 5–11

'Aquarius'

GRANDIFLORA ı PINK BLEND

Blending ice-cream-pink and candy-pink, the double, high-centred flowers of 'Aquarius' are medium-sized and often come in clusters, which may be thinned to increase the bloom size. The scent is only slight, but the flowers are borne in profusion on a taller than average bush with leathery, olive-green

'April Hamer'

'Aquarius'

TOP 'Ards Beauty'
BOTTOM 'Arianna'

foliage. They last very well in water. This is still, deservedly, a very popular variety.

ARMaq ı Armstrong, USA, 1971
('Charlotte Armstrong' × 'Contrast') × ('Fandango' × ['World's Fair' × 'Floradora'])
Repeat flowering ı *Slight fragrance*
HABIT Bush H/W 2m/1.5m (7ft/5ft) ı ZONES 5–11
🏵 Geneva Gold Medal 1970, All-America Rose Selection 1971

'Ards Beauty'

FLORIBUNDA ı MEDIUM YELLOW

This has proved to be a very good yellow rose, its large, double, scented flowers borne very freely on a compact bush with glossy, dark green foliage. 'Ards Beauty' took its raiser by surprise when it won the RNRS President's International Trophy for the best new rose of 1983. At the time, Patrick Dickson had only 15 plants in stock, having

'Aromatherapy'

not yet decided whether to introduce it. With rose-lovers clamoring for it, it was introduced in 1986. It was named for the breeder's home town in County Down.

DICjoy ı Dickson, Northern Ireland, UK, 1984
('Eurorose' × 'Whisky Mac') × 'Bright Smile'
Repeat flowering ı *Moderate fragrance*
HABIT Bush H/W 1m/60cm (3ft/2ft) ı ZONES 5–11
🏵 Royal National Rose Society President's International Trophy 1983

'Arianna'

HYBRID TEA ı PINK BLEND

Rose-pink suffused with salmon, the large, double flowers of 'Arianna' may be a little loosely formed for the exhibition bench, but they are fragrant, and borne with amazing freedom for a rose so large. The bush is rather open in habit, and the foliage is matt

'Arnold'

'Arthur Bell'

'Auckland Metro'

green. It likes a warm climate and makes a good garden rose – it is especially fine in the fall/autumn.

MEldali | Meilland, France, 1968
'Charlotte Armstrong' × ('Peace' × 'Michèle Meilland')
Repeat flowering | *Slight fragrance*
HABIT Bush H/W 1.5m/1m (5ft/3ft) | ZONES 5–11

'Arnold'

HYBRID RUGOSA | MEDIUM RED

'Arnoldiana', 'The Arnold Rose'

The result of crossing *R. rugosa* with an Old Garden Rose, this variety is a minor piece of rose history – not one that is grown for the beauty of its flowers. The large, upright bush is hardy and easy to grow, with mid-green, rather crinkly foliage, and bears clusters of smallish, single, bright crimson flowers in spring, with a few later blooms to follow.

Dawson, England, UK, 1893
R. rugosa × 'Général Jacqueminot'
Spring flowering | *Strong fragrance*
HABIT Bush H/W 1.5m/1.2m (5ft/4ft) | ZONES 4–11

'Aromatherapy'

HYBRID TEA | MEDIUM PINK

This showy, rich pink beauty starts from perfect pink buds that sweeten the air with a powerful aroma as they open. The flowers are extremely long-lasting when cut. The bush is upright, well branched and very free-blooming, with disease-resistant, semi-glossy, dark green foliage.

JAChonew | Zary, USA, 2005
Seedling × 'New Zealand'
Repeat flowering | *Strong, rose fragrance*
HABIT Bush H/W 1.8m/1.2m (6ft/4ft) | ZONES 5–11

'Arthur Bell'

FLORIBUNDA | MEDIUM YELLOW

As shapely as most Hybrid Teas, and nearly as large, the sweetly scented, semi-double flowers

of 'Arthur Bell' start out deep golden yellow but pale to primrose and cream almost as soon as they are fully blown. Some people find this a major fault, others find the contrast between the two tones of yellow charming, but everyone agrees that 'Arthur Bell' is one of the easiest yellow roses to grow, especially in a cool climate. The bush is on the tall side, and the foliage is large, dark and heavily veined. Arthur Bell was the maker of the Scotch whisky that bears his name.

McGredy, Northern Ireland, UK, 1965
'Clare Grammerstorf' × 'Piccadilly'
Repeat flowering | *Intense fragrance*
HABIT Bush H/W 110cm/60cm (3ft 6in/2ft) | ZONES 5–11
Belfast Fragrance (R. J. Frizzell Memorial) Award 1967, Royal Horticultural Society Award of Garden Merit 1993

'Auckland Metro'

HYBRID TEA | WHITE

'Metro', 'Precious Michelle'

Palest pink to almost white, the large, double flowers with their 26–40 petals are of unusual formation for a Hybrid Tea. 'Camellia-like', the catalogues say, and that is a fair description. The petals are arranged with perfect symmetry, the inner ones smaller than the outer, forming an almost flat flower. The scent is excellent

(in this regard, this variety is uncamellia-like), and the bushy plant is shorter than average and well covered in shiny, dark green leaves. It flowers almost as freely as a Floribunda. 'Auckland Metro' is known as 'Precious Michelle' in Australia, in memory of the young lady who is also commemorated by 'Michelle Joy'.

MACbucpal | McGredy, New Zealand, 1987
'Sexy Rexy' × (seedling × 'Ferry Porsche')
Repeat flowering | *Intense fragrance*
HABIT Bush H/W 1.8m/1.2m (6ft/4ft) | ZONES 5–11

'Augustine Guinoisseau'

HYBRID TEA | WHITE

'White La France'

The nickname says it all: 'Augustine Guinnoisseau' closely resembles its famous parent 'La France' except that its flowers are blush-white and have rather fewer petals. They are beautifully scented. This is a rose that needs the greatest of care if it is to give of its exquisite best. Even then, the plant will be on the small side. It dislikes wet weather.

Guinnoisseau, France, 1889
'La France' sport
Repeat flowering | *Strong fragrance*
HABIT Bush H/W 1.5m/1.2m (5ft/4ft) | ZONES 5–11

'Augustine Guinoiseau'

'Autumn'

HYBRID TEA | ORANGE BLEND

Blending rich tones of burnt orange, red and gold, the double, 70-petalled flowers are large and fragrant. The colors soften with age. The compact bush flowers abundantly in the spring but is less generous with its flowers in the fall/autumn. The foliage is glossy and dark green, but watch out for black spot. This variety is a sister-seedling of the same raiser's better-known 'President Herbert Hoover' (also included in this book).

Coddington, USA, 1928
'Sensation' × 'Souvenir de Claudius Pernet'
Repeat flowering | *Moderate fragrance*
HABIT Bush H/W 1.5m/1.2m (5ft/4ft) | ZONES 5–11

'Autumn Delight'

HYBRID MUSK | WHITE

'Autumn Delight' makes a compact bush like that of a large Floribunda. The almost thornless branches are nicely clad with leathery foliage, and bear large clusters of single-petalled cream flowers with maroon stamens and a fine fragrance. In the fall/autumn, the flowers are deeper in tone and the sprays of flowers huge – a real delight.

Bentall, England, UK, 1933
Parentage unknown
Repeat flowering | *Moderate fragrance*
HABIT Bush H/W 1.2m/1.2m (4ft/4ft) | ZONES 6–11

'Avignon'

FLORIBUNDA | MEDIUM YELLOW

'Avignon' seems to be on the verge of dropping out of the catalogues, which is a pity, as it is

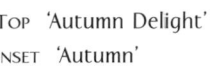

TOP 'Autumn Delight'
INSET 'Autumn'

'Avignon'

an attractive rose. The double flowers are a pleasing shade of cool yellow, which holds well. They are nicely shaped – not overly large, about 6cm (2½in) or so in diameter – and are carried in well-spaced clusters on a tallish, dark-leafed bush.

Cants, England, UK, 1974
'Allgold' × 'Zambra'
Repeat flowering | *Slight fragrance*
HABIT Bush H/W 1m/60cm (3ft/2ft) | ZONES 5–11

'Aztec'

HYBRID TEA | ORANGE RED

With its flowers of terracotta to brick-red, 'Aztec' was one of the first Hybrid Teas in this color range. It is still worth a look, as it makes a strong and healthy, if somewhat sprawling, bush, with olive-green leaves that tone well with the flowers. The double blooms are borne on rather weak stalks, but they have fine exhibition form. If the sprays of buds this variety often produces are thinned to singletons, the blooms can be very large. Try it as a standard, and the blooms will nod closer to eye level.

Swim, USA, 1957
'Charlotte Armstrong' × seedling
Repeat flowering | *Moderate fragrance*
HABIT Bush H/W 1.8m/1.2m (6ft/4ft) | ZONES 5–11

'Aztec'

'Azure Sea'

'Baby Faurax'

'Bahia'

'Azure Sea'

HYBRID TEA ı MAUVE

The word 'Azure' is mere wishful thinking
for this rose. It actually blends mauve with
varying amounts of pink. The large, double
blooms are nicely shaped but only lightly
scented. The bush is upright, with matt, dark
green foliage. Like most mauve Hybrid Teas,
it needs good cultivation to give of its best,
and the color is richest in the fall/autumn.

AROlala ı Christensen, USA, 1983
('Angel Face' × 'First Prize') × 'Lady X'
Repeat flowering ı *Slight fragrance*

HABIT Bush H/W 1.5m/1.2m (5ft/4ft) ı ZONES 5–11

'Baby Faurax'

POLYANTHA ı MAUVE

'Baby Faurax' is thought to be a dwarf sport
of the rambler 'Veilchenblau', which carries
some of the most convincing bluish tones
in the world of roses. While the blooms
of 'Veilchenblau' are very variable in color,
'Baby Faurax' is much more consistently

amethyst. It is a dwarf in an already dwarf
group, rarely growing more than 30cm
(12in) high. The dainty flowers, borne in
large clusters, are double and quite fragrant.
The foliage is a dull mid-green. It was named
for a Belgian nursery.

Lille, France, 1924
Parentage unknown
Repeat flowering ı *Moderate fragrance*

HABIT Bush H/W 30cm/30cm (12in/12in) ı ZONES 4–10

'Baccarà'

HYBRID TEA ı ORANGE RED

'Baccarat', 'Jacqueline'

For many years 'Baccarà' was the supreme
flower-shop rose; you hardly saw a florist's
window without a bunch of its mid-sized,
scarlet flowers, shapely and double, with
some 75 petals, on their unbelievably long
stems. The foliage is dark green and leathery.
Francis Meilland made a fortune from it, but
it was never much of a garden rose, even in
warm climates. Now it has been superseded
by such varieties as 'Mercedes' and 'Gabriella', which are more economical to grow,
but people still ask for it by name. There is
no scent to speak of.

MEIger ı Meilland, France, 1954
'Happiness' × 'Independence'
Repeat flowering ı *Slight fragrance*

HABIT Bush H/W 1.8m/1.2m (6ft/4ft) ı ZONES 5–11

'Baccarà'

'Bahia'

FLORIBUNDA ı ORANGE BLEND

The vermilion tone of 'Bahia' is made softer by
an overtone of old rose, which looks very much
better than it sounds against the dark green
foliage. The blooms are medium-sized and double, with a pleasantly informal, ruffled shape.
Alas, their color is not very stable; as they
age, the pink takes over and then fades, and
the spent flowers do not drop cleanly. But if
you are prepared to clean it up every few days
(and keep a spray gun handy in case of black

TOP 'Ballerina'
LEFT 'Barbra Streisand'
RIGHT 'Bantry Bay'
INSET 'Barbara Bush'

spot), 'Bahia' is a good, tall-growing rose.
The foliage is glossy, leathery and dark green.

Lammerts, USA, 1974
'Rumba' × 'Super Star'
Repeat flowering ı *Moderate, spicy fragrance*

HABIT Bush H/W 1.2m/1m (4ft/3ft) ı ZONES 5–11

All-America Rose Selection 1974

'Ballerina'

HYBRID MUSK ı MEDIUM PINK

Although 'Ballerina' is officially classed as
a Hybrid Musk, it is really more like an overgrown Polyantha with its big clusters of small
flowers and its lack of perfume. Perhaps it
should be classed as a Modern Shrub Rose,
as it has many admirers for its compact habit,
its lack of temperament (it is one of the easiest
of all roses to grow), and the extraordinary
freedom and continuity with which it bears
its pretty single flowers, soft pink with white
around the stamens. The mid-green foliage is
exceptionally healthy and disease-resistant.

Bentall, England, UK, 1937
Parentage undisclosed
Repeat flowering ı *No fragrance*

HABIT Bush H/W 1.5m/1.5m (5ft/5ft) ı ZONES 6–11

Royal Horticultural Society Award of Garden Merit 1993

'Bantry Bay'

LARGE FLOWERED CLIMBER ı MEDIUM PINK

The bright rose-pink flowers are shapely in
the bud, opening rather loosely and showing
a paler centre. They are only slightly fragrant,
but are borne in clusters freely throughout
the season. The plant is moderately vigorous
and rather shrubby in habit, with very glossy
leaves and the virtue of not usually becoming
bare of foliage low down.

McGredy, New Zealand, 1967
'New Dawn' × 'Korona'
Repeat flowering ı *Slight fragrance*

HABIT Bush H/W 3.5m/2.5m (12ft/8ft) ı ZONES 6–11

'Barbara Bush'

HYBRID TEA ı PINK BLEND

A lovely tribute to one of America's First
Ladies, this is an impressive plant that will
surprise everyone who grows it. The coral-
pink and ivory blooms are produced in
dozens on a stately, strong-growing plant.
The blooms are large and double, with 25–30
petals, and have a moderate damask fragrance.

They are very long-lasting, and are borne both
singly and in large clusters on a very vigorous
bush that is hardy and disease-resistant. The
foliage is glossy and dark green.

JACbush ı Warriner, USA, 1990
'Pristine' × 'Antigua'
Repeat flowering ı *Moderate, damask fragrance*

HABIT Bush H/W 1.8m/1.2m (6ft/4ft) ı ZONES 4–9

'Barbra Streisand'

HYBRID TEA ı LIGHT PINK

The famous Hollywood singer/actress
personally choose this rose to bear her name
on the basis of its color and fragrance. The
double, clean lavender blooms are highlighted
by a reddish hue along the petal edges; they
have impeccable exhibition form and a most
captivating fragrance. The flowers come
both singly and in candelabra-like clusters
on a medium-sized, upright plant that is a
good garden performer. The foliage is lush,
glossy and dark green.

WEKquaneze ı Carruth, USA, 1999
['Blue Nile' × ('Ivory Tower' × 'Angel Face')]
× 'New Zealand'
Repeat flowering ı *Strong rose and citrus fragrance*

HABIT Bush H/W 1.8m/1.2m (6ft/4ft) ı ZONES 5–11

Portland (Oregon, USA) Fragrance Award 2004, Rose
Hills (California) Fragrance Award 2004

'Baronne Edmond de Rothschild'

HYBRID TEA ı RED BLEND

'Baronne de Rothschild'

This is one of the more subtly toned bicolors
– deep pink, with an undertone of mauve,
and white. The flowers are large, double,
high-centred and very fragrant. The foliage
is bright green and glossy, and the bushes are
rather taller than the average. Sometimes it
is a little shy with its flowers. Keep an eye
out for black spot. Take care not to confuse
this variety with the older Hybrid Perpetual
'Baroness Rothschild', introduced in 1868.
'Baronne Edmond de Rothschild' came along
from the Meillands exactly 100 years later.
Baron Edmond de Rothschild is famous for
his Exbury Hybrid Rhododendrons.

MELgriso ı Meilland, France, 1968
('Baccará' × 'Crimson King') × 'Peace'
Repeat flowering ı *Intense fragrance*

HABIT Bush H/W 1.5m/1.2m (5ft/4ft) ı ZONES 5–11

Lyon Gold Medal 1968, Rome Gold Medal 1968,
Monza Fragrance Award 1969, Belfast Fragrance
(R. J. Frizzell Memorial) Award 1971

'Baronne Edmond de Rothschild'

'Basildon Bond'

'Basildon Bond'

HYBRID TEA ı APRICOT BLEND

Deep apricot-yellow, the shapely buds of
'Basildon Bond' open to loosely informal
double flowers, sweetly fragrant and set
against deep olive-green foliage with plum-
tinted young shoots. The flowers are borne
in clusters of 1–3. The bush is of average
height, its wood prickly. It is surprising that
this rose has found so little favor outside
Britain, where it was introduced in 1983.

HARjosine ı Harkness, England, UK, 1980
('Sabine' × 'Circus') × ('Yellow Cushion' ×
'Glory of Ceylon')
Repeat flowering ı *Moderate fragrance*

HABIT Bush H/W 1.5m/1.2m (5ft/4ft) ı ZONES 5–11

Belfast Gold Medal and Prize of the City of Belfast 1982

'Bassino'

SHRUB ı MEDIUM RED

'Suffolk'

Viewed as a single cluster, the small, single
flowers of 'Bassino' may look distinctly old
hat and unexciting; but when the prostrate
bush reaches its full spread of a metre (3ft)

'Bassino'

'Beauté'

HYBRID TEA ꞏ APRICOT BLEND

Beauty is the birthright of all roses, and it may seem presumptuous to single out one rose above all others to bear her name, but 'Beauté' is worthy of the compliment. Few roses have such blooms that hold their form until they drop. The foliage is large and a dark, dull green, the perfect setting for the huge and exquisite flowers, all apricot and cream. The bushes are apt to be on the low side, although not at all sparing with their flowers! The scent, although not strong, is pleasant.

Mallerin, France, 1953
'Madame Joseph Perraud' × seedling
Repeat flowering ꞏ *Moderate fragrance*
HABIT Bush H/W 1.4m/1m (4ft 6in/3ft) ꞏ ZONES 5–9

'Beautiful Britain'

FLORIBUNDA ꞏ ORANGE RED

The name is not quite as patriotic as it sounds: the rose was sponsored by the Keep Britain

or so and covers itself in brilliant red, the effect is striking indeed. The color seems all the more brilliant in contrast to the white centres of the flowers, and it holds without fading or going 'blue' no matter what the weather. This is one of the toughest and most useful of the new ground-covering roses. Flowering all season, it would make a pretty weeping standard. There is a slightly larger version, also by Kordes, called 'Royal Bassino'.

KORmixel ꞏ Kordes, Germany, 1988
('Sea Foam' × 'Red Max Graf') × seedling
Repeat flowering ꞏ *No fragrance*
HABIT Bush H/W 60cm/1.2m (2ft/4ft) ꞏ ZONES 4–11

RIGHT 'Bella Rosa'
TOP INSET 'Beauté'
BOTTOM INSET 'Beautiful Britain'

'Belle Époque'

Tidy organization. The raiser describes it as 'tomato-red', but it is usually distinctly orangered. There is little scent, but the individual flowers are small replicas of exhibition roses, and come in good sprays on an upright bush. The foliage is a glossy medium green. It is a very popular rose in the United Kingdom.

DICfire | Dickson, Northern Ireland, UK, 1983
'Red Planet' × 'Eurorose'
Repeat flowering | *Slight fragrance*

HABIT Bush H/W 1m/60cm (3ft/2ft) | ZONES 5–11

'Bella Rosa'

FLORIBUNDA | MEDIUM PINK

'Kordes's Rose Bella Rosa', 'KORwondis', 'Toynbee Hall'

The nursery industry groups a range of types under the omnibus term 'Patio Roses', all of which have in common short growth, making them suitable for edging a patio or growing in largish pots. Some are just overgrown Miniatures, but 'Bella Rosa' is the sort of rose the breeders ought to be aiming for. Short and spreading in growth, it has polished, dark green foliage. The very pretty double flowers are candy-icing pink, sometimes quite pale but at others a shade deeper. They are normal Floribunda size, and have perfect form but only a slight scent. It was introduced in 1982 by Reimer Kordes, who has also introduced a sport, 'White Bella Rosa'.

KORwunder | Kordes, Germany, 1981
Seedling × 'Träumeri'
Repeat flowering | *Slight fragrance*

HABIT Bush H/W 75cm/45cm (30in/18in) | ZONES 5–11

'Belle Époque'

HYBRID TEA | PINK BLEND

This two-toned beauty has inside petals of golden bronze, while the outside edges are deeper. It is quite an amazing sight as the long, pointed buds slowly unfurl to magnificent large, high-centred, double blooms. Free-flowering from spring through to the late fall/autumn, it is a tall, vigorous grower, with lush, dark green foliage that is normally disease-free and easy to maintain. This is a wonderful variety to plant en masse, providing spectacular quantities of flowers to cut and bring inside the home.

FRYyaboo/Fryer, England, UK, 1994
'Remember Me' × 'Simba'
Repeat flowering | *Moderate fragrance*

HABIT Bush H/W 1.5m/1.2m (5ft/4ft) | ZONES 5–11

'Belle Poitevine'

HYBRID RUGOSA | MEDIUM PINK

One of the smaller-growing Hybrid Rugosas, usually less than 2m (6ft) high and wide, 'Belle Poitevine' bears elegant, loosely double blooms in mid-pink, often flushed with mauve and sometimes entirely mauve. The cream stamens show the cool tones of the petals off to perfection, and the bush is typical Rugosa: strong and spiny, with lush, disease-proof foliage. It repeats its bloom very well.

Bruant, France, 1894
Parentage unknown
Repeat flowering | *Strong fragrance*

HABIT Bush H/W 1.8m/1.5m (6ft/5ft) | ZONES 3–11

Royal Horticultural Society Award of Garden Merit 1993

'Belle Portugaise'

'Belle Poitevine'

'Belle Portugaise'

LARGE FLOWERED CLIMBER | LIGHT PINK

'Belle of Portugal'

Like most of the hybrids of *R. gigantea*, this splendid rose is rather tender and at its best in mild climates. It has long been popular in California for its ease of growth, its great vigor and its lavish display in early summer, before most roses have started. The semidouble flowers are not especially scented, but they are very pretty, long-budded and silky, and tinted in pale pink and peach. They appear over several weeks. The slightly drooping foliage is olive-green.

Cayeux, Portugal, 1903
R. gigantea × 'Reine Marie Henriette'
Summer flowering | *Moderate fragrance*

HABIT Bush H/W 4.5m/3m (15ft/10ft) | ZONES 6–11

'Belle Story'

SHRUB | LIGHT PINK

Introduced in 1984 and named for one of the first nursing sisters who joined the Royal Navy, in 1864, 'Belle Story' has large, double,

'Belle Story'

'Bellona'

'Benjamin Franklin'

'Benson & Hedges Gold'

peony-like flowers in delicate tones of peach-pink. The bush is strong and branching, like a larger edition of 'Iceberg'. The foliage is a semi-glossy mid-green.

AUSelle ⦙ Austin, England, UK, 1985
('Chaucer' × 'Parade') × ('The Prioress' × 'Iceberg')
Summer flowering ⦙ *Intense fragrance*

HABIT Bush H/W 1.2m/1.2m (4ft/4ft) ⦙ ZONES 6–11

'Bellona'

FLORIBUNDA ⦙ MEDIUM YELLOW

Essentially a greenhouse rose for the cut-flower trade, 'Bellona' has medium-sized, double flowers in small clusters on very long stems. They are exceedingly shapely, open slowly, and retain their deep yellow color – set against glossy, green foliage – until they drop, but there is not much fragrance. In the garden this variety needs a warm and sunny spot to flower well. There are plenty of better yellow garden roses! 'Bellona' was the Roman goddess of war, whose priests marched in procession on state occasions, blowing golden trumpets as they went.

KORilona ⦙ Kordes, Germany, 1976
'New Day' × 'Minigold'
Repeat flowering ⦙ *Slight fragrance*

HABIT Bush H/W 105cm/75cm (3ft 6in/2ft 6in) ⦙ ZONES 5–11

'Benjamin Franklin'

HYBRID TEA ⦙ LIGHT PINK

The color is often described as 'dawn-pink', which is apt, as it is lit with gold and apricot. The bush is strong, with leathery, dark green

foliage. Exhibitors might complain about a shortage of petals, but really the only demerit of these large, double flowers is their very slight perfume.

Von Abrams, USA, 1969
Parentage undisclosed
Repeat flowering ⦙ *Slight fragrance*

HABIT Bush H/W 1.5m/1.2m (5ft/4ft) ⦙ ZONES 5–11

'Benson & Hedges Gold'

HYBRID TEA ⦙ YELLOW BLEND

'Benson & Hedges Gold' is a cross between 'Yellow Pages' and a seedling of 'Arthur Bell' and 'Cynthia Brooke' – three beautiful golden roses in one. Ovoid buds open to medium-sized, double, bright yellow blooms, sometimes with a flush of red. Like other newer yellow roses, this variety is fragrant.

MACgem ⦙ McGredy, New Zealand, 1979
'Yellow Pages' × ('Arthur Bell' × 'Cynthia Brooke')
Repeat flowering ⦙ *Moderate fragrance*

HABIT Bush H/W 1.5m/1.2m (5ft/4ft) ⦙ ZONES 5–11

🌹 Gold Star of the South Pacific, Hamilton (New Zealand) 1978

'Berlin'

SHRUB ⦙ ORANGE BLEND

Although classed as a Shrub Rose, 'Berlin' is like an exceptionally strong-growing Floribunda. The foliage is broad and glossy; the wood is dark and armed with red thorns; and the almost-single flowers, borne in large trusses, open a brilliant scarlet. They pale almost at once to cerise, the two tones

'Berlin'

together creating a brilliant effect. There is little scent, although the flowers are exceptionally resistant to bad weather. 'Berlin' is one of a series of so-called 'Park Roses' named for German cities.

Kordes, Germany, 1949
'Eva' × 'Peace'
Repeat flowering ı *Moderate fragrance*
HABIT Bush H/W 1.5m/1m (5ft/3ft) ı ZONES 5–11

'Berries 'n' Cream'

LARGE FLOWERED CLIMBER ı PINK BLEND

'Calypso', 'Climbing Berries 'n' Cream'

Lovers of Old Garden Roses will be instantly reminded of 'Rosa Mundi' (*R. gallica versicolor*). The double, ruffled flowers, with their 26–40 petals, are swirls of old rose and cream, with no two alike. They are borne in bountiful clusters – like miniature bouquets – on strong, thick canes and stems. In cooler climates, the cream color becomes more dominant.

POUlclimb ı Olesen, Denmark, 1999
'Evita' × seedling
Repeat flowering ı *Fresh-cut apple fragrance*
HABIT Climber H/W 3.5m/3m (12ft/10ft) ı ZONES 5–11

'Berries 'n' Cream'

'Better Homes and Gardens'

'Betty Boop'

'Better Homes and Gardens'

HYBRID TEA ı PINK BLEND

Rose-pink with an ivory reverse, the double flowers of this celebrity rose are not very large, but they are high-centred and mildly fragrant. The bush is a shade above average in height, and well clad with dark foliage. It is a pleasing rose, if perhaps not a distinguished one, although its parentage is aristocratic.

Warr ner, USA, 1976
'Super Star' × 'Peace'
Repeat flowering ı *Slight fragrance*
HABIT Bush H/W 1.5m/1.2m (5ft/4ft) ı ZONES 5–11

'Betty Boop'

FLORIBUNDA ı RED BLEND

'Centenary of Federation'

Named for a much-loved American animated cartoon character, this variety is well matched for color, vitality and sparkle. The low-growing plant tends to cover itself in early spring with medium-sized clusters of 5–8 single florets, making it an ideal choice for borders and sidewalks. The flowers are wonderfully long-lived, but they are inclined to fade after a few days of strong sunlight – in the process displaying a dramatic tapestry of colors. The foliage is glossy, dark green and disease-resistant. 'Betty Boop' was renamed

'Centenary of Federation' to honor the 100th anniversary of federation in Australia.

WEKplapic ı Carruth, USA, 1999
'Playboy' × 'Picasso'
Repeat flowering ı *Fruity fragrance*
HABIT Bush H/W 1m/1m (3ft/3ft) ı ZONES 5–11
🌹 All-America Rose Selection 1999

'Betty Prior'

FLORIBUNDA ı MEDIUM PINK

For many years this English-bred rose was one of the most popular of all roses in the United States, and is by no means out of

'Betty Prior'

favor there even now. At first sight you might wonder what the fuss is about: the flowers are just pink, single, and not especially fragrant. They are an attractive enough shade and come in graceful clusters against dull, mid-green foliage. Why so popular? This plant will grow anywhere, resisting cold, heat, disease and unskilled gardeners, to give abundant flowers right throughout the season. Who can deny it its place!

Prior, England, UK, 1935
'Kirsten Poulsen' × seedling
Repeat flowering ı *Moderate fragrance*

HABIT Bush H/W 1.2m/1m (4ft/3ft) ı ZONES 4–11

'Bewitched'

HYBRID TEA ı MEDIUM PINK

Clear pink, often with a suggestion of salmon, the large, double, high-centred flowers of 'Bewitched' are well scented and very long-lasting. This is an outstanding rose for a warm climate, holding its color in midsummer heat when so many roses become fleeting ghosts of themselves. 'Bewitched' does not have the iron constitution of its parent 'Queen Elizabeth', but it scores for softer color and its stronger fragrance. The flowers are borne singly, and the foliage is large, glossy and apple green, red-tinted when young.

Lammerts, USA, 1967
'Queen Elizabeth' × 'Tawny Gold'
Repeat flowering ı *Moderate, damask fragrance*

HABIT Bush H/W 1.8m/1.2m (6ft/4ft) ı ZONES 4–11

✿ All-America Rose Selection 1967, Dublin Gold Medal 1994

'Bienvenu'

GRANDIFLORA ı ORANGE BLEND

Despite its French name, this rose was bred in America. It is fairly typical of the Grandi-flora class, with large, double, high-centred flowers borne in small clusters on a taller

'Bewitched'

than average bush. Unusually for a rose of this burnt orange color, it is very fragrant. Introduced in 1969, 'Bienvenu' got lost in the crowd of orange-red roses of the 1970s and 1980s and is rarely catalogued today. Do not confuse it with 'Benvenuto', a Hybrid Tea Climber also included in this book.

Swim, USA, 1969
'Camelot' × ('Montezuma' × 'War Dance')
Repeat flowering ı *Strong fragrance*

HABIT Bush H/W 2m/1.5m (7ft/5ft) ı ZONES 5–11

'Big Ben'

HYBRID TEA ı DARK RED

This rose does poorly in hot climates, but in the cool summer of Vancouver, where it was

'Bill Warriner'

photographed, it looked outstanding. The blooms were of perfect form, velvety crimson, and very fragrant indeed, as one would expect from a child of its parents. The foliage is mid-green. 'Big Ben' is the famous clock tower of the Houses of Parliament in London.

Gandy, England, UK, 1964
'Ena Harkness' × 'Charles Mallerin'
Repeat flowering ı *Intense fragrance*

HABIT Bush H/W 1.5m/1.2m (5ft/4ft) ı ZONES 5–11

'Bienvenu'

'Big Ben'

'Bing Crosby'

'Bill Warriner'

FLORIBUNDA ı ORANGE PINK

Named in honor of the late master hybridizer
at Jackson & Perkins, who brought the world
so many great Floribundas over his 40-year
career, this lovely rose has proved a great
favorite among US gardeners. The bush is
constantly covered with very double, salmon-
coral flowers of perfect form. They are borne
both singly and in large clusters, and are very
long-lasting – perfect for flower arrangements.
The plant is medium to tall, upright and vigorous, with an abundance of glossy, dark
green, disease-resistant foliage.

JACsur ı Warriner and Zary, USA, 1998
'Sun Flare' × 'Impatient'
Repeat flowering ı *Slight, sweet fragrance*
HABIT Bush H/W 1.2m/1m (4ft/3ft) ı ZONES 5–9

'Bing Crosby'

HYBRID TEA ı ORANGE BLEND

Like many roses that straddle the boundary
between red and orange, 'Bing Crosby' varies
in tone with the soil and the weather. Sometimes almost pure deep orange, at other times
it is definitely red. The very double flowers
are borne mostly singly. The foliage is slightly
wrinkled and red in its youth, maturing to olive-
green. Introduced in 1981, this magnificent
bloom is happiest in a warm climate – it has
never found favor in Europe.

Weeks, USA, 1980
Seedling × 'First Prize'
Repeat flowering ı *Slight, spicy fragrance*
HABIT Bush H/W 1.5m/1.2m (5ft/4ft) ı ZONES 5–11
All-America Rose Selection 1981

'Bishop Darlington'

HYBRID MUSK ı APRICOT BLEND

'Bishop Darlington' conforms to expectations
for the Hybrid Musk class, being a fine, arching bush about 1.8m (6ft) tall with sprays of
8cm (3in) flowers. Shapely, coral-pink buds
open to large, semi-double, loosely informal
flowers in blush and cream. They are borne
all season and have a fruity scent. The foliage
is softly bronzed.

Thomas England, UK, 1926
'Aviateur Blériot' × 'Moonlight'
Repeat flowering ı *Moderate, fruity fragrance*
HABIT Bush H/W 1.8m/1.5m (6ft/5ft) ı ZONES 6–11

'Black Baccarà'

'Black Baccarà'

HYBRID TEA ı DARK RED

This unique rose has rich, velvety textured
blooms of a deep dark red; they have lots of
substance, and can last up to two weeks in
a vase. The flowers are small, with some
45 petals, and are borne both singly and
in small clusters. The plant is low-growing
but upright and bushy, with highly disease-
resistant, semi-glossy, dark green foliage.
It is an excellent variety for the front of
a rose bed or walkway, and would also
look lovely in a container on the patio.

MEIdebenne ı Meilland, France, 2001
Parentage unknown
Repeat flowering ı *No fragrance*
HABIT Bush H/W 1.8m/1.5m (6ft/5ft) ı ZONES 4–11

'Black Beauty'

HYBRID TEA ı DARK RED

A sport of the yellow Hybrid Tea 'Frisco',
this dazzling variety has attracted a good deal
of attention since its release. The medium-
sized, double blooms are a velvety red, turning to black as they age, with – here comes the
surprise – a yellow reverse (a characteristic

'Bishop Darlington'

'Black Beauty'

inherited from 'Frisco'). They are produced both singly and in good-sized clusters, and have an excellent vase life. The plant is of medium size and very free-blooming.

Delbard, France, 1973
'Frisco' sport
Repeat flowering ı *Light fragrance*

HABIT Bush H/W 1.5m/1.2m (5ft/4ft) ı ZONES 4–11

'Black Boy'

LARGE FLOWERED CLIMBER ı DARK RED

'Blackboy'

Striking easily from cuttings and almost inde-structible once established, 'Black Boy' has been popular in Australian gardens for so long that this name is apt to be attached to almost any dark red rose, climbing or not, whose real name has been forgotten! The large, semi-double flowers are in the 'decorative' Hybrid Tea style; they are dark crimson, although not usually dark enough to be called black. They are sweetly fragrant, and are produced freely (it seems on every twig) on a vigorous plant with dull green, slightly olive-toned foliage. Fall/autumn flowers are very rare.

Clark, Australia, 1919
'Étoile de France' × 'Bardou Job'
Summer flowering ı *Moderate fragrance*

HABIT Bush H/W 3m/1.8m (10ft/6ft) ı ZONES 6–11

'Black Cherry'

FLORIBUNDA ı DARK RED

Dark crimson buds with black tips swirl open to reveal sumptuous, cherry-red flow-ers, their velvety petals edged ever so slightly in dark chocolate. The flowers are of medium

ABOVE 'Black Boy'
INSET 'Black Cherry'

size and classically shaped, with some 25 petals. They are borne mainly in clusters on long, sturdy stems. The plant is medium-sized and vigorous, with a slightly spreading habit, and has the ability to repeat its bloom fast. The foliage is glossy, medium green and disease-resistant.

JACreflo ı Zary, USA, 2006
Parentage unknown
Repeat flowering ı *Light damask fragrance*

HABIT Bush H/W 1.2m/1m (4ft/3ft) ı ZONES 5–11

'Black Garnet'

HYBRID TEA ı DARK RED

Very dark red, almost black, the flowers of this unusual rose are medium-sized, double, and high-centred, and usually borne in threes. Most disappointingly, they have little fragrance. The plant is bushy, with lead-green foliage. While well regarded in the United States, 'Black Garnet', has found little favor else-where. It inherits from its parents a tendency to mildew in cool climates like those of Britain and northern Europe.

Weeks, USA, 1980
'Mister Lincoln' × 'Mexicana'
Repeat flowering ı *Slight, tea fragrance*

HABIT Bush H/W 1.5m/1.2m (5ft/4ft) ı ZONES 5–11

'Black Garnet'

'Black Magic'

'Blanc Double de Coubert'

'Black Magic'

HYBRID TEA ι DARK RED

Black buds open to reveal spellbinding velvety flowers of dark garnet with even darker edges, the flowers slowly unfurling to large, exhibition-style blooms. Long-lasting and borne on long, strong stems, they make wonderful cut flowers. The plant is tall and upright, with glossy, dark green, disease-resistant foliage. To some, this variety will bring back memories of a box of chocolates of the same name!

TANkalgic ι Tantau, Germany, 1997
'Red Velvet' × 'Cora Marie'
Repeat flowering ι *Sweet fragrance*
HABIT Bush H/W 1.8m/1.2m (6ft/4ft) ι ZONES 4–9

'Blanc Double de Coubert'

HYBRID RUGOSA ι WHITE

The raiser, Cochet-Cochet, claimed that 'Blanc Double de Coubert' ('Double White of Coubert') was a cross between *R. rugosa* and the Tea Rose 'Mademoiselle de Sombreuil', but few authorities have believed him; it looks to be purebred *R. rugosa*. The bush is a little less bushy and vigorous than the wild types, but it is still a handsome plant, with the characteristic spines and tough, brilliant green leaves. It bears clusters of ruffled flowers all season; they are touched with pink in the bud, but open glistening white. Alas, rain rots them, and in wet conditions the bushes have to be groomed to keep them presentable. There are no hips.

Cochet-Cochet, France, 1892
R. rugosa × 'Mademoiselle de Sombreuil'
Repeat flowering ι *Intense fragrance*
HABIT Bush H/W 1.5m/1.2m (5ft/4ft) ι ZONES 3–10

'Blaze'

LARGE FLOWERED CLIMBER ι MEDIUM RED

For many years 'Blaze' was the most popular climbing rose, at least in America. Gardeners loved its bright, blood-red color, its willingness to grow just about anywhere, and its resistance to mildew. The double flowers are middle-sized and come in clusters, and the foliage is mid-green. Its only fault was its reluctance to repeat bloom. But in 1950 Jackson & Perkins, the firm that introduced this rose, discovered a more continuously blooming clone. Originally called 'Blaze Superior', it has usurped the original in the catalogues and (usually) dropped the

'Blaze'

'Superior' from its name. The original was bred by a Mr Kallay of Painesville, Ohio.

Kallay, USA, 1932
'Paul's Scarlet Climber' × 'Grüss an Teplitz'
Repeat flowering ı *Slight fragrance*
HABIT Bush H/W 3.5m/3m (12ft/10ft) ı ZONES 6–11

'Blessings'

HYBRID TEA ı ORANGE PINK

Pink with a distinct overtone of salmon, the shapely, double flowers of 'Blessings' are scarcely large enough for exhibition, but they are borne in great profusion, often in small clusters, on a compact bush with dark foliage. They last well in water, and are scented as well. 'Blessings' is an excellent rose for a formal bed.

Gregory, England, UK, 1967
'Queen Elizabeth' × seedling
Repeat flowering ı *Moderate fragrance*
HABIT Bush H/W 1.5m/1.2m (5ft/4ft) ı ZONES 5–11
🌹 Royal Horticultural Society Award of Garden Merit 1993

'Blessings'

'Bloomfield Dainty'

HYBRID MUSK ı MEDIUM YELLOW

Some people report that as the canary-yellow, five-petalled flowers of 'Bloomfield Dainty' age, they pass to peach-pink; more often, though, they are just a straight yellow, with perhaps the merest touches of peach. The 5cm (2in) flowers, borne in small clusters all along the arching branches, are fragrant of musk, and dainty indeed. The foliage is a glossy green. The plant is not dainty, however, being a stalwart arching shrub reaching 2.5m (8ft) or more. It flowers repeatedly, and inherits its pollen parent's preference for a warm climate.

Thomas, England, UK, 1925
'Danäe' × 'Madame Edouard Herriot'
Repeat flowering ı *Moderate fragrance*
HABIT Bush H/W 2.5m/1.2m (8ft/4ft) ı ZONES 6–11

'Blossomtime'

LARGE FLOWERED CLIMBER ı MEDIUM PINK

Introduced in 1951 by an American called O'Neil who does not seem to have any other roses to his account, 'Blossomtime' was one of the first of the repeat-flowering climbers to be raised from 'New Dawn'. It remains one of the best of them, with its clusters of shapely, double flowers in two shades of pink, and is reminiscent of one of the older Hybrid Teas. Of pillar rose vigor, it makes a great display in early summer, with scattered flowers for the rest of the season.

BELOW LEFT 'Bloomfield Dainty'
BELOW RIGHT 'Blossomtime'

'Blue Moon'

The fragrance is delightful, the foliage mid-green and resistant to mildew.

O'Neal, USA, 1951
'New Dawn' × Hybrid Tea
Repeat flowering ı *Intense fragrance*
HABIT Bush H/W 3m/1.8m (10ft/6ft) ı ZONES 6–11

'Blue Moon'

HYBRID TEA ı MAUVE

'Mainzer Fastnacht', 'Sissi', 'TANnacht'

Not blue but a cold, pale lilac shade, sometimes warmed with a little pink, the blooms are only moderate in size, although double, well formed and very sweetly scented. The

'bbie James'

TOP 'Blue River'
BOTTOM 'Blue Nile'

'Blueberry Hill'

petals are thin. The plant is tall, with dull green foliage. Flower arrangers enjoy the long, slender stems, which are fairly free of thorns. Introduced in 1964, 'Blue Moon' is much the most popular of the 'blue' roses, both for its perfume and its willingness to grow and flower freely.

TANsi　ı　Tantau, Germany, 1965
'Sterling Silver' × seedling
Repeat flowering　ı　Intense fragrance
HABIT Bush H/W 1.5m/1.2m (5ft/4ft)　ı　ZONES 5–11

'Blue Nile'

HYBRID TEA　ı　MAUVE

'Nil Bleu'

The buds of 'Blue Nile' are long and elegant, opening to nicely formed flowers with more substance to the petals than is the case with most 'blue' roses. The double flowers are clear mauve and strongly fragrant. The plant is on the tall side and quite vigorous, with dull green foliage.

DELnible　ı　Delbard, France, 1981
('Holstein' × 'Bayadère') × ('Prélude' × 'Saint-Exupéry')
Repeat flowering　ı　Intense, fruity fragrance
HABIT Bush H/W 1.8m/1.2m (6ft/4ft)　ı　ZONES 5–11

'Blue River'

HYBRID TEA　ı　MAUVE

Lilac, and flushed at the petal edges with a deeper mauve, which passes to rose-pink in old age, 'Blue River' may lack the ethereal touch of so many mauve roses, but its stronger colors have more impact in the garden. It flowers quite freely on an average-sized bush with shiny, mid-green foliage. The flowers are double and richly fragrant, and very long-lasting when cut. They are of fine form, but early disbudding will be called for to have them large enough for the show bench.

KORsicht　ı　Kordes, Germany, 1984
'Blue Moon' × 'Zorina'
Repeat flowering　ı　Intense fragrance
HABIT Bush H/W 1.5m/1.2m (5ft/4ft)　ı　ZONES 5–11
👑 Baden-Baden Gold Medal 1975

'Blueberry Hill'

FLORIBUNDA　ı　MAUVE

This excellent garden variety will have great appeal to those rosarians who instantly fall in love with all mauve-colored roses. The large, semi-double flowers, borne mostly in clusters on long, strong canes, are consistent in both color and size in all climates. They have a wonderful sweet apple scent. The plant is rounded in shape and of medium height, with lots of glossy, dark green foliage.

WEKcryplag　ı　Carruth, USA, 1999
'Crystalline' × 'Playgirl'
Repeat flowering　ı　Moderate, sweet apple fragrance
HABIT Bush H/W 1.2m/1m (4ft/3ft)　ı　ZONES 5–9

'Bobbie James'

HYBRID WICHURANA　ı　WHITE

Its ancestry is unknown—speculation links it to both *R. moschata nepalensis* and *R. multiflora*. This is one of the best choices if you want a really vigorous, semi-double, white climbing

confusion with Meilland's 1958 Floribunda 'Bonica', which was scarlet. 'Bonica '82' bears its salmon-pink flowers in lavish profusion, blooming for months on end, and is very easy to grow. The foliage is a glossy green. Meilland, who introduced it in 1982, call it a 'Landscape Rose', claiming it to be virtually immune to diseases and to need no regular pruning.

MEIdomonac **⁝** Meilland, France, 1985
(*R. sempervirens* × 'Mademoiselle Marthe Caron')
× 'Picasso'
Repeat flowering **⁝** *No fragrance*

HABIT Bush H/W 1.5m/1.2m (5ft/4ft) **⁝** ZONES 4–11

🏵 All-America Rose Selection 1987, Royal Horticultural Society Award of Garden Merit 1993, World Federation of Rose Societies Hall of Fame 2003

'Bonnie Hamilton'

FLORIBUNDA **⁝** ORANGE RED

For all its merits, 'Bonnie Hamilton' has not achieved wide popularity, perhaps because it is only happy in the climate of its native Britain. Its lack of fragrance may also have told against it. In Britain it seems to be a desirable rose, its double flowers shapely, like small Hybrid Teas, its clusters nicely spaced, and its orange-to-red colors bright without being shrill. The plant appears to be strong and healthy, and the foliage is a pleasant dark green.

Cocker, Scotland, UK, 1976
'Anne Cocker' × 'Allgold'
Repeat flowering **⁝** *Slight fragrance*

HABIT Bush H/W 110cm/75cm (3ft 6in/2ft 6in) **⁝** ZONES 4–10

'Bonsoir'

HYBRID TEA **⁝** MEDIUM PINK

The beautifully shaped double blooms of 'Bonsoir' usually come in threes. They are of palest peach-pink, deeper in the heart of the flower, and sweetly fragrant. The exhibitor will want to disbud in order to show them at their full size, but in the garden they can be left to develop naturally. The bush is a little below average in height and very thorny, with fine dark foliage. It is sometimes rather shy with its flowers, whose beauty is easily ruined by a spell of wet weather.

DICbo **⁝** Dickson, Northern Ireland, UK, 1968
Parentage unknown
Repeat flowering **⁝** *Intense fragrance*

HABIT Bush H/W 1.5m/1.2m (5ft/4ft) **⁝** ZONES 5–11

TOP 'Bonnie Hamilton'
BOTTOM 'Bolero'
INSET 'Bonsoir'

rose that produces attractive clusters. Like its ancestors, the Himalayan Musks, it will smother a large house or a sizeable tree with glossy green foliage and, in early summer, clouds of deliciously fragrant blossoms. Introduced in 1960 by Graham Thomas, it was named for the Honorable Robert James and his garden, St Nicholas, in Yorkshire.

Sunningdale Nurseries, England, UK, 1961
Parentage unknown
Summer flowering **⁝** *Intense fragrance*

HABIT Bush H/W 9m/6m (30ft/20ft) **⁝** ZONES 6–11

'Bolero'

FLORIBUNDA **⁝** WHITE

The extraordinarily powerful fragrance of its white flowers is sure to earn 'Bolero' a place in rose history. The large, double flowers are borne in clusters and beautifully set off by the glossy, dark green foliage. The plant is vigorous, low-growing and bushy, with good disease resistance, and blooms freely throughout the season.

MEIdeweis **⁝** Meilland, France, 2005
'Fair Bianca' × seedling
Repeat flowering **⁝** *Old rose and spicy fragrance*

HABIT Bush H/W 1.2m/1m (4ft/3ft) **⁝** ZONES 5–11

'Bonica'

SHRUB **⁝** MEDIUM PINK

'Bonica '82', 'Demon'

You can just call it 'Bonica' – most catalogues do – but the full title, 'Bonica '82', avoids any

RIGHT 'Bon

'Bordure Rose'

'Borderer'

'Borderer'

POLYANTHA | PINK BLEND

With the rose industry getting quite excited over the novelty of dwarf-growing Floribundas, there is a certain mischievous pleasure in noting that 'Borderer' has been around since 1918! The bush is very compact, less than 50cm (20in) tall, with very glossy, dark green leaves, and smothers itself with semi-double, rose-pink flowers, ruffled and faintly scented, for months on end. The name is Australian and American rather than British English. 'Border' refers to a low row of plants edging a flowerbed, not the grand array of the English herbaceous border.

Clark, Australia, 1918
'Jersey Beauty' × unknown
Repeat flowering | *Slight fragrance*

HABIT Bush H/W 45cm/30m (18in/12in) | ZONES 4–10

'Brand

'Bordure Rose'

FLORIBUNDA | PINK BLEND

'Roslyne', 'Strawberry Ice'

The flowers are only semi-double, the better to show off the attractive effect of the wide rose-pink border to the cream petals. They are medium-sized, and carried in well-spaced clusters on a compact, dark-leafed bush. Whichever of its three names you find it under, this is a pretty garden rose, and long-lasting as a cut flower, too. Even the raiser, Georges Delbard, admits that it is scentless. The name 'Bordure Rose' is to be preferred, as it is both descriptive and the original name bestowed by Delbard in 1975.

DELbara ı Delbard, France, 1975
Seedling × 'Fashion'
Repeat flowering ı *No fragrance*

HABIT Bush H/W 1.2m/1m (4ft/3ft) ı ZONES 4–11

Baden-Baden Gold Medal 1973, Lyon Gold Medal 1974, Madrid Gold Medal 1974, West Flanders Gold Medal 1996

'Bow Bells'

SHRUB ı DEEP PINK

The name is a tribute to London's famous 'Bow Bells', the bells of the historic church of St Mary-le-Bow. Reminiscent of those of the classic Bourbon Rose 'Reine Victoria', the double blooms are a deep rich pink, fading graciously with age. They come in large clusters on a medium-sized bush well covered with attractive, deep green foliage. The cupped blooms of 'English Roses' are always accompanied by good fragrance, and 'Bow Bells' is no exception.

AUSbells ı Austin, England, UK, 994
('Chaucer' × 'Conrad Ferdinand Meyer') × 'Graham Thomas'
Repeat flowering ı *Moderate fragrance*

HABIT Bush H/W 1.2m/1m (4ft/3ft) ı ZONES 4–11

'Brandenburg'

HYBRID TEA ı ORANGE RED

The deep salmon-red petals are a shade deeper on the reverse, and some 40 of them build up into a big, exhibition-style flower. There is little scent. The flowers come on long stems, and the foliage is glossy and olive-green. This plant is not very free with its large, double blooms, and it has rather lost favor in recent years. It is happiest in a warm climate.

Kordes, Germany, 1965
('Spartan' × 'Prima Ballerina') × 'Karl Herbst'
Repeat flowering ı *Slight fragrance*

HABIT Bush H/W 1.8m/1.2m (6ft/4ft) ı ZONES 5–11

'Brandy'

HYBRID TEA ı APRICOT BLEND

The unusual deep apricot color softens a little as the flowers open. The blooms are rather loosely formed, with 25–30 petals, and have a pleasing fruity fragrance. They are freely borne, mostly singly, on a bush of average height with large, glossy leaves. Be warned,

BOTTOM 'Brass Band'
INSET 'Bow Bells'

'Brandenburg'

however, that the leaves are susceptible to black spot.

AROcad ı Swim and Christensen, USA, 1981
'First Prize' × 'Dr A. J. Verhage'
Repeat flowering ı *Slight, tea fragrance*

HABIT Bush H/W 1.5m/1.2m (5ft/4ft) ı ZONES 5–11

All-America Rose Selection 1982

'Brass Band'

FLORIBUNDA ı APRICOT BLEND

The eye-catching blooms have good form and lots of substance, with tones ranging from neon-bright orange to paler tones of apricot. They come mostly in good-sized clusters, but also singly, especially in warm climates. The bush is of medium height and rounded, with lush, bright green, highly disease-resistant foliage. Cool weather produces bigger, more intensely colored blooms.

JACofl ı Christensen, USA, 1993
'Gold Badge' × seedling
Repeat flowering ı *Moderate, fruity fragrance*

HABIT Bush H/W 1m/60cm (3ft/2ft) ı ZONES 5–11

All America Rose Selection 1995

'Bridal Pink'

FLORIBUNDA ı MEDIUM PINK

It is unusual for a bride to wear pink at her first wedding, but many brides choose to carry pink roses. In America, they will almost certainly be 'Bridal Pink', one of the country's leading cut-flower roses. This variety is less popular in Europe, where its soft candy-pink is less favored than the coral tones of roses such as 'Sonia'. The double flowers are borne both

'Bridal Pink'

'Bride's Dream'

'Bridal White'

'Brigadoon'

singly and in small clusters. The foliage is
dark green. 'Bridal Pink' is not a good rose
out of the glasshouse, except in warm climates.

JACbri ı Boerner, USA, 1967
'Summertime' seedling × 'Spartan' seedling
Repeat flowering ı *Spicy fragrance*
HABIT Bush H/W 1m/60cm (3ft/2ft) ı ZONES 5–11

'Bridal White'

FLORIBUNDA ı WHITE

A sport of the very successful 'Bridal Pink',
'Bridal White' is a very similar rose except
for its creamy white color and the fact that
it has acquired quite a few more petals along
the way. Like 'Bridal Pink', it is only worth
growing in the garden in the mildest climates,
but the blooms are very long-lasting.

JACwhy ı Warriner, USA, 1970
'Bridal Pink' sport
Repeat flowering ı *Slight fragrance*
HABIT Bush H/W 1m/60cm (3ft/2ft) ı ZONES 5–11

'Bright Be

'Bride's Dream'

HYBRID TEA ı LIGHT PINK

'Fairy Tale Queen', 'Märchenkönigin'

With its elegant, super-long, pastel pink
buds, borne mostly singly on low-thorned
stems, this variety does indeed make a lovely
bridal bouquet. The buds open to large, double, long-lasting blooms with outstanding

'Bright Melody'

'Britannia'

exhibition form – an improvement over its parent 'Royal Highness'. The plant is tall, upright and profuse-blooming, with lush, dark green, disease-resistant foliage.

KORoyness · Kordes, Germany, 1985
'Royal Highness' × seedling
Repeat flowering · *Light rose fragrance*
HABIT Bush H/W 1.8m/1.2m (6ft/4ft) · ZONES 5–11

'Brigadoon'

HYBRID TEA · PINK BLEND

Every so often a rose comes along that everyone instantly falls in love with. 'Brigadoon' is such a rose. The huge, very double blooms are of perfect shape, softly fragrant, and irresistible in their blending of softest pink, cream and coral. The foliage is a handsome dark olive-green, and the bush is a good grower.

JACpal · Warriner, USA, 1991
Seedling × 'Pristine'
Repeat flowering · *Tea rose fragrance*
HABIT Bush H/W 1.5m/1.2m (5ft/4ft) · ZONES 5–11
All-America Rose Selection 1992

'Bright Beauty'

HYBRID TEA · ORANGE RED

Delbard is one of France's leading rose-breeding families, with a penchant for excellent cut-flower varieties, and is usually one of the most conscientious about registering its new roses, often giving their ancestry unto the third and fourth generations. This time it seems to have slipped up. 'Bright Beauty' remains an orphan. It is a beautiful one, though, with large, beautifully formed flowers in brilliant coral, and glossy, healthy leaves. It does very well in warm climates.

Delbard, France, 1986
Parentage undisclosed
Repeat flowering · *Slight fragrance*
HABIT Bush H/W 1.5m/1.2m (5ft/4ft) · ZONES 5–11

'Bright Melody'

SHRUB · MEDIUM RED

'Bright Melody' is one of those roses that can be described as a light shade of red or a deep pink, depending on one's point of view. The double blooms, fairly large and of loose Hybrid Tea form, are carried singly or in bunches of up to 10 on an upright plant. The leaves are medium to large, and olive-green. Like just about all of Griffith Buck's creations, it is easy to grow and flowers right through the season.

Buck, USA, 1984
'Carefree Beauty' × ('Herz As' × 'Cuthbert Grant')
Repeat flowering · *Slight fragrance*
HABIT Bush H/W 1.2m/1m (4ft/3ft) · ZONES 5–11

'Britannia'

POLYANTHA · RED BLEND

While most early Polyanthas were of either Dutch or Belgian origin and named for the British market, this variety is from an English amateur breeder. Fortunately, although 'Britannia' has vanished from the rose catalogues, it is captured in various reference works, keeping its place in history. In the face of competition from shapely, fragrant Floribundas, even patriotism was not enough to keep people admiring its little single, cerise flowers with their startling white eyes. The foliage is a dull green.

Burbage, England, UK, 1929
'Coral Cluster' × 'Éblouissant'
Repeat flowering · *Slight fragrance*
HABIT Bush H/W 45cm/45cm (18in/18in) · ZONES 4–10

'Broadway'

HYBRID TEA · YELLOW BLEND

Where the sun strikes the yellow petals, it brushes them heavily with bright pink. When the outer petals are heavily flushed and the centre still yellow, the effect is very striking and theatrical indeed. The double blooms, with their 30–35 petals, are not especially large, but nicely scented. The bush is upright and perhaps a trifle taller than average. The foliage is medium to large, semi-glossy and dark green.

BURway · Perry, USA, 1985
('First Prize' × 'Gold Glow') × 'Sutter's Gold'
Repeat flowering · *Damask fragrance*
HABIT Bush H/W 1.5m/1.2m (5ft/4ft) · ZONES 5–11
All-America Rose Selection 1986

'Broadway'

'Brother Cadfael'

'Brother Cadfael'

SHRUB ı MEDIUM PINK

With its gigantic, globular, pink blooms, more like peonies than roses, there is little danger of confusing 'Brother Cadfael' with another variety. The stems are usually strong enough to support the resplendent flowers, and the dark green foliage is in good proportion to their size, giving a pleasing effect overall. The fragrance is reminiscent of old Bourbon Roses. 'Brother Cadfael' is named for the hero of Ellis Peters's medieval detective stories, set around Wolverhampton in England, home to David Austin and his nursery.

AUSglobe ı Austin, England, UK, 1994
'Charles Austin' × seedling
Repeat flowering ı *Old rose fragrance*
HABIT Bush H/W 1.2m/1m (4ft/3ft) ı ZONES 5–11

'Brown Velvet'

FLORIBUNDA ı RUSSET

'Colorbreak'

'A new color break!' the old-time rose catalogues used to say whenever a rose appeared that was faintly unusual. It is one of those catchphrases that is worn-out from overuse. But 'Brown Velvet', introduced in 1975, is something out of the ordinary, a combination of dark orange and brown, much richer and brighter than it might sound. The blooms are medium-sized and double, with some 35 petals. The bush is upright, and the growth is unusually strong for a novel color. 'Color breaks' are usually associated with sickly plants. The foliage is glossy and dark green. The scent is only slight.

MACultra ı McGredy, New Zealand, 1983
'Mary Sumner' × 'Kapai'
Repeat flowering ı *Slight fragrance*
HABIT Bush H/W 1m/60cm (3ft/2ft) ı ZONES 5–11
🏵 Gold Star of the South Pacific, Palmerston North (New Zealand) 1979

'Buff Beauty'

'Buccaneer'

GRANDIFLORA | MEDIUM YELLOW

Deep buttercup yellow, the ovoid buds of 'Buccaneer' open to loose, informal, double flowers of a slightly paler shade, the blossoms tending to come in small clusters. The dull, grey-green foliage is unusually resistant to diseases, making 'Buccaneer' one of the most reliable of yellow roses. Its height allows it to be grown as a Shrub Rose, or at the back of the bed with others of similar stature, like 'Alexander', 'Queen Elizabeth' or 'President Hoover'.

Swim, USA, 1952
'Geheimrat Duisberg' × ('Max Krause' × 'Captain Thomas')
Repeat flowering | *Moderate fragrance*

HABIT Bush H/W 2m/1.5m (7ft/5ft) | ZONES 5–11
☘ Geneva Gold Medal 1952

'Buff Beauty'

HYBRID MUSK | APRICOT BLEND

The Reverend Mr Pemberton would surely have chosen to dedicate this most delicious of Hybrid Musks to some lovely goddess. It came out in 1939, 13 years after his death, and is credited to Anne Bentall, the widow of his gardener. It is one of those roses that everyone loves. It has a pleasing, graceful habit, the branches arching beneath the weight of the clusters of blooms. The double flowers are filled with muddled petals and sweet fragrance, the color varying with the seasons from straw yellow to apricot, but always charming and distinctive. The foliage is dark green and handsome.

Bentall, England, UK, 1939
Possibly 'William Allen Richardson' × unknown
Repeat flowering | *Moderate fragrance*

HABIT Bush H/W 1.5m/1.5m (5ft/5ft) | ZONES 6–11
☘ Royal Horticultural Society Award of Garden Merit 1993

'Burma Star'

FLORIBUNDA | APRICOT BLEND

This older variety is still grown extensively throughout the world, but especially in the United Kingdom. The flowers are light apricot-yellow with a flush of buff-orange along the petal edges. Mostly borne in clusters, they are medium to large and somewhat informal in shape, with some 22 petals. The bush is strong-growing and upright; it is of above-average height and could grow taller in areas with warmer climates. A healthy-looking plant with large, glossy, dark green foliage, it is very suitable for a hedge as well as for planting in mixed borders. It was named for Britain's Burma Star Association (a welfare association for World War II veterans who served in Burma).

Cocker, Scotland, UK, 1974
'Arthur Bell' × 'Manx Queen'
Repeat flowering | *Moderate fragrance*

HABIT Bush H/W 110cm/1m (3ft 6in/3ft) | ZONES 4–11

LEFT 'Burma Star'
RIGHT 'Buccaneer'
BOTTOM 'Brown Velvet'

'Butterfly Wings'

'Burnaby'

'Cabana'

'Burnaby'

HYBRID TEA | WHITE

'Gold Heart', 'Golden Heart'

Cream, often deeper in the centre, but paling almost to white in hot weather, the double flowers of 'Burnaby' are sometimes very large indeed, which has made them a great favorite with rose-show addicts for many years. 'Burnaby' is less successful as a garden rose, however. Despite the handsome dark green foliage, the plants are leggy and often shy with their blooms, especially in the fall/autumn. Wet weather upsets the flowers a great deal. 'Burnaby' remains a classic exhibition rose to this day.

Eddie, Canada, 1954
'Phyllis Gold' × 'President Herbert Hoover'
Repeat flowering | Slight fragrance
HABIT Bush H/W 1.5m/1.2m (5ft/4ft) | ZONES 4–11
Portland (Oregon, USA) Gold Medal 1957

'Busy Lizzie'

FLORIBUNDA | MEDIUM PINK

The buds give the impression that the open flowers will be a much deeper pink than they actually are. The blooms are only semi-double, but the clusters are well arranged to show each flower off to advantage. They have a slight fragrance. This variety was much favored in England for its soft color and the fact that it makes a bushy, flower-covered plant. The foliage is mid-green. It appears now to be disappearing from the catalogues, presumably to make way for newer varieties whose plant patents are still in force.

HARbusy | Harkness, England, UK, 1971
('Pink Parfait' × 'Masquerade') × 'Dearest'
Repeat flowering | Slight fragrance
HABIT Bush H/W 1m/60cm (3ft/2ft) | ZONES 5–11

'Butterfly Wings'

FLORIBUNDA | PINK BLEND

One flower in a catalogue photograph does not do justice to this rose. You have to see a bush full of the delicate, almost single flowers to appreciate their subtle tones of cream and pale pink, admirably set off by the large, pale

'Calocarpa'

'Busy Lizzie'

green foliage. The flowers come in clusters and are scented, but this rose has come and virtually gone from the catalogues in only a short time. The child of aristocratic parents, it was raised by an amateur rosarian, W. D. Gobbee, in a suburban London garden.

Gobbee, England, UK, 1976
'Dainty Maid' × 'Peace'
Repeat flowering | Moderate fragrance
HABIT Bush H/W 1m/60cm (3ft/2ft) | ZONES 5–11

'Cabana'

HYBRID TEA | PINK BLEND

The unusually striped petals earned this rose America's prestigious Green Thumb Award in 2002. Long, pointed buds open to large, deep rose-pink blooms with some 30 petals, each bloom having its own distinctive, soft yellow markings. The flowers have a spicy fragrance and come on long, strong stems that are ideal for cutting. The plant is medium to tall and upright, with plentiful semi-glossy, dark green foliage, making it attractive even between bloom cycles.

JACepirt | Zary, USA, 2002
Parentage unknown
Repeat flowering | Spicy fragrance
HABIT Bush H/W 1.5m/1.2m (5ft/4ft) | ZONES 5–11

'Calocarpa'

HYBRID RUGOSA | MEDIUM PINK

'André', *R. rugosa calocarpa*, *R.* × *calocarpa*

The name is mock-classical Greek for 'beautiful fruit'. It is certainly appropriate, for 'Calocarpa' does give an abundant crop of typical, globular *R. rugosa* hips in the fall/autumn. It is effectively pure *R. rugosa*, although slightly smaller in growth than usual. The single

'Camelot'

flowers are rose-pink, without the usual Rugosa undertone of magenta. The mid-green foliage is slightly wrinkled. Like most of the tribe, it gives a display of yellow fall/autumn foliage to go with its attractive hips.

Bruant, France, before 1891
R. rugosa × *R. chinensis*
Repeat flowering ı *Slight fragrance*
HABIT Bush H/W 1.8m/1.5m (6ft/5ft) ı ZONES 5–10

'Camelot'

GRANDIFLORA ı ORANGE PINK

Borne both singly and in clusters, the flowers of 'Camelot' are medium-sized, double and cupped. Their color is an unfading coral-pink, strong rather than delicate, and they have a pleasing spicy fragrance. The plant is taller than average, with heavy, glossy foliage. 'Camelot' is an excellent rose both for garden display and for cutting. Its name reminds us of the idealism that blossomed during the days of President John F. Kennedy.

Swim and Weeks, USA, 1964
'Circus' × 'Queen Elizabeth'
Repeat flowering ı *Moderate, spicy fragrance*
HABIT Bush H/W 2m/1.5m (7ft/5ft) ı ZONES 5–11
🌹 All-America Rose Selection 1965

'Camphill Glory'

HYBRID TEA ı PINK BLEND

The double, pale yellow and pink flowers are large and of high-centred exhibition form.

'Camphill Glory'

They are borne singly, and have only a slight scent. The foliage is matt green, and the bush is of average height, dense and very prickly. 'Camphill Glory' has not been widely grown outside Britain, where it was introduced in 1982, but there it is much admired for its ability to withstand wet weather. The name honors the Camphill Village Trust, a charity that assists the mentally handicapped.

HARkreme ı Harkness, England, UK, 1980
'Elizabeth Harkness' × 'Kordes Perfecta'
Repeat flowering ı *Slight fragrance*
HABIT Bush H/W 1.8m/1.2m (6ft/4ft) ı ZONES 5–11

'Can Can'

HYBRID TEA ı ORANGE BLEND

'Can-Can'

Two roses bear this name, but spelled differently. 'Cancan' is a 1969 greenhouse variety in orange-red from the E. G. Hill Company in the United States. 'Can Can' is the coral-salmon Hybrid Tea shown here, introduced in 1982. It is not a straight coral, the large, double flowers being suffused with gold toward the base. Their intense fragrance will, perhaps, compensate the frustrated exhibitor for their

rather loose structure. The plant habit is bushy, and the foliage is large and glossy.

LEGglow ı LeGrice, England, UK, 1981
'Just Joey' × ('Superior' × 'M schief')
Repeat flowering ı *Intense fragrance*
HABIT Bush H/W 1.5m/1.2m (5ft/4ft) ı ZONES 5–11

'Canadian Centennial'

FLORIBUNDA ı ORANGE RED

'Canadian Centennial' is in fact an American rose, named to celebrate the 100th birthday of the Dominion of Canada in 1967. These days there does not seem to be even one patriotic Canadian nursery offering it. Let us remember it as a pleasing, orange-red Floribunda, with glossy foliage and some fragrance.

Boerner, USA, 1965
'Pinocchio' seedling × 'Spartan'
Repeat flowering ı *Moderate fragrance*
HABIT Bush H/W 110cm/1m (3ft 6in/3ft) ı ZONES 5–11

'Can Can'

'Canadian Centennial'

'Canadian White Star'

HYBRID TEA I WHITE

'Dr Wolfgang Pöschl', 'C.W.S.'

Long buds open to large, shapely, double flowers of glistening white, the sharply reflexing petals giving the bloom a starry outline. The scent is only slight. The plant is of average height, with glossy, dark green foliage. A fine rose for cool climates, and well regarded in the United States and Canada, 'Canadian White Star' is not often seen elsewhere.

Mander, Canada, 1980
'Blanche Mallerin' × 'Pascali'
Repeat flowering I Slight fragrance

HABIT Bush H/W 1.5m/1.2m (5ft/4ft) I ZONES 5–11

'Canary'

'Canadian White Star'

'Canary'

HYBRID TEA I YELLOW BLEND

The International Registration Authority for Roses (IRAR) prefers to use the codename TANcary to avoid confusion between this 1972 rose from Mathias Tantau and Patrick Dickson's 1929 Hybrid Tea of the same name. Tantau has not revealed the parents of his 'Canary', but it is a safe guess that it descends from 'Super Star', as it is effectively a yellow version of it, with similar vigorous growth and olive-green foliage, plum-tinted when young. The medium-sized, double blooms are similar, too, except that they are bright, deep yellow, becoming flushed with coral as they open. The fragrance is moderate. Dickson's rose, a clear yellow, is more deserving of the name 'Canary'.

TANcary I Tantau, Germany, 1976
Parentage undisclosed
Repeat flowering I Moderate fragrance

HABIT Bush H/W 1.5m/1.2m (5ft/4ft) I ZONES 5–11

'Candy Stripe'

'Candia'

HYBRID TEA I RED BLEND

'Candia' made its debut at the Chelsea Flower Show in 1982, where it was photographed, but Meilland did not get around to introducing it until 1987. Now it seems to be available only in Canada, Israel and (of all places!) Argentina. Such are the ins and outs of marketing a new rose. One cannot help wondering whether the rest of us are missing out on something pretty good; if 'Candia' can do well in cold Canada and warm, dry Israel, it should do well just about anywhere. The large, double flowers have superb shape and color but not a great deal of fragrance. The foliage is large and dark green.

MEIbiranda I Meilland, France, 1978
'Matador' × 'Super Star'
Repeat flowering I Slight fragrance

HABIT Bush H/W 1.5m/1.2m (5ft/4ft) I ZONES 5–11

'Candia'

'Candy Stripe'

HYBRID TEA I PINK BLEND

The deep rose-pink buds of 'Candy Stripe' are boldly slashed with blush-white, and open quite quickly to large, intensely fragrant flowers. The bush is slightly above average in height, with matt green leaves. The flowers are carried on long stems and are probably best enjoyed as cut flowers, as their bizarre, tulip-like stripes are apt to look a bit restless in the garden.

McCummings, USA, 1963
'Pink Peace' sport
Repeat flowering I Intense fragrance

HABIT Bush H/W 1.5m/1.2m (5ft/4ft) I ZONES 5–11

'Canterbury

SHRUB I MEDIUM PINK

This rose is not one of David Austin's more robust English Roses, making a smallish bush rather than a Shrub, but the flowers are lovely – large, fragrant and a glowing warm pink. Semi-double, with some 12 petals, they look most elegant against the dark green foliage. The ancient cathedral city of Canterbury was the goal of Chaucer's pilgrims, and is commemorated by several Austin roses.

AUScanterbury I Austin, England, UK, 1969
'Monique' × ('Constance Spry' × seedling)
Repeat flowering I Intense fragrance

HABIT Bush H/W 75cm/60cm (2ft 6in/2ft) I ZONES 5–11

'Canterbury'

'Carabella'

'Captain Harry Stebbings'

HYBRID TEA ı DEEP PINK

Deep pink, almost red, the double flowers of 'Captain Harry Stebbings' are very large and shapely. They have a very strong, fruity fragrance, and the foliage is dark green and glossy. To judge by its performance in Portland, Oregon, where it was photographed, it seems to be a desirable exhibition rose restricted to Californian climates. The raiser, retired Captain Stebbings of Santa Rosa, California, certainly seems to have faith in it, for he named it after himself.

Stebbings, USA, 1980
Sport from unnamed seedling
Repeat flowering ı Intense, fruity fragrance

HABIT Bush H/W 1.5m/1.2m (5ft/4ft) ı ZONES 5–11

'Captain Harry Stebbings'

'Cara Mia'

'Caramba'

'Cara Mia'

HYBRID TEA ı MEDIUM RED

'Danina', 'Dearest One', 'Maja Mauser', 'Natacha'

For a rose seen in relatively few gardens, this one has a lot of names. This reflects the popularity of 'Cara Mia' in the greenhouses of cut-flower growers. In the greenhouse, it is

a lavish producer of large, double, velvet-red blooms on long stems, set against dark green foliage. In the garden it is prone to sulk, except in a warm climate, like that of Australia or California. It is moderately fragrant.

McDaniel, USA, 1969
Parentage undisclosed
Repeat flowering ı Moderate fragrance

HABIT Bush H/W 1.5m/1.2m (5ft/4ft) ı ZONES 5–11

'Carabella'

FLORIBUNDA ı YELLOW BLEND

When this rose came out in 1960, it was almost completely ignored. But fashions change, and 'Carabella' now has a growing circle of admirers for the Wild Rose simplicity of its ivory and blush flowers, moderately fragrant and borne in immense sprays throughout the season. (Leave the late ones to ripen decorative hips.) The plant is larger than average for a Floribunda. Signs of disease on its glossy, light green leaves are very rare, even in a humid climate, where fungi flourish. It was named as an affectionate tribute to a member of the New South Wales Rose Society.

Riethmuller, Australia, 1960
'Gartendirektor Otto Linne' × seedling
Repeat flowering ı Moderate fragrance

HABIT Bush H/W 110cm/75m (3ft 6in/2ft 6in) ı ZONES 5–11

'Caramba'

HYBRID TEA ı RED BLEND

The bicolored flowers, bright scarlet-red and cream, are large and shapely, but have no scent.

English Roses

The term 'English Roses' was introduced by David Austin Roses of Wolverhampton in England to describe a new group of roses whose clan matriarch was born in 1961 from a cross between the 1845 Hybrid Gallica 'Belle Isis' and the twentieth-century Floribunda 'Dainty Maid'. The resulting rose, named 'Constance Spry', was assigned the international registered codename AUSfirst.

The best of two worlds

It was hoped that using a single-flowering Gallica as seed parent and a repeat-flowering Floribunda as pollen parent would result in a rose that combined the delicate charm, form and bouquet of an Old Garden Rose with the habit of repeat flowering inherited from a Modern Rose – at that time an unconventional approach to rose-breeding. The initial cross was not completely successful, for 'Constance Spry' was only summer flowering. In 1967, Austin introduced another summer-flowering shrub, 'Chianti', which he had hybridized by using as seed parent the 1948 prize-winning Floribunda 'Dusky Maiden' and as pollen-parent the Hybrid Gallica 'Tuscany'. The following year he introduced 'Shropshire Lass', born from 'Madame Butterfly', a classic early Hybrid Tea introduced in 1918, and 'Madame Legras de St Germain', an 1846 Alba. Alas, they, too, were only summer flowering.

Finally, building on this triumvirate of potential genetic material, Austin developed the first varieties that did indeed combine the charm, elegance, fragrance and form of Old Garden Roses with the Modern Rose's habit of repeat flowering. They were 'Wife of Bath' and 'Canterbury'. For 'Wife of Bath', he used the early 1890 Hybrid Tea 'Madame Caroline Testout' as seed parent, introducing pollen derived from a cross between the 1952 Floribunda 'Ma Perkins' and 'Constance Spry'. Similarly, 'Canterbury' was the result of a cross between a 1949 Hybrid Tea, 'Monique', and 'Constance Spry'.

It was after these successes that Austin adopted the term 'English Roses' to describe his new breed of roses – not a new classification, for they were Shrubs under the existing international registration scheme. By the time his 'Graham Thomas' and 'Mary Rose' were introduced at the Chelsea Flower Show of 1983, English Roses had won acceptance and popularity throughout the world. Since that time David Austin has introduced more than 200 varieties resulting from breeding programs based on his original concept of using a selected few Old Garden Roses. Additionally, he had experimented with two Species (Wild) Roses to augment his genetic pool. The list of roses he used in his program is surprisingly limited:

Species *R. macrantha* and *R. pimpinellifolia*
Bourbons 'Reine Victoria' and 'Louise Odier'
Hybrid Gallicas 'Duchess of Montebello' and 'Tuscany'
Hybrid Perpetual 'Baroness Rothschild'
Hybrid Rugosas 'Roseraie de l'Haÿ' and 'Conrad Ferdinand Meyer'
Noisettes 'Alister Stella Grey' and 'Blush Noisette'
Portland 'Comte de Chambord'

Building on success

The main thrust of his future developments was then directed toward breeding from the new varieties he had established. A review of the parents Austin chose for the large majority of his English Roses shows how successful his program of inbreeding was, resulting in a wide diversity of colors and flower forms.

David Austin has chosen to name most of his varieties after characters from *The Canterbury Tales*, his family members and historically significant people. Clearly, his most productive seed parents have been 'Charles Austin', 'Graham Thomas', 'Lillian Austin', 'Mary Rose', 'The Knight' and 'Wife of Bath'. As pollen parents, the most productive have been 'Constance Spry', 'Chaucer', 'Graham Thomas', 'Lillian Austin', 'Mary Rose' and 'The Squire'. It may be said of the well-known English gardener Graham Stuart Thomas that he was both a good mother and father to English Roses!

Top 'Crocus Rose'
Right 'Constance Spry'

ABOVE 'The Endeavour'
RIGHT 'Fair Bianca'
BELOW One of the gardens at David Austin's estate in Albrighton, England.

Other European hybridizers have built on Austin's pioneering work, introducing their own versions of English Roses and marketing them as 'Romanticas', 'Generosas' and 'Country Roses'. The sad part of this great story is that while David Austin has been awarded a range of honors for his work, English Roses are still classified as Shrubs. Perhaps some day the rose world will finally recognize the true significance of this evolutionary development in the history of the rose and give David Austin's lovely roses a class of their own.

English Roses

To the average home gardener, English Roses represent a group of repeat-flowering Shrub Roses with several highly desirable characteristics.

Beautiful flowers

The form and brilliance of the blooms are cloned directly from Old Garden Roses, retaining their best qualities. The flowers may be cupped, quartered or rosette-shaped, and come in a range of delightful colors – mostly pastels, although there are a few stunning dark reds. Light tends to bounce off the many small petals characteristic of these blooms and seems to be captured within the flower itself.

Pleasing growth habit and foliage

English Roses have a natural shrub-like growth that blends into the garden without overpowering companion plants. They create that perfect 'English garden' look, radiating peace and tranquility.

Fragrance

English Roses are first noticed for their elegance and delicate charm but their seductive perfume comes a close second. They come in a wide range of fragrances, from Tea Rose to musk, myrrh and many different fruit scents.

Cut flowers

English Roses make excellent cut flowers, both for the home and commercially, thanks to their unique bloom characteristics, their wide range of beautiful colors, their long, straight stems and their long-lasting qualities.

'Wife of Bath'

'Cathedral'

FLORIBUNDA | APRICOT BLEND

'Coventry Cathedral', 'Houston'

This rose is very variable in color: sometimes vividly orange-red, sometimes almost salmon-pink. It is common for the older flowers to fade almost to white, while retaining a rim of coral around each ruffled, almost transparent petal. The double flowers are borne in clusters on short stalks, so that the flowers sit among the glossy, olive-green leaves, making this a pretty garden plant. But 'Cathedral' is definitely a rose for cool climates. It is odd that it won the AARS award, as that usually implies that the winner will do well everywhere.

McGredy, New Zealand, 1975
'Little Darling' × ('Goldilocks' × 'Irish Mist')
Repeat flowering | *Slight, anise fragrance*

HABIT Bush H/W 1m/60cm (3ft/2ft) | ZONES 5–11

🌹 New Zealand International Rose Ground Trials Fragrance Award 1974, New Zealand International Rose Ground Trials Gold Medal 1974, All-America Rose Selection 1976

'Catherine Deneuve'

HYBRID TEA | ORANGE PINK

Long buds open to wide, ruffled flowers, not full enough for exhibition but very pretty and sweetly fragrant. They vary a little in color,

'Cathedral'

'Catherine Deneuve'

'Centenaire de Lourdes'

the basic coral tone being sometimes shaded with yellow or pink. The dark foliage sets the flowers off very well. The growth is average, and the flowers are freely borne on long stems for cutting. The rose is named for the well-known French actress.

MEIpraserpi | Meilland, France, 1981
Parentage undisclosed
Repeat flowering | *Strong fragrance*

HABIT Bush H/W 1.2m/1m (4ft/3ft) | ZONES 5–11

'Centenaire de Lourdes'

FLORIBUNDA | MEDIUM PINK

'Centennaire de Lourdes', 'Mrs Jones'

The semi-double, soft salmon-pink flowers are only slightly scented, but they are prettily shaped and borne in great abundance in clusters of 5–10. The bush is compact and tidy, with lush, dark green foliage. Despite its reputation for disliking heavy frost, which is unusual for a Floribunda, 'Centenaire de Lourdes' deserves to be more popular than

it is. Perhaps the name, commemorating the visions of St Bernadette in 1858, puts Protestant English-speaking gardeners off.

DELge | Delbard, France, 1958
'Frau Karl Druschki' × seedling
Repeat flowering | *Slight fragrance*

HABIT Bush H/W 1m/60cm (3ft/2ft) | ZONES 5–11

'Century Two'

HYBRID TEA | MEDIUM PINK

Opening from long buds, the double, strong pink flowers are of medium size and fragrant. They are borne singly, and last very well both on the bush and in the vase. The bush is of average height, with leathery, dull green leaves. 'Century Two' inherits much of its free-flowering habit from 'Duet' (one of its parents); it is at its best in a sunny climate.

Armstrong, USA, 1971
'Charlotte Armstrong' × 'Duet'
Repeat flowering | *Damask fragrance*

HABIT Bush H/W 1.5m/1.2m (5ft/4ft) | ZONES 4–11

'Century Two'

of fire vintage. The foliage is a slightly grey tone of matt green that shows the flowers off very nicely. It was introduced in 1984.

Weeks USA, 1983
Seedling × 'Louisiana'
Repeat flowering ı *Slight fragrance*

HABIT Bush H/W 1.5m/1.2m (5ft/4ft) ı ZONES 5–11

'Champion'

LARGE FLOWERED CLIMBER ı YELLOW BLEND

Blending cream, yellow and salmon-pink, the huge, double flowers are of perfect exhibition form and well scented, too. The bush is shorter than average, the foliage light green. Unfortunately, it is also susceptible to black spot. For such an enormous rose, 'Champion' flowers quite freely, but not really enough to make it a good garden rose. This is another one for the show-bench.

Fryer, England, UK, 1976
'Grandpa Dickson' × 'Whisky Mac'
Repeat flowering ı *Moderate fragrance*

HABIT Climber H/W 2.5m/1.8m (8ft/6ft) ı ZONES 5–11

'Chanelle'

FLORIBUNDA ı ORANGE PINK

It is often said that 'Chanelle' is virtually unique among Modern Roses in being immune to black spot. It has other charms, too. The double flowers are scented and prettily shaped, and come in delicate pastel shades of apricot and peach, with the occasional touch of coral. They are borne in clusters. The foliage is glossy, and the plant is strong and compact. The only demerit is that the stems are rather thorny.

McGredy, Northern Ireland, UK, 1959
'Ma Perkins' × ('Fashion' × 'Mrs William Sprott')
Repeat flowering ı *Moderate fragrance*

HABIT Bush H/W 1.2m/1m (4ft/3ft) ı ZONES 5–11

🌹 Madrid Gold Medal 1959

'Champion'

'Cerise Bouquet'

SHRUB ı DEEP PINK

This early-summer-flowering Shrub Rose is sheer delight, covering itself in its season with bouquets of semi-double, cerise blooms the size of a Floribunda. The flowers are sweetly fragrant, and the large shrub has the graceful, arching growth of its parent, the rare *R. multibracteata*. The dainty foliage is dark green. It is credited to Wilhelm Kordes, but he is on record as saying that it is not his, but one of Mathias Tantau's early *R. multibracteata* crosses in the line that led to 'Super Star'.

Kordes, Germany, 1958
R. multibracteata × 'Crimson Glory'
Summer flowering ı *Sweet fragrance*

HABIT Bush H/W 3.5m/3.5m (12ft/12ft) ı ZONES 5–11

🌹 Royal Horticultural Society Award of Garden Merit 1993

'Chablis'

HYBRID TEA ı WHITE

White overlaid with cream in the centre, the double flowers are fairly large and of fine exhibition form, with a slight scent. The color, however, lacks the undertone of green that one looks for in white wine, especially in a chablis

'Cerise Bouquet'

'Charisma'

'Charles Austin'

ABOVE 'Charles Dickens'
LEFT 'Charles Darwin'

'Charisma'

FLORIBUNDA ı RED BLEND

'Surprise Party'

This award-winning rose is a splendid plant, bushy and well clad with very glossy, dark, maroon-tinted foliage that grows right up into the clusters of smallish, very double flowers, the better to show off their dazzling colors – scarlet and gold, passing to solid scarlet as the blooms mature. It certainly makes a colorful display, but there is one fault (apart from its very slight fragrance): the spent flowers do not fall cleanly, and you have to pick them off or they spoil the effect.

JELroganor ı Jelly, USA, 1977
'Gemini' × 'Zorina'
Repeat flowering ı *Slight, fruity fragrance*

HABIT Bush H/W lm/60cm (3ft/2ft) ı ZONES 4–11

🏵 All-America Rose Selection 1978, Portland (Oregon, USA) Gold Medal 1978

'Charles Austin'

SHRUB ı APRICOT BLEND

One of the earlier 'English Roses', raised in 1973, 'Charles Austin' bears clusters of medium-sized, double blooms in apricot and yellow, with a bit of pink sometimes thrown in. Nicely formed in the old style, they are fragrant, too. The foliage is mid-green. It does repeat its bloom, but even David Austin admits that it needs encouraging with trimming and fertilizer after the first crop for the repeat to be generous.

AUSfather ı Austin, England, UK, 1981
'Chaucer' × 'Aloha'
Repeat flowering ı *Moderate fragrance*

HABIT Bush H/W 1.5m/1.2m (5ft/4ft) ı ZONES 4–11

'Charles Darwin'

SHRUB ı MEDIUM YELLOW

The deeply cupped blooms are perhaps the largest ever seen on an Austin English Rose! They start off as cupped and quickly change to shallower flowers, revealing a button eye. Attempts to describe the color of the blooms fall between yellow and yellow tending toward mustard. In full spring bloom, the bush is very attractive, with flowers at all stages. It is named after naturalist Charles Darwin, whose legendary treatise on evolution revolutionized modern thought.

AUSpeet ı Austin, England, 2002
Parentage unknown
Repeat flowering ı *Lemony fragrance*

HABIT Bush H/W 1.2m/110cm (4ft/3ft 6in) ı ZONES 5–11

'Charles Dickens'

FLORIBUNDA ı ORANGE PINK

Not surprisingly, novelist Charles Dickens had a rose named after him during his lifetime, a red Hybrid Perpetual. It seems to have been forgotten after his death, and it fell to Sam McGredy to make good the omission in 1970

'Charles Rennie Mackintosh'

'Charles Mallerin'

with this very attractive two-tone pink Floribunda. The semi-double flowers are faintly scented and are carried in neat sprays, displaying golden stamens when they open. The plant is a little below average height and has leathery foliage. It flowers early and continues late. The great novelist was the son of a mere naval clerk. His rose is of royal descent.

McGredy, New Zealand, 1970
'Paddy McGredy' × 'Elizabeth of Glamis'
Repeat flowering ı *Slight fragrance*

HABIT Bush H/W 1m/60cm (3ft/2ft) ı ZONES 5–11

'Charles Mallerin'

HYBRID TEA ı DARK RED

Of all the deep velvet-red, almost black, roses, 'Charles Mallerin' has the most sensational flowers, opening huge and ruffled from long, elegant buds. They hold their gorgeous color without fading or 'blueing' until the petals drop, and are intensely fragrant. The foliage is leaden green. Plant it at the back of the bed, prune lightly, and be lavish with water and fertilizer. Raised by Francis Meilland in 1947, it is named for his teacher, a retired engineer who also raised many lovely roses.

Meilland, France, 1951
('Glory of Rome' × 'Congo') × 'Tassin'
Repeat flowering ı *Intense fragrance*

HABIT Bush H/W 1.2m/1m (4ft/3ft) ı ZONES 5–11
🏵 Lyon Gold Medal 1947

'Charles Rennie Mackintosh'

SHRUB ı PINK BLEND

An arching shrub to about 1.5m (5ft), this 1988 David Austin creation bears largish, beautifully old-fashioned flowers in soft pink with strong undertones of lilac. The very double blooms come in small clusters, and are sweetly scented. The foliage is mid-green. Charles Rennie Mackintosh was the great Scottish architect, designer and artist of the early twentieth century.

AUSren ı Austin, England, UK, 1994
Seedling × 'Mary Rose'
Repeat flowering ı *Sweet fragrance*

HABIT Bush H/W 1.5m/1.2m (5ft/4ft) ı ZONES 4–11

'Charleston'

FLORIBUNDA ı YELLOW BLEND

The bright colors suggested the Roaring Twenties to the raiser, hence the name. Of all the yellow-turning-red Floribundas, this is probably still the brightest, there being little of the intermediate pink tones that dull the contrast between today's and yesterday's flowers in so many of the others. The double flowers come in clusters; the foliage is leathery and dark green. But it is only a rose for gardens where fungus diseases are no problem. There is a climbing form, which seems to be a bit more disease-resistant.

MEIridge ı Meilland, France, 1963
'Masquerade' × ('Radar' × 'Caprice')
Repeat flowering ı *Slight fragrance*

HABIT Bush H/W 1m/60cm (3ft/2ft) ı ZONES 5–11

'Charleston'

✓ 'Charlotte Armstrong'

HYBRID TEA ı DEEP PINK

There is scarcely an American rose in our gardens today that does not descend from 'Charlotte Armstrong'. She is desirable for her elegant buds and big, ruffled, double flowers, stained brilliant cerise, and also for her strong constitution. The leaves are leathery and matt green. Lack of scent is her only fault, but many of her descendants are strongly fragrant – 'Sutter's Gold', 'Tiffany', 'Double Delight' and 'Papa Meilland' among others. This rose is named for the mother of the founder of Armstrong Nurseries.

Lammerts, USA, 1940
'Soeur Thérèse' × 'Crimson Glory'
Repeat flowering ı *No fragrance*

HABIT Bush H/W 1.5m/1.2m (5ft/4ft) ı ZONES 4–11

All-America Rose Selection 1941, American Rose Society David Fuerstenberg Award 1941, Portland (Oregon, USA) Gold Medal 1941

'Chaucer'

SHRUB ı MEDIUM PINK

David Austin has expressed his surprise that 'Chaucer' should be repeat flowering, as neither of its parents is. Perhaps there are repeat-flowering ancestors lurking unknown on the family tree. 'Chaucer' makes a compact, very thorny bush to about 1m (3ft) tall, and bears clusters of full-petalled, intensely fragrant, soft pink flowers all season against medium green foliage. One might think of this variety as a Floribunda with Bourbon Rose flowers. It came out in 1970.

AUScon ı Austin, England, UK, 1981
Seedling × 'Constance Spry'
Repeat flowering ı *Intense fragrance*

HABIT Bush H/W 110cm/60cm (3ft 6in/2ft) ı ZONES 5–11

'Charlotte Armstrong'

'Chaucer'

'Cherish'

FLORIBUNDA ı ORANGE PINK

The double flowers are salmon-pink and shapely, if not very fragrant. They are borne in good-sized, nicely spaced clusters on a low-growing, dark-foliaged bush. Like 'Bridal Pink', they make long-lasting cut flowers. The name falls less strangely on the ear when one knows that it is one of a trio of Jackson & Perkins roses that won the AARS award in 1980: 'Love', 'Honor' and 'Cherish'.

JACsal ı Warriner, USA, 1980
'Bridal Pink' × 'Matador'
Repeat flowering ı *Slight fragrance*

HABIT Bush H/W 1m/60cm (3ft/2ft) ı ZONES 5–11

All-America Rose Selection 1980

'Cherry Brandy'

HYBRID TEA ı ORANGE BLEND

The cherry brandy we drink is usually deep cerise in color, nothing at all like this Hybrid Tea, whose double flowers are a blend of coral-pink and orange. Large, high-centred and quite fragrant, they are borne on a tall bush with dark olive-green foliage. Mathias Tantau has reused the name, as 'Cherry Brandy '85', for a 1985 introduction whose code-name is TANryrandy. From its official description it seems very similar, except that it is scentless.

Tantau, Germany, 1965
Parentage undisclosed
Repeat flowering ı *Moderate fragrance*

HABIT Bush H/W 1.5m/1.2m (5ft/4ft) ı ZONES 5–11

Belfast Gold Medal and Prize of the City of Belfast 1989

'Cherish'

'Cherry Parfait'

GRANDIFLORA ı ORANGE BLEND

The flowers put on quite a color display with their swirls of white petals with broad red edges shading darker as they age. The medium-sized blooms are fully double, and borne mostly in large clusters on a free-flowering bush. This variety is reminiscent of one of the world's favorite roses, 'Double Delight'. Not your typical tall Grandiflora, it is of medium height, broadly rounded and bushy, with healthy, deep green foliage. The plant performs beautifully all year, but the colors become more intense during very hot weather.

MEIsponge ı Meilland, France, 2003
'Jacqueline Nebout' × ('Anticipation' × 'Matangi')
Repeat flowering ı *Moderate fragrance*

HABIT Bush H/W 1.5m/1.2m (5ft/4ft) ı ZONES 5–11

All-America Rose Selection 2003

'Cherry-Vanilla'

'Cherry-Vanilla'

GRANDIFLORA ⏐ PINK BLEND

A softly colored blend of ice-cream-pink and cream, the double flowers of 'Cherry-Vanilla' are of good size and fairly fragrant. The bush is taller than average, with glossy foliage. The flowers tend to appear in small clusters, and 'Cherry-Vanilla' is thus classified as a 'Grandiflora' in the United States. It is happiest in a warm climate, where, with disbudding, the flowers can be enormous.

ARMilla ⏐ Armstrong, USA, 1973
'Buccaneer' × 'El Capitan'
Repeat flowering ⏐ *Moderate fragrance*

HABIT Bush H/W 1.5m/1.2m (5ft/4ft)   ZONES 5–11

'Cheshire Life'

HYBRID TEA ⏐ ORANGE RED

Bright and unfading orange-red, the double flowers of 'Cheshire Life' are medium to large and shapely, and stand up unusually well to wet weather. They are only faintly scented. The bush is a little lower than average, and densely covered with dark green leaves, reddish when young. It is well regarded in Britain as a bedding rose, but it has not found wide acceptance elsewhere. Perhaps the name is against it – 'Cheshire Life' does not suggest much to a gardener unfamiliar with the English insurance company that sponsored the rose.

Fryer, England, UK, 1972
'Prima Ballerina' × 'Princess Michiko'
Repeat flowering ⏐ *Slight fragrance*

HABIT Bush H/W 1.5m/1.2m (5ft/4ft) ⏐ ZONES 5–11

'Chester'

FLORIBUNDA ⏐ MEDIUM YELLOW

This is another rose that has lost the spotlight. It is possibly unknown in Australia, but this

semi-double rose has always looked good in England, with its golden yellow petals and matching stamens and glossy leaves. It does pale a little with age, but not excessively, and it seems to be disease-resistant. One wonders about its lack of popularity – perhaps 'Chester' just never got the right publicity. It was named for the ancient cathedral city where the raisers have their offices.

Bees, England, UK, 1976
'Arthur Bell' × 'Zambra'
Repeat flowering ⏐ *Slight fragrance*

HABIT Bush H/W 1m/60cm (3ft/2ft) ⏐ ZONES 5–11

TOP 'Cherry Brandy'
BELOW LEFT 'Cherry Parfait'
INSET 'Chester'
BOTTOM 'Cheshire Life'

'Chicago Peace'

HYBRID TEA | PINK BLEND

Discovered in Chicago, this is a sport from the universally admired 'Peace', and identical to its parent except for its greatly enriched coloring – a blend of carmine and coral-pink with gold. Some people prefer it to the parent. Others say it misses the delicate touch of 'Peace'; and the way the very double flowers fade to dull pink and cream almost as soon as they are fully open does not please everyone. To each his taste! The flowers are borne mostly singly; the glossy leaves, like those of 'Peace', are prone to black spot where summers are hot and humid.

JOHnago | Johnston, USA, 1962
'Peace' sport
Repeat flowering | Slight fragrance

HABIT Bush H/W 1.8m/1.2m (6ft/4ft) | ZONES 5–11
❀ Portland (Oregon, USA) Gold Medal, 1962

'Chihuly'

FLORIBUNDA | RED BLEND

The rose chosen to honor America's famous glass artist Dale Chihuly had to have impeccable style and an ever-changing array of flashy colors. This one has it all! As the sun hits the opening petals, they blush from subtly striped apricot-yellow to dazzling orange and deep red – a stunning sight against the deep dark green leaves and mahogany new growth. The plant is of medium height, bushy and

profuse-blooming, and stays healthy-looking all season long.

WEKscemala | Carruth, USA, 2004
'Scentimental' × 'Amalia'
Repeat flowering | Mild, tea fragrance

HABIT Bush H/W 1m/60cm (3ft/2ft) | ZONES 5–11

'China Doll'

POLYANTHA | MEDIUM PINK

Pretty as they are, the double, cupped, rose-pink flowers of 'China Doll' are not all that unusual. What makes this rose great is the way it blooms in such profusion. You would not think a rosebush only 30cm (1ft) or so tall could give so many flowers of reasonable

'Chinatown'   TOP INSET 'Chihuly'

'Chicago Peace'

'China Doll'

size – up to 6cm (2½in) in diameter – and in clusters of up to 15. The foliage is glossy and mid-green. Treat it well, and use it closely spaced as an edging plant to taller flowers, as a diminutive standard, or as a charming container plant.

Lammerts, USA, 1946
'Mrs Dudley Fulton' × 'Tom Thumb'
Repeat flowering ı *Tea fragrance*

HABIT Bush H/W 30cm/30cm (1ft/1ft) ı ZONES 4–10

'Chinatown'

FLORIBUNDA ı DEEP YELLOW

'Ville de Chine'

Enormously vigorous, 'Chinatown' is best treated as a Shrub Rose 1.8m (6ft) or so tall. It is apt to sulk if you prune it hard and try to force it into an ordinary rose bed. Its leaves are distinctive – light green, very

large and healthy, too. Some feel they are a bit coarse for the mid-sized, double flowers, which are frilly and carried in bold clusters, but if you plant it among other plants, this will not be so noticeable. The colour? The imperial yellow of the Chinese emperors.

Poulsen, Denmark, 1963
'Columbine' × 'Cläre Grammerstorf'
Repeat flowering ı *Intense fragrance*

HABIT Bush H/W 1.8m/1.2m (6ft/4ft) ı ZONES 5–11

🌹 (Royal) National Rose Society Gold Medal 1962, Royal Horticultural Society Award of Garden Merit 1993

'Chivalry'

HYBRID TEA ı RED BLEND

Scarlet and gold, the double flowers are large and nicely shaped, but even the raiser does not claim fragrance for them. The plant is a bit

'Chivalry'

taller than average, with glossy, dark green leaves, bronze-tinted when young. The flowers often come in clusters, but with disbudding they can be fit for the show bench. 'Chivalry' has the reputation of being one of the most reliable bicolored roses for cold climates.

MACpow ı McGredy, New Zealand, 1977
'Peer Gynt' × 'Brazilia'
Repeat flowering ı *No fragrance*

HABIT Bush H/W 1.5m/1m (5ft/3ft) ı ZONES 5–11

'Chris Evert'

HYBRID TEA ı ORANGE RED

'Raymond Kopa'

This extremely colorful rose was named for the world-famous tennis champion. The melon-orange and blushing red blooms are large, double and high-centred, and very long-lasting. The colors hold even in hot weather, but cool weather brings out the best in size. They are borne mostly one to a stem on a vigorous, upright bush that repeats extremely well. The reddish new foliage turns a healthy-looking deep green as it matures.

WEKjuvoo ı Carruth, USA, 1996
'Voodoo' × ('Katherine Loker' × 'Gingersnap')
Repeat flowering ı *Fruity fragrance*

HABIT Bush H/W 1.5m/1.2m (5ft/4ft) ı ZONES 4–9

'Chris Evert'

'Circus'

'Christian Dior'

HYBRID TEA ı MEDIUM RED

Stylish in its perfect form, its glowing blood-red color, its long, plum-colored, almost thornless stems, 'Christian Dior' is named for the great Parisian couturier. Alas, the flowers are scentless. The mid-green, elegantly cut foliage has to be protected from mildew and black spot, so it is primarily a rose for the exhibitor, although if you can keep it healthy it will flower quite freely. It was introduced in Europe in 1958 and in the United States in 1962.

MEllie ı Meilland, France, 1958
('Independence' × 'Happiness') × ('Peace' × 'Happiness')
Repeat flowering ı *Spicy fragrance*

HABIT Bush H/W 1.5m/1.2m (5ft/4ft) ı ZONES 5–11
🌹 Geneva Gold Medal 1958, All-America Rose Selection 1962

'Chrysler Imperial' ✓

HYBRID TEA ı DARK RED

Deep rich crimson with a sheen like velvet, the very double flowers of 'Chrysler Imperial' are

'Christian Dior'

'Chrysler Imperial'

beautifully high-centred and nicely fragrant. They are borne one to a stem, with matt, green foliage. This rose created a sensation when it came out, and it remains an excellent choice for warm climates. Cold is apt to cause the flowers to 'blue' and the plant to snuffle with mildew. Germain's, the introducers, wanted to call it 'Chrysler', but the car-makers objected to the use of their trademark.

Lammerts, USA, 1952
'Charlotte Armstrong' × 'Mirandy'
Repeat flowering ı *Intense fragrance*

HABIT Bush H/W 1.5m/1.2m (5ft/4ft) ı ZONES 4–11
🌹 Portland (Oregon, USA) Gold Medal 1951, All-America Rose Selection 1953, American Rose Society James Alexander Gamble Fragrance Medal 1965

'Circus'

FLORIBUNDA ı YELLOW BLEND

This is one of the classic Floribundas, but also one of the best reasons for buying your roses from a reputable grower! For there are two strains of 'Circus' about: the original, a neat bush with semi-glossy, dark green leaves and perfectly arranged clusters of ruffled, double flowers, at first buff-yellow, turning pink and coral-red as they develop; and an impostor, vigorous to the point of legginess, with colorless flowers that often do not open properly. Insist on getting Herbert Swim's 1956 original.

The fragrance is slight. 'Circus Parade' is a deeper-colored sport with more petals.

Swim, USA, 1956
'Fandango' × 'Pinocchio'
Repeat flowering | *Spicy fragrance*

HABIT Bush H/W 1m/60m (3ft/2ft) | ZONES 4–11

🏅 Geneva Gold Medal 1955, All-America Rose Selection 1956

'Circus Parade'

FLORIBUNDA | YELLOW BLEND

This sport from 'Circus' has deeper-colored flowers with more petals, set against dark foliage, and is a better buy if you are at all uncertain of getting the original strain of 'Circus' from your nursery. 'Circus Parade', however, lacks some of the subtlety of color of the original. For all its gaiety, it is not very fragrant.

Begonia and DeVor, USA, 1963
Sport from 'Circus'
Repeat flowering | *Slight fragrance*

HABIT Bush H/W 1m/60cm (3ft/2ft | ZONES 5–11

'City of Auckland'

'City of Auckland'

HYBRID TEA | ORANGE BLEND

A blend of old gold and orange, sometimes with a bit of pink thrown in, these flowers are large, double, pleasingly shaped and very fragrant. The plant is of average height, with medium green leaves. It is named for Sam McGredy's adopted home town. Although it is a popular rose in New Zealand, and McGredy's have used it for further breeding, it has not been much grown elsewhere.

MACtane | McGredy, New Zealand, 1981
'Benson & Hedges Gold' × 'Whisky Mac'
Repeat flowering | *Intense fragrance*

HABIT Bush H/W 1.5m/1.2m (5ft/4ft) | ZONES 5–11

'City of Belfast'

'Claire Rose'

'City of Belfast'

FLORIBUNDA | ORANGE RED

The double, cupped flowers are quite prettily shaped, with ruffled petals. They are orange-red, deepening and dulling with age. But the effect that matters is that of the huge trusses of blooms, borne very freely on an average-height bush with dark green leaves. The plant is hasty in repeating its bloom, and if the color suits your garden, it is a fine, showy garden rose. It was introduced in 1968, and the name commemorates the establishment of Belfast's Rose Trial Ground.

MACci | McGredy, New Zealand, 1981
'Evelyn Fison' × ('Circus' × 'Korona')
Repeat flowering | *Slight fragrance*

HABIT Bush H/W 1m/60cm (3ft/2ft) | ZONES 5–11

🏅 Royal National Rose Society Gold Medal and Presidents International Trophy 1967, Gold Star of the South Pacific, Palmerston North (New Zealand) 1969, Belfast Gold Medal 1970, The Hague Gold Medal 1976

'City of Leeds'

FLORIBUNDA | ORANGE PINK

Although it is more or less scentless, 'City of Leeds' can be a fine choice for creating a splash of strong coral-pink in the garden. The semi-double flowers are borne freely, in large clusters, on a dark-leafed, not too tall plant. They are medium-sized and nicely shaped, and hold their color without turning magenta. They need good weather to look their best, however, and are inclined to get marked by heavy rain

'Circus Parade'

'City of Leeds'

'Cocktail'

and bleached by hot sun. Definitely a rose for favored climates. It was introduced in 1966.

McGredy, Northern Ireland, UK, 1981
'Evelyn Fison' × ('Spartan' × 'Schweizergriiss')

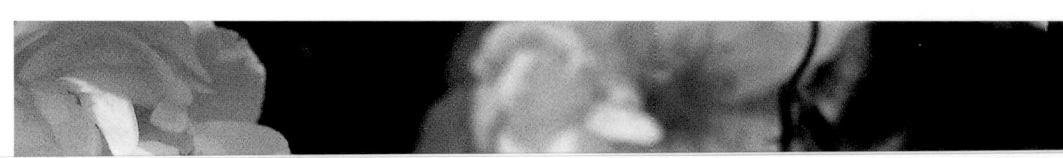

'Constance Spry'

'Coronado'

'Cornelia'

age. Still, it is an attractive, colorful rose, its large, shapely flowers borne in small clusters, and the foliage richly green and glossy on a tallish bush. One might wish for more fragrance, though.

HARtwiz ı Harkness, England, UK, 1986
'Amy Brown' × 'Judy Garland'
Repeat flowering ı *Slight fragrance*

HABIT Bush H/W 1m/60cm (3ft/2ft) ı ZONES 5–11

'Constance Spry'

SHRUB ı LIGHT PINK

Forgive it its single season of bloom; this is one of the most beautiful of all roses. It makes a very large shrub, its rather floppy branches best supported on a tripod or even trained as a climber. The broad, dark leaves are handsome, the flowers magnificent. Borne in clusters, they are huge, 12cm (5in) versions of the globular cabbage roses that you see on old chintzes and china, but not in the least blowsy. Double and richly fragrant, they are an exceptionally clear shade of pink, and after the great early summer show there are hips in the fall/autumn. Introduced by

David Austin in 1961, at the beginning of his career, this rose commemorates the great flower arranger Constance Spry, an ardent lover of Old Garden Roses.

AUSfirst ı Austin, England, UK, 1961
'Belle Isis' × 'Dainty Maid'
Summer flowering ı *Moderate, myrrh fragrance*

HABIT Bush H/W 1.8m/1.5m (6ft/5ft) ı ZONES 5–11

'Contempo'

FLORIBUNDA ı ORANGE BLEND

The flowers are 10cm (4in) or more in diameter, and but for their coming in clusters of half a dozen or more, might be mistaken for decorative Hybrid Tea Roses. They open slowly, so the contrast between the coral upper surface of the petals and the yellow underside is visible for quite a while. In cooler weather they soften to salmon-pink and cream. Indeed, this is a rose that is at its best in hot weather. The leaves are glossy and dark green. Perhaps the rather leggy habit has cost it admirers, for it is not seen all that often.

Armstrong, USA, 1971
'Spartan' × ('Goldilocks' × 'Fandango' × 'Pinocchio')
Repeat flowering ı *Moderate fragrance*

HABIT Bush H/W 1.2m/1m (4ft/3ft) ı ZONES 5–11

'Cornelia'

HYBRID MUSK ı PINK BLEND

One of the best-loved of Joseph Pemberton's Hybrid Musks, 'Cornelia' is also one of his last, having been introduced in 1925. The color of the flowers varies: sometimes soft, peachy pink, at others flushed with coral and much richer in effect. The flowers are small and borne in flattish sprays. They are always very fragrant, with the real scent of musk, and the bush is tall and graceful. With pruning, it can be held to about 1.5m (5ft), but it is flexible enough to train as a short pillar rose. Sometimes the blooms come in enormous clusters, two or three of which would fill the largest vase. The foliage is nicely bronze-tinted, glossy and leathery.

Pemberton, England, UK, 1925
Parentage unknown
Repeat flowering ı *Moderate fragrance*

HABIT Bush H/W 2.5m/1.5m (8ft/5ft) ı ZONES 6–11
🏆 Royal Horticultural Society Award of Garden Merit 1993

'Coronado'

HYBRID TEA ı RED BLEND

Deep shocking pink and gold, the bicolored flowers of 'Coronado' are too loosely formed

'Contempo'

flowers of 'Corso' are fairly large and of exhibition form, although their scent is only faint. The bush is tall, with glossy, dark foliage, which is not always as disease-free as it ought to be. This is a rose for cool climates; it sulks in a humid summer. It is an exceptionally fine rose for cutting.

Cocker, Scotland, UK, 1976
'Anne Cocker' × 'Dr A. J. Verhage'
Repeat flowering ⁞ *Slight fragrance*
HABIT Bush H/W 1.5m/1.2m (5ft/4ft) ⁞ ZONES 5–11

'Cotillion'

FLORIBUNDA ⁞ MAUVE

'Perfume Perfection', 'Serenissima'

This award-winning petite yet hardy Floribunda is full-petalled and comes in shades of soft lavender-pink. The English-style blooms

'Corso'

for exhibition, but they are double, very large and pleasantly fragrant. The foliage is a glossy green. Despite the disdain in which it is held by exhibitors, 'Coronado' has a reputation for being one of the easiest of bicolors to grow, and it seems a pity that it is not more widely available. It was introduced in 1960. Francisco Vásquez de Coronado was one of the more colorful figures in Spanish colonial history, and is much remembered in the American Southwest.

Von Abrams, USA, 1961
('Multnomah' × 'Peace') × ('Multnomah' × 'Peace')
Repeat flowering ⁞ *Moderate fragrance*
HABIT Bush H/W 1.5m/1.2m (5ft/4ft) ⁞ ZONES 5–11

'Corso'

HYBRID TEA ⁞ ORANGE BLEND

Orange, usually blended with yellow and sometimes touched with salmon-pink, the double

'Cotillion'

'Dr Darley'

'Dr Darley'

HYBRID TEA   I   MEDIUM PINK

The flowers are a strong, bright pink, large
and double, with some 35 petals, but 'Dr Darley'
does not seem to have made much of an impact
outside Britain, where it was introduced in
1982. Perhaps this is only because the color
lacks novelty – there are so many rose-pink
roses. In Britain it is still considered a desirable garden rose, the plant vigorous and the
dark foliage healthy. The flowers are usually
borne singly, and are only slightly scented.
Dr William Darley was a country GP who
courageously continued to care for the sick
after being himself crippled by polio.

HARposter   I   Harkness, England, UK, 1980
'Red Planet' × ('Carina' × 'Pascali')
Repeat flowering   I   *Slight fragrance*

HABIT Bush H/W 1.5m/1.2m (5ft/4ft)   I   ZONES 5–11

'Dr J. H. Nicolas'

LARGE FLOWERED CLIMBER   I   MEDIUM PINK

Not too rampant for a small garden, this rose
bears large, double, beautifully formed flowers
in soft rose-pink. They tend to come in threes
and are sweetly fragrant. Disbudding will bring
them to exhibition size. The plant may not make
the sheet of flowers in the garden that some of
the newer climbers do, but it flowers well both
in spring and in the fall/autumn, against leathery, dark green foliage. Jean Henri Nicolas was
a remarkable Frenchman, Chevalier of the

Legion of Honour, member of the Académie
Française and Director of Research at Jackson
& Perkins, who introduced this rose in his
memory in 1940.

Nicolas, USA, 1940
'Charles P. Kilham' × 'George Arends'
Repeat flowering   I   *Moderate fragrance*

HABIT Bush H/W 3m/1.8m (10ft/6ft)   I   ZONES 6–11

'Dublin Bay'

LARGE FLOWERED CLIMBER   I   MEDIUM RED

A rather stiff, shrubby plant that takes its time
to cover its allotted space, 'Dublin Bay' has
double flowers that are rather like smallish
Hybrid Teas, usually coming in small clusters.
As the sepals part, the flowers look as though
they will be very dark indeed, but they open
to a beautiful shade of blood-red that holds
without 'blueing' as they age. If not strongly
scented, they are pleasantly so; and although
their stems are not very long, the flowers last
very well in the vase. The leaves are glossy,
dark and disease-resistant. Sam McGredy has
said that he is especially proud of this rose,
as well he should be. It is a favorite climber
just about everywhere.

MACdub   I   McGredy, New Zealand, 1975
'Bantry Bay' × 'Altissimo'
Repeat flowering   I   *Moderate fragrance*

HABIT Climber H/W 3m/2.5m (10ft/8ft)   I   ZONES 5–11

🌹 Rose Introducers of New Zealand Auckland Rose
of the Year 1993, Royal Horticultural Society Award of
Garden Merit 1993

'Dublin Bay'

'Dr J. H. Nicolas'

'Duet'

'Duet'

HYBRID TEA ı MEDIUM PINK

Salmon-pink, flushed with rose and backed with orange-red, the double flowers of this All-America winner are not especially large or shapely; nor are they fragrant. What is remarkable about them is the extraordinary profusion in which they appear, usually in small clusters, on a compact, bronze-green bush. There are still few roses easier to grow or better able to keep up a grand display in the garden, and the flowers last well in water,

BELOW 'Duke of Windsor'
BELOW RIGHT 'Dutch Gold'

their rather unsubtle colors flattered by artificial light.

Swim, USA, 1960
'Fandango' × 'Roundelay'
Repeat flowering ı *Slight, tea fragrance*

HABIT Bush H/W 1.5m/1.2m (5ft/4ft) ı ZONES 5–11

All-america Rose Selection 1961

'Duke of Windsor'

HYBRID TEA ı ORANGE BLEND

'Herzog von Windsor'

Large, double and shapely, with 27 petals, and fragrant as well, the flowers are a

lustrous coral-orange, much like 'Super Star', but the plant is much more compact. Indeed, although a very vigorous rose, it is lower-growing than most Hybrid Teas and should be planted at the front of a mixed bed. The foliage is a dark, dull green, russet in its youth, and the branches are thorny. Good cultivation is called for, along with an alert eye for mildew and rust, but this is a worthy rose by which to remember the former King Edward VIII, a keen gardener and a lover of roses all his life.

Tantau, Germany, 1969
'Spartan' × 'Montezuma'
Repeat flowering ı *Intense fragrance*

HABIT Bush H/W 1m/1m (3ft/3ft) ı ZONES 6–11

Anerkannte Deutsche Rose (Germany) 1970

'Dutch Gold'

HYBRID TEA ı MEDIUM YELLOW

Deep yellow, sometimes with touches of orange, the double flowers of 'Dutch Gold' are fragrant, although not exceptionally so. What is remarkable about them is their enormous size. They are borne quite freely, one to a stem, on an upright bush with handsome, dark leaves. Still quite popular in Europe, this variety is at its best in a cool-summer climate. Dutch gold, a substitute for real gold leaf, tends to be brassier in tone than the real thing. Our rose, however, is named to celebrate its winning the gold medal at The Hague Rose Trials in 1978.

Wisbech Plant Co., England, UK, 1978
'Peer Gynt' × 'Whisky Mac'
Repeat flowering ı *Moderate fragrance*

HABIT Bush H/W 1.5m/1.2m (5ft/4ft) ı ZONES 6–10

The Hague Gold Medal 1978

'Earth Song'

'Earth Song'

GRANDIFLORA I DEEP PINK

One of the best-loved of the 80-odd roses bred by the legendary Griffith Buck to endure the fierce winters of the mid-west of the United States, 'Earth Song' bears large, double, elegantly ruffled flowers in a beautiful shade of deep rose. Nicely fragrant, they are borne abundantly all season on long stems and last well when cut. The glossy-leafed plant is very strong indeed and could almost be classed as a Shrub Rose. Naturally, its resistance to severe cold is exceptional, and so is its disease resistance. It does well in mild climates also.

Buck, USA, 1975
'Music Maker' × 'Prairie Star'
Repeat flowering I *Moderate fragrance*
HABIT Bush H/W 2m/1.5m (7ft/5ft) I ZONES 4–9

'Eclipse'

HYBRID TEA I LIGHT YELLOW

Just as well the 1930s are in fashion again, for if ever there was such a thing as an 'Art Deco rose' it would be this Jackson & Perkins masterpiece, created by their hybridist J. H. Nicolas and for many years the most popular yellow rose in the United States. The deep gold buds are extraordinarily long, and encased in narrow, branching sepals. The fragrant blooms are double and loosely constructed; the foliage is dark. Legend has it that it first bloomed on the day of an eclipse in 1932, hence its name.

Nicolas, USA, 1935
'Joanna Hill' × 'Frederico Casas'
Repeat flowering I *Moderate fragrance*
HABIT Bush H/W 1.5m/1.2m (5ft/4ft) I ZONES 6–11

 Portland (Oregon, USA) Gold Medal 1935, Rome Gold Medal 1935, Bagatelle (Paris) Gold Medal 1936, American Rose Society David Fuerstenberg Award 1938

'Eclipse'

'Editor McFarland'

HYBRID TEA I MEDIUM PINK

J. Horace McFarland was a master printer from Harrisburg, Pennsylvania, who in the 1920s and early 1930s edited the *Annual of the American Rose Society* and later became president of that organisation. McFarland is remembered chiefly for his magnum opus, *Modern Roses*, which is to the rose-lover what *Debrett* is to those interested in family lineages. For years and years, 'Editor McFarland' grew in every garden, a delight with its fine form, intense fragrance and freedom of bloom. But fashions change, and in these days of coral and orange, the deep rose-pink of the 'Editor' is not so popular. The foliage is leathery and mid-green.

Mallerin, France, 1931
'Pharisäer' × 'Lallita'
Repeat flowering I *Intense fragrance*
HABIT Bush H/W 1.5m/1.2m (5ft/4ft) I ZONES 5–11

'Eiffel Tower'

HYBRID TEA I MEDIUM PINK

'Eiffelturm', 'Tour Eiffel'

An appropriate name, for height is this rose's leading characteristic. The bush is very tall and

'Eiffel Tower'

upright, the slim stems are very long, and the elegant buds must be almost the longest of those of any rose. They are a lovely shade of cool rose, and although the double flowers are a little loose when fully open, they are of good size and last very well both on the plant and in the vase. The fragrance is superb. The foliage is leathery and mid-green. Warm, dry climates suit it best.

Armstrong and Swim, USA, 1963
'First Love' × seedling
Repeat flowering I *Intense fragrance*
HABIT Bush H/W 1.5m/1.2m (5ft/4ft) I ZONES 6–11
 Geneva Gold Medal 1963, Rome Gold Medal 1963

'Electron'

HYBRID TEA I DEEP PINK

'Mullard Jubilee'

Sam McGredy has recorded that when the Mullard Electronics Company offered him the then unheard-of fee of £10,000 for a new rose to celebrate their golden jubilee in 1970, they insisted that nothing less than a world-beater would do. And indeed the rose-pink 'Mullard Jubilee' proved to be just that, winning just about every high award

'Editor McFarland'

'Elegance'

'Elizabeth Arden'

TOP LEFT 'Elegant Beauty'
TOP RIGHT 'Electron
BOTTOM LEFT 'Elina'

there is, including the AARS under its catchier American name 'Electron'. It is indeed a first-rate rose, large, double and of exhibition form, beautifully fragrant, and freely borne – mostly singly – on a tall bush with outstandingly healthy, dark leaves. Cool climates seem to suit it best.

McGredy, Northern Ireland, UK, 1970
'Paddy McGredy' × 'Prima Ballerina'
Repeat flowering ı *Intense fragrance*

HABIT Bush H/W 1.5m/1.2m (5ft/4ft) ı ZONES 5–11

🌹 Royal National Rose Society Gold Medal 1969, The Hague Gold Medal 1970, Belfast Gold Medal 1972, All-America Rose Selection 1973, Portland (Oregon, USA) Gold Medal 1973

'Elegance'

LARGE FLOWERED CLIMBER ı MEDIUM YELLOW

The name describes it well. It has long, shapely buds and large, double, wide-open blooms of soft canary-yellow. They have a delicate fragrance. Although it is not repeat-blooming, its season is a long one, and a single plant will give hundreds of perfect, long-stemmed flowers. It is a very strong grower, with glossy leaves and many thorns. Raised by Dr and Mrs Walter Brownell of Long Island in their quest for roses that would endure their sub-arctic winters, it remains one of the easiest of yellow roses to grow.

Brownell, USA, 1937
'Glenn Dale' × ('Mary Wallace' × 'Miss Lolita Armour')
Summer flowering ı *Moderate fragrance*

HABIT Climber H/W 3m/2.5m (10ft/8ft) ı ZONES 6–11

'Elegant Beauty'

HYBRID TEA   LIGHT YELLOW

'Delicia', 'Kordes Rose Delicia'

This rose was originally bred for the greenhouse trade but also gives a good account of itself in the garden, at least in warm climates, for the bush is on the tender side. Although they have only about 20 petals, the flowers open very slowly and hold their perfect form for a long time; they are a beautiful clear shade of pale yellow, sometimes lightly touched with pink. The stems are long and the bush upright, with healthy, dark leaves. There isn't much scent, however.

KORgatum ı Kordes, Germany, 1982
'New Day' × seedling
Repeat flowering ı *Light fragrance*

HABIT Bush H/W 1.5m/1.2m (5ft/4ft) ı ZONES 7–11

'Elina'

HYBRID TEA ı LIGHT YELLOW

'Peaudouce'

The name to be preferred is 'Elina': 'Peaudouce', even if it is the name the raiser uses, is a brand of babies' diapers. That is where the commercial sponsorship of roses can lead! The rose itself is a beauty – large, very shapely indeed, and delicate in its tones of lemon and white. For a flower so large and pale, it is quite tolerant of wet weather. The bush is strong, with healthy, glossy leaves, and flowers freely. The only fault is a lack of scent.

DICjana ı Dickson, Northern Ireland, UK, 1984
'Nana Mouskouri' × 'Lolita'
Repeat flowering ı *Slight fragrance*

HABIT Bush H/W 1.8m/1.2m (6ft/4ft) ı ZONES 5–11

🌹 Gold Star of the South Pacific, Hamilton (New Zealand) 1987, Royal Horticultural Society Award of Garden Merit 1993, Portland (Oregon, USA) Gold Medal 1996, World Federation of Rose Societies Hall of Fame 2006

'Elizabeth Arden'

HYBRID TEA ı WHITE

It is fitting that a rose of such perfect complexion should bear the name of the woman

'Elizabeth Harkness'

'Elizabeth of Glamis'

who dedicated her long life to making other women beautiful. The darling of the 1930s, it is not often seen now; more's the pity, as sweetly scented white roses are still rare. The double blooms are large and of most perfect form, and the stems long and almost thornless. But the grey-green leaves may need protection against mildew, and the bush, which is only moderately sized, is inclined to be short-lived and dislikes very cold winters.

Prince, England, UK, 1929
'Edith Part' × 'Mrs Herbert Stevens'
Repeat flowering ı *Intense fragrance*
HABIT Bush H/W 1.2m/1.2m (4ft/4ft) ı ZONES 7–11

'Elizabeth Harkness'

HYBRID TEA ı LIGHT YELLOW

No doubt when Jack Harkness crossed 'Red Dandy' with 'Piccadilly' he was anticipating

'Ellen'

something dazzling, so it must have been a surprise when 'Elizabeth Harkness' opened its first, pastel-tinted blooms. They are enormous, shapely and blush-white with softest tints of apricot and pink at the centre, and fragrant, too. The bush is strong and free, with dark leaves, but (like many Harkness roses) it is happiest in a cool climate. It is an ideal rose for a bride to carry on her wedding day, and indeed it was named as a wedding present for the raiser's daughter.

Harkness, England, UK, 1969
'Red Dandy' × 'Piccadilly'
Repeat flowering ı *Moderate fragrance*
HABIT Bush H/W 1.5m/1.2m (5ft/4ft) ı ZONES 5–11

'Elizabeth of Glamis'

FLORIBUNDA ı ORANGE PINK

'Irish Beauty'

Elizabeth of Glamis is that expert rosarian the late Queen Mother, and when Sam McGredy dedicated this rose to her it was universally agreed to be worthy of her name. The double flowers, borne in clusters, are such a lovely blend of soft salmon shades, their shape so perfect from bud to petal fall, their scent so sweet – sweet enough for this to be the first Floribunda to win the RNRS's premier award for fragrance – and the olive-green leaves, red-tinted in youth, set them off perfectly. But alas, its constitution appears to be deteriorating, and these days it will certainly need protection from black spot and probably from rust.

MACel ı McGredy, Northern Ireland, UK, 1964
'Spartan' × 'Highlight'
Repeat flowering ı *Intense fragrance*
HABIT Bush H/W 1.2m/1m (4ft/3ft) ı ZONES 6–11
🌹 Royal National Rose Society President's International Trophy 1963, Copenhagen Gold Medal 1965

'Elizabeth Taylor'

HYBRID TEA ı DEEP PINK

The great actress was English-born, but her rose is American and is chiefly popular in that country. It is a superb flower in deep pink, sometimes with just a hint of mauve, large, double and shapely enough for exhibition, and well scented. The flowers are usually borne singly. The wickedly thorny bush is of average height and spreading habit, its leaves dark green and healthy. Miss Taylor appeared several times on a radio show that Stirling Macoboy produced back in the 1950s, and he was disappointed not to be able to include her rose in the first edition of this book. It is a pleasure to make good the omission now.

Weddle, USA, 1985
'First Prize' × 'Swarthmore'
Repeat flowering ı *Slight, spicy fragrance*
HABIT Bush H/W 1.5m/1.2m (5ft/4ft) ı ZONES 6–11

'Elle'

HYBRID TEA ı PINK BLEND

It sometimes takes a rose a little while to achieve fame outside the country of its birth. By the time 'Elle' won the AARS award in 2005, French gardeners had already been enjoying its deliciously citrus-scented flowers in their variable but *très belle* blends of cream, pink and apricot for six years. Cool weather sees them at their best, when they are very large and shapely enough for exhibition. The bush is strong and slightly spreading in habit, and its glossy leaves are disease-resistant. Altogether a stylish rose, well named for the leading French fashion magazine.

MEIbderos ı Meilland, France, 2003
'Purple Splendor' × ('Chicago Peace' × 'Tchin-Tchin')
Repeat flowering ı *Intense fragrance*
HABIT Bush H/W 1.5m/1.2m (5ft/4ft) ı ZONES 6–11
🌹 Bagatelle (Paris) Gold Medal 1999, Tokyo Fragrance Award 2000, All-America Rose Selection 2005

'Ellen'

SHRUB ı APRICOT BLEND

David Austin has banished 'Ellen' from his own catalogue, accusing it of lack of refinement and a habit of taking a mid-summer rest from flowering. But many rosarians disagree with him, citing the huge size of the fully double flowers; their informal, old-fashioned shape; their lovely shades of apricot and soft pink, sometimes with a curious tinge of russet; and their intense fragrance. The bush is on the tall side, with large, dark leaves and a good record of health. The name was a retirement present to an Austin employee, Ellen Drew.

AUScup । Austin, England, 1985
'Charles Austin' × seedling
Repeat flowering । *Intense fragrance*
HABIT Bush H/W 1.2m/1m (4ft/3ft) । ZONES 4–11

'Elveshörn'

SHRUB । MEDIUM PINK

Merit does not always translate into popularity. This rose is one of the toughest and easiest to grow of the 'Patio Roses', flourishing everywhere and smothering itself all season with elegant sprays of neatly formed, double flowers. Its faults in the public's eyes are: the name, easily confused with the much larger 'Elmshorn' (Reimer Kordes ought to have known better); the lack of gloss on the dark foliage; the lack of perfume; and the color of the flowers. Their brilliant cerise is uniform and unfading, but outside Germany, where the rose was raised in 1985, many people find it garish and refuse to buy it, which is a pity.

KORbotaf । Kordes, Germany, 1985
'The Fairy' × seedling
Repeat flowering । *Slight fragrance*
HABIT Bush H/W 1.2m/1m (4ft/3ft) । ZONES 5–11

TOP 'Elveshörn'
MIDDLE INSET TOP 'Elle'
MIDDLE INSET BOTTOM 'Elizabeth Taylor'

'Emanuel'

SHRUB । APRICOT BLEND

'Emmanuelle'

With this name David Austin has not sought biblical connections, but has chosen to honor David and Elizabeth Emanuel, the English couturiers best known for designing the wedding dress of the late Princess of Wales. Appropriately, the rose has ruffled flowers, taffeta-like in texture, blending shades of peach, pink and cream. They are very large and very fragrant, and are borne in small clusters in profusion all season, but the glossy, mid-green leaves are prone to black spot. It was introduced in 1985.

AUSuel । Austin, England, UK, 1992
('Chaucer' × 'Parade') × (seedling × 'Iceberg')
Repeat flowering । *Intense fragrance*
HABIT Bush H/W 1.2m/1m (4ft/3ft) । ZONES 5–11

'Ena Harkness'

HYBRID TEA । MEDIUM RED

For many years 'Ena Harkness' was Britain's leading red rose, and it is pleasing to note that it was raised by an amateur hybridist, a diamond cutter called Albert Norman, who named it after the wife of the owner of the firm who introduced it for him. In the cool climates it prefers, it can still be unsurpassed in its beautiful velvety colour and perfect form.

'Emanuel'

'Ena Harkness'

'Fire King'

'Fire King'

FLORIBUNDA ı ORANGE RED

Although 'Fire King' won the AARS award in 1960, many people think it is a little out-classed now, citing its increasing fondness for mildew, its rather leggy growth, and the way its double, brilliant scarlet blooms are apt to be disfigured by blackish edges to the petals. In its day it was a sensational rose, and if you see it in good form you can understand why it still has admirers: it can still put on a dazzling show. The flowers come in clusters; the foliage is leathery and dark green. With its musky scent, it is a fine rose for cutting.

MEIkans ı Meilland, France, 1959
'Moulin Rouge' × 'Fashion'
Repeat flowering ı *Musk fragrance*

HABIT Bush H/W 1.2m/1m (4ft/3ft) ı ZONES 5–11

🌹 All-America Rose Selection 1960

'First Edition'

FLORIBUNDA ı ORANGE PINK

'Arnaud Delbard'

The wide outer petals and shorter inner ones give the double flowers of this AARS winner unusual form, very like the dwarf Gumpo Azalea 'Balsaminiflora', which is similar in its spar-kling coral-rose shades, too. The rose is an erratic performer: in cooler climates it is compact and floriferous; in sultry climates it sulks. The foliage is glossy and mid-green. Perhaps Georges Delbard, the raiser, will favor us with a second edition, with similar charming flowers on a sturdier plant.

DELtep ı Delbard, France, 1976
('Zambra' × ['Orleans Rose' × 'Goldilocks']) ×
('Orange Triumph' seedling × 'Floradora')
Repeat flowering ı *Tea fragrance*

HABIT Bush H/W 1.2m/1m (4ft/3ft) ı ZONES 4–11

🌹 All-America Rose Selection 1977

'First Edition'

'First Love'

'First Love'

HYBRID TEA ı LIGHT PINK

'Premier Amour'

This romantically named Hybrid Tea remains one of the classic roses of the 1950s. It is loved for the elegance of its long buds (the semi-double blooms are a little thin when open) and for its beautiful color, softest pink with slightly deeper tones on the petal reverse. Scent is not really a feature, alas. 'First Love' is some-times said to be thornless. This is not true, although thorns are few and far between on the long, slim stems. The bush is on the tall side and upright in habit, free in its bloom and well clothed in pointed, light green leaves.

Swim, USA, 1951
'Charlotte Armstrong' × 'Show Girl'
Repeat flowering ı *Slight fragrance*

HABIT Bush H/W 1.5m/1.2m (5ft/4ft) ı ZONES 6–11

'First Prize'

HYBRID TEA ı PINK BLEND

For its lovely, high-centred blooms, 'First Prize' certainly deserves a first prize, and wins them regularly at rose shows in America; it also has the AARS award and the American Rose Soci-ety's gold medal to its credit. Although it has a reputation for tenderness, the plant is vig-orous and upright. The huge, double flowers, borne singly, are a blend of soft rose-pinks, touched with old ivory at their centres, and are fragrant. The foliage is leathery and dark green. There is a well-regarded climbing sport.

Boerner, USA, 1970
'Enchantment' seedling × 'Golden Masterpiece' seedling
Repeat flowering ı *Tea fragrance*

HABIT Bush H/W 1.5m/1.2m (5ft/4ft) ı ZONES 6–11

🌹 All-America Rose Selection 1970, American Rose Society Gold Medal 1971

'Fisherman's Friend'

SHRUB ı DARK RED

'Fisherman'

David Austin has the praiseworthy habit of auctioning the naming rights for some of his roses for British charities. In this case it was Children's Need, and the winner named the rose after a favorite brand of cough lozenges! It is not so strange, however, when you real-ize the lozenges are garnet-red, a shade fairly close to that of the rose. The very double flowers are among the biggest of the Austin

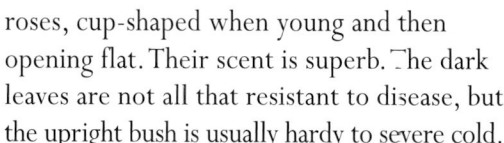

roses, cup-shaped when young and then opening flat. Their scent is superb. The dark leaves are not all that resistant to disease, but the upright bush is usually hardy to severe cold.

AUSchild ꟾ Austin, England, 1987
'Lilian Austin' × 'The Squire'
Repeat flowering ꟾ Strong, damask fragrance

HABIT Bush H/W 1.2m/1m (4ft/3ft) ꟾ ZONES 4–10

'Flamenco'

FLORIBUNDA ꟾ LIGHT PINK

A 1960 introduction, 'Flamenco' was one of Sam McGredy's first, marking the return of the McGredy firm to the new rose business after a long absence. The rose world seems to have regarded it as merely a taste of things to come, and even the McGredy catalogue no longer lists it. It is a rose for cool climates, like that of Portland, Oregon, where it was photographed, and where it makes a cheerful display with its double, coral-pink blooms, lit with touches of yellow and orange. The flowers are borne in clusters; the foliage is leathery and dark olive-green.

McGredy, Northern Ireland, UK, 1960
'Cinnabar' × 'Spartan'
Repeat flowering ꟾ Slight fragrance

HABIT Bush H/W 1.2m/1m (4ft/3ft) ꟾ ZONES 5–11

TOP 'Fisherman's Friend'
LEFT 'First Prize'
RIGHT 'Flamenco'

'Folksinger'

'Fragrant Cloud'

'Fountain'

'Fragrant Delight'

'Fourth of July'

which bears large, loosely formed, double flowers in shades of peach and yellow. They come in small clusters all season and are pleasingly fragrant. The foliage is a dark, leathery green.

Buck, USA, 1985
'Carefree Beauty' × 'Friesia'
Repeat flowering ı *Moderate fragrance*

HABIT Bush H/W 1.2m/1m (4ft/3ft) ı ZONES 4–11

'Fountain'

HYBRID TEA ı MEDIUM RED

'Fontaine', 'Red Prince'

The name 'Fountain' does not call to mind a red rose. Perhaps that is why this very good modern shrub rose has not become as popular as it deserves. The fact that it is virtually a Hybrid Tea, carrying its shapely, velvety, double flowers all season on a sturdy, head-

high shrub with leathery, dark green leaves, makes it all the more desirable. The flowers are strongly fragrant. The RNRS saw its merits in 1970, the year of its introduction, and gave it their top award, the President's Trophy.

Tantau, Germany, 1970
Parentage undisclosed
Repeat flowering ı *Intense fragrance*

HABIT Bush H/W 2m/1.2m (7ft/4ft) ı ZONES 5–11

🌼 Royal National Rose Society Gold Medal and President's International Trophy 1970, Anerkannte Deutsche Rose (Germany) 1971

'Fourth of July'

LARGE FLOWERED CLIMBER ı RED BLEND

'Crazy for You', 'Hanabi'

California's Tom Carruth has shown himself one of the virtuoso breeders of striped roses, winning his first AARS award in 1997 with the excellent Floribunda 'Scentimental' and following this two years later with 'Fourth of July', which is not only the first climber to win the coveted award for more than 20 years but the first striped climbing rose of the modern era. It is a typical modern climber, not overly vigorous and bearing its clusters of Floribunda-style flowers in profusion throughout the season. They are only barely semi-double, the better to show off their white stripes and splashes, which are laid over a bright red ground. Every flower is different; and backed by dark, disease-resistant leaves, they bring to mind fireworks bursting in the night sky.

WEKroalt ǀ Carruth, USA, 1999
'Roller Coaster' × 'Altissimo'
Repeat flowering ǀ *Apple fragrance*

HABIT Climber H/W 3m/2.5m (10ft/8ft) ǀ ZONES 5–11

✿ All-America Rose Selection 1999

'Fragrant Cloud'

HYBRID TEA ǀ ORANGE RED

'Duftwolke', 'Nuage Parfumé'

For many years after its introduction, this was the world's bestselling rose. The name is apt, as it is outstandingly fragrant. The double flowers are brick-red, and borne most singly. The foliage is a dark olive-green, red-tinted when young. Introduced in Europe in 1963, it was not brought to the United States (by Jackson & Perkins) until 1968. It does best in a sunny climate; in sunless ones the flowers can go a distressing shade of magenta as they age.

TANellis ǀ Tantau, Germany, 1967
Seedling × 'Prima Ballerina'
Repeat flowering ǀ *Intense, damask fragrance*

HABIT Bush H/W 1.5m/1.2m (5ft/4ft) ǀ ZONES 5–11

✿ Royal National Rose Society Gold Medal 1963 and President's International Trophy 1964, Portland (Oregon, USA) Gold Medal 1966, American Rose Society James Alexander Gamble Fragrance Medal 1970, World Federation of Rose Societies Hall of Fame 1981

'Fragrant Delight'

FLORIBUNDA ǀ ORANGE PINK

'Wisbech Rose Fragrant Delight'

The name promises perfume, and the coral and salmon flowers, shot with apricot, deliver it. With its upright habit, dark green foliage and huge sprays of double, nicely shaped flowers, 'Fragrant Delight' is a highly regarded bedding rose in Britain, where it was bred, but it does not seem to enjoy hotter climates.

Wisbech Plant Co., England, UK, 1978
'Chanelle' × 'Whisky Mac'
Repeat flowering ǀ *Intense fragrance*

HABIT Bush H/W 1.2m/1m (4ft/3ft) ǀ ZONES 5–11

✿ Geneva Gold Medal 1985

'Fragrant Gold'

HYBRID TEA ǀ DEEP YELLOW

'Duftgold', 'TANduft'

Pure yellow roses are apt to be stingy with their scent, but although this one's name exaggerates a bit, it is one of the better-scented yellow Hybrid Teas. Its semi-double flowers are shapely in the bud, opening quickly to rather loose, full blooms, and the rich color holds without fading to any great degree. The bush is on the short side, and well clothed in dark green foliage. An attractive garden rose rather than a prize-winner at shows.

TANducoft ǀ Tantau, Germany, 1981
Parentage undisclosed
Repeat flowering ǀ *Strong fragrance*

HABIT Bush H/W 1.5m/1.2m (5ft/4ft) ǀ ZONES 5–11

'Fragrant Hour'

HYBRID TEA ǀ ORANGE PINK

One of a dozen or so Modern Roses whose names promise fragrance, this is another that delivers, and it has the awards to prove it. High-pointed buds open to large, well-shaped, double blooms in a remarkable shade of bronze-pink. They are wonderfully fragrant and look very well against the light green foliage.

McGredy, New Zealand, 1973
'Arthur Bell' × ('Spartan' × 'Grand Gala')
Repeat flowering ǀ *Intense fragrance*

HABIT Bush H/W 1.5m/1.2m (5ft/4ft) ǀ ZONES 5–11

✿ Belfast Fragrance (R. J. Frizzell Memorial) Award 1975, Belfast Gold Medal and Prize of the City of Belfast 1975, American Rose Society James Alexander Gamble Fragrance Medal 1997

'Fragrant Plum'

HYBRID TEA ǀ MAUVE

Usually described as 'deep purple-rose', the double flowers are really rose-pink with overtones of lilac. As they age, they become deeper and more pink. But it is a handsome rose nevertheless, large, shapely and intensely fragrant. The flowers are borne both singly and in large clusters. It does best in a warm climate, where it makes a strong bush with glossy foliage. Give it a pale yellow or blush-pink rose for contrast.

AROplumi ǀ Christensen, USA, 1990
'Shocking Blue' × ('Blue Nile' × 'Ivory Tower')
Repeat flowering ǀ *Intense, fruity fragrance*

HABIT Bush H/W 1.5m/1.2m (5ft/4ft) ǀ ZONES 5–11

'Fragrant Gold'

'Fragrant Plum'

'Fragrant Hour'

'Frank Naylor'

SHRUB | RED BLEND

This rose makes a head-high shrub that is covered all season with sprays of smallish, almost single flowers in an unusual tone of dusky crimson, with gold around the stamens. The young foliage is plum-tinted and matures to a dark greyish green. Major-General Naylor was sometime President of the Royal National Rose Society. Breeder Jack Harkness has raised some other very attractive roses from this rose.

Harkness, England, UK, 1978
(['Orange Sensation' × 'Allgold'] × ['Little Lady' × 'Lilac Charm']) × (['Blue Moon' × 'Magenta'] × ['Cläre Grammerstorf' × 'Frühlingsmorgen'])
Repeat flowering | Musk fragrance

HABIT Bush H/W 1.8m/1m (6ft/3ft) | ZONES 5–11

'Franklin Englemann'

FLORIBUNDA | DARK RED

This Irish-raised rose is named for a German rose-grower. The double, blood-red flowers, like small Hybrid Teas in size and form, are borne in small clusters (but there are great numbers of them) on a tall, rather open bush with glossy, dark green leaves. It lacks scent,

'Frank Naylor'

which has told against its wider popularity, but it is still a fine garden rose and has proved useful as a parent. Herr Englemann had to endure the indignity of having his name misspelt as Engelmann when the rose was registered; it is given here with the correct spelling.

Dickson, Northern Ireland, UK, 1970
'Heidelberg' × ('Schlössers Brilliant' × seedling)
Repeat flowering | No fragrance

HABIT Bush H/W 1.2m/1m (4ft/3ft) | ZONES 5–11

'Frau Dagmar Hartopp'

HYBRID RUGOSA | LIGHT PINK

'Frau Dagmar Hastrup', 'Fru Dagmar Hastrup'

Call it by any one of its names (or just, affectionately, 'Frau Dagmar'), this is perhaps the best of all the Rugosas for a small garden. The blooms are single, sweetly fragrant and a most attractive shade of pale, cool pink. The later flowers are accompanied by deep crimson hips, which go perfectly with them. At the very end of the season there are fall/autumn plum tints in the rich green, wrinkled foliage. What more could one ask of a small shrub?

Hastrup, Germany, c. 1914
Parentage unknown
Repeat flowering | Sweet fragrance

HABIT Bush H/W 1m/1.2m (3ft/4ft) | ZONES 4–10

🌸 Royal Horticultural Society Award of Garden Merit 1993

'Frau Dagmar Hartopp'

'Frédéric Mistral'

'Fred Edmunds'

HYBRID TEA | ORANGE BLEND

'L'Arlésienne'

Oregon nurseryman Fred Edmunds seems to have stolen some of the glory from the Meilland family, who first called this lovely rose 'L'Arlésienne' (after Bizet's opera) in 1943. It is a loosely decorative rose of 25 petals, opening in cupped form from long, pointed buds. The coppery orange blooms, up to 13cm (5in) in diameter, develop a strong fragrance that helped it to earn its two awards. The bush has an open habit and healthy, glossy foliage.

Meilland, France, 1943
'Duquesa de Peneranda' × 'Marie Claire'
Repeat flowering | Intense fragrance

HABIT Bush H/W 1.5m/1.2m (5ft/4ft) | ZONES 5–11

🌸 Portland (Oregon, USA) Gold Medal 1942, All-America Rose Selection 1944

'Fred Loads'

SHRUB | ORANGE RED

This is a Shrub Rose for rose-lovers who appreciate bright colors in lavish quantity. Like a gigantic Floribunda in habit, 'Fred Loads' dazzles with great sprays of semi-double, lightly scented flowers in coral-orange, not unlike those of 'Super Star'

'Fred Loads'

(also known as 'Tropicana') in tone. The foliage is dark green and lush, and the plant is upright and grows very strongly. It needs something shorter to be planted in front of it, as most of the blooms come at the top of the bush. Raised by an English amateur raiser, it is named for a leading British gardening writer. There is a striped sport from 'Fred Loads' called 'Festival Fanfare'.

Holmes, England, UK, 1968
'Dorothy Wheatcroft' × 'Orange Sensation'
Repeat flowering ı *Slight fragrance*

HABIT Bush H/W 1.5m/1.2m (5ft/4ft) ı ZONES 5–11

Royal National Rose Society Gold Medal 1967, Royal Horticultural Society Award of Garden Merit 1993

'Fred Edmunds'

'Frédéric Mistral'

HYBRID TEA ı LIGHT PINK

'The Children's Rose'

This makes a very tall bush for the back of the bed, so tall indeed that it can be trained against a wall as a short climber, although it is rather tender and will need frost protection in places colder than zone 7. The double, soft pink flowers, borne mostly singly, are very fine indeed, shapely in the bud and opening large and lightly ruffled. Their fragrance is to die for. The foliage is dull green and healthy. The name commemorates the Nobel Prize-winning Provençal poet; in Australia it is named

'Franklin Englemann'

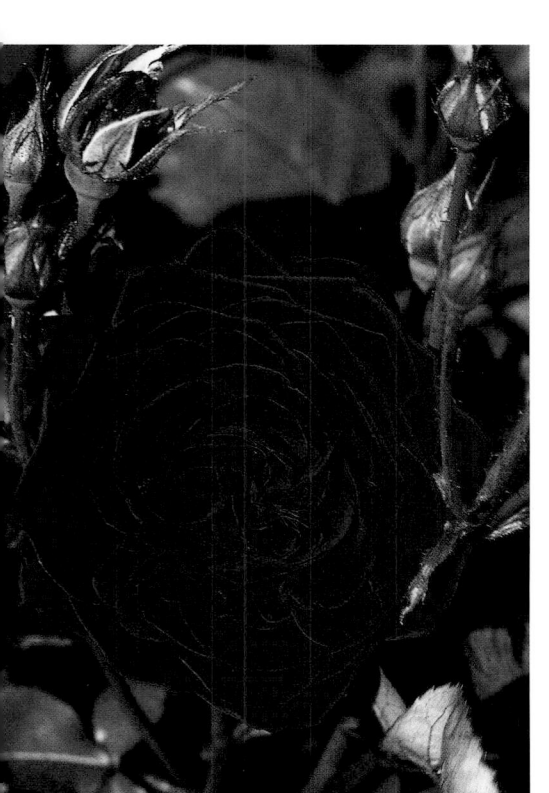

'Freedom'

'The Children's Rose', a portion of its royalties going to the support of children's hospitals.

MEItebros ı Meilland, France, 1998
('Perfume Delight' × 'Prima Ballerina') ×
'The McCartney Rose'
Repeat flowering ı *Intense, old rose fragrance*

HABIT Bush H/W 2m/1.2m (7ft/4ft) ı ZONES 6–10
Baden-Baden Fragrance Award 1993, Le Roeulx Fragrance Award 1994, Monza Fragrance Award 1994, Belfast Fragrance Award 1996

'Freedom'

HYBRID TEA ı DEEP YELLOW

You do not really need to know that 'Freedom' won the RNRS gold medal in 1983, although that is proof of its great performance over a number of years. Suffice to say that its double flowers are absolutely gorgeous. What a dazzling chrome yellow! And the color stays that way until the flowers actually fall.

'Frensham'

semi-double, warm crimson flowers set against matt, dark green foliage. Then, in the 1960s, cries of 'deterioration' and 'mildew' were heard, and 'Frensham' fell from favor. It seems that in recent years the mildew problem is lessening, heralding, one hopes, a revival of popularity for this lovely rose. Raised in 1946 by that remarkable English amateur breeder Albert Norman, its only fault is the faintness of its perfume.

Norman, England, UK, 1946
Seedling × 'Crimson Glory'
Repeat flowering ı *Slight fragrance*

HABIT Bush H/W 1.8m/1.2m (6ft/4ft) ı ZONES 5–11

'Friendship'

HYBRID TEA ı DEEP PINK

Not surprisingly given its parentage, 'Friendship' is richly fragrant. Tinted a rich raspberry pink, the 28 petals form a huge, cupped flower, sometimes 15cm (6in) across. The foliage is a dark green and the bush is vigorous. It almost goes without saying that it received the AARS award for 1979.

LINrick ı Lindquist, USA, 1978
'Fragrant Cloud' × 'Miss All-American Beauty'
Repeat flowering ı *Intense fragrance*

HABIT Bush H/W 1.5m/1.2m (5ft/4ft) ı ZONES 5–11
🌹 All-America Rose Selection 1979

It is a neat plant, dense, bushy and not too tall, freely blooming (although the flowers are by no means big) and clad in glossy, green foliage.

DICjem ı Dickson, Northern Ireland, UK, 1984
('Eurorose' × 'Typhoon') × 'Bright Smile'
Repeat flowering ı *Moderate fragrance*

HABIT Bush H/W 1m/1m (3ft/3ft) ı ZONES 6–11
🌹 Royal National Rose Society Gold Medal 1983

'French Lace'

FLORIBUNDA ı WHITE

What an appropriate name: the flowers are almost exactly the écru color of the best Vincennes lace. Often they are tinted with palest apricot; always they are of perfect exhibition form. The double flowers are rather large and the clusters small, but there is nothing delicate about the plant, which is strong and bushy. One might cavil about the lack of scent, and wish the small, dark

TOP 'French Lace'
BOTTOM INSET 'Friendship'

green leaves a bit larger. It is an excellent cut flower, as are its parents.

JAClace ı Warriner, USA, 1980
'Dr A. J. Verhage' × 'Bridal Pink'
Repeat flowering ı *Fruity fragrance*

HABIT Bush H/W 1.2m/1m (4ft/3ft) ı ZONES 5–11
🌹 All-America Rose Selection 1982, Portland (Oregon, USA) Gold Medal 1984

'Frensham'

FLORIBUNDA ı DARK RED

In cool climates 'Frensham' has long been an outstanding rose – taller than head-high and completely covered with clusters of

'Full Sail'

'Fyvie Castle'

'Full Sail'

HYBRID TEA | WHITE

'Land of the Long White Cloud', 'Long White Cloud', 'MAClanoflon'

Identical white sports of Sam McGredy's excellent pale pink Hybrid Tea 'Aotearoa' ('New Zealand') have occurred in several places, but the first to be discovered and propagated was in Sam's own nursery, so to him go the royalties! It is a fine double rose, borne mostly singly, with all the good qualities of its parent, including its beautiful honeysuckle fragrance. It isn't always pure white; in cool weather a faint pink blush sometimes appears, and like many white roses the flowers dislike heavy rain. The Maori name for their country is Aotearoa (pronounce each vowel separately), which means 'the land of the long white cloud'.

MAClanoflan | McGredy, New Zealand, 1998
'New Zealand' sport
Repeat flowering | *Honeysuckle fragrance*
HABIT Bush H/W 1.5m/1.2m (5ft/4ft) | ZONES 5–11

'Fyvie Castle'

HYBRID TEA | PINK BLEND

'Amberlight'

This rose appears to have dropped out of the lists in America, although it is still quite popular in Britain and in New Zealand. The double flowers are large and of perfect form, in a variable but lovely blend of soft shades of apricot and peach, deeper in cool weather. The scent is quite good, and the glossy, green foliage is very handsome, although not always as free of black spot as one would like. The bush is short and compact. Fyvie Castle stands near the Cocker nurseries outside Aberdeen.

COCbamber | Cocker, Scotland, UK, 1985
('Sunblest' × ['Sabine' × 'Dr. A. J. Verhage']) × 'Silver Jubilee'
Repeat flowering | *Moderate fragrance*
HABIT Bush H/W 1m/1.2m (3ft/4ft) | ZONES 6–11
🌹 Gold Star of the South Pacific, Hamilton (New Zealand) 1985

'Gabriella'

FLORIBUNDA | MEDIUM RED

'Gabrielle'

Bred for the florist's greenhouse and for many years one of the world's leading cut-flower varieties, this is an unreliable performer in the garden, where it is apt to be stingy with its double, dark orange flowers. Borne on long, thin stems (the small clusters are usually disbudded), they can last two weeks in water, but like most such roses they are almost without perfume. The foliage is a leathery olive-green. A sport from 'Mercedes', it was discovered by Lars Berggren, a Swedish cut-rose grower, and introduced by Kordes in 1977.

BERgme | Berggren, Sweden, 1977
'Mercedes' sport
Repeat flowering | *Slight fragrance*
HABIT Bush H/W 1.2m/1m (4ft/3ft) | ZONES 7–11

'Gallivarda'

HYBRID TEA | RED BLEND

'Galsar

Although this extraordinary Hybrid Tea is officially described as 'red with yellow reverse', it is often rather russet in tone and looks like a preview of the brown and ochre shades of more recent years. The buds of 'Gallivarda' are long and pointed, unfurling to large, high-centred blooms with 34 petals. The bush is vigorous and upright, with abundant glossy, green foliage, and may need protection where winters go below freezing.

Kordes, Germany, 1977
'Königin der Rosen' × 'Vienna Charm'
Repeat flowering | *Slight fragrance*
HABIT Bush H/W 1.5m/1.2m (5ft/4ft) | ZONES 7–11

'Garden Party'

HYBRID TEA | WHITE

This is still a popular show rose in America, despite some complaints about winter frost damage and too much mildew on its grey-green leaves. In warm climates it is glorious, very large, double, and opening high-centred and ruffled from long, shapely buds – and much better scented than it is usually said to be. The amount of pink on the petal edges varies with the season. Sometimes it is quite prominent, at others

'Gallivarda'

'Gabriella'

'Garden Party'

'Gene Boerner'

'George Burns'

FLORIBUNDA ¦ YELLOW BLEND

'George Burns Centennial'

Another fine striped rose from Tom Carruth. Named to celebrate the 100th birthday of the great Hollywood actor and comedian, it is a cheerful blend of red and yellow, the red more prominent in warm weather, the yellow in cool. Usually borne in rather small clusters, the informally shaped, double flowers are almost of Hybrid Tea size and nicely fragrant. The bush is compact and free-blooming, and

RIGHT 'George Burns'
BELOW 'Geraldine'

'Gene Boerner'

FLORIBUNDA ¦ MEDIUM PINK

This 1969 AARS winner was named by Jackson & Perkins in memory of their Director of Research, the raiser of so many beautiful roses, who died in 1966. Mid-pink, it rather resembles 'Queen Elizabeth' in color and in being a tall, sturdy bush, although the double flowers are somewhat shapelier. It is generally regarded as being not quite as good; the old flowers are apt to go spotty, and it is not nearly as robust and indestructible a plant. Yet, for all the odiousness of the comparison, 'Gene Boerner' is a good rose, and gives a long-lasting cut flower. The foliage is a glossy mid-green. The fragrance is only slight.

Boerner, USA, 1968
'Ginger' × ('Ma Perkins' × 'Garnette Supreme')
Repeat flowering ¦ *Slight fragrance*

HABIT Bush H/W 1.2m/1m (4ft/3ft) ¦ ZONES 4–11
All-America Rose Selection 1969

'Geranium'

the leaves are glossy and dark green, although perhaps not quite as resistant to black spot as they might be. Tom Carruth also named a rose for George Burns's wife and long-time co-star, Gracie Allen, this time a Floribunda in blended shades of pink. It was introduced in the same year, 1996.

WEKcalroc | Carruth, USA, 1996
'Calico' × 'Roller Coaster'
Repeat flowering | Strong, fruit and citrus fragrance
HABIT Bush H/W 1m/1m (3ft/3ft) | ZONES 5–11

'Geraldine'

FLORIBUNDA | ORANGE BLEND

'Orange' is a much-abused word in the rosarian's lexicon, having been pressed into duty to describe roses whose red petals are even the slightest bit on the scarlet side of crimson. 'Geraldine', however, is 'true' orange blended with lemon. The double flowers are shapely, carried on a compact, lush-leafed bush, and last well in the vase. It was raised by Devon rosarian Colin Pearce and named for his wife.

PEAhaze | Pearce, England, UK, 1982
Seedling × seedling
Repeat flowering | Slight fragrance
HABIT Bush H/W 1.2m/1m (4ft/3ft) | ZONES 5–11

'Geranium'

HYBRID MOYESII | MEDIUM RED

Selected by the Royal Horticultural Society at its garden at Wisley in 1938, this is probably the best of several named clones of *R. moyesii*

'Geranium Red'

for the average garden. It is much less gawky in habit; its hips are just magnificent; and the single flowers, borne in clusters, are a fine bright red, although rather lighter and less vinous than the wild species itself. It is still a big shrub: expect it to grow to 2.5m (8ft) high and almost as wide. It has dainty foliage of a dull medium green.

Royal Horticultural Society, England, UK, 1938
Hybrid form of *R. moyesii*
Spring flowering | Slight fragrance
HABIT Bush H/W 2.5m/1.8m (8ft/6ft) | ZONES 5–11

'Geranium Red'

FLORIBUNDA | ORANGE RED

With its multitude of petals, ruffled and quartered, 'Geranium Red' is reminiscent of an Old Garden Rose. One in modern dress, though, for the flowers, borne in clusters, are an intense, deep orange-red, brilliant without being strident, and becoming darker with age. The foliage is a leathery, dark olive-green, red-tinted when young. Few catalogues list it nowadays, but it is well worth seeking out for its unusual beauty and its intense, spicy fragrance. It will repay the best of care. Raised by Eugene Boerner in 1947, it is important historically, for it was the parent of 'Spartan' and through it has transmitted fragrance and a compact habit to many of the most desirable of today's Floribundas.

Boerner, USA, 1947
'Crimson Glory' × seedling
Repeat flowering | Intense, geranium fragrance
HABIT Bush H/W 1.2m/1m (4ft/3ft) | ZONES 4–11

'Gertrude Jekyll'

SHRUB | MEDIUM PINK

'AUSboard'

'Gertrude Jekyll' is one of the largest-flowered of the David Austin 'English Roses', its deep shocking pink blooms as large as those of any old Hybrid Perpetual. It is powerfully fragrant, too. The bush is upright, to about 1.5m (5ft), with mid-green leaves. It does repeat its bloom, but will benefit from encouragement to do so. Gertrude Jekyll was one of the most influential figures in English gardening in the twentieth century, and a lover of Old Garden Roses.

AUSbord | Austin, England, UK, 1986
'Wife of Bath' × 'Comte de Chambord'
Repeat flowering | Intense fragrance
HABIT Bush H/W 1.5m/1.2m (5ft/4ft) | ZONES 5–11

'Gertrude Jekyll'

'Gina Lollobrigida'

'Gina Lollobrigida'

HYBRID TEA | DEEP YELLOW

'Children's Rose', 'The Children's Rose'

You will be immediately struck by the gigantic size of the magnificent golden yellow blooms! Indeed, the flowers, normally borne one to a stem, have been likened to giant, yellow lollipops. Like the movie star this rose is named for, the very double flowers are of exceptional star quality. Their 70–90 petals contain a great deal of starch, making them resistant to dehydration in hot climates. In Britain this rose is sold as 'The Children's Rose', and the proceeds benefit one of the children's hospitals in London.

MEllivar | Meilland, France 1990
'Laura '81' × 'Cookies'
Repeat flowering | Slight fragrance
HABIT Bush H/W 1.8m/1.2m (6ft/4ft) | ZONES 4–11

'Ginger Rogers'

HYBRID TEA ׀ ORANGE PINK

'Salmon Charm'

Apart from her long-time dancing partner Fred Astaire, the only thing missing from this rose is any suggestion of ginger color! It is a uniform shade of salmon-pink from edge to edge. However, it was not named for its color, but to commemorate Miss Rogers's appearance on the London stage in 1969. Raised by Sam McGredy, it is a tallish grower with light green foliage and large, 30-petalled flowers with, yes, a touch of ginger in the fragrance.

McGredy, New Zealand, 1969
'Super Star' × 'Miss Ireland'
Repeat flowering ׀ *Moderate fragrance*

HABIT Bush H/W 1.5m/1.2m (5ft/4ft) ׀ ZONES 5–11

'Gingersnap'

FLORIBUNDA ׀ ORANGE BLEND

'Apricot Prince', 'Prince Abricot'

What a lot of 'apricots' there have been! 'Apricot Queen' in 1941 and 'Apricot Nectar' in 1966 were both AARS winners, and in 1978 'Apricot Prince' appeared.

'Glenfiddich'

The two award-winners are roses of delicate color, whereas this one is brilliant in orange and gold. Perhaps to emphasize this difference, Armstrong Nurseries rechristened it 'Gingersnap'. It is successful in warm climates, less so in muggy ones, at its best making a vigorous, upright bush bearing many clusters of double, lightly fragrant flowers, 10cm (4in) in diameter. It has glossy, dark green foliage.

AROsnap ׀ Delbard-Chabert, France, 1978
('Zambra' × ['Orange Triumph' × 'Floradora']) × ('Jean de la Lune' × ['Spartan' × 'Mandrina'])
Repeat flowering ׀ *Slight fragrance*

HABIT Bush H/W 1.2m/1m (4ft/3ft) ׀ ZONES 5–11

'Givenchy'

HYBRID TEA ׀ RED BLEND

'Paris Pink'

In the garden, 'Givenchy' is a deep cyclamen pink, lighter on the reverse. Indoors, it opens

'Gingersnap'

'Ginger Rogers'

'Glenara'

'Givenchy'

paler, with deeper shades around the edge. Like its parent 'Double Delight', it needs the sun on its petals for the strong tones to develop. The blooms are large, full-petalled and fragrant, and borne in sprays on an upright, bushy plant with dark green foliage. Hubert de Givenchy

'Glowing Peace'

is one of Paris's leading couturiers and makers of perfume.

AROdousra　ı　Christensen, USA, 1986
'Gingersnap' × 'Double Delight'
Repeat flowering　ı　*Spicy fragrance*
HABIT Bush H/W 1.5m/1.2m (5ft/4ft)　ı　ZONES 5–11

'Glenara'

CLIMBING HYBRID TEA　ı　DEEP PINK

This 1951 Australian creation must have been a particular favorite of Alister Clark's, for he named it after his Victorian home, Glenara. It is a charming rose, its semi-double flowers large and loosely shapely from long buds, in a pleasing shade of rose-pink. They are borne freely in early summer, with the odd flower to follow. The growth habit is moderate, and it is traditionally grown on a pillar. The foliage is large, leathery and dark green.

Clark, Australia, 1951
Parentage unknown
Repeat flowering　ı　*Slight fragrance*
HABIT Climber H/W 3m/2m (10ft/7ft)　ı　ZONES 5–11

'Glenfiddich'

FLORIBUNDA　ı　DEEP YELLOW

Deep old gold to amber – the color of a fine malt whisky, in fact, although it doesn't smell like one – 'Glenfiddich' bears smallish clusters of shapely, double blooms, 10cm (4in) in diameter, on an upright plant with glossy, dark green leaves. Its unusual color makes it very

popular, but – despite its sensitivity to severe frosts – it looks its best in cool climates. Hot sun bleaches the flowers to a rather ordinary lemon-yellow. It is a child of the Scotch whisky country, being a creation of Alec Cocker of Aberdeen.

Cocker, Scotland, UK, 1976
'Arthur Bell' × ('Circus' × 'Sabine')
Repeat flowering　ı　*Moderate fragrance*
HABIT Bush H/W 1m/1m (3ft/3ft)　ı　ZONES 5–11

'Glowing Peace'

GRANDIFLORA　ı　YELLOW BLEND

'MEIzoelo', 'Philippe Noiret'

Raised in France and blooming there in memory of the great French movie star Philippe Noiret, this AARS winner is being promoted elsewhere as a more colorful version of its great-grandparent 'Peace'. It isn't quite that – it is considerably smaller and less perfect in form, and often blooms in small clusters – but colorful it certainly is in its ever-varying blends of gold and amber and cantaloupe. The double flowers are long-lasting in the vase, although flower arrangers will find the stems a little short. The plant is bushy and well clothed with glossy, dark green leaves, but it will need winter protection in cold climates.

MEIzoele　ı　Meilland, France, 2001
'Sun King' × 'Roxane'
Repeat flowering　ı　*Light fragrance*
HABIT Bush H/W 1.2m/1m (4ft/3ft)　ı　ZONES 6–11
🌹 All-America Rose Selection 2001

'Godfrey Winn'

'Golden Celebration'

'Godfrey Winn'

HYBRID TEA | MAUVE

'Milas de Fortecruiba'

Originally, the Spanish raiser Pedro Dot had named this rose 'Milas de Fortecruiba' in honor of a Spanish celebrity, and it may never have bloomed outside of Spain if it had not been discovered by that great, bewhiskered English rosarian Harry Wheatcroft, who snapped up the rights to it and rededicated it to the British journalist, actor and radio personality Godfrey Winn, who died in 1971. In its time it was a leading mauve rose, but the intensely fragrant, globular, double blooms are not often

'Gold Badge'

seen these days. It prefers a warm, dry climate. The flowers are usually borne singly, and the foliage is leathery and dark green.

Dot, Spain, 1968
Parentage undisclosed
Repeat flowering | Intense fragrance

HABIT Bush H/W 1.5m/1.2m (5ft/4ft) | ZONES 6–11

'Gold Badge'

FLORIBUNDA | MEDIUM YELLOW

'Gold Bunny', 'Rimosa 79'

Most of the world calls it 'Gold Bunny', but the American name 'Gold Badge' is the officially registered name (apart from the codename). However you call it, it is an excellent rose, the double flowers fairly large, their golden yellow rich and bright, although the spent flowers do tend to hang

'Gold Medal'

'Golden Dawn'

'Golden Days'

on the bush a little long; dead-heading is called for. The fairly low-growing bush is very free with its blooms. The foliage is leathery and dark green. At its best in a warm climate, it does not seem to have found the success in foggy Britain (where it is accused of susceptibility to black spot) that it has found elsewhere.

MElgronuri · Paolino, France, 1978
'Rusticana' × ('Charleston' × 'Allgold')
Repeat flowering · Slight fragrance

HABIT Bush H/W 1m/1m (3ft/3ft) · ZONES 5–11

'Gold Medal'

GRANDIFLORA · MEDIUM YELLOW

'Golden Medal'

One would expect a gold medal to be larger than a gold badge, and indeed among roses this is so, although the double flowers of 'Gold Medal' are not exceptionally large. (Hence, perhaps, its American classification as a 'Grandiflora'.) It is a tall bush for the back of the bed, which it will brighten up with many long-lasting, golden flowers alloyed with copper on the petal edges. Although it has a reputation for tenderness, in warm climates it remains one of the very best

bright yellow roses. Borne on long stems, the flowers are long-lasting in the vase; and the dark green leaves are very disease-resistant for a yellow rose.

AROyqueli · Christensen, USA, 1982
'Yellow Pages' × ('Granada' × 'Garden Party')
Repeat flowering · Slight, fruity fragrance

HABIT Bush H/W 1.8m/1.2m (6ft/4ft) · ZONES 7–11
Gold Star of the South Pacific, Hamilton (New Zealand) 1983, Rose Introducers of New Zealand Gold Medal 1994

'Golden Celebration'

SHRUB · DEEP YELLOW

This is the largest and most spectacular of David Austin's yellow roses to date, and a glorious rival to his classic 'Graham Thomas', which it outclasses both in size and richness of color. The fragrance is equally fine. It is not quite so easy to grow, however, being more susceptible to black spot and more tender to cold. The very double flowers, borne in small clusters, are indeed so large and heavy that their stems have difficulty in holding them up, and after a shower of rain the slim branches can collapse under the weight. A discreet stake or two is a wise precaution. The bush is very tall, the leaves mid-green.

AUSgold · Austin, England, UK, 1993
'Charles Austin' × 'Abraham Darby'
Repeat flowering · Intense, tea fragrance

HABIT Bush H/W 1.8m/1.2m (6ft/4ft) · ZONES 7–11

'Golden Dawn'

HYBRID TEA · MEDIUM YELLOW

'Golden' is hardly the word: the scented, full-petalled flowers of 'Golden Dawn' are, in fact, a soft, pale yellow, sometimes blushed with pink on the outer petals. They are very nicely scented and carried on a rather short, bushy plant. The leaves are a distinctive grey-ish green. Sometimes the early flowers are spoilt by split centres, but usually the double blooms are as large and shapely as anyone could desire. For many years one of the leading yellow roses in Europe (until 'Peace' came along to steal its thunder), 'Golden Dawn' is of Australian origin, raised by Patrick Grant of Macksville, in northern New South Wales, and introduced in 1929.

Grant, Australia, 1929
'Elegante' × 'Ethel Somerset'
Repeat flowering · Strong fragrance

HABIT Bush H/W 1m/1m (3ft/3ft) · ZONES 7–11

'Golden Days'

HYBRID TEA · DEEP YELLOW

'RUgolda'

'Golden Days' is a rather uncommon rose that, like many yellow roses, varies in its depth of color with climate and season. It can be the deep yellow the catalogues promise, but it is equally likely to be much paler. Either way, it is a lovely, radiant color, well able to evoke the 'golden days' of heady youth. The scent is only slight, but the double flowers are quite large and shapely. The leaves are dark and have a good reputation for disease resistance. The raiser, a Dutchman, taking pity on foreigners' attempts to pronounce his first name, Ghijs, used to ask them to call him George.

RUggelda · De Ruiter, The Netherlands, 1982
'Peer Gynt' × seedling
Repeat flowering · Slight fragrance

HABIT Bush H/W 1.5m/1.2m (5ft/4ft) · ZONES 5–11

'Golden Delight'

FLORIBUNDA · MEDIUM YELLOW

Although somewhat overshadowed by its sister-seedling 'Allgold', 'Golden Delight' is still one of the best yellow Floribundas from the 1950s. It is more full of petals than 'Allgold', but it is paler in tone and not quite so vigorous and easy to grow. It scores over its rival in the fragrance department, however, and many rose-lovers preferred it for that reason. The flowers are borne in clusters, and the foliage is glossy and dark green.

LeGrice, England, UK, 1956
'Goldilocks' × 'Ellinor LeGrice'
Repeat flowering · Moderate fragrance

HABIT Bush H/W 1.2m/1.2m (4ft/4ft) · ZONES 6–11

'Golden Delight'

'Golden Giant'

'Golden Jubilee'

'Golden Gloves'

'Golden Holstein'

'Golden Masterpiece'

'Golden Giant'

HYBRID TEA ׀ DEEP YELLOW

'Fièvre d'Or', 'Goldrausch'

Although German-raised, 'Golden Giant' seems to be most often grown in warm climates these days – it is grown in India, and is still quite widely grown in Australia. It takes after its pollen parent 'Buccaneer' in being a real giant of a bush, towering over other plants in the rose garden, and in its matt, olive-green foliage, although its double flowers are both larger and more perfectly formed than those of 'Buccaneer'. At their best they can be huge, and they are pleasantly scented. The plant's disease resistance is very good. The German and French names both mean 'gold rush'.

KORbi ׀ Kordes, Germany, 1961
('Condesa de Sastago' × 'Walter Bentley') × 'Buccaneer'
Repeat flowering ׀ Moderate fragrance
HABIT Bush H/W 1.8m/1.2m (6ft/4ft) ׀ ZONES 5–11
Royal National Rose Society Gold Medal 1960

'Golden Gloves'

FLORIBUNDA ׀ DEEP YELLOW

The Golden Gloves award is one of the highest in amateur boxing, which would suggest that the raiser hoped for high awards for this rose; but alas it seems to have missed out. It is only available in Australia these days. The plant is bushy, the leaves bright green, and the double, bright yellow flowers, which come in small clusters, are shapely

like small Hybrid Teas. It does best in a warm, dry climate. There is a little scent.

Bear Creek Gardens, USA, 1991
('Friesia' × 'Katherine Loker') × 'Gingersnap'
Repeat flowering ׀ Slight fragrance
HABIT Bush H/W 1.2m/1m (4ft/3ft) ׀ ZONES 6–11

'Golden Holstein'

FLORIBUNDA ׀ DEEP YELLOW

'Kordes Rose Golden Holstein'

Back in 1939, Wilhelm Kordes named a red Floribunda 'Holstein' after the province of Germany where he lived. It is appropriate that his son Reimer should bestow the name on another rose, this time a golden one. It has just the same wide-open, semi-double flowers, but here they are a deep and dazzling yellow. For a rose raised in 1989, this was going against the fashion, which called for small, exhibition form flowers. The big clusters of blooms, backed up by dark green foliage on an easy-to-grow bush, are a splendid sight. The scent is mild.

KORtickel ׀ Kordes, Germany, 1989
Parentage undisclosed
Repeat flowering ׀ Slight fragrance
HABIT Bush H/W 1.2m/1m (4ft/3ft) ׀ ZONES 5–11
Dublin Gold Medal 1991

'Golden Ophelia'

'Golden Queen'

'Golden Ophelia'

HYBRID TEA ı MEDIUM YELLOW

In 1912, English hybridist William Paul selected a chance seedling to bear the name 'Ophelia'. It became one of the most famous roses of all time, and in the Colchester nursery of Benjamin Cant & Sons it added to its lustre by producing, in 1918, 'Golden Ophelia' – a seedling, not a sport – in pale creamy yellow, deepening at the centre. It was awarded the (then) NRS gold medal, and its delicately tinted flowers soon appeared in gardens and flower shops the world over. The foliage is a dark, glossy green, but there is little of the 'Ophelia' scent.

Cant, England, UK, 1918
'Ophelia' × 'Mrs Aaron Ward'
Repeat flowering ı *Slight fragrance*

HABIT Bush H/W 1.5m/1.2m (5ft/4ft) ı ZONES 5–11
(Royal) National Rose Society Gold Medal 1918

'Golden Queen'

HYBRID TEA ı ORANGE BLEND

Bred in Germany, 'Golden Queen' seems to have found its home away from home in New Zealand, where it was awarded a gold star in 1984 and was listed for many years by every one of that country's major rose nurseries. Classed in the United States as an 'orange blend', it looked more like an orange and pink blend (with hardly any gold!) when photographed in Christchurch in 1990 – but then some roses do vary very much from climate to climate. The foliage of 'Golden Queen' is glossy and dark green.

KORgitte ı Kordes, Germany, 1986
Parentage undisclosed
Repeat flowering ı *Slight fragrance*

HABIT Bush H/W 1.5m/1.2m (5ft/4ft) ı ZONES 5–11
Gold Star of the South Pacific, Hamilton (New Zealand) 1984

'Golden Jubilee'

HYBRID TEA ı MEDIUM YELLOW

You might occasionally come across 'Golden Jubilee', a Hybrid Tea raised by the American grower Jacobus in 1948, but the current holder of the name shown here, is a 1981 introduction from Alec Cocker of Aberdeen, who dedicated it to all long and happily married couples. (The American Rose Society suggests we use the codename 'COCagold' to save confusion.) It is a handsome, medium yellow bloom of 29 or 30 petals, exhaling the fragrance of tea, and is well set off by glossy, mid-green foliage.

COCagold ı Cocker, Scotland, UK, 981
'Peer Gynt' × 'Gay Gordons'
Repeat flowering ı *Tea fragrance*

HABIT Bush H/W 1.5m/1.2m (5ft/4ft) ı ZONES 5–11

'Golden Masterpiece'

HYBRID TEA ı MEDIUM YELLOW

This was one of the most desirable of yellow roses in the 1950s, and it has proved an important parent of yellow Hybrid Teas since. In cool, cloudy weather it can indeed be the splendid gold you see in the picture, but sunshine brings it out primrose. Never mind, the huge, double blooms, full of ruffled petals and softly fragrant, are still spectacular. They are borne one to a stem – if only the tall, glossy-leafed bush were a little more generous with them! In humid climates you may need to spray against black spot.

Boerner, USA, 1954
'Mandalay' × 'Golden Scepter'
Repeat flowering ı *Licorice fragrance*

HABIT Bush H/W 1.5m/1.2m (5ft/4ft) ı ZONES 5–11

'Golden Scepter'

HYBRID TEA ı DEEP YELLOW

'Spek's Yellow'

Strangely enough, this rose did not win a major award when it was introduced in 1950. Perhaps the judges faulted it for the loose, rather ragged form of its double blooms, but the public took it to heart and it became the most popular yellow rose for 20 years. The buds are long and pointed, and the deep, rich yellow pales only a little as the

ABOVE 'Golden Showers'
LEFT 'Golden Scepter'

flowers open. They are often borne in clusters, on a very tall, open bush with glossy, dark green foliage. Do not try to prune hard for bushiness or it will sulk. Jan Spek of Boskoop was the introducer; the raiser was Hans Verschuren.

Verschuren-Pechtold, The Netherlands, 1950
'Golden Rapture' × seedling
Repeat flowering ı *Moderate fragrance*

HABIT Bush H/W 1.5m/1.2m (5ft/4ft) ı ZONES 5–11

'Golden Showers'

LARGE FLOWERED CLIMBER ı MEDIUM YELLOW

This 1957 AARS winner remains one of the most popular of all yellow roses. True, the brilliant daffodil-yellow of the long buds is rather fleeting, and the wide, ruffled, double blooms are quite pale around their maroon stamens; but they still look stunning on long, almost black stems against the dark, shining green foliage. They are borne both singly and in clusters. 'Golden Showers' takes a year or

'Golden State'

'Golden Slippers'

two to settle in and start climbing, and even then it is only of moderate size. It always looks the picture of smartness and good health.

Lammerts, USA, 1956
'Charlotte Armstrong' × 'Captain Thomas'
Repeat flowering ı *Sweet fragrance*

HABIT Climber H/W 3m/1.8m (10ft/6ft) ı ZONES 6–11

🌹 All-America Rose Selection 1957, Portland (Oregon, USA) Gold Medal 1957, Royal Horticultural Society Award of Garden Merit 1993

'Golden Slippers'

FLORIBUNDA ı YELLOW BLEND

It is surprising how sometimes two raisers in different countries will come up with something quite new at the same time. In the same year that Gordon von Abrams in Oregon brought out 'Golden Slippers', Alain Meilland introduced the rather similar 'Zambra'. Both had a new color – clear, pale orange, with lemon on the reverse – both bear their flowers ('Golden Slippers' double, 'Zambra' semi-double) in typical Floribunda-style clusters,

'Golden Wings'

both have glossy, green foliage, and both were well received. Although 'Golden Slippers' still has its admirers, it is 'Zambra' that proved able to transmit its new color to improved descendants and so is better remembered.

Von Abrams, USA, 1961
'Goldilocks' × seedling
Repeat flowering ı *Moderate fragrance*

HABIT Bush H/W 1.2m/1m (4ft/3ft) ı ZONES 5–11

🌹 Portland (Oregon, USA) Gold Medal 1960, All-America Rose Selection 1962

'Golden State'

HYBRID TEA ı DEEP YELLOW

One of Francis Meilland's early successes, 'Golden State' was classified as 'deep yellow' in 1937, but it is definitely not deep yellow, as claimed in its youth. It is now almost cream, opening from pink-tinted buds. The foliage is still healthy, glossy, leathery and dark green, and the flowers are large, double and cupped. The 'Golden State' is California; Meilland named this rose with an eye to the American

'Golden Times'

market. Do not confuse this rose with a later rose of the same name.

Meilland, France, 1937
'Souvenir de Claudius Pernet' × ('Charles P. Kilham' × seedling)
Repeat flowering ı *Slight fragrance*

HABIT Bush H/W 1.4m/1m (4ft 6in/3ft) ı ZONES 5–11

🌹 Bagatelle (Paris) Gold Medal 1937, Portland (Oregon, USA) Gold Medal 1937

'Golden Times'

FLORIBUNDA ı MEDIUM YELLOW

Kordes's 'Golden Times' (with the codename KORtime) was for many years one of the favorites with the growers whose greenhouses supply the florists' shops. Introduced in 1976 (but not registered in America until 1985), it is not much of a garden rose. The rose described and shown here is the prior (and therefore legitimate) holder of the name, a much larger, double flower raised in 1970 by Alec Cocker and distributed by Wheatcroft Brothers. It has little fragrance, but the 40-petalled blooms can be 12cm (5in) wide and stand out dramatically against the abundant glossy, green foliage.

Cocker, Scotland, UK, 1970
'Fragrant Cloud' × 'Golden Splendour'
Repeat flowering ı *Slight fragrance*

HABIT Bush H/W 1.2m/1m (4ft/3ft) ı ZONES 5–11

'Golden Wings'

SHRUB ı LIGHT YELLOW

Any person who writes about the rose will, sooner or later, end up consulting Roy Shepherd's *History of the Rose*; and anyone who loves roses will, sooner or later, end up falling in

'Gordon's College'

FLORIBUNDA ı ORANGE PINK

'Braveheart'

Generations of the raiser's family have attended Robert Gordon's College in Aberdeen, which first opened its doors in 1750. With its 250th anniversary coming up, it was timely to dedicate a rose to it; and the family chose a very nice one, a headily scented Floribunda with shapely, coral flowers borne in sprays. Although the plant is not very tall, the double flowers are borne on long stems and last well in the vase. The foliage is dark green, and its disease resistance is said to be very good. There are grumblings in America about frost damage in severe winters, but Scotland isn't quite cold enough for that to be a problem there.

COCjabby ı Cocker, Scotland, 1992
'Abbeyfield Rose' × 'Roddy McMillan'
Repeat flowering ı *Strong fragrance*

HABIT Bush H/W 1m/1m (3ft/3ft) ı ZONES 6–11

'Grace de Monaco'

HYBRID TEA ı LIGHT PINK

As beautiful as the Hollywood star who became a real-life princess, 'Grace de Monaco' was named by Francis Meilland in 1956 as a wedding present to Grace Kelly. It bears big, shapely,

'Grace de Monaco'

'Goldmarie'

'Gordon's College'

love with 'Golden Wings', the only one of his rose creations still commonly met with. It is one of the most outstanding of all modern Shrub Roses: continuous in its flowering, delicious in its scent and golden colour, and perfect in its form, although the flowers are not always perfectly single. Sometimes they indulge in an extra petal or two. The plant is upright and bushy, and the foliage is matt and medium green.

Shepherd, USA, 1956
('Soeur Thérèse' × *R. pimpinellifolia* 'Altaica') ×
'Ormiston Roy'
Repeat flowering ı *Slight fragrance*

HABIT Bush H/W 1.5m/1.2m (5ft/4ft) ı ZONES 4–9

🌹 Royal Horticultural Society Award of Garden Merit 1993

'Goldmarie'

FLORIBUNDA ı DEEP YELLOW

'Goldmarie 82', 'Goldmarie Nirp'

The original 'Goldmarie' was a deep yellow Floribunda with slight scent, ruffled flowers and the bad habit of becoming blotched with red as the flowers aged. Its 1984 replacement from Reimer Kordes answers the same description, except that the red is simply a flush on the backs of the outside petals, which retain their clear gold until they drop. The bush is more compact, the foliage a paler green. The original 'Goldmarie' apparently played no part in the creation of the new one.

KORfalt ı Kordes, Germany, 1984
(['Arthur Bell' × 'Zorina'] × ['Honeymoon' ×
'Dr A. J. Verhage']) × (seedling × 'Friesia')
Repeat flowering ı *Slight fragrance*

HABIT Bush H/W 1.2m/1m (4ft/3ft) ı ZONES 5–11

🌹 Golden Rose of the Hague 1988

'Graceland'

'Graham Thomas'

a Bourbon in their cupped formation and its fine fragrance, it remains a classic rose. The plant is very tall, and in warm climates it is best treated as a moderate climber or pillar rose. The leaves are mid-green, the flowering profuse.

AUSmas ı Austin, England, UK, 1983
Seedling × ('Charles Austin' × 'Iceberg' seedling)
Repeat flowering ı Intense fragrance

HABIT Bush H/W 1.8m/1.2m (6ft/4ft) ı ZONES 5–11
Royal Horticultural Society Award of Garden Merit 1993

'Granada'

HYBRID TEA ı RED BLEND

'Donatella'

When the author was young, one of the world's best-loved roses was a sweetly scented cerise and gold Hybrid Tea of 1932 called 'Talisman'. Old-timers remember it fondly, but when its great-granddaughter 'Granada' came out in 1963, it vanished from the catalogues almost overnight. Similar in its blend of colors, 'Granada' is superior in size, in form, in freedom of bloom and in scent, too – it won the American Rose Society's Gamble Medal for fragrance in 1968. The double flowers are borne one to a stem. Its only fault is that the olive-green leaves are apt to get mildew in sunless climates, although in sunny ones it remains a favorite.

Lindquist USA, 1963
'Tiffany' × 'Cavalcade'
Repeat flowering ı Intense, damask fragrance

HABIT Bush H/W 1.5m/1.2m (5ft/4ft) ı ZONES 5–11
All-America Rose Selection 1964, American Rose Society James Alexander Gamble Fragrance Medal 1968

'Peace'-like blooms in softest rose-pink, one to a stem and as sweetly perfumed as a princess should be. The plant is vigorous, although not tall, with glossy, green foliage – not always as free from black spot as it might be – and few thorns. Plant it in the company of the later, and equally lovely, 'Princesse de Monaco'.

MEImit ı Meilland, France, 1956
'Peace' × 'Michèle Meilland'
Repeat flowering ı Intense fragrance

HABIT Bush H/W 1.5m/1.2m (5ft/4ft) ı ZONES 5–11

'Graceland'

HYBRID TEA ı MEDIUM YELLOW

There have been two roses named after the home of the late Elvis Presley, this one and a 'Patio Rose' raised in Britain in 1989. That one seems to have vanished without trace from the catalogues, and (despite its high awards) Bill Warriner's yellow Hybrid Tea is rather less popular than it used to be. It is still a good rose, though, double, nicely shaped and a pleasing shade of lemon-yellow. The flowers are borne singly, but have virtually no scent. The bush is strong, with light green leaves. It does best in warm climates.

JACel ı Warriner, USA, 1988
'New Day' × seedling
Repeat flowering ı No fragrance

HABIT Bush H/W 1.5m/1.2m (5ft/4ft) ı ZONES 6–11
All-America Rose Selection 1988, The Hague Gold Medal 1988

'Graham Thomas'

SHRUB ı DEEP YELLOW

The late Graham Stuart Thomas was one of the leading figures in the revival of interest in Old Garden Roses, on which he was arguably the world's leading authority. He frequently lamented the rarity of the ochre-toned yellow of such as 'Lady Hillingdon' among the Moderns. It was appropriate that David Austin dedicated the first of his yellow 'English Roses' to him, for it is ochre-yellow, at least in cool climates; in warm ones it is a more conventional gold and fades a little. With its double flowers like

'Granada'

The 'Peace' Rose

In 2005 a very special rose celebrated its diamond jubilee. 'Peace' was introduced to the American public on 29 April 1945, a date that also marked the fall of Berlin at the end of World War II. That same year, at a meeting of 50 delegations of the United Nations in San Francisco, the head of each delegation received a small vase containing a single 'Peace' rose, accompanied by a card bearing the following message:

> This is the 'Peace' rose which was christened at the Pacific Rose Society exhibition in Pasadena on the day Berlin fell. We hope that the 'Peace' rose will influence men's thoughts for everlasting world peace.

At that historic moment, 'Peace' had fame thrust upon it, but the truth was that it was already a great rose in its own right, representing a major breakthrough in hybridizing and setting a standard for perfect symmetry of bloom form, color, vigor and substance that remains unequalled today.

Birth of a special rose

The story begins at Antibes in the south of France, home to the now-famous rose-breeders the House of Meilland. In 1935, the then 23-year-old Francis Meilland executed his master pollinating stroke and gave birth to a wonderful new rose. He pollinated an unnamed seedling (number 3–35) with the Hybrid Tea 'Margaret McGredy'. The records show that 55 flowers were pollinated, from which emerged 52 hips, giving 800 seedlings. Of these 800 seedlings, 50 were propagated in 1936 for further trial. In the fall/autumn of 1936, Francis and his father, Antoine, were able to admire a bloom of 'Peace' for the very first time. Francis Meilland recounted the story in his article 'My Masterpiece', published in *The Rose Annual 1953* (National Rose Society of Great Britain, now the Royal National Rose Society):

It was not very sturdy, this little 3–35 plant, and there was nothing about it to attract attention. It was during the summer of 1936 that a few eyes were budded for the first time. Under the influence of extremely favourable weather conditions during that Autumn of 1936, these few buds produced flowers quite marvellous in shape and size with a greenish tinge, warming to yellow, and progressively impregnated with carmine round the edges of the petals.

This remarkable new rose was receiving great praise from visitors to Antibes. Fortunately, bud eyes were dispatched to the Conrad-Pyle Company, the American agents for Meilland, and also to Germany and Italy. When war broke out on 3 September 1939, communications ceased between rose-hybridizers. To commemorate the end of the suffering of World War II, the Conrad-Pyle Company decided to introduce the rose to American rose-growers under the name of 'Peace'. In Italy and Germany, it was known as 'Gioia' ('Joy') and 'Gloria Dei' respectively; in France it was named 'Madame A. Meilland' in memory of the raiser's late mother.

Regrettably, Francis Meilland died a young man at the age of 46, in 1958. Rose-hybridizing is often a long, slow process, requiring

many years of painstaking research before a masterpiece is created. 'Peace' was born right at the beginning of Francis Meilland's career and allowed his family to enjoy the royalty rewards of his efforts and to establish the House of Meilland as the premier rose-hybridizing company in France.

ABOVE LEFT 'Peace'
ABOVE RIGHT 'Chicago Peace'
RIGHT 'Michèle Meilland' is a cross between 'Joanna Hill' and 'Peace'.

Parentage of 'Peace'

From the time of its introduction, debate and discussion about the exact genealogy of 'Peace' has flourished in the rose world. Scholars have finally reached a consensus that the family tree as outlined in the diagram shown here is correct. It illustrates a highly complex genealogy, involving the use of many award-winning roses of the early twentieth century. Needless to say, the finest examples of 'Peace' have garnered many honors for their beauty and perfection.

Hybridized progeny of 'Peace'

The appearance of 'Peace' provoked a flurry of activity among rose-breeders anxious to use it in their breeding programs. Since 1945, the genetic material from 'Peace' has produced a staggering number of offspring – almost 500 in all! The rose registration data of the period 1950–1970 reveal that most amateur and professional hybridizers were quickly aware of the potential of 'Peace' and made many crosses to capitalize on its outstanding characteristics. A whole series of high-quality Hybrid Teas, using 'Peace' as both the seed parent and the pollen parent, was introduced, including 'Grace de Monaco' (Meilland, 1956), 'Gold Crown' (Kordes, 1961), 'Mischief' (McGredy, 1961), 'Memoriam' (Von Abrams, 1962) and 'Perfume Delight' (Weeks, 1984).

Many roses with 'Peace' as their pollen parent have been recognized as All-America Rose Selections winners, including 'Christian Dior', 'Garden Party' and 'Royal Highness'. Furthermore, there is no other cultivar in the history of the rose with a demonstrated list of sports comparable to those produced from 'Peace'. Since 1954, there have been 20 sports reported from 'Peace', of which 'Chicago Peace', 'Flaming Peace' and 'Speaker Sam' are the best known.

What makes it marvellous

What was so special about the 'Peace' rose? The first Hybrid Tea, 'La France', appeared in 1867. The early Hybrid Teas that followed in the late nineteenth and early twentieth centuries were small, and although they had pleasingly symmetrical flowers, they generally came on weak stems, causing the bloom heads to droop – all due to their inheritance from their frost-tender mothers, the Teas. In the early twentieth century, breeders began to

ABOVE The many descendants of 'Peace' include, from left to right, 'Pink Peace', 'Cannes Festival', 'Chanteclerc', 'Grand'mère Jenny' and 'Royal Highness'.

LEFT 'Astrée' is a cross between 'Peace' and 'Blanche Mallerin'.

take a keen interest in this class, and improving plant habit and vigor became the paramount concern. Many Hybrid Teas were much improved in stem strength over their early cousins, and provided a wider palette of colors than the early pinks. By the 1930s, rose-breeders had a good genetic pool to experiment with in their attempts to produce the ultimate Hybrid Tea. 'Peace' was the result of these intense experiments, depending on many older Hybrid Teas in its complex family tree. The plant was exceptionally vigorous and healthy. But the real achievement lay in the bloom. It was of magnificent size, almost 12–15cm (5–6in) in diameter, with the petals unfurling in a pleasingly symmetrical fashion, such that when the flower was two-thirds open, it displayed the ideal shape of a Hybrid Tea – the shape that rose-breeders had dreamed of for decades. What is more, the color was a delicate yellow brushed with raspberry-pink at the perimeter of each petal, the pink framing for the viewer the overall three-dimensional shape. Indeed, perfection had been attained!

Francis Meilland gave the world of roses a genetic treasure trove when he produced 'Peace'. The rich legacy of that discovery has inspired rose-breeders ever since to emulate the high standard set by 'Peace'. Today it is recognized as the world's favorite rose and is well deserving of the accolade 'The Rose of the Twentieth Century'.

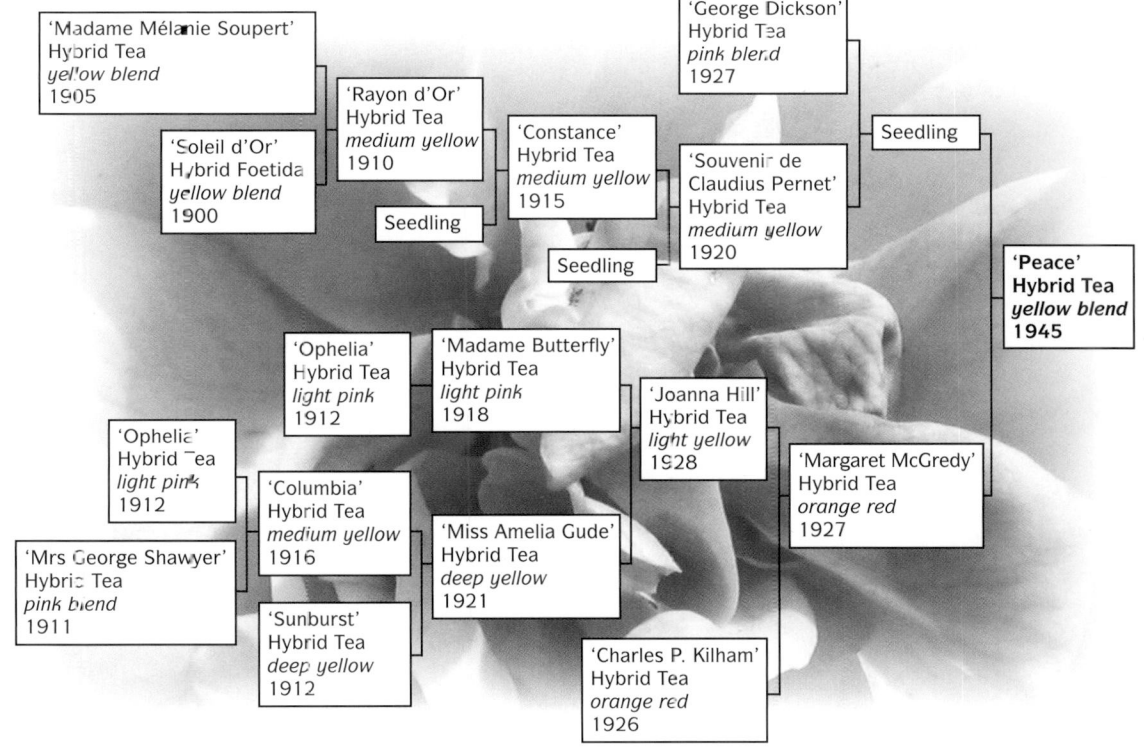

'Madame Mélanie Soupert'
Hybrid Tea
yellow blend
1905

'Soleil d'Or'
Hybrid Foetida
yellow blend
1900

'Rayon d'Or'
Hybrid Tea
medium yellow
1910

Seedling

'Constance'
Hybrid Tea
medium yellow
1915

'George Dickson'
Hybrid Tea
pink blend
1927

'Souvenir de Claudius Pernet'
Hybrid Tea
medium yellow
1920

Seedling

Seedling

'Ophelia'
Hybrid Tea
light pink
1912

'Madame Butterfly'
Hybrid Tea
light pink
1918

'Joanna Hill'
Hybrid Tea
light yellow
1928

'Peace'
Hybrid Tea
yellow blend
1945

'Ophelia'
Hybrid Tea
light pink
1912

'Columbia'
Hybrid Tea
medium yellow
1916

'Miss Amelia Gude'
Hybrid Tea
deep yellow
1921

'Margaret McGredy'
Hybrid Tea
orange red
1927

'Mrs George Shawyer'
Hybrid Tea
pink blend
1911

'Sunburst'
Hybrid Tea
deep yellow
1912

'Charles P. Kilham'
Hybrid Tea
orange red
1926

'Grand Hotel'

'Grande Amore'

'Grande Duchesse Charlotte'

'Grand Masterpiece'

'Grand Hotel'

LARGE FLOWERED CLIMBER ı MEDIUM RED

'Hotel Royal'

So mixed is the parentage of Modern Roses that the results of a particular cross can be difficult to predict. Sam McGredy, seeking the huge, fire-red flowers of 'Schlössers Brilliant' on a sturdier plant, crossed it with the modern Shrub Rose 'Heidelberg' and got 'Uncle Walter' in 1963. It was so vigorous that it was reclassified as a modern Shrub – and as the plant matured, the flowers shrank to middling size. Try again, thought Sam, and in 1972 the same cross produced 'Grand Hotel'. The double flowers are what was hoped for – large, brilliantly red and shapely – but this time the plant is an out-and-out climber. Grow it for exhibition; it repeats quite well. The foliage is dark green and susceptible to black spot.

MACtel ı McGredy, New Zealand, 1972
'Schlössers Brilliant' × 'Heidelberg'
Repeat flowering ı *Slight fragrance*

HABIT Climber H/W 2.5m/1.2m (8ft/4ft) ı ZONES 6–11

'Grand Masterpiece'

HYBRID TEA ı MEDIUM RED

This rose is becoming hard to find now, although its luminous colour, large size and perfect form still earn it admirers, especially among exhibitors. There is little fragrance, but the stems are long, a characteristic American show judges admire, and the double flowers are borne quite freely on a bush of average height. The leaves are mid-green, and like those of so many red roses may need protection from mildew.

JACpie ı Warriner, USA, 1978
Seedling × 'Tonight'
Repeat flowering ı *Slight fragrance*

HABIT Bush H/W 1.5m/1.2m (5ft/4ft) ı ZONES 5–11

'Grand Siècle'

HYBRID TEA ı PINK BLEND

'Grand Age', 'Great Century', 'Greatest Century'

English-speaking rosarians have never paid the attention they should to the creations of the French breeders André Chabert

'Grand Siècle'

and Pierre Delbard. Just look at the picture of 'Grand Siècle'. What a grand century it would be if more roses like this were introduced! First placed before the public in 1977, the double flowers of 'Grand Siècle' are of remarkable coloring – pastel pink with touches of cream – beautiful shape and good size. The fragrance is light, the bush strongly branching, with mid-green foliage. After a few years out of the catalogues, it is enjoying new popularity in Australia.

DELegran ı Delbard-Chabert, France, 1986
(['Queen Elizabeth' × 'Provence'] × ['Michèle Meilland' × 'Bayadère']) × (['Voeux de Bonheur' × 'Meimet'] × ['Peace' × 'Dr Debat'])
Repeat flowering ı *Slight fragrance*

HABIT Bush H/W 1.5m/1.2m (5ft/4ft) ı ZONES 5–11

'Grande Amore'

HYBRID TEA ı DARK RED

'Kordes Rose Grande Amore'

Kordes has released two roses of this name, both red – a large mid-crimson Hybrid Tea in 1968 and a darker, smaller one intended for greenhouse growers in 2004. The richly scented original is shown here. Its classic, urn-shaped buds open to exhibition-quality blooms, which are borne freely and in quick succession on a compact plant with leathery, dusky green foliage. Give it the best of cultivation – it deserves it.

KORliegra ı Kordes, Germany, 1968
Parentage undisclosed
Repeat flowering ı *Slight fragrance*

HABIT Bush H/W 1.5m/1.2m (5ft/4ft) ı ZONES 5–11

'Grand'mère Jenny'

exhibitors. Like its parent, it has little fragrance, its stems are long, and the double flowers are long-lasting, holding their shape to the very end. The bush is strong, if a little on the short side, and the dark green leaves have a good record of health.

Ballin, USA, 1991
'Cleo' sport
Repeat flowering ɪ *Light fragrance*

HABIT Bush H/W 1.2m/1.2m (4ft/4ft) ɪ ZONES 7–11

'Green Fire'

FLORIBUNDA ɪ DEEP YELLOW

Sometimes, in cool weather, there is a touch of green in the heart of these flowers, but most days 'Green Fire' appears clear yellow. The 8cm (3in) flowers, borne in clusters, have 13 petals and open to show golden stamens. The shrub is bushy, with glossy, green foliage. The whole effect is rather like a slightly paler but larger-flowered 'Allgold'. 'Green Fire' is hard to find now, but if you don't insist on your Floribundas having flowers like small exhibition Hybrid Teas, it is well worth seeking out. Warm climates suit it best.

Swim, USA, 1958
'Goldilocks' × seedling
Repeat flowering ɪ *Slight fragrance*

HABIT Bush H/W 1.2m/1m (4ft/3ft) ɪ ZONES 5–11

'Grande Duchesse Charlotte'

HYBRID TEA ɪ MEDIUM RED

Fame is as fleeting in the world of roses as elsewhere: around the end of World War II, the constant winner of gold medals was 'Grande Duchesse Charlotte', raised by Ketten Brothers of the tiny duchy of Luxembourg and named, patriotically, for their then ruler. Alas, it is now but a memory, like the grand lady herself. Which is a pity, as there has never been a rose quite like it: long buds open to huge, 25-petalled blooms in a unique shade of hot red, and the foliage is glossy and dark green. It still survives in collections of AARS winners (it won in 1943), and the nursery trade should revive it.

Ketten, Luxembourg, 1942
Parentage unknown
Repeat flowering ɪ *Slight fragrance*

HABIT Bush H/W 1.5m/1.2m (5ft/4ft) ɪ ZONES 5–11
🏅 Rome Gold Medal 1938, Portland (Oregon, USA) Gold Medal 1941, All-America Rose Selection 1943

'Grand'mère Jenny'

HYBRID TEA ɪ YELLOW BLEND

'Grem'

'Peace' is known as 'Madame A. Meilland' in France in memory of the mother of the raiser,

Francis Meilland. 'Grand'mère Jenny', a seedling of 'Peace' and not unlike it in color, takes the family history back a generation, to the raiser's grandmother. It is a smaller, looser flower than its parent (23 petals against 43), the yellow and pink tones more pronounced, the scent stronger, and the bush more slender in habit, with glossy, dark green foliage. Some people find it more refined and elegant. It was raised in 1950 and is, of course, adorned with gold medals.

Meilland, France, 1950
'Peace' × ('Jul en Potin' × 'Sensation')
Repeat flowering ɪ *Moderate fragrance*

HABIT Bush H/W 1.5m/1.2m (5ft/4ft) ɪ ZONES 6–11
🏅 (Royal) National Rose Society Gold Medal 1950, Rome Gold Medal 1955

'Great Scott'

HYBRID TEA ɪ MEDIUM PINK

'Great Scott!' Is that what Don and Paula Ballin exclaimed when they saw a bush of the pale pink 'Cleo' in their garden suddenly bearing a flower of deeper, luminous rose-pink? History doesn't say, but the sport was carefully propagated and the new rose introduced. It is not very widely available, but its perfect form and lovely color have won it a faithful following among American

'Great Scott'

'Green Fire'

'Greensleeves'

'Greensleeves'

FLORIBUNDA ı WHITE

Few flower arrangers can resist green flowers, and while there have been some rather pleasant pale green Hybrid Teas bred for the greenhouse growers recently, they all seem to go plain white in the garden. 'Green-sleeves', despite its age, is one of the very few that performs out of doors, although even so it is an erratic performer in the gar-den – the bush is on the leggy side, the dark green leaves are prone to black spot and mil-dew, and the semi-double flowers are apt to go blotchy in rain or hot sun. They are pink in the bud, but if cut when half-open they will open palest green in the vase and hold their rare tint for days. Then all is forgiven!

HARlenten ı Harkness, England, UK, 1980
('Rudolph Timm' × 'Arthur Bell') × (['Pascali' ×
'Elizabeth of Glamis'] × ['Sabine' × 'Violette Dot'])
Repeat flowering ı *Slight fragrance*
HABIT Bush H/W 1.2m/1m (4ft/3ft) ı ZONES 5–11
❀ Rome Gold Medal 1979

'Guinée'

'Grey Dawn'

FLORIBUNDA ı MAUVE BLEND

Is this unique rose a Floribunda? Or is it a Hybrid Tea? It depends on which catalogue you are reading. Whatever it is, it is a beautiful rose, officially classed as a mauve blend. In reality it appears rather as if a grey shadow has been cast over tints of palest pink and gold. The blooms have 45 petals and are of medium

size, and lightly fragrant. The foliage is a glossy green and the plant is bushy, with straight, smooth stems for the flower arranger.

LeGrice, England, UK, 1975
'Brownie' × 'News'
Repeat flowering ı *Moderate fragrance*
HABIT Bush H/W 1.2m/1m (4ft/3ft) ı ZONES 5–11

'Grootendorst Supreme'

HYBRID RUGOSA ı DARK RED

This is a sport from 'F. J. Grootendorst', which some people prefer to the original, as the flowers are a much more attractive shade of dark garnet-red. They are just as prettily fringed, but they are a shade smaller, and most growers report that it is not as vigorous and easily grown as its parent. Like its parent, it is scentless.

Grootendorst, The Netherlands, 1936
'F. J. Grootendorst' sport
Repeat flowering ı *No fragrance*
HABIT Bush H/W 1.2m/1m (4ft/3ft) ı ZONES 4–10

'Gruss an Aachen'

FLORIBUNDA ı LIGHT PINK

How to classify this old and famous rose, a cross between a Hybrid Perpetual and a Polyantha? Prune it as a Floribunda and it can be used as a bedding rose. Or you might prefer to go lightly with the shears and allow it to make a smallish Shrub, like one of the 'English Roses'. But do not forgo the pleasure of its pearly pink and cream flowers, full-petalled like an Old Garden Rose and quite deliciously fragrant. The very double flowers are born in clusters; the foliage is leaden green. The German raiser named it in tribute to the ancient cathedral city, the imperial capital of Charlemagne.

Geduldig, Germany, 1909
'Frau Karl Druschki' × 'Franz Deegen'
Repeat flowering ı *Sweet fragrance*
HABIT Bush H/W 45cm/45cm (18in/18in) ı ZONES 4–11

'Guinée'

CLIMBING HYBRID TEA ı DARK RED

There is no color more desired in roses than the deepest of velvety reds, but none that the rose seems less willing to offer. Few of the darkest red roses are really good 'doers'. 'Guinée' is one of the most reliable of them.

'H. C. Andersen'

'Grey Dawn'

At its best, there are few roses to match the lovely form, sweet scent and almost-black coloring of its double flowers, but it is only of fairly modest vigor, and unless you treat it well there will be no repeat flowers. The foliage is olive-green. It was a 1938 triumph for Charles Mallerin. The name is intended to suggest Darkest Africa, not golden guineas!

Mallerin, France, 1938
'Souvenir de Claudius Denoyel' × 'Ami Quinard'
Repeat flowering ı *Intense fragrance*
HABIT Climber H/W 3m/1.8m (10ft/6ft) ı ZONES 5–11
Lyon Prix de La Rose Parfumée 1938

'Gruss an Aachen'

'H. C. Andersen'

FLORIBUNDA ı DARK RED

'America's Choice', 'Hans Christian Andersen', 'Touraine'

The great Danish author of children's stories was a great lover of the rose, which features in many of his tales. Sadly, he never had a garden of his own; but we who have one may honor his memory by growing his rose, which ranks among the very best of the red Floribundas. Usually borne in quite large sprays, the smallish flowers are clear blood-red without the hardness of tone that spoils some others, and it holds clean until the petals drop. The semi-double blooms are neatly shaped and show their stamens, and the bush is well clad with handsome, bronze-tinted foliage. Its disease resistance is very good.

POULander ı Poulsen, Denmark, 1986
'Royal Occasion' × seedling
Repeat flowering ı *Slight fragrance*
HABIT Bush H/W 110cm/75cm (3ft 6in/2ft 6in) ı ZONES 5–11

'Hanayome'

HYBRID TEA ı LIGHT PINK

'Flowery Bride'

Nothing is more frustrating than to see a beautiful rose at a flower show and not be able to find out anything about it. I was much taken with this softly fragrant, pastel-pink rose at the rose show in Osaka, Japan, but it wasn't listed in any of the Japanese catalogues

'Grootendorst Supreme'

that I consulted. All I could learn at the time was that the name had something to do with 'a flower in a dream' – beautifully apt for a rose of such delicacy. The foliage is leathery, not dream-like at all, and the flowers would indeed be an exhibitor's dream. In fact, the Japanese name translates as 'the bride', after the heroine of a popular *manga* called *Bara no Hanayome*, 'The Bride of the Rose'.

Keihan, Japan, 1970
'Michèle Meilland' × 'Anne Letts'
Repeat flowering ı *Moderate fragrance*
HABIT Bush H/W 1.2m/1m (4ft/3ft) ı ZONES 6–11

'Hanayome'

'Happy'

'Hansa'

'Happiness'

'Handel'

LARGE FLOWERED CLIMBER ı RED BLEND

'Haendel'

Sam McGredy once remarked that of all the fine roses he had raised, 'Handel' was a special favorite. It is easy to see why: it is a very pretty and distinctive rose, white with a touch of cream at the centre and a piping of hot pink around the outside of each petal. The Floribunda-style flowers only just count as double, and they do not have much scent, but you cannot have everything! The olive-green, glossy-leafed plant takes its time to

build up its branches – you could not call it rampageous – and also to settle down to flowering freely. Be patient, and keep an eye out for black spot.

MACha ı McGredy, Northern Ireland, UK, 1965
'Columbine' × 'Heidelberg'
Repeat flowering ı *Slight fragrance*

HABIT Climber H/W 2.5m/1.8m (8ft/6ft) ı ZONES 6–11

🏵 Portland (Oregon, USA) Gold Medal 1975, Royal Horticultural Society Award of Garden Merit 1993

'Hannah Gordon'

FLORIBUNDA ı PINK BLEND

'Raspberry Ice'

Reimer Kordes named this rose in tribute to a popular British television star, but as she isn't very well known overseas, some United States and Australian nurseries prefer the name 'Raspberry Ice'. There are three other roses of that name, however, so let us stick with Miss Gordon! Whatever you call it, this is a fine and popular rose, strong in growth, healthy in its leathery foliage and abundant in bloom. Borne in medium-sized clusters, the long-lasting flowers are a little reminiscent of 'Handel' in their pink-edged white petals, although they are more double and not quite so elegantly formed. They have little scent.

KORweiso ı Kordes, Germany, 1983
Repeat flowering ı *Slight fragrance*

HABIT Bush H/W 1m/1m (3ft/3ft) ı ZONES 6–11

'Hansa'

HYBRID RUGOSA ı MEDIUM RED

How you rate this Hybrid Rugosa will depend very much on the severity of your winters. In places like the Mid-West of the United States and in Canada it is much admired for its extreme hardiness and its double flowers of purple-red. In milder places its legginess of habit (unusual in a Rugosa) and its habit of fading in hot sun have cost it admirers. The foliage is bright green and wrinkled. It flowers quite freely all season and is sweetly fragrant, with the characteristic Rugosa note of cloves.

Schaum and Van Tol, The Netherlands, 1905
Parentage unknown
Repeat flowering ı *Intense, clove-rose fragrance*

HABIT Bush H/W 1.2m/1m (4ft/3ft) ı ZONES 3–10

'Happiness'

HYBRID TEA ı MEDIUM RED

'Rim', 'Rouge Meilland'

As the world's bestselling crimson flower-shop rose for more than 20 years, 'Rouge Meilland' must have made a fortune for the

'Hannah Gordon'

Meilland family. No wonder they recycled the name in 1984 after the patent (and the royalties!) finished. It will save confusion if we all agree to use the American name 'Happiness' for the 1948 original, which is still around, its flat, 38-petalled flowers as warm and unfading a crimson as ever, the stems as long, the bush as tall. The foliage is dark sage-green. Like all greenhouse roses, it needs a warm climate to grow well out of doors, and there is little scent.

Meilland, France, 1954
('Rome Glory' × 'Tassin') × ('Chas P. Kilham' × ['Chas P. Kilham' × 'Capichine Chambard'])
Repeat flowering ı *Sight fragrance*

HABIT Bush H/W 1.5m/1m (5ft/3ft) ı ZONES 5–11

'Happy'

POLYANTHA ı MEDIUM RED

'Alberich'

In 1954, the Dutch hybridist De Ruiter brought out a series of dwarf roses that he called 'Compacta Roses', seven of them named for the Seven Dwarfs (but none for Snow White!). They are mostly dull reds

and pinks. Some say 'Happy' is the only one worth growing: it bears as many clusters of tiny crimson flowers as can be crammed onto the bush, but they are quite scentless. The foliage is a dull green. All are derived from 'Robin Hood', and were originally christened in German: 'Geisebrecht', 'Degenhard', 'Burkhard' and so on. Neither true Miniatures nor Polyanthas, they are now largely ignored.

De Ruiter, The Netherlands, 1954
Parentage undisclosed
Repeat flowering ı *No fragrance*

HABIT Bush H/W 45cm/30cm (18in/1ft) ı ZONES 5–10

'Harmonie'

HYBRID TEA ı ORANGE PINK

There are many fine roses in the salmon-pink to coral color group these days, and this one seems to be getting lost in the crowd. Still, it remains a good rose, large and high-centred with some 20 petals, very fragrant, and carried on long stems for cutting. The bush is strong, the lightly polished foliage mid-green.

KORtember ı Kordes, Germany, 1981
'Fragrant Cloud' × 'Uwe Seeler'
Repeat flowering ı *Intense, fruity fragrance*

HABIT Bush H/W 1.5m/1.2m (5ft/4ft) ı ZONES 6–11

🌹 Baden-Baden Gold Medal 1981

'Harry Wheatcroft'

HYBRID TEA ı YELLOW BLEND

'Caribia', 'Harry'

As flamboyant as the bewhiskered rose-lover and nurseryman for whom it is named (and in whose nursery it arose as a sport from 'Piccadilly' in 1972), 'Harry Wheatcroft' now blooms in his memory – he died in 1975. It is striped in scarlet and gold, and has the same large flowers and glossy, green foliage of 'Piccadilly'. From his base in Nottingham, Harry Wheatcroft travelled the world seeking new roses to introduce to rose-lovers in the United Kingdom; he used often to misquote Thomas Gray: 'Full many a flower is born to blush unseen – but not if I can help it!' The flowers are most brilliant and last longest in cool-summer climates.

Wheatcroft, England, UK, 1972
'Piccadilly' sport
Repeat flowering ı *Slight fragrance*

HABIT Bush H/W 1.5m/1.2m (5ft/4ft) ı ZONES 6–9

'Headliner'

HYBRID TEA ı PINK BLEND

Appropriately named, 'Headliner' is an eye-catching rose, white stained with deep pink at the petal edges, the pink taking over as the

'Harry Wheatcroft'

'Harmonie'

'Handel'

flower ages, rather in the manner of 'Double Delight', although this rose is both lighter in tone and much less fragrant. Large and with 40 petals, it is suitable for exhibition. The bush is strong and upright, with medium green foliage. Do not confuse this rose with 'Headline', a yellow-blend Hybrid Tea raised in Australia by George Dawson in 1970.

JACtu ı Warriner, USA, 1985
'Love' × 'Color Magic'
Repeat flowering ı Slight fragrance
HABIT Bush H/W 1.5m/1.2m (5ft/4ft) ı ZONES 6–11

'Headliner'

'Heart of Gold'

HYBRID TEA ı APRICOT BLEND

There were already two similarly named roses when this rose was introduced in 2003, but as the name celebrates the centenary of the charity Rotary International, which receives a portion of the profits, the choice is understandable. It is a handsome flower, large and shapely, in an attractive blend of peach and gold with the occasional touch of bronze. The bush is strong, the leaves dark and glossy, and its disease resistance is said to be very good. The other two roses are

'Heidesommer'

'Gold Heart', a yellow Hybrid Tea (McGredy, 1998), and an American-raised pink-blend variety, 'Heart o' Gold' (Dykstra, 1997).

COCtarlotte ı Cocker, Scotland, 2003
'Queen Charlotte' × 'Shirley Spain'
Repeat flowering ı Slight fragrance
HABIT Bush H/W 1.5m/1.2m (5ft/4ft) ı ZONES 6–10

'Heirloom'

'Heart of Gold'

'Helen Traubel'

'Heidesommer'

FLORIBUNDA ı WHITE

'Cevennes'

The breeders of Ground Cover Roses have a way to go before they achieve plants that can challenge *Hypericum calycinum* or the creeping junipers in usefulness. The roses are still deciduous (which means winter weeds can grow among their branches) and thorny (which makes them a trial to pull out). But Reimer Kordes's 'Heidesommer' comes as close as any yet to the ideal, making a low, spreading bush densely clad with shining, dark green leaves, against which the clusters of little white flowers positively sparkle. They appear all season, and have an elusive scent.

KORlirus ı Kordes, Germany, 1985
'The Fairy' × seedling
Repeat flowering ı *Intense fragrance*

HABIT Ground cover H/W 1.2m/1.2m (4ft/4ft) ı ZONES 5–11

'Heirloom'

HYBRID TEA ı MAUVE

The name might suggest a modern rose in the antique style after the manner of one of David Austin's, but the semi-double flowers are fairly conventional Hybrid Teas. They do, however, suggest a nineteenth-century rose in their delicious fragrance and in their colour, which varies between deep mauve and cool pink. Large and well filled with petals, they are freely borne on long stems on an upright bush with matt, green leaves that are rather prone to mildew. Warm climates suit it best.

JACloom ı Warriner, USA, 1972
Seedling × seedling
Repeat flowering ı *Intense, sweet fragrance.*

HABIT Bush H/W 1.5m/1.2m (5ft/4ft) ı ZONES 7–11

'Helmut Schmidt'

'Heritage'

'Helen Traubel'

HYBRID TEA ı PINK BLEND

Barely double with only 23 petals (although they form long buds and elegant, open blooms, borne one to a stem), 'Helen Traubel' is a star, even among the many famous roses from the garden of Californian Herbert Swim. It is of lovely coloring, a luminous blend of pink and apricot, and fragrant, too. The bush is tallish, with matt, leathery, green leaves and slender stems, and is both free-blooming and easy to grow. But a rose named for a celebrated opera star must be allowed a touch of temperament: 'Helen Traubel' resents hard pruning and is said to be difficult to propagate.

Swim, USA, 1951
'Charlotte Armstrong' × 'Glowing Sunset'
Repeat flowering ı *Strong, tea fragrance*

HABIT Bush H/W 1.2m/1m (4ft/3ft) ı ZONES 7–11

Rome Gold Medal 1951, All-America Rose Selection 1952

'Helmut Schmidt'

HYBRID TEA ı MEDIUM YELLOW

'Goldsmith', 'Simba'

The name of the great German statesman, a patron of the arts and lover of gardens, is appropriate for this noble rose, which remains one of the best-regarded pure yellow Hybrid Teas. Its double flowers are shapely and sweetly (if not powerfully) scented, and are borne in clusters on long stems. They last very well in the vase. The upright bush is strong and free-blooming, and the foliage is matt and dark green, with a good reputation for resistance to black spot.

KORbelma ı Kordes, Germany, 1979
'New Day' × seedling
Repeat flowering ı *Moderate fragrance*

HABIT Bush H/W 1.5m/1.2m (5ft/4ft) ı ZONES 6–11

Geneva Gold Medal 1979

'Heritage'

SHRUB ı LIGHT PINK

David Austin once nominated 'Heritage' as perhaps his favorite of all his 'English Roses', for its perfect Old Garden Rose form, opening cupped from shapely buds, for its delicate tones of pink and for its strong fragrance. The flowers are certainly lovely, and the well-branched bush with small, semi-glossy, dark green leaves is excellent, flowering freely all season. Although on the tall side, it remains bushy in warm climates.

AUSblush ı Austin, England, UK, 1985
Seedling × ('Wife of Bath' × 'Iceberg')
Repeat flowering ı *Intense, lemon fragrance*

HABIT Bush H/W 1.5m/1.2m (5ft/4ft) ı ZONES 6–11

'Hero'

SHRUB | MEDIUM PINK

It is a pity that 'Hero' is such a leggy grower – although you can get over its legginess by planting it in a group or using it as a small climber – for its double flowers are very pretty, deeply cup-shaped, fragrant and a lovely shade of clear pink. The foliage is semi-glossy and mid-green. Hero was, confusingly to modern ears, the *girl* for whom the Greek hero Leander swam the Hellespont.

AUShero | Austin, England, UK, 1983
'The Prioress' × seedling
Repeat flowering | *Intense fragrance*
HABIT Bush H/W 1.5m/1.2m (5ft/4ft) | ZONES 5–11

TOP LEFT 'High Esteem'
TOP RIGHT 'Hiroshima's Children'
BOTTOM LEFT 'Hero'
INSET 'Home & Garden'

'High Esteem'

HYBRID TEA | PINK BLEND

Peterson & Deering (the distributors of this large, exhibition-style rose) certainly showed their faith in the product when they named it 'High Esteem' and proceeded to charge $10 a plant, an unheard of price back in 1961. It is a huge bloom with some 50 petals, shapely

'Hoagy Carmichael'

'Hobby'

and fragrant, in an attractive medium pink with a silvery reverse, but the compact plant, with leathery, green leaves, is not all that free-flowering or particularly tolerant of cold winters. Grow it only for the show bench!

Von Abrams, USA, 1961
('Charlotte Armstrong' × 'Madame Henri Guillot') × ('Multnomah' × 'Charles Mallerin')
Repeat flowering ǀ *Fruity fragrance*

HABIT Bush H/W 1.2m/1m (4ft/3ft) ǀ ZONES 6–11

'Hiroshima's Children'

FLORIBUNDA ǀ YELLOW BLEND

This name commemorates 40 years of devotion by Dr Tomin Hamada to the victims of the atomic attacks of World War II on Japan. This is one of the loveliest of all the exhibition-style Floribundas, its medium-sized, double flowers, in their small clusters, being exquisite in their perfect form. They combine shades of cream and pale coral, the blend varying with the season. Lightly scented, 'Hiroshima's Children' is a delightful rose for cutting, but some say that it is not a terribly easy rose to grow to perfection. The bush is of open habit, with matt, green foliage.

HARmark ǀ Harkness, England, UK, 1985
Parentage undisclosed
Repeat flowering ǀ *Slight fragrance*

HABIT Bush H/W 1m/60cm (3ft/2ft) ǀ ZONES 5–11

'Hoagy Carmichael'

HYBRID TEA ǀ MEDIUM RED

When Stirling Macoboy photographed this rose it was still new and untried, although it was obvious that the very large size and perfect form of its double, rose-red flowers were the stuff of which exhibitors' dreams

were made. They still are, but exhibitors can be a fickle lot – especially when it comes to red roses – and 'Hoagy Carmichael' is dropping out of the catalogues now. The foliage is a dull mid-green and the bush needs winter protection in all but mild climates. There is little scent. Sam McGredy is obviously one of the many fans of the great American songwriter.

MACtitir ǀ McGredy, New Zealand, 1990
Parentage unknown
Repeat flowering ǀ *Slight fragrance*

HABIT Bush H/W 1.5m/1.2m (5ft/4ft) ǀ ZONES 7–11

'Hobby'

FLORIBUNDA ǀ ORANGE PINK

Though rarely seen now – current taste finds the individual blooms rather uninteresting, and there are many other Floribundas of similar color – 'Hobby' is still able to bring a generous splash of neon-like color to the garden with its sprays of deep rose-pink to coral flowers. The bush is upright, and the foliage dark green. There is very little scent. Herr Tantau has recycled the name for a pink 'Patio Rose' introduced in 2001.

TANob ǀ Tantau, Germany, 1955
('Schweizergrüss' × 'Red Favourite') × 'Käthe Divigneau'
Repeat flowering ǀ *Slight fragrance*

HABIT Bush H/W 1m/60cm (3ft/2ft) ǀ ZONES 6–11

'Hocus Pocus'

HYBRID TEA ǀ RED BLEND

This is essentially a greenhouse rose, and there are contradictory reports on its performance in the garden, some saying that although the bush is a bit leggy, it does quite

well and flowers freely, others that it sulks and gets mildew and black spot. Everyone agrees that the dark red flowers with their irregular stripes and splashes of pale yellow are unusual and eye-catching – and that they have no scent. They aren't especially large, but they are nicely shaped and last a very long time in the vase.

KORpocus ǀ Kordes, Germany, 2001
'Frisco' sport
Repeat flowering ǀ *No fragrance*

HABIT Bush H/W 1.2m/1m (4ft/3ft) ǀ ZONES 7–11

'Home & Garden'

FLORIBUNDA ǀ MEDIUM PINK

'Sister's Fairy Tale', 'Sister's Vigorosa'

The raiser describes the flowers as 'nostalgic', and indeed in their graceful clusters they do remind us of an Old Garden Rose with their full-petalled, informal shape and clear pink coloring – although not in scent. There isn't any! But the bush is thoroughly modern – compact, very free-blooming and with polished, dark green leaves, said to be outstandingly resistant to mildew and black spot. The only serious fault (apart from lack of scent) is that the flowers are rather fleeting in mid-summer heat. A cool-summer climate seems indicated. It is named for a European homemaking magazine.

KORgrasotra ǀ Kordes, Germany, 2002
Parentage undisclosed
Repeat flowering ǀ *No fragrance*

HABIT Bush H/W 1.2m/1m (4ft/3ft) ǀ ZONES 6–11

'Hocus Pocus'

'Honey Dijon'

'Honey Perfume'

'Honey Favorite'

'Honey Dijon'

GRANDIFLORA ı RUSSET

A curious name – does the raiser mean to
invite comparisons with 'Gloire de Dijon',
or was he thinking of Dijon mustard? Usually
borne in small clusters, the sweetly scented,
double flowers can be mustard-yellow, and
they can be the soft buff shade of 'Gloire de
Dijon' – but at their best (in cool weather)
they are a most unusual shade we might
describe as beige. It is the sort of color
flower arrangers adore. Usually borne in
small clusters, the flowers are not especially
large, but they are of good, high-centred
form and borne on long stems. The bush is
on the tall side, the foliage dark green and
with a good reputation for disease resistance.

WEKsproulses ı Sproul, USA, 2004
'Stainless Steel' × 'Singin' in the Rain'
Repeat flowering ı Sweet, fruity fragrance

HABIT Bush H/W 1.2m/1m (4ft/3ft) ı ZONES 6–11

'Honey Favorite'

HYBRID TEA ı LIGHT PINK

'Honey Favourite'

Introduced by Gordon Von Abrams in 1962,
this is a sport from the same raiser's 'Pink
Favorite' of 1956. It shares its parent's glossy,
disease-free leaves, good form and preference
for a cool climate, but scores over it, in the
opinion of many, for its delicacy of color.

The name promises a tone of yellow or at
least apricot, but in fact 'Honey Favorite'
is a soft pink, with just a touch of primrose
at the heart of the flower. The scent is only
slight, alas, but it is a good rose, undeserv-
edly neglected.

Von Abrams, USA, 1962
'Pink Favorite' sport
Repeat flowering ı Slight fragrance

HABIT Bush H/W 1.5m/1.2m (5ft/4ft) ı ZONES 6–11

'Honey Perfume'

FLORIBUNDA ı APRICOT BLEND

'Pam Golding'

An AARS winner from Jackson & Perkins in
the currently fashionable tones of old gold
and apricot. The informally styled flowers
are large for a Floribunda and borne usually
in smallish clusters. They are at their best
early and late in the season; in mid-summer
heat they soon fade almost to white. The
name overstates the fragrance, although it
is still quite pleasing, with, indeed, a note
of honey. The bush is upright and prolific,
with glossy, dark green leaves that some
reports suggest are not always quite as
resistant to black spot as they might be.

JACarque ı Zary, USA, 2004
Seedling × 'Amber Queen'
Repeat flowering ı Moderate, spicy fragrance

HABIT Bush H/W 1m/60cm (3ft/2ft) ı ZONES 6–11

🏵 All-America Rose Selection 2004

'Honeyflow'

'Honeyflow'

FLORIBUNDA I PINK BLEND

Raised by Australia's Frank Reithmuller in 1957, 'Honeyflow' is very like his more popular 'Carabella' in its light green, almost thornless bush, iron constitution and huge sprays of single blooms, which are white with just a hint of pink. 'Carabella' is a more positive color, although still pale, and so is more popular, but 'Honeyflow' scores in having the stronger perfume. It really does smell of honey. If not dead-headed, it has pretty orange hips in autumn.

Riethmuller, Australia, 1957
Parentage unknown
Repeat flowering I *Moderate, honey fragrance*
HABIT Bush H/W 1.5m/1.5m (5ft/5ft) I ZONES 6–11

'Hot Chocolate'

'Honor'

HYBRID TEA I WHITE

'Michèle Torr', 'Honour'

The second alphabetically of the three roses with which Bill Warriner and Jackson & Perkins swept the AARS awards in 1980 – 'Love', 'Honor' and 'Cherish' – 'Honor' has the largest flowers, in white with just a hint of lemon at the centre. With 23 petals they only just qualify as double, but they are of beautiful high-centred form and borne on long stems. 'Honor' remains a popular

exhibition rose in the United States, but Australian exhibitors complain that it opens too quickly and wish it had a few more petals. The bush is tall and upright, with dark green leaves and a reputation for tenderness to severe cold. The light fragrance is more noticeable in the vase than in the garden.

JAColite I Warriner, USA, 1980
Parentage undisclosed
Repeat flowering I *Slight fragrance*
HABIT Bush H/W 1.5m/1.2m (5ft/4ft) I ZONES 7–11
🏵 Portland (Oregon, USA) Gold Medal 1978, All-America Rose Selection 1980

'Hot Chocolate'

FLORIBUNDA I RUSSET

1986 was something of an *annus mirabilis* for amateur rose-breeders in New Zealand – Pat Stevens brought out 'Big Purple', and his colleague J. W. Simpson introduced 'Hot Chocolate'. Both were brand-new colors, one purple, the other a deep, rich orange, so dark that it can be fairly described as a velvet brown. The color, as with so many unusually toned roses, is best in the cool weather at either end of the season; hot summer pales it into ordinariness. The foliage is leathery, the growth acceptable, but the perfume is only slight.

SIMcho I Simpson, New Zealand, 1986
Parentage undisclosed
Repeat flowering I *Slight fragrance*
HABIT Bush H/W 1m/60cm (3ft/2ft) I ZONES 6–11
🏵 Gold Star of the South Pacific, Hamilton (New Zealand) 1986

'Honor'

'Hot Cocoa'

'Ice White'

'Ian Thorpe'

'Hot Cocoa'

FLORIBUNDA ˙ RUSSET

'Hot Chocolate', 'Kiwi', 'Nubya'

Take care not to confuse this rose with the previous one! The raisers describe it as 'smoky chocolate', but the American Rose Society has hit it in one – 'russet'. It only shows its unusual brown tones in cool weather; in mid-summer the flowers are apt to be plain brick-red. There are plenty of them through the season, however, and they are always nicely shaped and long-lasting on the bush and in the vase. The glossy-leafed bush is upright and its disease resistance is rated excellent, although winter protection will most likely be needed in cold climates. The European name 'Nubya' honors a beautiful Swiss pop singer.

WEKpaltlez ˙ Carruth, USA, 2003
('Playboy' × 'Altissimo') × 'Livin' Easy'
Repeat flowering ˙ Old rose fragrance

HABIT Bush H/W 1.5m/1m (5ft/3ft) ˙ ZONES 7–11

🏵 All-America Rose Selection 2003

'Ian Thorpe'

HYBRID TEA ˙ RUSSET

'Estelle', 'Estelle de Meilland'

Meilland created quite a stir a few years ago with a greenhouse rose in a unique combination of warm, soft brown with cream on the reverse called 'Leonidas'. The flower arrangers immediately fell in love with it, but in the garden it is usually a more conventional orange-red and the bush is an uncertain performer.

Similar in color, 'Ian Thorpe' ('Estelle' in Europe and the United States) is said to be a much better garden rose. It still needs the best of cultivation; but at their best in spring and the fall/autumn the flowers can be sensational – large and shapely enough for exhibition and of a startling color. Australian Olympic swimming champion Ian Thorpe has requested that the sale of his rose will benefit the foundation he has set up to assist underprivileged young people.

OLIjbrau ˙ Olij, The Netherlands, 1999
'Fantazia' × 'Madelon'
Repeat flowering ˙ Slight fragrance

HABIT Bush H/W 1.2m/1m (4ft/3ft) ˙ ZONES 7–11

'Ice White'

FLORIBUNDA ˙ WHITE

'Vision Blanc'

What Sam McGredy was hoping for when he introduced 'Ice White' in 1966 was a shorter, more manageable version of

'Iceberg', the world's bestselling white rose. He has certainly achieved that, although the public continues to prefer 'Iceberg'. The exhibitors, however, give the nod to this one, as the double flowers are larger and more classically formed and the clusters are symmetrical and beautifully spaced. The foliage is glossy, a little darker than that of 'Iceberg'; the scent is only faint. What is astonishing is how it came about – all of its parents are orange-toned!

McGredy, Northern Ireland, UK, 1966
'Madame Léon Cuny' × ('Orange Sweetheart' × 'Tantau's Triumph')
Repeat flowering ˙ Slight fragrance

HABIT Bush H/W 1m/1m (3ft/3ft) ˙ ZONES 6–11

🏵 Portland (Oregon, USA) Gold Medal 1970

'Iceberg'

FLORIBUNDA ˙ WHITE

'Fée des Neiges', 'Schneewittchen'

Everywhere roses are gown, 'Iceberg' is a bestseller, and deservedly so. It makes a tall, not too prickly bush, with healthy, light green leaves, and covers itself all season with large and small clusters of nicely shaped, double blooms. They are fragrant but not always stark white; cool weather often brings out a touch of pale pink. Prune it lightly. The only fault is that the flowers are not very long-lasting when cut. There is a splendid climbing version, and the bush is a very good choice for growing as a standard – but do buy from reliable suppliers

who select their budwood carefully or the flowers may be inferior and the leaves less disease-resistant than they should be. Two sports have been introduced recently, both from Australia: 'Brilliant Pink Iceberg' and 'Burgundy Iceberg'.

KORbin | Kordes, Germany, 1958
'Robin Hood' × 'Virgo'
Repeat flowering | *Good, fruity fragrance*

HABIT Bush H/W 1.2m/1m (4ft/3ft) | ZONES 6–11

World Federation of Rose Societies Hall of Fame 1983

'Iced Ginger'

FLORIBUNDA | ORANGE BLEND

If there is one thing the Irish agree on, on both sides of the border, it is a good rose. There was never any doubt that in 'Iced Ginger' Pat Dickson of County Down had a world-beater. Not a big rose, with some 45 petals, and cursed with an ungainly bush, it is nevertheless enchanting in its blends of pink and copper, and sweetly fragrant. The foliage is broad and olive-green but susceptible to black spot. It often flowers in clusters, and is thus sometimes listed as a Floribunda.

Dickson, Northern Ireland, UK, 1971
'Anne Watkins' × seedling
Repeat flowering | *Moderate, sweet fragrance*

HABIT Bush H/W m/60cm (3ft/2ft) | ZONES 5–11

'Iced Parfait'

FLORIBUNDA | LIGHT PINK

The great English hybridist Albert Norman once said that the genes of Modern Roses are such a mixed-up lot that the laws of heredity are more a consolation in explaining the failure of a cross than in predicting success. Sister Mary Xavier of Launceston in Tasmania must have had some help from above, because her cross between 'Pink Parfait' and 'Iceberg' came out just as one would expect. The picture tells all! The double blooms, borne in clusters, are a blend of very pale pinks, set against the light green foliage. 'Iced Parfait' has inherited its parents' reliability, too. It was featured on an Australian postage stamp in 2000.

Xavier, Australia, 1972
'Pink Parfait' × 'Iceberg'
Repeat flowering | *Moderate, fruity fragrance*

HABIT Bush H/W 1m/60cm (3ft/2ft) | ZONES 6–11

'Iced Parfait'

ABOVE 'Iced Ginger'
BELOW 'Iceberg'

'Innoxa Femille'

'Ingrid Bergman'

'Impatient'

FLORIBUNDA ı ORANGE RED

This 1984 AARS winner seems to be little known outside the United States, and even there it is less widely available than it used to be. At first sight it is just another bright orange-red Floribunda, but it is a strong plant with healthy, dark green foliage, and the flowers are given subtlety by the touch of yellow at the petal bases. They are about 8cm (3in) across, semi-double and shapely, and carried in small clusters. There is little scent. The branches are wickedly thorny, a cause of impatience in its admirers. It does very well in hot climates.

JACdew ı Warriner, USA, 1982
'America' × seedling
Repeat flowering ı *Slight fragrance*
HABIT Bush H/W 1.2m/60cm (4ft/2ft) ı ZONES 6–11
🌹 All-America Rose Selection 1984

'Impatient'

'Inner Wheel'

'Ingrid Bergman'

HYBRID TEA ı DARK RED

This lovely rose is dedicated to the memory of the Academy Award-winning Swedish actress. She was controversial in her lifetime, but there has never been any controversy about her rose, which has won award after award and remains a great favorite everywhere. The flowers are large, very double, perfectly formed and rich in colour, not losing their color or going magenta in midsummer heat, as so many red roses do. They are borne singly, on long stems and last very well in the vase. One might wish for more scent, but the bush

is strong and the glossy, dark green leaves are resistant to mildew and black spot.

POUlman ı Poulsen, Denmark, 1984
'Precious Platinum' × seedling
Repeat flowering ı *Light, spicy fragrance*
HABIT Bush H/W 1.5m/1.2m (5ft/4ft) ı ZONES 6–11
🌹 Belfast Gold Medal and Prize of the City of Belfast 1985, Madrid Gold Medal 1986, Golden Rose of The Hague 1987, World Federation of Rose Societies Hall of Fame 2000

'Inner Wheel'

FLORIBUNDA ı PINK BLEND

These dainty flowers are most unusual in their two-tone color, blending pale candy-pink with coral, and the sprays of blooms are borne on a low, bushy plant with good, dark green foliage. There is not much scent, but since its introduction 'Inner Wheel' has been well received as a decorative garden rose. It was named in honor of the Association of Rotarians' Ladies, a worldwide community service group.

FRYjasso ı Fryer, England, UK, 1984
'Pink Parfait' × 'Picasso'
Repeat flowering ı *Slight fragrance*
HABIT Bush H/W 1m/60cm (3ft/2ft) ı ZONES 5–11

'Innoxa Femille'

HYBRID TEA ı DARK RED

The British like to think of themselves as above crass commercialism, but ever since the 1970s many British rose-breeders have actively sought commercial sponsors for their roses, the idea being that the sponsors would use the rose in their own advertising, to everyone's profit. Witness the very clumsily named 'Innoxa Femille', which was sponsored by a cosmetics company. The double, dark crimson flowers, borne mostly singly but sometimes in small clusters, are well formed, and the bush is vigorous and resistant to mildew, with leathery, dark green leaves and plenty of prickles. The scent is only slight.

HARprincely ı Harkness, England, UK, 1983
'Red Planet' × 'Eroica'
Repeat flowering ı *Slight fragrance*
HABIT Bush H/W 1.5m/1.2m (5ft/4ft) ı ZONES 5–11

'International Herald Tribune'

FLORIBUNDA ı MAUVE

'Violetta', 'Viorita'

With its low growth and massive sprays of small, rather shapeless, double flowers,

'International Herald Tribune'

'International Herald Tribune' is more like
a Polyantha than a Floribunda. It would look
decidedly old hat if it were not for its most
attractive deep violet color, unusual among
Modern Roses, and its pleasant scent.
The foliage is semi-glossy and dark green.
For all its shortness, it is quite a strong
grower, but give it a sunny spot where
the sun can light it up. It was sponsored
by a leading British newspaper.

HARquantum ı Harkness, England, UK, 1984
Seedling × (['Orange Sensation' × 'Allgold'] ×
R. californica)
Repeat flowering ı Moderate, fruity fragrance
HABIT Bush H/W 60cm/60cm (2ft/2ft) ı ZONES 6–11
Tokyo Gold Medal 1982, Geneva Gold Medal and
Golden Rose 1983, Monza Gold Medal 1984

'Intrigue'

FLORIBUNDA ı MAUVE

In the old days, 'Intrigue' would probably
have been classed as a decorative Hybrid Tea,
for its clusters are small and its double flowers
large and loose in structure. They are fragrant,
borne on long stems for cutting, and are indeed
intriguing in color – deep magenta, paling only
slightly as they age. The bush is of average height,

'Intrigue'

with dark, plum-tinted leaves. Do not confuse
this 1984 introduction from Jackson & Perkins
with Kordes's 1978 red Floribunda, codename
KORlech. You will find that one here, too,
under its original name, 'Lavaglut'.

JACum ı Warriner, USA, 1982
'White Masterpiece' × 'Heirloom'
Repeat flowering ı Intense, citrus fragrance
HABIT Bush H/W 1m/60cm (3ft/2ft) ı ZONES 6–11
All-America Rose Selection 1984

'Invincible'

FLORIBUNDA ı DARK RED

'Fennica', 'Runtru'

This Dutch-bred, dark crimson rose
never became popular in Australia or
the United States, but it is still admired in
Europe. The double flowers are fairly large,
10cm (4in) in diameter, carried in sprays
on good stems for cutting, and last well in
the vase. The tall bush is compact, unlike
some red Floribundas, and mildew (the curse
of so many red roses) is not a problem. The
foliage is a dark bronze-green. Have Australians and Americans been missing out on an
excellent rose?

RUnatru ı De Ruiter, The Netherlands, 1983
'Rubella' × 'National Trust'
Repeat flowering ı Slight fragrance
HABIT Bush H/W 1m/60cm (3ft/2ft) ı ZONES 6–10

'Invincible'

'Irene of Denmark'

'Irish Elegance'

'Irish Fireflame'

'Irene of Denmark'

FLORIBUNDA ı WHITE

'Irene au Danmark', 'Irene von Dänemarck'

Until 'Iceberg' came along, 'Irene of Denmark' was widely regarded as the best white Floribunda available, and although no longer easy to find would still be a good choice if 'Iceberg' is too tall for you. The double flowers are smallish, but full of petals and fragrance, and the compact plant is strong and floriferous, with bright green leaves, which may need protection from black spot. It was raised by the Danish pioneer of Floribundas, Svend Poulsen, in 1948. Its heritage is a blend of Polyantha, Noisette and Hybrid Tea.

Poulsen, Denmark, 1948
'Orléans Rose' × ('Madame Plantier' × 'Edina')
Repeat flowering ı *Strong, fruity fragrance*
HABIT Bush H/W 1m/60cm (3ft/2ft) ı ZONES 6–10

'Irish Elegance'

HYBRID TEA ı ORANGE BLEND

During the reign of King Edward VII there was a vogue in Britain for single-flowered Hybrid Teas. 'Irish Elegance' is a fine example

raised by Alex Dickson, better known for his huge, many-petalled exhibition roses. It is a beauty, its long buds opening to wide, softly fragrant blossoms in soft tea-rose-yellow, just faintly brushed with pink. 'Bronze', the old catalogues said, and that is not a bad description. The bush is tall, the foliage semi-glossy. Check carefully when you buy — too many nurseries confuse this rose with 'Irish Fireflame'.

Dickson, Northern Ireland, UK, 1905
Parentage unknown
Repeat flowering ı *Moderate, tea fragrance*
HABIT Bush H/W 1.5m/1.2m (5ft/4ft) ı ZONES 7–11

'Irish Fireflame'

HYBRID TEA ı ORANGE BLEND

Another of Alex Dickson's singles, and a lovely companion to 'Irish Elegance'. Add 'Mrs Oakley Fisher' and 'Dainty Bess' and you have a delightful quartet for a period garden. The buds of 'Irish Fireflame' are indeed like brilliant scarlet flames, but they open to soft coral-pink. Of all the group, it is the most fragrant. The glossy-leafed bush is compact and free, the blooms coming in large clusters. Alas, Dickson's had a fire in their offices in 1921 and the records of the breeding of their roses up to then were all destroyed.

Dickson, Northern Ireland, UK, 1914
Parentage unknown
Repeat flowering ı *Strong, fruity fragrance*
HABIT Bush H/W 1.5m/1.2m (5ft/4ft) ı ZONES 6–11

'Irish Gold'

'Irish Gold'

HYBRID TEA ı MEDIUM YELLOW

'Grandpa Dickson'

Pat Dickson named this rose for his grandfather, a notable raiser of big, many-petalled exhibition roses (as were his father and grandfather before him), and indeed it is the sort of big, shapely flower that show judges adorn with blue ribbons. The American name 'Irish Gold' overstates the color: the flowers are rarely deeper than lemon-yellow and often show touches of pink. They are only slightly fragrant, and need protection against both rain and hot sun. The foliage is glossy and dark green, but the upright bushes are apt to be

'Iskra'

'Isabelle de France'

'Ivory Tower'

'Iskra'

CLIMBING FLORIBUNDA | MEDIUM RED

'MEIhaiti , 'Sparkling Scarlet'

Perhaps better known as 'Sparkling Scarlet', which describes its color exactly, 'Iskra' bears clusters of Floribunda-style flowers on a rather bushy climbing plant, well clothed with large, semi-glossy foliage. It is not overly vigorous, but repeats its bloom very well and makes quite a splash of color in the garden. It is a nice surprise to find the flowers fragrant, unusually so for a rose of this color.

MEIhati | Meilland, France, 1970
'Danse des Sylphes' × 'Zambra'
Repeat flowering | Moderate, fruity fragrance

HABIT Bush H/W 2.5m/1.8m (8ft/6ft) | ZONES 5–11

'Ivory Fashion'

FLORIBUNDA | WHITE

Eugene Boerner must have got a bit of a surprise when the marriage of two salmon roses gave birth to an ivory-white one. It would have been a very pleasant surprise, for 'Ivory Fashion' proved good enough to win the 1959 AARS award. In cool weather there are subtle hints of amber and palest pink. In all weather the semi-double flowers, borne in clusters, are elegant and shapely, the open blooms crowned by their crimson anthers, and there is fragrance as well. For all its elegance, it is an erratic performer, sometimes bushy and full of dark greyish green foliage, sometimes inclined to be straggling in its growth and shy with its flowers, but no one who has grown it once will willingly do without it again.

Boerner, USA, 1958
'Sonata' × 'Fashion'
Repeat flowering | Moderate, fruity fragrance

HABIT Bush H/W 1.2m/1m (4ft/3ft) | ZONES 6–10

All-America Rose Selection 1959

'Ivory Tower'

HYBRID TEA | WHITE

Raised by Reimer Kordes in Germany but now apparently available only in America, this upright-growing Hybrid Tea is one for connoisseurs. Its ivory-white is not a best-selling color in the rose world, but in this case it is saved from monotony by shadings of light pink and palest yellow. The long buds open to large, double, well-scented flowers, shapely enough for exhibition and long-lasting both on the bush and when cut. The foliage is glossy, dark green and corrugated. The bush will need winter protection in cold climates.

Kordes, Germany, 1979
'Königin der Rosen' × 'King's Ransom'
Repeat flowering | Light, tea fragrance

HABIT Bush H/W 1.2m/1m (4ft/3ft) | ZONES 7–11

'Jacqueline Nebout'

FLORIBUNDA | MEDIUM PINK

'City of Adelaide', 'Sanlam Roos'

Meilland originally dedicated this rose to Mme Jacqueline Nebout to celebrate her outstanding

on the small side and short-lived. For all its beauty, this rose is really only for the exhibitor. It prefers a cool-summer climate.

Dickson, Northern Ireland, UK, 1966
('Kordes's Perfecta' × 'Governador Braga da Cruz') × 'Piccadilly'
Repeat flowering | Moderate fragrance

HABIT Bush H/W 1.2m/1m (4ft/3ft) | ZONES 6–11

Royal National Rose Society President's International Trophy 1965, Belfast Gold Medal and Prize of the City of Belfast 1968, Portland (Oregon, USA) Gold Medal 1970

'Isabelle de France'

HYBRID TEA | ORANGE RED

An uncommon Hybrid Tea dating from 1956, 'Isabelle de France' is treasured by those who grow it, but it rarely appears in catalogues these days. The long, elegant buds open to double flowers of unusual coloring, a vermilion-scarlet with almost black tips to the petals. The flowers are long-lasting. The growth is vigorous, but perhaps its slightness of fragrance and proneness to black spot and mildew have told against it. The foliage is a leathery green.

Mallerin, France, 1956
'Peace' × ('Madame Joseph Perraud' × 'Opéra')
Repeat flowering | Slight fragrance

HABIT Bush H/W 1.4m/110cm (4ft 6in/3ft 6in) | ZONES 6–9

'Ivory Fashion'

'Jacqueline Nebout'

'Jadis'

'Jean du Tilleux'

work in developing and expanding the green spaces of the city of Paris, but we feel she would not have been offended to learn that in Australia it is named to mark the first Rose Festival to be held in Adelaide, a city also famous for its parklands. It is a charming flower, as elegantly shapely as a Hybrid Tea but carried in small clusters, and a pleasing shade of warm pink, which deepens in the fall/autumn. Lightly but pleasantly scented, the blooms are borne on long stems for cutting. The bush is compact, with glossy leaves and a good reputation for disease resistance.

MEIchoiju   ı   Meilland, France, 1989
Repeat flowering   ı   Mild fragrance

HABIT Bush H/W 1m/60cm (3ft/2ft)   ı   ZONES 6–11

🌹 Dublin Gold Medal 1988

'Jadis'

HYBRID TEA   ı   MEDIUM PINK

'Fragrant Memory'

'Jadis' is French, and means 'the old days', but this is an American rose raised by Bill Warriner for Jackson & Perkins in 1974, and later reintroduced by them as 'Fragrant Memory', for the benefit of those whose French is a little shaky. Either name is appropriate, for in its exquisite color – lilac washed over rose-pink – and intense perfume, 'Jadis' is indeed evocative of Old Garden Roses. But the form is modern, high-centred and full-petalled, and the bush is upright, with large, leathery, light green

'Jardins de Bagatelle'

leaves. You might have to watch out for mildew, something it inherits from both its parents.

JACdis   ı   Warriner, USA, 1974
'Chrysler Imperial' × 'Virgo'
Repeat flowering   ı   Intense fragrance

HABIT Bush H/W 1.5m/1.2m (5ft/4ft)   ı   ZONES 5–11

🌹 Monza Fragrance Award 1972

'Jardins de Bagatelle'

HYBRID TEA   ı   WHITE

'Queen Silvia', 'Sarah'

The 1986 creation of one of the world's leading rose hybridists, Marie-Louisette Meilland, 'Jardins de Bagatelle' is a wonderfully feminine bloom in palest cream flushed with delicate pink and yellow, large and very double, and sweetly fragrant, too. Like many pale roses,

it dislikes heavy rain. The bush is sturdy, with broad, glossy, medium green foliage. The Palace of Bagatelle in Paris, built by the Comte d'Artois, owes its inspiration to Queen Marie-Antoinette. It is in its beautiful gardens that the famous competition for new roses is held each year. It seems a pity that 'Jardins de Bagatelle' has not won the gold medal there, although it did win the award for perfume in 1984.

MEImafris   ı   Meilland, France, 1986
('Queen Elizabeth' × 'Elegy') × 'Laura '81'
Repeat flowering   ı   Intense fragrance

HABIT Bush H/W 1.4m/1m (4ft 6in/3ft)   ı   ZONES 6–11

🌹 Bagatelle (Paris) Fragrance Award 1984, Geneva Gold Medal 1984, Genoa Gold Medal 1986, Madrid Fragrance Award 1986, Poitiers Gold Medal 1986

'Jean du Tilleux'

HYBRID TEA | MEDIUM PINK

Sometimes a new rose will come from distinguished parents but seem to combine the wrong features. 'Jean du Tilleux' has inherited a good plant and nicely shaped, double flowers from the dark red 'King of Hearts', but it has failed to acquire the many petals and sweet scent of 'Golden Masterpiece'. Still, it is an attractive, long-budded flower in strawberry-pink fading to lavender, and the foliage is lush and dark green. The name honors a self-taught American ceramicist, famous for her porcelain roses.

Winchel, USA, 1980
'King of Hearts' × 'Golden Masterpiece'
Repeat flowering | *Slight fragrance*
HABIT Bush H/W 1.2m/1m (4ft/3ft) | ZONES 7–11

'Jennifer Hart'

HYBRID TEA | DARK RED

Only in California could a rose be named after a fictional character in a hit television series, and that is where 'Jennifer Hart' was raised. The perpetrators of the gimmick were Armstrong Nurseries in 1981. It is quite an attractive variety, though, with high-centred, double blooms of rich ruby-red with a sweet, tea fragrance. They are borne on a medium-height, bushy plant with semi-glossy, mid-green foliage. Alas, both *Hart to Hart* and the rose are almost forgotten now.

AROart | Swim and Christensen, USA, 1981
'Pink Parfait' × 'Yuletide'
Repeat flowering | *Slight, tea fragrance*
HABIT Bush H/W 1.2m/1m (4ft/3ft) | ZONES 6–11

'Jennifer Hart'

'Jens Munk'

'Jessie Mathews'

'Jens Munk'

HYBRID RUGOSA | MEDIUM PINK

When in the late 1960s Dr Felicitas Svejda of the Canadian Department of Agriculture embarked on a program of breeding roses able to endure that country's sub-arctic winters, she decided to draw attention to their hardiness by giving them the names of the pioneering explorers who had opened Canada up to European settlement. This one, the second to be introduced, honors the Danish captain who in 1619 attempted to discover a route through the legendary North-West Passage. Nicely fragrant, its double, clear cool pink flowers are of medium size and informal shape, and are borne almost continuously all season. The iron-hardy bush is arching in habit, with the wrinkled leaves of *R. rugosa*. A slight tendency to mildew is its only fault.

Svejda, Canada, 1974
'Schneezwerg' × 'Frau Dagmar Hartopp'
Repeat flowering | *Strong, spicy fragrance*
HABIT Bush H/W 1.2m/1m (4ft/3ft) | ZONES 2–8

'Jessie Mathews'

HYBRID TEA | YELLOW BLEND

The delicate blooms of 'Jessie Mathews' are more likely to display themselves in clusters in the style of a Floribunda. Individually they are quite large, with 35 petals of pale yellow, with picotee edges in warm pink. This rose was introduced in 1982 in memory of the charming star of English musical comedy, who lived in Australia for some years. The plant is dense and bushy, the foliage light green. A rose of such charm deserves to be, like Jessie's theme song, 'Evergreen'.

BEEjes ı Bees, England, UK, 1982
'Ernest H. Morse' × 'Rosenella'
Repeat flowering ı *Slight fragrance*

HABIT Bush H/W Xm/Xm (Xft/Xft) ı ZONES X–XI

'Johann Strauss'

'John Cabot'

'Jocelyn'

'Jocelyn'

FLORIBUNDA ı RUSSET

This is a rose more for the flower arranger than the garden, for its matt mahogany and purple tones do not show up well in the garden, and in hot weather it is apt simply to be deep pink. It is a reasonably healthy grower, however, with attractive, dark green leaves. Borne in small clusters, the blossoms are full of petals, although one could wish they were also full of fragrance. Try it in the cutting garden and in arrangements with russet and grey-green leaves. It was a 1970 introduction from E. B. LeGrice, a specialist in the unusual.

LeGrice, England, UK, 1970
Parentage undisclosed
Repeat flowering ı *Slight fragrance*

HABIT Bush H/W 1m/60cm (3ft/2ft) ı ZONES 6–11

'Johann Strauss'

SHRUB ı PINK BLEND

'Forever Friends', 'Johann Straus', 'MEIoffic', 'Sweet Sonata'

Every reference book tells a different story about the parentage, but never mind. Breeding will out, as they say; and this is an aristocratic rose indeed, a worthy tribute to the great master of the Viennese waltz. Medium-sized and borne in Floribunda-like sprays, the flowers open from elegant buds to informally old-fashioned flowers, well filled with petals and with a light lemon-verbena scent; they are a very pretty shade of soft pink, sometimes lightly touched with apricot, and sometimes deepening to porcelain-pink. The bush is strong, upright and prolific, and the dark leaves have a very good reputation for resistance to black spot.

MEIoffi ı Meilland, France, 1994
'Flamingo' × ('Pink Wonder' × 'Tip Top')
Repeat flowering ı *Lemon-verbena fragrance*

HABIT Bush H/W 1.5m/1.2m (5ft/4ft) ı ZONES 6–11

'John Clare'

'John Cabot'

HYBRID KORDESII ı MEDIUM RED

Another of Felicitas Svejda's 'Explorer Series', this time named for the great British sea-captain who discovered Newfoundland in 1497. It is one of those roses that can be grown either as a large shrub or a climber of moderate size; either way it is an outstanding rose for very cold climates. The double, informally styled flowers can be called deep pink or light red at the viewer's discretion; they are borne all season in small clusters and are very pleasingly, if not intensely, fragrant. The matt, dark green leaves are notably disease-resistant. The later flowers will be most abundant if the plant is fertilized generously as the first flush fades.

Svejda, Canada 1978
R. kordesii × ('Masquerade' × *R. laxa*)
Repeat flowering ı *Moderate fragrance*

HABIT Bush H/W 1.5m/1.2m (5ft/4ft) ı ZONES 3–10

'John Clare'

SHRUB ı DEEP PINK

One of the few David Austin roses to be deficient in fragrance, 'John Clare' makes up for that by the sheer abundance of its flowers; none of the tribe flowers more generously or continuously. The very double flowers are the color of a Ceylon ruby, not quite red, not quite pink, and are of medium size and pleasantly informal shape. They usually come in small sprays, on a spreading bush with good, dark green leaves and few thorns. It was named on behalf of the John Clare Society after their hero, the nineteenth-century poet who has been called 'England's most articulate village voice'.

AUScent ı Austin, England, UK, 1997
('Wife of Bath' × seedling)
Repeat flowering ı *Slight fragrance*

HABIT Bush H/W 1.5m/1.2m (5ft/4ft) ı ZONES 6–11

'John F. Kennedy'

HYBRID TEA ı WHITE

'JFK', 'President John F. Kennedy'

When after President Kennedy's tragic death Jackson & Perkins offered to name a rose in his memory, Mrs Kennedy requested that it be a white one. Jackson & Perkins had a real beauty for her, with majestic blooms nearly 14cm (5½in) across, high-centred and shapely, with a delightful touch of lime-green at the flower's heart. They are fragrant, too. Alas,

'John F. Kennedy'

'Jolly Roger' is not one of them, however, but a Floribunda of 1973 from Armstrong Nurseries. It has jolly orange-red flowers, semi-double, scarcely fragrant, and borne in clusters on a low bush with wrinkled, green leaves. It has not won the lasting admiration of rose-lovers and is little grown now. It was photographed in the Huntington Gardens in California, where it was in fine form.

Armstrong, USA, 1973
'Spartan' × 'Angelique'
Repeat flowering ı *Slight fragrance*
HABIT Bush H/W 1m/60cm (3ft/2ft) ı ZONES 6–11

'Johnnie Walker'

'Johnnie Walker'

HYBRID TEA ı APRICOT BLEND

'Arthur Bell', 'Glenfiddich', 'Johnnie Walker' – the Scotch whisky drinker could plant quite a big bed with roses named for his favorite tipple! 'Johnnie Walker' is the latest of the three, yellow like the others, but a difficult color to describe. Buff? Apricot gold? Or just the clear amber of a very fine whisky? There are only 20 petals, but they build up into a large and beautifully formed bloom, lavishly endowed with fragrance. The bush is compact, and the leaves are mid-green. It was an early success for Gareth Fryer, who has since established himself as one of Britain's leading rose breeders.

FRYgran ı Fryer, England, UK, 1983
'Sunblest' × ('Arthur Bell' × 'Belle Blonde')
Repeat flowering ı *Intense fragrance*
HABIT Bush H/W 1.2m/1m (4ft/3ft) ı ZONES 6–10

'Jolly Roger'

FLORIBUNDA   ORANGE RED

There was in the 1930s a group of roses bearing pirate names – 'Captain Kidd', 'Doubloons' and 'Long John Silver' among them – all hybrids of *R. setigera* raised by M. H. Horvath of Ohio.

'Jolly Roger'

it is beginning to show its age and there are reports that the plant is not as strong as it was and the leathery leaves not as resistant to mildew as they used to be. At its best it can still be wonderful, but it needs good, rich soil and winter protection in cold climates.

Boerner, USA, 1965
Seedling × 'White Queen'
Repeat flowering ı *Moderate fragrance*
HABIT Bush H/W 1.5m/1.2m (5ft/4ft) ı ZONES 7–11

'Josephine Bruce'

HYBRID TEA ı DARK RED

Introduced as long ago as 1949, and often criticized for its sprawling growth and fondness for mildew, 'Josephine Bruce' is still much admired. The attraction is the color of the flowers: few red roses are so deep and velvety. There are only 24 petals, but they make up a big, high-centred flower that opens slowly.

'Josephine Bruce'

'Joybells'

The foliage is a dark olive-green and may need protection from mildew. Some people claim that it is intensely fragrant; others find its scent only slight. Perhaps, as happened with 'Ena Harkness', there are two strains of 'Josephine Bruce'?

Bees, England, UK, 1949
'Crimson Glory' × 'Madge Whipp'
Repeat flowering ı *Slight fragrance*

HABIT Bush H/W 1.2m/1m (4ft/3ft) ı ZONES 6–10

'Joseph's Coat'

LARGE FLOWERED CLIMBER ı RED BLEND

There are several climbers in the 'Masquerade' colors of yellow turning red, including a climbing sport of 'Masquerade' itself, but many people think that 'Joseph's Coat', raised by Herbert Swim as long ago as 1964, is still the best of them. True, it is not very rampant (with careful pruning it can be grown as a large shrub) and it rarely makes a great mass of color, but there seem to be at least a few Floribunda-style clusters of double blooms all season, and they are prettily shaped and clear in tone and do not go blotchy with age. The foliage is glossy and mid-green, tinted reddish when young, and is susceptible to black spot. Joseph, in the Old Testament story, had a coat of many colors, and the name is appropriate for the rose.

Armstrong, USA, 1964
'Buccaneer' × 'Circus'
Repeat flowering ı *Slight fragrance*

HABIT Climber H/W 2.5m/1.8m (8ft/6ft) ı ZONES 6–11

🌹 Bagatelle (Paris) Gold Medal 1964

'Joybells'

FLORIBUNDA ı MEDIUM PINK

'Cubana', 'Joy Bells'

In the shape of its two-toned pink, nicely perfumed flowers, this rose is a model for breeders to follow. The flowers are completely regular and imbricated like a formal double camellia. Several flowers displayed together look most attractive. ('English Miss' is another, newer, rose of the same shape.) The plant is strong, with glossy leaves, the variety's only fault being that its branches are excessively thorny.

There is also a red and yellow Hybrid Tea called 'Joybells', raised by Kordes. Do not confuse the two.

Robinson, England, UK, 1961
Seedling × 'Fashion'
Repeat flowering ı *Moderate fragrance*

HABIT Bush H/W 1m/60cm (3ft/2ft) ı ZONES 5–11

'Joyfulness'

HYBRID TEA ı APRICOT BLEND

'Frohsinn '82'

Mathias Tantau has sown confusion here by christening two roses 'Frohsinn' and allowing English-speaking customers to translate them both as 'Joyfulness'. The first was an apricot-toned Floribunda of 1961, a rose rarely seen now; the other is our present subject, also known as 'Frohsinn'82'. It bears wide, Grandiflora-style flowers in a variable blend of peach and coral. Lightly scented, they open from long, elegant buds. It is a rose very much to the American taste, and it is a little surprising that it is not more widely available there. Perhaps its rather leggy growth and the susceptibility of its glossy leaves to black spot have been against it. In the warm climates that it prefers it is a lovely rose for cutting and for exhibition.

TANsinnroh ı Tantau, Germany, 1984
'Horstman's Jubläumsrose' × 'Circus'
Repeat flowering ı *Slight fragrance*

HABIT Bush H/W 1.5m/1.2m (5ft/4ft) ı ZONES 7–11

'Jude The Obscure'

'Joseph's Coat'

'Joyfulness'

'Judy Garland'

'Jude The Obscure'

SHRUB ı MEDIUM YELLOW

A favorite among David Austin's fans, although it is really only worth growing in a warm, sunny climate – let rain or even heavy dew fall on the young flowers and they will 'ball' and refuse to open, and it is never a long-lasting cut flower. But where it does well it can be glorious: large, deeply cupped like an old Centifolia, and a most beautiful shade of clear, soft yellow deepening to gold at the flower's heart and sometimes touched with pink or apricot. The scent is delightful, with notes of fruit and sweet wine. The bush is strong and the leathery leaves have an excellent

reputation for resistance to black spot and mildew.

AUSjo ı Austin, England, 1997
'Abraham Darby' × 'Windrush'
Repeat flowering ı *Guava and sweet wine fragrance*
HABIT Bush H/W 1.5m/1.2m (5ft/4ft) ı ZONES 6–11
🏵 Monza Fragrance Award 1996

'Judy Garland'

FLORIBUNDA ı YELLOW BLEND

The flowers open deep yellow, and as they develop a band of orange-red appears at the

edge of each petal, gradually spreading over the entire surface like a curtain being slowly drawn across a stage. Large and shapely, with 35 petals, they come in small clusters on an upright bush, and are lovely for cutting, as they hold their form until they drop. The foliage is glossy and dark green. Raised in England and named in memory of the great but tragic movie star, 'Judy Garland' has been very well received elsewhere, particularly in Japan and in India.

HARking ı Harkness, England, UK, 1977
(['Super Star' × 'Circus'] × ['Sabine' × 'Circus']) × 'Pineapple Poll'
Repeat flowering ı *Slight fragrance*
HABIT Bush H/W 1m/60cm (3ft/2ft) ı ZONES 5–11

'Julia Child'

FLORIBUNDA ı MEDIUM YELLOW

The late Julia Child, the award-winning cook, author and television personality who intro- duced a generation of Americans to the delights

'Julia Child'

of classic French cuisine, adored cooking with butter, so it is appropriate that the rose she chose to bear her name should be described as 'butter-yellow' – and be an award-winner itself. It is a truly delicious color, too, although like many yellow roses it varies from pale to deep according to the season. The old-fashioned, ruffled flowers are very nicely scented and borne abundantly all season in smallish clusters on a strong bush with glossy, dark green leaves and an excellent reputation for disease resistance.

WEKvossutono ı Carruth, USA, 2006
(['Voodoo' × *R. soulieana* derivative] × 'Summer Wine') × 'Top Notch'
Repeat flowering ı *Strong, licorice candy and spice fragrance*

HABIT Bush H/W 1.2m/1m (4ft/3ft) ı ZONES 5–11

🌹 All-America Rose Selection 2006

'Julia's Rose'

HYBRID TEA ı RUSSET

Very aptly named for the doyenne of flower arrangers, Julia Clements, 'Julia's Rose' hit the world of floral art like a stroke of lightning when it was introduced in 1976. Its color is unique, an indescribable blend of *café au lait* and lavender, and its stems are long and smooth. The flowers are small and double, and the foliage is olive-green, red-tinted when young. This is a rose for the rose enthusiast, needing protection from disease. The beautiful color only develops fully in cool weather; at the height of summer it is just pale pink. Alas, little of the scent of 'Blue Moon' has been passed on.

Wisbech Plant Co., USA, 1976
'Blue Moon' × 'Dr A. J. Verhage'
Repeat flowering ı *Slight fragrance*

HABIT Bush H/W 1.2m/1m (4ft/3ft) ı ZONES 5–11

'Just Joey'

'Julie Delbard'

FLORIBUNDA ı APRICOT BLEND

You do not often see this rose outside France, where it was introduced in 1976, but it is well liked there for its very pretty pink and apricot flowers and its compact growth. It seems to be at its best in the sunny climate of the south. Despite their lack of perfume, the large, double flowers are excellent for cutting, being long-lasting. The foliage is olive-green, red-tinted when young.

DELjuli ı Delbard, France, 1986
('Zambra' × ['Orange Triumph' × 'Floradora']) × (['Orléans Rose' × 'Goldilocks'] × ['Bettina' × 'Henri Mallerin'])
Repeat flowering ı *No fragrance*

HABIT Bush H/W 1m/60cm (3ft/2ft) ı ZONES 6–11

🌹 Madrid Gold Medal 1976

'Julien Potin'

HYBRID TEA ı LIGHT YELLOW

'Golden Pernet'

'Julien Potin' was one of the first so-called 'Pernetianas' (a term reserved for the early yellow Hybrid Teas) to be a reliable garden rose, although rosarians of the day found it gave its best blooms on the side shoots. Winner of the gold medal in Portland, it is still available in France and worth growing in a cool, dry climate, for its double, primrose-yellow blooms are large and perfectly formed, and the foliage is a glossy green; but you may have to watch out for black spot. It was named for a leading French horticulturist, who was famous for his work with orchids, especially *Potinara*.

Pernet-Ducher, France, 1927
'Souvenir de Claudius Pernet' × seedling
Repeat flowering ı *Moderate, fruity fragrance*

HABIT Bush H/W 1.2m/1m (4ft/3ft) ı ZONES 6–11

🌹 Portland (Oregon, USA) Gold Medal 1929

'Julie Delbard'

'Julien Potin'

'Julia's Rose'

'Just Joey'

HYBRID TEA ı ORANGE BLEND

The Essex city of Colchester is famous
in history as the seat of the warrior queen
Boadicea, but for the past century it has
also been famous for its roses, especially
a long succession of beauties from the old
firm of Benjamin Cant & Sons, now known
as Cants of Colchester. Star among them all,
perhaps, is 'Just Joey', raised by Roger Pawsey
and named in affectionate tribute to his wife,
Joanna. The bush is only moderate in size,
but the richly scented, double flowers, with
their distinctive frilled petals, can be enormous,
and they are of a unique color, a blend of
coppery shades with apricot. It has broad,
olive-green foliage, which will need protection
from black spot in muggy-summer climates.
Winter protection is called for in cold ones.

Cants, England, UK, 1972
'Fragrant Cloud' × 'Dr A. J. Verhage'
Repeat flowering ı *Intense, spicy fragrance*

HABIT Bush H/W 1.2m/1.2m (4ft/4ft) ı ZONES 7–10

Royal Horticultural Society Award of Garden Merit
1993, World Federation of Rose Societies Hall of Fame 1994

'Kabuki'

HYBRID TEA ı DEEP YELLOW

'Golden Prince'

'Kabuki' is sometimes claimed (although not
by the raiser, Marie-Louisette Meilland, who
knows better) to be superior to 'Peace'. It is
not. Sure, the flowers are nearly as big as those
of 'Peace'; the foliage is just as glossy and handsome; and the buds are longer and slimmer.
But their deep gold fades rapidly as the flower

'Kabuki'

opens, and they lack the touches of pink that
make 'Peace' so lovely, even when it is pale.
It is usually not so free with its blooms either,
and it is not always free from black spot. Still,
it is a handsome rose, rarely seen now.

MEIgold ı Mei land, France, 1968
('Monte Carlo' × 'Bettina') × ('Peace' × 'Soraya')
Repeat flowering ı *Moderate fragrance*

HABIT Bush H/W 1.2m/1m (4ft/3ft) ı ZONES 7–10

'Kardinal'

HYBRID TEA ı MEDIUM RED

'Kardinal 85', 'Kordes Rose Kardinal'

This is the third rose of the name, all red
of course, the color of a cardinal's robes; but
as the other two seem to have vanished from
the catalogues, you aren't likely to be offered
the wrong one when you ask for the 'Kardinal' you saw adorned with blue ribbons at
the flower show. Originally bred for the
greenhouse cut-flower trade, it took a few
years to escape into the garden, where exhibitors seized on it with delight for the immac-
ulate form of its double flowers and its lovely
cherry-red color, which shows up beautifully
under artificial light. That the flowers have
almost no scent did not matter! It makes

'Kardinal'

a tall (and rather prickly) bush and flowers
quite freely on long, straight stems, but to
have the blooms up to exhibition size it
needs generous feeding. The leathery,
dark green leaves rate highly for black
spot resistance, a bit lower for mildew.
It does best in warm climates.

KORlingo ı Kordes, Germany, 1985
Seedling × 'Flamingo'
Repeat flowering ı *Slight fragrance*

HABIT Bush H/W 1.5m/1.2m (5ft/4ft) ı ZONES 7–11

The Rose in America

IT IS SAID THAT COLUMBUS'S SAILORS, ON THE POINT OF MUTINY AFTER WEEKS OF SAILING INTO THE UNKNOWN, WERE GIVEN THE COURAGE TO GO ON BY THE SIGHT OF A FLOATING ROSE BRANCH, WHICH SHOWED THEM THAT LAND WAS NEAR.

Whether or not this is a true story, there were certainly many roses awaiting them in the New World. Some 20 species are native to North America, among them such beautiful roses as *R. virginiana*, *R. californica* and *R. setigera*. The pioneers reported that the Indians transplanted bushes from the wild to adorn their villages, and some of the settlers followed suit, the native roses mingling happily in their gardens with roses brought from Europe.

That was in what is now the eastern United States. To the south, in present-day Mexico, the Aztecs practised a form of horticulture as sophisticated as that of Europe, if not more so. Curiously, the rose does not appear to have featured in their gardens. Perhaps the few species native to Mexico were not flamboyant enough for Aztec taste – in contrast to the dahlia, the African Marigold and the zinnia – but at least the rose was spared being used in the service of the bloodthirsty Aztec gods.

A European passion for flowers

With Christianity, the rose came to Mexico. The most revered shrine in all of the Americas, that of Our Lady of Guadeloupe, was established in 1521 on a spot that, so it is said, the Virgin Mary marked as her own with roses – and today roses are as cherished in Mexican gardens as they are everywhere.

ABOVE The Wild Roses of North America are second to none in beauty. Here is the 'Prairie Rose', *R. setigera*, as depicted by the great American naturalist and artist John James Audubon (1785–1851) in his *Birds of America*. The bird perching in the branches is the Seaside Finch.

BELOW 'American Pillar' owes much of its hardiness to the native 'Prairie Rose', *R. setigera*.

ABOVE The famous International Rose Gardens in Washington Park, in Port and, Oregon, occupy a fine site with extensive views over the city. For many years it was the city government's policy to plant rosebushes along the streets, gaining Portland the title of the Rose City.

The United States led the world in granting royalties to the creators of new and improved varieties of plants, who hitherto had had to practise their art for love and little money. 'New Dawn', introduced in 1931, holds Plant Patent No. 1.

The early colonists of the United States brought the English passion for flowers with them. George Washington and Thomas Jefferson are only the most prominent of a number of colonial gardeners whose gardens are preserved today; both carried on correspondence with fellow enthusiasts in Europe, and many a new plant blossomed for the first time in America in Washington's garden at Mount Vernon or Jefferson's at Monticello. (It was a two-way traffic – American plants like phlox, clarkias and magnolias enjoyed quite a vogue in Europe at the end of the eighteenth century.)

Jefferson, who once wrote that 'the greatest service that can be rendered to any country is to add a useful plant to its culture', no doubt took an interest in the Rose Garden of the White House, although he did not establish it – it dates from 1800, during John Adams's presidency. Neither large nor, as rose gardens go, especially interesting, it is the most famous rose garden in America, visited by an endless list of the world's distinguished and powerful. Not that most of them go to see the roses!

There are many splendid rose gardens in both the United States and Canada, where visitors can feast their senses on roses to their heart's content. Most interesting, perhaps, are the 24 test gardens of the All-America Rose Selections (AARS), where new roses are tested for two years before they are introduced to commerce. The roses chosen by a panel of judges as the best of the year are given the coveted AARS award, which virtually guarantees sales for the fortunate hybridists. Roses that receive the AARS award account for some 18 million of the 40-odd million rosebushes sold each year in the United States. This is not surprising, considering that they include such all-time greats as 'Peace', 'Super Star' (known in America as 'Tropicana') and 'Queen Elizabeth'.

The American Rose Society

The fact that the majority of ARS winners are American is in no way a reflection on the judges' impartiality; American hybridists are some of the most skilful in the world. Even the British take notice when a new rose appears from the hand of an American expert, and by international consent a new rose should be registered with the American Rose Society (ARS) for its codename to be legally protected.

Founded in 1892, the ARS is the largest, but not the oldest, rose society in the world – the distinction of being the oldest belongs to Britain's Royal National Rose Society – and one of the most dedicated. In addition to maintaining the registers of new roses (which it publishes in its *Annual* and from time to time in the rose-lover's bible, *Modern Roses*), it maintains one of the world's largest rose gardens at Shreveport, Louisiana, and acts as a clearing house for information about roses. Its 15,000 members by no means comprise all the rose-lovers of America. There are many smaller local societies and groups dedicated to special interests such as Old Garden Roses and Miniatures and Mini-Flora.

Several American states have chosen roses as their symbol: the best known are the 'Cherokee Rose' of Georgia, the 'Prairie Rose' of North Dakota, and the District of Columbia's 'American Beauty'. New York chose simply 'the rose' as its symbol, and the whole United States followed suit, choosing the rose as the national flower. Is it not a hopeful sign when the most powerful nation on earth, whose ferocious eagle has traditionally offered the arrows of war as well as the olive branch of peace, should choose the rose of love as its symbol?

'Karen Blixen'

'Katherine Loker'

'Karl Herbst'

'Karlsruhe'

'Karl Herbst'

HYBRID TEA | MEDIUM RED

'Red Peace'

Herr Herbst was Wilhelm Kordes's right-hand man for many years, and he is said to have been much amused to hear the hybridists nickname his rose 'the old bull' for the potency of its pollen. Its descendants are too numerous to mention, and it is as a stud that this rose will be chiefly remembered. At their best, the enormous, very double, fire-red flowers can be formidable on the show bench; but it is a difficult rose to grow to perfection, the flowers only coming perfectly formed at the end of the season and easily damaged both by rain and hot sunshine. The tall, prickly bush is not over-generous in producing them, either, although the dark green leaves are quite disease-resistant.

Kordes, Germany, 1950
'Independence' × 'Peace'
Repeat flowering | Moderate, tea fragrance
HABIT Bush H/W 1.5m/1.2m (5ft/4ft) | ZONES 6–11

'Karlsruhe'

HYBRID KORDESII | DEEP PINK

Wilhelm Kordes never disclosed the parentage of 'Karlsruhe', which he introduced in 1957, but it is safe to say that it was bred from *R. kordesii*, the fertile seedling of 'Max Graf' that was given the status of a 'hybrid Species' and that Herr Kordes used extensively as a parent of cold-tolerant, repeat-flowering climbers. This one makes a moderate-growing plant, with shiny, mid-green leaves and very double, deep pink flowers, filled with petals (if not with fragrance) in the Old Garden Rose style. It makes a great show in summer and a lesser one in the fall/autumn. The city of Karlsruhe, founded in 1715, is near Heidelberg; it was rebuilt after being almost totally destroyed during World War II.

Kordes, Germany, 1957
Probably *R. kordesii* × unknown
Repeat flowering | Slight fragrance
HABIT Bush H/W 3m/2.5m (10ft/8ft) | ZONES 6–11

'Katherine Loker'

FLORIBUNDA | MEDIUM YELLOW

Both this rose's parents are best known as greenhouse roses, and it seems their offspring 'Katherine Loker' is also best as a greenhouse florist's rose, except in very warm

'Karen Blixen'

HYBRID TEA | WHITE

'Roy Black', 'Silver Anniversary'

One of the best-scented white Hybrid Teas, and a fine rose for exhibition, although when the many-petalled flowers are fully blown they are rather pleasingly muddled and old-fashioned in form. They are of good size – so large, indeed, that unless you feed the bush well they can be a bit heavy for their slim stems – and like many white roses they don't like prolonged rain – but those are the only faults. The bush is strong and prolific, with glossy, disease-resistant leaves. Perhaps better known by her nom-de-plume Isaak Dinesen, the Danish writer Karen Blixen chronicled her years as a farmer in Kenya in her book *Out of Africa*, which became a hit movie.

POUlari | Poulsen, Denmark, 1995
Seedling × seedling
Repeat flowering | Strong fragrance
HABIT Bush H/W 1.2m/1m (4ft/3ft) | ZONES 6–11

climates. The double, bright yellow flowers are shapely and long-lasting, and the plant appears strong. The foliage is leathery and dark green. Not easy to find these days, this rose is still worth a second look; it is well thought of in California. The scent is only slight.

AROkr | Swim and Christensen, USA, 1978
'Zorina' × 'Dr A. J. Verhage'
Repeat flowering | Slight fragrance

HABIT Bush H/W 1m/60cm (3ft/2ft) | ZONES 7–11

'Kathleen'

HYBRID MUSK | LIGHT PINK

'Kathleen' can be thought of as a sister to 'Ballerina'. It has similar large clusters of small,

'Keepsake'

'Kerryman'

single flowers, but it is a slightly bigger, more sprawling shrub, and the almost-white blooms, opening from pink buds, are sweetly fragrant of musk. Its admirers (and there are many) compare them to apple blossom. The flowers are followed, without prejudice to the later blooms, by sprays of orange hips, and the sight of both together is very pretty indeed. The foliage is dark green.

Pemberton, England, UK, 1922
'Daphne' × 'Perle des Jardins'
Repeat flowering | Sweet, musk fragrance

HABIT Bush H/W 2.5m/1.2m (8ft/4ft) | ZONES 6–11

'Keepsake'

FLORIBUNDA | DEEP PINK

'Esmeralda', 'Kordes's Rose Esmeralda'

When Reimer Kordes introduced this rose, it was hailed as an improved version of Meilland's 'Eden Rose', and it does resemble the older rose in its lovely, full-bodied form and its beautiful color, clear deep pink with lighter tints and gold at the flower's heart. It isn't quite so powerfully scented, but it scores over its rival in being more bushy and in its stronger resistance to mildew. The stems are long and the flowers long-lasting in the vase. Which to choose? The one your trusted rose nursery offers.

KORmalda | Kordes, Germany, 1981
Seedling × 'Red Planet'
Repeat flowering | Moderate, damask fragrance

HABIT Bush H/W 1.5m/1.2m (5ft/4ft) | ZONES 5/6–11

🌹 New Zealand International Rose Ground Trials Fragrance Award 1981, Portland (Oregon, USA) Gold Medal 1987

'Kathleen'

'Kerry Gold'

FLORIBUNDA | YELLOW BLEND

Introduced by Pat Dickson in 1967, 'Kerry Gold' still looks pretty good, with its flowers of deep yellow, often set off by splashes of red on the outside petals, against dark green foliage. The clusters are large, and the bush is compact and healthy. This rose likes a cool climate. It is losing popularity in the face of competition from the many more recent yellow Floribundas, many of which surpass 'Kerry Gold' in scent. Despite what many experts claim, if there is a choice of fragrant roses in a particular color, the most sweetly scented will be the better seller.

Dickson, Northern Ireland, UK, 1967
'Circus' × 'Allgold'
Repeat flowering | Slight fragrance

HABIT Bush H/W 1m/60cm (3ft/2ft) | ZONES 6–9

'Kerryman'

FLORIBUNDA | PINK BLEND

The Irish tell Kerryman jokes the way the rest of the world tell Irish and Polish jokes; but this 1971 Sam McGredy introduction is nothing to laugh at. It bears quite large, 10cm (4in) flowers in a blend of pinks with salmon, shapely and in nicely spaced clusters,

'Kerry Gold'

and there is a soft fragrance. The bush is of medium height, but alas, the shiny, dark green foliage is apt to get black spot. Treat the rose kindly! It is a sister seedling of 'Molly McGredy'. It seems to be only available in Britain these days.

McGredy, New Zealand, 1971
'Paddy McGredy' × ('Madame Léon Cuny' × 'Columbine')
Repeat flowering ı *Slight fragrance*
HABIT Bush H/W lm/60cm (3ft/2ft) ı ZONES 6–11

'Kim'

FLORIBUNDA ı MEDIUM YELLOW

There are not many yellow dwarf Floribundas – 'Patio Roses', as they are often called – and 'Kim' is as nice as any. Its flowers are shapely

'Kiss of Fire'

'King's Ransom'

and astonishingly large for so small a plant; they are often brushed with pink, and last very well in water. The foliage is small, matt and light green. There is some scent. Plant it as an edging for taller roses, to mask bare legs, or in a container. Named in memory of Master Kim Mulford, it was raised by Jack Harkness and introduced in 1971. The raisers still offer it, but it seems to have disappeared from the American and Australian catalogues. A pity.

Harkness, England, UK, 1971
('Orange Sensation' × 'Allgold') × 'Elizabeth of Glamis'
Repeat flowering ı *Slight fragrance*
HABIT Bush H/W lm/60cm (3ft/2ft) ı ZONES 7–10

'King's Ransom'

HYBRID TEA ı DEEP YELLOW

Exhibitors are inclined to criticize 'King's Ransom' for floppiness in the open bloom, but its long buds are elegant indeed (fit companions, in the arrangement pictured here, for the shapely 'Virgo'). The name might imply a deeper color than it is, but it is still a beautiful, luminous yellow and it fades but little in the sun. The flowers are double; the bush is sturdy and upright; the light green leaves are glossy and quite resistant to black spot, although not always to mildew. Winner of the 1962 AARS award, it was for many years the leading yellow garden rose. It is not quite that now, although it still has its admirers and has proved an important parent of yellow roses.

Morey, USA, 1961
'Golden Masterpiece' × 'Lydia'
Repeat flowering ı *Moderate, tea fragrance*
HABIT Bush H/W 1.5m/1.2m (5ft/4ft) ı ZONES 7–10
 All-America Rose Selection 1962

'Kiss'

FLORIBUNDA ı ORANGE PINK

'Kordes Rose Kiss'

Primarily a cut-flower variety, 'Kiss' is one of those Floribundas where the individual blooms in the cluster often have stems long enough to be cut separately; or, should the florist choose, the blooms can be treated as a small bouquet on the one stem. Individually, the flowers are not very large, but they are very shapely indeed and last a long time in the vase. Their color is pale salmon-pink, and the scent is only slight. The bush is tall, with dark green leaves, and very prolific – in the greenhouse anyway; it does not seem to be sold as a garden rose these days.

KORikis ı Kordes, Germany, 1988
Parentage undisclosed
Repeat flowering ı *Slight fragrance*
HABIT Bush H/W lm/60cm (3ft/2ft) ı ZONES 5–11

'Kiss of Fire'

FLORIBUNDA ı RED BLEND

Jean Gaujard's aptly named 'Kiss of Fire' seems to be catalogued only in Canada these days. The blooms are large and shapely, in golden yellow, with a brushing of flame around the petal edges, and the foliage is handsomely

RIGHT 'Kiss'
INSET 'Kim'

glossy. If it will grow in both hot India, where it was photographed, and cold Canada, then it should do well just about anywhere. It is somewhat reminiscent of 'Peace' and 'Double Delight', two favorite roses.

Gaujard, France, 1960
Parentage unknown
Repeat flowering ı *Slight fragrance*

HABIT Bush H/W 1m/60cm (3ft/2ft) ı ZONES 6–11

'Knock Out'

SHRUB ı RED BLEND

'Madraz', 'Purple Meidiland'

A rose that American gardeners have taken to their hearts, as well they might, for it is an immensely tough, easy-to grow rose, hardy to cold and heat, strongly resistant to disease, and a lavish producer of flowers all season. Of moderate size and only just semi-double, the blooms are described as 'fluorescent red', sometimes with a touch of purple, and they drop their spent petals cleanly. The plant is the right size for most gardens – strong enough to be effective, not so strong as to be overwhelming. The only criticism so far is a lack of scent. It was a great triumph for its amateur raiser, Bill Radler of Greenfield, Wisconsin, when he won the 2000 AARS award with this rose – but he did it again in 2007 with the coral-to-orange 'Rainbow Knock Out'. It is a seedling; the various pink versions of 'Knock Out' are sports of the original.

RADrazz ı Radler, USA, 2000
('Carefree Beauty' × seedling) × ('Razzle Dazzle' × seedling)
Repeat flowering ı *No fragrance*

HABIT Bush H/W 1.2m/1m (4ft/3ft) ı ZONES 4–11

🌹 All-America Rose Selection 2000, Anerkannte Deutsche Rose (Germany) 2002, American Rose Society David Fuerstenberg Award 2003, Monza Gold Medal 2003, Portland (Oregon, USA) Gold Medal 2003, American Rose Society Members' Choice 2004

'Kordes's Perfecta'

HYBRID TEA ı PINK BLEND

'Perfecta'

When it is grown well, this rose lives up to its name – it is indeed perfection. The blooms are huge, their 70 petals arranged with flawless symmetry, and their color is meltingly lovely, cream overlaid with cyclamen pink; and they are fragrant, too! Alas, such perfection is only usual in the fall/autumn, and then only in mild, dry weather; rain soon ruins everything.

The bush is lush in growth and very prickly, and the foliage is glossy and very dark green, with plum tints when young. It is liable to black spot. This is not an easy rose to grow and only exhibitors should try – but they can hardly do without it!

KORalu ı Kordes, Germany, 1957
'Golden Scepter' × 'Karl Herbst'
Repeat flowering ı *Strong, fruity fragrance*

HABIT Bush H/W 1.2m/1.2m (4ft/4ft) ı ZONES 6–9

🌹 (Royal) National Rose Society Gold Medal and President's International Trophy 1957, Portland (Oregon, USA) Gold Medal 1958

'Korona'

FLORIBUNDA ı ORANGE RED

For years, 'Korona' was the leading orange-red rose, and it is by no means a back number yet. The double flowers are as dazzling as ever, although they do tend to dull with age, and the growth is tall and healthy, with flowers borne abundantly in great clusters. The foliage is a matt olive-green. Apart from its lack of scent, its only other faults are its occasional slowness in repeating bloom and the informal shape of the individual flowers, a bit old-fashioned in these days of perfectly formed Floribundas.

KORnita ı Kordes, Germany, 1955
'Obergärtner Wiebicke' × 'Independence'
Repeat flowering ı *Slight fragrance*

HABIT Bush H/W 1m/60cm (3ft/2ft) ı ZONES 5–11

'Knock Out'

'Korona'

'Kordes's Perfecta'

'La Jolla'

HYBRID TEA ۱ PINK BLEND

The 65-petalled 'La Jolla' is a splendid rose
for a hot, dry climate – the photograph was
taken in the gardens of the Indian Rose Society
in Delhi. The blooms are very large, sometimes too large and heavy for the slim stems,
and shapely. They blend pink with cream and
gold toward the centre, all overlaid with deeper
veining. The bush is upright, with ample dark
green leaves. It is named for the Californian
town whose inhabitants pronounce it 'La Hoya'.

Swim, USA, 1954
'Charlotte Armstrong' × 'Contrast'
Repeat flowering ۱ *Moderate fragrance*
HABIT Bush H/W 1.5m/1.2m (5ft/4ft) ۱ ZONES 5–11

'La Sevillana'

FLORIBUNDA ۱ ORANGE RED

Oh, wow. Not another hard-toned, red Floribunda with smallish, semi-double flowers
in big clusters and no scent? Well, yes; but
what has made this rose a worldwide hit is
not the originality of its flowers – although
they neither fade nor cling to their dead
petals, and they are elegantly arranged in
their clusters – but the excellence of the

'La Jolla'

'La France'

'La France'

HYBRID TEA ۱ LIGHT PINK

No patriotic Frenchman would give a name
like this to a rose unless it was sensational,
and back in 1867, 'La France' certainly was.
It was the first of a new class, the Hybrid Teas,
which combined the grace and elegance of
the Teas with the vigor and hardiness of the
Hybrid Perpetuals. Alas, its constitution has
deteriorated with age and it is no longer an
easy rose to grow; but its exquisite double,
soft pink flowers, full of petals and the sweetest
perfume, captivate everyone still. The foliage
is semi-glossy and mid-green and will probably need protection against black spot and
rust these days.

Guillot, France, 1867
Probably 'Madame Victor Verdier' × 'Madame Bravy'
Repeat flowering ۱ *Intense, damask fragrance*
HABIT Bush H/W 1m/60cm (3ft/2ft) ۱ ZONES 5–11

'La Sevillana'

'Lady Curzon'

'Lady'

'Lady Elsie May'

'Lady Godiva'

plant. Bushy, almost shrubby in habit, it is well clad in disease-proof, bronze-tinted foliage and flowers with amazing freedom right through the season. No Modern Rose is easier to grow, and it really comes into its own when planted in a big bed or as a hedge, its color glowing in the sunlight. Its bright pink sport, 'Pink La Sevillana', is just as good.

MEIgekanu ۱ Meilland, France, 1978
(['MEIbrim × 'Jolie Madame'] × ['Zambra' × 'Zambra']) × (['Super Star' × 'Super Star'] × ['Poppy Flash' × 'Rusticana'])
Repeat flowering ۱ No fragrance

HABIT Bush H/W 1.2m/1.2m (4ft/4ft) ۱ ZONES 6–11

Anerkannte Deutsche Rose (Germany) 1979, Orléans Gold Medal 1980

'Lady'

HYBRID TEA ۱ MEDIUM PINK

Bred by Herb Swim's old partner Ollie Weeks from Georges Delbard's lavender 'Song of Paris' and Swim's pastel pink 'Royal Highness', the romantically named 'Lady' is a delightful double, pink rose in the manner of the beauties of the 1920s, its 35 petals slightly deeper on the reverse. The bush is pure 1980s – compact, with strong, mid-green foliage – and both parents have contributed their fragrance. But the lady has vanished from the catalogues and now

lingers only in a few public gardens that conserve old varieties.

Weeks, USA, 1933
'Song of Paris' × 'Royal Highness'
Repeat flowering ۱ Moderate fragrance

HABIT Bush H/W 1.2m/1m (4ft/3ft) ۱ ZONES 5–11

'Lady Curzon'

HYBRID RUGOSA ۱ MEDIUM PINK

Another modern Shrub Rose that is vigorous enough to train as a climber, 'Lady Curzon', left to itself, will mound up its prickly branches into a bush much wider than tall. In early summer it covers itself for several weeks with highly fragrant, single flowers in a pleasing shade of mid-pink, with just a hint of salmon. The foliage is glossy, wrinkled and mid-green. It would look stunning if allowed to trail among upright blue flowers like delphiniums or campanulas. Lady Curzon was the beautiful American-born Vicereine of India, Mary, Baroness Curzon of Kedleston.

Turner, England, UK, 1901
R. macrantha × R. rugosa rubra
Summer flowering ۱ Strong, spicy fragrance

HABIT Bush H/W 1m/1.8m (3ft/6ft) ۱ ZONES 5–10

'Lady Elsie May'

SHRUB ۱ ORANGE PINK

'Angelisa', 'ANCelsie'

Best known for his 'Flower Carpet' series of Ground Cover Roses, Werner Noack has been aiming for higher things! Though she comes from ground-cover bloodlines, 'Lady Elsie May' is no prostrate ground cover but a waist-high Shrub Rose, in habit like an unusually bushy Floribunda. The double, coral-pink

flowers are in the Floribunda style, too, borne on stems long enough for cutting and lasting well in the vase. They have little scent, but they are borne very freely all season and the glossy leaves are said to be exceptionally disease-resistant. In 2005 it won one of the highest awards in the rose world, the AARS.

NOAelsie ۱ Noack, Germany, 2005
'Repandia' × 'Gruss an Angelin'
Repeat flowering ۱ Light fragrance

HABIT Bush H/W 1.2m/1m (4ft/3ft) ۱ ZONES 4–11

All-America Rose Selection 2005

'Lady Godiva'

HYBRID WICHURANA ۱ LIGHT PINK

Introduced in 1908, 'Lady Godiva' is a sport from 'Dorothy Perkins', described in the catalogues of the day as, would you believe it, 'flesh-colored'. Apart from its color, which many people preferred to the original, it is

Africa and Italy, and it won high awards on its introduction in 1982. The double flowers are a delight, soft coral in color, large in size, beautifully shaped, and fragrant as well. They come on long, straight stems for cutting, on tall bushes with shiny, dark green foliage. It is from Meilland, of course, and although the parentage is undeclared, it is a safe bet that its ancestors are Meilland roses, too.

MEIalzonite ı Meilland, France, 1986
Parentage undisclosed
Repeat flowering ı *Strong, fruity fragrance*

HABIT Bush H/W 1.2m/1m (4ft/3ft) ı ZONES 5–11

🌹 Gold Star of the South Pacific, Palmerston North (New Zealand) 1982

'Lady Huntingfield'

'Lady Rose'

HYBRID TEA ı ORANGE PINK

'Kordes's Rose Lady Rose'

Reimer Kordes might have named 'Lady Rose' after a real-life lady, or maybe he just wanted to draw our attention to the fact that there is something that is very feminine in the big, shapely, sweetly scented, double flowers, despite the brightness of their orange-pink color. There is certainly nothing delicate about the bush, which is on the tall side and rudely healthy, with glossy, dark green foliage.

KORlady ı Kordes, Germany, 1979
Seedling × 'Träumerei'
Repeat flowering ı *Strong, spicy fragrance*

HABIT Bush H/W 1.5m/1.2m (5ft/4ft) ı ZONES 5–11

🌹 Lyon Prix de La Rose Parfumée 1979, Belfast Gold Medal and Prize of the City of Belfast 1981

'Lady Meilland'

exactly the same. You do not often see it now, and it is mainly remembered for being the parent of the very popular Polyantha 'The Fairy', which, although it is supposed to be a sport from 'Lady Godiva', looks nothing like it. The foliage is small, glossy and dark green.

Paul, England, UK, 1908
'Dorothy Perkins' sport
Summer flowering ı *Slight fragrance*

HABIT Bush H/W 1.2m/1m (4ft/3ft) ı ZONES 7–11

'Lady Huntingfield'

HYBRID TEA ı MEDIUM YELLOW

The roses from Australian hybridist Alister Clark are suddenly right back in fashion, along with anything else of the romantic, old-fashioned persuasion. There is nothing old-fashioned about this rose, however. Its blends of apricot and yellow are right up to date, although it was introduced back in 1937! It is a sturdy plant, with glossy, dark green foliage, and the double flowers are large, shapely and deliciously fragrant. It is much

liked in Australia and New Zealand – and perhaps it will soon be admired elsewhere in the world.

Clark, Australia, 1937
'Busybody' × seedling
Repeat flowering ı *Strong, tea fragrance*

HABIT Bush H/W 1.2m/1m (4ft/3ft) ı ZONES 5–11

'Lady Meilland'

HYBRID TEA ı ORANGE PINK

Why has this lovely rose not found favor in the United States? It is still firmly entrenched in the catalogues in countries as far apart as Australia, France, New Zealand, South

'Lady Rose'

'Lady Seton'

HYBRID TEA | LIGHT PINK

Lady Seton was the married name of Julia Clements, the doyenne of British flower arrangers, and she must have been delighted to discover that her namesake rose is a very good one for cutting, the elegant flowers being borne on long, slim stems and lasting well. They are not especially large, but they are high-centred and shapely and a pleasing clear rose-pink with just a suggestion of salmon. The bush is on the tall side, with semi-glossy, mid-green leaves; but the variety's chief attraction has always been its delightful scent. Alas, that hasn't been enough to keep it in the catalogues forever, and it is a rare rose now.

McGredy, Northern Ireland, UK, 1966
'Ma Perkins' × 'Mischief'
Repeat flowering | *Intense fragrance*

HABIT Bush H/W 1.5m/1m (5ft/3ft) | ZONES 5–10

Royal National Rose Society Clay Vase for fragrance 1964

'Lady Seton'

'Lagerfeld'

GRANDIFLORA | MAUVE

'Starlight'

How does one tempt the public to buy a series of new roses as a matched set? Armstrong Nurseries hit on one answer in 1986, with a trio named for Paris couturiers – their 'French collection' of 'Givenchy', 'Lanvin' and 'Lagerfeld'. (Meilland had already taken the most famous, 'Christian Dior'.) 'Lagerfeld' is, appropriately, one of the most stylish of the 'blue' large-flowered modern roses. Its double, pale mauve flowers, borne in sprays, are large, shapely and fragrant, and its bush as strong as any of them, tall and with leaden green foliage. (You may need to watch out for black spot in humid climates.) As a bonus, the end-of-season flowers are followed by large, orange hips.

AROlaqueli | Christensen, USA, 1986
'Blue Nile' × ('Ivory Tower' × 'Angel Face')
Repeat flowering | *Intense fragrance*

HABIT Bush H/W 1.8m/1.2m (6ft/4ft) | ZONES 5–11

'Laminuette'

FLORIBUNDA | RED BLEND

'La Minuette', 'Minuette'

'I often see this rose at my local florist, and more than once have brought home a bunch

'Lagerfeld'

so I could take its portrait – but something always prevented me. It was in Canada that I finally managed to capture on film its shapely flowers, their white petals daintily rimmed in cherry-red.' So wrote the author in the first edition of this book. He would have a harder time finding it now, although it is still around and still worth growing in the garden. The bush is compact, with glossy, dark green leaves; the flowers are double; and although the stems won't be as long as they are in the greenhouse, it remains a delightful rose for cutting. There is little scent.

LAMinuette | Lammerts, USA, 1969
'Peace' × 'Rumba'
Repeat flowering | *Slight fragrance*

HABIT Bush H/W 1m/60cm (3ft/2ft) | ZONES 5–11

'Laminuette'

'Lancôme'

HYBRID TEA | DEEP PINK

The famous Parisian firm of Lancôme was founded in 1936 by Armand Pétitjean, an ardent rose-lover, who chose a rose as his firm's emblem. It is appropriate that the firm should have a rose with its name, but ironic that it should be almost fragrance-free. Introduced in Europe in 1973, it was bred for the greenhouse, and its ability to bloom in winter at lower temperatures than most others guaranteed it a long run in the flower shops.

'Lancôme'

'Lanvin'

It does well in the garden also, the tall, almost thornless bush bearing its shapely, double, high-centred flowers of deep fuchsia-pink freely. The foliage is leathery and dark green. It was introduced into commerce as a garden rose in 1986.

DELboip ı Delbard-Chabert, France, 1986
('Dr Albert Schweitzer' × ['Michèle Meilland' × 'Bayadère']) × ('MEImet' × 'Présent Filial')
Repeat flowering ı *Slight fragrance*

HABIT Bush H/W 1.5m/1.2m (5ft/4ft) ı ZONES 5–11

'Las Vegas'

'Lanvin'

HYBRID TEA ı LIGHT YELLOW

'Lanvin' is another in the series that Armstrong Nurseries named for Paris couturiers – their 'French Collection'. It is a vigorous grower, bearing large, stylish, double blooms in a medium yellow that holds well in the sun. It is a pleasing rose for cutting, as the flowers, borne in sprays, have long, slim stems, but it does not have much fragrance; but then the clear yellows, as a rule, are not noteworthy in this respect. The foliage is semi-glossy and dark green, red-tinted when young. Exhibitors should find it worth adding to their collections. It does best in a mild climate.

AROlemo ı Christensen, USA, 1986
Seedling × 'Katherine Loker'
Repeat flowering ı *Moderate fragrance*

HABIT Bush H/W 1.5m/1.2m (5ft/4ft) ı ZONES 5–11

'Las Vegas'

HYBRID TEA ı ORANGE BLEND

The glitzy colors of orange-red and gold certainly suit a rose named for America's gambling and showbiz paradise, but it is a German rose, from Kordes in 1981, and its parents are German, too. The glossy green foliage and brown prickles form an effective background to the dazzling double blooms, which, unusually for a bicolored rose, are nicely fragrant. They often come three to a stem. And to complete the picture, the rose won a gold medal in Genoa – a long way indeed from Las Vegas! Mildew resistance is excellent, black spot resistance average.

KORgane ı Kordes, Germany, 1981
'Ludwigshafen am Rhein' × 'Feuerzauber'
Repeat flowering ı *Moderate fragrance*

HABIT Bush H/W 1.5m/1.2m (5ft/4ft) ı ZONES 5–11

🌹 Genova (Genoa, Italy) Gold Medal 1985, Portland (Oregon, USA) Gold Medal 1988

'Lavaglut'

FLORIBUNDA ı DARK RED

'Intrigue', 'Lava Flow', 'Lavaglow'

This remains one of the most highly rated of the red Floribundas, its color dark and smouldering, its flowers attractively camellia-shaped, the plant compact and floriferous. Many roses of this color tend to scorch in hot sun, but not this one! The shiny, dark green foliage does have the fault of being slightly susceptible to black spot, and a sunny climate suits it best. The German name, meaning 'Lava Glow', is most appropriate; calling it 'Intrigue' confuses it with the excellent purple American rose of that name.

KORlech ı Kordes, Germany, 1978
'Gruss an Bayern' × seedling
Repeat flowering ı *Slight fragrance*
HABIT Bush H/W 1m/1m (3ft/3ft) ı ZONES 5–11

'Lavender Dream'

SHRUB ı MAUVE

Raised as long ago as 1984, this rose has taken some years to become as widely known as its merits deserve. It is an excellent shrub, abundantly vigorous but not growing so big that it takes up half the garden, well clothed in excellent mid-green foliage and smothering itself in flowers all season. Borne in elegant sprays, they are neither large nor double; but they have the charm of a Wild Rose, and their lovely, soft shades of rose and mauve are lit up by golden stamens. Lack of scent is the only demerit.

INTerlav ı Ilsink, The Netherlands, 1984
'Yesterday' × 'Nastarana'
Repeat flowering ı *No fragrance*
HABIT Bush H/W 1.2m/1m (4ft/3ft) ı ZONES 4–11
❀ Anerkannte Deutsche Rose (Germany) 1987

'Lavender Lassie'

HYBRID MUSK ı MAUVE

Wilhelm Kordes described this rose as a Hybrid Musk. Many people think it is not quite shrubby enough to be thus described. It is more like a tall-growing Floribunda; and the flowers are hardly lavender. Rather they are rose-pink, with just a hint of mauve, at least in warm climates. (Apparently, it is more mauve in Germany.) However, 'Lavender Lassie' is a very attractive rose, tough and easy to grow, and bears its clusters of many-petalled and strongly fragrant blooms with freedom all season. The foliage is dull green, with a good reputation for disease resistance.

Kordes, Germany, 1960
'Hamburg' × 'Madame Norbert Lavavasseur'
Repeat flowering ı *Intense fragrance*
HABIT Climber H/W 2.5m/1.8m (8ft/6ft) ı ZONES 6–11
❀ Royal Horticultural Society Award of Garden Merit 1993

LEFT 'Lavender Dream'
TOP INSET 'Lavender Lassie'
BOTTOM INSET 'Lavaglut'

in growth, to 9m (30ft) high and wide on a wall, it bears large, deliciously fragrant, golden yellow flowers in profusion early in the season and intermittently afterwards. The flowers have only about 15 petals, but are most elegantly formed. The foliage is glossy and bright green. This rose has a complicated history. It was raised in about 1920 by Joseph Pernet-Ducher, who sold his only plant to Major Lawrence Johnston for his famous garden at Hidcote Manor in Gloucestershire, England. The Major subsequently introduced it to commerce in 1923.

Pernet-Ducher, France, 1923
'Madame Eugène Verdier' × *R. foetida persiana*
Repeat flowering ı *Moderate fragrance*

HABIT Climber H/W 9m/9m (30ft/30ft) ı ZONES 6–9

'Le Rouge et le Noir'

HYBRID TEA ı DARK RED

Stendahl's eerie novel about the Vatican is probably less well known these days than the red and black of the roulette wheel, but either source for the name suggests the dramatic beauty of this beautifully scented rose. The petals are such a deep (although vivid) shade of cardinal-red that they often have a black sheen to them. It is reputed to be a very reliable performer. It has dark green leaves, red-tinted when young.

DELcart ı Delbard, France, 1973
Parentage undisclosed
Repeat flowering ı *Strong, rose and vanilla fragrance*

HABIT Bush H/W 1.4m/110cm (4ft 6in/3ft 6in) ı ZONES 5–11

ABOVE 'Le Rouge et le Noir'
INSET 'Lemon Honey'

'Lavender Pinocchio'

FLORIBUNDA ı MAUVE

This was the first of the mauve Floribundas to be introduced, and in many ways it is still among the best, provided you don't insist on your mauve roses being blue! The color is not a straight lavender, but pleasingly mixed with *café au lait* tones. The double flowers have a pleasant shape and good fragrance, and are beautifully arranged in the cluster, and the rather short bush is as robust as any of the mauve roses, with matt leaves. The rather odd name makes sense when you realize that the rose was intended to be a lavender version of the popular 'Pinocchio'.

Boerner, USA, 1948
'Pinocchio' × 'Grey Pearl'
Repeat flowering ı *Moderate, fruity fragrance*

HABIT Bush H/W 1m/60cm (3ft/2ft) ı ZONES 5–11

'Lawrence Johnston'

LARGE FLOWERED CLIMBER ı MEDIUM YELLOW

'Hidcote Yellow'

This is one of the outstanding climbing roses, at least where black spot is not a worry. Strong

'Lavender Pinocchio'

'Lawrence Johnston'

'Len Turner'

'Leander'

'Leander'

SHRUB ı APRICOT BLEND

David Austin has been criticized for bringing too many very similar 'English Roses' onto the market. 'Leander' is a case in point, as it is very like its parent 'Charles Austin'. It has slightly smaller flowers, however, and is a much larger grower, to 2.5m (8ft) tall in mild-winter climates. The apricot-yellow of the flowers is very unusual among the big Shrub Roses. The double blooms are borne in wide sprays, and make a fine sight in early summer, but there are not as many to follow as one might like. The foliage is mid-green and smooth. The rose was named for the lover of Hero.

AUSlea ı Austin, England, UK, 1983
'Charles Austin' × seedling
Repeat flowering ı *Moderate fragrance*
HABIT Bush H/W 2.5m/1.5m (8ft/5ft) ı ZONES 5–11

'Lemon Honey'

FLORIBUNDA ı LIGHT YELLOW

Although this is an Irish-bred rose, by Pat Dickson, it appears to be available only in New Zealand. The rest of us have been missing out on a most attractive rose. The flowers of 'Lemon Honey' are large enough to pass for Hybrid Teas, shapely, softly scented and of lovely pastel coloring – a pale lemon-yellow and cream. The bush appears to be healthy, with dark green foliage.

DICkindlel ı Dickson, Northern Ireland, UK, 1986
Parentage undisclosed
Repeat flowering ı *Good, fruity fragrance*
HABIT Bush H/W lm/60cm (3ft/2ft) ı ZONES 5–11

'Len Turner'

FLORIBUNDA ı RED BLEND
'Daydream'

This really is a distinctive rose with its double, red and white flowers, carried in clusters on a very bushy plant with glossy, dark green foliage. It is a splendid rose for cutting, but the stems are not very long. Forget the name 'Daydream', which has been used several times before, and remember the sterling service of Len Turner, secretary to the Royal National Rose Society for nearly 20 years. His rose appears to be only available in Britain these days.

DICjeep ı Dickson, Northern Ireland, UK, 1984
'Electron' × 'Eyepaint'
Repeat flowering ı *Slight fragrance*
HABIT Bush H/W lm/60cm (3ft/2ft) ı ZONES 5–11

'Leonard Dudley Braithwaite'

SHRUB ı DARK RED
'Braithwaite', 'L. D. Braithwaite'

The dedicatee is the raiser's father-in-law, who is just as happy for his rose to be known by his initials as by his full name. Either way, this is a fine rose: many people think it is the best red 'English Rose' so far. It is not dark, dark red but clear crimson – rich, glowing and unfading – and its fragrance is very good indeed. Borne usually in small clusters, the very double flowers are of good size and pleasing Old Garden Rose form, and they are borne with great freedom on a compact shrub that does not try to become a climber in warm climates. The foliage is dark green and resistant to mildew.

AUScrim   I   Austin, England, 1993
'Mary Rose' × 'The Squire'
Repeat flowering   I   Strong, old-rose fragrance
HABIT Bush H/W 1.2m/1.2m (4ft/4ft)   I   ZONES 4–11

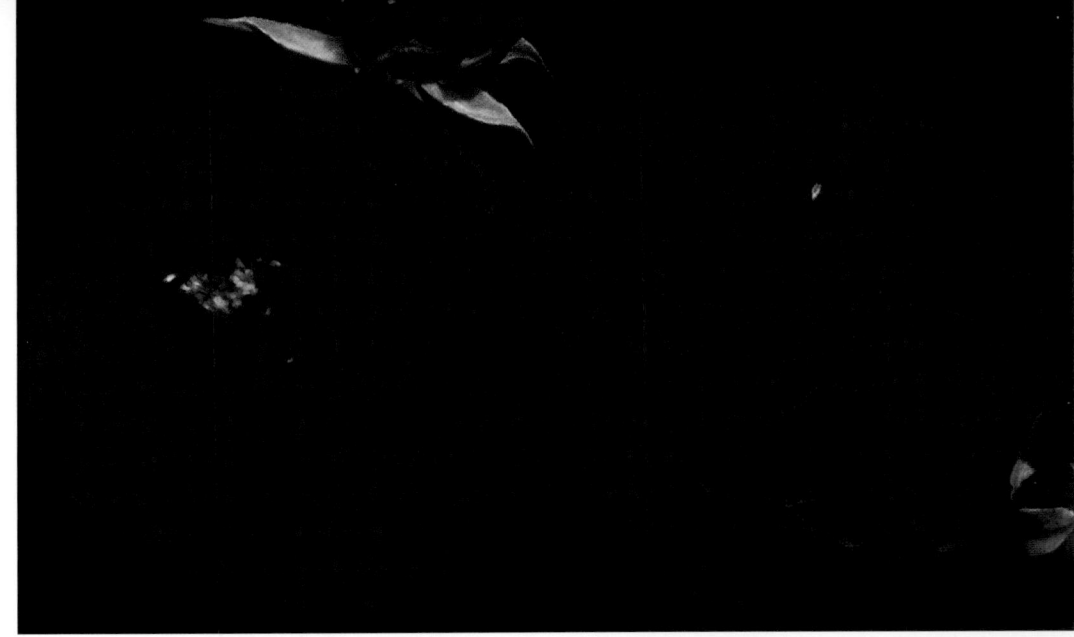

'Leonard Dudley Braithwaite'

'Leonardo da Vinci'

FLORIBUNDA   I   LIGHT PINK

'Leonard de Vinci', 'Leonardo Da Vinci'

In a photograph, or in a vase at a flower show, the clear rose-pink flowers with their many swirled petals may suggest one of David Austin's 'English Roses'; but 'Leonardo da Vinci' is not an Old Garden Rose in modern dress. In its bushy growth, its glossy foliage and the way it blooms in clusters all season (and its rather faint scent) it is a normal Floribunda – it is only when the flowers open to reveal the informally quartered arrangement of their petals that they suggest the roses of yesteryear. Would the great Renaissance artist whose name they bear be pleased with them? We think he would; this is a very good rose.

MEIdeauri   I   Meilland, France, 1994
'Sommerwind' × ('Milrose' × 'Rosamunde')
Repeat flowering   I   Slight fragrance
HABIT Bush H/W 1.2m/1m (4ft/3ft)   I   ZONES 5–11
🌹 Monza Gold Medal 1993

'Leonardo da Vinci'

'Let Freedom Ring'

HYBRID TEA   I   MEDIUM RED

Every so often American hybridists are seized with patriotic fervor. 'V for Victory', 'Purple Heart' and 'American Flagship' appeared during World War II and this one's name was one of the rallying cries of the Iraq War. It is a good rose in an attractive shade of strawberry-red, large, high-centred and shapely, and borne freely on very long stems for cutting. The bush is tall and upright, the foliage dark green and said to be very disease-resistant. Cool climates suit it best.

WEKearman   I   Carruth, USA, 2005
'Prima Donna' × 'Touch of Class'
Repeat flowering   I   Slight, tea fragrance
HABIT Bush H/W 1.8m/1.2m (6ft/4ft)   I   ZONES 5–11

'Lilac Charm'

FLORIBUNDA   I   MAUVE

A rose for favored climates, as it objects to cold and rain, but a charming one indeed, its single flowers of palest mauve set off by crimson stamens and an elusive fragrance. It is not a very strong grower, needing the best of care, but it flowers quite freely, in clusters, against dull, dark green foliage. Cut it young: the color is richer indoors. It was introduced by E. B. LeGrice in 1962.

In 1968, LeGrice introduced 'Silver Charm'; bred from 'Lilac Charm', it is very like it. Some people find it a stronger grower.

LeGrice, England, UK, 1962
'Lavender Pinocchio' × seedling of *R. californica*
Repeat flowering   I   Moderate fragrance
HABIT Bush H/W 1m/60cm (3ft/2ft)   I   ZONES 5–11

'Lilac Dawn'

FLORIBUNDA   I   MAUVE

Despite its fragrance and its mauve flowers being a rather richer tone than is usual, 'Lilac Dawn' seems to have dropped out of the catalogues, perhaps because its flowers, which are often more pink than mauve, just are not 'blue'

'Lilac Charm'

'Let Freedom Ring'

'Lilian Austin'

'Lilli Marleen'

'Lilac Time'

enough. The double flowers are borne in clusters, and the foliage is a leathery light green.

Swim and Weeks, USA, 1964
'Lavender Pinocchio' × 'Frolic'
Repeat flowering ⋅ *Lilac fragrance*

HABIT Bush H/W 1m/60cm (3ft/2ft) ⋅ ZONES 5–11

'Lilac Time'

HYBRID TEA ⋅ MAUVE

Ever since hybridists have been creating roses, they have been playing games on a hopeful public with names that suggest that the rose in question is blue, or at least purple. Take 'Lilac Time', for example. All that you usually see in the rose, at least in warm climates, is a sort of off-pink. Still, it is a pretty rose, informally shaped, with 33 petals and a sweet fragrance, and it still has its admirers. The plant is strong and free, with dull, light green foliage.

McGredy, New Zealand, 1956
'Golden Dawn' × 'Luis Brinas'
Repeat flowering ⋅ *Strong fragrance*

HABIT Bush H/W 1.5m/1.2m (5ft/4ft) ⋅ ZONES 5–11

'Lilac Dawn'

'Lilian Austin'

SHRUB ⋅ ORANGE PINK

You can bet that when a raiser names a rose for his mother, he regards it highly. So it is no surprise that 'Lilian Austin' is one of the most desirable of David Austin's 'English Roses', with big, full-petalled blooms in soft salmon-pink, with plenty of fragrance. The bush is compact and free with its flowers, and the glossy foliage is ample and healthy.

It was introduced in 1973 and remains very popular.

AUSmound ⋅ Austin, England, UK, 1981
'Aloha' × 'The Yeoman'
Repeat flowering ⋅ *Moderate fruity fragrance*

HABIT Bush H/W 1.2m/1.2m (4ft/4ft) ⋅ ZONES 5–11

'Lilli Marleen'

FLORIBUNDA ⋅ MEDIUM RED

'Lili Marlene', 'Lilli Marlene'

Almost everywhere you go in Europe, you will see this rose, in great beds at the public parks, in smaller ones at the service station, in twos and threes in front gardens. Everywhere it will be making an eye-catching splash of red. The foliage is leathery and dark green, and the bush is of average height, sending up its clusters of flowers with abandon. Although the double flowers are neither large nor scented, they are a real, true red, with no purple or orange in it. It is as memorable as the song for which it was named. It was one of Reimer Kordes's early successes.

KORlima ∣ Kordes, Germany, 1959
('Our Princess' × 'Rudolph Timm') × 'Ama'
Repeat flowering ∣ *Moderate fragrance*

HABIT Bush H/W 1.2m/1.2m (4ft/4ft) ∣ ZONES 5–11

'Limelight'

'Limelight'

HYBRID TEA ∣ LIGHT YELLOW

'Golden Medallion'

In cool weather, the young flowers sometimes show a suggestion of lime-green, but usually 'Limelight' is a straight yellow, deep and brilliant. It is a very good yellow rose, too, especially for a humid-summer climate, the foliage being dark, glossy and resistant to black spot. The large, shapely, double blooms are freely borne and very nicely scented. Do not confuse this variety with 'St Patrick', which is sold as 'Limelight' in New Zealand.

KORikon ∣ Kordes, Germany, 1984
'Peach Melba' × seedling
Repeat flowering ∣ *Strong, tea-rose fragrance*

HABIT Bush H/W 1.5m/1.2m (5ft/4ft) ∣ ZONES 5–11

'Lincoln Cathedral'

HYBRID TEA ∣ ORANGE BLEND

'Sarong'

Mr G. W. T. Langdale of Lincoln certainly believed in supporting his local cathedral, for he named his new rose after it. Introduced in 1985 and winning the RNRS gold medal in that year, it was the only rose Mr Langdale had developed up to that time. Still available in England, although not elsewhere, it is a large, exhibition-style flower

'Liselle'

ABOVE 'Linda Campbell'
INSET 'Lissy Horstmann'

'Lincoln Cathedral'

'Little Purple'

(with 35 petals) and fragrant, showing up well against dark, bronze-green foliage.

RULis · Fryer, England, UK, 1982
'Whisky Mac' × 'Matador'
Repeat flowering · Moderate fragrance
HABIT Bush H/W 1.5m/1.2m (5ft/4ft) · ZONES 5–11

'Lissy Horstmann'

HYBRID TEA · MEDIUM RED

'Lissy Horstmann' might be a little short on petals, only 25, but everything else about it is first-rate – the glowing crimson color, the long buds, the strong, upright bush, and above all the intense perfume. The foliage is matt and dark green. A fine rose for cutting, it was raised in 1943 by Mathias Tantau senior, the father of the raiser of 'Fragrant Cloud', 'Blue Moon' and many other excellent roses. A rare rose indeed now, but one well worth seeking out if you live in a warm climate.

Tantau, Germany, 1943
'Hadley' × 'Heros'
Repeat flowering · Intense, damask fragrance
HABIT Bush H/W 1.4m/110cm (4ft 6in/3ft 6in) · ZONES 5–11

'Little Darling'

FLORIBUNDA · YELLOW BLEND

Although 'Little Darling' has never achieved elsewhere the popularity it enjoys in the United States, it is a reliable and most attractive rose. Its double, salmon-pink and gold flowers are very prettily shaped, and are carried in good clusters all the season, exuding a spicy fragrance. The bush, although not especially tall, is shrubby and spreading, the foliage leathery and healthy. It can be used as a moderate-sized shrub in a mixed planting or as a 1m (3ft) tall flowering hedge. It has been much used as a parent by American hybridists.

Duehrsen, USA, 1956
'Captain Thomas' × ('Baby Chateau' × 'Fashion')
Repeat flowering · Moderate, spicy fragrance
HABIT Bush H/W 1.5m/1.2m (5ft/4ft) · ZONES 5–11

🌹 Portland (Oregon, USA) Gold Medal 1958, American Rose Society David Fuerstenberg Award 1964

'Little Darling'

with 28 petals in a blend of pink and apricot. The foliage is lush and glossy, as you would expect from the parentage.

GLAnlin · Langdale, England, UK, 1985
'Silver Jubilee' × 'Royal Dane'
Repeat flowering · Slight fragrance
HABIT Bush H/W 1.2m/1m (4ft/3ft) · ZONES 5–11

🌹 Royal National Rose Society Gold Medal 1985

'Linda Campbell'

HYBRID RUGOSA · MEDIUM RED

'Tall Poppy'

When Ralph Moore introduces one of the by-products of his lifelong quest for better Miniatures, the rose world sits up and takes notice – it is bound to be a fine and distinctive rose. Like this one, which is a handsome, spreading shrub, with much of *R. rugosa*'s hardiness and disease resistance, although its grey-green foliage is less quilted and the semi-double flowers are Floribunda-like and borne in elegant sprays. They are a fine shade of crimson with none of the Rugosa tendency to magenta – but with none of its scent, either. The name honors a distinguished and much-loved American rosarian, a former Director of the American Rose Society.

MORten · Moore, USA, 1990
'Anytime' × 'Rugosa Magnifica'
Repeat flowering · No fragrance
HABIT Bush H/W 1.8m/1.2m (6ft/4ft) · ZONES 3–10

'Liselle'

HYBRID TEA · ORANGE BLEND

'Royal Romance'

The Dutch raiser, De Ruiter, preferred to name this 1980 introduction 'Liselle', but when Fryer's introduced it to the United Kingdom two years later, it became 'Royal Romance' in honor of the Duke and Duchess of York. Its peach and titian flowers echoed the color of the duchess's hair. The double flowers are of good size, excellent shape

'Little Purple'

FLORIBUNDA · MAUVE

'Love Potion', 'Purple Puff'

This rose is listed under the name the raiser originally gave it, but he changed his mind and rechristened it 'Love Potion', a much

'Living Fire'

'Lolita'

happier choice. In any case, it is hardly a Floribunda version of the popular 'Big Purple'. Its small, perfectly formed blooms are more reminiscent of 'Paradise', but in richer dress of deep lilac with burgundy-red edges to the petals. There is fragrance, too, and the foliage is dark and leaden green, rather like that of 'Paradise'. It is a very pretty rose to introduce into a mixed planting of roses and perennials, but watch out for black spot.

JACsedi | Christensen, USA, 1994
Seedling × 'Dilly Dilly'
Repeat flowering | Moderate fragrance

HABIT Bush H/W 1m/60cm (3ft/2ft) | ZONES 5–11

'Liverpool Echo'

FLORIBUNDA | ORANGE PINK

'Liverpool'

Another rose that is perhaps more suited to cool climates than hot, 'Liverpool Echo' bears beautifully spaced clusters of double, soft salmon-pink flowers, their many petals beautifully arranged, on a bushy plant of average height, with dark green leaves. The perfection of its clusters makes it very popular with exhibitors, but it is also well liked as a garden rose. Named for the British newspaper, it seems to be only available in Britain and New Zealand these days.

McGredy, Northern Ireland, UK, 1971
('Little Darling' × 'Goldilocks') × 'München'
Repeat flowering | Slight fragrance

HABIT Bush H/W 1m/60cm (3ft/2ft) | ZONES 5–11

🏆 Portland (Oregon, USA) Gold Medal 1979

'Livin' Easy'

FLORIBUNDA | ORANGE BLEND

'Fellowship'

Although Jack Harkness introduced this rose in Britain in 1992, American rose-lovers had to wait until 1996, when it arrived in the United States adorned with a new American name and the AARS award. Never mind, this is an excellent rose, one of the easiest of all the apricot-to-orange roses to grow. The bush is tall, strong and prolific, and although its branches are very thorny, they are well clothed in glossy, unusually disease-resistant foliage. The attractively ruffled, double flowers are large for a Floribunda, the clusters correspondingly small. Pleasantly scented, the flowers vary with the season from apricot and gold to orange and gold, and they do not fade with age. They last very well in the vase.

HARwelcome | Harkness, UK, 1992
'Southampton' × 'Remember Me'
Repeat flowering | Moderate, fruity fragrance

HABIT Bush H/W 1m/60cm (3ft/2ft) | ZONES 5–11

🌹 Royal National Rose Society Gold Medal 1990, All-America Rose Selection 1996

'Living Fire'

FLORIBUNDA | ORANGE BLEND

The double flowers of 'Living Fire' are not very large, but they are nicely shaped, vivid in their orange-red color, and rich with fragrance. The foliage is a particularly dark green, setting them off very well. British-bred, it is only available in that country now. Do not confuse it with 'Living', a now rare Hybrid Tea of similar color raised by Walter Lammerts back in 1957.

Gregory, England, UK, 1972
'Super Star' × seedling
Repeat flowering | Moderate fragrance

HABIT Bush H/W 1m/60cm (3ft/2ft) | ZONES 5–11

'Lolita'

HYBRID TEA | APRICOT BLEND

'LitaKOR'

In Vladimir Nabokov's novel *Lolita*, Humbert Humbert had a rather prickly time with a young lady, and perhaps this influenced Reimer Kordes when he named this rose after her in 1973. It is very prickly, like most seedlings from 'Colour Wonder'. Everyone loves the double flowers, with their radiant blends of apricot and gold, their perfect form

'Long Tall Sally'

and their seductive fragrance. The foliage
is glossy and dark green, and may need
watching for black spot.

KORlita ׀ Kordes, Germany, 1973
'Colour Wonder' × seedling
Repeat flowering ׀ *Moderate fragrance*

HABIT Bush H/W 1.5m/1.2m (5ft/4ft) ׀ ZONES 5–11

'Long Tall Sally'

SHRUB ׀ LIGHT PINK

Stirling Macoboy would have enjoyed this
rose, for when Little Richard appeared on his
radio show back in 1956 to sing his great hit
'Long Tall Sally', it was the start of a lifelong
friendship. The name is apt; although it is officially classed as a Shrub, the plant produces
long, tall shoots and can equally well be
enjoyed as a moderate climber or a pillar rose.
The flowers, in their large and small sprays,
are very pretty, almost single, and borne very
freely indeed in spring, more sparingly thereafter. They aren't quite white, being tinted
peach and apricot in the bud and opening
faintly blushed with pink, and they are pleasingly scented. The large, dark green leaves
have a good reputation for disease resistance.

WEKajazoul ׀ Carruth, USA, 1999
'All That Jazz' × *R. soulieana* derivative
Repeat flowering ׀ *Moderate fragrance*

HABIT Bush/climber H/W 3m/1.8m (10ft/6ft) ׀ ZONES 5–11

'L'Oréal Trophy'

HYBRID TEA ׀ ORANGE BLEND

'Alexis'

This 1981 sport from 'Alexander' resembles
its parent in its vigorous, tall habit, its tendency
to produce petals with scalloped edges, and
its preference for a cool climate. In hot areas
the flowers are apt to be undersized. The color
is a pale orange, almost apricot, as against the
vivid scarlet of 'Alexander'. The foliage is glossy
and dark green. 'L'Oréal Trophy' was sponsored
by a cosmetics manufacturer.

HARlexis ׀ Harkness, England, UK, 1981
'Alexander' sport
Repeat flowering ׀ *Moderate fragrance*

HABIT Bush H/W 1.8m/1.2m (6ft/4ft) ׀ ZONES 5–10

🌹 Bagatelle (Paris) Gold Medal 1982, Belfast Gold
Medal and Prize of the City of Belfast 1984, West
Flanders Gold Medal 1986

TOP 'Livin' Easy'
INSET 'Liverpool Echo'
RIGHT 'L'Oréal Trophy'

'Los Angeles Beautiful'

GRANDIFLORA ı YELLOW BLEND

For the vigor of its growth and its tendency to bloom in clusters, 'Los Angeles Beautiful' is classed as a Grandiflora in the United States. The double flowers are rather like those of its parent 'Queen Elizabeth' in size and shape. They derive their prettily blended tones of yellow and coral from the other parent, 'Rumba'. Unfortunately, neither parent was able to give them much in the way of perfume. The bush has leathery leaves. Although it is rarely seen now, it is still worth planting in warm climates – like that of Los Angeles.

Lammerts, USA, 1967
'Queen Elizabeth' × 'Rumba'
Repeat flowering ı *Slight fragrance*

HABIT Bush H/W 1.8m/1.2m (6ft/4ft) ı ZONES 5–11

'Louise Estes'

HYBRID TEA ı PINK BLEND

Louise Estes is a watercolorist from Alabama who has long specialized in painting roses. Large, double and of classic high-centred form, her rose is a regular prize-winner on American show benches, although Australian and New Zealand exhibitors don't seem to

'Love & Peace'

'Los Angeles Beautiful'

have discovered it yet. Pleasingly fragrant, it is a most attractive blend of rose-pink and white. The bush is of average height, slightly spreading, and repeats its bloom faster than many big, full-petalled roses do. The matt, mid-green foliage has an excellent reputation for disease resistance.

Winchel, USA, 1991
Seedling × 'Miss Canada'
Repeat flowering ı *Moderate, fruity fragrance*

HABIT Bush H/W 1.5m/1.2m (5ft/4ft) ı ZONES 5–10

'Love'

GRANDIFLORA ı RED BLEND

Jackson & Perkins may be one of the oldest rose-growers in the United States, but even

ABOVE 'Love Story'
LEFT INSET 'Love'
RIGHT INSET 'Louise Estes'

they were not old-fashioned enough to call their trio of 1980 AARS winners 'Love', 'Honor' and 'Obey' – the third is 'Cherish'. 'Love', classed as a Grandiflora in the United States, is a little short in growth for that class. Most would be content to have it as a Hybrid Tea. It is a nice rose, its medium-sized, double flowers shapely and distinctive in their crimson

'Loving Memory'

and white colors. Unlike many bicolors, the contrast holds for the life of the flower. The foliage is leathery and dark green, with a good reputation for disease resistance.

JACtwin ⏐ Warriner, USA, 1980
Seedling × 'Red Gold'
Repeat flowering ⏐ *Slight fragrance*
HABIT Bush H/W 1.5m/1m (5ft/3ft) ⏐ ZONES 5–11
🌺 Monza Gold Medal 1977, All-America Rose Selection 1980, Portland (Oregon, USA) Gold Medal 1980

'Love & Peace'

HYBRID TEA ⏐ YELLOW BLEND

The name invites comparison with its parent 'Peace', and indeed it takes after it in its glossy leaves and the style of its flowers, although their blends of yellow and pink are rather richer, especially in sunny weather, which brings out the pink tones. Although it sometimes opens rather loosely, at its best it can be a winner on the show bench. And as the stems are long and the flowers long-lasting, it is a fine rose for cutting. The plant is on the tall side and is reputed to be unusually winter-hardy for a Hybrid Tea. The chief demerits are the rather mild fragrance and an occasional tendency to black spot.

BAIpeace ⏐ Lim and Twomey, USA, 2002
Seedling × 'Peace'
Repeat flowering ⏐ *Light fragrance*
HABIT Bush H/W 1.5m/1.2m (5ft/4ft) ⏐ ZONES 4–11
🌺 All-America Rose Selection 2002

'Love Story'

HYBRID TEA ⏐ ORANGE BLEND

Mathias Tantau named this rose to cash in on the success of the hit movie *Love Story*, which

was released in 1970. The well-formed, double flowers are orange, and the bush is strong, with glossy foliage; but there is little fragrance, which is rather unromantic! It has virtually disappeared from the catalogues, and Herr Tantau recycled the name in 1990 for a red Floribunda.

TANvery ⏐ Tantau, Germany, 1974
Parentage undisclosed
Repeat flowering ⏐ *Slight fragrance*
HABIT Bush H/W 1.2m/1m (4ft/3ft) ⏐ ZONES 6–10

'Lovely Lady'

HYBRID TEA ⏐ MEDIUM PINK

'Dickson's Jubilee'

When a firm like Dickson's names one of its roses in honor of its 150th birthday, you can be sure it will be worth growing. It seems that commercial considerations took over, as the star of 1986 was rechristened 'Lovely Lady' to entice a public ignorant of rose history. Under either of its names it is a delightful rose, large, double and shapely, of soft coral and salmon-pink coloring, and full of the fragrance that so many Modern

Roses miss out on. It is a bushy plant, with glossy, mid-green foliage.

DICjubell ⏐ Dickson, Northern Ireland, UK, 1986
'Silver Jubilee' × ('Eurorose' × 'Anabell')
Repeat flowering ⏐ *Strong fragrance*
HABIT Bush H/W 1.5m/75cm (5ft/3ft 6in) ⏐ ZONES 5–11

'Loving Memory'

HYBRID TEA ⏐ MEDIUM RED

'Burgund '81', 'Red Cedar'

This is one of those roses that, while not a bestseller, has a devoted following. Popular in Europe and well liked in Australia, it is a leading exhibition rose in New Zealand. It is only in America that it seems to be neglected. Perhaps its lack of scent – always a serious demerit in a red rose – is the problem, for it is a good, strong grower, the glossy leaves are resistant to mildew, and the blood-red flowers are one and all large and shapely.

KORgund ⏐ Kordes, Germany, 1983
Seedling × seedling of 'Red Planet'
Repeat flowering ⏐ *Slight fragrance*
HABIT Bush H/W 1.5m/1.2m (5ft/4ft) ⏐ ZONES 5–11
🌺 Dublin Gold Medal 1981

'Lovely Lady'

'Luis Brinas'

'Lustige'

'Luis Brinas'

HYBRID TEA | ORANGE BLEND

The name of Pedro Dot (1885–1976), Spain's master hybridist, is not seen in the catalogues as often as some others these days, but his roses are generally still worth a second look. Take 'Luis Brinas' as an example. Its coppery buds, long and elegant, open to loosely formed, orange and coral blooms, set off by shiny, green foliage. The flowers are deliciously fragrant, too. Its only fault is a decided preference for sunny climates; in humidity it gets black spot.

Dot, Spain, 1934
'Madame Butterfly' × 'Federico Casas'
Repeat flowering | *Strong, fruity fragrance*

HABIT Bush H/W 1.2m/1m (4ft/3ft) | ZONES 6–10

'Lustige'

HYBRID TEA | RED BLEND

'Jolly'

Don't mistranslate the name as 'lusty', but think rather of the 'merry' widow of Franz Lehar's famous operetta *Die Lustige Witwe*. Still, there is certainly something lusty about the plant of this rose, which is a tall, bushy grower, with large, leathery, glossy foliage, and something very merry about the large, double flowers, brightly beautiful in their coppery red color, fine shape and fascinating fragrance. It was raised by Reimer Kordes in 1973, from two favorite roses. Oddly enough, in America it is known by its German name rather than as 'Jolly'.

LuKOR | Kordes, Germany, 1973
'Peace' × 'Brandenburg'
Repeat flowering | *Moderate fragrance*

HABIT Bush H/W 1.5m/1.2m (5ft/4ft) | ZONES 5–11

'Lynn Anderson'

HYBRID TEA | PINK BLEND

'Oh My God'

Fancy calling a rose 'Oh My God'! Much better to stick with Lynn Anderson, the popular American singer whose great hit was 'I never promised you a rose garden'. Some say that should be this rose's theme song, too. They concede that it is a strong, cold-hardy bush, that the leaves are large, healthy and handsome, and that the way the shapely, double flowers blend white and rose-pink is most attractive – but, they say,

'Lyon Rose'

the flowers aren't all that large to begin with, and the enormous leaves make them look undersized and skimpy. Others do not find this a problem, and they seem to be in the majority. Despite its rather mild fragrance, it is popular rose.

WEKjoe | Winchel, USA, 1993
Seedling × 'Gold Medal'
Repeat flowering | *Slight fragrance*

HABIT Bush H/W 1.5–1.8m/1.2 m (5–6ft/4ft) | ZONES 5–11

'Lyon Rose'

HYBRID TEA | ORANGE PINK

'The Lyons Rose'

Joseph Pernet-Ducher won the nickname the 'Wizard of Lyon', and his roses the now-obsolete title 'Pernetiana', from his huge success in creating yellow roses. 'Lyon Rose' was one of his triumphs, not yellow this time, but a then-new blend of shrimp-pink and coral, its double blooms globular and full-petalled, with a rather sharp scent inherited from *R. foetida persiana*. Despite its only moderate vigor and susceptibility to black spot, its color won it the Bagatelle gold medal in 1909 and great popularity. The foliage is shiny and dark green.

Pernet-Ducher, France, 1907
'Madame Mélanie Soupert' × seedling of 'Soleil d'Or'
Repeat flowering | *Moderate fragrance*

HABIT Bush H/W 1.5m/1.2m (5ft/4ft) | ZONES 5–11
Bagatelle (Paris) Gold Medal 1909

'Ma Perkins'

FLORIBUNDA | PINK BLEND

Novelty is no criterion of excellence. 'Ma Perkins', although raised in 1952, remains one of the best pink Floribundas, its double flowers as shapely and fragrant as ever, its blend of pale peach and coral as appealing. The plant is compact and easily grown, although you might sometimes have to guard against mildew, and the matt, dark green foliage makes a lovely foil for the delicate flowers. It never makes a great mass of bloom, but from one end of the season to the other there always seem to be a few exquisite flowers to admire. It was named after a popular broadcaster, no relation to the Perkins family of Jackson & Perkins.

Boerner, USA, 1952
'Red Radiance' × 'Fashion'
Repeat flowering | *Moderate fragrance*

HABIT Bush H/W 1m/60cm (3ft/2ft) | ZONES 5–11
All-America Rose Selection 1953

'Madame Abel Chatenay'

HYBRID TEA I PINK BLEND

Every rose-lover has some great favorite from childhood. The author's was 'Madame Abel Chatenay', which he vividly remembered growing in his mother's garden in Hobart in the early 1930s. The foliage is bronze, and the double flowers are a delight in their blend of soft pinks that rose-lovers used to call 'chatenay-pink'. Raised by Joseph Pernet-Ducher in 1895, it became a great favorite with the greenhouse growers, and just before World War I it was estimated that two out of three roses sold in British flower shops were 'Chatenay'. Its only fault is that the bushes are short-lived.

Pernet-Ducher, France, 1895
'Dr Grill' × 'Victor Verdier'
Repeat flowering I Strong, tea fragrance

HABIT 3ush H/W 75cm/30cm (3ft 6in/2ft 6in) I ZONES 5–11

'Lynn Anderson'

'Ma Perkins'

'Madame Abel Chatenay'

'Madame Butterfly'

HYBRID TEA I LIGHT PINK

One of the world's best-loved roses in the years between the wars was the creamy pink and sweetly fragrant 'Madame Butterfly', a sport from William Paul's 'Ophelia', discovered in 1916 in the nurseries of E. G. Hill & Company

'Madame Butterfly'

'Madame Caroline Testout'

'Madame G. Forest-Colchomet'

'Madame Edouard Herriot'

of Indiana. The florists were soon growing it by the millions, and its blooms filled silver rose bowls everywhere. A few years later along came a climbing sport, and history repeated itself – there was hardly a fence or pergola in the civilized world not adorned with 'Madame Butterfly'. It is no period piece, however, as it remains one of the loveliest and most reliable pale pink roses. The foliage is matt and dark green. The name, of course, honors the beautiful heroine of Puccini's opera.

Hill, USA, 1918
'Ophelia' sport
Repeat flowering ı *Strong, damask fragrance*
HABIT Bush H/W 1.5m/1.2m (5ft/4ft) ı ZONES 5–11

'Madame Caroline Testout'

HYBRID TEA ı MEDIUM PINK

'Caroline Testout'

For many years, it is said, you could not go very far in Portland, Oregon, without encountering 'Madame Caroline Testout'. It was planted

in thousands all along the city's streets, and won Portland the title of America's Rose City. It was another triumph for Joseph Pernet-Ducher of Lyon, who had raised it in 1890 and named it for a Paris fashion designer. Appropriately, the double blooms are described as 'satin-pink', the perfect color for 1890. The plant is strong and long-lived, and there is an excellent climbing sport, too. The foliage is rich green and smooth. It was photographed in Osaka on the occasion of its centenary, looking as radiant as ever.

Pernet-Ducher, France, 1890
'Madame de Tartas' × 'Lady Mary Fitzwilliam'
Repeat flowering ı *Moderate fragrance*
HABIT Bush H/W 75cm/30cm (3ft 6in/2ft 6in) ı ZONES 5–11

'Madame Edouard Herriot'

HYBRID TEA ı ORANGE BLEND

'Daily Mail Rose'

'Madame Edouard Herriot' created a double sensation in 1913. Firstly for its altogether new color, flame paling to coral-pink, and secondly for winning the £1000 prize offered by the London *Daily Mail* for a new rose to bear the newspaper's name. But the raiser, Joseph Pernet-Ducher, had already named it for the wife of the man who shortly after became the prime minister of France! Supported by

the National Rose Society, Pernet-Ducher kept his prize, and the rose its original name. It is best grown as a climber these days, and its loosely semi-double blooms, glossy foliage and zigzag branches are as distinctive as ever.

Pernet-Ducher, France, 1913
'Madame Caroline Testout' × Hybrid Tea
Repeat flowering ı *Moderate fragrance*
HABIT Bush H/W 110cm/1m (4ft 6in/3ft) ı ZONES 5–11

'Madame G. Forest-Colchomet'

HYBRID TEA ı DEEP PINK

This glowing rose appears to be the earliest rose from the great amateur hybridist Charles Mallerin. That is its only claim to fame, as no modern catalogue lists it and it survives only in museum gardens like that of the Roseraie de l'Haÿ, where it was photographed. Launched in 1928, it is nearly double, rich carmine in color and strongly fragrant. The foliage is dull green and prone to mildew. Its parent, 'Hadley', was a leading dark red rose in the early 1920s.

Mallerin, France, 1928
'Hadley' sport
Repeat flowering ı *Intense, damask fragrance*
HABIT Bush H/W 75cm/30m (3ft 6in/2ft 6in) ı ZONES 5–11

'Madame Georges Delbard'

HYBRID TEA ı DARK RED

'Madame Delbard'

For many years this has been the world's leading red cut-flower rose, which must have given great satisfaction to 'Papi' Delbard, who introduced it in 1979 and named it for his wife. It has the reputation of being one of the relatively few greenhouse roses that does well in the garden, at least in warm climates. The bush is upright, with handsome, medium green foliage, and the double flowers of velvety dark crimson are of exhibition quality. Unfortunately, they have missed out on fragrance.

DELadel | Delbard, Georges, 1982
[('Super Star' × 'Samourai') × ('Super Star' × ('Rome Glory' × 'Impeccable'))]
Repeat flowering | *Almost no fragrance*
HABIT Bush H/W 1.5m/1.2m (5ft/4ft) | ZONES 5–11

'Madame Joseph Perraud'

HYBRID TEA | YELLOW BLEND

'Sunburst'

On Joseph Pernet-Ducher's death in 1928, his business passed on to Jean Gaujard, who released 'Madame Joseph Perraud' in 1934.

Some people think it was in fact one of the last creations of the 'Wizard of Lyon'. It was popular for some years in America as 'Sunburst', but like so many of the early yellow Hybrid Teas it is best in a warm, dry climate, where black spot is not a problem. The large, double flowers are of handsome shape, their old gold color lightly touched with salmon. The foliage is glossy and dark green.

Gaujard, France, 1934
'Julien Potin' × seedling
Repeat flowering | *Moderate fragrance*
HABIT Bush H/W 1.2m/1m (4ft/3ft) | ZONES 5–11
Bagatelle (Paris) Gold Medal 1934, Lyon Gold Medal 1934

'Madame Louis Laperrière'

HYBRID TEA | MEDIUM RED

'Madame Louise Laperrière'

The English might well counter Napoleon's remark that they are a nation of shopkeepers with the observation that France is full of rose-breeders, all naming their creations after their wives! Let us not begrudge Mme Louis Laperrière of Chesnes her modicum of fame, however. Her rose has long been regarded in Europe as one of the better velvety red roses, in the manner of 'Etoile de Hollande'. Her husband introduced it in 1951, and it won the Bagatelle gold medal. It has beautiful fragrance, and does best in cool climates. The foliage is leathery and mid-green.

Laperrière, France, 1951
'Crimson Glory' × seedling
Repeat flowering | *Intense, damask fragrance*
HABIT Bush H/W 1.4m/1m (4ft 6in/3ft) | ZONES 5–11
Bagatelle (Paris) Gold Medal 1950

LEFT INSET 'Madame Georges Delbard'
RIGHT INSET 'Madame Joseph Perraud'
BELOW 'Madame Louis Laperrière'

'Mademoiselle Cécile Brünner'

POLYANTHA | LIGHT PINK

'Cécile Brünner', 'Mignon', 'Sweetheart Rose'

'Cécile Brünner' (most people drop the formal 'Mademoiselle') has been one of the world's favorite roses ever since Joseph Pernet-Ducher and his mother-in-law introduced it in 1881, naming it after the young daughter of a colleague, the Swiss rosarian Ulrich Brünner. Everyone knows its fragrant little blush-pink flowers, unfolding from the most exquisitely shapely buds and set against small, light green leaves; but buy with care. The original is shorter than the average bush, like a China Rose in habit but bearing its flowers in Floribunda-like sprays — but there is a much bigger-growing version, a sport, that often impersonates it in nurseries. A desirable rose in its own right,

'Madras'

it goes by the names 'Bloomfield Abundance' and 'Spray Cécile Brünner'. Almost identical in leaf and flower, it is sometimes called 'Bloomfield Abundance', despite the existence of another rose of that name. It is a desirable Shrub Rose in its own right.

Ducher, France, 1881
Said to be double-flowered Multiflora × 'Souvenir d'un Ami'
Repeat flowering | *Moderate fragrance*
HABIT Bush H/W 1.2m/60cm (4ft/2ft) | ZONES 4–10

World Federation of Rose Societies Old Rose Hall of Fame 1988, Royal Horticultural Society Award of Garden Merit 1993

'Mademoiselle Cécile Brünner', Climbing

CLIMBING POLYANTHA | LIGHT PINK

'Mademoiselle Cécile Brünner, Climbing', 'Mignon, Climbing', 'Sweetheart Rose, Climbing'

The much-loved 'Mademoiselle Cécile Brünner' is just as lovely in its very vigorous climbing version, which originated in California in 1894. Forgive it its lack of repeat-flowering for the sake of its health, its ease of culture and the lavishness with which it blooms in early summer. Do not be surprised if the flowers are a trifle darker and larger than on the bush. They are still most exquisite. The foliage is the same as the parent's, small and mid-green.

Hosp, USA, 1894
'Mademoiselle Cécile Brünner' sport
Summer flowering | *Moderate fragrance*
HABIT Bush H/W 7.5m/6m (25ft/20ft) | ZONES 5–11

BELOW 'Magenta'

TOP LEFT 'Mademoiselle Cécile Brünner'
LEFT 'Mademoiselle Cécile Brünner', Climbing

'Maggie Barry'

'Mahina '81'

'Magic Mountain'

'Magenta'

FLORIBUNDA ⁞ MAUVE

'Kordes's Magenta'

A strong and prolific grower, almost a Shrub Rose – it will grow 1.8m (6ft) tall if lightly pruned – 'Magenta' bears sweetly fragrant blooms of Old Garden Rose form and petal-lage. The name suggests the color, on the border between pink and mauve, although it is much gentler than the magenta dye is apt to be in fabrics and 1960s wallpapers. Plant it in a mixed border, with suitable perennials to mask its bare lower stems. The foliage is broad, leathery and dark green.

Kordes, Germany, 1954
Yellow Floribunda × 'Lavender Pinocchio'
Repeat flowering ⁞ *Intense, fruity fragrance*

HABIT Bush H/W 1.8m/1m (6ft/3ft) ⁞ ZONES 5–11

'Magic Mountain'

FLORIBUNDA ⁞ YELLOW BLEND

Hardly mountainous in its growth – indeed, the bushes are on the low side – 'Magic Mountain' has generous clusters of quite large, full-petalled flowers blending yellow and red, the red taking over as the flower ages. Its chief claim to fame among hordes of similarly hued roses is that it is more fragrant than most. The foliage is glossy, leathery and dark green. It is an Armstrong Nurseries introduction of 1973, a period when Thomas Mann's novel of the same name was enjoying renewed popularity.

Armstrong, USA, 1973
'Circus' × 'Texan'
Repeat flowering ⁞ *Slight fragrance*

HABIT Bush H/W 1m/60cm (3ft/2ft) ⁞ ZONES 5–11

'Madras'

HYBRID TEA ⁞ PINK BLEND

It is most frustrating for those of us who follow form when a rose-breeder tells us that the parentage of his latest creation is 'seedling × seedling'. This is the case with 'Madras', introduced by Bill Warriner in 1981. The double blooms are stunning, wherever they came from, perfect in form, rich in fragrance, and gorgeous in their deep, glowing pink with suggestions of purple at the petal edges and gold at the base. The foliage is a leathery green and abundant. 'Madras' should have become popular, but it vanished from the catalogues rather quickly.

Warriner, USA, 1981
Seedling × seedling
Repeat flowering ⁞ *Moderate fragrance*

HABIT Bush H/W 1.2m/1.2m (4ft/4ft) ⁞ ZONES 5–11

'Maggie Barry'

HYBRID TEA ⁞ PINK BLEND

There are two celebrities called Maggie Barry – one a Los Angeles fashion designer, the other the presenter of New Zealand's best-rated gardening show and a friend of the raiser. It is the latter, of course, to whom Sam McGredy dedicated this rose. Although not strongly scented, it is a bright and handsome rose, opening from long, coral buds to large, high-centred blooms with scalloped petals in a pleasing two-tone blend of coral and salmon-pink. The bush is of average height, with rather pale green leaves and a very good reputation for both disease resistance and freedom of bloom.

MACoborn ⁞ McGredy, New Zealand, 1995
'Louise Gardener' × 'West Coast'
Repeat flowering ⁞ *Slight fragrance*

HABIT Bush H/W 1.5m/1.2m (5ft/4ft) ⁞ ZONES 5–10

'Mahina '81'

HYBRID TEA ⁞ APRICOT BLEND

Not all of Francis Meilland's roses repeated the sensational success of 'Peace'. One such was 'Mahina' of 1956, a lovely flower in an unusual, almost-orange shade. It never caught the public's fancy – too much black spot, it is said – and after Francis's tragic death from cancer in 1958, his family decided to try again with the same parents. The result was 'Mahina 81', and it is a beauty, with great, sumptuous, peaches-and-cream flowers as silken as peonies and fragrant, too. The foliage is dark green. It was photographed in Kyoto, but it seems not to have caught the fancy of the rest of the world.

Meilland, France, 1981
Parentage undeclared
Repeat flowering ⁞ *Moderate fragrance*

HABIT Bush H/W 1.5m/1.2m (5ft/4ft) ⁞ ZONES 5–11

'Maid of Honour'

HYBRID TEA ı YELLOW BLEND

'Maid of Honor'

One expects a maid of honor to be feminine and fragrant, and 'Maid of Honour' certainly lives up to expectations with its shapely, sweetly scented blooms in blends of ivory and cream, sometimes blushed with pink. The bush is no swooning maiden, though. It is tall and upright, with foliage that is bold and leathery. It is the creation of a relatively small concern, the Von C. Weddle family of New Albany, Indiana, who introduced it in 1984. Do not confuse it with Kordes's earlier coral Flori-bunda of the same name.

Weddle, Bush, 1986
'Folklore' × seedling
Repeat flowering ı *Sweet fragrance*

HABIT Bush H/W 1.5m/1.2m (5ft/4ft) ı ZONES 5–11

'Maigold'

SHRUB ı DEEP YELLOW

'Maygold'

'Maigold' is another of those accommodating roses that can be grown either as a climber or a large shrub. Either way it is a delight, with exceptionally handsome, luxuriant green foliage as well as marvellous flowers, semi-double and richly fragrant, in old gold. Through its father it has inherited the *R. pimpinellifolia* habit of early blooming, but do not expect more than the occasional flower after the gorgeous spring display. Cool climates suit it best.

Kordes, Germany, 1953
'Poulsen's Pink' × 'Frühlingstag'
Spring flowering ı *Intense, spicy fragrance*

HABIT Shrub/climber H/W 3.5m/2.5m (12ft/8ft) ı ZONES 5–11

🌹 Anerkannte Deutsche Rose (Germany) 1953

'Maid of Honour'

'Maigold'

'Malaga'

CLIMBING HYBRID TEA ı DEEP PINK

Deep coral-pink, 'Malaga' bears its double blooms on and off all season on a shortish climber with glossy green leaves, bronze when young. So far so ordinary, but the nice thing about this rose is its really excellent fragrance, a quality not overly abundant among the repeat-flowering modern climbers. The foliage is glossy and dark green. It was named for the Spanish resort.

McGredy, New Zealand, 1971
('Hamburger Phoenix' × 'Spectacular') × 'Copenhagen'
Repeat flowering ı *Intense fragrance*

HABIT Climber H/W 2.5m/1.2m (8ft/4ft) ı ZONES 5–11

'Malaga'

'Manou Meilland'

HYBRID TEA ⏐ MAUVE

All stars must start to shine some time. In the case of 'Manou Meilland', that was in 1979. 'Manou' is the family nickname for Marie-Louisette Meilland, and you know that when a rose bears the name of a family member, the Meillands are pretty proud of it. Well they might be, for the rose is a stunner: large, double and shapely, a glowing deep pink, and borne freely on a healthy bush. The foliage is leathery and dark green. A lack of fragrance is its only fault. It does best in mild-winter climates.

MEItulimon ⏐ Meilland, France, 1979
('Baronne Edmond de Rothschild' × 'Baronne Edmond de Rothschild') × ('Ma Fille' × 'Love Song')
Repeat flowering ⏐ *Slight fragrance*

HABIT Bush H/W 1.5m/1.2m (5ft/4ft) ⏐ ZONES 5–11

Madrid Gold Medal 1978, Gold Star of the South Pacific, Palmerston North (New Zealand) 1980

'Manuela'

HYBRID TEA ⏐ MEDIUM PINK

Mathias Tantau's 'Manuela' would seem to bear out the rose-growers' belief that cool pink roses are difficult to sell. It has never been popular outside Germany and the United Kingdom, where it was championed by the late Harry Wheatcroft. Yet it is a very good rose, its color enlivened by a hint of salmon, its flowers large, double and high-centred,

'Marx Queen'

and the bush vigorous and well clad with leathery leaves. Perhaps it was just not novel enough.

Tantau, Germany 1968
Parentage undisclosed
Repeat flowering ⏐ *Moderate fragrance*
HABIT Bush H/W 1.5m/1.2m (5ft/4ft) ⏐ ZONES 5–11

'Manx Queen'

FLORIBUNDA ⏐ ORANGE BLEND

'Isle of Man'

Long one of the leading yellow-flushed-red Floribundas, 'Manx Queen' has rather lost popularity in the face of many newcomers, but it is still a pretty rose, bearing its flowers freely on a compact, dark-leafed bush. Individually, the semi-double blooms, borne in large clusters, are perhaps not very exciting, being somewhat shapeless and scentless. Its virtue is its bright color. A 1963 Dickson creation, it appears to be only available in the United Kingdom now.

Dickson, Northern Ireland, UK, 1963
'Shepherd's Delight' × 'Circus'
Repeat flowering ⏐ *Moderate fragrance*
HABIT Bush H/W 1m/60cm (3ft/2ft) ⏐ ZONES 5–11

'Manou Meilland'

'Manuela'

'Margaret Merril'

FLORIBUNDA ⏐ WHITE

For all its popularity in Britain and the United States, this rose has never been a hit in Australia, probably because it prefers cooler climates. Where it flourishes it is one of the

'Marguerite Hilling'

loveliest of roses, its double flowers perfectly
formed and very sweetly fragrant, their whiteness warmed with a faint pink glow. Give it
the best of everything. The foliage is glossy
and dark green, and can be susceptible to
black spot. It is named for Margaret Merril,
the fictitious beauty adviser for the Oil of
Ulan company.

HARkuly ı Harkness, England, UK, 1977
('Rudolph Timm' × 'Dedication') × 'Pascali'
Repeat flowering ı *Strong, sweet, spicy fragrance*

HABIT Bush H/W 1.2m/1m (4ft/3ft) ı ZONES 5–11

🏵 Geneva Gold Medal 1978, Monza Fragrance Award
1978, Rome Gold Medal 1978, New Zealand International
Rose Ground Trials Gold Medal 1982, Rose Introducers
of New Zealand Gold Medal 1991, Rose Introducers of
New Zealand Fragrance Award 1992

'Marguerite Hilling'

SHRUB ı MEDIUM PINK

'Pink Nevada'

Pink sports from the blush-white 'Nevada',
one of the most widely admired of all Shrub
Roses, have occurred in several places, but
the privilege of naming and introducing
the first one fell to Thomas Hilling in 1959.
'Marguerite Hilling' has all the good qualities
of its parent, making a large, graceful and very
flowery shrub, but the blooms are a beautiful
cool pink, paling gradually to white in the centre.
It can also be trained to a pillar, grown as
a climber or planted to make a hedge. Like
'Nevada', it needs regular removal of the

'Margaret Merril'

old branches to maintain its youthful vigor
and beauty. The foliage is pale green.

Hilling, England, UK, 1959
'Nevada' sport
Repeat flowering ı *Slight fragrance*

HABIT Bush H/W 2.5m/2m (8ft/7ft) ı ZONES 5–11

'Marilyn Monroe'

'Mariandel'

'Mariandel'

FLORIBUNDA ı MEDIUM RED

'Carl Philip', 'Christian IV', 'The Times Rose', 'Timeless Beauty'

What a multiplicity of names! They indicate the enthusiasm with which this rose was marketed everywhere when it was new. With considerable and sustained success, it might be added, except in the United States. It is even in growth, with dark, mahogany-tinted foliage to set off the semi-double, blazing red flowers, and both fuller-petalled and more interesting individually than many such roses bred for the impact of their massed color. There is not much in the way of perfume, but it remains a very good rose.

KORpeahn ı Kordes, Germany, 1986
'Tornado' × 'Redgold'
Repeat flowering ı *Slight fragrance*

HABIT Bush H/W 1m/60cm (3ft/2ft) ı ZONES 5–11
❀ Royal National Rose Society Gold Medal and President's International Trophy 1982, The Hague Gold Medal and Golden Rose 1990

'Marijke Koopman'

HYBRID TEA ı MEDIUM PINK

The long-stemmed beauties in the photograph are just the sort of rose a flower arranger dreams of – and American exhibitors, too, although Australian judges, less impressed by long stems than their American counterparts, would like them to have more petals. Still, even if the open flowers are a little thin, they

'Marijke Koopman'

are a beautiful shade of bright, medium pink with a touch of gold at the base. The flowers are double, and borne in clusters. The bush is strong, and the fragrance just fine. The foliage is leathery and dark green. The rose was named in memory of a young lady tragically killed in a car crash, the daughter of a friend of the raiser. Cool climates suit it best.

Fryer, England, UK, 1979
Parentage undisclosed
Repeat flowering ı *Moderate fragrance*

HABIT Bush H/W 1.5m/1.2m (5ft/4ft) ı ZONES 5–11
❀ The Hague Gold Medal and Golden Rose 1978

'Marilyn Monroe'

HYBRID TEA ı APRICOT BLEND

It was probably inevitable that catalogue writers would be unable to resist describing the rose named in memory of the great movie star as a 'blonde beauty' – but in fact it varies with the season from peaches and cream to apricot, and the opening flowers often show a tint of pale green that would have any blonde rushing to the beauty parlor in dismay. Still, that is one of this rose's charms, and exhibitors have not been slow to admire the shapeliness of the blooms, which are carried on long, straight stems. The tall, slightly spreading bush is wickedly thorny, but it is free-blooming and well clothed in healthy, dark green leaves, and carries its flowers on long stems. There is not a lot of scent, however.

WEKsunspat ı Carruth, USA, 2002
'Sunset Celebration' × 'St Patrick'
Repeat flowering ı *Mild fragrance*

HABIT Bush H/W 1.5m/1.2m (5ft/4ft) ı ZONES 4–11

The Search for the Blue Rose

THE DUTCH MARINERS WHO IN THE SEVENTEENTH CENTURY WERE THE FIRST EUROPEANS TO LAND ON THE AUSTRALIAN CONTINENT WERE GREETED WITH DERISION BACK HOME WHEN THEY REPORTED SIGHTING BLACK SWANS IN NEW HOLLAND. HAD THEY FOUND BLUE ROSES, HOWEVER, THEY WOULD NOT ONLY HAVE BEEN BELIEVED, THEY WOULD HAVE BEEN THOUGHT TO HAVE DISCOVERED A NEW EDEN!

It is odd how people have always dreamed of blue roses. In all the centuries when there were no yellow roses, or flame ones, no one seemed to miss them. Blue roses, however, captured people's imagination. Legend is full of them: a blue rose plays a major role in Rimsky-Korsakov's fairytale opera *Sadko*, and we read in the *Arabian Nights* of magicians who turn roses blue, usually in return for the favors of some virtuous maiden. The thirteenth-century Arabian botanist Ibn el-Awam listed a blue rose among those in his garden, although nobody has seen it since; modern scholars have concluded that it was probably the blue form of *Hibiscus syriacus*, the Rose of Sharon (and no relation of the rose).

Shades of blue

As long ago as the beginning of the nineteenth century, an 'azure' rose was announced as having just arrived from China. Great was the disappointment when it flowered crimson! Perhaps it was just an innocent mistake made in translating the Chinese label – classical Chinese has no word for 'blue'. In fact, there are many purple and lilac roses among the Old Garden Roses – 'Cardinal de Richelieu', 'Reine des Violettes', 'Belle Poitevine', to name but a few – and in 1909 the rambler 'Veilchenblau' appeared with the by then customary fanfare. As its violet flowers fade, they sometimes turn a clear

An arrangement of the first rose with the transgenic blue gene as displayed at the 14th World Rose Convention in Osaka, Japan, in May 2006. Rather than a true blue, the petal color is more a bluish violet. Release of this cultivar for future breeding in Japan is restricted until effects on native Wild Roses has been fully evaluated.

lilac – probably the closest to blue any rose had come until the Modern Rose 'Rhapsody in Blue' appeared in 1999. With its sumptuous clusters of smoke blue/purple blend flowers, this variety caused quite a sensation in the rose world – but a true blue rose it is not. Some Hybrid Tea Roses come in lilac tones, but names such as 'Blue Moon', 'Shocking Blue' and 'Azure Sea' are, it must be said, rather optimistic, however lovely the roses themselves may be. A true blue rose still eludes us.

TOP LEFT 'Neptune'

RIGHT The 'blue rose of the Arabs' is almost certainly *Hibiscus syriacus*, often called the Rose of Sharon, although it is unrelated to the rose.

'Blue Moon' is the most popular of the mauve roses, but its name promises much more than it delivers; it is really pinkish lilac.

TOP 'Blueberry Hill'

ABOVE Purple roses have been with us for a long time: 'Cardinal de Richelieu' dates from 1840.

RIGHT 'Dioressence'

The science of color

Every child who has ever played with a paintbox knows that red plus blue equals purple. Surely, if hybridists could eliminate the red from purple roses, blue would remain? The answer from botanists is a stern 'No!' They tell us that the pigment that makes flowers blue, delphinidin, is absent from the rose, and indeed from all its relatives in the Rosaceae, too. The mauve roses derive their color from the breakdown of the red pigment cyanidin in combination with tannins. Which makes sense — who has not seen a red or pink rose slowly turn purplish with age? The modern mauves often have a greyish or even brownish cast — 'sullied colors', as the great Irish hybridist Alexander Dickson called them. So it seems that our purple and lilac roses are just reds and pinks suffering from premature old age, and no amount of crossing will make them any bluer than they are.

Of course, there is always the million-to-one chance that a mutation will produce a delphinidin-bearing rose, just as a chance mutation some 60 years ago gave the rose the scarlet pigment pelargonidin, which is responsible for the color of such roses as 'Independence', 'Super Star' and 'Alexander' — but don't hold your breath waiting for this to happen. It is somewhat frustrating to find that not all blue flowers owe their color to delphinidin; the brilliantly pure blue of the cornflower is due to cyanidin, the same pigment that makes the rose red. Cyanidin can be either red or blue, depending on the acidity or alkalinity of the flower's sap and the various sugars with which it combines — so, as there are both pink and crimson cornflowers, it seems that all we have to do to breed a blue rose is to persuade the rose to arrange its sap accordingly.

Isolating the blue gene

All we have to do! That is a bigger task than its sounds, for the conditions within the flower are controlled by the DNA in its chromosomes, and so far no one has succeeded in altering the DNA of roses. In 1990, Suntory (Japan) and Florigene Ltd (Australia) began a joint research project to create a blue rose. By 1995 they had successfully created a violet variety of a carnation — which they named 'Moondust' and which is now on sale in Australia and Japan. In 2004, they succeeded in transferring the blue gene that leads to the production of delphinidin to roses, but the resulting rose was more of a bluish violet than blue, in spite of the strong presence of delphinidin. However, under the Cartagena Protocol, an international agreement on biosafety that forms a supplement to the Convention on Biological Diversity, the possible effects of this transgenic technique on Wild Roses in Japan must be evaluated before it can be released for commercial use. It is anticipated that no major effect on Wild Roses will be detected. In the meantime, what is sig-nificant is that the blue gene has been successfully transferred to a rose, whose progeny will have the ability to display a whole new range of colors when they are used in breeding programs.

Scientists will continue to research methods of improving the blue coloration in roses in the hope that this will produce a genuinely blue rose, and future generations may well enjoy an as yet undreamed-of palette of rose colors. Of course, many traditionalists will argue that roses were never meant to be blue — that 'Roses are red, Violets are blue', and that that is the natural way and how things should stay.

'Rhapsody in Blue'

'Marina'

'Marita'

'Marina'

FLORIBUNDA | ORANGE BLEND

It is hard to say whether this 1981 AARS winner was named for the heroine of Shakespeare's *Pericles* or the boat harbors so filled with status symbols in modern life. It is a desirable rose, despite its somewhat thorny branches, for its small clusters of shapely, double flowers of salmon-orange, lit with gold, and its handsomely bronze-tinted foliage. It holds its shape and color well, on the plant or as a cut flower. Introduced by Reimer Kordes in 1974, it was not introduced to the United States until later – hence the date of the AARS award.

RinaKOR | Kordes, Germany, 1974
'Colour Wonder' × seedling
Repeat flowering | *Moderate fragrance*

HABIT Bush H/W 1m/60cm (3ft/2ft) | ZONES 5–11

🌹 All-America Rose Selection 1981

'Marita'

FLORIBUNDA | ORANGE BLEND

This little-known rose is nonetheless very distinctive, with its petals quilled almost like a cactus dahlia. They are a warm salmon-pink

'Marjory Palmer'

with touches of gold, and carried on a tall, open-growing bush with dark green leaves. There is no scent. Introduced by John Mattock, the Oxford rose-grower, in 1961, it seems to survive only in museum gardens nowadays.

Mattock, England, UK, 1961
'Masquerade' × 'Serenade'
Repeat flowering | *No fragrance*

HABIT Bush H/W 1m/60cm (3ft/2ft) | ZONES 5–11

'Marjorie Fair'

SHRUB | RED BLEND

'Red Ballerina', 'Red Yesterday'

The alternative name is not in honor of Soviet dancers, but alludes to the similarity

of 'Marjorie Fair' to its popular parent 'Ballerina'. It makes an easy-care, lavish-flowering bush with great sprays of single flowers all season, but it has not proved as popular as 'Ballerina'; the carmine and white flowers lack delicacy. The small foliage is bright green. The fair Marjorie was a childhood friend of the raiser, Jack Harkness.

HARhero | Harkness, England, UK, 1978
'Ballerina' × 'Baby Faurax'
Repeat flowering | *Slight fragrance*

HABIT Bush H/W 1.2m/1m (4ft/3ft) | ZONES 5–11

🌹 Rome Gold Medal 1977, Bagatelle (Paris) Landscape Prize 1988, Royal Horticultural Society Award of Garden Merit 2002

'Marjory Palmer'

POLYANTHA | MEDIUM PINK

One of the more notable Australian-bred roses, raised by Alister Clark in 1936, 'Marjory Palmer' was one of the most popular Floribundas for many years, holding its own against highly publicized introductions from other countries. It is still a good rose, endowed with excellent glossy foliage, and bearing its double blooms very freely, in large and small clusters. They are not especially shapely, and their deep rose-pink color

'Marjorie Fair'

is no longer fashionable. The rose may yet prove of use to a modern hybridist looking for fresh blood. There is a pale pink sport named 'Alister Clark'.

Clark, Australia, 1936
'Jersey Beauty' × unknown
Repeat flowering ı *Strong, fruity fragrance*
HABIT Bush H/W 1m/1m (3ft/3ft) ı ZONES 4–10

'Marlena'

FLORIBUNDA ı MEDIUM RED

'Marlena' was introduced in 1964, and so is an old lady as Modern Roses go, but some people think that it remains one of the best red Floribundas. Still popular in Europe, it is certainly outstanding among the low growers, the bushes smothering themselves with semi-double flowers of an especially fine color, dark red yet brilliant. The foliage is dark green

'Marlena'

and glossy. It was raised by Reimer Kordes, and apparently the name is a tribute to that great star Marlene Dietrich, who was awarded the red ribbon of the Legion of Honor for her work for Free France in World War II.

Kordes, Germany, 1964
'Gertrud Westphal' × 'Lili Marleen'
Repeat flowering ı *Slight fragrance*
HABIT Bush H/W 1m/60cm (3ft/2ft) ı ZONES 5–11
🌹 Baden-Baden Gold Medal 1962, Belfast Dani Award 1966

'Marmalade'

HYBRID TEA ı ORANGE BLEND

'Marmalade' by name, marmalade in color; the long, pointed buds open to 30-petalled

'Marmalade'

'Marmalade Skies'

blooms in bright orange with yellow on the reverse. The fragrance is reminiscent of tea. The bush is upright, the foliage large and dark green. Borne on long stems, the strongly scented flowers are excellent for cutting. A rare rose now, although it can still be found in the United States.

Swim and Ellis, USA, 1977
'Arlene Francis' × 'Bewitched'
Repeat flowering ı *Intense, tea fragrance*

HABIT Bush H/W 1.5m/1.2m (5ft/4ft) ı ZONES 5–11

'Mary MacKillop'

'Marmalade Skies'

FLORIBUNDA ı ORANGE BLEND

'Tangerine Dream'

'Picture yourself on a boat by the river / With tangerine trees and marmalade skies' sang the Beatles back in 1967; and this award-winning rose would be a good choice to bring a splash of sunset color to the garden. (The boat and the river are optional!) Although they have virtually no scent, the coral-to-orange flowers are nicely shaped, borne in well-spaced clusters, and long-lasting both on the plant and in the vase. The bush is compact and prolific, with good glossy foliage and a good reputation for disease resistance. It is said to put up with more shade than most roses do.

MEImonblan ı Meilland, France, 2001
('Tamango' × 'Parador') × 'Patricia'
Repeat flowering ı *Slight fragrance*

HABIT Bush H/W 1.2m/1m (4ft/3ft) ı ZONES 5–10

🌸 All-America Rose Selection 2001

'Mary MacKillop'

HYBRID TEA ı PINK BLEND

'Mother Mary McKillop'

Mother Mary MacKillop dedicated her life to educating children in Australia's outback, and her reward is that she is set to become Saint Mary of the Cross, Australia's first saint. The rose dedicated to her is a charmer, with fragrant, shell-pink blooms with deeper touches. Perfectly formed, they are of medium size and are borne in clusters of up to half a dozen on a sturdy, glossy-leafed bush. For some reason its American raisers did not introduce it at home, but their Australian agent, Valerie Swane, fell in love with it and included it in her catalogue. It is still much admired in Australia and New Zealand.

Armstrong Nurseries, USA, 1989
Parentage undisclosed
Repeat flowering ı *Moderate fragrance*

HABIT Bush H/W 1.2m/1.2m (4ft/4ft) ı ZONES 6–10

'Mary Rose'

'Mary Rose'

SHRUB ı MEDIUM PINK

David Austin has written that 'Mary Rose' comes close to his ideal in the breeding of his English Roses. It has much of the charm of an Old Garden Rose, with the reliably repeat-flowering habit of a Modern Rose. Unfortunately, the very double, rose-pink flowers do not have any perfume, but they are very lovely. The bush is sturdy and not too large, and it flowers freely all season. A bush in full bloom is quite a feature in a mixed planting. The foliage is matt and

'Masquerade'

mid-green. It was introduced in 1983, the year that Henry VIII's flagship *Mary Rose* was raised from the sea.

AUSmary ⏐ Austin, England, UK, 1983
Seedling × 'The Friar'
Repeat flowering ⏐ *Intense fragrance*

HABIT Bush H/W 1.2m/1.2m (4ft/4ft) ⏐ ZONES 5–11

Royal Horticultural Society Award of Garden Merit 2002

'Masquerade'

FLORIBUNDA ⏐ RED BLEND

Rose-growers today are apt to dwell on the faults of 'Masquerade': the spottiness of the dying flowers, the dull, dark olive-green foliage and the lack of perfume. It is difficult to remember the sensation it created when Jackson & Perkins introduced this semi-double rose back in 1949. It was a first – a rose that opened bright yellow, then gradually turned salmon-pink, then red. There are many roses like 'Masquerade' today, most indeed descended from it, but for a bright show in the garden, 'Masquerade' can still hold its own; and if its leaves are dull, they are also disease-resistant. Do not confuse Boerner's original with Kordes's 2004 pink and white greenhouse Hybrid Tea 'Masquerade'.

Boerner, USA, 1949
'Goldilocks' × 'Holiday'
Repeat flowering ⏐ *Slight fragrance*

HABIT Bush H/W 1.2m/1m (4ft/3ft) ⏐ ZONES 5–11

(Royal) National Rose Society Gold Medal 1952

'Matangi'

FLORIBUNDA ⏐ RED BLEND

Sam McGredy's 'Hand-painted Roses' are often more curious than beautiful, but not 'Matangi'. This is a rose of real distinction and character, its basic vermilion tone softened and brightened by the palest pink, with which the petals are so liberally brushed. The double flowers are very nicely shaped, too, borne in abundance on a strong, healthy plant with small, dark green foliage. The only fault is the lack of pronounced fragrance. The name comes from an old Maori song. It means a breeze, the breeze that will waft departing friends back home.

MACman ⏐ McGredy, New Zealand, 1974
Seedling × 'Picasso'
Repeat flowering ⏐ *Slight fragrance*

HABIT Bush H/W 1m/60cm (3ft/2ft) ⏐ ZONES 5–11

Bagatelle (Paris) Gold Medal 1974, Rome Gold Medal 1974, Royal National Rose Society President's International Trophy 1974, Belfast Dani Award 1976, Portland (Oregon, USA) Gold Medal 1982, Royal Horticultural Society Award of Garden Merit 2002

'Medallion'

'Max Graf'

'Matthias Meilland'

FLORIBUNDA | MEDIUM RED

At first sight, this might seem just another bright red Floribunda, but it has its admirers for its low, bushy growth and general air of neatness – not to mention the fact that the raiser, Alain Meilland, named it for his son. Meilland is not in the habit of naming roses for members of the family unless he thinks

they are pretty good. The double flowers are smallish, the clusters large, and the foliage is mid-green. 'Matthias Meilland' was introduced in 1985 in France, and in 1988 in the United States.

MEIfolio | Meilland, France, 1988
'Madame Charles Sauvage' × 'Fashion' × ('Poppy Flash' × 'Parador')
Repeat flowering | *No fragrance*
HABIT Bush H/W 1m/60cm (3ft/2ft) | ZONES 5–11

'McGredy's Ye

'Matthias Meilland'

'Max Graf'

HYBRID RUGOSA | PINK BLEND

James H. Bowdich of Connecticut appears to have no other roses to his credit, and he can hardly have made his fortune from this 1919 introduction. 'Max Graf' was grown by few nurserymen then. Now ground covers are fashionable, and 'Max Graf' is admired for its shiny foliage and dense, trailing habit. Its only fault is its spring-only flowering season, although the single, rose-pink blossoms appear for many weeks. Yet Mr Bowdich will be remembered as long as roses are grown, for 'Max Graf', in the hands of Wilhelm Kordes, gave rise to the highly cold- and disease-resistant *R. kordesii*, which, married to Modern Roses, has brought

'Meg'

forth both the excellent 'Kordesii' climbers and a still-evolving race of disease-resistant bush and Shrub roses.

Bowditch, USA, 1919
R. rugosa × *R. wichurana*
Spring flowering ı *Slight fragrance*
HABIT Ground cover H/W 60cm/2.5m (2ft/8ft) ı ZONES 4-10

'McGredy's Yellow'

HYBRID TEA ı MEDIUM YELLOW

'Every flower, large or small, of perfect form,' proclaimed McGredy's catalogue back in 1934, announcing their new 'McGredy's Yellow'. They then go on to describe it as buttercup-yellow, a considerable exaggeration. Light lemon-yellow would be more accurate in cool climates; in hot ones it could be very pale indeed. The foliage is bronze-green. Alas, the rose has deteriorated with age and it takes real skill now to grow it to its former perfection. The raiser was the father of the present Sam McGredy.

McGredy, New Zealand, 1933
'Mrs Charles Lamplough' × ('The Queen Alexandra Rose' × 'J. B. Clark')
Repeat flowering ı *Slight fragrance*
HABIT Bush H/W 1.2m/1m (4ft/3ft) ı ZONES 5-11

'Medallion'

HYBRID TEA ı APRICOT BLEND

Everything about 'Medallion' is king-size. The plant is tall, the foliage big and leathery, and the double flowers enormous. Too large, really, for their slender stems. After a shower

of rain they hang their heads and you have to lift them up to appreciate their delightful light apricot color and soft fragrance.

Warriner, USA, 1973
'South Seas' × 'King's Ransom'
Repeat flowering ı *Moderate fragrance*
HABIT Bush H/W 1.2m/1m (4ft/3ft) ı ZONES 5-11
Portland (Oregon, USA) Gold Medal 1972, All-America Rose Selection 1973

'Meg'

CLIMBING HYBRID TEA ı APRICOT BLEND

This rose is rather stiff and thorny in its growth, so that it can be most uncomfortable to prune and train; it is not very fragrant, and, despite what the books will tell you, it is stingy with its repeat blooms. Nonetheless, 'Meg' is one of the most admired of modern climbing roses for the sheer elegance of its single, peach-toned flowers, opening wide from their long buds to show their crimson stamens. The flowers are borne in clusters against glossy, dark green foliage. 'Meg' is best trained to a

tripod or given some support and allowed to make a vast and spreading shrub. The raiser was an amateur, and this appears to be his only introduction.

Gosset, England, UK, 1954
'Paul's Lemon Pillar' × 'Madame Butterfly'
Repeat flowering ı *Moderate fragrance*
HABIT Bush H/W 2.5m/1.2m (8ft/4ft) ı ZONES 5-11

'Megiddo'

FLORIBUNDA ı ORANGE RED

Megiddo is in Palestine and has been the scene of two famous battles: one around 1470 BC, when the Pharaoh Thutmose III vanquished the Hittites; and another in AD 1918, when the British under Lord Allenby defeated the Turks. It is predicted to be the scene of another, even greater, battle, the Armageddon that will bring the final triumph of good over evil. But it is Lord Allenby's victory that is commemorated by this fiery rose, which bears large sprays of double, bright scarlet flowers on a strong-growing, upright plant with large,

'Megiddo'

'Memento'

matt, olive-green foliage. Despite being introduced in 1970 (which in the highly competitive world of scarlet Floribunda breeding seems nearly as long ago as ancient Egypt), it remains popular for its great freedom of bloom.

Gandy, England, UK, 1970
'Coup de Foudre' × 'Saint-Agaro'
Repeat flowering · Slight fragrance

HABIT Bush H/W 1m/60cm (3ft/2ft) · ZONES 5–11

'Memento'

FLORIBUNDA · RED BLEND

In Britain, where 'Memento' was bred, it is regarded as one of the very best of all bedding roses. Its habit is neat, its foliage is sage-green, handsome and disease-resistant, and its clusters of double blooms are perfectly spaced and borne abundantly, whatever the weather. The rest of the world has largely ignored it. Even in Britain its admirers are likely to wish it was more popular, blaming its somewhat indeterminate color, neither red, deep pink, nor truly coral. Whatever, I find it bright and cheerful.

DICbar · Dickson, Northern Ireland, UK, 1978
'Bangor' × 'Anabell'
Repeat flowering · Slight fragrance

HABIT Bush H/W 1m/60cm (3ft/2ft) · ZONES 5–11
🌸 Royal Horticultural Society Award of Garden Merit 2002

'Memoire'

'Memoire'

HYBRID TEA · WHITE

'Ice Cream', 'Memory'

Top-quality white exhibition roses have always been rare, scented ones even rarer, so it is not surprising that down-under exhibitors and their European colleagues have taken this rose so firmly to their hearts. Softened by a touch of ivory at its heart, it is a splendid flower, large and high-centred, with its many petals arranged in perfect symmetry and reflexing gracefully. Although not especially tall, the bush is vigorous, well clothed in healthy, dark leaves, and flowers with unusual freedom

for a rose so large and full-bodied. It is a fine rose for cutting, too, the stems being long and straight.

KORzuri · Kordes, Germany, 1992
Parentage undisclosed
Repeat flowering · Strong, tea rose fragrance

HABIT Bush H/W 1.2m/1m (4ft/3ft) · ZONES 4–10
🌸 Royal Horticultural Society Award of Garden Merit 2001, Belfast Gold Medal 1992

'Memorial Day'

HYBRID TEA · MEDIUM PINK

'Heaven Scent', 'Parfum de Liberté'

The last Monday in May is Memorial Day, the day on which Americans remember their war dead. In much of the country, it comes at the peak of the spring rose season, and that weekend many an exhibitor will be staging this big, orchid-pink rose and dreaming of blue ribbons. He or she may well get them, too, for it is a superb flower, large, full-petalled, of perfect, high-centred form and carried proudly on long, almost thornless stems. As Australians and New Zealanders remember their dead

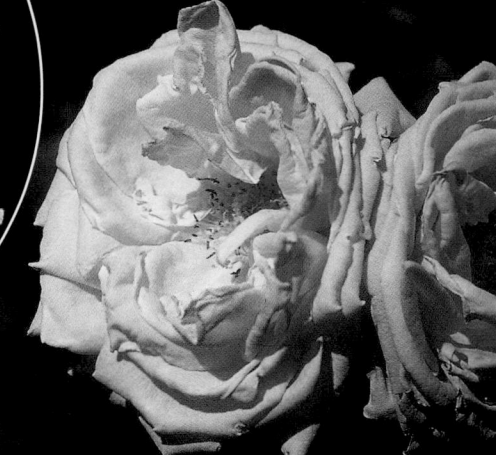

'Memoriam'

'Memorial Day'

'Mercedes'

on Anzac Day, 25 April, the American name has little significance for them, and down under the rose is called 'Heaven Scent' for its superb fragrance. The bush is tall and prolific, with healthy, mid-green leaves.

WEKblunez ı Carruth, USA, 2004
'Blueberry Hill' × 'New Zealand'
Repeat flowering ı *Strong, damask fragrance*

HABIT Bush H/W 1.5m/1.2m (5ft/4ft) ı ZONES 4–10

🏵 All-America Rose Selection 2004

'Memoriam'

HYBRID TEA ı LIGHT PINK

I have never seen this variety make a big, free-blooming bush, but it is indispensable for the exhibitor, as the softly scented flowers are very large and of most perfect form, with some 55 petals. It dislikes wet weather. The foliage is leathery and dark green. It was named in memory of Gordon van Abrams's wife.

Von Abrams, USA, 1961
('Blanche Mallerin' × 'Peace') × ('Peace' × 'Frau Karl Druschki')
Repeat flowering ı *Moderate fragrance*

HABIT Bush H/W 1.5m/1.2m (5ft/4ft) ı ZONES 5–11

🏵 Portland (Oregon, USA) Gold Medal 1960

'Mercedes'

FLORIBUNDA ı ORANGE RED

'Merko'

In the garden, 'Mercedes' is just another scarlet rose, its double flowers shapely, their color bright, the plants upright, and the foliage leathery and dark green. In a greenhouse, it is a different story: there it has few rivals for its freedom of flowering, its length of stem, or its ability to last and last when it is cut. For years and years it was one of the roses most commonly met with in florists' shops. Mercedes is a common girl's name in Europe, and this 1974 Reimer Kordes

'Merci'

creation has nothing to do with German motor cars. It is quite without scent.

MerFOR ı Kordes, Germany, 1974
'Anabell' × seedling
Repeat flowering ı *Slight fragrance*

HABIT Bush H/W 1.2m/1m (4ft/3ft) ı ZONES 5–11

'Merci'

FLORIBUNDA ı MEDIUM RED

Despite its name, this is an American rose, from Bill Warriner of Jackson & Perkins. It used to be widely grown in the United States for its vigor, resistance to disease and freedom of bloom, and is still available there; but it has rarely been seen elsewhere. Perhaps it is the color of the double flowers, which are a medium shade of crimson. Europe and Australia tend to like red Floribundas to be dark or flaming. Fond of warm climates, it looks its best in California. The foliage is leathery and dark green.

Warriner, USA, 1974
Parentage undisclosed
Repeat flowering ı *Slight fragrance*

HABIT Bush H/W 1m/60cm (3ft/2ft) ı ZONES 5–11

'Michelangelo'

'Michelangelo'

HYBRID TEA ı MEDIUM YELLOW

'Gracious Queen'

There are two roses called 'Michelangelo' — a 1997 striped Floribunda from Sam McGredy (codename MACtemaik) and this one, which is one of Meilland's 'Romantica' collection. It is a Hybrid Tea in its growth, being tall and strong, with healthy, dark green leaves, and the flowers open from sculptured, Hybrid Tea-style buds. Fully blown, their many petals are swirled and ruffled in the old style. They are a beautiful rich yellow, as clear and vivid

as Michelangelo's colors on his Sistine Chapel ceiling, whose cleaning and restoration this rose celebrates. They are very well scented, too, with a top note of lemon. It flourishes best in warm climates.

MEItelov ı Meilland, France, 1997
('Natilda' × 'Parador') × 'Helmut Schmidt'
Repeat flowering ı *Lemony fragrance*
HABIT Bush H/W 1m/60cm (3ft/2ft) ı ZONES 4–10
🌹 Monza Gold Medal 1997, Bagatelle Fragrance Award 2001

'Michelle Joy'

HYBRID TEA ı ORANGE PINK

'Michelle Joy' should please the exhibitor for the fine symmetry of its flowers, which vary in color with the season. Sometimes they are quite a pale shade of coral-pink, at other times much deeper. The bush is strong and free with its blooms, and the dark green foliage is glossy. It appears likely to do best in a warm climate. Raised by Jack Christensen in California, it was named in memory of Michelle Joy Cowley of Queensland. Mr Christensen does not seem to have introduced it in the United States, probably because exhibitors in America would prefer a longer, slimmer bud and more fragrance.

AROshrel ı Christensen, USA, 1991
Seedling × 'Shreveport'
Repeat flowering ı *Slight fragrance*

HABIT Bush H/W 1.5m/1.2m (5ft/4ft) ı ZONES 5–11

'Midas Touch'

HYBRID TEA ı DEEP YELLOW

When the gods gave King Midas the gift of having everything he touched turn to gold, things went badly awry, but Jack Christensen had no such troubles – 'Midas Touch' was an immediate hit and remains among the leading yellow Hybrid Teas. Although the flowers are not huge or very double, they are shapely both in bud and when fully open, and their beautiful chrome-yellow fades but little as they age. The plant is strong, with glossy, dark green foliage; and while it has sometimes been accused of being a little tender to cold, it is among the better-rated yellows for resistance to black spot. The scent is quite good.

JACtou ı Christensen, USA, 1992
'Brandy' × 'Friesensöhne'
Repeat flowering ı *Moderate, fruity fragrance*

HABIT Bush H/W 1.5m/1.2m (5ft/4ft) ı ZONES 4–11

All-America Rose Selection 1994

'Mikado'

HYBRID TEA ı RED BLEND

'Koh-Sai', 'Kohsai'

Gilbert and Sullivan's character may have been a figure of fun rather than a king of beauty, but his name is both Oriental and familiar to Western ears, just right for a Japanese rose (from the late Seizo Suzuki) destined for the Western market. 'Koh-Sai' is Japanese for 'harmonious friendship', which is appropriate, too, for a rose that has won high awards in the West. The double blooms are large, to 12cm (5in) in diameter, well formed, and of brilliant red with yellow on the reverse and at the centre. The dark green foliage is glossy. There is little scent, but its disease resistance is exceptional for a rose in this color group.

Suzuki, Japan, 1987
'Duftwolke' × 'Kayayaki'
Repeat flowering ı *Slight fragrance*

HABIT Bush H/W 1.5m/1.2m (5ft/4ft) ı ZONES 6–11

All-America Rose Selection 1988

'Milestone'

HYBRID TEA ı RED BLEND

'Milestone' is a spectacular rose, the coloring of its 45 petals almost three-dimensional. The flowers are basically a dense medium red, silvery on the reverse and shading lighter toward the centre, the whole show darkening with age – just what one would expect from its parentage. The foliage is large, half-glossy and medium green. The scent is only slight.

JACes ı Warriner, USA, 1983
'Sunfire' × 'Spellbinder'
Repeat flowering ı *Slight fragrance*

HABIT Bush H/W 1.5m/1.2m (5ft/4ft) ı ZONES 5–11

'Miriam'

HYBRID TEA ı YELLOW BLEND

The Book of Exodus talks about Miriam the Prophetess taking a timbrel in her hand and dancing, which is certainly a picture suggestive of the bright cheerfulness of this rose. 'Miriam' was, however – more prosaically, yet more affectionately – named for a lady of Sam McGredy's acquaintance. In the garden, the shapely, double blooms can be a very bright combination of gold and carmine. Cut them young for the house and they open to the more delicate tones you see in the photograph. The foliage is glossy and dark green.

MACsupcat ı McGredy, New Zealand, 1989
'Sexy Rexy' × 'Yabadabadoo'
Repeat flowering ı *Slight fragrance*

HABIT Bush H/W 1.5m/1m (5ft/3ft) ı ZONES 5–11

'Miriam'

'Milestone'

'Miss Alice'

'Mister Lincoln'

'Mission Bells'

'Miss Alice'

SHRUB | LIGHT PINK

The catalogues promise a low bush for the front of the bed. It isn't *that* short, but it is one of the more compact and bushy of David Austin's creations. Borne freely all season, its flowers are charming in their clear soft pink, their neat Old Garden Rose form, and in their light, sweet fragrance with its top note of lily of the valley. The foliage is mid-green and has a good reputation for disease resistance. Miss Alice de Rothschild created the beautiful garden at her family's home, Waddeston Manor in Buckinghamshire. Her rose is a bit prickly – but then so was she. She once shouted at her friend Queen Victoria to stop treading on her pansies!

AUSjake | Austin, England, 2001
'Mary Rose' × seedling
Repeat flowering | *Moderate, sweet fragrance*

HABIT Bush H/W 1m/1m (3ft/3ft) | ZONES 6–11

'Miss All-American Beauty' ✓

HYBRID TEA | DEEP PINK

'Maria Callas'

Unlike the great diva for whom it was originally named, 'Miss All-American Beauty' is not at all temperamental. Renamed for the

American marketplace, it is one of the easiest of the exhibition-style roses to grow, bearing enormous, highly fragrant, brilliant pink flowers with great freedom. The foliage is large, leathery and dark green. Like Miss Callas, who was half-Greek, it is no real all-American. It was raised in France, by Alain Meilland. It did, however, win the AARS award in 1968, three years after it came out in Europe.

MEIdaud | Meilland, France, 1965
'Chrysler Imperial' × 'Karl Herbst'
Repeat flowering | *Moderate fragrance*

HABIT Bush H/W 1.5m/1.2m (5ft/4ft) | ZONES 5–11

🌹 Portland (Oregon, USA) Gold Medal 1966,
All-America Rose Selection 1968

'Mission Bells'

HYBRID TEA | PINK BLEND

For many years one of the most popular roses, 'Mission Bells' began to lose ground to brighter colored, more exciting roses in the 1970s, but it is so easy to grow, especially in humid climates, that a revival should be considered. The reward will be large, double, warm pink blooms, opening informal and deliciously fragrant from long, pointed buds, on long, almost thornless stems. The foliage is soft and dark green.

Morris, USA, 1949
'Mrs Sam McGredy' × 'Mälar-Ros'
Repeat flowering | *Strong, tea-rose fragrance*

HABIT Bush H/W 1.5m/1.2m (5ft/4ft) | ZONES 5–11

🌹 All-America Rose Selection 1950

BELOW 'Mister Chips'
INSET 'Modern Art'

'Miss All-American Beauty'

'Mojave'

'Mister Chips'

HYBRID TEA ၊ YELLOW BLEND

James Hilton's lovable schoolmaster Mr Chips from the classic movie, starring Robert Donat, might not have been Irish, but the rose certainly is, raised by Patrick Dickson in 1970. It is rather like 'Peace' in color, but richer, in light yellow shaded with orange and cerise, all trimmed with raspberry-pink. The form is closer to the exhibition ideal, with a high centre and reflexing petals. The foliage is a glossy and dark green. Cool-summer climates suit it best.

Dickson, Northern Ireland, UK, 1970
'Irish Gold' × 'Miss Ireland'
Repeat flowering ၊ *Slight fragrance*

HABIT Bush H/W 1.5m/1.2m (5ft/4ft) ၊ ZONES 5–11

'Mister Lincoln'

HYBRID TEA ၊ DARK RED

'Mister Lincoln' has been one of the world's favorite red roses for very many years. Sure, the English may sniff about mildew and 'blueing', but give it a reasonable amount of sunshine and the plant will be as tall and clean as the great man in whose memory it is named, and the color will be perfect, deep and velvety. The urn-shaped buds open rather flat, but what is that to set beside the pleasure of cutting armloads of long-stemmed, double,

richly fragrant beauties from each bush? The foliage is matt, leathery and dark green.

Swim and Weeks, USA, 1964
'Chrysler Imperial' × 'Charles Mallerin'
Repeat flowering ၊ *Intense fragrance*

HABIT Bush H/W 1.8m/1.2m (6ft/4ft) ၊ ZONES 5–11

All-America Rose Selection 1965, American Rose Society James Alexander Gamble Fragrance Medal 2003

'Modern Art'

HYBRID TEA ၊ RED BLEND

'Prince de Monaco'

'Hand-painted Roses' are no longer Sam McGredy's exclusive property. Here is one from Pernille Olesen (nee Poulsen), the fourth generation of the Poulsen family to grow roses. It is a safe guess that the McGredy strain is in the two unnamed seedlings that gave rise to 'Modern Art', introduced in 1983. Its blooms are full-sized Hybrid Teas, double, shapely and high-centred, in orange-red with a white reverse. The deeper 'brush marks' are most evident in a cool climate. The foliage is healthy and dark green, the growth bushy.

POUlsart ၊ Pernille & Mogens, Denmark, 1985
Seedling × seedling
Repeat flowering ၊ *Slight fragrance*

HABIT Bush H/W 1.5m/1.2m (5ft/4ft) ၊ ZONES 5–11

Rome Gold Medal 1984

'Mojave'

HYBRID TEA ၊ ORANGE BLEND

In the 1950s, 'Charlotte Armstrong' × 'Signora' was one of Herbert Swim's most fertile crosses. It yielded 'Sutter's Gold' as well as this brilliant rose, introduced in 1954. Long buds in deep, pure orange open rather loosely to large, double blooms in apricot, orange and red — the rich colors of a desert sunset. (Pronounce the name as 'Mohahvee' in the Californian manner.) The blooms are fragrant, the foliage is gleaming; and although the flowers are not especially long-lasting in the vase, the stems are long, slim and almost thornless.

'Charlotte Armstrong' × 'Signora'
Repeat flowering ၊ *Moderate fragrance*

HABIT Bush H/W 1.5m/1.2m (5ft/4ft) ၊ ZONES 5–11

Bagatelle (Paris) Gold Medal 1953, Geneva Gold Medal 1953, All-America Rose Selection 1954

'Molly McGredy'

FLORIBUNDA ၊ RED BLEND

High awards from the expert judges do not always translate into adoration from the public. Sam McGredy considered this rose good enough to name for his sister, and the RNRS gave it its top award in 1968, when it was exhibited prior to being released commercially the following year. The deep pink and white is not

'Mon Cheri'

HYBRID TEA ⁚ RED BLEND

Rather resembling a deeper-colored 'Double Delight', 'Mon Cheri' is in fact descended from that rose. It shows it in the semi-glossy, mid-green foliage, and in the way the high-centred, double blooms, which start out medium pink lit with yellow at the petal bases, gradually become suffused with dark red, but not in its scent, which is only moderate. The bush is of medium height and upright. The oddly ungrammatical French name (correctly *Mon Cher* or *Ma Chérie*) is

LEFT 'Molly McGredy'
INSET 'Moondance'
ABOVE 'Moonstone'

the favorite color combination of most rose-buyers, however, no matter how shapely the flowers and how perfect the bush. A lack of strong perfume has not helped, either, but it is indeed a very good rose. The large, double blooms are borne in trusses. The foliage is glossy and dark green.

MACmo ⁚ McGredy, New Zealand, 1969
'Paddy McGredy' × ('Madame Léon Cuny' × 'Columbine')
Repeat flowering ⁚ *Slight fragrance*

HABIT Bush H/W 1m/60cm (3ft/2ft) ⁚ ZONES 5–11

❀ Royal National Rose Society Gold Medal and President's International Trophy 1968, Belfast Dani Award 1971, Portland (Oregon, USA) Gold Medal 1971

that of a brand of chocolates that come in a red and white wrapper.

AROcher ⁚ Christensen, USA, 1981
('White Satin' × 'Bewitched') × 'Double Delight'
Repeat flowering ⁚ *Moderate, spicy fragrance*

HABIT Bush H/W 1.4m/1m (4ft 6in/3ft) ⁚ ZONES 5–11

❀ All-America Rose Selection 1982

'Moondance'

FLORIBUNDA ⁚ WHITE

The envelope please . . . and the 2007 AARS award goes to Keith Zary for 'Moondance'! By the time the Academy Awards come around each year, the public has already had the opportunity to see the winning movies for themselves, but the awards for new roses are almost all made before they are introduced, and we the

rose-buying public must place our faith in the expertise and integrity of the judges. At the time of writing 'Moondance' is still brand-new. Will we agree with the judges' verdict and take it to our hearts? It certainly looks promising, with its shapely, ivory flowers, its pleasing raspberry fragrance and its glossy, dark green leaves.

JACtanic ⁚ Zary, USA, 2007
'Princess Alice' × 'Iceberg'
Repeat flowering ⁚ *Slight fragrance*

Habit Bush H/W 1.5m/1m (5ft/3ft) ZONES 5–11

'Moonstone'

HYBRID TEA ⁚ WHITE

'Cadillac DeVille'

'Moonstone' has rapidly become a great favorite with exhibitors, who rave about its large size and the perfect symmetry with which its 40 petals are arranged. It isn't really white, however: the edges of the petals are washed with varying amounts of rose-pink, and the general effect in the garden is of delicate, fresh pink. The scent could be stronger, but the plant is tall, upright and free-blooming, and the very glossy leaves have an excellent reputation for disease resistance. A very fine rose for cutting, it does best in warm, sunny climates; the flowers can 'ball' in cool, wet weather.

WEKcryland ⁚ Carruth, USA, 1999
'Crystalline' × 'Lynn Anderson'
Repeat flowering ⁚ *Mild, tea rose fragrance*

HABIT Bush H/W 1.5m/1.2m (5ft/4ft) ⁚ ZONES 4–11

'Mon Cheri'

'Morgengruss'

HYBRID KORDESII ı ORANGE PINK

'Morning Greeting'

Many of Wilhelm Kordes's 'Kordesii' climbers
come in the strong colors that sell so well in
Germany. 'Morgengruss' is an exception.
Long, shapely buds open to ruffled blooms,
not overlarge but carried in graceful sprays,
in all the pale pinks and corals of the sunrise.
They are fragrant, too, and borne freely all
season on strong, although not rampageous,
plants with glossy, dark green foliage. Introduced in 1962, it is a rose that deserves wider
attention than it gets. It has a reputation
for hardiness.

Kordes, Germany, 1962
Parentage undisclosed
Repeat flowering ı Intense fragrance
HABIT Climber H/W 3m/1.8m (10ft/6ft) ı ZONES 5–11

'Morgengruss'

'Morning Jewel'

LARGE FLOWERED CLIMBER ı MEDIUM PINK

A repeat-flowering climber from the late Alec
Cocker, with medium-sized Hybrid Tea-style
flowers in rich pink, nicely shaped although
not very double, and nicely scented although
not powerfully. The plant is quite vigorous,
although not very large – it is about the right
size for growing around the door of a single-
storey house or on a tripod in the garden.

ABOVE 'Morning Jewel'
RIGHT 'Mother's Love'

'Mount Shasta'

'Moth'

'Mount Hood'

The flowers usually come in small clusters, the repeat flowering is very good, and it has the good habit of not bearing its flowers mainly on its highest branches. The foliage is dark green, and disease resistance is said to be very good. Cool climates suit it best.

Cocker, Scotland, UK, 1968
'New Dawn' × 'Red Dandy'
Repeat flowering · *Moderate fragrance*

HABIT Climber H/W 2.5m/1.8m (8ft/6ft) · ZONES 5–11

Anerkannte Deutsche Rose (Germany) 1975, Royal Horticultural Society Award of Garden Merit 1993

'Moth'

SHRUB · MAUVE

This is a rather pretty David Austin rose, its petals wide and fluttering, as befits its name. The name does not come from the insect that eats holes in sweaters but from one of the fairies who attend Titania in Shakespeare's *A Midsummer Night's Dream*. The bush is compact for a Shrub Rose, and the soft pink flowers settle on its branches like a flight of butterflies. The foliage is soft green, the flowers fragrant.

Austin, England, UK, 1983
Parentage undisclosed
Repeat flowering · *Slight fragrance*

HABIT Bush H/W 1.2m/1m (4ft/3ft) · ZONES 5–11

'Mother's Love'

HYBRID TEA · LIGHT PINK

Although raised in France (by Louisette Meilland), this rose is grown only in Australia, where a portion of its profits is donated to the Nursing Mother's Association of Australia. The rest of the world is missing out on a fine rose: large, shapely, borne on long stems and a most lovely shade of tender, pale pink. It is deliciously fragrant, too, with the true old rose scent. The bush is tall and strong, the dark green leaves resistant to black spot and mildew.

MEIpikon · Meilland, France, 1999
('Baronne Edmond de Rothschild' × 'Madame Hilda Neumann') × 'Natilda'
Repeat flowering · *Strong, damask fragrance*

Habit Bush H/W 1.8m/1.2m (6ft/4ft) ZONES 7–11

'Mount Hood'

HYBRID TEA · WHITE

'Christine Horbiger', 'Foster's Melbourne Cup', 'Foster's Wellington Cup'

Forget the horses and the punters, let alone the crowd drinking Australia's famous lager. Think rather of the ladies in the Members Enclosure showing off their new dresses and pretty hats. The rose is just as pretty, all cream and blush ruffles, set off by dense, glossy green foliage, bronze when young and olive-green at maturity. The double flowers are quite large and nicely scented, and the bush is compact and floriferous. A lifelong lover of white daffodils, Sam McGredy borrowed the name of one of the most famous, 'Mount Hood', for this rose's rather tardy American release.

MACmoutoo · McGredy, New Zealand, 1988
'Sexy Rexy' × 'Pot o' Gold'
Repeat flowering · *Moderate fragrance*

HABIT Bush H/W 1.5m/1.2m (5ft/4ft) · ZONES 7–11

Gold Star of the South Pacific, Hamilton (New Zealand) 1991, All-America Rose Selection 1996

'Mount Shasta'

GRANDIFLORA · WHITE

'Mount Shasta' is tall and upright, with distinctive greyish leaves, but it does not bear its large, double, high-centred blooms freely enough to avoid being upstaged by 'Pascali', another white seedling of 'Queen Elizabeth', which came out at the same time and took the rose world by storm. Yet, although 'Pascali' is the better rose overall, 'Mount Shasta' has by no means disappeared from the catalogues. Many exhibitors prefer it, as it is a purer white and a bigger flower – and size always impresses the judges. It does best in warm climates.

Swim and Weeks, USA 1963
'Queen Elizabeth' × 'Blanche Mallerin'
Repeat flowering · *Moderate fragrance*

HABIT Bush H/W 1.8m/1m (6ft/3ft) · ZONES 5–11

'Mountbatten'

FLORIBUNDA | MEDIUM YELLOW

Very tall and vigorous, 'Mountbatten' is a good choice for the back of the rose bed or for bringing a splash of soft yellow to the mixed border. It does not usually produce large clusters of blooms, but the individual double flowers in their small sprays are quite big, nicely formed and softly scented. The foliage is leathery and olive-green. 'Mountbatten' would make an appropriate companion for 'Alexander' and, like it, honors the memory of a notable British serviceman. The patriotic raiser of both was Jack Harkness.

HARmantelle | Harkness, England, UK, 1982
'Peer Gynt' × (['Anne Cocker' × 'Arthur Bell'] × 'Southampton')
Repeat flowering | *Moderate fragrance*
HABIT Bush H/W 1m/60cm (3ft/2ft) | ZONES 5–11
🏵 Belfast Dani Award 1984

'Mrs Wakefield Christie-Miller'

'Mrs Sam McGredy'

'Mrs Oakley Fisher'

'Mountbatten'

'Mrs Anthony Waterer'

'Mrs Anthony Waterer'

HYBRID RUGOSA | DARK RED

Introduced in 1898 by the great British nursery John Waterer & Sons, 'Mrs Anthony Waterer' has always been admired for the clarity of its crimson, the elegantly cupped form of its semi-double flowers and its intense fragrance. Do not be carried away by its Hybrid Rugosa classification. Its *R. rugosa* blood is a little far back, and it is, in effect, a vigorous (and thorny) Hybrid Perpetual. Grow it in the same way, pegging down the long shoots, and do not expect the later display to be as lavish as the early summer one. The foliage is bright green and quilted.

Waterer, England, UK, 1898
R. rugosa × 'Général Jacqueminot'
Repeat flowering | *Intense fragrance*
HABIT Bush H/W 1.2m/1.5m (4ft/5ft) | ZONES 5–10

'Mrs Oakley Fisher'

HYBRID TEA ı DEEP YELLOW

'Mrs Oakley Fisher' is one of the most delightful of all the delightful single Hybrid Teas that were fashionable in the 1920s. The buds are deep orange, and they open to beautiful single, apricot-yellow flowers that are quite fragrant. The bush is vigorous, usually blooming in small clusters, and the foliage dark green. It likes to be pruned lightly, when it will make a head-high, open shrub.

Cant, England, UK, 1921
Parentage unknown
Repeat flowering ı Strong, tea fragrance
HABIT Bush H/W 1.8m/1.2m (6ft/4ft) ı ZONES 5–11
🏵 Royal Horticultural Society Award of Garden Merit 1993

'Mrs Sam McGredy'

HYBRID TEA ı ORANGE PINK

It is said that when Sam McGredy III decided to name a rose for his wife, she rejected his choice and insisted instead on a rose he was not even considering introducing. 'Mrs Sam McGredy' turned out to be one of the all-time greats. Its young foliage is perhaps the most richly purple of any rose, maturing to bronze-green, and the young flowers a still unique color of copper-red, paling to salmon-pink as the huge, shapely, double blooms open. It is fragrant, too. If only it were a stronger grower! Grow the climbing sport.

McGredy, New Zealand, 1929
('Donald McDonald' × 'Golden Emblem') × (seedling × 'The Queen Alexandra Rose')
Repeat flowering ı Moderate, tea rose fragrance
HABIT Bush H/W 1.5m/1.2m (5ft/4ft) ı ZONES 5–11
🏵 Portland (Oregon, USA) Gold Medal 1956

'Mrs Wakefield Christie-Miller'

HYBRID TEA ı PINK BLEND

They don't name them like that any more! It is probably nearer the truth that modern owners of such names are apt to say, 'Oh, do call me Fiona'. There was no such informality in 1909, when Sam McGredy II introduced 'Mrs Wakefield Christie-Miller' to the public. Her recent revival was originally due to her having masqueraded for a while as the long-lost 'Lady Mary Fitzwilliam', but she is a delight in her own right, the large, double, fragrant, two-toned pink blooms just like the kind you see on Edwardian chintzes. The growth is moderate, and some

pampering will be appreciated. The foliage is leathery and light green.

McGredy, New Zealand, 1909
Parentage unknown
Repeat flowering ı Strong, rose fragrance
HABIT Bush H/W 1m/1m (3ft/3ft) ı ZONES 5–11

'Nana Mouskouri'

FLORIBUNDA ı WHITE

Named for the celebrated Greek singer, this variety is considered by many aficionados to be the perfect Floribunda. Pink buds open slowly to double, creamy white flowers that become almost pure white during hot summer days. The blooms are borne in small to medium-sized clusters that practically cover the entire bush. The plant is vigorous, with excellent resistance to mildew and black spot.

Dickson, Northern Ireland, UK, 1975
'Redgold' × 'Iced Ginger'
Repeat flowering ı Moderate fragrance
HABIT Bush H/W 1m/60cm (3ft/2ft) ı ZONES 5–11

'Nancy Hayward'

LARGE FLOWERED CLIMBER ı MEDIUM RED

The perfect climber to train over balcony railings, this eye-catching variety has big, single-petalled roses in strawberry-red fading to carmine. The show starts in late winter and by spring is guaranteed to stop the passing traffic. It is repeated several times until the fall/autumn. The flowers last very well in the vase, and their only fault is a lack of perfume. The mid-green foliage and growth betray this plant's descent from *R. gigantea*. Like most *R. gigantea* hybrids, it is rather tender.

Clark, Australia, 1937
'Jessie Clark' × unknown
Repeat flowering ı Slight fragrance
HABIT Climber H/W 3m/2.5m (10ft/8ft) ı ZONES 6–11

'Nana Mouskouri'

'Nancy Hayward'

'National Trust'

'Natilda'

'Neue Revue'

'Natilda'

HYBRID TEA ı ORANGE RED BLEND

'Laura '81'

The flowers are very handsome, large, full-petalled, and a gentle blend of salmon and cream. They are lightly fragrant, and sometimes come several together. The foliage is semi-glossy and fresh green.

MEIdragelac ı Meilland, France, 1985
('Pharaoh' × 'Colour Wonder') × (['Suspense' ×
'Suspense'] × 'King's Ransom')
Repeat flowering ı *Slight fragrance*

HABIT Bush H/W 1.5m/1.2m (5ft/4ft) ı ZONES 5–11

'National Trust'

HYBRID TEA ı DARK RED

'Bad Nauheim', 'Nationalstolz'

If 'National Trust' had scent, it would be the near-perfect red rose, its color brilliant, its form excellent, and its compact bush easy to grow and very free with its bloom. Nonetheless it is one of the best red roses for bedding. The blooms have 50-plus petals, and the foliage is leathery and dark green. No doubt it has found its way into many gardens looked after by the original National Trust – a body founded in England in 1895 to care for the nation's heritage – and into the gardens of the many National Trusts that have followed in other countries. Bad Neuheim is a famous spa in Germany, and it is appropriate that this rose grows very well there.

McGredy, New Zealand, 1970
'Evelyn Fison' × 'King of Hearts'
Repeat flowering ı *Slight fragrance*

HABIT Bush H/W 1.5m/1.2m (5ft/4ft) ı ZONES 5–11

'National Velvet'

HYBRID TEA ı DARK RED

Elizabeth Taylor made her debut in the movie of this name, which told the story of a young English girl who, disguised as a jockey, won the Grand National in 1944. It was not until 1988 that Larry Burks of Tyler, Texas, raised the rose he named to commemorate this event. Appropriately, the semi-double flowers are velvet-red, opening loose and informal, the way some camellias do. The glossy foliage is like that of a camellia, too. There is not enough scent to be remarkable. Tyler sometimes calls itself the rose capital of the world, because many of the big American wholesale rose-growers have their nurseries there.

BURalp ı Burks, USA, 1988
'Poinsettia' × 'National Beauty'
Repeat flowering ı *Slight fragrance*

HABIT Bush H/W 1.5m/1.2m (5ft/4ft) ı ZONES 5–11

'National Velvet'

'Nevada'

pink and red with touches of coral, and, unusually for such a dazzler, very fragrant. The name honors the well-known German magazine.

KORrev ı Kordes, Germany, 1962
'Colour Wonder' × unknown
Repeat flowering ı *Intense fragrance*
HABIT Bush H/W 1.5m/1.2m (5ft/4ft) ı ZONES 5–11

'Nevada'

SHRUB ı WHITE

One of the best-loved of all the Shrub Roses (officially it is a Hybrid Moyesii), 'Nevada' makes a tall, bushy plant, its arching branches wreathed in early summer with big, wide-open, single blooms of a pink so pale that from a distance it passes for white. The pale green foliage has many leaflets. Rarely without flowers until the late fall/autumn, 'Nevada' comes as close as any rose to uniting the grace of a Wild Rose with the flowers and repeat-flowering habit of a Modern Rose. Pedro Dot registered it as 'La Giralda' × *R. moyesii*, but the pundits have disputed that ever since.

'Neptune'

HYBRID TEA ı MAUVE

The big, double flowers are of soft lavender tinged with just a touch of purple and have a powerful, sweet fragrance. Exhibitors recognize their show-winning potential, but this variety also performs well in the home garden. The plant is vigorous, upright and bushy, with lots of large, glossy foliage, and blooms abundantly. It performs best in cooler temperatures.

WEKhilpurnil ı Carruth, USA, 2003
('Blueberry Hill' × 'Stephen's Big Purple') × 'Blue Nile'
Repeat flowering ı *Sweet fragrance*
HABIT Bush H/W 1.5m/1.2m (5ft/4ft) ı ZONES 5–11

'Neue Revue'

HYBRID TEA ı RED BLEND

'News Review'

It is odd that Reimer Kordes introduced 'Neue Revue' in 1962, but held back its parent, 'Colour Wonder' (aka 'Königin der Rosen'), until 1964. 'Neue Revue' shows its parentage in its thorniness and its glossy, dark green leaves, but also in the soft wood that it inherits from its grandfather 'Perfecta', which makes it a rather unreliable performer. This is a pity, as the blooms can be sensational – large, double and perfectly formed, a rich blend of gold,

'Neptune'

'New Year'

It has been suggested that it
derives from *R. pimpinellifolia*.

Dot, Spain, 1927
Registered as 'La Giralda' × *R. moyesii*
Repeat flowering ⊦ *Slight fragrance*

HABIT Bush H/W 2.5m/2m (8ft/7ft) ⊦ ZONES 5–11
✿ Royal Horticultural Society Award of Garden Merit 1993

'New Dawn'

LARGE FLOWERED CLIMBER ⊦ LIGHT PINK

'Everblooming Dr W. Van Fleet', 'The New Dawn'

'New Dawn', introduced in 1930, is often
claimed to be the first repeat-flowering climbing
rose. This is not true, as many of the Noisettes
and Climbing Bourbons flower all season.
They do not like cold, however. 'New Dawn'
is a cold-hardy rose and has proved able to
transmit its repeat-flowering habit to many
lovely descendants. It will reach 3m (10ft)
or so on a wall, but it is also lovely when
allowed to grow as a large shrub. The very
double blooms, cameo-pink fading to flesh-
white, are borne both singly and in clusters.
The foliage is glossy and dark green. A sport
from the once-blooming but otherwise
identical 'Dr W. Van Fleet', it was discovered in a Connecticut nursery. It holds the
first plant patent issued in the United States.

Somerset Roses, USA, 1930
'Dr W. Van Fleet' sport
Repeat flowering ⊦ *Sweet fragrance*

HABIT Climber H/W 6m/3m (20ft/10ft) ⊦ ZONES 6–11
✿ World Federation of Rose Societies Hall of Fame 1997

'New Day'

HYBRID TEA ⊦ MEDIUM YELLOW

'Mabella'

Call it by either name – 'New Day' is the
officially registered one, 'Mabella' the one
the greenhouse growers use – this is one
of the outstanding yellow roses, and a great
exception to the rule that first-rate greenhouse roses are second-rate in the garden.
It is a particularly reliable bush, even in the
hot, humid or cold climates that so many
yellow roses dislike, and the double flowers
are large, shapely, brilliant in color and
seemingly immune to weather damage.
The foliage is glossy and dark green.
It was raised by Reimer Kordes in 1977,
from two very much older yellow roses.

KORgold ⊦ Kordes, Germany, 1977
'Arlene Francis' × 'Roselandia'
Repeat flowering ⊦ *Intense fragrance*

HABIT Bush H/W 1.4m/1m (4ft 6in/3ft) ⊦ ZONES 5–11

ABOVE 'New Dawn'
INSET 'New Zealand'

'New Year'

GRANDIFLORA ⊦ ORANGE BLEND

'Arcadian', 'MACneweye'

A Grandiflora introduced by Sam McGredy
in 1982, 'New Year' does not seem to have
been a worldwide hit, despite winning the
1987 AARS award. The double flowers are
large and shapely, and a delightful blend
of clear orange and yellow. They have only
20 petals, and some say that they open too
quickly in hot weather. The bush is tall and
shrubby, with dark green foliage, and it
flowers freely enough that the quick
opening can be forgiven.

MACnewye ⊦ McGredy, New Zealand, 1983
'Mary Sumner' × seedling
Repeat flowering ⊦ *Slight fragrance*

HABIT Bush H/W 1.8m/1.2m (6ft/4ft) ⊦ ZONES 5–11
✿ All-America Rose Selection 1987

although they come in clusters, are quite large and open wide from long buds. The color is very distinctive: a bright magenta-purple, redder in the bud and softening with age. The rose is fragrant, too, and a good grower, with olive-green foliage. It has the enviable characteristic of performing well in poor soils, and can also be grown in a container or planted as a hedge. A very desirable rose, it was raised by E. B. LeGrice and introduced in 1968.

LEGnews ı LeGrice, England, UK, 1968
'Lilac Charm' × 'Tuscany Superb'
Repeat flowering ı Moderate fragrance

HABIT Bush H/W 1m/60cm (3ft/2ft) ı ZONES 5–11

'Nicole'

FLORIBUNDA ı WHITE

White, sometimes with a golden light in the depths, the petals are edged with a distinct

ABOVE 'Nicole'
INSET 'New Day'
BELOW RIGHT 'News'

'New Zealand'

HYBRID TEA ı LIGHT PINK

'Aotearoa', 'Aotearoa-New Zealand'

Long buds open to enormous, shapely, double flowers that are richly fragrant and of a delightful soft pink color. The glossy-leafed bush is strong and healthy. This rose is known in New Zealand as 'Aotearoa', the Maori name for New Zealand, which means 'Land of the Long White Cloud'. The Maori name was bestowed on the rose in honor of New Zealand's sesquicentenary year in 1990. Sam McGredy must have great faith in his creation, as he is on record as saying that new pink roses are the most difficult for the hybridist to sell, the color lacking novelty.

MACgenev ı McGredy, New Zealand, 1989
'Harmonie' × 'Auckland Metro'
Repeat flowering ı Honeysuckle fragrance

HABIT Bush H/W 1.5m/1.2m (5ft/4ft) ı ZONES 5–11

✿ New Zealand International Rose Ground Trials Fragrance Award 1990, Rose Introducers of New Zealand Auckland Rose of the Year 1990/Fragrance Award 1990/Gold Medal 1990

'News'

FLORIBUNDA ı MAUVE

Although it is always classed as a Floribunda, had 'News' come out earlier than it did, it would probably have been classed as a decorative Hybrid Tea, for its semi-double flowers,

'Northern Lights'

band of cherry-pink. There are 35 of them, building up a nicely shaped flower with a slight fragrance. The foliage is dark green, and the plant is strong. 'Nicole' was raised by Reimer Kordes and introduced in 1975. It is not widely grown, but it is a good rose for cutting, perhaps more people should try it. Do not confuse it with 'Nicola', a deep pink Floribunda from Gandy's, introduced in 1980, or with 'Nicole Debrosse', a red Hybrid Tea from France, introduced in 1962.

KORicole ı Kordes, Germany, 1985
Seedling × 'Bordure Rose'
Repeat flowering ı Slight fragrance

HABIT Bush H/W 1.2m/1.2m (4ft/4ft) ı ZONES 5–11

'Northern Lights'

HYBRID TEA ı YELLOW BLEND

The blooms are super-large, with some 50 petals, classically high-centred, and of a lemony yellow with a suffusion of rose-pink on the outer petals. They are borne mostly one to a stem and later in the season in small clusters, and are very long-lasting. The plant is tall and upright, and as it is of Scottish ancestry, you can be sure it is hardy!

Cocker, Scotland, 1969
'Fragrant Cloud' × 'Kingcup'
Repeat flowering ı Intense fragrance

HABIT Bush H/W 1.2m/1m (4ft/3ft) ı ZONES 4–11

'Norwich Castle'

FLORIBUNDA I ORANGE BLEND

The tallish, upright bush bears shiny, dark green leaves and clusters of slightly fragrant, pleasantly shapely, double flowers that – according to the raiser, English rose-grower and writer Peter Beales – are the color of an excellent beer! Introduced in 1980, this rose was named for the great Norman castle (now a museum) that dominates the East

BELOW LEFT 'Nymphenburg'
INSET 'Oklahoma'
BELOW RIGHT 'Norwich Castle'

Anglian capital of Norwich, where Peter Beales's nursery is located.

Beales, England, UK, 1980
('Whisky Mac' × 'Arthur Bell') × seedling
Repeat flowering I *Fruity fragrance*

HABIT Bush H/W 1m/60cm (3ft/2ft) I ZONES 5–11

'Nymphenburg'

HYBRID MUSK I ORANGE PINK

The palace and gardens of the Nymphenburg, just on the outskirts of Munich, are a German tourist attraction. The rose is worthy of the name. Its fat buds open to mid-sized, semi-double flowers of a beautifully ruffled shape in exquisite shades of salmon, peach and gold. They are deliciously fragrant, and are borne all season in large and small clusters. The shrub is large, but open and lax in habit. Many of its admirers prefer to see it trained as a pillar rose. The foliage is glossy, olive-green and lightly rugose.

Kordes, Germany, 1954
'Sangerhausen' × 'Sunmist'
Repeat flowering I *Moderate fragrance*

HABIT Bush H/W 1.8m/1.2m (6ft/4ft) I ZONES 6–11

'Oklahoma'

HYBRID TEA I DARK RED

The black rose seems to be as much desired by some people as the elusive blue one. 'Oklahoma' is about as close to black as they come. Sometimes its crimson is so dark that you do not notice the flowers until you are right next to the bush. The double blooms are large and globular, sometimes too much so for shapeliness, and richly fragrant. The dark green foliage is leathery. 'Oklahoma' needs a temperate climate – the flowers scorch in hot areas and turn magenta in cold. It is a very tall grower. It was raised by Herbert Swim and Ollie Weeks in 1963. The name is apt: 'Oklahoma' means 'the red man's land'.

Swim and Weeks, USA, 1964
'Chrysler Imperial' × 'Charles Mallerin'
Repeat flowering I *Intense fragrance*

HABIT Bush H/W 1.5m/1.2m (5ft/4ft) I ZONES 5–11

🌹 Tokyo Gold Medal 1963

The Fragrance of Roses

THE FRAGRANCE OF THE ROSE HAS ALWAYS BEEN ONE OF THE MAIN QUALITIES THAT HAS DRAWN US TO THE FLOWER. THE PERSIAN POET HA'AFIZ SPEAKS OF HAVING BEEN 'LURED IN TO THE GARDEN BY THE SCENT OF ROSES', WHERE HE FOUND COMFORT FROM THE FEVER OF UNREQUITED LOVE; AND THE GREEKS BELIEVED THAT EROS CARELESSLY SPILT SOME OF THE NECTAR OF THE GODS ON A ROSE, THEREBY GIVING THE FLOWER ITS SWEET PERFUME.

If he did, he must have been careless with several vintages, for the rose offers not just one perfume but many. Think of the pure, soft sweetness of the Damasks and the Centifolias; of the warmer fragrance of the Teas, which does vaguely resemble that of a fresh packet of China tea; of the sharper, more piercing scents of such Modern Roses as 'Fragrant Cloud' and 'Double Delight'. Then there is the intense, musk-like fragrance of some of the ramblers, such as *R. filipes*, *R. moschata* and *R. multiflora*. Their scent is exhaled not by the petals, as is the case with other roses, but by the stamens. A note of musk can be detected in the scent of many of their descendants, such as the Hybrid Musk Roses and some Floribunda Roses, like 'Elizabeth of Glamis'. The scents of roses are as varied as their colors. It is a shame we cannot photograph them!

Unfortunately, there are many roses Eros seems to have missed. 'They don't smell like they used to!' is one of the commonest remarks made about roses. Even allowing for the elusiveness of scent, which varies with the weather, the time of day, the age of the flower and the sensitivity of one's nose, this does seem to be true. Relatively few Modern Roses have the rich fragrance characteristic of the old French roses.

The elusive gift of fragrance

After denying the obvious for many years, hybridists are now actively seeking to improve things, but they are not finding the process at all easy. For one thing, fragrance appears to be what geneticists call a 'recessive character', which makes it difficult for a hybridist to plan for. Crossing two fragrant parents is as likely as not to result in a brood of scentless seedlings, and a rose that is itself scentless may yet be able to give the gift to its children and grandchildren. 'Charlotte Armstrong', the parent of 'Sutter's Gold', 'Tiffany' and 'Mojave', and grandmother to 'Chrysler Imperial', 'Mister Lincoln' and 'Double Delight', is one such, and 'Dr A. J. Verhage' another. The family trees of fragrant Hybrid Tea Roses will often show the names of the same few roses: some examples are 'Ophelia', 'Crimson Glory', 'Signora' and, further back, 'Lady Mary Fitzwilliam'. Indeed, it was Wilhelm Kordes's belief that 'Lady Mary' was the most potent of all perfume donors that led to the revival of this almost-extinct old variety.

The business is complicated by the fact that breeders are usually looking for other things as well as perfume. For a new rose to be successful, it must score highly for shape, color, vigor, disease resistance and what have you, and not all these desirable characteristics appear to be compatible with rich fragrance. The priceless gift of repeated flowering, for instance, comes from the China Rose, which is only mildly fragrant at best, and many of its early crosses with the old European roses were scarcely fragrant. Tough, long-lasting petals seem less able to release their scent than those more delicate, which is why the cast-iron varieties you find in the florist's tend to have only the vague smell that all growing plants have. The search for new colors has not helped, either. Some think it fortunate that the Species (Wild) Rose *R. foetida persiana* ('Persian Yellow') proved unable to transmit its heavy odor along with its golden color, but as a rule there has to be a suffusion of red on the petals of a yellow rose if there is to be scent as well. 'Sutter's Gold' is an example; 'Sunsprite' is an exception. The earlier orange-red varieties tended to scentlessness, but there are now fragrant roses in this color class – 'Dolly Parton' and the duller-toned 'Fragrant Cloud' are as strong and sweet as any of the dark reds and rich pinks with which fragrance is traditionally associated.

ABOVE LEFT 'Madame Creux' (tea rose fragrance)

ABOVE RIGHT 'Talisman' (sweet rose fragrance)

'Double Delight' (spicy fragrance)

'Sheila's Perfume' (fruity fragrance)

'Sutter's Gold' (fruity fragrance with cherry and cognac undertones)

ABOVE *On the terrace of the Monte Carlo Casino gardens*, c. 920 (chromolithograph).

BELOW The flat, quartered flowers characteristic of the Old Garden Roses are far more efficient at releasing their fragrance than the fewer-petalled blooms of Modern Roses. 'Baronne Prévost', with its classic 'old rose' fragrance, is a typical example.

'English Roses'

David Austin's strategy in creating 'English Roses' was to marry Old Garden Roses, with their classical – if somewhat narrow – range of fragrances, with Modern Roses, which feature a much broader and more novel range of perfumes. The resulting off-spring display an even wider and more diverse group of fragrances. Examples include:

'Evelyn' – fresh peaches and apricot

'Golden Celebration' – sauterne wine and strawberry

'Jude The Obscure' – guava and sweet white wine

'Mary Rose' – honey and almond blossom

The secrets of scent

Recent research into rose fragrance has finally uncovered many of its secrets, as well as providing a classification scheme to conveniently subdivide fragrance into five major groups. Instead of analyzing distilled rosewater or extracts from petals using solvents, which often resulted in compounds being degraded, Dr Ivon Flament of the Firmenich Company in Geneva, Switzerland, has developed a gentler method of examining the volatile components of roses. The vapors from a rose are captured from the air directly above the rose while it is still growing. Essentially, the fragrant compounds are drawn off from the airspace above the blooms and trapped in a charcoal filter for later analysis in the laboratory. One advantage of this method is that the chemist can measure the changes in fragrance composition as the rose grows, opens and finally drops its petals. The resulting new chemical data reveal that rose fragrance can be attributed to five major groups of chemical compounds associated with distinctive fragrances, as shown in the sidebar. This research may well help hybridizers to breed for fragrance. In the meantime, rose-lovers continue to lament the lack of perfume in many Modern Roses – indeed, 'Where has all the fragrance gone?'

'Perdita' (myrrh fragrance)

The five main fragrance groups

Hydrocarbon group

The group of cultivars derive their fruity odors from complex hydrocarbons such as terpenic, homoterpenic and sesquiterpenic compounds (which comprise more than 40 per cent of the fragrance content), with a small contribution from esters. Examples are 'Charles de Gaulle', 'Monika' and 'Sonia'. A study of the parentage of this group has revealed no common ancestor responsible for passing on these fragrances.

Alcohol group without orcinol dimethyl ether

These cultivars reveal the role of essential alcohols such as phenylethanol, citronellol, nerol and geraniol (which comprise 35 to 85 per cent of the fragrance content) in providing a range of fragrances from honey to balsamic to lemon to resinous. They include such classic roses as *R. rugosa rubra*, *R. muscosa purpurea* (an alternative name for an old mauve hybrid of 'Centifolia Muscosa'), *R. gallica*, *R. damascena* and 'Rose à Parfum de l'Haÿ'. The parents of these old roses are unknown, but a few Modern Roses that descend from them have been analyzed and have been shown to display similar fragrances with a similar chemical composition, indicating that this range of fragrances can be transmitted.

Alcohol group with orcinol dimethyl ether

Three varieties Flament studied, 'Châtelaine de Lullier', 'Margaret Merril' and 'Westerland', possess a combination of fragrances derived partly from the above two groups but to a major extent from phenols and the aromatic ethers group (see below), including a significant contribution from a powerful odor called orcinol dimethyl ether, which is detected mainly in modern hybrids. In effect they combine elements of the old and the new.

Esters group

This group consists mainly of modern Hybrid Teas developed by Meilland and Herbert Swim. These roses have a range of fruity scents, comprising esters (more than 30 per cent), alcohols (less than 25 per cent) and orcinol dimethyl ether (less than 30 per cent). Among them is perhaps the most fragrant rose of the modern era, 'Fragrant Cloud'. All the roses in this group have their own distinctive fragrance.

Aromatic ethers group

The modern Hybrid Teas have a diverse range of fragrances. These have been found to contain more than 40 per cent of orcinol dimethyl ether, with a small amount of hydrocarbons. They exemplify modern efforts to introduce fragrance into new roses. Examples are the famous 'Papa Meilland' (classic rose with a lemon-peel note); 'White Success' (jasmine-like); 'Gina Lollobrigida' (honey); 'Sylvia' (aka 'Congratulations'; lemony); and 'Youki San' (resinous).

'Old John'

'Old John'

FLORIBUNDA ı ORANGE BLEND

This rose is a tribute to the great English rosarian John Mattock. The flowers are a bright mid-orange with an orange-red reverse, full-petalled and about 7cm (2.5in) in diameter. They are borne in large clusters on a medium-sized, upright plant with attractive, glossy, dark green foliage. They are moderately fragrant. With its free-blooming habit and long-lasting flowers, it is an ideal specimen for a mass planting in the landscape.

DICwilllynilly ı Dickson, Northern Ireland, 1999
'Sunseeker' × 'New Horizon'
Repeat flowering ı *Moderate fragrance*
HABIT Bush H/W 1m/60cm (3ft/2ft) ı ZONES 4–10

'Oldtimer'

HYBRID TEA ı ORANGE BLEND

'Coppertone', 'Old Time'

The rarely used name 'Coppertone' describes the color of this rose very well. It is a sort of coppery tan color, with orange highlights. The blooms are very large, with slightly reflexed petals, and the foliage is glossy and mid-green. Reimer Kordes has not revealed the parentage, but it is evident that he intended this 1966 introduction as an improvement on his sensational 1963 'Vienna Charm'. They are certainly alike. Most people, however, find 'Oldtimer' a little easier to grow and the plants longer-lived.

KORol ı Kordes, Germany, 1969
Parentage undisclosed
Repeat flowering ı *Slight fragrance*
HABIT Bush H/W 1.5m/1m (5ft/3ft) ı ZONES 5–11

'Oldtimer'

'Olé'

GRANDIFLORA ı ORANGE RED

This Grandiflora might equally well be regarded as a 'decorative' Hybrid Tea, for its double flowers are informal and ruffled, and of good size, 10cm (4in) or more in diameter – although they are borne on a shortish plant and in clusters, in the manner of a Floribunda. There is only moderate scent, but the color is stunning: brilliant, warm crimson with a distinct overlay of orange. Like its parents, it is best in a warm climate, where it has proved resistant to mildew. The foliage is glossy and olive-green. One would not think that people would confuse *Olé!*, a Spanish phrase of public rejoicing, with the more intimate French *Oh la la!*, but this rose is often confused with Tantau's 'Ohlala'.

Armstrong, USA, 1964
'Roundelay' × 'El Capitan'
Repeat flowering ı *Moderate fragrance*
HABIT Bush H/W 1.8m/1.2m (6ft/4ft) ı ZONES 5–11

'Oph

'Olé'

'Olympic Torch'

'Olympiad' ✓ pp 384–5

HYBRID TEA ı MEDIUM RED

'Olympiode'

Adopted as the official flower of the 1984 Los Angeles Olympics, this rose came to California from New Zealand, where it was raised by Sam McGredy. It is a medal-winner in its

'Olympiad'

own right, winning the 1984 AARS award. The blooms are large, double, well shaped – if a trifle flat – and a brilliant, unfading red. They are borne mostly singly on a plant that is exceptionally sturdy and easy to grow, with disease-resistant, olive-green foliage. A lack of fragrance is its only demerit. Do not confuse this one with an earlier 'Olympiad', raised in 1931 by Pernet-Ducher and also known as 'Madame Raymond Gaujard'. It was a red blend.

MACauck ‖ McGredy, New Zealand, 1982
'Red Planet' × 'Pharaoh'
Repeat flowering ‖ Slight fragrance

HABIT Bush H/W 1.5m/1.2m (5ft/4ft) ‖ ZONES 5–11

All-America Rose Selection 1984, Portland (Oregon, USA) Gold Medal 1985

'Olympic Torch'

HYBRID TEA ‖ RED BLEND

'Sacred Fire', 'Sei-Ka', 'Seika'

Seizo Suzuki made a most spectacular debut in the world of international rose-breeding in 1966 with this large and shapely rose. Literally meaning 'sacred fire', *sei-ka* is the Japanese name for the Olympic torch, so in both languages the rose honors Japan's hosting of the Olympic Games in Tokyo. Fittingly, each bloom combines the Japanese national colors, red and white, with just a touch of Olympic gold at the flower's heart. The bush is strong and upright, with polished green leaves. It performs best in warm climates. There is not much fragrance.

Suzuki, Japan, 1966
'Rose Gaujard' × 'Crimson Glory'
Repeat flowering ‖ Slight fragrance

HABIT Bush H/W 1.5m/1.2m (5ft/4ft) ‖ ZONES 5–11

Gold Star of the South Pacific, Hamilton (New Zealand) 1972

'Opening Night'

'Opening Night'

HYBRID TEA ‖ DARK RED

The blooms are sumptuous: large, very double and of a brightly glowing, velvety deep red, with a mild but attractive fruity scent. The petals have lots of substance, so the flowers last well both on the bush and when cut. They are borne mostly singly on a medium-sized, upright, bushy plant that is clothed with abundant semi-glossy, dark green foliage. Healthy and easy to maintain, this variety is a good all-around performer.

JAColber ‖ Zary, USA, 1998
'Olympiad' × 'Ingrid Bergman'
Repeat flowering ‖ Mild, fruity fragrance

HABIT Bush H/W 1.5m/1.2m (5ft/4ft) ‖ ZONES 4–11

All-America Rose Selection 1998

'Ophelia'

HYBRID TEA ‖ LIGHT PINK

'Ophelia' turned up as a foundling at the English nursery of William Paul in 1912. For a couple of years it was ignored, but by the 1920s it had become a favorite. 'The Queen Mother of Roses', it was called, for not only did it produce no less than 36 sports, including such beauties as 'Madame Butterfly' and 'Lady Sylvia', but it was also used by every

'Orange Juice'

hybridist to create yet more beautiful roses. It remains as lovely as always, its medium-sized, double blooms of blush-white exquisitely formed and very fragrant. The bush is as easy to grow as ever, with leathery, dark green foliage. The climbing sport is exceptionally fine, too.

Paul, England, UK, 1912
[Possibly a chance seedling of an 'Antoine Rivoire' sport]
Repeat flowering ‖ Moderate fragrance

HABIT Bush H/W 1.4m/1m (4ft 6in/3ft) ‖ ZONES 5–11

'Orange Juice'

FLORIBUNDA ‖ ORANGE BLEND

'Lady Glencora'

This is one of those in-between roses with large, double, exhibition-form flowers in

'Orient Express'

'Oriental Charm'

'Othello'

with 'Cocorico' and 'Sarabande', which are not unlike it but much more red. They will flatter the orange tones in 'Orangeade', and together they create a smouldering effect.

McGredy, New Zealand, 1959
'Orange Sweetheart' × 'Independence'
Repeat flowering | *Slight fragrance*

HABIT Bush H/W 1m/60cm (3ft/2ft) | ZONES 5–11

🌹 (Royal) National Rose Society Gold Medal 1959, Portland (Oregon, USA) Gold Medal 1965

'Oranges 'n' Lemons'

SHRUB | ORANGE BLEND

'Papagena'

Most modern striped roses are color variations on the theme of red or pink and white, and when Sam McGredy brought out 'Oranges 'n' Lemons', it was quite a stunning innovation. Its flowers are gloriously striped in coral-orange and yellow, the precise blend varying with the season but always eye-catching. Sometimes listed as a Floribunda, it is really a Shrub Rose and might even be classed as a Hybrid Musk, as along with the tall, arching growth it has the musk scent, if not powerfully. But none of the Hybrid Musks of the Reverend Pemberton is as dazzling as this! The bronze-tinted foliage sets the vivid colors off perfectly. Its vigor and general good health make it a fine candidate for inclusioin in a hot-colored garden,

ABOVE 'Orangeade'
RIGHT 'Oregold'

'Oranges 'n' Lemons'

fairly small clusters. The color is officially described as 'clear orange', but it varies a bit. Sometimes it is exactly the color of orange juice, at others there is a good deal of yellow in it. There is not much fragrance, but the plant seems good, with dark green foliage and unusual, bright red thorns.

AROraju | Christensen, USA, 1986
'Katherine Loker' × 'Gingersnap'
Repeat flowering | *Slight fragrance*

HABIT Bush H/W 1m/60cm (3ft/2ft) | ZONES 5–11

'Orangeade'

FLORIBUNDA | ORANGE RED

When Sam McGredy introduced this rose in 1959, it created quite a sensation. 'Orangeade' remains one of the best of the dazzling roses. Its orange-red color is less unusual now than it was then, but the grace of its clusters of almost-single flowers remains unique, and the glossy-leafed, thorny plant is as strong as ever. Try it in a mixed planting

in the company of such gaudy plants as scarlet cannas, red-hot pokers and purple foliage.

MACoranlem ı McGredy, New Zealand, 1994
'New Year' × ('Freude' × seedling)
Repeat flowering ı *Slight, fruity fragrance*
HABIT Bush H/W 1.8m/1.5m (6ft/5ft) ı ZONES 6–10

'Oregold'

HYBRID TEA ı DEEP YELLOW

'Anneliesse Rothenberger', 'Miss Harp', 'Silhouette'

Not a rose for places with muggy summers, when it is apt to go into shock and refuse to grow, 'Oregold' – winner of the 1975 AARS award – is a gorgeous sight where conditions suit it. The double blooms are then large, high-centred and a glorious deep buttercup-yellow, with a light fragrance. The foliage is glossy and dark green.

TANolg ı Tantau, Germany, 1975
'Piccadilly' × 'Colour Wonder'
Repeat flowering ı *Slight fragrance*
HABIT Bush H/W 1.5m/1.2m (5ft/4ft) ı ZONES 5–11
🌹 All-America Rose Selection 1975

'Orient Express'

HYBRID TEA ı ORANGE RED

The great popularity of Mathias Tantau's 'Whisky Mac' sent hybridists searching for a similarly beautiful old-gold flower on a less

temperamental plant. One of the contenders is Christopher Wheatcroft's 'Orient Express'. It is a good, reliable grower, and the double blooms are lovely, high-centred and fragrant, but they are a deeper color than 'Whisky Mac', more of an orange tone, with yellow on the reverse. The foliage is bronze-green. It was named for the famous train that takes travellers from Paris to Venice in absolute luxury.

Wheatcroft, England, UK, 1978
'Sunblest' × seedling
Repeat flowering ı *Intense fragrance*
HABIT Bush H/W 1.4m/1m (4ft 6in/3ft) ı ZONES 5–11

'Oriental Charm'

HYBRID TEA ı MEDIUM RED

Lovers of single roses should clamor now for the reintroduction of 'Oriental Charm', despite its faintly twee name, for it is a beauty. It is not quite single, having a few petals beyond the canonical five, but the color is rich and unusual – orange-red, heavily veined with crimson, and set off by golden stamens. The glossy-leafed bush is tall and free-blooming, the blooms slightly fragrant and excellent for cutting. It was raised, from very mixed ancestry, by Carl Duehrsen.

Duehrsen, USA, 1960
('Charlotte Armstrong' × 'Gruss an Teplitz') ×
('Madame Butterfly' × 'Floradora')
Repeat flowering ı *Slight fragrance*
HABIT Bush H/W 1.4m/1m (4ft 6in/3ft) ı ZONES 5–11

'Paddy McGredy'

'Othello'

SHRUB ı MEDIUM RED

Aptly named for Shakespeare's Moor, 'Othello' is one of the darkest of the David Austin roses, its big, well-filled flowers reminiscent of the dark red Hybrid Perpetuals. They vary in color, from light to deep crimson, frequently adding an overlay of purple. It is, as one expects of a red rose, richly fragrant. The bush is strong and upright to about 1.5m (5ft), its faults being an abundance of thorns and that bane of dark red roses, a need for protection from mildew. The foliage is leathery and mid-green. It was introduced in 1986.

AUSlo ı Austin, England, UK, 1990
'Lilian Austin' × 'The Squire'
Repeat flowering ı *Intense fragrance*
HABIT Bush H/W 1.5m/1.2m (5ft/4ft) ı ZONES 5–11

'Paddy McGredy'

FLORIBUNDA ı MEDIUM PINK

Sam McGredy has written that when this rose was still unnamed, it was suggested he call it 'New Look', as it was just about the first Floribunda to have flowers of exhibition form on a not-too-tall bush. When it came out in 1962, it bore the name of Sam's younger sister, 'Paddy McGredy'. The double flowers are a deep coral-rose, almost red, and make a bright show when in full flush, as they almost cover the plant. The foliage is leathery and

'Paddy Stephens'

'Paloma'

'Pania'

'Paloma'

HYBRID TEA ı WHITE

'Paloma' is Spanish for 'dove', an appropriate name for this elegant rose, whose large, double, high-centred, white blooms open to show red stamens against grey-green foliage. It was raised by Herbert Swim and Ollie Weeks and introduced in 1968 after Swim had set up in partnership with Weeks under the name Swim & Weeks Wholesale Rose Growers.

Swim and Weeks, USA, 1968
'Mount Shasta' × 'White Knight'
Repeat flowering ı Slight fragrance
HABIT Bush H/W 1.2m/1m (4ft/3ft) ı ZONES 5–11

'Pania'

HYBRID TEA ı LIGHT PINK

Named in honor of a heroine of Maori legend, 'Pania', bred in Ireland and released in 1968, marks the beginning of Sam McGredy's love affair with New Zealand, where he moved in 1972. Slightly fragrant, the blooms blend delicate salmon-pink and cream with deeper shadings toward the petal edges, and the bush is healthy and full of bloom. The foliage is leathery.

McGredy, Northern Ireland, UK, 1968
'Paddy McGredy' × ('Kordes's Perfecta' ×
'Montezuma')
Repeat flowering ı Slight fragrance
HABIT Bush H/W 1.5m/1m (5ft/3ft) ı ZONES 5–11

'Paola'

HYBRID TEA ı MEDIUM RED

With this 1982 introduction, Mathias Tantau shows yet again how well plum-tinted foliage

'Papa Meilland'

olive-green. There are few flowers in between the peak flowerings, and the color tends to bleach in hot weather. This is definitely a cool-climate rose.

MACpa ı McGredy, Northern Ireland, UK, 1962
'Spartan' × 'Tzigane'
Repeat flowering ı Moderate fragrance
HABIT Bush H/W 1m/60cm (3ft/2ft) ı ZONES 5–11

'Paddy Stephens'

HYBRID TEA ı ORANGE BLEND

At first sight, 'Paddy Stephens' looks to be a straight coral-pink, much in the manner of the old (and always lovely) 'Mission Bells',

but it is really a blend of bright pinks with coral and gold. Large and shapely, the double flowers are pleasantly scented. The foliage is dark and glossy, and the bush has the reputation of being free-flowering. It was named for the raiser's friends Patrick and Patricia Stephens, long-time stalwarts of the New Zealand Rose Society.

MACclack ı McGredy, New Zealand, 1991
'Solitaire' × {(('Tombola' × {Elizabeth of Glamis' ×
('Circus' × 'Golden Fleece')}] × 'Mary Sumner') ×
unknown}
Repeat flowering ı Slight fragrance
HABIT Bush H/W 1.5m/1.2m (5ft/4ft) ı ZONES 5–11
🌹 Rose Introducers of New Zealand Gold Medal 1992

'Paola'

'Paradise'

shows off a deep but bright red rose. 'Paola' has little scent but, as I saw it in New Zealand, all the makings of a fine, colorful garden rose, its 20 or so petals holding their ruffled shape until they drop. Tantau has not told us the parentage, but at a guess 'Fragrant Cloud' must appear somewhere in this rose's family tree.

TANaloap ı Tantau, Germany, 1982
Parentage undisclosed
Repeat flowering ı *Slight fragrance*
HABIT Bush H/W 1.4m/1m (4ft 6in/3ft) ı ZONES 5–11

'Papa Meilland'

HYBRID TEA ı DARK RED

'MEIcesar'

Great publicity attended the introduction of 'Papa Meilland' in 1963. We were promised nothing less than the finest red rose ever. At its best, 'Papa Meilland' is indeed glorious, its double blooms dark and velvety, with a wonderful fragrance. In cool climates, however, like Britain's, the bush is a mildew-smothered runt, and in very hot places the flowers can scorch. The foliage is leathery,

mat: and leaden green. It still has enough ardent admirers for the 1988 World Rose Convention to have declared it 'the world's favorite rose'. It was raised by Alain Meilland and named in tribute to his grandfather.

MEIsar ı Meilland, France, 1963
'Chrysler Imperial' × 'Charles Mallerin'
Repeat flowering ı *Very intense fragrance*
HABIT Bush H/W 1.5m/1.2m (5ft/4ft) ı ZONES 5–11
❀ Geneva Fragrance Award 1963, American Rose Society James Alexander Gamble Fragrance Medal 1974, World Federation of Rose Societies Hall of Fame 1988

'Parade'

LARGE FLOWERED CLIMBER ı DEEP PINK

'Parade' makes a cheerful display with its biggish, informal, double blooms of deep, strong pink. They are pleasingly fragrant and come on long stems for cutting, which is unusual for a climber. It repeats its bloom very well, although not very continuously. There is apt to be a flowerless period between flushes, but that is the case with many climbers. They rarely bloom as continuously as the best bush roses do. The foliage is glossy, and the plant grows quite well in the shade.

Boerner, USA, 1953
Seedling of 'New Dawn' × 'Climbing World's Fair'
Repeat flowering ı *Moderate fragrance*
HABIT Climber H/W 3m/2.5m (10ft/8ft) ı ZONES 6–11
❀ Royal Horticultural Society Award of Garden Merit 1993

'Paradise'

HYBRID TEA ı MAUVE

'Burning Sky'

'Paradise' is as dramatic in color as a set for a grand opera. Each of its 28 lavender petals

is bordered in ruby-red. True, the contrast fades as the flower ages, but when the large and shapely bloom is at its best, there is nothing quite like it. It is a tall and easily grown bush, doing well everywhere. The foliage is a dark grey-green. Raised by Ollie Weeks and introduced in 1977, it won the AARS award in 1979.

WEZeip ı Weeks, USA, 1978
'Swarthmore' × seedling
Repeat flowering ı *Moderate fragrance*
HABIT Bush H/W 1.5m/1.2m (5ft/4ft) ı ZONES 5–11
❀ All-America Rose Selection 1979, Portland (Oregon, USA) Gold Medal 1979

'Parure d'Or'

LARGE FLOWERED CLIMBER ı YELLOW BLEND

A 'parure' is the name for a suite of matching jewelry – necklace, earrings, maybe a tiara – such as the celebrated set featuring emeralds that belonged to the Empress Joséphine. 'Parure d'Or', the rose, adorns itself with sprays of lovely golden yellow flowers touched with red and orange, set against dark green leaves.

'Parure d'Or'

'Parade'

It varies in the number of petals, sometimes being almost single and at others quite double.

DELmir ı Delbard–Chabert, France, 1968
('Queen Elizabeth' × 'Provence') × (seedling of 'Sultane' × 'Madame Joseph Perraud')
Repeat flowering ı *Slight fragrance*

HABIT Climber H/W 3m/1.8m (10ft/6ft) ı ZONES 6–11

🌹 Bagatelle (Paris) Gold Medal 1968

'Pascali' ✓   *good to cut*

HYBRID TEA ı WHITE

'Blanche Pasca'

When it was introduced in 1963, 'Pascali' created a mild sensation in the rose world by winning an award in every competition for new roses in Europe. This is most unusual, especially for a white rose. It then went on to win the 1969 AARS award and entered the WFRS Hall of Fame in 1991. It is firmly established as the world's favorite white Hybrid

'Patricia'

Tea, a triumph for its Belgian breeder, Louis Lens. True, the double blooms are not very large, and they have a hint of cream at the centre, but they are of most perfect form, they stand up to wet weather, and they are borne in profusion on a tall, healthy bush, as you would expect from this plant's parentage. The foliage is leathery and dark green.

LENip ı Lens, Belgium, 1963
'Queen Elizabeth' × 'White Butterfly'
Repeat flowering ı *Slight fragrance*

HABIT Bush H/W 1.2m/1m (4ft/3ft) ı ZONES 5–11

🌹 Portland (Oregon, USA) Gold Medal 1967, All-America Rose Selection 1969, World Federation of Rose Societies Hall of Fame 1991

'Passionate Kisses'

ABOVE 'Paul Shirville'
'RIGHT 'Patrician'

'Passionate Kisses'

FLORIBUNDA | MEDIUM PINK

'Jardins de France'

The fresh salmon-colored blooms, almost porcelain-looking, blend well into any landscape, and this rose is a perfect companion plant in mixed perennial beds. The medium-sized flowers are multi-petalled, with good, high-centred form and thick, starchy petals that are long-lasting both when cut and on the bush. They are borne in large clusters — each stem a ready-made bouquet — making them perfect for enjoying indoors. The plant is medium-sized, round and bushy, with dense, dark green foliage that stays healthy all year long.

MEIzebul | Meilland, France, 2003
'Celine Delbard' × 'Natilda'
Repeat flowering | Slight fragrance

HABIT Bush H/W 1m/1m (3ft/3ft) | ZONES 5–11

Bagatelle (Paris) Gold Medal 1998, Dublin Gold Medal 1998

'Patricia'

FLORIBUNDA | APRICOT BLEND

'Kordes's Rose Patricia'

Modern Roses XI, the Bible of those who seek knowledge of the ancestors of roses, states that 'Patricia' is a sport from 'Elizabeth of Glamis'. No doubt that is correct; and so here we have a sport that was content to change not merely the color of its flowers (to a richer salmon-pink, paler on the reverse), but their shape (the petals reflex more sharply); the foliage (which is broader and a deeper green); and the habit of the bush (which is taller and more upright). The perfume, although pleasing, is not quite as good. Although Reimer Kordes marketed 'Patricia' mainly as a greenhouse rose, it performs well as a garden rose in warm climates.

KORpatri | Kordes, Germany, 1972
'Elizabeth of Glamis' sport
Repeat flowering | Moderate fragrance

HABIT Bush H/W 1m/60cm (3ft/2ft) | ZONES 5–11

Orléans Gold Medal 1979

'Patrician'

HYBRID TEA | MEDIUM RED

There are a few parents that turn up again and again, among them 'Fragrant Cloud' and 'Chrysler Imperial'. Here we have the two getting together once again. The parentage of 'Patrician' is given as 'Fragrant Cloud' × 'Proud Land', and 'Proud Land' is a seedling of

'Chrysler Imperial'. The result is a tall, upright bush with large, very fragrant, double blooms. The official description is 'cardinal-red', and for once it is exactly right. The foliage is large and dark red.

Warriner, USA, 1977
'Fragrant Cloud' × 'Proud Land'
Repeat flowering | Intense fragrance

HABIT Bush H/W 1.5m/1.2m (5ft/4ft) | ZONES 5–11

'Paul Shirville'

HYBRID TEA | ORANGE PINK

'Heart Throb', 'Saxo'

The elegant double flowers are classically formed and a pretty shade of rosy salmon-pink. They are borne in profusion against a canopy of shiny, dark green foliage, compensating for the fact that the plant is markedly spreading in habit, giving it a shrub-like quality. The rose was named as a surprise present for a noted design engineer on the occasion of his retirement. In New Zealand it is sold as 'Heart Throb' in aid of The National Heart Foundation.

HARqueterwife | Harkness, England, UK, 1981
'Compassion' × 'Mischief'
Repeat flowering | Sweet fragrance

HABIT Bush H/W 1.2m/1m (4ft/3ft) | ZONES 5–11

American Rose Society Edland Fragrance Medal 1982

'Paul Transon'

LARGE FLOWERED CLIMBER | ORANGE PINK

The large, double flowers have old-fashioned form and are borne mostly in small clusters of 3–5. The bush grows very tall, to more than 3m (10ft) in warm areas, and has lax, arching stems that can be trained up arches, tall pillars, pergolas and similar structures.

An established plant is quite a spectacular sight, especially during the first burst of color in early spring, when its bright coppery pink blooms will practically cover the entire bush. Thereafter it flowers intermittently, but the glossy, dark green foliage remains lush, attractive and healthy-looking.

Barbier, France, 1900
R. wichurana × 'L'Idéal'
Once flowering | Slight, apple fragrance

HABIT Climber H/W 3m/2.5m (10ft/8ft) | ZONES 6–11

Royal Horticultural Society Award of Garden Merit 1993

'Paulii'

SHRUB | WHITE

R. rugosa repens alba, R. × paulii

Although this rose is often credited to the English hybridist William Paul, of 'Paul's Scarlet' fame, there is doubt about its origin. It appears to be a cross between *R. rugosa* and *R. arvensis*. Its admirers think it one of the best Ground Cover Roses, pointing to its vigor and its splendid show of scented, white roses in summer. One famous rosarian, on the other hand, has described it as being

INSET 'Paul Transon'
RIGHT 'Pascali'

'Pearly Gates'

'Peggy Lee'

'Penelope'

'Peer Gynt'

'Pearly Gates'

LARGE FLOWERED CLIMBER | MEDIUM PINK

'Pearly Gates, Climbing'

The flowers have some 35 petals and are a pure, pastel, angelic pink, possessing all the charms of their mother, 'America'. The canes arch beautifully out to 3m (10ft) or so, bearing stems strong enough to support the bountiful clusters of flowers. This sport was discovered by Larry Meyer and introduced by Weeks Roses Inc. If you wanted a rose to grace the gates of heaven, you need look no further!

WEKmeyer | Meyer, USA, 1999
'America' sport
Repeat flowering | *Strong, rose and spice fragrance*

HABIT Bush H/W 3m/1.8m (10ft/6ft) | ZONES 5–10

'Peer Gynt'

HYBRID TEA | YELLOW BLEND

Reimer Kordes must have had Grieg's popular music in mind rather than Ibsen's weirdly gloomy play when he named this deep yellow rose in 1968. It is popular in Europe, but in a warm and humid climate it does not do very well. The blooms are large and very full of petals, and open flat. Warm weather brings a touch of coral-pink to the petal edges. The foliage is leathery and olive-green. It has itself been much used for breeding. The fragrance is delicate.

KORol | Kordes, Germany, 1968
'Colour Wonder' × 'Golden Giant'
Repeat flowering | *Slight fragrance*

HABIT Bush H/W 1.5m/1.2m (5ft/4ft) | ZONES 5–11

🌹 Belfast Gold Medal and Prize of the City of Belfast 1970

'Peggy Lee'

HYBRID TEA | LIGHT PINK

This is a splendid sport from 'Century Two'. It occurred in the garden of John R. Feigel, in Evansville, Illinois, and was distributed by Armstrong Nurseries in 1983. It resembles its parent in its good habit and its shapely, scented blooms. They are in one of the late Miss Lee's favorite colors: soft, pale pink. The foliage is glossy and olive-green.

AROfeigel | Feigel, USA, 1982
'Century Two' sport
Repeat flowering | *Moderate fragrance*

HABIT Bush H/W 1.5m/1.2m (5ft/4ft) | ZONES 5–11

'Penelope'

HYBRID MUSK | LIGHT PINK

Like most of the Hybrid Musks from the Reverend Mr Pemberton, 'Penelope' can be either disciplined into a Floribunda-sized bush or (more attractively) trimmed only lightly. Its branches are well clad with dark green foliage, and bear clusters of semi-double flowers in huge abundance in early summer, after which 'Penelope' is often inclined to take a nap before the fall/autumn flowers appear. The blooms are then succeeded by beautiful salmon-pink hips. There are many who regard this 1924 seedling of 'Ophelia' as one of the most satisfying of all shrub roses.

Pemberton, England, UK, 1924
'Ophelia' × seedling or possibly 'William Allen Richardson' or 'Trier'
Repeat flowering ı *Moderate fragrance*
HABIT Bush H/W 1.5m/1.2m (5ft/4ft) ı ZONES 6–11
🌹 Royal Horticultural Society Award of Garden Merit 1993

'Perdita'

SHRUB ı APRICOT BLEND

This 1983 David Austin creation looks more like a bushy Floribunda than an English Rose. In any case it is a very pretty rose, with small clusters of very double, cupped flowers in pale peach-pink, and it is pleasingly fragrant. Growing to just over 1m (3ft) tall, it would be a good choice for a mixed bed with perennials. The foliage is dark green. It is named for the heroine of Shakespeare's *The Winter's Tale*.

AUSperd ı Austin, England, UK, 1992
'The Friar' × (seedling × 'Iceberg')
Repeat flowering ı *Intense fragrance*
HABIT Bush H/W 110cm/75cm (3ft 6in/2ft 6in) ı ZONES 5–11

'Perfect Moment'

HYBRID TEA ı RED BLEND

'Jack Dayson'

This 1989 introduction from Reimer Kordes certainly stands out in the crowd. Each petal is half golden yellow and half tangerine-red, and the double blooms are large and of perfect form, set against leathery, dark green foliage. The flowers are borne both singly and in small clusters. Roses of such startling color are not always of strong constitution, so it is good to hear that the AARS judges gave 'Perfect Moment' high marks for disease resistance and winter hardiness when they gave it their award for 1991.

KORwilma ı Kordes, Germany, 1989
'New Day' × seedling
Repeat flowering ı *Slight fragrance*
HABIT Bush H/W 1.5m/1.2m (5ft/4ft) ı ZONES 5–11
🌹 All-America Rose Selection 1991

'Perfume Delight'

HYBRID TEA ı MEDIUM PINK

The perfume of 'Perfume Delight' is very variable; sometimes it is rich and sweet, sometimes, in hot weather, only faint. It is a big, nicely shaped, double flower, in vivid deep pink with overtones of purple, set against

'Perfect Moment'

'Perfume Delight'

'Perle d'Or'

glossy, dark green foliage. It is a delight for flower arrangers, as the stems are long.

Weeks, USA, 1973
'Peace' × (['Happiness' × 'Chrysler Imperial'] × 'El Capitan')
Repeat flowering ı *Sweet fragrance*
HABIT Bush H/W 1.5m/1.2m (5ft/4ft) ı ZONES 5–11
🌹 All-America Rose Selection 1974

'Perle d'Or'

POLYANTHA ı YELLOW BLEND

'Yellow Cécile Brünner'

'Perle d'Or' is sometimes called the yellow 'Cécile Brünner', but it is actually a rather soft peaches-and-cream color. It does resemble 'Mademoiselle Cécile Brünner' in its sprays of small, exquisitely perfect buds, carried throughout the season. It is quite as distinctive and lovely, and just as easy to grow. It is beautifully perfumed, even more so than 'Mademoiselle Cécile Brünner'. The foliage is a rich green. Perhaps if modern breeders would like to try similar crosses, we might have more of these delightful beauties.

Rambaux, France, 1884
Polyantha × 'Madame Falcot'
Repeat flowering ı *Intense fragrance*
HABIT Bush H/W 1.2m/60cm (4ft/2ft) ı ZONES 4–10
🌹 Royal Horticultural Society Award of Garden Merit 1993

'Perdita'

'Pernille Poulsen'

'Peter Frankenfeld'

'Phoenix'

'Peter Mayle'

'Pernille Poulsen'

FLORIBUNDA | MEDIUM PINK

The semi-double, coral-pink flowers tend to open quickly and turn pale with age, but they have a little fragrance and are among the first of the Modern Roses to bloom in the spring, a foretaste of pleasures to follow. The bush is of average height, with mid-green foliage. Raised by Niels Poulsen, 'Pernille Poulsen' bears the name of his eldest daughter, now a notable hybridist herself.

Poulsen, Denmark, 1965
'Ma Perkins' × 'Columbine'
Repeat flowering | Moderate fragrance
HABIT Bush H/W 1m/60cm (3ft/2ft) | ZONES 5–11

'Peter Frankenfeld'

HYBRID TEA | DEEP PINK

Reimer Kordes is apparently a follower of show business and is fond of dedicating roses, such as 'Peter Frankenfeld', to entertainers he admires. Named in tribute to the German comedian, it does them both proud. The blooms are large, of perfect exhibition form and of deep rose-pink, set against semi-glossy, olive-green foliage. They are only mildly fragrant, but this variety is one of the most reliable and free-blooming of exhibition-style roses. It has been a real winner since its introduction, and it does especially well in rather difficult humid climates.

Kordes, Germany, 1966
Parentage undisclosed
Repeat flowering | Slight fragrance
HABIT Bush H/W 1.5m/1.2m (5ft/4ft) | ZONES 5–11

'Peter Mayle'

HYBRID TEA | DEEP PINK

'Lempicka', 'Lolita', 'Mainauduft'

With its intense, old rose fragrance, this variety is sure to appeal to rose-lovers of a romantic persuasion. The blooms are large, up to 13cm (5in) in diameter, with strong petals and long stems that are perfect for cutting. Extremely vigorous, this rose survives the hottest and most humid summers without injury. The foliage is glossy, deep green and healthy, and covers the plant throughout the season. The rose is named for the bestselling British author, who is famous for his series of books about his life in Provence, France.

MEIzincaro | Meilland, France, 2001
('Miss All-America Beauty' × 'Papa Meilland') × 'Susan Hamphire'
Repeat flowering | Intense fragrance
HABIT Bush H/W 1.5m/1.2m (5ft/4ft) | ZONES 5–11

'Pfälzer Gold'

HYBRID TEA | DEEP YELLOW

The official description of this 1981 introduction from Mathias Tantau has it as 'deep yellow', but whenever I have seen it the shapely blooms have been lemon-yellow, with the outer petals paler from the sunshine. It is a most attractive and unusual effect. The bush is tall, upright and glossy-leafed, and the flowers are long-lasting in the vase. They are quite scentless, however.

TANälzergo | Tantau, Germany 1982
Parentage undisclosed
Repeat flowering | No fragrance
HABIT Bush H/W 1.5m/1.2m (5ft/4ft) | ZONES 5–11

'Phoenix'

HYBRID TEA | DEEP PINK

'Phoenix' has double, high-centred blooms, light cerise in color and heavily fragrant. The bush is vigorous, and the foliage is glossy and olive-green. It is named for the capital city of Arizona, its sponsor.

Armstrong, USA, 1973
'Manitou' × 'Grand Slam'
Repeat flowering | Moderate fragrance
HABIT Bush H/W 1.5m/1.2m (5ft/4ft) | ZONES 5–11

'Picasso'

'Piccadilly'

'Picotee'

'Pfälzer Gold'

'Picture'

'Picasso'

FLORIBUNDA ı PINK BLEND

It seems that Sam McGredy initially started raising seedlings from the shrub rose 'Frühlingsmorgen' for the sake of its hardiness and disease resistance. But he soon discovered that it was able to transmit to Modern Roses the marbled and variegated colors of its ancestor *R. pimpinellifolia*. The result was what he has called his 'Hand-painted Roses'. 'Picasso', which came out in 1971, was the first of them. Although its foliage is dull and the semi-double flowers are small and scentless, the mixture of pink, red and white on each petal can be very striking.

MACpic ı McGredy, New Zealand, 1971
'Marlena' × ('Evelyn Fison' × ['Frühlingsmorgen' × 'Orange Sweetheart'])
Repeat flowering ı *No fragrance*
HABIT Bush H/W lm/60cm (3ft/2ft) ı ZONES 5–11
🏅 Belfast Dani Award 1973, New Zealand International Rose Ground Trials Gold Medal 1973

'Piccadilly'

HYBRID TEA ı RED BLEND

Raised by Sam McGredy and introduced in 1960, 'Piccadilly' soon gained the reputation of being the most reliable of the red and yellow bicolors – much to the embarrassment of the London judges, who, noting that it was too lightly built for exhibition, did not give it a gold medal. It did win in Madrid and Rome, however. There is a big planting of these scarlet and gold roses not far from Piccadilly Circus in London, in front of Christopher Wren's Church of St James. The flowers are double,

the foliage glossy and dark green, with red tints in its youth.

MACar ı McGredy, Northern Ireland, UK, 1971
'McGredy's Yellow' × 'Karl Herbst'
Repeat flowering ı *Slight fragrance*
HABIT Bush H/W .5m/1.2m (5ft/4ft) ı ZONES 5–11
🏅 Madrid Gold Medal 1960, Rome Gold Medal 1960

'Picotee'

FLORIBUNDA ı RED BLEND

In horticulture, a picotee is a carnation with a white or cream flower more or less heavily edged with red or pink. Although 'Picotee', the rose, hardly has enough petals (about 24) to pass for a carnation, it does have the characteristic color pattern, in white and pink. The foliage is glossy and dark green. Raised by Frank Raffel of Stockton, California, it has not been widely distributed. It looked most attractive in Pasadena's Huntington Gardens, where it was photographed. The Huntington people say it performs well. Do not confuse this Floribunda with a Miniature of the same name.

Raffel, USA, 1960
'Little Darling' × 'Gertrude Raffel'
Repeat flowering ı *Slight fragrance*
HABIT Bush H/W lm/60cm (3ft/2ft) ı ZONES 5–11

'Picture'

HYBRID TEA ı LIGHT PINK

The story goes that Sam McGredy III, father of the present Sam, having sent one of his new seedlings to the RNRS's trial ground, decided not to introduce it after all. He threw out his plants, and then had to ask for his own rose back when the judges gave it a prize! Introduced in 1932 as 'Picture', it was for a long time one of the most widely loved pink roses, for its soft color warmed with salmon, its perfect shape and its delicate scent. The double flowers are not large, but the plant makes up for that by producing them in large numbers. The foliage is glossy and dark green. Alas, its vigor seems to be declining, and it is not often seen now.

McGredy, Northern Ireland, UK, 1932
Parentage undisclosed
Repeat flowering ı *Slight fragrance*
HABIT Bush H/W 1.5m/1.2m (5ft/4ft) ı ZONES 5–11

'Pink Chiffon'

'Pimlico'

'Pierre de Ronsard'

'Pierre de Ronsard'

LARGE FLOWERED CLIMBER ı PINK BLEND

'Eden', 'Eden Climber', 'Grimpant Pierre de Ronsard'

Best known for his romantic sonnets, France's 'prince of poets' was a keen gardener, and it is appropriate that he be commemorated by a rose. 'Pierre de Ronsard' bears large, softly fragrant blooms, full of petals like an old Tea Rose, pale pink, deepening markedly in the centre. The plant is of pillar-rose vigor, and

can also be used as a free-standing shrub. Almost thornless, it has lush, glossy, bright green foliage and blooms freely and repeatedly.

MEIviolin ı Meilland, France, 1987
('Danse des Sylphes' × 'Haendar') × 'Pink Wonder, Climbing'
Repeat flowering ı Slight fragrance

HABIT Climber H/W 3m/2.5m (10ft/8ft) ı ZONES 6–11

🌸 World Federation of Rose Societies Hall of Fame 2006

'Pimlico'

FLORIBUNDA ı MEDIUM RED

'Pimlico '82'

One would expect a rose called after one of London's riverside suburbs to be English-raised and sold in that country. In fact, this is a French rose, from Meilland, and despite winning an award in Belfast in 1983, it now seems to be available only in France. It is quite a good red Floribunda, its double flowers wide and bright, its foliage glossy and dark green.

MEIdujaran ı Meilland, France, 1980
('Tamango' × 'Fidelio') × ('Charleston' × 'Lili Marleen')
Repeat flowering ı No fragrance

HABIT Bush H/W 1m/60cm (3ft/2ft) ı ZONES 5–11

🌸 Belfast Dani Award 1983

'Piñata'

'Piñata'

LARGE FLOWERED CLIMBER ı YELLOW BLEND

'Piñata' is in fact Japanese, despite its Spanish (or rather, Californian) name. It was introduced in the United States by Jackson & Perkins, but was raised by Seizo Suzuki in 1978. It is one of the most dazzling of the modern climbers, covering itself several times each season with sprays of double blooms in blends of yellow and scarlet, the scarlet taking over as they age. The plant is not over-vigorous, and has plenty of olive-green leaves. There is little scent, as is so often the case with brilliantly colored flowers.

Suzuki, Japan, 1978
Parentage undisclosed
Repeat flowering ı Slight fragrance

HABIT Climber H/W 3m/1.8m (10ft/6ft) ı ZONES 6–11

'Pink Chiffon'

FLORIBUNDA ı LIGHT PINK

The palest of pinks, the flowers of 'Pink Chiffon' are filled with silky petals, almost in the Old Garden Rose style. They are sweetly fragrant, and carried in good-sized clusters on a rather low, spreading bush with dark green foliage. This variety needs a dry climate, for the delicate blossoms are easily damaged by rain. It is one of the great Modern Roses – the flowers are irresistible.

Boerner, USA, 1956
'Fashion' × 'Fantasia'
Repeat flowering ı Intense fragrance

HABIT Bush H/W 1m/60cm (3ft/2ft) ı ZONES 5–11

'Pink Favorite'

HYBRID TEA ı MEDIUM PINK

'Pink Favourite'

'Pink Favorite' is best grown in cool climates. Where summers are hot, the double blooms tend to be on the small side and their already dark pink deepens into hardness, assorting oddly with the highly polished, dark green foliage. The foliage is outstandingly resistant to fungal diseases, so this is a good rose to grow where they are troublesome. In cool climates, the blooms are superlative. There is little scent.

Von Abrams, USA, 1956
'Juno' × ('Georg Arends' × 'New Dawn')
Repeat flowering ı *Slight fragrance*
HABIT Bush H/W 1.5m/1.2m (5ft/4ft) ı ZONES 5–11
Portland (Oregon, USA) Gold Medal 1957

'Pink Garnette'

FLORIBUNDA ı DEEP PINK

This is a pink sport from 'Garnette', introduced by Jackson & Perkins in 1951. Like its parent, it has clusters of small, scentless flowers that are notable for lasting forever in the vase no matter how the florist treats them. It is not much of a garden rose, being subject to mildew. There are several pink sports from 'Garnette', of varying colors. The foliage is dull and dark green.

Schneeberg, USA, 1950
'Garnette' sport
Repeat flowering ı *No fragrance*
HABIT Bush H/W 1m/60cm (3ft/2ft) ı ZONES 5–11

'Pink Grootendorst'

HYBRID RUGOSA ı MEDIUM PINK

A sport from 'F. J. Grootendorst', 'Pink Grootendorst' is the most popular of the fringe-petalled Grootendorst roses. The very double flowers are a pretty shade of candy-pink, with just a hint of salmon; and the sturdy, chest-high bush is rarely without a cluster or two from spring until late in the fall/autumn. The foliage is bright green and quilted, with a tendency to look pallid. Like all the Hybrid Rugosas, it is an easy rose to grow. It is scentless. Pronounce the name 'Grote-en-dorst', in the Dutch fashion.

Grootendorst, The Netherlands, 1923
'F. J. Grootendorst' sport
Repeat flowering ı *No fragrance*
HABIT Bush H/W 1.2m/1m (4ft/3ft) ı ZONES 4–10

TOP LEFT 'Pink Favorite'
TOP RIGHT 'Pink Garnette'
ABOVE 'Pink Grootendorst'

'Pink Parfait'

'Pink Parfait'

GRANDIFLORA ı PINK BLEND

Double and perfectly formed, these 8cm (3in) blooms are a confection of soft pinks, growing paler toward the centre, where they are often touched with apricot and cream. They have a soft, fruity fragrance, and are borne very freely in small and biggish clusters on a medium-sized, even-growing bush with mid-green leaves and elegantly thin, almost thornless stems. No rose is perfect, and 'Pink Parfait' has the fault of its color bleaching in hot weather. Cut it young, or plant it where there will be a little afternoon shade. It is still one of the loveliest pink roses ever raised. One of Herbert Swim's greatest triumphs, it was introduced in 1961, to be honored with a string of awards.

Swim, USA, 1960
'First Love' × 'Pinocchio'
Repeat flowering ı *Slight fragrance*

HABIT Bush H/W 1.5m/1.2m (5ft/4ft) ı ZONES 5–11

🏅 Baden-Baden Gold Medal 1959, Portland (Oregon, USA) Gold Medal 1959, All-America Rose Selection 1961, (Royal) National Rose Society Gold Medal 1962

'Pink Peace'

'Pink Peace'

HYBRID TEA ı MEDIUM PINK

Why Francis Meilland, or his United States agent, Robert Pyle, should have given this 1959 introduction such a name escapes most people, for it resembles its grandparent 'Peace' not in the least. It is, however, a very good rose, the tall, matt-foliaged bushes easy to grow and flowering with great freedom. The double blooms can be huge, if a little loosely formed, and they are intensely fragrant. 'Dusty

'Pink Perpétue'

pink', the catalogues say, and there is indeed something muted in their deep color, each petal showing a very narrow edge of paler pink. A rose for warm climates, 'Pink Peace' remains very popular in the United States.

MEIbil ı Meilland, France, 1959
('Peace' × 'Monique') × ('Peace' × 'Mrs John Laing')
Repeat flowering ı *Intense fragrance*

HABIT Bush H/W 1.5m/1.2m (5ft/4ft) ı ZONES 5–11

🏅 Geneva Gold Medal 1959, Rome Gold Medal 1959

'Pink Pillar'

'Playgirl'

'Playboy'

'Pink Perpétue'

LARGE FLOWERED CLIMBER · MEDIUM PINK

Introduced in 1965, 'Pink Perpétue' was one of the first of the modern repeat-flowering, not too vigorous climbers to become widely popular. It is strange how long it took gardeners generally to latch onto them. It remains a good one, reliable in its repeat flowering and lavish with its clusters of blooms – double, nicely fragrant, in a pleasing shade of bright rose-pink – set against glossy, light green foliage. It was raised by the English nurseryman Walter Gregory, and the rather odd English-French name is meant to recall 'Félicité Perpétue'.

Gregory, England, UK, 1965
'Spectacular' × 'New Dawn'
Repeat flowering · *Moderate fragrance*

HABIT Climber H/W 3m/1.8m (10ft/6ft) · ZONES 6–11

'Pink Pillar'

LARGE FLOWERED CLIMBER · APRICOT BLEND

The name does not do it justice. The loosely informal blooms with their scalloped petals blend every shade of pink, coral and apricot, and they have a pleasing fragrance, too. But it is apt in warning that the growth is really too lax to make a satisfactory shrub; train 'Pink Pillar' as a pillar or a moderate climber. Like most of the roses from Mr and Mrs Brownell of Long Island, it has the reputation of being extremely resistant to cold winters.

Brownell, USA, 1940
Parentage unknown
Repeat flowering · *Moderate fragrance*

HABIT Climber H/W 3m/2.5m (10ft/8ft) · ZONES 6–11

'Playboy'

FLORIBUNDA · RED BLEND

'Cheerio'

The almost single, scarlet and gold flowers are quite large and come in well-spaced clusters, but there is only a little fragrance. They certainly make a bright display, and the plant is strong, with dark green foliage. Perhaps the name 'Playboy' was sponsored by the magazine, or maybe it is just a tribute to the gaiety of the rose. It seems to have turned off the British – this Scottish-bred rose is much more popular in America than at home.

Cocker, Scotland, UK, 1976
'City of Leeds' × ('Chanelle' × 'Piccadilly')
Repeat flowering · *Slight fragrance*

HABIT Bush H/W 1.2m/1m (4ft/3ft) · ZONES 4–10

'Playgirl'

FLORIBUNDA · MEDIUM PINK

'Playgirl' is a very feminine, although hardly demure, flower in bright pink. Its five petals make up a shapely bloom, carried usually in sprays of five or so. It has little scent, but the plant is free-flowering, upright in growth and not very thorny. The foliage is semi-glossy and mid-green.

MORplag · Moore, USA, 1986
'Playboy' × 'Angel Face'
Repeat flowering · *Slight fragrance*

HABIT Bush H/W 1m/60cm (3ft/2ft) · ZONES 4–10

'Pleasure'

FLORIBUNDA · MEDIUM PINK

'Pleasure' won the 1990 AARS award for Jackson & Perkins. It has proved to be one of the very best pink Floribundas, its flowers – borne in sprays of 3–7 – large, double and ruffled and the color warm, shot with coral and salmon. In the United States it is praised for its strong resistance to mildew and rust, and for its abundant flowering. There is not much in the way of fragrance. The foliage is mid-green.

JACpif · Warriner, USA, 1988
('Merci' × 'Fabergé') × 'Intrigue'
Repeat flowering · *Slight fragrance*

HABIT Bush H/W 1m/60cm (3ft/2ft) · ZONES 5–11

🌹 All-America Rose Selection 1990

'Polarstern'

HYBRID TEA · WHITE

'Evita', 'Polar Star'

The name conjures up a vision of pristine white flowers reminiscent of polar icecaps, and that is exactly what you see! The creamy white buds open to reveal large, high-centred, pure white blooms of exhibition quality. Unlike most white Hybrid Teas, the flowers are unaffected by rain or inclement weather. While white is not a color to amaze, it is a necessary contrast in a garden to show off the brighter, richer colors. Bloom production is excellent and the repeat cycle is fast.

TANlarpost · Tantau, Germany, 1983
Parentage unknown
Repeat flowering · *Slight fragrance*

HABIT Bush H/W 1.5m/1.2m (5ft/4ft) · ZONES 5–11

'Polo Club'

HYBRID TEA · YELLOW BLEND

'Polo Club' could hardly be mistaken for any other rose, and it is surprising that it is not more widely grown. The petals are an unusual spoon shape; there are about 25 of them, making up a prettily shaped flower. The color is striking: each brilliant yellow petal is edged with red, and the pattern holds without the red taking over as the flower ages. The bush is

'Pleasure'

'Polarstern'

'Polo Club'

'Poppy Flash'

'Polynesian Sunset'

'Ponderosa'

tall and upright, with semi-glossy, dark green foliage, and produces its mid-sized blooms in small clusters all season.

AROtigy ⏐ Christensen, USA, 1986
'Gingersnap' × 'Young Quinn'
Repeat flowering ⏐ *Slight fragrance*

HABIT Bush H/W 1.4m/1m (4.5ft/3ft) ⏐ ZONES 5–11

'Polynesian Sunset'

HYBRID TEA ⏐ ORANGE PINK

In Polynesia the sunset is usually deep rose, passing to lilac – nothing like this 1965 rose from Eugene Boerner. Perhaps the coral tone of the double flowers suggests the association with Polynesia. The blooms are not of classical form, but they are decorative and borne in abundance on a good bush, with leathery foliage. The fragrance is fruity.

Boerner, USA, 1965
Seedling of 'Diamond Jubilee' × 'Hawaii'
Repeat flowering ⏐ *Fruity fragrance*

HABIT Bush H/W 1.4m/110cm (4ft 6in/3ft 6in) ⏐ ZONES 5–11

'Portrait'

'Ponderosa'

FLORIBUNDA ⏐ ORANGE RED

This is one of those roses whose value lies in the profuse display of bright color it gives in the garden rather than in the beauty of its individual blooms. The double, sharp orange-red flowers are smallish, with very little scent, and are set against very dark green foliage that has red tints when young. They are borne in abundance on a conveniently dwarf bush, not unlike that of its parent 'Marlena'. It is not quite as easy to grow as that rose is, though. 'Ponderosa' is still popular in Germany, but less so elsewhere.

KORpon ⏐ Kordes, Germany, 1970
Seedling × 'Marlena'
Repeat flowering ⏐ *Very slight fragrance*

HABIT Bush H/W 1m/60cm (3ft/2ft) ⏐ ZONES 5–11

'Poppy Flash'

FLORIBUNDA ⏐ ORANGE RED BLEND

'Rusticana'

This rose is one of the nicer of the 'screaming orange' Floribundas, the double flowers being lightened by a touch of gold. They go redder

'Pot o' Gold'

as they age, so a bush in full bloom displays subtly varied colors against its mid-green leaves. Individually, the blooms are nicely shaped, but it is as a provider of color in the garden that 'Poppy Flash' is notable. The growth is both strong and even, and there is an excellent climbing sport available. Scent is not its strong point.

MElléna ⏐ Meilland, France, 1971
('Dany Robin' × 'Fire King') × ('Alain' × 'Mutabilis')
Repeat flowering ⏐ *Slight, fruity fragrance*

HABIT Bush H/W 1m/60cm (3ft/2ft) ⏐ ZONES 6–11

'Portrait'

HYBRID TEA ⏐ PINK BLEND

'Stéphanie de Monaco'

Every rose-lover who dabbles in the art of hybridization dreams of raising a prize-winner. Imagine the thrill it must have been for Carl Meyer in 1972 to hear that his 'Portrait' was the first amateur-raised rose to win the coveted AARS award. He deserved it – this is a lovely rose in two tones of pink, shapely, double, fragrant and a very good grower. The foliage is leathery and dark green. The recipe for success was deceptively simple: cross two excellent roses.

MEYpink ⏐ Meyer, USA, 1971
'Pink Parfait' × 'Pink Peace'
Repeat flowering ⏐ *Moderate fragrance*

HABIT Bush H/W 1.5m/1.2m (5ft/4ft) ⏐ ZONES 5–11

🌹 All-America Rose Selection 1972, American Rose Society David Fuerstenberg Award 1972

'Pot o' Gold'

HYBRID TEA ⏐ MEDIUM YELLOW

In Ireland, it is said that if you can catch a leprechaun, he has to give you a pot of gold for his freedom. Rose-lovers do not have to wait for the elusive Wee Folk, they can have the joy of this golden rose from Pat Dickson.

Its double blooms are mid-sized – usually coming in threes – and of bright color, with good form and fragrance. The bush is spreading and healthy, with mid-green leaves.

DICdivine ı Dickson, Northern Ireland, UK, 1980
'Eurorose' × 'Whisky Mac'
Repeat flowering ı *Intense fragrance*

HABIT Bush H/W 1.4m/1m (4ft 6in/3ft) ı ZONES 5–11

'Poulsen's Bedder'

FLORIBUNDA ı LIGHT PINK

'Poulsen's Grupperose'

This is a lovely rose, with nicely formed sprays of semi-double flowers – ruffled, slightly scented, and tinted a lovely shade of powder-pink. By current standards it would not be called a good bedding rose; although it flowers freely enough, its growth is too tall. The foliage is olive-green.

Poulsen, Denmark, 1948
'Orléans Rose' × 'Talisman'
Repeat flowering ı *Slight fragrance*

HABIT Bush H/W 1m/60cm (3ft/2ft) ı ZONES 5–11

'Pounder Star'

HYBRID TEA ı MEDIUM RED

'Karma'

The flowers are medium red and open wide from long, pointed buds. There are only 20 petals, but they hold long enough for this to be a good exhibition rose. The bush is compact, the foliage is dark green, and the fragrance is old rose to sometimes spicy. It was introduced in 1982 by Sam McGredy.

MACnic ı McGredy, New Zealand, 1981
'John Waterer' × 'Kalahari'
Repeat flowering ı *Old rose fragrance*

HABIT Bush H/W 1.5m/1.2m (5ft/4ft) ı ZONES 5–11

'Prairie Fire'

SHRUB ı MEDIUM RED

This is a Shrub Rose of considerable vigor. Raised at the University of Minnesota, 'Prairie Fire' has apparently inherited its wild parent's exceptional resistance to disease and frost. The semi-double flowers are borne in large clusters of 35–50. The foliage is glossy and olive-green.

Phillips, USA, 1960
'Red Rocket' × *R. arkansana*
Repeat flowering ı *Moderate fragrance*

HABIT Bush H/W 1.5m/1.2m (5ft/4ft) ı ZONES 5–11

TOP 'Poulsen's Bedder'
INSET 'Precious Platinum'

'Precious Platinum'

HYBRID TEA ı MEDIUM RED

'Opa Pötschke , 'Red Star'

'Precious Platinum' may seem an odd name for a red rose, but Pat Dickson was loath to miss out on the sponsorship of a firm of refiners of precious metals. It is one of the best of all red roses. The double flowers are large and of beautiful form and color, and the bush is well clad in glossy foliage, resisting the mildew that plagues most red roses. The color holds without blueing, in all climates. All one could wish for is more perfume. Do not confuse it with a much older 'Red Star', the parent of some of the earliest Floribundas.

Dickson, Northern Ireland, UK, 1974
'Red Planet' × 'Franklin Englemann'
Repeat flowering ı *Slight fragrance*

HABIT Bush H/W 1.5m/1.2m (5ft/4ft) ı ZONES 4–10

'Pounder Star'

'Prairie Fire'

'Pretty Lady'

'President Leopold Senghor'

'President Heidar Aliyev'

HYBRID TEA | RED BLEND

Named in honor of the President of Azerbaijan for his peacekeeping efforts in the former Soviet Union, and to celebrate the first Western Oil production from the Caspian Sea, this rose is a strong, upright grower with an abundance of very glossy, dark green, disease-resistant foliage. The very double flowers have classical form and come in tones of salmon-red; they are very long-lasting, both on the bush and in the vase. This variety is a direct offspring of the famous 'Silver Jubilee', also bred by Cocker.

COCosimber | Cocker, Scotland, UK, 1998
'Silver Jubilee' × 'Remember Me'
Repeat flowering | Light fragrance
HABIT Bush H/W 1.5m/1.2m (5ft/4ft) | ZONES 4–11

'President Herbert Hoover'

HYBRID TEA | PINK BLEND

'President Hoover'

The politicians of his day were not very fond of President Hoover, blaming him – unfairly,

as it now appears – for the Great Depression and forcing his resignation from office. Neither are most nursery proprietors fond of the rose that L. B. Coddington named for him in 1930. Their complaint is that it rarely makes the kind of multi-branched plant that their customers expect. This is no sign of weakness, for it makes an exceptionally tall, healthy bush, with sparse, leathery, dark green foliage. The double flowers are a splendid melange of orange, pink and gold, opening paler; they are very large, and have a strong, spicy fragrance. One of the classic Hybrid Teas, it is still popular in Australia, where Mr Hoover spent some time as a young mining engineer.

Coddington, USA, 1930
'Sensation' × 'Souvenir de Claudius Pernet'
Repeat flowering | Spicy fragrance
HABIT Bush H/W 1.5m/1.2m (5ft/4ft) | ZONES 5–11

'President Leopold Senghor'

HYBRID TEA | DARK RED

'President L. Senghor'

This is a splendid red rose, dark and handsome. Its long buds open to large, double blooms, shapely and fragrant; the plant is bushy, with glossy, dark green foliage. The name honors the widely acclaimed poet and philosopher, the first African to be elected to the Académie Francaise, who served for 20 years as president of Senegal and wrote his country's national anthem, 'Le Lion Rouge' ('The Red Lion').

MElluminac | Meilland, France, 1979
(['Samourai' × 'Samourai'] × ['Crimson Wave' × 'Crimson Wave']) × (['Pharaoh' × 'Pharaoh']) × ('Pharaoh' × 'Pharaoh')
Repeat flowering | Moderate fragrance
HABIT Bush H/W 1.5m/1.2m (5ft/4ft) | ZONES 5–11

'Pretty Jessica'

'Pretty Jessica'

SHRUB | DEEP PINK

This is almost a dwarf version of a David Austin 'English Rose', growing to less than 1m (3ft). The flowers have Old Garden Rose form – globular, filled with petals and sweetly scented – and are of an old-fashioned soft pink, with no hint of salmon. The raiser finds the mid-green foliage a little sparse, which is a fair criticism, if a minor one. 'Pretty Jessica' was introduced in 1983. David Austin named it for Portia's confidante in Shakespeare's *The Merchant of Venice*.

AUSjess | Austin, England, UK, 1992
Seedling × 'Wife of Bath'
Repeat flowering | Intense fragrance
HABIT Bush H/W 1m/60cm (3ft/2ft) | ZONES 5–11

'Pretty Lady'

FLORIBUNDA | LIGHT PINK

This is an excellent rose that will perform consistently throughout the year with minimum fuss, not being susceptible to most of the diseases that affect other roses. The semi-double, cream-colored flowers come in clusters, and are long-lasting. The bush is of medium size and rounded, with plenty of glossy, dark green foliage. It was raised by amateur British breeder Len Scrivens, who prides himself on producing disease-resistant varieties.

SCRivo | Scrivens, England, UK, 1997
Seedling × [R. davidii elongata × seedling] × (['Royal Dane' × 'Alpine Sunset'] × 'Freedom')
Repeat flowering | Slight fragrance
HABIT Bush H/W 1m/60cm (3ft/2ft) | ZONES 5–11

'Prima Ballerina'

HYBRID TEA | DEEP PINK

'Première Ballerine', 'Primaballerina'

'Prima Ballerina' was a slow starter. When Mathias Tantau introduced it in 1957, it was obvious that it was a beautiful flower – large, double, of most elegant form, intensely fragrant, and of a lively deep pink. The foliage is leathery and light green. It took the rose-buying public some years to realize what a star performer it really was and to start queuing up at the box office. Surprisingly, it has never been a bestseller in America, although it is

RIGHT 'President Herbert Ho
LEFT INSET 'President Heidar A
RIGHT INSET 'Prima Balle

great fault, but all else is good news: the strong growth, the bushy habit, and the extraordinary brilliance of the semi-double flowers, still the most dazzling of the orange-red group, and not dulled by the carmine flush characteristic of the old blooms. It does, indeed, grow very well in Japan. The foliage is glossy and mid-green.

Dickson, Northern Ireland, UK, 1966
'Circus' × 'Spartan'
Repeat flowering ı *Slight fragrance*
HABIT Bush H/W 1m/60cm (3ft/2ft) ı ZONES 5–11

'Princess Nobuko'

HYBRID TEA ı MEDIUM PINK

This rose was sponsored by the Royal National Rose Society to mark its Alliance of Friendship with the Japan Rose Society, whose patron, Her Imperial Highness Nabuko, Princess Tomohito of Mikasa, is the wife of the Emperor's nephew. The classically formed blooms are a delicate light pink, multi-petalled

'Princess Nobuko'

and nicely scented. The plant is medium to tall, upright and bushy, with large, very glossy, medium green foliage that stays healthy all year.

COClistine ı Cocker, Scotland, UK, 2002
'Pristine' × 'National Trust'
Repeat flowering ı *Moderate fragrance*
HABIT Bush H/W 1.5m/1.2m (5ft/4ft) ı ZONES 4–10

'Princess of India'

HYBRID TEA ı RED BLEND

'Indian Princess'

This rose is indeed of Indian origin, raised by Delhi's Dr B. P. Pal. The large, double flowers are strawberry-red, deeper on the outer petals, and highly fragrant. Both of its parents are

'Princess of India'

'Princesse de Monaco'

susceptible to mildew, so it is pleasing to find that 'Princess of India' has a reputation for being resistant to the disease. The foliage is smooth and dark green.

Pal, India, 1980
'Super Star' × 'Granada'
Repeat flowering ı *Intense fragrance*
HABIT Bush H/W 1.5m/1.2m (5ft/4ft) ı ZONES 5–11

'Princess of Wales'

FLORIBUNDA ı WHITE

When Jack Harkness was asked to name a rose after the much-loved Princess Diana to honor her work for charity, he would hardly have dared offer her one that wasn't first-rate, and so 'Princess of Wales' has proved to be. It is a strong but short-growing bush, well furnished with glossy, dark green leaves, which make a perfect backdrop for the sprays of prettily shaped flowers. Often tinted peach and cream in the bud, they open white and last very well in the vase. Disease resistance and freedom of bloom are outstanding. It made its debut at the Hampton Court Flower show only a few months before Diana's untimely death.

HARdinkum ı Harkness, England, UK, 1997
Parentage undisclosed
Repeat flowering ı *Moderate fragrance*
Habit: Bush H/W 1m/60cm (3ft/2ft) ı ZONES 5–11
🏵 Royal Horticultural Society Award of Garden Merit 2001

'Princesse de Monaco'

HYBRID TEA ı WHITE

'Grace Kelly', 'Princess Grace', 'Princess of Monaco'

One of the world's favorite roses, this rose is as beautiful and elegant as the princess herself was. The double blooms are large, shapely and fragrant, and the bush is easy to grow and has glossy, dark green leaves. The color is exquisitely delicate, ranging from white to ivory

'Priscilla Burton'

and shading to warm pink at the edges. It holds until the petals drop. Francis Meilland raised 'Grace de Monaco' back in 1955. This variety is from his widow, Marie-Louisette, and was introduced in 1981.

MEImagarmic | Meilland, France, 1982
'Ambassador' × 'Peace'
Repeat flowering | Moderate fragrance

HABIT Bush H/W 1.5m/1.2m (5ft/4ft) | ZONES 4–10

'Promise'

'Princess of Wales'

'Prominent'

'Priscilla Burton'

FLORIBUNDA | RED BLEND

Raiser Sam McGredy has described his 'Priscilla Burton' as 'something of a chameleon', and this semi-double rose does vary remarkably in its colors. At its best it is an indescribable blend of light and dark pinks with white, but it can also come as straight pale pink or mix a great deal of red into its complexion. The plant, though, is uniformly vigorous and healthy, and the foliage is dark green. 'Priscilla Burton' was named for the wife of the chairman of Fison's, the British garden products firm.

MACrat | McGredy, New Zealand, 1978
'Old Master' × seedling
Repeat flowering | Moderate fragrance

HABIT Bush H/W 1m/60cm (3ft/2ft) | ZONES 5–11

Royal National Rose Society President's International Trophy 1976, Madrid Gold Medal 1978

'Pristine'

HYBRID TEA | WHITE

Fragrance is an elusive thing to describe, but at least most of us can tell whether a rose is fragrant or not. 'Pristine' is an anomaly. It won the Edland Fragrance Medal, the premier RNRS award for fragrance, but many people find it almost scentless. Even Bill Warriner, who raised it, describes the scent as 'light'. Everyone agrees on the beauty of the double flowers, with their sculptured petals and their ethereal white-ness, and on the sturdiness and reliability of the bush. The foliage is glossy and dark green.

JACpico | Warriner, USA, 1978
'White Masterpiece' × 'First Prize'
Repeat flowering | Slight fragrance

HABIT Bush H/W 1.8m/1.2m (6ft/4ft) | ZONES 5–11

Royal National Rose Society Edland Fragrance Medal 1979, Portland (Oregon, USA) Gold Medal 1979, Rome Gold Medal 1980

'Prominent'

GRANDIFLORA | ORANGE RED

'Korp'

The double flowers are large and shapely, although the clusters are small, and the bush is tall and floriferous. The color is such that the rose is indeed prominent in the garden — a hot orange-red, in the style of 'Alexander' or 'Super Star'. It holds very well, too, without fading or going purple, and there is some

'Pristine'

scent. The foliage is olive-green. Raised by Reimer Kordes and introduced in 1971, it did not find its way to the United States until 1977, when it was introduced and adorned with the AARS award.

KORp | Kordes, Germany, 1971
'Colour Wonder' × 'Zorina'
Repeat flowering | Slight fragrance

HABIT Bush H/W 1.5m/1.2m (5ft/4ft) | ZONES 5–11

Portland (Oregon, USA) Gold Medal 1975, All-America Rose Selection 1977

'Promise'

HYBRID TEA | LIGHT PINK

'Poesie'

In life, a promise comes before the ceremony at which you vow to 'love, honor and cherish', and so it was in Jackson & Perkins's catalogues. 'Promise' was introduced in 1976, and was followed in 1980 by the 'Love', 'Honor' and 'Cherish' trio of AARS winners. 'Promise' has not proved as popular as they have, but it is quite a good rose, with very large, double blooms of fine, high-centred form, in a pleasing light pink with a touch of coral to it. The bush is strong and on the tall side. The foliage is glossy and dark green, and the scent is, well, just a promise.

JACis | Warriner, USA, 1976
'South Seas' × 'Peace'
Repeat flowering | Slight fragrance

HABIT Bush H/W 1.5m/1.2m (5ft/4ft) | ZONES 5–11

'Prosperity'

'Purple Tiger'

'Prosperity'

HYBRID MUSK ı WHITE

A classic rose dating from the early twentieth century, and raised by an English pioneer in rose-breeding, 'Prosperity' is still widely grown and still highly desirable for its creamy white buds flushed with pale pink, which open to small, semi-double, pure ivory-white flowers. The weight of the clusters, particularly when wet, can sometimes give the plant an arching appearance; but when it is given space to spread, this plant's sprawling habit adds to its attractiveness.

Pemberton, England, UK, 1919
'Marie-Jeanne' × 'Perle des Jardins'
Repeat flowering ı *Moderate fragrance*
HABIT Bush H/W 1.5m/1.2m (5ft/4ft) ı ZONES 5–11
✿ Royal Horticultural Society Award of Garden Merit 1994

'Prospero'

SHRUB ı DARK RED

Even the raiser admits that this is a difficult rose to grow, lacking vigor, as the very dark roses so often do. If you would like a bit of a challenge, the mid-sized, double, deep crimson and purple blooms are beautifully quartered, borne repeatedly and richly

'Prospero'

'Proud Titania'

fragrant. The foliage is matt and dark green. It is a plant that needs the best of everything. Raised by David Austin, it was introduced in 1982.

AUSpero ı Austin, England, UK, 1983
'The Knight' × seedling
Repeat flowering ı *Intense fragrance*
HABIT Bush H/W 1m/60cm (3ft/2ft) ı ZONES 5–11

'Proud Titania'

SHRUB ı WHITE

One of the smaller of David Austin's 'English Roses', this rose is named for Shakespeare's fairy queen. The double blooms are full and quartered in the Old Garden Rose manner, white with just a hint of peach at the centre,

and fragrant. They are borne repeatedly on a compact bush 1m (3ft) tall, with semi-glossy, medium green foliage.

AUStania ı Austin, England, UK, 1983
Seedling × seedling
Repeat flowering ı *Intense fragrance*
HABIT Bush H/W 1m/60cm (3ft/2ft) ı ZONES 5–11

'Purple Splendour'

FLORIBUNDA ı MAUVE

'News' brought the rich purple of the Old Garden Roses into the Moderns. 'Purple Splendour' presents it in a yet clearer and deeper shade, and the flowers are both smaller and fuller of petals. It is, in fact, a more conventional Floribunda than 'News', from which it was bred, but it has never been quite as popular, perhaps for that very reason. It is a good rose, the plant strong and upright, with matt foliage, but there is little scent. It was one of E. B. LeGrice's last successes — he died in 1977.

LeGrice, England, UK, 1976
'News' × 'Overture'
Repeat flowering ı *Slight fragrance*
HABIT Bush H/W 1m/60cm (3ft/2ft) ı ZONES 5–11

'Purple Tiger'

FLORIBUNDA ı MAUVE

'Impressionist'

Lovers of rich purple and mauve roses will find this magnificent variety irresistible. The petals are eye-catchingly striped in purple and white, the colors becoming darker and more pronounced as the bloom ages. Of average size, the double flowers come mostly in attractive, tight clusters. They are very

'Queen Elizabeth'

'Queen Mary 2'

long-lasting and excellent for cutting. The plant is free-blooming and quite vigorous, with healthy, glossy, dark green foliage.

JACpurr ı Christensen, USA, 1991
'Intrigue' × 'Pinstripe'
Repeat flowering ı *Old-rose fragrance*

HABIT Bush H/W 1m/60cm (3ft/2ft) ı ZONES 5–11

'Queen Elizabeth'

GRANDIFLORA ı MEDIUM PINK

'Queen of England', 'The Queen Elizabeth Rose'

The WFRS, in 1980, declared 'Queen Elizabeth' the world's favorite rose. It is a little too tall for some. The outrageous height of the bush is a result of this variety's enormous vitality – 'Queen Elizabeth' seems to flourish anywhere. Long, high-centred buds open to large, double blooms of a clear, bright pink, produced both singly and in clusters. The foliage is glossy, leathery and dark green. The archetype of the American Grandifloras, it was raised in 1954 by California's Walter Lammerts and won just about every top award, including the AARS award.

Lammerts, USA, 1954
'Charlotte Armstrong' × 'Floradora'
Repeat flowering ı *Moderate fragrance*

HABIT Bush H/W 1.8m/1.2m (6ft/4ft) ı ZONES 5–11

🌹 Portland (Oregon, USA) Gold Medal 1954, All-America Rose Selection 1955, (Royal) National Rose Society Gold Medal and President's International Trophy 1955, American Rose Society Gertrude M. Hubbard Award 1957, Golden Rose of The Hague 1968, World Federation of Rose Societies Hall of Fame 1978

'Queen Margrethe'

SHRUB ı LIGHT PINK

'Dronning Margrethe', 'Enchantment'

Another of the currently popular 'Patio Roses', 'Queen Margarethe' is classed as

'Queen Margrethe'

a Shrub, but it is more like an enlarged Miniature, growing to about 110cm (2ft 5in) tall, with glossy, dark green leaves and perfectly formed flowers in proportion. The double blooms, borne in small clusters, are the prettiest shade of pale pink and delicately scented. It was raised in 1991 by the Poulsen company and named in honor of the Queen of Denmark, which suggests that its Danish raiser must have thought very highly of it.

POUlskov ı Olesen, Denmark, 1991
Seedling × 'Egeskov'
Repeat flowering ı *Apple fragrance*

HABIT Bush H/W 110cm/60cm (2ft 6in/2ft) ı ZONES 5–11

🌹 Gold Star of the South Pacific, Palmerston North (New Zealand) 1992

'Queen Mary 2'

HYBRID TEA ı WHITE

This striking, pure white Hybrid Tea is deserving of its spectacular name. The long, tapered buds open to large, high-centred,

'Purple Splendour'

white flowers with thick petals. They are long-lasting both on the bush and when cut, and have a distinctive, strong fragrance of sweet rose and banana. With excellent disease resistance and winter hardiness, this exceptional rose would make a wonderful addition to almost any garden. It is named for the luxury Cunard Line cruise ship *Queen Mary 2*, which was launched in the spring of 2004.

MEIfaissell ı Meilland, France, 2004
Parentage undisclosed
Repeat flowering ı *Rose and banana fragrance*

HABIT Bush H/W 1.2m/1m (4ft/3ft) ı ZONES 5–10

'Queen Mother'

'Radox Bouquet'

'Queen Mother'

FLORIBUNDA ı LIGHT PINK

'Queen Mum'

This extremely vigorous, free-flowering, low-growing plant makes a good ground cover once established. The semi-double flowers, borne mostly in large clusters, are a lovely confection of bright pink. The initial flowering in the spring can be an almost overwhelming sight, and it is followed by a good second crop. The growth habit is wide and dense, and the foliage is glossy, dark green and healthy. It was named in honor of the 90th birthday of the late Queen Elizabeth The Queen Mother.

KORquemu ı Kordes, Germany, 1991
Parentage undisclosed
Repeat flowering ı *Slight fragrance*

HABIT Ground cover H/W 1.2m/1.2m (4ft/4ft) ı ZONES 4–11

'Radox Bouquet'

FLORIBUNDA ı MEDIUM PINK

'Rosika'

Richly fragrant (although hardly of bath salts!), the flowers of 'Radox Bouquet' are softly pink and full-petalled – almost, but not quite, in the Old Garden Rose style. The bush is modern, rather upright, and well clothed in shiny leaves. Raised in England by Jack Harkness, it is highly regarded there. It is probably happiest in a cool climate; in humid climates, black spot can be a problem.

HARmusky ı Harkness, England, UK, 1980
('Alec's Red' × 'Piccadilly') × ('Southampton' × ['Cläre Grämmerstorf' × 'Frühlingsmorgen'])
Repeat flowering ı *Moderate fragrance*

HABIT Bush H/W 1m/60cm (3ft/2ft) ı ZONES 6–9

🌹 Geneva Fragrance Award 1980, Belfast Fragrance (R. J. Frizzell Memorial) Award 1983

'Rainbow Sorbet'

FLORIBUNDA ı YELLOW BLEND

This exotic-looking Floribunda is reminiscent of the popular rose 'Playboy', from which it descends. The medium to large, double blooms

'Raspberry Ice'

come in clusters, initially in shades of bright yellow, orange and red, and finishing a stunning yellow-pink blend. The flowers are carried on long, strong stems for cutting. The growth habit is upright and vigorous, and the plant is healthy and easy to maintain.

BAIprez ı Lim, USA, 2006
Parentage unknown
Repeat flowering ı *No fragrance*

HABIT Bush H/W 1m/60cm (3ft/2ft) ı ZONES 4–10

🌹 All-America Rose Selection 2006

'Ramona'

'Ralph's Creeper'

'Ralph's Creeper'

SHRUB ı RED BLEND

'Chunga Creepy', 'Creepy', 'Glowing Carpet', 'Highveld Sun'

This is not named after just any old Ralph, but after Ralph Moore, California's master of Miniatures. It is, in fact, one of his seedlings, although it is not a Miniature but a ground cover. The leaves are glossy and very dark indeed, the better to set off the Floribunda-size, semi-double blooms in brilliant scarlet and gold. The flowers have a distinctly apple-blossom scent. The parentage is undisclosed, but as Ralph Moore rarely releases the by-products of his search for better Miniatures, I should think he was rather taken by this one, as I was.

MORpapplay ꞁ Moore, USA, 1988
'Papoose' × 'Playboy'
Repeat flowering ꞁ *Apple-blossom fragrance*

HABIT Ground cover H/W 1.5m/1.5m (5ft/5ft) ꞁ ZONES 5–11

'Ramona'

SHRUB ꞁ MEDIUM RED

'Red Cherokee'

A sport from 'Pink Cherokee' that occurred in the California nursery of Dietrich and Turner in 1913, 'Ramona' is exactly like its parent except for its much deeper color. The single flowers are not quite red – cerise would be a better description – with a more muted tint on the reverse of the petals. The plant flowers early and long, with the occasional flower in the fall/autumn. Like all the 'Cherokee' roses, it dislikes extreme cold. The foliage is polished and dark green.

Dietrich and Turner, USA, 1913
'Pink Cherokee' sport
Repeat flowering ꞁ *Slight fragrance*

HABIT Rambler H/W 3m/2.5m (10ft/8ft) ꞁ ZONES 7–11

'Raspberry Ice'

FLORIBUNDA ꞁ RED BLEND

'Tabris'

Although this rose was raised by Reimer Kordes and introduced in 1986, the Kordes catalogue does not list it. Presumably it was sold to another firm to distribute, or else, as occasionally happens, one of Kordes's agents thought more highly of its pink and white flowers and bushy habit than the raiser did. The foliage is semi-glossy and dull green. The name 'Raspberry Ice' was aimed at the

'Rainbow Sorbet'

'Raubritter'

American market, but it is also known as 'Tabris', after the city in Iran from which the fine Tabriz carpets come.

KORtabris ꞁ Kordes, Germany, 1989
Parentage undisclosed
Repeat flowering ꞁ *Slight fragrance*

HABIT Bush H/W 1.2m/1.2m (4ft/4ft) ꞁ ZONES 4–10

🌹 Rose Introducers of New Zealand Gold Medal 1994, Portland (Oregon, USA) Gold Medal 1995

'Raubritter'

SHRUB ꞁ LIGHT PINK

'Macrantha Raubritter'

'Raubritter' is one of the most popular of the modern Shrub Roses, both for its unusual cascading habit – which makes it an attractive ground cover – and for its unique flowers. Double but on the small side, the flowers come in lovely bunches and are of most unusual form, the shell-shaped petals making a perfect pale pink sphere. They are extremely long-lasting, both individually and in clusters on the bush. The plant will eventually spread to more than 1.8m (6ft) wide, but is rarely more than 1m (3ft) tall. Watch it for black spot, and do not expect much in the way of scent. The foliage is matt, leathery and pale green. It was raised by that master of the unusual, Wilhelm Kordes.

Kordes, Germany, 1936
'Daisy Hill' × 'Solarium'
Repeat flowering ꞁ *Moderate fragrance*

HABIT Ground cover H/W 1m/1.8m (3ft/6ft) ꞁ ZONES 5–11

'Red Coat'

'Red Coat'

FLORIBUNDA ꞁ MEDIUM RED

'Redcoat'

'Red Coat' is a semi-double 'English Rose', and it could just as well be classed simply as a modern Shrub Rose – along with, for example, Kordes's so-called 'Park Roses', which it resembles. With light pruning, it makes a 1.5m (5ft) tall shrub. Disciplined a bit more, it can be treated as a tallish bush rose. Either way it makes quite a show all season, when it is covered with clusters of slightly scented blooms. The flowers are quite large, opening bright red and rapidly passing to a softer shade. The foliage is matt and dark green. David Austin, the raiser, thinks highly of 'Red Coat' as a flowering hedge, and as such it is a kind of updated 'Gloire des Rosomanes'. It was introduced in 1973.

Austin, England, UK, 1981
Seedling × 'Golden Showers'
Repeat flowering ꞁ *Slight fragrance*

HABIT Bush H/W 1.5m/1.2m (5ft/4ft) ꞁ ZONES 5–11

'Regensberg'

have impeccable form and good substance. They usually appear in medium-sized clusters. The bush is vigorous and upright, and well covered with deep green foliage. Introduced by Pat Dickson in 1967, this Floribunda rightly deserves the many accolades it has received in various rose trials. In humid climates, however, black spot can be a problem.

DICor ı Dickson, Northern Ireland, UK, 1971
(['Karl Herbst' × 'Masquerade'] × 'Faust') ×
'Piccadilly'
HABIT Bush H/W 1m/60cm (3ft/2ft) ı ZONES 6–11
🌹 Portland (Oregon, USA) Gold Medal 1969,
All-America Rose Selection 1971

'Remember Me'

'Red Success'

HYBRID TEA ı RED BLEND

Had Meilland introduced 'Red Success' in 1956 instead of 1976, it would probably have been called 'Orange Success', for the red does lean very strongly toward orange. The outer petals are usually a darker shade than the inner, and the whole flower tends to go darker and redder with age. There are some 40–45 petals, arranged beautifully symmetrically, making this a fine show rose. There is little scent, but the bush is tall and free-flowering, and the olive-green leaves blend well with the flowers. This variety definitely prefers a warm climate.

MEIrodium ı Paolino, Italy, 1976
('Super Star' × 'MEIalto') × (['MEIbrem' × 'Zambra']
× 'Super Star')
Repeat flowering ı *Slight fragrance*
HABIT Bush H/W 1.5m/1.2m (5ft/4ft) ı ZONES 5–11

'Redgold'

FLORIBUNDA ı YELLOW BLEND

'Alinka', 'Red Gold', 'Rouge et Or'

The double flowers are a golden yellow, their edges just lightly brushed with deep pink, and

'Redgold'

a sport. Present-day rose-lovers do not care for the rather dull green leaves or the cabbage-like, incurving form of the flowers. For many years, though, 'Radiance' (introduced in 1904 by John Cook of Baltimore) and 'Red Radiance', which came along in 1916, were the bestselling roses in the United States, thanks to their cast-iron constitutions, lavish blooming and fine fragrance. Old-fashioned they may be, but they remain among the easiest of all Hybrid Teas to grow.

Gude Bros, USA, 1916
'Radiance' sport
Repeat flowering ı *Moderate fragrance*
HABIT Bush H/W 1.5m/1.2m (5ft/4ft) ı ZONES 5–11

'Red Success'

'Regensberg'

FLORIBUNDA ı PINK BLEND

'Buffalo Bill', 'Young Mistress'

It would not be quite accurate to call this rose 'shocking pink', even though it is one of the most eye-catching of roses in the garden. The brilliant pink is, in fact, splashed and washed over a lighter ground, which shows through here and there. The petals are edged with white, and the flowers have a white eye, with yellow stamens. This is one of Sam McGredy's

'Renae'

'Hand-painted Roses', and one of the very best of them, for the flowers are large, up to 11cm (4½in) across, shapely and double, with 21 petals. Their fragrance is moderate, and they are carried in abundance on a very dwarf but healthy bush of 'Patio Rose' dimensions. The foliage is glossy and bright green. Introduced in 1979, this was the first rose that Sam McGredy raised in New Zealand after he moved there from Northern Ireland. The name is a compliment to the flower painter Lotte Gunthardt, who had already had a rose named for her. Regensberg in Switzerland is her home town.

MACyoumis · McGredy, New Zealand, 1979
'Geoff Boycott' × 'Old Master'
Repeat flowering · *Moderate fragrance*
HABIT Bush H/W 1m/60cm (3ft/2ft) · ZONES 5–11

'Rio Samba'

'Remember Me'

HYBRID TEA · ORANGE BLEND

The first variety bred and introduced by Anne Cocker, wife of Alec Cocker of 'Silver Jubilee' fame, this is an attractive rose with good form and novel color. The blooms are of coppery orange irradiated with yellow. They are large and moderately full, and are borne both singly and in Floribunda-size clusters. The plant is upright and strong-growing, with abundant large, disease-resistant foliage. In very hot climates, the blooms may be smaller, although the colors become more intense.

COCdestin · Cocker, Scotland, 1984
'Ann Letts' × ('Dainty Maid' × 'Pink Favorite')
Repeat flowering · *Fruit and spice fragrance*
HABIT Bush H/W 1.5m/1.2m (5ft/4ft) · ZONES 4–11
🌹 Belfast Gold Medal 1986

'Renae'

CLIMBING FLORIBUNDA · MEDIUM PINK

Introduced in 1954, 'Renae' is an unexpected offshoot of Ralph Moore's search for beautiful Miniatures. To all intents it is a repeat-flowering rambler, with very flexible branches and bunches of small, double, well-scented, pale pink blooms on and off all season. It is reminiscent of a more elegant 'Dorothy Perkins', without the mildew. It makes a first-rate weeping standard and has no thorns – one of its chief selling points. Do not expect it to grow as large as the old 'Dorothy'-type ramblers

Moore, USA, 1954
'Étoile Luisante' × 'Sierra Snowstorm'
Repeat flowering · *Intense fragrance*
HABIT Climber H/W 2.5m/1.2m (8ft/4ft) · ZONES 5–11

'Rhapsody in Blue'

'Rhapsody in Blue'

FLORIBUNDA · MAUVE

'Fantasia'

The closest anyone has yet come to a nearly-blue rose, this unusual variety from British amateur breeder Frank Colishaw has created quite a sensation in the rose world. Large clusters of semi-double, smoke blue/purple blend blooms, about 6cm (2½in) in diameter, are borne on long, strong stems. As with most purples, the color fades with age, particularly in very strong sunlight, but the varying color tones that result give the flowers added chromatic charm. The plant habit varies with climate. 'Rhapsody in Blue' is best grown in cooler climates; it can often sulk, and even defoliate, in hot-summer climates, where black spot can also be a problem.

FRAntasia · Colishaw, England, 1999
'Summerwine' × ('International Herald Tribune' × ['Blue Moon' × 'Montezuma'} × {'Violacea' × 'Montezuma'}])
Repeat flowering · *Sweet, spicy fragrance*
HABIT Bush H/W 1.2m/1m (4ft/3ft) · ZONES 5–11

'Rio Samba'

HYBRID TEA · YELLOW BLEND

A stunning rose in terms of both color and bloom production, this variety is truly a landscaper's dream. The pointed buds open to double, bright yellow flowers edged with orange, borne singly but mostly in large clusters. While a single plant will attract attention, a mass planting will set the landscape ablaze! The plant is medium and upright,

'Risqué'

'Rob Roy'

'Rockin' Robin'

'Rockin' Robin'

SHRUB ׀ RED BLEND

The very double blooms (40–45 petals) are ruffled, and are striped and splashed in vivid shades of pink, red and white. They are borne in large sprays that continue to bloom for weeks, providing color in the garden over a long period. The plant is of medium size and has a rounded habit – giving it a fountain-like appearance, dripping with color. In cooler climates, the bush may grow taller. The foliage is glossy and disease-resistant.

WEKboroco ׀ Carruth, USA, 1997
'Bonica' × 'Roller Coaster'
Repeat flowering ׀ *Mild, apple fragrance*
HABIT Bush H/W 1.5m/1.2m (5ft/4ft) ׀ ZONES 4–11

and very little care and maintenance is needed during the blooming season. It does, however, prefer cooler climates; in hot climates, the color fades and the plant is susceptible to black spot.

JACrite ׀ Warriner, USA, 1991
Seedling × 'Sunbright'
Repeat flowering ׀ *Slight fragrance*
HABIT Bush H/W 1.5m/1.2m (5ft/4ft) ׀ ZONES 5–11
🏵 All-America Rose Selection 1993

'Risqué'

GRANDIFLORA ׀ RED BLEND

'Risqué' makes an excellent garden rose, holding its tomato-red color well, without fading or going magenta. The double blooms open very prettily to show yellow stamens. The fragrance is only slight, and the foliage is medium-sized and dark green.

Weeks, USA, 1985
'Bob Hope' × seedling
Repeat flowering ׀ *Slight fragrance*
HABIT Bush H/W 1.8m/1.2m (6ft/4ft) ׀ ZONES 5–11

'Rob Roy'

FLORIBUNDA ׀ DARK RED

Long, shapely buds open to rather loose, double flowers carried in small trusses on a tall and healthy bush. This rose's greatest asset is its warm, crimson color – rich and velvety – and its greatest drawbacks are its only slight fragrance and its preference for a cool climate. The foliage is leathery and dark green. Raised by Alec Cocker of Aberdeen, it was named, patriotically, for Sir Walter Scott's legendary hero.

CORob ׀ Cocker, Scotland, UK, 1970
'Evelyn Fison' × 'Wendy Cussons'
Repeat flowering ׀ *Slight fragrance*
HABIT Bush H/W 1m/60cm (3ft/2ft) ׀ ZONES 5–11

'Robusta'

SHRUB ׀ MEDIUM RED

'Kordes Robusta', 'Kordes's Rose Robusta'

Most hybrids of *R. rugosa* tend to take after it quite strongly, but this Kordes introduction shows its *R. rugosa* ancestry chiefly in its prickliness and the leathery quality of its dark green leaves. Otherwise, it is a fairly typical (and good) Shrub Rose, raising upright branches to about 1.5m (5ft) high and crowned with trusses of single, brilliant red flowers all through the season. Alas, there is little of the clove-like *R. rugosa* fragrance.

KORgosa ׀ Kordes, Germany, 1979
R. rugosa regeliana × unknown
Repeat flowering ׀ *Slight fragrance*
HABIT Bush H/W 1.5m/1.2m (5ft/4ft) ׀ ZONES 4–10

'Rocky'

'Roman Holiday'

'Rosabell'

'Robusta'

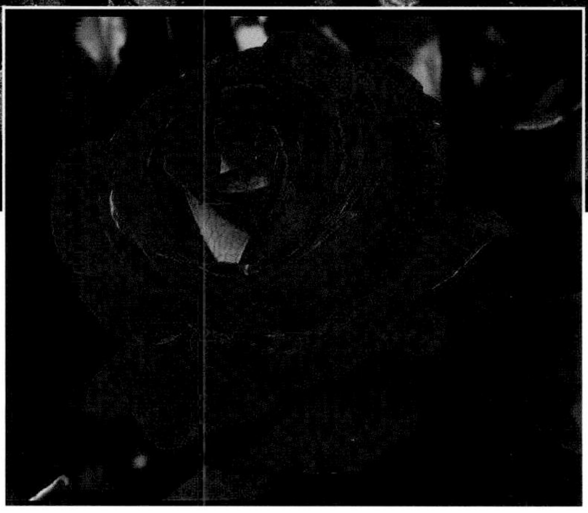

'Rocky'

SHRUB ⎪ ORANGE BLEND

'Blushing Maid'

This 1979 rose from Sam McGredy is named
for the Sylvester Stallone movies. Derived from
Sam's 'Hand-painted Roses' breeding line, it
is in effect an overgrown Floribunda, bearing
its clusters of shapely, double flowers – coral-
orange with a white reverse – all season on
a tall bush with dark green foliage.

MACkepa ⎪ McGredy, New Zealand, 1979
'Liverpool Echo' × ('Evelyn Fison' × ['Orange
Sweetheart' × 'Frühlingsmorgen'])
Repeat flowering ⎪ *Slight fragrance*

HABIT Bush H/W 1.2m/1m (4ft/3ft) ⎪ ZONES 5–11

'Ronald Reagan Rose'

'Roman Holiday'

FLORIBUNDA ⎪ RED BLEND

Although it won the AARS award in 1967,
the year after its introduction, 'Roman Holiday'
has dropped out of the catalogues. This is a
shame, as it still looks pretty good, its compact plant, with glossy, dark green leaves, still
flaunting clusters of double blooms in a festive
blend of red and orange with flashes of gold.
They are fragrant, too. Admittedly, it was
never as good in cold or humid climates.

LINro ⎪ Lindquist, USA, 1966
('Pinkie' × 'Independence') × 'Circus'
Repeat flowering ⎪ *Moderate fragrance*

HABIT Bush H/W 1m/60cm (3ft/2ft) ⎪ ZONES 5–11
All-America Rose Selection 1967

'Ronald Reagan Rose'

HYBRID TEA ⎪ RED BLEND

This majestic rose is of striking and unusual
color, and pays tribute to one of America's
most popular presidents – and the man responsible for declaring the rose the national floral
emblem of the United States. The blooms
start off as whitish pink buds edged with
red – giving just a hint of the luminous color
within – and as the petals unfold to huge
flowers, they magically transform to rich red
with a crisp white reverse. The long-lasting,
long-stemmed flowers are breathtaking in
floral arrangements. The plant is tall and
upright, with glossy, dark green foliage,
and repeats its bloom well.

JACtanre ⎪ Zary, USA, 2003
Parentage undisclosed
Repeat flowering ⎪ *Light, sweet fragrance*

HABIT Bush H/W 1.8m/1.2m (6ft/4ft) ⎪ ZONES 4–10

'Rosabell'

FLORIBUNDA ⎪ MEDIUM PINK

'Rosabell' looks to be a charmer, with large
sprays of smallish flowers – full-petalled and
neatly formed – in a lovely shade of soft pink.
The bush is low-growing, with glossy leaves,
and the general effect is one of an updated
Polyantha. This variety is part of a trend away
from the traditional Floribundas, with exhi-
bition-type flowers. There is not a great deal
of fragrance.

COCceleste ⎪ Cocker, Scotland, UK, 1988
('National Trust' × 'Wee Man') × 'Darling Flame'
Repeat flowering ⎪ *Slight fragrance*

HABIT Bush H/W 1.2m/1m (4ft/3ft) ⎪ ZONES 5–11

The Rose in India

It is said that Brahma the Creator, wishing to endow the goddess Lakshmi with loveliness beyond that of any other being, gathered the essence of a myriad roses and bestowed it upon her. It may seem ungrateful of her, after that, to have adopted the lotus and not the rose as her favorite emblem, but perhaps she was being considerate toward her worshippers, for it is difficult to grow roses in most of Hindu India. The climate is too tropical and sweltering, although Wild Roses grow in the Himalayas.

The rose and the Mogul empire

It was not until the advent of Islam, and especially the rise of the Mogul emperors in the early sixteenth century, that the rose came into its own in Indian gardens. Babur, the Persian founder of the Mogul dynasty, seems not to have been overly enchanted with the land he had conquered. In a famous passage in his diaries, he laments, among other things, the scarcity of beautiful gardens in Hindustan and the ignorance of Indian gardeners. A keen and knowledgeable gardener himself, he set about raising standards, establishing gardens in the Persian manner throughout his domains. To furnish them, he brought many trees and flowers from Persia and Ferghana: cypresses and almonds, pomegranates and roses. Just what roses they were, no one seems to remember, but they may well have included 'Summer Damask' (also known as the 'Damask Rose' and *R. gallica damascena*), which is a native of Asia Minor. Always prized for its fragrance, it is still the most important source of attar of roses.

Thereby hangs a tale. It seems that Babur's grandson Jahangir (another great gardener) was boating one day with his empress, the beautiful and clever Nur Jahan, on a lake in one of the royal gardens. Such was the luxury of the Mogul court that the entire surface of the water had been floated with fresh roses. The empress, noticing that the flowers were making the water oily, scooped some of the oil up. It proved to be powerfully scented of roses. Thus, it is said, was attar of roses invented, and the delighted emperor showered riches and honor on his wife for her discovery. The source of this story is impeccable: Jahangir's own autobiography. Apparently he was unaware that the Persians had already been making attar of roses for more than a hundred years.

Indian rose gardens today

Nur Jahan's niece Arjumand Begum is known to history as Mumtaz Mahal, the favorite wife of Jahangir's son Shah Jahan, who built the Taj Mahal at Agra in her memory. Surely no monument ever raised by man is lovelier than this. Among the flowers that bloom in marble on its walls are roses. The gardens of the Taj used to be famous for living roses, too, but they have been less in evidence in more recent years. A little to the north, however, in Delhi, is the garden of the Indian Rose Society, which has some very beautiful roses indeed.

Top It would be pleasing to think that the woman in this Indian miniature is none other than the Empress Nur Jahan, but the strictness of purdah in the Mogul court has deprived us of an authentic likeness of her. No mere artist would have been allowed to look upon her unveiled face.

Left Roses are among the flowers that bloom in marble on the walls of the Taj Mahal, which was built between 1631 and 1648 by Shah Jahan in memory of his favorite wife, Mumtaz.

The climate of the Indian plains is such that roses there reverse their usual seasons, resting during the scorching summer heat and blooming during the cooler days of winter. These roses are in the gardens of the Rashtrapati Bhavan in Delhi, the great palace built by Sir Edwin Lutyens in the 1920s for the British Viceroy and now the official residence of the president of India.

The summer heat of the Indian plains is such as to send roses into a state of shock; unusually, therefore, roses in India are at their best in winter. Many European and American roses do well in India, and they are joined by roses bred for local conditions, notably those bred by Dr P. B. Pal. Among them are such beauties as the red Hybrid Tea 'Princess of India' and 'Raja of Nalagarh', an orange-red Hybrid Tea. Also found here are such gallant old-timers as 'Crimson Glory' and 'Maréchal Niel', the latter still the best climbing rose for Indian conditions, according to Dr Pal.

RIGHT It was a convention throughout Islam to portray a ruler or other notable smelling a rose, as in this portrait of the Indian Emperor Shah Jahan. The image suggested that these mighty warriors also cultivated the arts of peace.

Farther to the north, roses abound in the Vale of Kashmir, where they are grown commercially for export to the flower shops of Europe. Babur and Nur Jahan would surely have approved, and they would also have been delighted by the roses in the great Mogul gardens of the Shalimar and the Nishat Bagh in Kashmir. This was the region where, 2300 years ago, the armies of Alexander the Great arrived – and East met West for the first time. Is it fanciful to imagine that those two goddesses of beauty, Aphrodite and Lakshmi, each associated with the rose, linger jointly in the beauty and fragrance of flowers?

ABOVE No status-conscious Maharajah felt his palace complete without a suite of silver-plated furniture. With the reduction in princely fortunes since Independence, pieces like this side chair with its all-over pattern of rose buds often appear in sales-rooms and antique shops.

LEFT *Rosa moschata*, which is native to Persia (modern-day Iran) and also to Madeira, North Africa and Spain, is said to be the rose that led Nur Jahan to 'discover' attar of roses. It is powerfully fragrant.

INSET 'Raja of Nalagarh'

are borne all season. They are deep purple-crimson and fragrant. The foliage is light green and rugose. The plant's only omission is a lack of hips. The later displays are more abundant if you are generous with watering during hot weather, but this variety does have a tendency to sulk in subtropical climates.

Cochet-Cochet, France, 1901
Seedling of, or sport from, unknown hybrid of
R. rugosa
Repeat flowering ┊ *Intense fragrance*
HABIT Bush H/W 1.8m/1.5m (6ft/5ft) ┊ ZONES 4–9

RIGHT 'Royal Albert Hall'
BELOW 'Royal Dane'

'Rosy Cheeks'

HYBRID TEA ┊ RED BLEND

Anderson's Rose Nurseries are an Aberdeen firm with the laudable habit of only cataloguing roses with good fragrance. Naturally, one

would expect a rose of their own introduction to be beautifully scented, and 'Rosy Cheeks' does not disappoint. The blooms are very large indeed – some 18cm (7in) in diameter – of perfect exhibition form (with 35 petals), and a pleasing shade of cerise with yellow on the reverse. The foliage is glossy. Like its pollen parent, 'Irish Gold', it is happiest in a coolish climate.

Anderson, Scotland, UK, 1975
Unknown × 'Irish Gold'
Repeat flowering ┊ *Intense fragrance*
HABIT Bush H/W 1.2m/1m (4ft/3ft) ┊ ZONES 5–11

'Rosy Cushion'

SHRUB ┊ LIGHT PINK

Interplant of the Netherlands market this as a Ground Cover Rose. In fact, it is not dense enough in growth for this purpose. The low, spreading shrub, with glossy, dark green leaves, does become a mound of pretty, single, pink and cream flowers several times each season, so the name 'Rosy Cushion' is apt enough.

'Rosy Cushion'

'Rosy Cheeks'

The flowers are borne in clusters, and there is little scent.

INTerall | Ilsink, The Netherlands, 1979
'Yesterday' × seedling
Repeat flowering | Slight fragrance

HABIT Ground cover H/W 1m/1.2m (3ft/4ft) | ZONES 5–11

Royal Horticultural Society Award of Garden Merit 1993

'Rouge Royale'

'Rouge Royale'

HYBRID TEA | DEEP RED

'Caruso', 'Rouge Royal', 'Royal Red'

The deep burgundy-red buds open to reveal perfectly quartered, old-fashioned blooms of bright raspberry-red. The flowers are large and sturdy, with up to 80 petals, and come singly and, occasionally, in small clusters. They hold up well in rain and heat, and have a strong, sweet fragrance of citrus and fresh, ripe berries. The plant is vigorous, tallish and upright in habit, and has a fast bloom cycle.

MEIkarouz | Meilland, France, 2000
'Charlotte Rampling' × ('Ambassador' × Fiorella')
Repeat flowering | Strong, citrus and berry fragrance

HABIT Bush H/W 1.5m/1.2m (5ft/4ft) | ZONES 5–11

Buenos Aires Fragrance Award 2000, Le Roeulx Fragrance Award 2000, Saverne Fragrance Award 2000, Rose Hills (California) Gold Medal and Fragrance Award 2003

'Royal Albert Hall'

HYBRID TEA | RED BLEND

London's great concert hall is built in dark red bricks adorned with yellow terracotta and is crowned with a green copper dome. It is not surprising that the rose named in its honor is a bicolor in red and yellow, with bright green leaves. A creation of Alec Cocker of Aberdeen, it is a big, double flower of fine exhibition form, with good fragrance, and is also a good performer in the garden. It is becoming rare now, but it still has

'Royal Gold'

a good reputation in the United Kingdom as a show rose.

Cocker, Scotland, UK, 1972
'Fragrant Cloud' × 'Postillion'
Repeat flowering | Intense fragrance

HABIT Bush H/W 1.5m/1.2m (5ft/4ft) | ZONES 5–11

'Royal Dane'

HYBRID TEA | ORANGE BLEND

'Troika'

This rose looks good from the moment it starts to grow in spring. Its young foliage is plum-red and brilliantly glossy, maturing to dark green. It flowers early, too, the blooms large and richly fragrant, in a melange of orange and copper with touches of cerise. It grows best, and is most richly colored, in cool climates.

POUrridor | Poulsen, Denmark, 1971
('Super Star' × [Baccarà' × 'Princess Astrid']) × 'Hanne'
Repeat flowering | Intense fragrance

HABIT Bush H/W 1.5m/1.2m (5ft/4ft) | ZONES 5–11

Royal Horticultural Society Award of Garden Merit 1993

'Royal Gold'

LARGE FLOWERED CLIMBER | MEDIUM YELLOW

If you want to grow a deep, deep yellow rose for exhibition, then this is it. It is pleasantly fragrant, too. Plant it only if you live in a warm, dry climate, for it languishes and takes black spot where summers are humid; and where winters are cold, it is apt to be frosted. In warm climates, 'Royal Gold' makes a strong pillar rose, flowering quite freely all season – both singly and in clusters – the beautiful color of its double blooms well set off by glossy, slightly grey-toned foliage.

Morey, USA, 1957
'Climbing Goldilocks' × 'Lydia'
Repeat flowering | Fruity fragrance

HABIT Climber H/W 3m/2.5m (10ft/8ft) | ZONES 6–11

'Royal Highness'

HYBRID TEA | LIGHT PINK

'Königliche Hoheit'

This is a rose for a sunny climate; rain damages its silken petals. That is the only reservation.

'Royal Highness'

'Royal Highness', the winner of the 1963 AARS award, is one of the great roses of the 1960s. Carried on long, almost thornless stems, the double blooms are large, of most perfect, high-centred form, and of the most beautiful pale, luminous pink – ethereal without being at all wishy-washy. They are fragrant, too. The plant is bushy and of average height, with splendid, glossy foliage. This rose was a triumph for its raisers. It is, however, essentially a show rose now, and in humid climates is susceptible to black spot if not sprayed regularly.

Swim and Weeks, USA, 1962
'Virgo' × 'Peace'
Repeat flowering | *Intense fragrance*

HABIT Bush H/W 1.5m/1.2m (5ft/4ft) | ZONES 5–11

🏅 Portland (Oregon, USA) Gold Medal 1960, Madrid Gold Medal 1962, All-America Rose Selection 1963, American Rose Society David Fuerstenberg Award 1964

'Royal Sunset'

LARGE FLOWERED CLIMBER | APRICOT BLEND

After the acclaim that greeted 'Royal Gold' in 1957, Jackson & Perkins introduced several more 'Royal' climbers of Dr Dennison Morey's breeding. 'Royal Sunset' of 1960 is probably the best. 'Sunset' describes the copper, flame and apricot colors well – although the colors are usually soft rather than blazing – and the double blooms are large and shapely. The foliage is leathery. Like 'Royal Gold', 'Royal Sunset' is not a rose for humid climates. It has some of its pollen parent's fine fragrance.

Morey, USA, 1960
'Sungold' × 'Sutter's Gold'
Repeat flowering | *Fruity fragrance*

HABIT Climber H/W 3m/2.5m (10ft/8ft) | ZONES 6–11

🏅 Portland (Oregon, USA) Gold Medal 1960

'Royal William'

'Royal Sunset'

'Sabrina'

'Royal William'

HYBRID TEA | DARK RED

'Duftzauber '84', 'Fragrant Charm'

This rose was introduced in 1983, when Britain was celebrating the birth of Prince William. The Palace apparently declined to

'Rubaiyat'

approve the name, as 'Royal William' can also be seen as commemorating the tricentenary of the so-called Glorious Revolution of 1688, when England's James II was overthrown by a union of Parliamentarians and William III of Orange-Nassau. It is a fine red rose – dark, velvety and fragrant, with some 35 petals – and is borne on a strong, bushy plant with semi-glossy, dark green foliage. The blooms vary with the season; in the cool climates this variety prefers, they are large and shapely. The German name, 'Duftzauber', was originally used for a lighter red Kordes rose of 1969; it means 'scented magic'.

KORzaun | Kordes, Germany, 1984
'Feuerzauber' × seedling
Repeat flowering | *Moderate fragrance*

HABIT Bush H/W 1.5m/1.2m (5ft/4ft) | ZONES 4–11

🏅 Royal Horticultural Society Award of Garden Merit 1993, Royal National Rose Society Rose of the Year 1987

'Rubaiyat'

HYBRID TEA | DEEP PINK

The color – on the border between pink and red, like a Ceylon ruby – is one that nature must think suits the rose, for there are many that wear it. One of the very best is 'Rubaiyat', raised by the father of the present Sam McGredy in 1946. Long buds open wide to large, decorative, double blooms. The plant is tall and strong, with leathery, dark green foliage, and blooms freely all season. It won the AARS award for 1947, but, alas, is now prone to mildew if not sprayed regularly.

McGredy, New Zealand, 1946
('McGredy's Scarlet' × 'Mrs Sam McGredy') × (seedling × 'Sir Basil McFarland')
Repeat flowering | *Intense fragrance*

HABIT Bush H/W 1.5m/1.2m (5ft/4ft) | ZONES 5–11

🏅 Portland (Oregon, USA) Gold Medal 1944, All-America Rose Selection 1947

'Rumba'

FLORIBUNDA · RED BLEND

'Rhumba'

If only 'Rumba' would shed its dead flowers, it would be an ideal garden rose. The neat little blooms are double and carried in huge clusters; the bush is compact and the foliage glossy; and the reddish young leaves and very dark green mature ones make a perfect background for the flowers' bright colors. The blooms start out yellow, rapidly becoming flushed with orange and red, and look as attractive in the vase as in the garden. There are so many that deadheading is quite a job, and you will need to keep an eye out for black spot in humid climates.

Poulsen, Denmark, 1958
'Masquerade' × ('Poulsen's Bedder' × 'Floradora')
Repeat flowering · *Spicy fragrance*

HABIT Bush H/W 1m/60cm (3ft/2ft) · ZONES 5–11

'Sabrina'

HYBRID TEA · APRICOT BLEND

Sabrina was a blonde bombshell of the 1950s, and in 1960 Alain Meilland dedicated a big crimson and gold rose to her. You do not see it much now, which is a pity, as the gaudiness is offset by fine fragrance. In 1977 the Meilland firm reused the name. The new 'Sabrina' is essentially a greenhouse rose, with shapely, double blooms in a shade described as apricot-orange. It is very long-lasting in the vase, but scentless, and only reliable as a garden rose in warm climates. The foliage is glossy and rich green, with plum tints in the young growth.

MEIgandor · Meilland, France, 1977
('Sweet Promise' × 'Golden Garnette') × (['Zambra' × 'Suspense'] × ['King's Ransom' × 'Whisky Mac'])
Repeat flowering · *Slight fragrance*

HABIT Bush H/W 1.5m/1m (5ft/3ft) · ZONES 5–11

'Sally Holmes'

SHRUB · WHITE

'Sally Holmes' is a much-admired rose for the great beauty of its almost single, ivory-white flowers, large and slightly fragrant. They are sometimes borne in huge, tightly packed clusters, and sometimes in smaller, more widely spaced clusters, which show off the beauty of the flowers to better advantage. Some thinning of the buds in the larger trusses can improve the appearance. The foliage is glossy and dark green. 'Sally Holmes' was

'Sally Holmes'

'Salmon Sorbet'

'Rumba'

raised by an English amateur hybridist. It will grow to 4m (12ft) tall, with heavy canes that tend to bend outwards, like a rambler.

Holmes, England, UK, 1976
'Ivory Fashion' × 'Ballerina'
Repeat flowering · *Slight fragrance*

HABIT Rambler H/W 3.5m/3m (12ft/10ft) · ZONES 5–1

Monza Gold Medal 1979, Rome Gold Medal 1979, Portland (Oregon, USA) Gold Medal 1993

'Salmon Sorbet'

FLORIBUNDA · PINK BLEND

A very pretty striped rose from Armstrong Nurseries in California, 'Salmon Sorbet' displays its coral and white blooms – usually with a few stripes of pale pink thrown in – in small clusters on a lowish, compact bush. The size of the bush is a great asset, making it easier to place the rose in the garden and to arrange companion plantings that it will not upstage. The scent is a pleasing bonus. The foliage is leathery and dark green.

Armstrong, USA, 1991
Parentage undisclosed
Repeat flowering · *Slight fragrance*

HABIT Bush H/W 1m/60cm (3ft/2ft) · ZONES 5–11

'San Francisco'

HYBRID TEA ı MEDIUM RED

This rose was photographed in the public rose gardens in Oakland, across the bay from its namesake city. The large flowers, 10–13cm (4–5in) in diameter, are usually borne in clusters, opening sometimes high-centred, sometimes cupped, from ovoid buds, and have a stronger fragrance than is usual for roses of their bright red color. The bush is strong and healthy, with leathery, dark green foliage.

Lammerts, USA, 1962
'Dean Collins' × 'Independence'
Repeat flowering ı *Moderate fragrance*

HABIT Bush H/W 1.4m/1m (4ft 6in/3ft) ı ZONES 5–11

'Sangria'

FLORIBUNDA ı ORANGE RED

The name dates this rose, because sangria, a Spanish drink blending red wine and fruit juice, was a fad of the 1960s. It is fairly rare now, and so is the rose, a Meilland introduction of 1966. This is a colorful garden rose, with large trusses of smallish, semi-double

'Sangria'

'San Francisco'

'Santa Fé'

'Santa Maria'

flowers with ruffled petals and little fragrance. The color is officially described as orange-red, but it actually blends red with orange – and so the name is appropriate. The foliage is dark green.

MEIestho ı Meilland, France, 1966
'Fire King' × ('Happiness' × 'Independence')
Repeat flowering ı *No fragrance*

HABIT Bush H/W 1m/60cm (3ft/2ft) ı ZONES 5–11

'Santa Catalina'

CLIMBING FLORIBUNDA ı LIGHT PINK

From a cross of the deep pink Floribunda 'Paddy McGredy' and the red Shrub Rose 'Heidelberg', one would expect a dark-toned rose. Sam McGredy must have been surprised when 'Santa Catalina' turned out to be pale pink – with just the occasional deeper flush – and a climber as well, although a shrubby one. It blooms well all season; the flowers are almost of Hybrid Tea size and fragrant; and the foliage is notably glossy and dark green. Some find the foliage too glossy and think it is inclined to upstage the delicate tones of the flowers.

McGredy, Northern Ireland, UK, 1970
'Paddy McGredy' × 'Heidelberg'
Repeat flowering ı *Slight fragrance*

HABIT Climber H/W 2m/1.2m (7ft/4ft) ı ZONES 5–11

'Santa Fé'

HYBRID TEA ı ORANGE PINK

'All the health and vigor of its mother "Super Star" and the charming grace of its father "Mischief",' enthused the McGredy catalogue when Sam introduced 'Santa Fé' in 1967. Regrettably, it has not inherited the beautiful luminosity of color of either of its parents: it is a rather bland shade of deep salmon-pink. The bush is a good grower, nevertheless, with leathery, bronze-green leaves, and the flowers are large and quite shapely enough for exhibition. It likes a cool climate. There is no fragrance.

McGredy, New Zealand, 1967
'Mischief' × 'Super Star'
Repeat flowering ı *No fragrance*

HABIT Bush H/W 1.4m/1m (4ft 6in/3ft) ı ZONES 5–11

'Santa Maria'

FLORIBUNDA ı MEDIUM RED

The Columbus quincentennial in 1992 might have created a revival of interest in this 1969 McGredy creation, which bears the name of the largest of the three ships Christopher Columbus used on his first voyage across the Atlantic in 1492 – if only the rose had been available! It has disappeared from the world's catalogues. Anyone who manages to find it will be rewarded by masses of bright orange-red flowers, which are borne in trusses on a compact bush with dark green foliage, maroon-tinted in its youth.

McGredy, New Zealand, 1969
'Evelyn Fison' × ('Ma Perkins' × 'Moulin Rouge')
Repeat flowering ı *Slight fragrance*

HABIT Bush H/W 1m/60cm (3ft/2ft) ı ZONES 5–11

'Santa Catalina'

'Sarabande'

'Sarabande'

FLORIBUNDA ı ORANGE RED

'MEIrabande'

This is one of the great Meilland roses, notable for its flaming scarlet color, its healthy and even growth, its resistance to disease and its abundant flowering. It won the AARS in 1960, but the rise of Floribundas with exhibition-style flowers since then has robbed it of popularity, for its flowers are almost single. They are very elegant, they open slowly and they last well in the vase. The foliage is semi-glossy and mid-green. The sarabande is an old Spanish dance.

MEIhand ı Meilland, France, 1957
'Cocorico' × 'Moulin Rouge'
Repeat flowering ı Slight fragrance

HABIT Bush H/W 1m/60cm (3ft/2ft) ı ZONES 5–11

🏆 Bagatelle (Paris) Gold Medal 1957, Geneva Gold Medal 1957, Portland (Oregon, USA) Gold Medal 1958, All-America Rose Selection 1960

'Sarah Arnot'

HYBRID TEA ı MEDIUM PINK

Hailed in Britain when it was introduced in 1957 as one of the most perfect Hybrid Tea Roses since the war, 'Sarah Arnot' has never found the same favor elsewhere, possibly because it inherits from 'Ena Harkness' a preference for cool climates. At its best it is indeed a lovely rose, large, double, shapely and fragrant, and a beautiful shade of rose-pink. The plant is bushy, with handsome green foliage.

Croll, Scotland, UK, 1957
'Ena Harkness' × 'Peace'
Repeat flowering ı Fragrant

HABIT Bush H/W 1.2m/1m (4ft/3ft) ı ZONES 5–1

🏆 (Royal) National Rose Society Gold Medal 1958

'Sarah Van Fleet'

'Sarah Arnot'

'Sarah Van Fleet'

HYBRID RUGOSA ı MEDIUM PINK

Although 'Sarah Van Fleet' is about as bushy as a bush can be, it grows to 1.8–2.5m (6–8ft) tall and it is not always clad with foliage to the base. Plant it at the back of the border, with other plants in front to hide its legs, and you can enjoy the bronze young leaves, which mature light green, and the masses of loosely double, scented blooms in pale, cool pink. Although some authorities dispute the stated parentage, it looks to be halfway between a Rugosa and a Hybrid Tea, and has inherited much of the Rugosa habit and toughness. It flowers all season.

Van Fleet, USA, 1926
R. rugosa × 'My Maryland'
Repeat flowering ı Intense fragrance

HABIT Bush H/W 1.8–2.5m/1.2–1.5m (6–8ft/4–5ft) ı ZONES 4–10

'Saratoga'

'Saratoga'

FLORIBUNDA ı WHITE

The AARS winner for 1964, and for a while one of the most popular white roses, 'Saratoga' has since lost ground to 'Iceberg'. But it remains a desirable rose, less robust than 'Iceberg' perhaps, but with larger individual blooms – shapely, fragrant and often brushed with cream in the bud. The foliage is glossy, leathery and mid-green. Saratoga is a town in New York's Hudson Valley, the site of a famous engagement in the American War of Independence, and a place where the raiser liked to spend his holidays.

Boerner, USA, 1963
'White Bouquet' × 'Princess White'
Repeat flowering ı Intense fragrance

HABIT Bush H/W 1m/60cm (3ft/2ft) ı ZONES 5–11

🏆 All-America Rose Selection 1964

'Satchmo'

'Scarlet Knight'

'Satchmo'

FLORIBUNDA ı ORANGE RED

Although Sam McGredy considers that his 'Satchmo' of 1970 has been superseded by its seedling 'Trumpeter' (1977) – also named in honor of the great jazz musician Louis Armstrong – the older rose still has plenty of admirers for its bright scarlet color, its shapely clusters of double flowers and its freedom of bloom. It is a compact and healthy grower, with shiny, bright green foliage, plum-tinted in its youth. Its faults, admittedly minor, are a tendency for the old flowers to darken

'Scarlet Queen Elizabeth'

unevenly and a certain slowness in repeat flowering. There is not much fragrance.

McGredy, New Zealand, 1970
'Evelyn Fison' × 'Diamant'
Repeat flowering ı *Slight fragrance*

HABIT Bush H/W 1m/60cm (3ft/2ft) ı ZONES 5–11

🌹 The Hague Gold Medal 1970

'Savoy Hotel'

HYBRID TEA ı LIGHT PINK

'Integrity', 'Vercors', 'Violette Niestlé'

The large, double blooms are light pink, but they have a vibrancy unusual for such a subtle color thanks to the darker, deeper pink on the undersides of the petals. As the flowers open further, these darker tints serve to accentuate their form – a visual effect (seen in the photograph) that is part of this variety's charm. The bush is vigorous and well clothed in dark green foliage. It was named to celebrate the centenary of the famous London hotel.

HARvintage ı Harkness, England, UK, 1987
'Silver Jubilee' × 'Amber Queen'
Repeat flowering ı *Slight fragrance*

HABIT Bush H/W 1.4m/1m (4ft 6in/3ft) ı ZONES 5–11

🌹 Dublin Gold Medal 1988, Dortmund Gold Medal 1991, Royal Horticultural Society Award of Garden Merit 1994, Portland (Oregon, USA) Gold Medal 1998

'Scarlet Knight'

GRANDIFLORA ı MEDIUM RED

'Samourai'

This rose was originally named for Japan's knights of old, which is not as odd as it might seem, for many of the samurai passed their time in between heroic deeds by cultivating

flowers, especially the Higo camellias. As its American name, 'Scarlet Knight', implies, the big, completely flat flowers are pure scarlet, taking on velvety, darker tones in the sun. The bush is of average height, sturdy and – despite a slight tendency to mildew – a very reliable performer. The handsome foliage is leathery and bright green. 'Scarlet Knight' won the AARS award in 1968. There is only a faint scent.

MEIelec ı Meilland, France, 1966
('Happiness' × 'Independence') × 'Sutter's Gold'
Repeat flowering ı *Slight fragrance*

HABIT Bush H/W 1.5m/1.2m (5ft/4ft) ı ZONES 5–11

🌹 Madrid Gold Medal 1966, All-America Rose Selection 1968

'Scharlachglut'

SHRUB ı DARK RED

'Scarlet Fire', 'Scarlet Glow'

The admirers of 'Scharlachglut' enthuse over its summer display of dazzling, velvet-red blooms, large and perfect in their five-petalled symmetry. Its detractors point out that it is a very large and thorny shrub, growing to at least 2.5m (8ft) each way; that there is little scent; and that the space it occupies could be given to two or three more compact, and repeat-flowering, Shrub Roses. It all depends on how much space you have. The foliage is ashen green, and there are fine hips in the fall/autumn.

Kordes, Germany, 1952
'Poinsettia' × 'Alika'
Summer flowering ı *Slight fragrance*

HABIT Bush H/W 2.5m/2.5m (8ft/8ft) ı ZONES 5–11

'Scarlet Queen Elizabeth'

FLORIBUNDA ı ORANGE RED

'That's just what it is,' burbled the catalogues in 1963, 'the wonderful "Queen Elizabeth" in red.' Well, that is what it is not. It is certainly as vigorous and as easy to grow, but where 'Queen Elizabeth' is upright, 'Scarlet Queen Elizabeth' is lax in its growth. The double, orange-red flowers are smaller and shapeless. They look well, however, against the bronze-green leaves, which retain the mahogany tint of youth well into old age. Although quite scentless, this is a good rose for a position where you want a really hot-colored shrub.

DICel ı Dickson, Northern Ireland, UK, 1963
('Korona' × seedling) × 'Queen Elizabeth'
Repeat flowering ı *Slight fragrance*

HABIT Bush H/W 1m/60cm (3ft/2ft) ı ZONES 5–11

🌹 The Hague Gold Medal and Golden Rose of The Hague 1973

'Scharlachglut'

'Savoy Hotel'

'Scentimental'

'Scentimental'

FLORIBUNDA ı RED BLEND

'Street Parade'

The large blooms are fully double and wonderfully striped, and each is as unique as a snowflake. Some flowers are more burgundy splashed with white; others, more cream swirled with red – all on the same vigorous plant. They are borne prolifically in small clusters, have a good, spicy fragrance, and are long-lasting. The plant is of medium size and rounded habit, with glossy, dark green foliage that stays healthy and is easy to maintain. It performs best in terms of bloom color and size in moderate temperatures.

WEPplapep ı Carruth, USA, 1997
'Playboy' × 'Peppermint Twist'
Repeat flowering ı *Strong, spicy fragrance*
HABIT Bush H/W 1.2m/1m (4ft/3ft) ı ZONES 5–11
🌹 All-America Rose Selection 1997

'Schneezwerg'

HYBRID RUGOSA ı WHITE

'Snow Dwarf', 'Snowdwarf'

Do not be misled by the name: this is a tall rose. Pruning will keep it shorter and compact.

It is a very popular shrub with landscape designers in Europe, as it combines toughness and hardiness with a long flowering season and a surprisingly dainty appearance. The foliage is a lush, bright green and not as rugose as that of most Hybrid Rugosas. 'Schneezwerg' is at its best in the fall/autumn, when the semi-double, shining white flowers, with their golden stamens, are accompanied by round, orange hips. The flowers are borne in clusters, and the smallish, dark leaves turn gold before they fall for the winter.

Lambert, Germany, 1912
Possibly *R. rugosa* × Polyantha hybrid
Repeat flowering ı *Slight fragrance*
HABIT Bush H/W 1.5m/1.2m (5ft/4ft) ı ZONES 4–10
🌹 Royal Horticultural Society Award of Garden Merit 1993

'Schweizer Gold'

HYBRID TEA ı LIGHT YELLOW

'Swiss Gold'

Raised by Reimer Kordes in 1972 and subsequently distributed by Adolph Horstmann,

Top 'Schneezwerg'
Above 'Schweizer Gold'

'Schweizer Gold' combines good, high-centred form and long petals in a large, mid-yellow bloom that deepens in color toward the centre. The matt, light green foliage is plentiful, the bush strong. The fragrance is quite good. This is a rose for cooler climates, like Baden-Baden, where it won the gold medal in 1972.

Kordes, Germany, 1975
'Peer Gynt' × 'King's Ransom'
Repeat flowering ı *Moderate fragrance*
HABIT Bush H/W 1.4m/1m (4ft 6in/3ft) ı ZONES 5–11
🌹 Baden-Baden Gold Medal 1972

'Sea Pearl'

'Sea Pearl'

FLORIBUNDA ꞏ PINK BLEND

'Flower Girl'

'Sea Pearl' remains popular in Europe, and the ARS rates it highly. It has never really been a hit in Australia, probably because its delicate coral-pink and cream colors bleach under the hot sun. The long, shapely buds open to quite large, double blooms, usually in clusters of five or so; there is some fragrance; and the bush is tall and strong, with dark green foliage. In the old days it would probably have passed for a decorative Hybrid Tea, and it is indeed the child of two Hybrid Teas.

Dickson, Northern Ireland, UK, 1964
'Kordes's Perfecta' × 'Montezuma'
Repeat flowering ꞏ *Slight fragrance*

HABIT Bush H/W 1m/60cm (3ft/2ft) ꞏ ZONES 4–11

❀ Belfast Fragrance (R. J. Frizzell Memorial) Award 1966

'Seagull'

HYBRID WICHURANA ꞏ WHITE

From the time of its introduction by the English grower Pritchard in 1907 until the establishment of 'Sander's White' as the public's favorite, 'Seagull' was unquestionably the best white rambler available. It is effectively a single-petalled version of *R. multiflora*, with that Wild Rose's ability to do well in difficult conditions. It has fresh green foliage and a strong, sweet perfume. In its summer season, the vigorous plant covers itself with huge trusses of blooms, their petals not so full as to hide their almost-orange stamens. It was not derived from a thornless form of *R. multiflora*, however, and there are prickles!

Pritchard, England, UK, 1907
R. multiflora × 'Général Jacqueminot'
Summer flowering ꞏ *Sweet fragrance*

HABIT Rambler H/W 7.5m/4.5m (25ft/15ft) ꞏ ZONES 6–11

'Seagull'

'Seashell'

'Seashell'

HYBRID TEA ꞏ ORANGE PINK

Despite winning the 1976 AARS award, 'Seashell' has been criticized for its susceptibility to black spot. There has been nothing but praise for its blooms, however, which are large, double and beautifully formed, the petals overlapping with the regularity of the tiles on a roof. The color is lovely, a clear shade of coral-pink, sometimes deeper at the petal edges, lit with gold. There is a slight tea fragrance. The foliage is glossy and dark green. It was created by Reimer Kordes and introduced in 1974.

KORshel ꞏ Kordes, Germany, 1976
Seedling × 'Colour Wonder'
Repeat flowering ꞏ *Slight fragrance*

HABIT Bush H/W 1.4m/1m (4ft 6in/3ft) ꞏ ZONES 5–11

❀ All-America Rose Selection 1976

'Secret'

HYBRID TEA ꞏ PINK BLEND

It is no secret that this rose has classical form and a seductive fragrance. But its fine attributes do not end there. The color is magnificent: creamy yellow suffused with pinks that often

vary with the season and the weather. The plant is easy to grow and very prolific, and the flowers, borne both singly and in small clusters, have exceptional vase life.

HILaroma ꞏ Tracy, USA, 1994
'Pristine' × 'Friendship'
Repeat flowering ꞏ *Spicy fragrance*

HABIT Bush H/W 1.5m/1.2m (5ft/4ft) ꞏ ZONES 4–11

❀ All-America Rose Selection 1994, Portland (Oregon, USA) Gold Medal 1998, American Rose Society James Alexander Gamble Fragrance Medal 2002

'Sheer Elegance'

'Sheer Bliss'

'Serenade'

HYBRID TEA ꞏ ORANGE BLEND

The books always describe 'Serenade' as coral-orange, which suggests something in the manner of 'Super Star', but it is really a much more delicate color than that, a blend of coral-pinks. The blooms are neither large nor full of petals, but they are produced with freedom over a long season, on a sturdy bush with matt foliage, richly bronzed in its youth. 'Serenade' was introduced in 1949, and you may have to search the catalogues to find it now.

Boerner, USA, 1949
'Sonata' × 'R.M.S. Queen Mary'
Repeat flowering ꞏ *Slight fragrance*

HABIT Bush H/W 1.4m/1m (4ft 6in/3ft) ꞏ ZONES 5–11

'Sexy Rexy'

FLORIBUNDA | MEDIUM PINK

'Heckenzauber', 'Sexy Hexy'

Fancy calling an innocently blushing rose like this 'Sexy Rexy'! Forget the name and admire the perfect symmetry of the double flowers, their delicate shell-pink color, their elusive scent, and the freedom with which the short, neat bush bears large clusters of them. The foliage is glossy and bright green, with red tints when young.

MACrexy | McGredy, New Zealand, 1984
'Seaspray' × 'Dreaming'
Repeat flowering | *Slight fragrance*

HABIT Bush H/W 110cm/1m (3ft 6in/3ft) | ZONES 5–11

New Zealand International Rose Ground Trials Gold Medal 1984, Golden Prize of the City of Glasgow 1989, Portland (Oregon, USA) Gold Medal 1990, Rose Introducers of New Zealand Gold Medal 1990, Rose Introducers of New Zealand Auckland Rose of the Year 1991

'Sheer Bliss'

HYBRID TEA | WHITE

The double blooms are delightful, whether in their long and elegant youth or when they have opened out to silky looseness. They are the palest of pale pinks – almost white – but shaded deeper in their hearts, and there is a most pleasing spicy fragrance. The bush is strong and dense, with matt, dark green foliage and brown prickles. 'Sheer Bliss' makes a lovely cut rose and looks superb arranged in a silver vase.

JACtro | Warriner, USA, 1985
'White Masterpiece' × 'Golden Masterpiece'
Repeat flowering | *Spicy fragrance*

HABIT Bush H/W 1.5m/1.2m (5ft/4ft) | ZONES 5–11

Tokyo Gold Medal 1984, All-America Rose Selection 1987

'Sheer Elegance'

HYBRID TEA | ORANGE PINK

The AARS award should be a guarantee that a rose will do well just about anywhere, but

'Sheer Elegance', the 1991 winner, seems to be establishing a marked preference for cooler climates. Where it does well, it justifies its name. The blooms are shapely indeed, with strongly reflexed petals, and of pale rose-pink, the petal edges darkening a little as the flower matures. The bush is strong, with leathery foliage.

TWObe | Twomey, USA, 1989
'Pristine' × 'Fortuna'
Repeat flowering | *Musk fragrance*

HABIT Bush H/W 1.4m/1m (4ft 6in/3ft) | ZONES 5–11

All-America Rose Selection 1991, Portland (Oregon, USA) Gold Medal 1994

'Sheila's Perfume'

FLORIBUNDA | YELLOW BLEND

The Sheila in question is an Englishwoman, the wife of the raiser, John Sheridan. 'Sheila's Perfume' is much praised as one of the few bicolored roses with a strong scent. It is not a classic bicolor, but rather yellow with a red border. It is a nice variety nonetheless, bearing large, shapely, double flowers on an upright bush with handsome, plum-tinted, dark-green leaves.

HARshery | Sheridan, England, UK, 1982
'Peer Gynt' × ('Daily Sketch' × ['Paddy McGredy × 'Prima Ballerina'])
Repeat flowering | *Intense fragrance*

HABIT Bush H/W 1.2m/1m (4ft/3ft) | ZONES 5–11

Glasgow Tollcross Fragrance Award 1989, Gold Star of the South Pacific, Hamilton (New Zealand) 1993, American Rose Society James Alexander Gamble Fragrance Medal 2005

'Serenade'

RIGHT 'Sexy Rexy'
BELOW 'Secret'

'Sheila's Perfume'

'Sherry'

'Sherry'

FLORIBUNDA · RUSSET

The name is appropriate: the semi-double, brownish orange flowers are like an *amoroso* sherry in color. The golden stamens save them from dullness in the garden, but this is essentially a rose for the flower arranger. The blooms are borne in clusters on a tallish bush with dark green foliage, but 'Sherry' is an erratic performer, sometimes magnificent, at others spindly and shy with its blooms. It is a sister of the better-known 'Orangeade'.

McGredy, Northern Ireland, UK, 1960
'Independence' × 'Orange Sweetheart'
Repeat flowering · Slight fragrance
HABIT Bush H/W 1m/60cm (3ft/2ft) · ZONES 5–11

'Shocking Blue'

FLORIBUNDA · MAUVE

The color is shocking indeed, but it is more magenta than blue. The double flowers are of fine shape and good size, and are very heavily perfumed as well. Disbudded, this variety is a popular florist's rose. The bush is on the tall side, with shiny, dark green leaves. It has the reputation of being both prolific and continuous in its flowering. 'Shocking Blue' may lack

'Showbiz'

the ethereal touch of such roses as 'Blue Moon', but it is a fine rose nevertheless.

KORblue · Kordes, Germany, 1974
Seedling × 'Silver Star'
Repeat flowering · Intense fragrance
HABIT Bush H/W 1.2m/60cm (4ft/2ft) · ZONES 5–11

'Shot Silk'

HYBRID TEA · PINK BLEND

Alex Dickson, father of Patrick, was once asked which of his roses was his favorite. The reply was unhesitating: 'Shot Silk'. The bush is attractive for its shining, emerald-green foliage alone, and the many flowers are of great beauty in their neat shape, their brilliant pink underlaid with gold, and their rich fragrance. The climbing sport is still popular and worthwhile.

Dickson, Northern Ireland, UK, 1924
'Hugh Dickson' × 'Sunstar'
Repeat flowering · Intense fragrance
HABIT Bush H/W 1.4m/1m (4ft 6in/3ft) · ZONES 5–11
🏵 (Royal) National Rose Society Gold Medal 1923

'Showbiz'

FLORIBUNDA · MEDIUM RED

'Bernhard Daneke Rose', 'Ingrid Weibull'

'Showbiz' won the AARS award for 1985 and has been busy ever since building a reputation as one of the best of all roses for making what a decorator would call 'a strong red statement'. It is a low bush, with glossy, dark green foliage, that covers itself with masses of smallish, fluorescent red flowers. It is quick to repeat. It is a little like 'Europeana', but the color is not nearly so dark, nor does it have the striking young foliage. It does appear to be unusually resistant to mildew, the scourge of the red Floribundas.

TANweieke · Tantau, Germany, 1983
Parentage undisclosed
Repeat flowering · No fragrance
HABIT Bush H/W 1m/60cm (3ft/2ft) · ZONES 5–11
🏵 All-America Rose Selection 1985

'Showoff'

HYBRID TEA · RED BLEND

'Show Off'

'Showoff' was raised in 1986 by Jack Christensen, but it now seems to have vanished from the catalogues. Is it perhaps that Christensen never got around to introducing it? The double blooms are as red as red can be, with silver blended into the reverse of their 35 petals, and they are large, brilliant and shapely, if not very fragrant. The bush is of average height, with dark green leaves. Do not confuse this rose with an earlier 'Show Off', a red climber of 1952.

AROwago · Christensen, USA, 1986
'Typhoo Tea' × 'Snowfire'
Repeat flowering · Slight fragrance
HABIT Bush H/W 1.2m/1m (4ft/3ft) · ZONES 5–11

'Showoff'

'Shreveport'

GRANDIFLORA | ORANGE BLEND

The ARS has its offices in Shreveport, Louisiana, in the midst of gardens that are planted with many thousands of roses. The 'Shreveport' rose, named in its honor, is German-bred by Reimer Kordes. It won the 1982 AARS award as a Grandiflora – the shapely, double blooms do tend to come in small clusters. They are a blend of orange and salmon-pink, have a light tea fragrance, and are borne on a strong but not overly tall bush with dark olive-green foliage. It is an excellent rose for cutting.

KORpesh | Kordes, Germany, 1981
'Zorina' × 'Uwe Seeler'
Repeat flowering | *Tea fragrance*
HABIT Bush H/W 1.5m/1.2m (5ft/4ft) | ZONES 5–11
All-America Rose Selection 1982

'Shropshire Lass'

SHRUB | LIGHT PINK

In the old days, 'Shropshire Lass' would have been called a 'Hybrid Alba'. Its raiser, David Austin, classes it with his 'English Roses',

although it is not repeat flowering. It would make a pleasing companion for his 'Constance Spry'. Like it, it can be grown as a large shrub or as a climber, but it is more compact in growth, with lush, mid-green foliage, and the flowers are a trifle smaller and almost single. They are blush-white. The fragrance is sweet, and the plant tough and hardy. With this 1968 creation, Austin honors the English county where he has lived all his life.

Austin, England, UK, 1968
'Madame Butterfly' × 'Madame Legras de Saint-Germain'
Summer flowering | *Moderate fragrance*
HABIT Climber H/W 1.8m/1.8m (6ft/6ft) | ZONES 5–11

BELOW 'Shot Silk'
INSET 'Shropshire Lass'

'Shocking Blue'

'Sierra Glow'

HYBRID TEA | PINK BLEND

A blend of sunset-pinks, the 30-petalled blooms of 'Sierra Glow' open from long buds. They are borne – on fine, long stems for cutting – on a vigorous and prolific bush with leathery, mid-green foliage. Raised by Walter Lammerts, this variety was popular in the United States in the 1950s and early 1960s, but you do not often see it now. It came from the same cross, but in the reverse order, that produced Dr Lammerts's epoch-making 'Charlotte Armstrong'.

Lammerts, USA, 1942
'Crimson Glory' × 'Soeur Thérèse'
Repeat flowering | *Moderate fragrance*
HABIT Bush H/W 1.4m/1m (4ft 6in/3ft) | ZONES 5–11

'Sierra Glow'

'Shreveport'

'Signature'

HYBRID TEA | DEEP PINK

'Juanita'

Long, pointed, wine-red buds unfurl to high-centred, deep-pink blooms swirled with cream. The flowers are large, with good, classical shape, and the petals have lots of substance and do not burn even in the heat of summer. They are borne mostly one to a stem, with occasional medium-sized clusters, on an attractive bush clothed with very dark green foliage that can sometimes be susceptible to mildew.

JACnor | Warriner, USA, 1998
'Honor' × 'First Federal Renaissance'
Repeat flowering | *Fruity fragrance*

HABIT Bush H/W 1.5m/1.2m (5ft/4ft) | ZONES 5–10

'Silent Night'

HYBRID TEA | YELLOW BLEND

The name has nothing to do with Christmas carols. Raiser Sam McGredy's sponsor for this 1969 introduction was a British maker of mattresses. The flowers are profuse – large and nicely formed, their color a soft yellow tinted pink – and the foliage is dark green, with a hint of red when young. 'Silent Night' won the Geneva gold medal in 1969.

McGredy, New Zealand, 1969
'Daily Sketch' × 'Hassan'
Repeat flowering | *Slight fragrance*

HABIT Bush H/W 1.4m/1m (4ft 6in/3ft) | ZONES 5–11
🏵 Geneva Gold Medal 1969

'Silk Hat'

HYBRID TEA | MAUVE

'AROsilma'

A gentleman's silk hat is usually black, but this rose is a mixture of American Beauty red and cream. It was raised by Jack Christensen in 1985, and it is a beauty. The 50-petalled blooms are of exhibition form, and are produced by

'Silver Lining'

'Signature'

'Silk Hat'

a bushy yet upright plant with large, mid-green leaves. The fragrance is good.

AROsilha | Christensen, USA, 1986
'Ivory Tower' × ('Night 'n' Day' × 'Plain Talk')
Repeat flowering | *Moderate fragrance*

HABIT Bush H/W 1.4m/1m (4ft 6in/3ft) | ZONES 5–11

'Silent Night'

'Silver Jubilee'

HYBRID TEA | PINK BLEND

In earlier days there was a pale yellow Hybrid Tea called 'Silver Jubilee', which was introduced by Alex Dickson in 1937. The universally admired modern bearer of the name came from another Alexander, Alexander (Alec) Cocker, in 1977. Its only fault is the lack of a good scent. The double flowers, in a lovely blend of soft pinks, are large, high-centred and shapely, and the bush is excellent, compact yet very strong, with luxuriant, glossy, bright-green foliage. It is

'Silver Jubilee'

'Silver Moon'

strongly disease-resistant. These are good habits derived ultimately from the climber *R. kordesii*, which lies in the background of one of it parents, 'Parkdirektor Riggers'. Many rosarians consider 'Silver Jubilee' to be the finest Hybrid Tea since 'Peace'.

Cocker, Scotland, UK, 1978
(['Highlight' × 'Colour Wonder'] × ['Parkdirektor Riggers' × 'Piccadilly']) × 'Mischief'
Repeat flowering ǀ *Slight fragrance*

HABIT Bush H/W 1.2m/1m (4ft/3ft) ǀ ZONES 5–11

🌹 Royal National Rose Society President's International Trophy 1977, Belfast Gold Medal and Prize of the City of Belfast 1980, Portland (Oregon, USA) Gold Medal 1981, Royal Horticultural Society Award of Garden Merit 1993

'Silver Lining'

HYBRID TEA ǀ PINK BLEND

The name describes it well, but the color of 'Silver Lining' varies very much with the seasons. Sometimes it is an overall silvery pink, at others much brighter, so that it is almost a pink and silver bicolor. But the perfect form is constant, and so is the sweet fragrance. (This is an outstanding exhibition rose.) The bush

is sturdy, with polished, dark green foliage, and for such a large rose it flowers very freely. It was raised in 1958 by Alex Dickson and was one of his last triumphs in a long career. In the hands of his son Patrick, 'Silver Lining' has given rise to a fine line of red Hybrid Teas, from 'Red Devil' to 'Precious Platinum'.

Dickson, Northern Ireland, UK, 1958
'Karl Herbst' × seedling of 'Eden Rose'
Repeat flowering ǀ *Intense fragrance*

HABIT Bush H/W 1.4m/1m (4ft 6in/3ft) ǀ ZONES 5–11

🌹 Portland (Oregon, USA) Gold Medal 1964

'Silver Moon'

LARGE FLOWERED CLIMBER ǀ WHITE

'The perfect choice,' wrote Peter Mallins of Brooklyn Botanic Garden, 'if you want to slipcover a barn with roses.' Indeed it would be, for 'Silver Moon' is one of the most vigorous of all climbing roses, even outgrowing 'Mermaid'. It flowers only in the spring but is then a lovely sight, with hundreds of double, ivory flowers shining against the dark green foliage. It is fragrant, too. It is not for climates with cold and frosty winters, however.

Van Fleet, USA, 1910
Thought to be (*R. wichurana* × 'Devoniensis') × *R. laevigata*
Spring flowering ǀ *Slight fragrance*

HABIT Climber H/W 3m/1.8m (10ft/6ft) ǀ ZONES 6–11

'Simplicity'

FLORIBUNDA ǀ MEDIUM PINK

Jackson & Perkins, the introducers, used to advertise 'Simplicity' as the 'blooming fence', and it is indeed a very even, bushy and free-blooming Floribunda. A number of bushes planted a bit closer together than normal make a very nice, chest-high hedge. The foliage is a rather pale green, the flowers semi-double and soft pink – very pleasing in the mass, although individually they are neither especially shapely nor fragrant. They are, however, large, 8–10cm (3–4in) in diameter. The bush is said not to need careful pruning, just trimming. Bill Warriner followed up this 1978 introduction with 'White Simplicity' and the ruby-red 'Bloomin' Easy'.

JACink ǀ Warriner, USA, 1978
'Iceberg' × seedling
Repeat flowering ǀ *Slight fragrance*

HABIT Bush H/W 1.2m/1m (4ft/3ft) ǀ ZONES 4–10

🌹 Monza Gold Medal 1976

'Singin' in the Rain'

FLORIBUNDA ǀ APRICOT BLEND

'Love's Spring', 'Spek's Centennial'

Exquisite golden apricot flowers with a coppery-shaded reverse grace an upright, bushy plant that is almost always in bloom. Most of the clusters have only 3–5 blooms, but they are very shapely and – unlike most roses of this color, which shudder at the first frost – quite hardy. They are ideal for cutting. 'Singin' in the Rain' is an outstanding garden performer, healthy and very easy to grow.

MACivy ǀ McGredy, New Zealand, 1994
'Sexy Rexy' × 'Pot O' Gold'
Repeat flowering ǀ *Sweet, musk fragrance*

HABIT Bush H/W 1m/60cm (3ft/2ft) ǀ ZONES 5–11

🌹 Royal National Rose Society Gold Medal 1991, All-America Rose Selection 1995

'Singin' in the Rain'

'Simplicity'

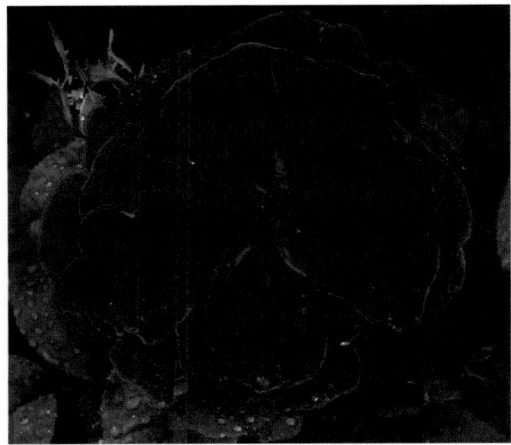

'Sir Edward Elgar'

'Sir Walter Raleigh'

'Sir Edward Elgar'

SHRUB ι MEDIUM RED

'Edward Elgar'

David Austin describes the color of this variety as a beautiful cerise-crimson rivalling 'Gertrude Jekyll', particularly if grown in warmer climate zones. He is not wrong. The flowers are large and cupped, giving an attractive 'domed rosette' appearance. The foliage is semi-glossy and mid-green. The rose is named for the great English composer of the *Enigma Variations*, *The Dream of Gerontius* and *Land of Hope and Glory*.

AUSprima ι Austin, England, 1995
'Mary Rose' × 'The Squire'
Repeat flowering ι *Intense fragrance*

HABIT Bush H/W 1.2m/60cm (4ft/2ft) ι ZONES 5–11

'Sir Walter Raleigh'

SHRUB ι MEDIUM PINK

David Austin has said of 'Sir Walter Raleigh' that it is the nearest he has been able to get to a repeat-flowering version of 'Constance Spry'. This exaggerates its merits somewhat, as the flowers are nothing like as gorgeous as those of that much-admired rose. They are,

however, large, double and pleasingly formed, sweetly fragrant, and a clear rose-pink with just a hint of coral. The tallish bush, with luxuriant green foliage, certainly does flower throughout the season. Introduced in 1985, this rose was named to commemorate the founding in 1776 of Virginia, the first English-speaking colony in America, in which Sir Walter played a leading role.

AUSspry ι Austin, England, UK, 1994
'Lilian Austin' × 'Chaucer'
Repeat flowering ι *Intense fragrance*

HABIT Bush H/W 1.5m/1m (5ft/3ft) ι ZONES 5–11

'Smoky'

HYBRID TEA ι RED BLEND

'Smoky ox-blood red, shaded burgundy,' reads the official description, so the name is apt for this French-bred rose, which Jackson & Perkins introduced in America in 1968. The name is a familiar one in American folklore. You will either love or hate this rose, with its curious scent of licorice, but it is quite a good grower and it is sure to be a conversation piece with visitors. The double blooms are of good size and form, and the foliage is leathery.

Combe, France, 1968
Parentage undisclosed
Repeat flowering ι *Licorice fragrance*

HABIT Bush H/W 1.2m/1m (4ft/3ft) ι ZONES 5–11

'Smooth Sailing'

GRANDIFLORA ι WHITE

A rose of interesting breeding, inheriting its perfect form and glossy foliage from 'Pink Favorite' and its delicate color from its mother, 'Little Darling', which also gave it its outstanding quality – its complete lack of thorns. In its turn, it has given Harvey

'Snowfire'

Davidson of California a whole series of thornless Hybrid Teas, all with 'smooth' in their name: 'Smooth Angel', 'Smooth Prince' and so on.

Davidson, USA, 1977
'Little Darling' × 'Pink Favorite'
Repeat flowering ι *Slight fragrance*

HABIT Bush H/W 1.5m/1.2m (5ft/4ft) ι ZONES 5–11

'Snowfire'

HYBRID TEA ι RED BLEND

'Snowfire' certainly produces a spectacular flower: large and double (sometimes enormous), of perfect exhibition form and of startling color. The upper surface of the petals is dark red, the underside brilliantly white, the white showing through as a fine, white edge to the red. There are mixed reports on the plant, some finding it satisfactory, others complaining that it does not grow strongly and is prone to mildew. The foliage is leathery and dark green.

Kordes, Germany, 1970
'Detroiter' × 'Liberty Bell'
Repeat flowering ι *Slight fragrance*

HABIT Bush H/W 1.4m/1m (4ft 6in/3ft) ι ZONES 5–11

'Soleil'

'Smooth Sailing'

'Snowline'

'Snowline'

FLORIBUNDA | WHITE

'Edelweiss'

Both names overstate the whiteness of the double flowers, which are creamy rather than snowy, but they do warn that this attractive rose is one for cool climates. There it makes a compact bush, its olive-green leaves almost hidden by the clusters of shapely, full-petalled flowers. Where summers are warm and humid, however, it is apt to grow leggy and become shy with its blooms. There is a pleasant, musky scent.

Poulsen, Denmark, 1970
Parentage undisclosed
Repeat flowering | *Musk fragrance*

HABIT Bush H/W 1m/60cm (3ft/2ft) | ZONES 5–11

🌹 Anerkannte Deutsche Rose (Germany) 1970

'Softly Softly'

FLORIBUNDA | PINK BLEND

This rose gives Jack Harkness the distinction of being the first hybridizer to name a rose after a television series. *Softly, Softly* was certainly very popular at the time the rose came out, in 1980. It is one of those roses that can be called a Hybrid Tea or a Floribunda at one's pleasure. The double blooms are not overlarge and tend to be borne in clusters. They are a blend of soft pinks. The foliage is leathery and olive-green.

HARkotur | Harkness, England, UK. 1977
'White Cockade' × (['Highlight' × 'Colour Wonder]) × ['Parkdirektor Riggers' × 'Piccadilly'])
Repeat flowering | *Slight fragrance*

HABIT Bush H/W 1m/60cm (3ft/2ft) | ZONES 5–11

'Softly Softly'

'Smoky'

'Soldier Boy'

LARGE FLOWERED CLIMBER | MEDIUM RED

If you find the popular 'Altissimo' strident but like the idea of a single-flowered red climber, take a look at this 1953 LeGrice creation. It is not as free with its later blooms as 'Altissimo', but the color is softer – crimson rather than scarlet – and the flowers are lit up by their yellow stamens. It is of pillar rose dimensions, but, alas, it has not inherited the sweet fragrance of 'Guinée'. The foliage is glossy and emerald-green. If you fancy a still deeper red single climber, seek out the crimson-maroon 'Sweet Sultan', which is much admired in Britain.

LeGrice, England, UK, 1953
Seedling × 'Guinée'
Repeat flowering | *Slight fragrance*

HABIT Climber H/W 3m/1.8m (10ft/6ft) | ZONES 6–11

'Soldier Boy'

'Soleil'

FLORIBUNDA | ORANGE RED

Not the golden color of the sun at noon but rather the fiery red it shows at sunset, 'Soleil' displays symmetrical, double flowers in clusters on a neat and low-growing plant. One would think it might have become a fashionable 'Patio Rose', but it was before its time, having been introduced in 1958. It was raised by Charles Mallerin, the well-known amateur French

'Sonia'

'Sonia Rykiel'

breeder, every one of whose roses is distinct and beautiful. The foliage is a clear green.

MALso ı Mallerin, France, 1958
Parentage undisclosed
Repeat flowering ı *Slight fragrance*

HABIT Bush H/W 1m/60cm (3ft/2ft) ı ZONES 5–11

'Sonia'

GRANDIFLORA ı PINK BLEND

'Sonia Meilland', 'Sonja', 'Sweet Promise'

Probably still the world's most popular greenhouse rose – its salmon-pink blooms

seemingly part of the furniture in every florist's window – 'Sonia' also has a very good reputation as a garden rose. However, the plant is very thorny, the stems are much shorter in the garden than in the greenhouse, and in hot climates the blooms fade markedly in the summer sunshine. The bush is tall and vigorous, with glossy, dark green foliage, and the double flowers are on the small side but very shapely. 'Sonia' must have made a fortune for the Meilland family.

MEIhelvet ı Meilland, France, 1974
'Zambra' × ('Baccarà' × 'White Knight')
Repeat flowering ı *Fruity fragrance*

HABIT Bush H/W 1.5m/1.2m (5ft/4ft) ı ZONES 5–11

'Sonia Rykiel'

SHRUB ı ORANGE PINK

With its delicate, strongly perfumed flowers of old-fashioned quartered form, 'Sonia Rykiel' is one of a series of French roses marketed under the name 'Generosa' that

'Soraya'

'Sophy's Rose'

seeks to emulate the success of David Austin's 'English Roses'. The blooms are large and many-petalled, and are borne both singly and in small clusters – usually on straight stems, although in young plants the weight of the blooms often causes the stems to bend. A stake or two will therefore be necessary during the first three years, or until the stems are strong enough to hold their own. The plant's growth habit is medium and wide, but the blooms are less than profuse. The rose was named for the daringly original Paris fashion designer and perfumier.

MASdogui ı Guillot-Massad, France, 1995
Parentage unknown
Repeat flowering ı *Strong, old rose fragrance*

HABIT Bush H/W 1.4m/1m (4ft 6in/3ft) ı ZONES 5–11

'Sophy's Rose'

SHRUB ı RED BLEND

The lovely red-purple flowers, medium-sized and very double, are shaped broad and flat like rosettes. Borne in small clusters, they are freely produced throughout the season on a vigorous, strong, bushy plant. The foliage is semi-glossy and mid-green, and has good disease resistance. With its moderate stature, profusion of blooms and lovely color, this is an ideal variety to incorporate into an English garden landscape.

AUSlot ı Austin, England, 1999
'Prospero' × seedling
Repeat flowering ı *Moderate fragrance*

HABIT Bush H/W 1m/75cm (3ft/2ft 6 in) ı ZONES 4–11

'South Seas'

'Souvenir de Philémon Cochet'

'Southern Belle'

'Southampton'

'Soraya'

HYBRID TEA ı ORANGE BLEND

'MEljenor'

Soraya was a former empress of Iran, divorced by the last reigning Shah and supplanted by Farah Diba, who also had a rose named for her, Delbard's 'Impératrice Farah' of 1992, a pink blend very different from 'Soraya', which is one of the most elegant of all the orange-red Hybrid Teas. Its smouldering color is brilliant yet subtle; its form double, cupped and symmetrical; its plant strong and glossy-leafed. The scent is not very strong.

MEjenor ı Meilland,, France, 1955
('Peace' × 'Floradora') × 'Grand'mère Jenny'
Repeat flowering ı *Slight fragrance*

HABIT Bush H/W 1.5m/1m (5ft/3ft) ı ZONES 5–11

'South Seas'

HYBRID TEA ı ORANGE PINK

'Mers du Sud'

This is a rose that has had mixed receptions in different countries, some people raving about the enormous, double, coral-pink blooms that open wide and ruffled from urn-shaped buds, others finding them loose and blowsy. The bush is of a size to match, but for all its height and vigor it is sometimes rather shy with its flowers. The scent is only moderate. The foliage is broad, semi-glossy and dark green.

Morey, USA, 1962
'Rapture' × seedling of Climbing Hybrid Tea
Repeat flowering ı *Moderate fragrance*

HABIT Bush H/W 1.2m/1m (4ft/3ft) ı ZONES 5–11

'Southampton'

FLORIBUNDA ı APRICOT BLEND

'Susan Ann'

Soft orange veering toward apricot, and often flushed with coral-red, the double flowers of 'Southampton' are pleasantly shapely and carried in moderate-sized clusters. They are fragrant, too. The bush is tallish and spreading, and the glossy, bronze-green foliage is among the healthiest for this color group. An English-raised rose that is very well regarded in Britain, 'Southampton' has not

fared well in hotter climates. The color tends to fade in strong sunshine.

Harkness, England, UK, 1971
('Ann Elizabeth' × 'Allgold') × 'Yellow Cushion'
Repeat flowering ı *Moderate fragrance*

HABIT Bush H/W 1m/60cm (3ft/2ft) ı ZONES 5–11

🌹 Belfast Dani Award 1974, Royal Horticultural Society Award of Garden Merit 1993

'Southern Belle'

HYBRID TEA ı PINK BLEND

The hibiscus 'Southern Belle' is known for its absolutely enormous flowers, but the rose of the same name is of only moderate size – much more suitable for a young lady to wear in her hair while entertaining a gentleman caller on the verandah of some stately mansion. The flowers are deep pink with a white reverse, and prettily shaped, and come in small clusters on an upright bush with semi-glossy foliage. There is very little in the way of fragrance.

Swim and Ellis, USA, 1981
'Pink Parfait' × 'Phoenix'
Repeat flowering ı *Slight fragrance*

HABIT Bush H/W 1.5m/1m (5ft/3ft) ı ZONES 5–11

'Souvenir de Philémon Cochet'

HYBRID RUGOSA ı WHITE

Introduced in 1899, this sport from 'Blanc Double de Coubert' resembles its parent in everything except its greatly increased complement of petals. The white flowers are so double that they sometimes open as perfect spheres, somewhat like double hollyhocks. The plant is not quite as free with its flowers as its parent is. Philémon Cochet was the raiser's brother. The foliage is light green and rugose.

Cochet-Cochet, France, 1899
'Blanc Double de Coubert' sport
Repeat flowering ı *Slight fragrance*

HABIT Bush H/W 1.5m/1.2m (5ft/4ft) ı ZONES 5–10

'Sparrieshoop'

'Souvenir de Pierre Leperdrieux'

'Souvenir de Pierre Leperdrieux'

HYBRID RUGOSA ı MEDIUM RED

It is surprising that this 1895 Hybrid Rugosa is not better known. It has all the group's good habits – the lush, light-green, rugose foliage, the bushy growth and the strong, clove-like fragrance – and bears large flowers – almost single, with only seven or eight petals – in a pleasant shade of cerise with undertones of purple, their cream stamens lighting up the centres. There are often hips in the fall/autumn, too.

Cochet-Cochet, France, 1895
Parentage unknown
Repeat flowering ı *Strong fragrance*

HABIT Bush H/W 1.5m/1.2m (5ft/4ft) ı ZONES 5–10

'Sparrieshoop'

SHRUB ı LIGHT PINK

'Sparrieshoop', named for the village where the Kordes family has its nurseries, is sufficiently long-limbed that it can be trained as a short climber, but it is also handsome as a big, spreading shrub. The young shoots are bronze, the mature leaves glossy and dark green. Sweetly fragrant, the flowers are apple-blossom-pink and come in large clusters all season. They are not quite single, having just one or two extra petals.

Kordes, Germany, 1953
('Baby Château' × 'Else Poulsen') × 'Magnifica'
Repeat flowering ı *Intense fragrance*

HABIT Bush H/W 1.5m/1.2m (5ft/4ft) ı ZONES 4–11
🌹 Portland (Oregon, USA) Gold Medal 1971

'Spartan'

FLORIBUNDA ı ORANGE RED

'Aparte'

When Jackson & Perkins introduced 'Spartan' in 1955, they gave it the most elaborate and expensive publicity ever mounted for a new

'Spartan'

'Spellbinder'

'Spellbound'

rose, including colored pages in *Time* and the *Saturday Evening Post*. Rumor had it that as 'Spartan' had been pipped at the post for the AARS award, Jackson & Perkins were determined to outsell the winner. With hindsight, perhaps it should have won, for it was, and still is, a stunning rose. The bush is tall and strong, with glossy, olive-green foliage, strongly red-tinted in its youth, and produces its double flowers, singly and in clusters, in great abundance. The flowers are strongly fragrant, too, but above all else their color was new and sensational – a vivid coral tone, not quite orange, not quite deep enough to be red. 'Spartan' has been a prolific parent.

Boerner, USA, 1955
'Geranium Red' × 'Fashion'
Repeat flowering ı *Intense fragrance*

HABIT Bush H/W 1m/60cm (3ft/2ft) ı ZONES 5–11
🌹 Portland (Oregon, USA) Gold Medal 1955, American Rose Society David Fuerstenberg Award 1959

'Spellbinder'

HYBRID TEA ı PINK BLEND

'Oratorio'

There are conflicting reports about the constitution of this rose, some saying that it is vigorous and healthy, others that it is sickly. So it would be wise to ask how it does in your area before planting it. The flowers are unique, and well deserving of the name. Officially described as ivory to crimson, they in fact blend cream, pale yellow, pink and red, all marbled and brocaded together in the manner of a variegated camellia. Completing the resemblance, the large, double flowers open quite flat. Their fragrance is only slight. The dark green foliage is thick-textured and distinctively pointed.

WARdido ı Warriner, USA, 1975
'South Seas' × seedling
Repeat flowering ı *Slight fragrance*

HABIT Bush H/W 1.2m/1m (4ft/3ft) ı ZONES 5–11

'Spellbound'

HYBRID TEA | ORANGE PINK

The color is best described as somewhere between deep coral and coral-pink, and the graceful, double blooms are a delight both in the landscape and in the vase. Like its popular parents, this outstanding variety makes a fine exhibition rose as well. The plant is upright, hardy and vigorous, with good disease resistance and a plentiful supply of semi-glossy foliage.

JACpribe | Zary, USA, 2006
'Ingrid Bergman' × 'Pristine'
Repeat flowering | *Spicy fragrance*
HABIT Bush H/W 1.2m/1m (4ft/3ft) | ZONES 5–1

'Stainless Steel'

'St Patrick'

'St Patrick'

HYBRID TEA | YELLOW BLEND

'Irish Luck', 'Limelight', 'Saint Patrick'

This is one of the few yellow roses that consistently does best in hot weather, when its green undertones become more noticeable. A favorite among floral arrangers, the classically formed blooms are big, multi-petalled and very long-lasting. They are produced quite freely throughout the season, mostly singly but occasionally in small clusters, on an upright, medium-sized bush with healthy, grey-green foliage and a slight tendency to spread. 'St Patrick' was bred by an amateur

'Stadt den Helder'

rose-grower in California and given a code-name in honor of his grand-daughter Amanda.

WEKamanda | Strickland, USA, 1999
'Brandy' × 'Gold Medal'
Repeat flowering | *Light fragrance*
HABIT Bush H/W 1.5m/1.2m (5ft/4ft) | ZONES 4–11

All-America Rose Selection 1996, American Rose Society David Fuerstenberg Award 2000

'Stadt den Helder'

FLORIBUNDA | MEDIUM RED

'Stadt den Helder' is a fairly typical bright red Floribunda, its double flowers slightly fragrant and carried in large clusters. Dutch-raised, it is a rose for very cool climates, such as in

Canada. Den Helder is a seaport in the Netherlands, notable for the presence of a naval base, a weather observatory, a zoological station and a lighthouse. The foliage is large, matt and dark green.

INTerhel | Interplant, The Netherlands, 1979
'Amsterdam' × ('Olala' × 'Diablotin')
Repeat flowering | *Slight fragrance*
HABIT Bush H/W 1m/60cm (3ft/2ft) | ZONES 5–11

'Stainless Steel'

HYBRID TEA | MAUVE

This tall, vigorous variety does exceptionally well in all climates. The flowers live up to the name, being of a unique silvery grey-lavender color. They have excellent form, and are borne both singly and in large clusters on very tall, straight stems. They make excellent cut flowers, with a long vase life, and, like most lavender roses, they are also strongly fragrant. The bush is well covered all season with large, healthy, deep green foliage.

WEKblusi | Carruth, USA, 1991
'Blue Nile' × 'Silverado'
Repeat flowering | *Intense, rose fragrance*
HABIT Bush H/W 2m/1.2m (7ft/4ft) | ZONES 4–11

'Starry Night'

SHRUB | WHITE

'Starry Night' won Pierre Orard of France the AARS award in 2002. This low-growing

'Starry Night'

Shrub Rose is strongly inclined to bloom all at once, producing a multitude of perfectly formed, single-petalled, white blooms against a canopy of luscious green foliage. Some gardeners have even mistaken this stunning plant for a member of the dogwood family!

ORAwichkay ι Orard, France, 2002
'Anisley Dickson' × *R. wichurana*
Repeat flowering ι *Slight fragrance*

HABIT Bush H/W 110cm/1m (3ft 6in/3ft) ι ZONES 4–11

All-America Rose Selection 2002

'Stephanie Diane'

HYBRID TEA ι MEDIUM RED

'Stephanie Diane' is only moderately vigorous, but exhibitors will be interested in it for the large size and perfect form of its 50-petalled, brilliant red flowers. Their color looks especially good under artificial light, and they open very evenly and slowly when cut. It is of good breeding, but it has inherited little of the perfume of 'Fragrant Cloud'. Introduced in 1971 by Bees of Chester, it seems to be popular mainly in the United Kingdom. A cool climate would seem indicated. The foliage is leathery and olive-green.

Bees, England, UK, 1971
'Fragrant Cloud' × 'Cassandra'
Repeat flowering ι *Slight fragrance*

HABIT Bush H/W 1.5m/1.2m (5ft/4ft) ι ZONES 5–11

'Stephen's Big Purple'

'Stephanie Diane'

'Sue Lawley'

'Stephen's Big Purple'

HYBRID TEA ι MAUVE

'Big Purple', 'Nuit d'Orient', 'Stephens' Rose Big Purple'

This rose comes from New Zealand, but not from the hand of Sam McGredy. It was raised by Pat Stephens, a stalwart of the New Zealand Rose Society. Its name describes it exactly: the blooms are big, full-bodied and purple. The color does vary, however: in hot weather the flowers incline toward crimson, and they never reach the deep intensity of such Old Garden Roses as 'Cardinal de Richelieu'. Love or hate the color, this is an outstanding rose, vigorous, free and intensely fragrant. The foliage is leathery and very dark green.

STEbigpu ι Stephens, New Zealand, 1985
Seedling × 'Purple Splendour'
Repeat flowering ι *Intense fragrance*

HABIT Bush H/W 1.5m/1.2m (5ft/4ft) ι ZONES 5–11

'Sue Lawley'

FLORIBUNDA ι RED BLEND

'Spanish Shawl'

Here we have yet another of Sam McGredy's 'Hand-painted Roses', this time in bright red, with a pink or cream border and centre. The flowers are not overstuffed with petals, so they show their pattern well, and are carried in clusters of seven or so on a compact bush with heavy, dark green foliage. It was bred from several generations of unnamed 'hand-painted' seedlings and named for a popular British television star on the occasion of the arrival of her first-born.

MACspash ι McGredy, New Zealand, 1980
(['Little Darling' × 'Goldilocks'] × [('Evelyn Fison' × ('Coryana' × 'Tantau's Triumph')] × ['John Church' × 'Elizabeth of Glamis']]) × ('Evelyn Fison' × ['Orange Sweetheart' × 'Frühlingsmorgen'])
Repeat flowering ι *Slight fragrance*

HABIT Bush H/W 1m/60cm (3ft/2ft) ι ZONES 5–11

New Zealand International Rose Ground Trials Gold Medal 1981

'Sue Ryder'

FLORIBUNDA ı ORANGE PINK

This rose has been well received in Britain but is hardly known elsewhere. It is really an exhibitor's rose, because it can produce the loveliest sprays of shapely, double, faintly scented blooms in orange and gold, but it is sometimes rather shy with them. The foliage is semi-glossy and mid-green. It was named in honor of Lady Ryder and her many years of work in assisting the homeless and unfortunate.

HARlino ı Harkness, England, UK, 1980
'Southampton' × seedling
Repeat flowering ı *Slight fragrance*

HABIT Bush H/W 1m/60cm (3ft/2ft) ı ZONES 5–11

'Summer Days'

HYBRID TEA ı LIGHT YELLOW

Large and high-centred, the blooms of 'Summer Days' are a refreshing pale yellow, suggestive of the soft light of an English summer. The flowers are semi-double, with 36 petals, and up to 9cm (3½in) in diameter. The plant is on the tall side, with glossy, mid-green foliage, and is quite vigorous.

Bees, England, UK, 1976
'Fragrant Cloud' × 'Dr A. J. Verhage'
Repeat flowering ı *Moderate fragrance*

HABIT Bush H/W 1.4m/1m (4ft 6in/3ft) ı ZONES 5–11

'Summer Dream'

HYBRID TEA ı APRICOT BLEND

This was Jackson & Perkins's Rose of the Year for 1987. The large, double blooms are balanced by the delicacy of their coloring, a blend of soft pinks and peach tones. They are of fine, high-centred form and good, if light, fragrance. The long stems often display two or three blooms together. The foliage is mid-green.

JACshe ı Warriner, USA, 1986
'Sunshine' × seedling
Repeat flowering ı *Fruity fragrance*

HABIT Bush H/W 1.4m/1m (4ft 6in/3ft) ı ZONES 5–11
❀ Rose Introducers of New Zealand Gold Medal 1998

'Summer Fashion'

FLORIBUNDA ı YELLOW BLEND

'Arc de Triomphe'

There are quite a few Floribundas that start out yellow and pass to red as they age. Here

is one whose colors are in a softer key. 'Summer Fashion' opens pale lemon-yellow, fading almost as soon as the flowers are fully blown to ivory-white and then gradually becoming suffused with soft rose-pink. Borne usually in small clusters, they are double, nicely formed and fragrant. The foliage is large and mid-green.

JACale ı Warriner, USA, 1986
'Precilla' × 'Bridal Pink'
Repeat flowering ı *Moderate fragrance*

HABIT Bush H/W 1m/60cm (3ft/2ft) ı ZONES 5–11

ABOVE 'Summer Days'
LEFT 'Summer Fashion'
BELOW 'Sue Ryder'

'Summer Dream'

'Summer Sunshine'

HYBRID TEA | DEEP YELLOW

'Soleil d'Été'

'Summer Sunshine' has long had the solid reputation of being one of the more reliable yellow roses for humid climates, where yellow roses often languish. It is a tendency inherited, way back, from *R. foetida persiana* ('Persian Yellow'). The color of the double blooms is exceptionally deep and shining, and fades but little as the bloom ages, but the spent petals often do not drop cleanly. The plant is on the short side, but usually has a plentiful

'Summer Sunshine'

'Sunday Best'

'Sunny Honey'

'Sundowner'

supply of rather thin branches clad in semi-glossy, dark green foliage. The scent is light but pleasant.

Swim, USA, 1962
'Buccaneer' × 'Lemon Chiffon'
Repeat flowering | *Slight fragrance*

HABIT Bush H/W 1.4m/1m (4ft 6in/3ft) | ZONES 5–11

'Sun Flare'

FLORIBUNDA | MEDIUM YELLOW

'Sunflare'

Rose-breeders like the publicity that a topical name can bring to a new rose, but 1983, the year 'Sun Flare' won the AARS award, was not a notable year for solar activity. It is an appropriate name for the pale, luminous yellow of the double flowers, 10cm (4in) in diameter, displayed on a fashionably low and spreading bush in clusters of up to a dozen. There is a pleasant fragrance, officially described as 'licorice-like' but more suggestive of a nice old vermouth to some. The foliage is small and glossy.

JACjem | Warriner, USA, 1981
'Sunsprite' × seedling
Repeat flowering | *Slight fragrance*

HABIT Bush H/W 1m/60cm (3ft/2ft) | ZONES 4–11

🌹 Bagatelle (Paris) Gold Medal 1981, Tokyo Gold Medal 1981, All-America Rose Selection 1983, Portland (Oregon, USA) Gold Medal 1985

'Sunblest'

HYBRID TEA | DEEP YELLOW

'Landora'

There are other yellow roses with larger or shapelier blooms, deeper and brighter colors, and stronger growth, but 'Sunblest' is still perfectly acceptable in each department. It is a good, reliable rose and very popular. While

not outstandingly fragrant, it is pleasingly so, and the clear yellow blooms stand out well. Gold medals have been awarded in Japan and New Zealand. The foliage is glossy and dark emerald-green.

Tantau, Germany, 1970
Seedling × 'King's Ransom'
Repeat flowering | *Slight fragrance*

HABIT Bush H/W 1.5m/1.2m (5ft/4ft) | ZONES 5–11

🌹 Tokyo Gold Medal 1971, Gold Star of the South Pacific, Palmerston North (New Zealand) 1971

'Sunblest'

'Sunday Best'

LARGE FLOWERED CLIMBER | RED BLEND

At first sight 'Sunday Best' looks like an improved version of 'Nancy Hayward'. The single flowers are as large, if not larger, and a more brilliant color, bright red fading to crimson. They are a trifle more fragrant, although that is not saying much. It loses out to its rival in not being as early in bloom and not being repeat flowering. That said, it can be a striking rose, the plant tall and vigorous enough to clad the facade of a two-storey house. In its season it makes a splendid display. The foliage is pale green and wrinkled.

Clark, Australia, 1924
'Frau Karl Druschki' × seedling
Repeat flowering | *Slight fragrance*

HABIT Climber H/W 3m/2.5m (10ft/8ft) | ZONES 5–11

'Sundowner'

GRANDIFLORA | APRICOT BLEND

'MACche'

In Australia and New Zealand a sundowner is an itinerant worker with the bad habit of turning up late in the working day. Sam McGredy has said that he followed the usage of the rest of the world, for whom a sundowner is a refreshing drink after a hard day's work.

'Sun Flare'

The name is apt for the sunset colors. The shapely, double blooms open brilliant coral and gold, passing to salmon-pink and cream. They are sweetly fragrant. The bush is tall, with leathery, olive-green foliage. 'Sundowner' won the 1979 AARS award, but you might have to watch out for mildew.

MACcheup ı McGredy, New Zealand, 1978
'Bond Street' × 'Peer Gynt'
Repeat flowering ı *Intense fragrance*
HABIT Bush H/W 1.5m/1.2m (5ft/4ft) ı ZONES 5–11
All-America Rose Selection 1979

'Sunny Honey'

FLORIBUNDA ı YELLOW BLEND

'Sunny Honey' retains its place in the catalogues only in New Zealand. The double flowers are delightful in their blend of peach and yellow, flushed with red on the backs of the petals, and they are fragrant, too. The foliage is dark green.

Dickson, Northern Ireland, UK, 1972
'Happy Event' × 'Elizabeth of Glamis'
Repeat flowering ı *Moderate fragrance*
HABIT Bush H/W 1m/60cm (3ft/2ft) ı ZONES 5–11

'Sunny June'

SHRUB ı DEEP YELLOW

At first sight 'Sunny June' is so like the better-known 'Golden Wings' that more than one nursery has got them muddled. 'Sunny June'

'Sunny June'

is really better trained to a pillar or as a short climber, whereas 'Golden Wings' is the better choice as a free-standing shrub, and it is rather more tolerant of cold winters. 'Sunny June' is a shade brighter in tone, but a touch smaller and less fragrant. It has a charming habit of closing up for the night. The foliage is semi-glossy and bright green. The two roses are not related.

Lammerts, USA, 1952
'Crimson Glory' × 'Captain Thomas'
Repeat flowering ı *Spicy fragrance*
HABIT Climber H/W 2m/1.2m (7ft/4ft) ı ZONES 5–11

'Sunset Celebration'

HYBRID TEA ı APRICOT BLEND

'Chantoli', 'Exotic', 'Warm Wishes'

The large, double blooms illuminate the garden with their creamy apricot to warm amber-pink tones. Packed with petals and poised on long, elegant stems, the flowers are large and long-lasting, with a delicious scent of fresh peaches and apricots. The plant is of medium height, bushy, and well clothed with shiny, healthy, dark green foliage, making it attractive even between bloom cycles. It is an excellent garden variety for its ease of maintenance and clean growing habit.

FRYxotic ı Fryer, England, 1999
'Pot o' Gold' × seedling
Repeat flowering ı *Peach and apricot fragrance*
HABIT Bush H/W 1.5m/1.2m (5ft/4ft) ı ZONES 5–11
Gold Medal and Prize of the City of Belfast 1996, Rose Introducers of New Zealand Gold Medal 1996, Golden Rose of The Hague 1997, All-America Rose Selection 1998

'Sunset Jubilee'

HYBRID TEA ı PINK BLEND

The jubilee in question was that of America's *Sunset* magazine, and the flowers are appropriately in sunset tones of pink with an undertone of coral. They are large, double and high-centred, opening to show their stamens. The bush is described as vigorous, with leathery, light green foliage. Introduced in 1973, 'Sunset Jubilee' appears to have

'Sunset Celebration'

'Sunset Jubilee'

'Sutter's Gold'

vanished from the catalogues. Even *Sunset* does not include it in their latest rose book. The fragrance is only slight.

Boerner, USA, 1973
'Kordes's Perfecta' × seedling of 'Pink Duchess'
Repeat flowering ⏐ *Slight fragrance*

HABIT Bush H/W 1.5m/1.2m (5ft/4ft) ⏐ ZONES 5–11

'Sunsilk'

FLORIBUNDA ⏐ MEDIUM YELLOW

With its large, shapely, double blooms, 'Sunsilk' might pass for a small Hybrid Tea, but they come in quite adequate clusters. The color is a lovely pale, clear yellow. It is less attention-grabbing than the deeper yellows like 'Sunsprite', perhaps, but a most useful blending color in the garden and the vase, and one that is surprisingly rare in flowers. The scent is only slight, the growth average, the foliage mid-green. Forget about shampoo and think of sunshine and silky petals instead.

Fryer, England, UK, 1974
'Pink Parfait' × seedling of 'Redgold'
Repeat flowering ⏐ *Slight fragrance*

HABIT Bush H/W 1m/60cm (3ft/2ft) ⏐ ZONES 5–11

🌹 Belfast Gold Medal and Prize of the City of Belfast 1976

'Sweet Afton'

'Sweet Surrender'

'Sunsprite'

FLORIBUNDA ⏐ DEEP YELLOW

'Friesia'

By whichever name you know it, this is one of the outstanding yellow roses anywhere, its color clear and almost unfading, its double flowers neatly formed, carried in large, well-spaced clusters, and fragrant, too. It might have been nice if the young leaves had a tint of bronze, but they are unusually healthy, shiny and dark green. Friesia (Friesland) is

'Sunsilk'

a province of the Low Countries, famous for dairying. This was one of the first roses to be given a 'codename', and the Royal National Rose Society in Britain often still uses it. 'Sunsprite', the American name, is most apt.

KORresia ⏐ Kordes, Germany, 1977
Seedling × 'Spanish Sun'
Repeat flowering ⏐ *Intense fragrance*

HABIT Bush H/W 110cm/1m (3ft 6in/3ft) ⏐ ZONES 5–11

🌹 New Zealand International Rose Ground Trials Gold Medal 1975, American Rose Society James Alexander Gamble Fragrance Medal 1979

'Super Star'

HYBRID TEA ⏐ ORANGE RED

'Orienta', 'Tropicana'

This is one of the classic roses of the mid-twentieth century. Its reputation is legendary. 'Super Star' – known in America as 'Tropicana' – is grown throughout the civilized world. The blooms are large, fully double and shapely, and their warm coral-orange color represented a major color breakthrough for Germany's Mathias Tantau. They have an intense fragrance, sweet and fruity. When 'Super Star' entered the rose world, it stimulated rose-breeding to a new level of activity, adding to the genetic pool established by 'Peace'. The flowers are borne singly on long stems, with glossy foliage that is sometimes susceptible to mildew. This is a variety that earns a place in any garden.

TANorstar ⏐ Tantau, Germany, 1960
(Seedling × 'Peace') × (seedling × 'Alpine Glow')
Repeat flowering ⏐ *Intense, fruity fragrance*

HABIT Bush H/W 1.5m/1.2m (5ft/4ft) ⏐ ZONES 4–11

🌹 Geneva Gold Medal 1960, (Royal) National Rose Society Gold Medal and President's International Trophy 1960, Portland (Oregon, USA) Gold Medal 1961, All-America Rose Selection 1963, American Rose Society Gold Medal 1967

'Sutter's Gold'

HYBRID TEA ⏐ ORANGE BLEND

'Sutter's Gold' demonstrates how elegance and reliability can outweigh a lack of exhibition form. Since it was introduced by Herbert Swim in 1950, it has been adorned with the AARS and other awards and has become one of the best-loved Modern Roses. True, the gold-touched scarlet of the buds pales in the open blooms, which are only semi-double and rather fleeting in hot weather. But they are stylish and richly fragrant, and are generously given from early in the season until the end of it. The plant is tall – a bit leggy, perhaps – but has polished, very dark green leaves and

'Super Star'

'Sunsprite'

few thorns. The name commemorates the first discovery of gold in California, in 1848, on the site of a sawmill jointly owned by Captain John Sutter and James Marshall.

Swim, USA, 1950
'Charlotte Armstrong' × 'Signora'
Repeat flowering ׀ *Intense fragrance*

HABIT Bush H/W 1.5m/1.2m (5ft/4ft) ׀ ZONES 5–11

🏵 Portland (Oregon, USA) Gold Medal 1946, Bagatelle (Paris) Gold Medal 1948, Geneva Gold Medal 1949, All-America Rose Selection 1950, American Rose Society James Alexander Gamble Fragrance Medal 1965

'Sweet Afton'

HYBRID TEA ׀ WHITE

Named for the old Scottish folksong, 'Sweet Afton' is a rose of lyrical beauty. The blooms are of the softest coloring – almost white, blushing pale pink toward the centre – and very sweetly fragrant. They are large, double and classically formed. The bush is tall and spreading, but apparently susceptible to black spot. The foliage is glossy and dark green.

Armstrong and Swim, USA, 1964
('Charlotte Armstrong' × 'Signora') × ('Alice Stern' × 'Ondine')
Repeat flowering ׀ *Intense fragrance*

HABIT Bush H/W 1.2m/1m (4ft/3ft) ׀ ZONES 5–11

🏵 Geneva Fragrance Award 1964

'Sweet Surrender'

HYBRID TEA ׀ MEDIUM PINK

A rose with an outrageously romantic name like this had better be fragrant, and 'Sweet Surrender' certainly is that. The color is a tender shade of rose-pink, with that sheen that rose catalogues love to call 'silvery', and the buds are long, in the manner favored in America. Indeed, this is an American rose, from Ollie Weeks in 1983, and it won the AARS award that year. The bush is strong and upright, and the foliage is dark green.

Weeks, USA, 1983
Seedling × 'Tiffany'
Repeat flowering ׀ *Tea fragrance*

HABIT Bush H/W 1.5m/1.2m (5ft/4ft) ׀ ZONES 5–11

🏵 All-America Rose Selection 1983

The Power of Red Roses

ROSES ARE RED,

VIOLETS ARE BLUE,

SUGAR IS SWEET;

AND SO ARE YOU

The first line of the familiar quatrain – which many people think derives from lines in Sir Edmund Spenser's epic poem of 1590, 'The Faerie Queene' – reflects the popular belief that the 'arche-typal rose', the one true rose, is red. And when we think of red roses, our imagination conjures up not just any red but a brilliant, velvety red; a scarlet red that excites the passions and draws the viewer to come, look and inhale the sensual fragrance; the red of rubies, the red of blood. No other color in the horticultural world has the same power to evoke such deep-felt emotions.

It will therefore come as a surprise to many people to learn that red roses do not occur naturally. Strange as it may seem, a true red color is not found among Wild (Species) Roses. Non-cultivated Species Roses cover a color range from white to light pink, with the occasional yellow or deep pink. Red was a later development. It is generally accepted that Modern Roses are the result of breeding from six important Species Roses: *R. foetida*, *R. gallica*, *R. damascena*, *R. gigantea*, *R. moschata* and *R. chinensis*. Variations in color often occurred in the course cross-pollination over several thousands of years, and such roses were then propagated, adding to the available genetic pool. Gradually, the brilliant reds we know today emerged.

From 'Slater's Crimson China' to 'General Jack'

In 1790, a repeat-flowering red China Rose, given the name 'Slater's Crimson China', appeared. Also known as 'Old Crimson China' and *R. chinensis semperflorens*, this red rose had the ability to transmit its crimson color to its progeny. Fortuitously, this variety arrived in Europe just as nineteenth-century botanists were beginning to recognize the benefits of planning parenthood through deliberate hybridizing rather than leaving it to Mother Nature. But there was a major genetic impediment. 'Slater's Crimson China' was what is known as a triploid, which means it has three sets of chromosomes. Such organisms are usually infertile. In other words, it seemed to be a mule in a world of mares. Persistence finally proved it was not completely sterile, however, and a few seedlings were produced. Significantly, a cross of (*R. damascena* × *R. gallica*) × 'Slater's Crimson China' produced the historically important rose the 'Duchess of Portland' – also called the 'Portland Rose' – which later gave

its name to the once-popular class. Perhaps the most recognizable surviving variety of Portland Roses today is 'Rose du Roi' (1815), known for its bright red color. Subsequent crosses of Portland Roses with Hybrid Chinas were later crossed with Bourbons to produce the precursors of our modern Hybrid Teas, the Hybrid Perpetuals (c. 1837). Among these offspring was a variety with a bright red color that was named 'Général Jacqueminot' (1853) – nicknamed 'General Jack' by the trade. This rose has had a strong influence on the development of modern red Hybrid Teas.

Twentieth-century developments

Over the years, many people have enjoyed the fragrant, deep-red Hybrid Tea called 'Mister Lincoln', which was hybridized by Ollie Weeks of California in 1964. Few, however, know the story of how close this variety came to a frozen death. Weeks's choice of the two good red roses 'Charles Mallerin' and 'Chrysler Imperial' as parents was an obvious one, and several other hydribizers were simultane-ously pursuing this same course. Weeks harvested a few thousand seeds from his cross and placed them in a refrigerator to lie dor-mant. However, they were all frozen! Somehow, about 160 seeds survived this near-death experience and were successfully germi-nated. Amazingly, from those 160 survivors were born not only 'Mister Lincoln' but another great red Hybrid Tea, 'Oklahoma'. Other hybridizers replicated this cross, but only one other great red resulted – 'Papa Meilland', which came from Meilland in 1963.

Another variety that has had a significant influence on today's red roses is 'Baby Chateau', introduced by Kordes in 1936 while he was attempting to improve upon a near-black, crimson Hybrid Tea called 'Chateau de Clos Vougeot'. Regrettably, it turned out to be a Floribunda and not a Hybrid Tea, but the significance of this event in

TOP 'Kardinal'

RIGHT 'Papa Meilland'

The rise and rise of red roses

The following roses have significantly contributed to the development and character of red roses.

'Old Crimson China' (c.1790)
Perhaps the first rose to bring the desirable red color range to modern breeding programs.

'Général Jacqueminot' (1853)
The rose generally declared to be the precursor of modern red roses. Its characteristics, both good and bad, are still evident in its numerous progeny.

'Crimson Glory' (1935)
Notable for its damask fragrance and glorious color, its influence on twentieth-century breeding programs is as important as that of 'Général Jacqueminot' in the nineteenth century.

'Charles Mallerin' (1951)
Although it never became popular on its own account, its influence on modern Hybrid Teas was pivotal.

'Independence' (1951)
The Floribunda that gave us the direct link to the red pigmentation pelargonidin, bringing scarlet color to Modern Roses.

'Chrysler Imperial' (1952)
A classic red rose whose own popularity has diminished, but it brought style and fragrance into nine breeding lines of the late twentieth century.

'Christian Dior' (1958)
This rose has been popular ever since it was introduced, in spite of its propensity to suffer from mildew and black spot.

'Papa Meilland' (1963)
Admired for its form, color and fragrance, its faults are an ungainly habit and limited adaptability to hot and cold climates.

'Mister Lincoln' (1964)
Rose-growers worldwide have adored this rose for its romance and powerful fragrance ever since it was introduced.

'Red Devil' (1970)
This robust variety has gained an excellent reputation as an exhibition rose in England.

'Uncle Joe' (1971)
Undeniably a great exhibition rose in hot and humid climates.

'Olympiad' (1984)
Having survived the test of time, this rose represents all the best qualities found in red roses and has earned its place among the great red roses.

ABOVE 'Loving Memory'
LEFT 'Mister Lincoln'

the history of red roses is that it introduced into the gene pool the chemical pigmentation pelargonidin, which among things gives geraniums their orange-red color. This gigantic step forward added to the color palette of red roses, which until that time had only the red pigmentation cyanicin in their genetic inheritance. It was a master achievement for Willi Kordes, but one acknowledged only long after the discovery. 'Baby Chateau' has continued to influence Hybrid Teas via a subsequent Floribunda Kordes bred from it, 'Independence' (1951).

A major step forward in developing red roses was the appearance of 'Olympiad', hybridized by Sam McGredy in New Zealand in 1982 using two great red roses, 'Red Planet' and 'Pharaoh'. Some growers bemoan its lack of any notable fragrance, while others cannot understand why fragrance is mandatory in red roses, for the color is sheer magic. 'Olympiad' has now displaced the mighty 'Mister Lincoln' as America's favorite red.

And the best reds? Opinions vary. In his book *Complete Rose Growing*, the famous English hybridizer Edward LeGrice stated that the great difficulty in hybridizing red roses is preserving the rich red color and powerful damask perfume without inducing weak necks. LeGrice believed that it was impossible to combine all the desirable qualities of red roses in one rose. His choices for best reds were 'Red Lion', 'Alec's Red', 'Ernest H. Morse', 'National Trust', 'Red Devil', 'Chrysler Imperial', 'John Waterer' and 'Papa Meilland'. English horticulturalist Harry Wheatcroft, in his book *In Praise of Roses*, said that he had never grown a red rose that lived up to his ideal. Wheatcroft's selection of the best reds included 'Alec's Red', 'Ernest H. Morse', 'Papa Meilland' and 'Red Planet'.

There is enough variety on the menu of red roses to suit every taste.

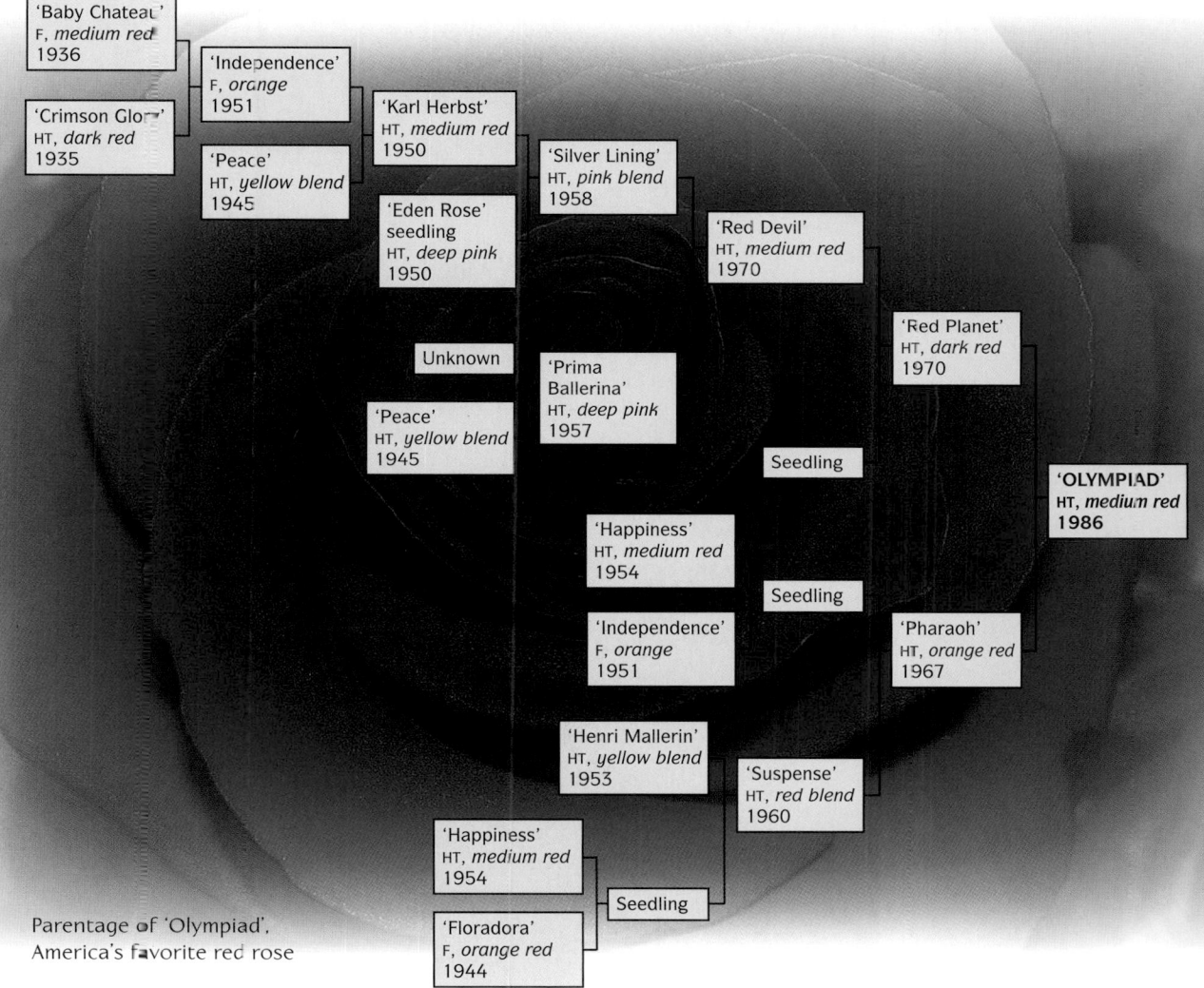

'Baby Chateau'
F, *medium red*
1936

'Independence'
F, *orange*
1951

'Crimson Glory'
HT, *dark red*
1935

'Karl Herbst'
HT, *medium red*
1950

'Peace'
HT, *yellow blend*
1945

'Silver Lining'
HT, *pink blend*
1958

'Eden Rose' seedling
HT, *deep pink*
1950

'Red Devil'
HT, *medium red*
1970

'Red Planet'
HT, *dark red*
1970

Unknown

'Prima Ballerina'
HT, *deep pink*
1957

'Peace'
HT, *yellow blend*
1945

Seedling

'OLYMPIAD'
HT, *medium red*
1986

'Happiness'
HT, *medium red*
1954

Seedling

'Independence'
F, *orange*
1951

'Pharaoh'
HT, *orange red*
1967

'Henri Mallerin'
HT, *yellow blend*
1953

'Suspense'
HT, *red blend*
1960

'Happiness'
HT, *medium red*
1954

Seedling

'Floradora'
F, *orange red*
1944

Parentage of 'Olympiad', America's favorite red rose

'Sweet Vivien'

'Sweet Vivien'

FLORIBUNDA ı PINK BLEND

This is a rose of unusual breeding, and it is
a real charmer. The flowers have just a few
petals too many to be quite single, but that
does not detract from the freshness of their
apple-blossom coloring. Leave the latest blooms
on the plants and they will be followed by large,
pear-shaped hips. The plant is low-growing
and very bushy, the foliage dark green and
quite exceptionally resistant to disease. The
perfume is rather faint. 'Sweet Vivien' was
introduced in 1961 by Frank Raffel, a rose-
grower from Stockton, California. It has never
been as widely distributed as it deserves to be.

Raffel, Bush, 1961
'Little Darling' × R. odorata
Repeat flowering ı *Slight fragrance*

HABIT Bush H/W 1m/1m (3ft/3ft) ı ZONES 5–11

'Sweetheart'

HYBRID TEA ı MEDIUM PINK

'Mademoiselle Cécile Brünner' is sometimes
called the 'Sweetheart Rose', but this Hybrid
Tea from Alec Cocker is nothing like it. The
blooms are several times as large, rose-pink
with yellow at the petal base, and – despite
their 50-odd petals and their high centre – not
quite so exquisitely perfect in shape. The bush
is upright, with large, mid-green foliage, but
it is inclined to be shy of blooming. The fragrance
is notable. This is an exhibitor's rose, and one
for cool climates.

COCapeer ı Cocker, Scotland, UK, 1980
'Peer Gynt' × ('Fragrant Cloud' × 'Gay Gordons')
Repeat flowering ı *Moderate fragrance*

HABIT Bush H/W 1.4m/1m (4ft 6in/3ft) ı ZONES 5–11
🌹 Belfast Fragrance Award 1982

'Sweetheart'

'Sylvia'

'Sylvia'

HYBRID TEA ı ORANGE PINK

'Congratulations', 'Kordes's Rose Sylvia'

Reimer Kordes insists that 'Sylvia' (known in
America as 'Congratulations') is a Floribunda.
Everyone else says No: it is a Hybrid Tea –
and a big one, too. Either way, it is one of
the loveliest of pink roses – of tender color
(warmed with just a hint of coral), of perfect
form and with a delightful fragrance. The foliage is semi-glossy and olive-green. The double
blooms are very freely produced, and it is a
well-regarded florist's rose. Congratulations
to Kordes are indeed in order. As 'Sylvia',
this variety has become a favorite exhibition
rose in New Zealand.

KORlift ı Kordes, Germany, 1979
'Carina' × seedling
Repeat flowering ı *Moderate fragrance*

HABIT Bush H/W 1.5m/1.2m (5ft/4ft) ı ZONES 5–11
🌹 Anerkannte Deutsche Rose (Germany) 1977

'Sympathie'

HYBRID KORDESII ı MEDIUM RED

Most of the climbers descended from R. kordesii
are like Floribundas in their blooms, but 'Sympathie' is as large as a Hybrid Tea, shapely,
and a beautiful, deep crimson. It is fragrant,
too, and it is surprising that it is not better
known. Perhaps its moderate growth, to 3m
(10ft) or so, makes it sound weak. It is in fact
a strong and healthy grower, with glossy,

'Tahitian Su

'Taihape Sunset'

'Sympathie'

bright green foliage, and the repeat bloom is excellent.

Kordes, Germany, 1964
'Wilhelm Hausmann' × 'Don Juan'
Repeat flowering ⫶ *Intense fragrance*

HABIT Climber H/W 3m/2.5m (10ft/8ft) ⫶ ZONES 4–11

🌹 Anerkannte Deutsche Rose (Germany) 1966

'Tahitian Sunset'

HYBRID TEA ⫶ APRICOT BLEND

Its unusual tie-dyed coloring and lavish fragrance have already earned this beauty many awards, including a gold medal at the Rose Hills international rose trials. The large blooms have good, high-centred form and come in a most attractive color combination of peach, apricot, yellow and pink. They have a pleasing licorice scent. The plant is a prolific bloomer, providing color and fragrance all season. It is tall, vigorous and well balanced, with excellent resistance to diseases, especially black spot.

JACgodde ⫶ Zary, USA, 2006
Seedling × 'Sun Goddess'
Repeat flowering ⫶ *Licorice fragrance*

HABIT Bush H/W 1.5m/1.2m (5ft/4ft) ⫶ ZONES 4–11

🌹 All-America Rose Selection 2006, Rose Hills (California) Gold Medal 2006

'Talisman'

'Taihape Sunset'

HYBRID TEA ⫶ ORANGE BLEND

Reimer Kordes's great friend and colleague Sam McGredy probably named this rose. It is catalogued only in New Zealand, where the name would hardly raise eyebrows or twist tongues the way it might in Germany. The elegantly shaped blooms are of a dazzling sunset-orange backed with yellow, and positively glow against the dark, purple-toned foliage. They have a slight scent.

KORlinde ⫶ Kordes, Germany, 1987
Parentage undisclosed
Repeat flowering ⫶ *Slight fragrance*

HABIT Bush H/W 1.4m/1m (4ft 6in/3ft) ⫶ ZONES 5–11

'Takao'

HYBRID TEA ⫶ YELLOW BLEND

This rose by the Japanese raiser Okamoto is a beauty, with large, shapely, double blooms whose pointed petals reflex most elegantly. They have the fragrance of a Damask Rose and start life deep yellow, gradually becoming entirely scarlet. The foliage is medium-sized and mid-green. Introduced in 1975, 'Takao' was exported to America, but it gained only limited success with exhibitors there because it tends to be highly susceptible

'Takao'

to powdery mildew. It is named for an area in Kyoto famous for its fall/autumn foliage.

Okamoto, Japan, 1975
('Masquerade' × 'Lydia') × ('Montezuma' × 'Miss Ireland')
Repeat flowering ⫶ *Damask fragrance*

HABIT Bush H/W 1.4m/1m (4ft 6in/3ft) ⫶ ZONES 5–11

'Talisman'

HYBRID TEA ⫶ YELLOW BLEND

In most catalogues today 'Talisman' has given way to its great-grandchild 'Granada', but there are many old rosarians who ask for it still. It remains an easy rose to grow, the bolt-upright bushes bearing their medium-sized, rather flat, double blooms with great freedom. When it came out in 1929, there was nothing quite like its scarlet and gold brilliance, and the Montgomery Rose Company, its raisers, asked and got six times the price of other roses for it. For many years one of the leading florist's roses, it has inherited the tendency of 'Ophelia' to produce sports – no fewer than 39 of them. The foliage is semi-glossy and light green.

Montgomery, USA, 1929
'Ophelia' × 'Souvenir de Claudius Pernet'
Repeat flowering ⵏ *Moderate fagrance*

HABIT Bush H/W 1.2m/1m (4ft/3ft) ⵏ ZONES 5–11

'Tamora'

SHRUB ⵏ APRICOT BLEND

Reminiscent of the old Gallica roses, 'Tamora' produces an abundance of very symmetrical, deeply cupped, apricot-pink blooms (with 60-plus petals) on very thorny stems. The plant habit is compact and not too tall, making it suitable for a small garden or to incorporate into an existing landscape. It was named for Queen Tamora of the barbaric Goths in Shakespeare's *Titus Andronicus*.

AUStamora ⵏ Austin, England, UK, 1992
'Chaucer' × 'Conrad Ferdinand Meyer'
Repeat flowering ⵏ *Strong, myrrh fragrance*

HABIT Bush H/W 1m/60cm (3ft/2ft) ⵏ ZONES 4–11

'Tamora'

'Tequila Sunrise'

'Teasing Georgia'

'Teasing Georgia'

SHRUB ⵏ YELLOW BLEND

The deep to light yellow blend flowers are elegantly formed and fully cupped, with honey-colored centres framed by lighter outer petals. The blooms are some 7.5cm (3in) in diameter and have 100-plus petals, and are borne mostly in small clusters on long, strong, stems. The plant is medium to tall, depending on climate conditions, with mid-green foliage. An excellent landscape variety, it can easily be pruned as a shrub or trained on a trellis or pillar. It was named for Ulrich Meyer – after his wife, Georgia – both of whom are media celebrities in Germany.

AUSbaker ⵏ Austin, England, UK, 1998
'Charles Austin' × seedling
Repeat flowering ⵏ *Moderate fragrance*

HABIT Bush H/W 1.2m/1.2m (4ft/4ft) ⵏ ZONES 5–11

🌹 Royal National Rose Society Edland Fragrance Medal 2000

'Tequila'

FLORIBUNDA ⵏ ORANGE BLEND

At first sight this is just another yellow-turning-red Floribunda, but it is not quite just this. The basic color is actually an orange, with yellow at the heart, and the carmine stain that

'Tequila'

develops as the double flowers age never quite takes them over. The effect in the garden is thus of a mixture of orange and coral flowers, set against dark green, red-tinted foliage, on a bush of average height. Introduced in 1982 by Marie-Louisette Meilland, it has happily not inherited the fault of 'Rumba' of clinging to its dead flowers.

MEIgavesol ⵏ Meilland, France, 1982
'Poppy Flash' × ('Rumba' × ['Meikim' × 'Fire King'])
Repeat flowering ⵏ *Slight fragrance*

HABIT Bush H/W 1m/60cm (3ft/2ft) ⵏ ZONES 5–11

'Tequila Sunrise'

HYBRID TEA ⵏ RED BLEND

'Beaulieu'

The bright and cheerful colors of this variety – yellow edged with red – and its ability to bloom profusely in all kinds of weather make it a great garden rose. The double flowers are medium-sized, rounded and firm, their broad petals full of substance. Borne both singly and in candelabra-like clusters, they make good cut flowers. The plant is a vigorous grower, well suited to beds, borders or hedges – where it will provide the perfect backdrop for a glass of tequila as the sun sets!

DICobey | Dickson, Northern Ireland, UK, 1989
'Bonfire Night' × 'Freedom'
Repeat flowering | Slight fragrance

HABIT Bush H/W 1.5m/1.2m (5ft/4ft) | ZONES 5–11

Dublin Gold Medal 1987, Royal National Rose Society Gold Medal 1988, Gold Medal and Prize of the City of Belfast 1991

'The Dark Lady'

'Texas Centennial'

HYBRID TEA | RED BLEND

Just about every garden used to have a bush of 'Texas Centennial', seemingly always adorned with large, strongly fragrant blooms in beautiful blends of pink and strawberry-red. It can still cause a sensation, and like 'President Herbert Hoover', from which it is a sport, it is one of those roses that seems to do well everywhere. The foliage is semi-glossy and dark green. The introducer was A. F. Watkins of the Dixie Rose Nursery. He and his company are long gone, but they will continue to be remembered for this beautiful rose, introduced in 1935.

Watkins, USA, 1935
'President Herbert Hoover' sport
Repeat flowering | Intense fragrance

HABIT Bush H/W 1.5m/1.2m (5ft/4ft) | ZONES 5–11

Portland (Oregon, USA) Gold Medal 1935

'The Dark Lady'

SHRUB | DARK RED

'Dark Lady'

The dark crimson flowers are rather loosely formed and open wide to reveal their 100-plus petals. David Austin describes them as having a special quality all of their own and as being reminiscent of the flowers of tree peonies, as seen on some fabrics and wallpapers. The bush is of medium height and spreading habit. One of Austin's Shakespeare roses, it is named for the mysterious Dark Lady of the sonnets.

AUSbloom | Austin, England, 1994
'Mary Rose' × 'Prospero'
Repeat flowering | Strong fragrance

HABIT Bush H/W 1m/110cm (3ft/3ft 6in) | ZONES 5–11

'The Doctor'

HYBRID TEA | MEDIUM PINK

'The Doctor' was Dr J. H. Nicolas, the Director of Research for Jackson & Perkins, but the rose was introduced by Howard & Smith – an exemplary courtesy from one raiser to a rival. Many people still consider its cool, clear color to be the loveliest of any pink rose. The enormous, high-centred blooms are fragrant indeed. It is no longer an easy rose to grow, however, needing extra care and protection from disease. The foliage is a soft leaden green.

'Texas Centennial'

'The Doctor'

Howard, USA, 1936
'Mrs J. D. Eisele' × 'Los Angeles'
Repeat flowering | Intense fragrance

HABIT Bush H/W 1.4m/1m (4ft 6in/3ft) | ZONES 5–11

'The Fairy'

POLYANTHA | LIGHT PINK

'Fairy', 'Feerie'

During all the years that Polyanthas have been out of fashion, 'The Fairy' has retained the affection of rose-lovers. Few roses are easier to grow. The short but spreading bushes are

'The Fairy'

'The Flower Arranger'

'The Prioress'

densely clad in glossy, dark green, disease-proof leaves and adorned for most of the year with clusters of small, neat, double flowers in a lovely shade of clear pink. Their only fault is that they fade in hot weather. 'The Fairy' is still one of the best low-growing roses, and the parent of many of the better Ground Cover Roses.

Bentall, England, UK, 1932
'Paul Crampel' × 'Lady Gay'
Repeat flowering ∣ *Slight fragrance*

HABIT Bush H/W 60cm/1.2m (2ft/4ft) ∣ ZONES 4–11

🌹 Royal Horticultural Society Award of Garden Merit 1993

'The Flower Arranger'

FLORIBUNDA ∣ APRICOT BLEND

This English-raised rose has not been much grown elsewhere. Its peach and apricot flowers are semi-double, nicely shaped and borne in well-spaced clusters. They are, as befits a rose named for the silver jubilee of the National Association of Flower Arrangers, fine cut flowers. The bush is upright and bushy, with large, glossy, dark green foliage. The scent is only slight.

FRYjam ∣ Fryer, England, UK, 1984
Seedling × seedling
Repeat flowering ∣ *Slight fragrance*

HABIT Bush H/W 1m/60cm (3ft/2ft) ∣ ZONES 5–11

'The Miller'

SHRUB ∣ MEDIUM PINK

This rose is the first, alphabetically, of a series of David Austin roses named for characters in *The Canterbury Tales*. 'The Miller' bears medium-sized, double flowers, rose-pink and slightly fragrant, in sprays, like a compromise between

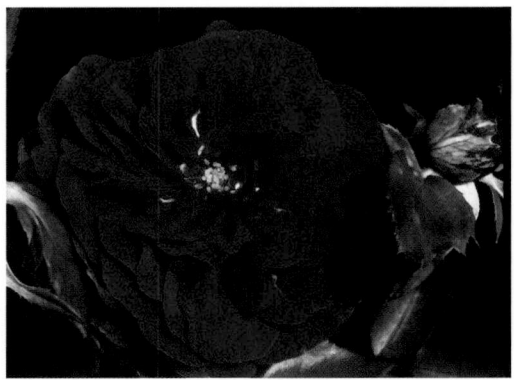

'The Prince'

'The Miller'

'The Squire'

a Floribunda and a Bourbon Rose. The bush is head-high, but it can be held at a little over 1m (3ft) with firm pruning, and it flowers repeatedly. The foliage is mid-green. Introduced in 1970, the rose is surpassed in quality by several of Austin's later introductions. However, its reputation for good performance in difficult conditions earns it a place here.

Austin, England, UK, 1981
'Baroness Rothschild' × 'Chaucer'
Repeat flowering ∣ *Moderate fragrance*

HABIT Bush H/W 1.8m/1.4m (6ft/4ft) ∣ ZONES 5–11

'The Prince'

SHRUB ∣ DARK RED

The marvellous, very double blooms are perhaps the darkest of David Austin's 'English Roses', opening as cupped rosettes of deep crimson and blending quickly into a rich, royal purple. The saturating fragrance is that of old Gallica roses, and the foliage is a complementary dark green. This is a variety with a lot of character, but it needs a few years to establish itself before it performs at its peak.

AUSvelvet ∣ Austin, England, 1993
'Lilian Austin' × 'The Squire'
Repeat flowering ∣ *Strong fragrance*

HABIT Bush H/W 1m/60cm (3ft/2ft) ∣ ZONES 5–11

'The Prioress'

SHRUB ∣ LIGHT PINK

'The Prioress' makes a rather slender bush with double, cupped blooms in pearly pink, moderately fragrant and borne repeatedly. It is really more like a Floribunda in its habit than a Shrub. The foliage is mid-green.

Austin, England, UK, 1969
'La Reine Victoria' × seedling
Repeat flowering ∣ *Moderate fragrance*

HABIT Bush H/W 1m/60cm (3ft/2ft) ∣ ZONES 5–11

'The Squire'

SHRUB | DARK RED

Very dark red roses are difficult for the raiser to come up with. The color is associated with reluctant growth, as though nature would prefer to do without it. 'The Squire' is one of the few David Austin roses that needs coddling. It will, however, make quite a sturdy, if somewhat leggy, bush, and produces flowers of deepest crimson, perfectly cupped and quartered, and very fragrant. Do not expect them in lavish quantity. The foliage is dark green and rough-textured.

AUSire | Austin, England, UK, 1976
'The Knight' × 'Château de Clos Vougeot'
Repeat flowering | *Intense fragrance*

HABIT Bush H/W 1m/60cm (3ft/2ft) | ZONES 4–11

'The Yeoman'

SHRUB | ORANGE PINK

This is a lovely rose, with its wide, informal, double blooms of soft pink, shaded and flushed with apricot, and its strong fragrance. It is not one of the sturdiest of the David Austin roses, needing good care to give of its best. Where it flourishes, it makes a bushy plant to about 1.5m (5ft) tall, flowering very freely in early summer and quite well later. The foliage is mid-green. With regular Floribunda-type pruning, it can be used as a bedding rose.

Austin, England, UK, 1969
'Ivory Fashion' × ('Constance Spry' × 'Monique')
Repeat flowering | *Intense fragrance*

HABIT Bush H/W 1.5m/1m (5ft/3ft) | ZONES 5–11

RIGHT 'Tiffany'
BELOW 'Thérèse Bugnet'

'The Yeoman'

'Thérèse Bugnet'

HYBRID RUGOSA | MEDIUM PINK

The quilted, grey-green foliage is the first clue that this plant belongs to the Rugosa family. The long, lilac buds open to reveal lovely rose-pink blooms – large, scented and with 35–40 petals – which pale as they age. This is a hardy variety, with the Rugosas' unsurpassed resistance to disease, and does not need spraying; in fact, it sulks if it is treated. It is usually grown as a medium-sized shrub and remains a firm favorite with the rose-buying public. The breeder named it for his daughter.

Bugnet, France, 1950
(IR. acicularis × R. rugosa kamtchatica] ×
[R. amblyotis × R. rugosa plena]) × 'Betty Bland'
Repeat flowering | *Spicy fragrance*

HABIT Bush H/W 1.2m/1.2m (4ft/4ft) | ZONES 4–11

'Tiffany'

HYBRID TEA | PINK BLEND

This 1955 AARS winner from Bob Lindquist is a favorite pink rose. Its cool, silvery color is made luminous by a glow of yellow at the heart, and the long buds open to wide, elegant, double flowers. It is a grandchild of 'Talisman', from which it inherits upright growth, olive-green foliage and delightful fragrance. It is an easy rose to grow, being of sturdy disposition. The ARS gave it the Gamble Medal for fragrance in 1962, and it will probably be around for many years yet.

Lindquist, USA, 1954
'Charlotte Armstrong' × 'Girona'
Repeat flowering ı *Intense fragrance*

HABIT Bush H/W 1.2m/1m (4ft/3ft) ı ZONES 5–11

Portland (Oregon, USA) Gold Medal 1954, All-America Rose Selection 1955, American Rose Society David Fuerstenberg Award 1957, American Rose Society James Alexander Gamble Fragrance Medal 1962

'Tiki'

FLORIBUNDA ı PINK BLEND

The double flowers of 'Tiki' are fairly large, to 9cm (3½ in), shapely and slightly fragrant. The color is a blend of salmon-pink and coral-pink – deeper on the outside of the bloom, paler at the heart, rather in the manner of 'Pink Parfait'. They tend to come in clusters, and are borne on a sturdy bush with glossy, dark green foliage. 'Tiki' has never been nearly as popular as its sister seedling 'Violet Carson'. It was named by Sam McGredy on

the occasion of a 1964 visit to New Zealand, where he subsequently settled.

McGredy, Northern Ireland, UK, 1964
'Madame Léon Cuny' × 'Spartan'
Repeat flowering ı *Slight fragrance*

HABIT Bush H/W 1m/60cm (3ft/2ft) ı ZONES 5–11

'Tineke'

HYBRID TEA ı WHITE

This variety was initially grown as a green-house flower for the florist trade and was subsequently found to perform equally well in the garden. It is a regular winner on the show bench. Long, pointed buds with green tints unfurl to classically formed, double flowers of creamy white. Borne singly on strong stems, they last well both on the bush and in the vase, and are nicely complemented by semi-glossy, dark green foliage. The plant is very vigorous, growing to above-average height, especially in hot climates.

Select Roses BV, The Netherlands, 1989
Seedling × seedling
Repeat flowering ı *Light fragrance*

HABIT Bush H/W 1.5m/1.2m (5ft/4ft) ı ZONES 5–11

'Tintinara'

HYBRID TEA ı ORANGE RED

The double blooms are fairly large and usually borne in clusters, more like a Grandiflora than a Hybrid Tea. The outer petals are a highly unusual color of poppy-red, and the inner

petals are of light porcelain-pink. The flowers are high-centred, becoming more cupped as they slowly open. There is only a slight fragrance. The plant is tall, upright and very free-blooming, ideal for bedding, borders or even hedges. 'Tintinara' has the distinction of having been pipped at the post for 'Golden Rose of The Hague' no fewer than three times!

DICuptight ı Dickson, Northern Ireland, UK, 1999
'Melody Maker' × seedling
Repeat flowering ı *Slight fragrance*

HABIT Bush H/W 1.8m/1.2m (6ft/4ft) ı ZONES 5–11

The Hague Gold Medal 1994, Casino of Baden-Baden Award 1997, Rose Introducers of New Zealand Gold Medal 1999

'Titian'

FLORIBUNDA ı DEEP PINK

'Titian' is classed officially as a Floribunda, but in Australia, where it was raised and introduced in 1950, its vigor is such that it is always grown as a large shrub or trained as a pillar rose. Few roses can outdazzle it when it is in

'Tony Jacklin'

'Tineke'

'Tiki'

'Tintinara'

'Toprose'

'Titian'

'Top Notch'

full bloom, covered from top to bottom with large, lightly fragrant flowers. Their color is extraordinary: close up they are deep pink, but at a little distance the sun lends them such brilliance that they seem scarlet, and their tone intensifies with age. One of the healthiest and easiest of all roses to grow, it was raised by Frank Riethmuller of Sydney, apparently from the Kordes Shrub Rose strain. The foliage is soft green. A very vigorous climbing sport appeared in Germany in 1964.

Riethmuller, Australia, 1950
Parentage unknown
Repeat flowering ı *Slight fragrance*

HABIT Bush H/W 1.5m/1.2m (5ft/4ft) ı ZONES 5–11

'Today'

GRANDIFLORA ı ORANGE BLEND

The double flowers of 'Today' are, perhaps, a bit too small to be in proportion to the very strong, tall bush, but people made this same complaint about 'Pascali' and it was a great hit. Everything else is good news: the blooms are shapely and long–lasting; they hold their bright orange and yellow until they drop, without going red or purple; and they harmonize perfectly with the bronze-green foliage. The scent is quite good.

MACcompu ı McGredy, New Zealand, 1989
('Typhoo Tea' × ['Yellow Pages' × 'Kabuki']) × (['Yellow Pages' × 'Kabuki'] × ['MACjose' × 'Typhoon'])
Repeat flowering ı *Slight fragrance*

HABIT Bush H/W 1.8m/1.2m (6ft/4ft) ı ZONES 5–11

'Tony Jacklin'

FLORIBUNDA ı ORANGE PINK

One of the shapeliest of all the exhibition-style Floribundas, and fragrant as well, 'Tony

Jacklin' has double flowers of a lovely soft shade of coral, luminous without being harsh. The clusters are not large, but nicely spaced, and the bush is strong and healthy, with semi-glossy, olive-green foliage. This variety deserves more attention than it gets; in humid climates, however, it is prone to mildew. It is named for the English golfer.

McGredy, New Zealand, 1972
Parentage undisclosed
Repeat flowering ı *Slight fragrance*

HABIT Bush H/W 1m/60cm (3ft/2ft) ı ZONES 5–11

✿ Madrid Gold Medal 1972, Portland (Oregon, USA) Gold Medal 1986

'Top Notch'

FLORIBUNDA ı APRICOT BLEND

'Florida', 'Matawhero Magic', 'Simply The Best'

The flowers are of a lovely, non-fading apricot color, medium in size, high-centred and fully double. They are long-lasting and freely produced throughout the year, and come both singly and in small clusters on a medium, upright, vigorous bush. Healthy and easy to maintain, 'Top Notch' is an excellent bedding rose and also makes a most attractive container specimen.

MACamster ı McGredy, New Zealand, 2003
'New Year' × 'Singin' in the Rain'
Repeat flowering ı *Moderate, fruit and anise fragrance*

HABIT Bush H/W 1m/60cm (3ft/2ft) ı ZONES 5–11

'Today'

'Toprose'

FLORIBUNDA ı DEEP YELLOW

'Dania', 'Roche du Theil', 'Top Rose'

The double, high-centred flowers come in large clusters and are of a brilliant and unyielding deep yellow. They have lots of substance, giving them a long vase life. The plant is of upright habit, and the mid-green foliage is large, tough and extremely disease-resistant. This outstanding rose would look wonderful in a mass planting, and is also ideal for borders or walkways, or as a container specimen.

COCgold ı Cocker, Scotland, 1991
(['Chinatown' × 'Golden Masterpiece'] × 'Adolf Horstmann') × 'Yellow Pages'
Repeat flowering ı *Slight fragrance*

HABIT Bush H/W 1m/60cm (3ft/2ft) ı ZONES 4–11

✿ Baden-Baden Gold Medal 1987

'Torvill & Dean'

HYBRID TEA | PINK BLEND

The British team of Jayne Torvill and Christopher
Dean skated their way to Olympic gold medals
and the adulation of millions. Their rose may
not be quite such a medal-winner, but it has
many admirers for its fine form and the way
pink and gold dance together across the petals.
The plant is strong and upright, with glossy,
dark green foliage. The fragrance is only slight,
and this variety has inherited a preference for
cool climates from its parents.

LANtor | Sealand, England, UK, 1985
'Irish Gold' × 'Alexander'
Repeat flowering | Slight fragrance

HABIT Bush H/W 1.5m/1.2m (5ft/4ft) | ZONES 5–11

'Touch of Class'

HYBRID TEA | ORANGE PINK

'D'Eleganta', 'Maréchal le Clerc'

The name is pure American; indeed, 'Touch
of Class' won the AARS award for 1986. It is,
however, of French origin, coming from the
long-established breeder Michel Kriloff of
Antibes; and in Europe it is just as likely to

'Touch of Class'

TOP 'Torvill & Dean'
ABOVE LEFT 'Träumerei'
ABOVE RIGHT 'Tournament of Roses'

be found as 'Maréchal le Clerc'. It is a very
fine rose, the large, double flowers shapely
and distinctive in their blends of pink and
coral, which grow more delicate toward the
heart of the flowers. The bush is tall and strong,
with semi-glossy, dark green foliage. Much
prized for exhibition and for cutting, it has
two faults: only slight fragrance and a predi-
lection for mildew.

KRIcarlo | Kriloff, France, 1984
'Micaela' × ('Queen Elizabeth' × 'Romantica')
Repeat flowering | Slight fragrance

HABIT Bush H/W 1.5m/1.2m (5ft/4ft) | ZONES 5–11

🌹 All-America Rose Selection 1986, Portland (Oregon,
USA) Gold Medal 1988

'Tournament of Roses'

GRANDIFLORA | MEDIUM PINK

'Berkeley', 'Poesie'

The double blooms are quite large, of fine
form, and often come in small clusters – hence
the American classification of Grandiflora.

The color is light pink, deeper on the petal reverse. This variety is reminiscent of the Hybrid Tea 'Madame Abel Chatenay' but with a touch of coral, although its scent is nowhere near as strong. The bush is tallish, with glossy leaves. It won the AARS award in 1989.

JACient ı Warriner, USA, 1988
'Impatient' × seedling
Repeat flowering ı *No fragrance*

HABIT Bush H/W 1.5m/1.2m (5ft/4ft) ı ZONES 4–11

✿ All-America Rose Selection 1989

'Träumerei'

FLORIBUNDA ı ORANGE BLEND

Dreaming', 'ReiKOR', 'Reverie'

This relatively little-known rose is one of the most outstanding of the larger-flowered Floribundas, its coral-orange flowers shapely, long-lasting on the bush and in the vase, and intensely fragrant. The bush is free-blooming and compact, with glossy, olive-green foliage. According to Kordes's Australian agent it makes a good companion plant for 'Sunsprite'. 'Träumerei' (or 'Dreaming') is one of the best-loved piano pieces of Robert Schumann.

KORrei ı Kordes, Germany, 1974
'Colour Wonder' × seedling
Repeat flowering ı *Intense fragrance*

HABIT Bush H/W 1m/60cm (3ft/2ft) ı ZONES 5–11

'Traviata'

HYBRID TEA ı DARK RED

The music-loving Alain Meilland has named two roses to celebrate Verdi's glorious opera *La Traviata*. The first in 1962 was a fragrant red-and-white Hybrid Tea now almost

'Traviata'

forgotten – a pity, as scented bicolors are still rare. The second is the crimson one in the photograph, which came out in 1998. It is a large flower, very double and well filled with petals in the nineteenth-century style,

well endowed with fragrance and lasting well in the vase. The bush is on the tall side, with glossy, dark green leaves and a very good reputation for disease resistance.

MEllavio ı Meilland, France, 1998
('Porta Nigra' x 'Paolo') × 'William Shakespeare'
Repeat flowering ı *Strong, apple fragrance*

HABIT Bush H/W 1.5 m/1m (5ft/3ft) ZONES 7–11

'Tribute'

HYBRID TEA ı DEEP PINK

'Tribute' gets a demerit for lacking the strong fragrance that one expects from a rose with its bright cerise coloring. Otherwise, it is a fine rose, its long buds opening to large, double flowers, ruffled and informal. They are borne singly on a sturdy bush of upright habit, with large foliage.

JACrose ı Warriner, USA, 1983
Seedling × seedling
Repeat flowering ı *Slight fragrance*

HABIT Bush H/W 1.4m/1m (4ft 6in/3ft) ı ZONES 5–11

'Tribute'

Tropicana = Super Star (handwritten)

'Trumpeter'

FLORIBUNDA ı ORANGE RED

Named, like its seed parent, 'Satchmo', in honor of the late Louis Armstrong, 'Trumpeter' is regarded by many people as the very best of the orange-red Floribundas. The flowers are medium-sized, neatly formed – without being especially shapely – and only slightly scented, but they are borne in great abundance and hold their jazzy color until they drop, without fading, burning, or turning purple. The foliage is glossy and mid-green.

MACtrum ı McGredy, New Zealand, 1977
'Satchmo' × seedling
Repeat flowering ı *Slight fragrance*

HABIT Bush H/W 1m/60cm (3ft/2ft) ı ZONES 4–11

❀ Gold Star of the South Pacific 1977, Royal National Rose Society Rose of the Year 1977, Portland (Oregon, USA) Gold Medal 1981, Royal National Rose Society James Mason Medal 1981, Royal Horticultural Society Award of Garden Merit 1993

'Troilus'

'Tuscan Sun'

'Troilus'

SHRUB ı APRICOT BLEND

One of the largest of David Austin's 'English Roses', this 1983 introduction is capable of producing some sumptuous flowers – huge, full of petals and with intense fragrance. They are a lovely shade of buff, paler on the outer petals. Often they come in clusters, when the individual blooms are not quite so large. The bush is moderate in growth, to about 1.2m (4ft), and sturdy, with broad, Hybrid Tea-style, mid-green foliage. It is named for the hero of Shakespeare's tragedy of the Trojan War, *Troilus and Cressida*.

AUSoil ı Austin, England, UK, 1992
('Duchesse de Montebello' × 'Chaucer') × 'Charles Austin'
Repeat flowering ı *Intense fragrance*

HABIT Bush H/W 1.2m/1m (4ft/3ft) ı ZONES 5–11

'Trumpeter'

'Tuscan Sun'

FLORIBUNDA ı ORANGE BLEND

The color of the blooms lives up to the name – an eye-catching deep apricot with a blush of bronze on the outer surface of the petals, ageing to an unusual coppery pink. Blossoming in generous clusters on long, sturdy stems, the flowers are very long-lasting and good for cutting. The plant is vigorous and free-blooming, with an upright, well-branched habit, and the foliage is glossy and dark green, with excellent disease resistance.

JACthain ı Zary, USA, 2005
'Singin' in the Rain' × seedling
Repeat flowering ı *Light, spicy fragrance*

HABIT Bush H/W 1m/60cm (3ft/2ft) ı ZONES 5–11

'Typhoon'

'Uncle Joe'

'Typhoon'

HYBRID TEA ı ORANGE BLEND

'Taifun'

The odds on getting a marketable rose from a batch of seedlings are thousands to one against. How much longer they must be against getting two from the same seed pod. That is what happened to Reimer Kordes in 1972 with 'Adolf Horstmann' and 'Typhoon'. The two are very much alike, 'Typhoon' having less yellow in its copper-gold-pink blend than its sibling. The bush is strong and healthy, with semi-glossy, olive-green foliage. The double flowers are so resistant to bad weather that, as Sam McGredy has said, it would take quite a storm to flatten them – hence the name.

Kordes, Germany, 1972
'Dr A. J. Verhage' × 'Colour Wonder'
Repeat flowering ı *Intense fragrance*

HABIT Bush H/W 1.5m/1.2m (5ft/4ft) ı ZONES 4–11

'Tyriana'

HYBRID TEA ı DEEP PINK

The name derives from Tyrian purple, a purple-red dye originally derived from a marine snail and greatly prized by the ancient Romans, who used it for ceremonial robes. The 40-petalled

'Tyriana'

flowers are of a deep rose-pink, a color in between red and purple. They are borne on an upright bush with leathery, dark green leaves. 'Tyriana' was raised by Meilland in 1963 and its spectacular coloring should have won it enduring fame, but it has vanished from the catalogues. It was photographed in the collection of the Roseraie de l'Haÿ, near Paris.

Meilland, France, 1963
('Happiness × 'Independence') × 'Paris-Match'
Repeat flowering ı *Moderate fragrance*

HABIT Bush H/W 1.2m/1m (4ft/3ft) ı ZONES 5–11

'Uncle Joe'

HYBRID TEA ı DARK RED

'El Toro', 'Gladiator', 'Toro'

This resplendent, multi-petalled variety thrives best where summers are hot and humid, and is a great favorite among gardeners in the southern states of the United States. It performs well throughout the growing season, the dark red blooms coming singly on long, strong stems. Ideal for cutting, the flowers have a long vase life and a hint of fragrance. The plant is tall, upright and very vigorous, with large, leathery, dark green foliage.

Kern Rose Nursery, USA, 1972
('Mirandy' × 'Charles Mallerin') × seedling
Repeat flowering ı *Slight fragrance*

HABIT Bush H/W 1.5m/1.2m (5ft/4ft) ı ZONES 5–11

'Uncle Sam'

HYBRID TEA ı DEEP PINK

'Uncle Sam wants YOU!' the army recruitment posters used to tell young Americans, but it seems that American rose-lovers no longer want 'Uncle Sam'. This 1965 creation from Bill Warriner has disappeared from the

catalogues. It is worth recording, however, for its large, long-budded flowers of a glowing, deep pink – not the rose-buyer's favorite color, admittedly. The bush is tallish, the foliage matt and deep green but not very luxuriant.

Warriner, USA, 1965
'Charlotte Armstrong' × 'Heart's Desire'
Repeat flowering ı *Moderate fragrance*

HABIT Bush H/W 1.4m/1m (4ft 6in/3ft) ı ZONES 5–11

'Uncle Walter'

HYBRID TEA ı MEDIUM RED

'A real man's rose,' said Sam McGredy in 1963 when he dedicated 'Uncle Walter' to his uncle, Walter Johnson, who ran the McGredy nurseries after Sam McGredy III's death. It is certainly virile in its growth, and is better regarded as a Shrub Rose than a bush rose. Try it as a red companion for 'Queen Elizabeth'. The double, blood-red blooms are of perfect exhibition form, but they need a cool climate to achieve any size. In Australia they are rarely more than 8cm (3in) in diameter. The foliage is glossy and olive-green, with red tints in its youth. The scent is only slight, but the brilliant color is quite unfading.

MACon ı McGredy, New Zealand, 1963
'Detroiter' × 'Heidelberg'
Repeat flowering ı *Slight fragrance*

HABIT Bush H/W 1.4m/1m (4ft 6in/3ft) ı ZONES 5–11

'Uncle Walter'

'Uncle Sam'

'UNICEF'

'UNICEF'

FLORIBUNDA · ORANGE BLEND

The holly-like foliage, very glossy and dark green, is a perfect backdrop for the luminous, multi-petalled, orange-gold flowers. The blooms are of good form, and in the bud stage have a slight hint of red at the petal edges. The plant is upright, very bushy and well furnished with foliage. It is very free-flowering all season and appears to be disease-resistant. Born of two excellent Cocker roses, it has retained the best characteristics of both.

COCjojo · Cocker, Scotland, 1993
'Anne Cocker' × 'Remember Me'
Repeat flowering · *No fragrance*

HABIT Bush H/W 1m/60cm (3ft/2ft) · ZONES 5–11

'Vesper'

'Valencia'

HYBRID TEA · APRICOT BLEND

'New Valencia', 'Valeccia', 'Valencia '89'

With its massive, saucer-sized blooms of light copper-yellow, this rose is very popular world-wide. The pointed buds unfurl slowly to multi-petalled blooms that fade but little as they age. The flowers are borne on long, strong stems on a plant with strong canes, upright growth and lovely deep green foliage with good disease resistance. Unfortunately, Kordes have reused this name several times in the past, causing some confusion with the rose-buying public

KOReklia · Kordes, Germany, 1989
Parentage unknown
Repeat flowering · *Light fragrance*

HABIT Bush H/W 1.5m/1.2m (5ft/4ft) · ZONES 5–11

🌹 Durbanville (South Africa) Gold Medal 1988, Royal National Rose Society Edland Fragrance Medal 1989, Royal Horticultural Society Award of Garden Merit 2002

'Vendôme'

LARGE FLOWERED CLIMBER · MEDIUM RED

As this splendid example at the Roseraie de l'Haÿ shows, this is a lovely rose for growing on a tall, free-standing pillar or tripod, which it will clothe from top to bottom with flowers for several weeks during the main rose season. They do pale a little as they age, but that only adds subtlety to the effect, and the foliage is good and usually free from mildew. There is little scent. Alas, 'Vendôme' has vanished from the catalogues, and its name has been recycled for a pink Floribunda — but perhaps we should not mourn its passing too much. Anyone wishing to create a pillar of roses in a modern garden can now choose from so many fine repeat-blooming climbers, which come in a variety of colors that the designers of the Roseraie could only dream of.

Parentage unknown
Summer flowering · *Slight fragrance*

HABIT Bush H/W 3m/2.5m (10ft/8ft) · ZONES 5–11

LEFT 'Vendôme'
BELOW 'Veterans' Honor'

'Via Mala'

'Victor Hugo'

'Valencia'

'Vesper'

FLORIBUNDA I ORANGE BLEND

In a photograph this lovely rose might look
to be just another salmon-pink flower, but
in real life it is a very distinct color that can
only be described as pastel-orange. The color
shows up very well under artificial light, which
makes 'Vesper' a desirable rose for cutting.
The double flowers are borne in clusters on
a sturdy bush with small, blue-grey foliage.
It seems to be a better rose in a cool climate,
though; hot sun can fade the flowers to
a 'nothing' pink.

LeGrice, England, UK, 1966
Parentage undisclosed
Repeat flowering I *Slight fragrance*

HABIT Bush H/W 1m/60cm (3ft/2ft) I ZONES 5-11

'Veterans' Honor'

HYBRID TEA I DARK RED

'City of Newcastle Bicentenary', 'Five-Roses
Rose', 'Lady in Red'

Patriotically named by its American raiser to
celebrate the courage and dedication shown
by his country's men and women in the armed
services, this rose is known by several names
in other countries. No matter: by whatever
name you call it, this is a very fine rose indeed.
The flowers are very large and shapely, opening

blood-red and later acquiring overtones of
pastel pink. They last well both in the vase
and on the bush, which is tall, healthy and
prolific, with dark foliage and a reputation
for doing well in hot climates. The scent is
light but sweet.

JACopper I Zary, USA, 1999
'Showstopper' × seedling
Repeat flowering I *Raspberry fragrance*

HABIT Bush H/W 1.5m/1.2m (5ft/4ft) I ZONES 5-11

'Via Mala'

HYBRID TEA I WHITE

Quite what Reimer Kordes expected from this
1977 cross of his mauve 'Silver Star' – rarely
seen now – and the bright yellow 'Peer Gynt'
is hard to imagine. The result is a most attractive
white rose. The blooms are double (33 petals),
high-centred and shapely, opening from long
buds, and the bush is upright, with glossy,
leathery, dark green leaves. The scent is
only slight, and you may find the blooms
need protection from prolonged wet weather
– a common failing of white roses, with their
delicate petals.

VIAkor I Kordes, Germany, 1977
'Silver Star' × 'Peer Gynt'
Repeat flowering I *Slight fragrance*

HABIT Bush H/W 1.5m/1.2m (5ft/4ft) I ZONES 5-11

'Victor Borge'

HYBRID TEA ORANGE BLEND

'Medina', 'Michael Crawford'

Orange is not the most popular color among
rose-growers, because it is not an easy one

'Victor Borge'

to combine with other colors in the garden,
especially reds and pinks. The blooms of
'Victor Borge' may change a few minds,
being a most appealing salmon-orange shade
with just a touch of peach – almost good
enough to eat! The double flowers are elegant
and well formed, and the plant is vigorous
and well shaped, with dark green foliage.

POUlvue I Poulsen, Denmark, 1991
Parentage unknown
Repeat flowering I *Slight fragrance*

HABIT Bush H/W 1.4m/1.2m (4ft 6in/4ft) I ZONES 5-10

'Victor Hugo'

HYBRID TEA I DARK RED

'Dreams Come True', 'Senator Burda',
'Spirit of Youth'

The rose illustrated is not Ernest Schwartz's
dark red Hybrid Perpetual of 1884 but a newer
one from Marie-Louisette Meilland, introduced in 1985. It is as dramatic as the great

French writer and patriot himself. The dark red flowers are huge, with a brilliant depth of color, and the foliage is leathery and mid-green. It is widely listed in France, but outside that country it is virtually unknown to date. The scent is good.

MEIvestal ɪ Meilland, France, 1988
('Karl Herbst' × ['Royal Velvet × 'Suspense'])
× 'Erotika'
Repeat flowering ɪ *Intense fragrance*
HABIT Bush H/W 1.5m/1.2m (5ft/4ft) ɪ ZONES 5–11

'Victoria Gold'

FLORIBUNDA ɪ DEEP YELLOW

Bred from two famous parents, this variety has inherited good characteristics from both. The blooms are fairly small, about 7.5cm (3in) in diameter, with petals of an intense golden yellow that deepens toward the edge. Borne in small clusters, they are high-centred and tightly formed, making them long-lasting and very good for cutting. The plant is tall and very bushy, with glossy, dark green, disease-resistant foliage. 'Victoria Gold' was

'Ville d'Angers'

'Victoria Gold'

introduced by the Rose Society of Victoria, Australia, in celebration of its centenary.

WELgold ɪ Welsh, Australia, 1999
'Gold Medal' × seedling of 'Gold Badge'
Repeat flowering ɪ *No fragrance*
HABIT Bush H/W 1m/60cm (3ft/2ft) ɪ ZONES 5–11

'Victoriana'

FLORIBUNDA ɪ ORANGE BLEND

The late E. B. LeGrice had a talent for raising roses in unusual colors, and this variety – one of his last – is one of the most extraordinary of all. The shapely, double blooms combine deep orange and brown, with distinct flushes of purple. The reverses of the petals are white. They are sweetly scented, and the bush, although not tall, is vigorous enough, with dark olive-green leaves. Flower arrangers are apt to fall in love with it at first sight.

LeGrice, England, UK, 1977
Parentage undisclosed
Repeat flowering ɪ *Slight fragrance*
HABIT Bush H/W 1m/60cm (3ft/2ft) ɪ ZONES 5–11

'Victoriana'

'Violet Carson'

'Ville d'Angers'

HYBRID TEA ɪ MEDIUM RED

Introduced in 1934, this French-bred rose was very popular in its day. Its cerise color was considered clear and bright, its petals were elegantly and regularly arranged, and it was well regarded as a bedding and general garden rose. It has lost popularity, and is now only seen in the collection of rose antiques at the Roseraie de l'Haÿ. It is not particularly fragrant, and compared with the lusty, glossy sturdiness of the post-World War II roses raised from 'Peace', its matt-leafed bush tends to look rather thin.

Delaunay, France, 1934
'Souvenir de Georges Pernet' × 'Souvenir de Claudius Denoyel'
Repeat flowering ı *Slight fragrance*

HABIT Bush H/W 1.4m/1m (4ft 6in/3ft) ı ZONES 5–11

'Violet Carson'

FLORIBUNDA ı ORANGE PINK

One of the leading characters in the early days of *Coronation Street* (which first went to air in Britain in 1960 and is one of the world's longest-running television 'soaps') was 'that dreadful woman' Ena Sharples, played by the late Violet Carson, who was

'Virgo'

'Violina'

a keen rose-lover away from the cameras. 'Violet Carson', the rose, bears the prettiest flowers imaginable. They are softly fragrant, of perfect form – like miniature exhibition roses – and of soft salmon-pink, with cream on the reverse. They come in good-sized clusters on an average-sized bush adorned with glossy, dark olive-green foliage, strikingly plum-colored in its youth.

MACio ı McGredy, New Zealand, 1964
'Madame Léon Cuny' × 'Spartan'
Repeat flowering ı *Moderate fragrance*

HABIT Bush H/W 1m/60cm (3ft/2ft) ı ZONES 5–11

'Violina'

HYBRID TEA ı PINK BLEND

Elegant long, pointed buds open to large, multi-petalled, shell-pink blooms. The flowers are borne singly on long stems, and are long-lasting both on the bush and in the vase. They are also intensely fragrant. A profuse bloomer all season long, the plant is vigorous and well branched, with large, glossy, mid-green foliage. This variety has a high resistance to both black spot and powdery mildew.

TANanilov ı Tantau, Germany, 1998
Parentage undisclosed
Repeat flowering ı *Intense fragrance*

HABIT Bush H/W 1.4m/1m (4ft 6in/3ft) ı ZONES 5–11
🏵 Monza Gold Medal 1998

'Vision'

'Virgo'

HYBRID TEA ı WHITE

'Virgo Liberationem'

For many years after its introduction in 1947, 'Virgo' was *the* white rose, loved for the purity of its color – warmed by just a suggestion of ivory at the heart – and for the supreme elegance of the way in which the shell-shaped petals unfold from the long buds. The open blooms, however, are rather flat. It is a rose that needs good cultivation, being only moderately vigorous and rather subject to mildew on its leaden green leaves. Wet weather spots the delicate petals. 'Pascali' may be more reliable, but a vase of perfect blooms of 'Virgo' is loveliness indeed. It is one of the jewels of Charles Mallerin's art as a hybridist.

Mallerin, France, 1947
'Blanche Mallerin' × 'Neige Parfum'
Repeat flowering ı *Slight fragrance*

HABIT Bush H/W 1.4m/1m (4ft 6in/3ft) ı ZONES 5–11

'Vision'

HYBRID TEA ı ORANGE PINK

'Benoni '75'

There are two roses of this name: one, a pink and gold Hybrid Tea, came from Pat Dickson in 1967. The rose shown here is the second one, which was introduced 10 years later by Niels Poulsen. It is a pleasing salmon-red rose, best in a cool climate (the 22 petals open rather too quickly in hot weather), its warm color well set off by shiny, dark green foliage. The scent from 'Vision', regrettably, is only slight.

POUloni ı Poulsen, Denmark, 1977
Parentage undisclosed
Repeat flowering ı *Slight fragrance*

HABIT Bush H/W 1.2m/1m (4ft/3ft) ı ZONES 5–11

'Viva'

'Vogue'

'Viva'

FLORIBUNDA ı DARK RED

This 1974 Jackson & Perkins introduction, raised by Bill Warriner, is no longer as widely grown as it used to be. It is still a handsome rose, the double flowers of deep velvet-red almost of Hybrid Tea size and beautifully formed. The plant is tallish and healthy, with glossy, dark green foliage, and usually well furnished with blooms. Perhaps the lack of strong fragrance, a quality expected in a rose of this color, has lost this rose admirers.

JACiv ı Warriner, USA, 1974
Seedling × seedling
Repeat flowering ı *Slight fragrance*

HABIT Bush H/W 1m/60cm (3ft/2ft) ı ZONES 5–11

Vogue

HYBRID TEA ı PINK BLEND

Back in the 1950s, the name 'Vogue' belonged to a popular Floribunda from Eugene Boerner, a sister seedling of 'Fashion' and very like it but a much deeper shade of coral. It is rarely seen now, and if you ask your florist for a bunch for your mother's birthday, he or she will offer you the shapely pink-and-silver Hybrid Tea in the photograph, which came from France in 1997 – and the flowers will probably have come from Ecuador, where the new 'Vogue' is popular with the greenhouse growers for its long stems and pretty color. Essentially a greenhouse rose, it is an indifferent performer in the garden.

PEKcourofondu ı Pekmez, France, 1997
Parentage undeclared
Repeat flowering ı *No fragrance*

HABIT Bush H/W 1.5m/1m (5ft/3ft) ı ZONES 6–11

'Voluptuous'

'Voodoo'

'Vol de Nuit'

HYBRID TEA ⏐ MAUVE

'Night Flight'

'Vol de Nuit' is one of the loveliest of the mauve Hybrid Teas, its color richer than most, and it is often warmed with pink. The double blooms are of good size and shape; the scent is excellent; and the plant is as strong as any of its color. (Many mauves are of only moderate vigor.) The foliage is matt and light green. The name is from the novel by Antoine de Saint-Exupéry, after whom the raiser, Georges Delbard, had already named a mauve rose.

DELrio ⏐ Delbard, France, 1983
('Holstein' × ['Bayadere' × 'Prelude']) × Saint-Exupéry
Repeat flowering ⏐ *Intense fragrance*
HABIT Bush H/W 1.4m/1m (4ft 6in/3ft) ⏐ ZONES 5–11
💮 Rome Gold Medal 1970

'Voluptuous'

HYBRID TEA ⏐ DEEP PINK

The very name conjures up visions of buxom blossoms! 'Voluptuous' does not disappoint, with its beautiful, exceptionally large blooms – high-centred and multi-petalled – their satiny petals of deep fuchsia-pink. Long-lasting both on the bush and in the vase, they come mostly one to a stem and occasionally

'Vol de Nuit'

in candelabra-like clusters of up to 10 florets. The plant is tall, upright and well branched, with glossy, dark green, disease-resistant foliage.

JACtour ⏐ Zary, USA, 2005
'Tournament of Roses' × 'Trumpeter'
Repeat flowering ⏐ *Light fragrance*
HABIT Bush H/W 1.4m/1m (4ft 6in/3ft) ⏐ ZONES 5–11
💮 Monza Gold Medal 1998

'Voodoo'

HYBRID TEA ⏐ ORANGE BLEND

If you are set on having the rare combination of brilliant color and rich fragrance, then 'Voodoo' is for you. Its blend of red, coral and gold stands out in the garden, and the fragrance is excellent. The bush is vigorous, with glossy, dark green foliage. If it has a fault, it is that the leaves could be a little bigger. It dislikes cool, sunless climates, but the color is better if it is grown in part-shade. It was

raised in California, under the hand of Jack Christensen, and won the 1986 AARS award.

AROmiclea ⏐ Christensen, USA, 1984
(['Camelot' × 'First Prize'] × 'Typhoo Tea') × 'Lolita'
Repeat flowering ⏐ *Sweet fragrance*
HABIT Bush H/W 1.5m/1.2m (5ft/4ft) ⏐ ZONES 5–11
💮 All-America Rose Selection 1986

'Waiheke'

GRANDIFLORA ⏐ ORANGE PINK

'Waikiki'

This is a most handsome rose, its large, semi-double blooms opening from long and elegant buds. The flowers are bicolored – coral with cream petal reverses – and come both in small clusters and singly on a tall bush. They have a light, spicy fragrance. The foliage is glossy and dark green.

MACwaike ⏐ McGredy, New Zealand, 1986
'Tony Jacklin' × 'Young Quinn'
Repeat flowering ⏐ *Spicy fragrance*
HABIT Bush H/W 1.8m/1.2m (6ft/4ft) ⏐ ZONES 5–11

'Warrawee'

HYBRID TEA ⏐ MEDIUM PINK

Mrs Harding Fitzhardinge named this rose for the Sydney suburb where she lived and gardened, and for many years it was one of

'Warrawee'

'Waiheke'

the most popular of pale pink roses in Australia, admired for the Tea Rose delicacy of its flowers and its ability to flourish in the acid, sandy soils of coastal New South Wales. The double blooms are high-centred and shapely, opening to reveal golden stamens, and exhale a sweet fragrance. The petals are a delicate shell-pink, a shade deeper on the reverse. The foliage is matt and dull green, and the bush is of average height. Introduced in 1935, it remains a rose of quiet refinement. The old growers say it likes fairly hard pruning.

Fitzhardinge, Australia, 1935
'Padre' × 'Rev. F. Page-Roberts'
Repeat flowering ı *Moderate fragrance*

HABIT Bush H/W 1.2m/1m (4ft/3ft) ı ZONES 5–11

'Wedding Day'

LARGE FLOWERED CLIMBER ı WHITE

'English Wedding Day'

This is an outstanding rose, widely admired for its ability to bloom freely and, later in the season, to show off its spectacular orange-red

'Westerland'

hips. The flowers are single-petalled, with colors of yellow to white, flushed with pink. They are borne in huge clusters on a very vigorous climber/rambler that send outs shoots up to 6m (20ft) long. An excellent variety to grow against trees or to cover a woodshed, it can perform well in any location, whether full sun or partly shaded.

Stern, England, 1950
R. sinowilsonii × unknown
Repeat flowering ı *Intense, citrus fragrance*

HABIT Rambler H/W 6m/5m (20ft/15ft) ı ZONES 5–11

'Wendy Cussons'

HYBRID TEA ı MEDIUM RED

That it has been possible to give the parents of so many of the roses in this book is a tribute to the dedication of their raisers. Keeping track of thousands of seeds and seedlings throughout the development of a new rose is a meticulous and expensive business. Walter Gregory,

'Western Sun'

although one of England's most successful rose-breeders, frankly admitted that he could not afford to do this, and that although the books give the parents of 'Wendy Cussons' as 'Independence' × 'Eden Rose', he could not guarantee it. No matter, this almost red rose is just about perfect – in a cool climate like Britain's. In warmer areas it grows so vigorously that many of its double flowers come malformed. The foliage is leathery and mid-green.

Gregory, England, UK, 1963
Believed to be 'Independence' × 'Eden Rose'
Repeat flowering ı *Intense fragrance*

HABIT Bush H/W 1.4m/1m (4ft 6in/3ft) ı ZONES 5–11

🏵 (Royal) National Rose Society Gold Medal and President's International Trophy 1959, Golden Rose of The Hague 1964, Portland (Oregon, USA) Gold Medal 1964

'Westerland'

SHRUB ı APRICOT BLEND

'KORlawe'

For many years this fragrant climber, with its bright apricot-orange flowers, went largely unnoticed. Then in the 1990s it was rediscovered serving as both a shrub and a climber depending on how it was trained to grow. The canes of this vigorous plant can reach up to 3m (10ft) in length, and bear large clusters of strongly fragrant blooms with 18–25 petals. The foliage is glossy, dark green and highly disease-resistant.

KORwest ı Kordes, Germany 1969
'Friedrich Worlein' × 'Circus'
Repeat flowering ı *Strong, spice and rose fragrance*

HABIT Bush H/W 3m/2.5m (10ft/8ft) ı ZONES 5–11

🏵 New Zealand International Rose Ground Trials Fragrance Award 1973, Anerkannte Deutsche Rose (Germany) 1974, Royal Horticultural Society Award of Garden Merit 1993

'Western Sun'

HYBRID TEA ı DEEP YELLOW

When Wilhelm Kordes introduced 'Golden Sun' ('Goldene Sonne') in 1957, it was acclaimed for its color – it is still the most luminous yellow of any rose – and deplored for the unreliability of its growth. Svend Poulsen promptly used its pollen on 'Golden Scepter', and gave us 'Western Sun' in 1965. It has much of 'Golden Sun's' wonderful color, but is a more reliable performer. It remains one of the better very deep yellow roses, even though it does like a bit of pampering. The double blooms are large and high-centred,

'Wendy Cussons'   RIGHT 'Wedding

'Whisky Mac'

'Whisper'

'White Delight'

'White Grootendor

the bush on the short side, with glossy, dark green leaves. The scent is only slight.

Poulsen, Denmark, 1965
Seedling of 'Golden Scepter' × 'Golden Sun'
Repeat flowering | *Slight fragrance*

HABIT Bush H/W 1.4m/1m (4ft 6in/3ft) | ZONES 5–10

'Whisky Mac'

HYBRID TEA | YELLOW BLEND

'Whisky'

One famous rosarian has described 'Whisky Mac' as the triumph of beauty over common sense. Everyone who grows it grizzles about its need to be pampered, but forgives it its unreliability for the sake of its wonderful flowers – when they consent to appear. Large, double, shapely and sweetly perfumed, they are of a unique, irresistible, almost indescribable color: deep gold, burnt orange or the color of a fine malt whisky? Even given the best of

everything, the bush is short-lived. The foliage is glossy and dark green. For all its faults, Mathias Tantau must have known it would be a best-seller when he introduced it in 1965.

TANky | Tantau, Germany, 1967
Parentage undisclosed
Repeat flowering | *Intense fragrance*

HABIT Bush H/W 1.4m/1m (4ft 6in/3ft) | ZONES 5–11

'Whisper'

HYBRID TEA | WHITE

Pointed, ovoid, greenish white buds open to huge, perfectly formed, clear ivory blooms. They are freely produced throughout the growing season and stay fresh for a long time, both on the bush and when cut. The

plant is vigorous – with a healthy, robust appearance – and the foliage is semi-glossy, dark green and disease-resistant.

DICwisp | Dickson, Northern Ireland, UK, 2003
'Solitaire' × 'Elina'
Repeat flowering | *Musk fragrance*

HABIT Bush H/W 1.4m/1m (4ft 6in/3ft) | ZONES 5–11

🌹 All-America Rose Selection 2003

'White Delight'

HYBRID TEA | WHITE

Jackson & Perkins's Rose of the Year for 1990 might be better named 'Off-White Delight', for there are distinct blushes of ivory and coral. The effect is delightful. The blooms are of good size and shape, borne on long, straight stems for cutting, and the bush flowers in profusion. Jackson & Perkins claim it is unusually quick to repeat. The foliage is glossy and dark green. The fragrance is slight.

JACglow | Warriner, USA, 1989
'White Masterpiece' × 'Futura'
Repeat flowering | *Slight fragrance*

HABIT Bush H/W 1.4m/1m (4ft 6in/3ft) | ZONES 5–11

'White Flower Carpet'

FLORIBUNDA ı LIGHT PINK

'Emera Blanc', 'Opalia', 'Schneeflocke', 'Snowflake'

The third of Werner Noack's 'Flower Carpet' series to appear, the white version was greeted with wide acclaim and high honors at the trial grounds. Many consider it the best of the group, citing its very pretty, pure white flowers and the health of its shining, dark leaves. Others grumble that the sprays of flowers are apt to grow on long, upright stems, making the plant rather taller than a true ground cover should be, and find their whiteness a little stark, especially when the plant is in full bloom and the foliage almost completely hidden. Still, it is a very popular rose.

NOAschnee ı Noack, Germany, 1991
'Flower Carpet' × 'Margaret Merril'
Repeat flowering ı Slight fragrance

HABIT Ground cover H/W 1m/1m (3ft/3ft) ı ZONES 5–11
Royal National Rose Society Gold Medal 1991,
Golden Rose of The Hague 1995

'White Grootendorst'

HYBRID RUGOSA ı WHITE

'White Grootendorst' came out in 1962, a sport from 'Pink Grootendorst'. It exactly resembles this rose in its fringed flowers and its ease of growth, and occasionally the half-open flowers will be tinged with palest pink. It is surprising that it has not become as well known as the others in the 'Grootendorst' set. In some ways it is the prettiest, and it would

look most attractive planted in tandem with the pink variety – maybe as a waist-high hedge – to flower from spring to the fall/autumn. It is just as resistant to extreme cold. The foliage is light green and quilted.

Eddy, USA, 1962
'Pink Grootendorst' sport
Repeat flowering ı Slight fragrance

HABIT Bush H/W 1.2m/1m (4ft/3ft) ı ZONES 4–10

'White Lightnin''

GRANDIFLORA ı WHITE

'White Lightnin'' won the AARS award partly on the strength of its fragrance, which is unusually intense for a pure white rose. It has other good qualities, too: the bush is sturdy and reliable, with glossy, dark green foliage, and the flowers are borne freely, both one at a time and in small clusters. The 30 petals are most attractively ruffled, and the color is clean and clear. The flowers are quite large, about 9cm (3½in) in diameter.

AROwhif ı Swim and Christensen, USA, 1980
'Angel Face' × 'Misty'
Repeat flowering ı Intense, citrus fragrance

HABIT Bush H/W 1.5m/1.2m (5ft/4ft) ı ZONES 5–11
All-America Rose Selection 1981

'White Masterpiece'

HYBRID TEA ı WHITE

'White Masterpiece' gives just about the largest blooms of any white rose: 15cm (6in)

'White Flower Carpet'

'White Masterpiece'

in diameter as a matter of course, and even bigger if you pamper it. It should be pampered, for it is not very free with its huge flowers, and in hot, humid weather the glossy, mid-green leaves are prone to fungus diseases. It is really one for the exhibitor, who will be quite enchanted with its perfect form and the delightful greenish glow in the flower's heart. The judges will not be giving it points for perfume, though.

JACmas ı Boerner, USA, 1969
Seedling × seedling
Repeat flowering ı Slight fragrance

HABIT Bush H/W 1.4m/1.2m (4.5ft/4ft) ı ZONES 5–11

'White Meidiland'

SHRUB ı WHITE

'Alba Meidiland', 'Blanc Meillandécor', 'Super Swany'

Meilland have introduced a series of 'Meidiland' roses, designed not so much for home gardens as for landscapers to grow on the verges

'White Lightnin''

'White Simplicity'

of roads or in parks. 'White Meidiland', introduced in 1987, is perhaps the most attractive. It makes a densely prostrate, sprawling bush, covering itself several times through the season with clusters of smallish, ivory-white flowers. The foliage is glossy and bright green. Its scent is a good point; many of the new Ground Cover Roses lack it. Meilland claim that the plants in the series need little care, can be pruned with a lawnmower set high every two or three years, and will put up with people walking on them!

MEIcoublan ⏐ Meilland, France, 1986
'Temple Bells' × 'MEIgurami'
Repeat flowering ⏐ *Slight fragrance*

HABIT Bush H/W 1.5m/1.2m (5ft/4ft) ⏐ ZONES 5–11

'White Simplicity'

FLORIBUNDA ⏐ WHITE

Bill Warriner scored quite a hit in 1979 with 'Simplicity', designed as an easy-care rose for people with little time for gardening. He followed it up with the red 'Bloomin' Easy' and, in 1991, with 'White Simplicity', to give a more or less matched set in pink, red and white. Some may find the white the nicest of the three; its compact habit, shining foliage and pure white flowers are a little reminiscent of its great-grandparent 'Iceberg', which was introduced in 1958 by Reimer Kordes. This variety is ideal to plant as a hedgerow.

JACsnow ⏐ Warriner, USA, 1991
'Sun Flare' × 'Simplicity'
Repeat flowering ⏐ *Slight fragrance*

HABIT Bush H/W 110cm/1m (3ft 6in/3ft) ⏐ ZONES 5–11

'White Spray'

FLORIBUNDA ⏐ WHITE

The incredible popularity of 'Iceberg' has led to other white Floribundas being neglected, despite their merits. This one, introduced in 1968, is a case in point. Compared with 'Iceberg', it is a more compact and upright grower, and the individual blooms are rather larger and more in the Hybrid Tea mould, with firm petals. They are creamy white in the bud, open snow-white, and are fragrant. They come in small clusters on long stems for cutting. The foliage is matt and mid-green.

LeGrice, England, UK, 1968
Seedling × 'Iceberg'
Repeat flowering ⏐ *Moderate fragrance*

HABIT Bush H/W 1m/60cm (3ft/2ft) ⏐ ZONES 5–10

'White Meidiland'

'White Spray'

'White Success'

'Wife of Bath'

'Wiener Charme'

'Wiener Charme'

HYBRID TEA I ORANGE BLEND

'Charme de Vienne', 'Charming Vienne', 'Vienna Charm'

'Wiener Charme' is one of those infuriating roses that is utterly gorgeous but temperamental to grow. Humidity will cause it to snuffle with black spot and mildew, and cold cuts it back. It is only in a warm, dry climate that you can rely on the tall, lanky bush giving anything like a generous number of its huge blooms in their unique color. The color was well described by the raiser, Reimer Kordes, as 'somewhere between copper and pure gold'. The buds are long, the open blooms loose, and they are fragrant. The foliage is glossy and dark green.

KORschapat I Kordes, Germany, 1963
'Chantré × 'Golden Sun'
Repeat flowering I *Moderate fragrance*
HABIT Bush H/W 1.5m/1.2m (5ft/4ft) I ZONES 5–11

'White Success'

HYBRID TEA I WHITE

The large blooms are very double (about 55 petals) and classically formed, and are borne mostly singly on long, strong stems. This variety thrives best in hot-summer climates, as heat helps the flowers to open properly. The plant is strong and vigorous, with healthy, semi-glossy, dark green foliage.

JELpirofor I Jelly, England, 1985
'Bridal Pink' × seedling
Repeat flowering I *No fragrance*
HABIT Bush H/W 1.4m/1m (4ft 6in/3ft) I ZONES 5–11

'Wife of Bath'

SHRUB I PINK BLEND

'The Wife of Bath'

One of the shorter growers among David Austin's roses, 'Wife of Bath' rarely tops 1m (3ft) in height, making a twiggy bush filled with small sprays of sweetly fragrant blooms. They open loose and cupped from fat buds to a pretty, old-fashioned color scheme of pale pink with much deeper tones in their centres. It repeats its bloom very well, and has the reputation of being an easy rose to grow. It is named for the liberated lady of Chaucer's *The Canterbury Tales*.

AUSwife I Austin, England, UK, 1969
'Madame Caroline Testout' × ('Ma Perkins' × 'Constance Spry')
Repeat flowering I *Intense fragrance*
HABIT Bush H/W 1m/60cm (3ft/2ft) I ZONES 5–11

'Wild Blue Yonder'

GRANDIFLORA I MAUVE

This new variety from Tom Carruth is a real eye-catcher with its unique color and camellia-like form. The wavy, velvet-like petals are of a warm wine-purple color overlaid on rich lavender. The fragrance is delicious, a blend of sweet citrus and rose. The flowers are borne in clusters and are freely produced all year on a medium-sized, upright plant that has a tendency to spread a little later in the season. The flowers are more deeply colored in cooler temperatures.

WEKisosblip I Carruth, USA, 2006
(['International Herald Tribune' × R. soulieana derivative'] × ['Sweet Chariot' × 'Blue Nile']) × ('Blueberry Hill' × 'Stephen's Big Purple')
Repeat flowering I *Sweet, citrus and rose fragrance*
HABIT Bush H/W 1.5m/1.2m (5ft/4ft) I ZONES 5–11
🌹 All-America Rose Selection 2006

'Wild Blue Yonder'

a genius in nautical astronomy, who in 1616, on a voyage in search of the North-West Passage, sailed further north in Arctic waters than anyone else ever had – a record that would hold for the next 236 years.

Svejda, Canada, 1983
Seedling of *R. kordesii*
Repeat flowering ı *Mild fragrance*
HABIT Bush H/W 2.5m/1.8m (8ft/6ft) ı ZONES 3–10

'William Shakespeare 2000'

SHRUB ı DARK RED

'New William Shakespeare', 'William Shakespeare III'

This newer variety supersedes the 'William Shakespeare' introduced in 1987 and is probably the best crimson 'English Rose' David Austin has so far produced. The deeply cupped flowers are a vibrant, velvety crimson with an indescribable sheen when young, ageing gracefully to an equally rich royal purple. The flowers are borne on strong, straight stems for cutting. It is a wonder that this rose was not called 'Romeo' in harmony with the codename.

AUSromeo ı Austin, England, UK, 2000
Repeat flowering ı *Strong fragrance*
HABIT Bush H/W 110cm/75cm (3ft 6in/2ft 6in) ı ZONES 5–11

'Winchester Cathedral'

SHRUB ı WHITE

'Winchester Cathedral' was introduced in 1988, the 900th anniversary of the Norman cathedral of Winchester, the cathedral with

ABOVE 'William Baffin'
RIGHT 'William Shakespeare 2000'

'Will Scarlet'

HYBRID MUSK ı MEDIUM RED

'Will Scarlet' is a sport from 'Skyrocket' (aka 'Wilhelm'), which Wilhelm Kordes introduced in 1934. It is identical to its parent except that it is a little more fragrant and much brighter in color. The foliage is large, glossy and leathery. It is a cheerful red rose, softening in tone as the flowers age. The name also connects it with 'Robin Hood', its grandparent.

Hilling, England, UK, 1948
'Skyrocket' sport
Repeat flowering ı *Moderate fragrance*
HABIT Bush H/W 1.5m/1.2m (5ft/4ft) ı ZONES 6–11

'William Baffin'

HYBRID KORDESII ı DEEP PINK

This variety is the most vigorous of the very hardy 'Explorer Series', and still as pretty as a picture. The tall, upright form allows it to be used as a climber – to 2.5–3m (8–10ft) high – or a dense shrub. The semi-double, bright pink blooms are produced prolifically all season. This rose is well known for its survival rate in even the severest of Canadian winters. It is named in honor of William Baffin,

'Will Scarlet'

'Winchester Cathedral'

'Wini Edmunds'

'Winning Colors'

the longest nave in England. It conforms pretty well to the David Austin style, with full-petalled, quartered blooms and quite good fragrance. The flowers are white, and the shrub is bushy and compact, flowering all season. The foliage is mid-green and lush.

AUScat · Austin, England, UK, 1995
'Mary Rose' sport
Repeat flowering · *Moderate fragrance*
HABIT Bush H/W 1.2m/1.2m (4ft/4ft) · ZONES 5–11

'Wini Edmunds'

HYBRID TEA · RED BLEND

Raised by Sam McGredy and named as a surprise present for the wife of his American agent, Fred Edmunds, 'Wini Edmunds' is certainly a striking flower, blood-red with a white reverse. Large, double and shapely, it would make a fine candidate for prizes on the show bench. Judging from the parentage, it is probably happiest in cool climates. This is fitting, as the Edmunds nursery is in Oregon. The foliage is glossy, leathery and dark green.

McGredy, New Zealand, 1973
'Red Lion' × 'Hanne'
Repeat flowering · *Moderate fragrance*
HABIT Bush H/W 1.4m/1m (4ft 6in/3ft) · ZONES 5–11

'Winning Colors'

GRANDIFLORA · ORANGE BLEND

'Winning Colors' was introduced in a very limited way in 1989 and marked the debut of rose-breeder Jerry Twomey, who went on to raise the AARS winners 'Sheer Elegance' and 'All That Jazz' and has more recently developed a range of easy-care roses trademarked 'Dream Roses'. It is really best treated as a Hybrid Tea, as the clusters are rather small. Its gold and scarlet colors are spectacular, and with disbudding it makes a knockout exhibition rose. It is pleasantly but not outstandingly fragrant. The foliage is very glossy and dark green.

TWOwin · Twomey, USA, 1989
'Gingersnap' × 'Marina'
Repeat flowering · *Musk fragrance*
HABIT Bush H/W 1.5m/1.2m (5ft/4ft) · ZONES 5–11

'Wise Portia'

SHRUB · MAUVE

One of the shorter growers among David Austin's 'English Roses', rarely touching 1m (3ft) in height, 'Wise Portia' bears large blooms filled with petals and fragrance in the

'Wise Portia'

Old Garden Rose manner. They vary a bit with the season. At their best they are a rich, deep pink, flushed with purple and mauve. Give this rose favored treatment to see it at its best. The foliage is matt and mid-green. The very model of wisdom and sagacity, Portia is the heroine of Shakespeare's *The Merchant of Venice*.

AUSport · Austin, England, UK, 1983
'The Knight' × seedling
Repeat flowering · *Intense fragrance*
HABIT Bush H/W 75cm/75cm (2ft 6in/2ft 6in) · ZONES 5–11

'Woburn Abbey'

FLORIBUNDA | ORANGE BLEND

Up until 1960, real orange-juice orange was unknown as a rose color except as a fleeting tint in blends like 'Signora', so it was remarkable when the color suddenly appeared in three new roses: 'Zambra' (France) and 'Golden Slippers' (United States), both in 1961, and then 'Woburn Abbey' a year later. Most rose-lovers quickly decided that 'Woburn Abbey' was the best of them. Of the three, it is the strongest and the most disease-resistant. The double flowers are borne in clusters, and the foliage is leathery and mid-green, with red tints. Much to everyone's surprise, this variety was raised by two English gardeners, G. Sidey and A. Cobley, who dabbled with a cross that had previously yielded nothing for professional rose-breeders.

Sidey and Cobley, England, UK, 1962
'Masquerade' × 'Fashion'
Repeat flowering | *Moderate fragrance*
HABIT Bush H/W 1m/60cm (3ft/2ft) | ZONES 5–11

'Woman and Home'

HYBRID TEA | ORANGE BLEND

The name will seem less sexist when one remembers that the rose was sponsored by the popular English women's magazine of that name. 'Woman and Home' bears large, double, regularly shaped blooms on a good bush with glossy, dark green foliage. The color, officially described as orange, is really only so in the young bud. The blooms open a blended coral-pink. The fragrance is only slight. This rose was raised by Walter Gregory of Nottingham and seems happiest in an English-style cool climate.

Gregory, England, UK, 1976
'Apricot Silk' × seedling of 'Piccadilly'
Repeat flowering | *Slight fragrance*
HABIT Bush H/W 1.4m/1m (4.5ft/3ft) | ZONES 5–10

'Yabadabadoo'

'Woburn Abbey'
'World Peace'

'World Peace'

HYBRID TEA | PINK BLEND

Presumably named as an expression of aspiration and hope, 'World Peace' has double flowers of remarkable color – they are basically straw-colored, but heavily and variably overlaid with a melange of tones from pink to maroon and red, with a bit of gold and coral thrown in. The foliage is dark green, the plant bushy, and the fragrance mildly fruity.

BURworre | Perry, USA, 1987
'First Prize' × 'Gold Glow'
Repeat flowering | *Fruity fragrance*
HABIT Bush H/W 1.4m/1m (4ft 6in/3ft) | ZONES 5–11

'Yabadabadoo'

HYBRID TEA | DEEP YELLOW

Fred Flintstone would yell 'yabadabadoo' when something pleased him. Sam McGredy was probably trying to tell us that this is a most pleasing rose. Whether the rest of the world has been all that excited about it is hard to say, because one does not come across it very

'Woman and Home'

often in gardens or catalogues It is a good, bushy grower, with semi-glossy, mid-green leaves, and the flowers are a lovely shade of deep yellow. They are large but rather short on petals (20) and perfume.

MACyaba | McGredy, New Zealand, 1981
'Yellow Pages' × 'Bonfire Night'
Repeat flowering | *Slight fragrance*
HABIT Bush H/W 1.4m/1m (4ft 6in/3ft) | ZONES 5–11

*Ah, no man
knows, through what
wild centuries roves
back the rose.*

WALTER DE LA MARE
(1873–1956)

INDEED — THE FOSSIL RECORD SHOWS THAT ROSES BLOSSOMED FOR MANY MILLIONS OF YEARS BEFORE THERE WERE HUMANS TO ADMIRE THEM. YET THERE WERE NONE ADORNING THE LANDS SOUTH OF THE EQUATOR UNTIL EUROPEAN SETTLERS BROUGHT THEM THERE — TO SOUTH AMERICA IN THE SIXTEENTH CENTURY, TO SOUTHERN AFRICA IN THE SEVENTEENTH CENTURY, AND FINALLY TO AUSTRALIA AT THE END OF THE EIGHTEENTH CENTURY.

It is recorded that when the First Fleet stopped at Cape Town on its way from Britain to Botany Bay, it picked up seeds and plants and livestock for the new colony. While the emphasis, naturally enough, was on plants that would provide food, it is not too far-fetched to imagine that a rosebush or two also found its way aboard. In a very strange land just about as far from home as it was possible to travel, the sight of a rose would have been a comforting reminder of home.

Roses in colonial gardens

The difficulties of establishing the new colony were very great, but by the early years of the nineteenth century they had been largely overcome and the colonists were able to congratulate themselves on their neat houses, each with its own garden. Modest these gardens may have been, most of them, but they shaped the ideal that has been espoused ever since — Australians have always been reluctant apartment dwellers. Gardens flourished in the virgin soil and mild climate, and every visitor, and every letter to relatives in England, spoke of them abounding with fruits that were luxuries at home — peaches, oranges, figs, melons, passionfruit, and grapes ripe with the promise of fine Australian wine.

The gardens abounded in flowers, too; and while some English favorites like primroses and bluebells found the climate a bit warm for their liking, everyone remarked on the beauty of the roses. No part of Australia is cold enough for roses to need winter protection, and the tender China and Tea Roses were great favorites, flowering all year and growing so luxuriantly that people made hedges of them. (In recent years an internationally important reference collection of frost-tender roses has been established at Carrick Hill in Adelaide in collaboration with the South Australian state government.)

Homesick colonials could not resist bringing out the dog rose (*R. canina*) and the scented-leafed sweet briar (*R. eglanteria*) also. Useful as these two were for making prickly enclosures for stockyards, they have gone feral in much of south-eastern Australia and been demoted to the status of weeds.

Nurseries sprang up to import and grow plants of all types, including the latest roses. In return they sent examples of the indigenous flora to Europe, where one of the leading enthusiasts was none other than the Empress Joséphine, who was very proud of her fine collection of Australian plants — and of the black swans on her lake at Malmaison.

TOP LEFT 'Crown Princess Mary', raised by Andrew Ross and named for the Australian-born Crown Princess of Denmark.

ABOVE RIGHT 'Amazing Grace', a new Hybrid Tea from Adelaide's Andrew Ross.

LEFT 'Burgundy Iceberg', a sport from 'Iceberg', from Swanes Nurseries in Sydney.

Antipodes

ABOVE Alister Clark's 'Black Boy', still a classic red climbing rose.

ABOVE RIGHT Clark's 'Nancy Hayward', photographed in mid-winter on Stirling Macoboy's balcony in Sydney.

A shrinking world

In the meantime, British settlers, led by missionaries keen to spread Christianity among the Maori, were arriving in New Zealand also. By 1840, when the treaty of Waitangi was signed, there were many flourishing homesteads there, with roses in their gardens. Very fine they were too, by all accounts; to this day the New Zealanders boast with some justice of growing the finest roses in the world.

With the advent of the steamship and the opening of the Suez Canal (in 1869) the long voyage to the Antipodes became a lot faster and easier. When a new rose made a splash in Europe or America, it wasn't long before Australian and New Zealand gardeners were trying it out. Not all proved suitable for the generally warmer climates and the different soils, of course; but many did, and then as now the rose-loving visitor could find many a familiar flower in gardens down under.

Roses from down under

For a long time the traffic in new roses was one-way, north to south. Then, in the late 1880s, the climbing sport of 'Souvenir de la Malmaison' was discovered in a Sydney garden and sent in triumph to Europe, where it made its debut in 1893. It didn't remain the only rose born down under for long, however. Early in the twentieth century Alister Clark began raising fine new roses in his garden just outside Melbourne. He raised conventional Hybrid Teas aplenty, but he is chiefly remembered for his work with the subtropical *R. gigantea*, which gave rise to such roses as 'Lorraine Lee' and 'Nancy Hayward', still classics in their home country. They inherit their Burmese ancestor's dislike of cold, but where winters are mild they remain unique. They are sensational in California.

Clark was followed by other talented amateurs, such as Patrick Grant and Frank Riethmuller, and more recently by Eric Welsh in Australia and Pat Stephens in New Zealand. Although some of their roses were quite successful overseas (such as Grant's 'Golden Dawn' and Riethmuller's 'Titian'), they were greatly outnumbered by successful roses from Europe and America. By the 1950s, air transport had made importing roses easy – budwood took only a couple of days to arrive from the breeder, and a new rose could be on the market within a year or two of its homeland debut.

Antipodean roses today

In 1972, the great Irish hybridist Sam McGredy moved his business lock, stock and barrel to New Zealand, and the world took notice of roses from down under as never before. He has retired now; but others, like Frank Schuurman and George Thomson in Australia, have taken up the good work. The passing of laws giving plant-breeders copyright in their creations, such as their overseas colleagues have long enjoyed, will ensure that they get a return for their efforts – and it has encouraged the major international breeders to appoint local agents. They send their promising seedlings to Australia and New Zealand for trial so that only those most suited to local conditions will be introduced, and introduced without delay. With very active Rose Societies in both countries – and with trial grounds in Adelaide, in South Australia, and in Palmerston North and Hamilton, in New Zealand – the rose-lovers of the Antipodes no longer need feel that they live on the far outskirts of the world. Not of the world of roses, anyway!

RIGHT The pillar rose 'Titian', by Frank Riethmuller of Sydney.

BELOW Patrick Grant's fragrant 'Golden Dawn'.

'Yankee Doodle'

HYBRID TEA | YELLOW BLEND

It would be appropriate for 'Yankee Doodle' to be an All-American production, and it is indeed an AARS winner, for 1976. But it is, in fact, a German rose, raised by Reimer Kordes. It is a splendidly vigorous plant, easy to grow and resistant to disease. The color of the flowers is admirable, yellow with flushes of peach and carmine. Their shape has rosarians sharply divided, some finding it full-petalled in the Old Garden Rose style, others describing it as overstuffed and shapeless. The foliage is glossy and light green. The scent is elusive but sometimes described as tea.

YanKOR | Kordes, Germany, 1965
'Colour Wonder' × 'King's Ransom'
Repeat flowering | *Tea fragrance*

HABIT Bush H/W 1.5m/1.2m (5ft/4ft) | ZONES 5–11
All-America Rose Selection 1976

'Yellow Butterfly'

SHRUB | LIGHT YELLOW

Ralph Moore is best known for his Miniatures, in the breeding of which he has used some unusual parents. He rarely introduces a rose that is not a Miniature. When he does introduce such a rose, you can be sure it is pretty good. 'Yellow Butterfly' is that. It is a sprawling shrub, with glossy leaves, bearing single, wide-open, golden yellow flowers all season. One is reminded of Roy Shepherd's classic 'Golden Wings', and Moore's choice of codename invites the comparison. To my eye, 'Yellow Butterfly' does not suffer by it, which is praise indeed.

MORwings | Moore, USA, 1989
'Ellen Poulsen' × 'Yellow Jewel'
Repeat flowering | *No fragrance*

HABIT Bush H/W 1.5m/1.2m (5ft/4ft) | ZONES 5–11

'Yellow Button'

'Yellow Button'

SHRUB | YELLOW BLEND

Hardly a tall shrub – at most 1m (3ft) in height – 'Yellow Button' nonetheless has a graceful, arching habit rather than the stiffer, more upright growth of a bush rose. The flowers are distinctive: not overlarge, borne in small clusters, and full of petals arranged in old-style quarterings. Their color varies: it is sometimes pale yellow,

'Yellow Butterfly'

'Yellow Pages'

'Yankee Doodle'

at other times deeper, but the richer tones in the centre are fairly constant. The foliage is a rather light green. 'Yellow Button' flowers profusely in early summer and again later.

Austin, England, UK, 1975
'Wife of Bath' × 'Chinatown'
Repeat flowering ı *Slight fragrance*

HABIT Bush H/W 1m/60cm (3ft/2ft) ı ZONES 5–11

'Yellow Charles Austin'

SHRUB ı LIGHT YELLOW

At first glance the name makes little sense, because 'Charles Austin' is itself yellow, albeit a blended yellow with flushes of apricot and pink. This sport is a clear lemon-yellow, and some people prefer it to the original. Introduced by David Austin in 1979, 'Yellow Charles Austin' resembles the original apart from its color, and like it will grow to more than head-high. They both benefit from fairly firm pruning, or they get leggy and less likely to repeat. The foliage is mid-green.

Austin, England, UK, 1981
'Charles Austin' sport
Repeat flowering ı *Slight fragrance*

HABIT Bush H/W 1.8m/1.2m (6ft/4ft) ı ZONES 5–11

'Yellow Pages'

HYBRID TEA ı YELLOW BLEND

The Yellow Pages are a worldwide institution, but don't expect to find advertisements on the petals of this rose! The blooms of 'Yellow Pages' are, as you would expect, deep yellow. Both parents tend to have red flushes on their petal edges; 'Yellow Pages' eliminates these, but keeps the fine fragrance of 'Arthur Bell'. It is a good yellow rose for bedding, its only fault being that the glossy, dark green foliage is a bit on the small side.

McGredy, New Zealand, 1971
'Arthur Bell' × 'Peer Gynt'
Repeat flowering ı *Moderate fragrance*

HABIT Bush H/W 1.4m/1m (4ft 6in/3ft) ı ZONES 5–11

'Yellow Ribbons'

SHRUB ı DEEP YELLOW

Within the classification of Shrub there are a number of varieties best described as Ground Cover Roses or, as the English would prefer, 'prostrate shrubs'. This variety fits that description to a tee. The plant crowds out the weeds for those who find hand-weeding a chore.

'Yellow Charles Austin'

The large, non-fading, yellow blooms are borne in clusters and last for weeks, providing a carpet of bright color 30–45cm (12–18in) off the ground. The plant sprawls about 1m (3ft) in all directions.

CHEwpatyel ı Warner, England, 2005
'Sweet Magic' × 'Pathfinder'
Repeat flowering ı *Light, fresh fragrance*

HABIT Ground cover H/W 45cm/1m (18in/3ft) ı ZONES 4–11
❀ Rose Hills (California) Gold Medal 2005

'Yellow Ribbons'

'Yesterday'

'Yesterday'

POLYANTHA ı MEDIUM PINK

'Tapis d'Orient'

Most Polyanthas are period pieces, but this
is modern, having been introduced by Jack
Harkness in 1974. It is a charmer, making
a lowish bush (although it occasionally sends
up a shoot or two taller than the rest), with
dainty, semi-double flowers that come in graceful sprays. The flowers are mid-pink with a
suggestion of lilac and, best of all, fragrant.
The foliage is small, glossy and bright green.

Harkness, England, UK, 1974
('Phyllis Bide' × 'Shepherds' Delight') × 'Ballerina'
Repeat flowering ı *Slight fragrance*

HABIT Bush H/W 1.2m/1.2m (4ft/4ft) ı ZONES 4–10

🌹 Monza Gold Medal 1974, Baden-Baden Gold Medal
1975, Anerkannte Deutsche Rose (Germany) 1978

'Yorkshire Bank'

HYBRID TEA ı WHITE

'True Love'

If ever there was a rose with two weirdly
assorted names, it is this one. Who associates
romance with a bank – unless, perhaps, a river-
bank. It is a pity that 'Yorkshire Bank' seems

'Yorkshire Bank'

'Zambra'

to be the most used name, as it really is quite
a romantic flower, in palest, mother-of-pearl
tints of pink and peach. The flowers are large,
with 36 petals, and are shapely and fragrant.
The bush is on the tall side, as one might
expect from the parentage. The foliage is
bright green.

RUTrulo ı De Ruiter, The Netherlands, 1979
'Pascali' × 'Peer Gynt'
Repeat flowering ı *Moderate fragrance*

HABIT Bush H/W 1.4m/1m (4ft 6in/3ft) ı ZONES 5–11

🌹 Geneva Gold Medal 1979, Gold Star of the South
Pacific, Palmerston North (New Zealand) 1979

'Yves Piaget'

'Young at Heart'

HYBRID TEA | APRICOT BLEND

'Young at Heart' is grown exclusively in Australia and New Zealand, where it was sponsored by the National Heart Foundation. In the United States, where it was raised by Armstrong Nurseries, it would be classed as a Grandiflora, despite its only average height, as the shapely, high-centred flowers are of medium size and come in clusters as well as singly. Pleasantly fragrant, they are an attractive shade of peach to apricot, sometimes veering toward light pink. The glossy, dark green foliage sets them off well. 'Young at Heart' was introduced as Australian 'Rose of the Year' in 1989.

Armstrong Nurseries, USA, 1988
Parentage undisclosed
Repeat flowering | *Slight fragrance*

HABIT Bush H/W 1.5m/1m (5ft/3ft) | ZONES 5–11
Australian 'Rose of the Year' 1989

'Yves Piaget'

HYBRID TEA | DEEP PINK

'Queen Adelaide', 'The Royal Brompton Rose'

In this rose, Marie-Louisette Meilland has tried to bring to a modern Hybrid Tea some of the full-petalled style of the Old Garden Roses of Queen Adelaide's day. The blooms are full-petalled and globular, and of a deep shade of Old Garden Rose pink, paling as they age. The plant is modern, however – bushy and upright, with large, glossy, dark green foliage, which is, unfortunately, rather prone to black spot. Introduced in 1983, this rose was named for a leading Swiss rosarian.

MEIvildo | Meilland, France, 1985
(['Pharaoh' × 'Peace'] × ['Chrysler Imperial' × 'Charles Mallerin']) × 'Tamango'
Repeat flowering | *Intense fragrance*

HABIT Bush H/W 1.5m/1.2m (5ft/4ft) | ZONES 6–11
Geneva Gold Medal and Fragrance Award 1982, LeRoeulx Gold Medal and Fragrance Award 1982, Bagatelle (Paris) Fragrance Award 1992

'Zambra'

FLORIBUNDA | ORANGE BLEND

'Magic Fire'

The success of 'Woburn Abbey' has not quite upstaged 'Zambra', which still has many admirers and has proved an important parent. The flowers have only about 12 petals, but they are arranged in beautiful clusters, and their pure orange, lightened with lemon

'Zorina'

around the stamens, is perfectly set off by glossy, bronze-green foliage. If only it were not so very prone to black spot. Raised in 1961 by Alain Meilland, it is named after an ancient Spanish dance. Much to Meilland's embarrassment, apparently, *la zambra* is colloquial in parts of Italy for what in Australia is called a 'dunny'.

MEIalfi | Meilland, France, 1961
('Goldilocks' × 'Fashion') × ('Goldilocks' × 'Fashion')
Repeat flowering | *Sweet fragrance*

HABIT Bush H/W 1m/60cm (3ft/2ft) | ZONES 5–11
Bagatelle (Paris) Gold Medal 1961, Rome Gold Medal 1961, Baden-Baden Gold Medal 1993

'Zorina'

FLORIBUNDA | ORANGE RED

This is one of those roses that is not often seen these days. Its name will bring back memories to some of the famous Hollywood ballerina and actress. It has proved a valuable parent, giving its offspring great strength of petal, lovely form and, considering its own slightly brash coral-orange, unexpectedly delicate colors. Perhaps its most distinctive contribution is the shape of its clusters: each double flower has a long stem of its own, so

that the inflorescence is not so much a bunch as a bouquet. The foliage is leathery and dark green. Primarily a greenhouse rose, 'Zorina' is fine in the garden in a hot climate.

Boerner, USA, 1963
Seedling of 'Pinocchio' × 'Spartan'
Repeat flowering | *Moderate fragrance*

HABIT Bush H/W 1m/60cm (3ft/2ft) | ZONES 5–11
Rome Gold Medal 1964

'Young at Heart'

miniatures and mini-flora

Suppose we made this cross
Another one not yet tried
Interesting things can happen
But we are never satisfied

So we try and try again
Many kinds o'er the years
Big ones, little ones too
Frustrating at times to tears

'OUR SPECIALTY' BY RALPH S. MOORE

424-447

miniatures and mini-flora

Anyone who has been to Disneyland or Disneyworld usually comes away humming the lilting melody of the theme song 'It's a Small World'. Well, you are about to learn about another small world, and a most delightful one it is – that of Miniature Roses, sometimes referred to as 'baby roses' or 'fairy roses'.

Stories about the origins of Miniature Roses have been greatly embellished over time. While the botanical evidence strongly supports the view that miniature rose strains originated in China, no miniature rose species have been found growing in the wild. It is generally agreed that modern Miniature Roses were developed from cultivated selections that were grown by seed and that self-pollinated. These cultivars were mostly single-petalled (5–12 petals), although some were double-petalled (13–24 petals), and they were mainly in the color range from white to deep pink. Cuttings from these seedlings were then propagated, and so the process of planned parenthood began. The resulting cultivars were introduced to Europe by seafaring traders, who transported plants from the Orient via Mauritius in the Indian Ocean.

The earliest miniatures

Many rose aficionados are of the view that modern Miniatures were largely developed from 'Rouletii' (Centifolia Minima, *R. rouletii*). In fact, the history of miniature roses goes back at least to the early nineteenth century, when Britain virtually dominated the seas. In 1810 the British captured the tiny island of Mauritius from the French. During the British occupation, botanists reported finding a plant bearing tiny roses. Soon afterwards various forms of this

variety were growing in gardens in England and a number of European countries. Because of their relatively small size, many plants were grown in containers as prized specimens.

The first known illustration and description of a miniature rose was published in England in 1815 in *Curtis's Botanical Magazine*. The magazine's editor, John Sims, referred to it as *R. semperflorens* var. *minima* and also as 'Miss Lawrance's [sic] Rose'. (Mary Lawrence was a noted floral artist of the time.) There are also anecdotal reports that miniature roses existed in France before 1810, suggesting that the French had already taken specimens back to Europe.

ABOVE 'Life Lines' (Climbing Miniature: Sproul, USA, 2004)
OPPOSITE 'Little Artist' (McGredy, New Zealand, 1982)

The next chapter in the story is well documented. In 1917, Swiss Army officer Colonel Roulet told his friend Henri Correvon, a Swiss plant expert, of a wonderful little baby rose he had seen growing in pots on a windowsill. He later published a detailed account of the discovery in *The Gardener's Chronicle* of 9 December 1922. Correvon named the variety *R. rouletii* in his friend's honor, and by making it known he gave breeders all over the world access to the genes that would allow them to breed miniature roses.

Important parents of modern Miniatures

While *R. rouletii* played a significant role in the development of modern Miniature Roses, so, too, did a number of other cultivars:

R. chinensis minima ('Angel Rose')

Although it has never been found growing in the wild, most botanists agree that this species (not regarded as a true wild species) originated in China, where hybrid forms such as 'Pompon de Paris' (introduced in Europe in 1839) and 'Rouletii' are considered to be closely related to it.

R. multiflora ('Multiflora Japonica')

This Species Rose is largely responsible for injecting vigor and the ability to bear multi-floret sprays into Miniatures. Its genes were introduced mainly via the light pink Polyantha 'Mademoiselle Cécile Brünner' (1881), which is descended from *R. multiflora*, as evidenced by its role as seed parent to Dot's 'Perla de Montserrat' (1945), De Vink's 'Cinderella' (1953) and Morey's 'Baby Betsy McCall' (1969).

R. roxburghii ('Chestnut Rose')

This small but hardy Species Rose from Japan and China was bred into Miniatures mainly by Ralph Moore of California, who introduced it via 'Floradora', a cinnabar-red Floribunda bred by Germany's Mathias Tantau in 1944 ('Baby Chateau' × *R. roxburghii*).

R. rugosa ('Hedgehog Rose')

The use of this hardy Rugosa species from Japan and China as a pollen parent with *R. acicularis* resulted in the Hybrid Rugosa 'Thérèse Bugnet' (1950). The latter has been much used to impart the vigor and disease resistance of *R. rugosa* to Miniatures.

R. acicularis ('Arctic Rose')

Via 'Thérèse Bugnet', a cross involving *R. acicularis* and *R. rugosa*, the cold-hardy shrub *R. acicularis* has introduced vigor and winter hardiness into the Miniature line.

R. wichurana ('Memorial Rose')

Known for its bountiful sprays of fragrant, pure white florets and phenomenal vigor, this cold-hardy rambler was employed extensively by Ralph Moore to inject into his Miniature breeding line strong vigor, ensuring ease of propagation via cuttings, and the latent genes that make possible the future development of both miniature climbers and miniature ground covers.

'Oakington Ruby' (1933)

Discovered by a Mr Bloom in an old garden in Oakington, near Cambridge, in England, this variety was used by Ralph Moore in the

breeding of some of his most important early Miniatures, including 'Janna' (1970), 'Yellow Jewel' (1973) and 'Windy City' (1974).

'Tom Thumb' (aka 'Peon', 1936)

The first rose-breeder to experiment successfully with 'Rouletii' was the Dutch nurseryman Jan de Vink. In 1936, he married it with the orange Polyantha 'Gloria Mundi' and produced 'Tom Thumb', a semi-double deep crimson with a white centre, following up with 'Pixie', 'Midget', 'Red Imp' and 'Cinderella', among many others. The significance of 'Tom Thumb' lies in its offspring: 'Sweet Fairy' (Jan de Vink, 1946); 'Baby Masquerade' (Mathias Tantau, 1955); 'Si' (probably the smallest Miniature to date: Pedro Dot, 1957); and 'Rosmarin' (Wilhelm Kordes, 1965).

The 'Father of Modern Miniature Roses'

As these building blocks were set in place, the breeding of Miniatures quickly gained pace. In 1940, Spain's Pedro Dot, already renowned for his many Hybrid Tea creations, introduced the first yellow Miniature, 'Baby Gold Star'. The first real commercial success was Francis Meilland's orange-red 'Starina' of 1965, which was one of the first roses to gain election to the American Rose Society Miniature Hall of Fame, in 1999. But while the Europeans were among the first to realize the potential of Miniatures, the title of the 'Father of Modern Miniature Roses' undoubtedly falls to Ralph Moore of Visalia, California. Through his wisdom and insight over an astonishing 60 years of experimentation, Miniature Roses have gained popularity, form, color, beauty and, above all, a place in rose history. His pioneering work in producing well over 500 varieties has bequeathed a huge genetic treasure trove to the rose-breeders of the twenty-first century.

Miniatures have rapidly gained in popularity, and by the 1990s the Miniature Rose classification was well established, with more than 1800 registrations. Also in the 1990s, the introduction of the sister classification Mini-Flora (roses with slightly larger florets and foliage) had immediate acceptance, resulting in more than 250 registrations. Largely thanks to the wonderful work of Ralph Moore, amateur Miniature Rose hybridizers have sprung up everywhere, for the facilities required to pursue an active program are simple – your own backyard!

'Amber Star'

'American Rose Centennial'

'Amy Grant'

'Amber Star'

MINIATURE ı ORANGE BLEND

'Brittany's Glowing Star'

Tall and vigorous, 'Amber Star' blooms profusely throughout the season and would make a pleasing addition to any garden. The orange and yellow flowers – with just a hint of pink during cooler weather – are classically shaped, and are borne both singly and in small clusters on straight stems. The foliage is medium green and has good resistance to most diseases.

MANstar ı Mander & Pazdzierski, Canada, 1999
'Glowing Amber' sport
Repeat flowering ı *Slight fragrance*

HABIT Bush H/W 60cm/30cm (2ft/1ft) ı ZONES 5–10

'American Rose Centennial'

MINIATURE ı PINK BLEND

'ARS Centennial'

Named to mark the 100th anniversary of the American Rose Society, 'American Rose Centennial' produces a profusion of double, creamy white blooms edged with soft pink.

The flowers have excellent classical shape, but lack the long stems needed to win 'Best in Show'. The foliage remains lush and dark green throughout the year, and has good resistance to fungal diseases. This is a very easy rose to grow and maintain, making it ideal for borders or containers.

SAVars ı Saville, USA, 1991
'High Spirits' × 'Rainbow's End'
Repeat flowering ı *Slight fragrance*

HABIT Bush H/W 45cm/30cm (18in/12in) ı ZONES 5–11

'Amy Grant'

MINI-FLORA ı LIGHT PINK

Named after a well-known Country/Gospel singer in the United States, 'Amy Grant' is a very vigorous, profuse-blooming variety. The large, double flowers are borne both one to a stem and in large clusters and are very long-lasting, making them suitable for exhibition and for cutting for the home. As with most white or light-colored flowers, however, the petals are easily marred by overhead watering or even morning dew. The plant is quite tall and disease-resistant, and is well covered with dark green foliage throughout the season.

TUCkamy ı Tucker, USA, 1998
'Loving Touch' × 'White Masterpiece'
Repeat flowering ı *Slight fragrance*

HABIT Bush H/W 1m/60cm (3ft/2ft) ı ZONES 5–10

'Andie MacDowell'

MINI-FLORA ı ORANGE RED

A lovely tribute to a well-known movie star, this variety produces vivid, bright orange blooms with a lighter-colored reverse. They are borne mostly in medium to large clusters but occasionally on individual stems. The flowers are high-centred, with enough petals

'Andie MacDowell'

---

to ensure that the rose holds its shape well, and have a slight fragrance. The plant is tall and quite vigorous, although the dark green foliage can be susceptible to mildew.

MICandie ı Williams, USA, 2003
Parentage unknown
Repeat flowering ı *Slight fragrance*

HABIT Bush H/W 45cm/30cm (18in/12in) ı ZONES 5–11
🌹 Award of Excellence for Miniature Roses 2004

'Angela Rippon'

MINIATURE ı MEDIUM PINK

'Ocarina'

An ocarina is a type of ancient flute native to Latin America and other parts of the world, but when Fryer's of Cheshire introduced this De Ruiter creation to Britain in 1978, they thought it better named for Angela Rippon, a well-known television personality at that time. By whichever name you know this rose, its salmon-pink blooms are outstanding. It is still one of the top-rated Miniatures almost everywhere. The foliage is dark green.

OcaRU ı De Ruiter, The Netherlands, 1978
'Rosy Jewel' × 'Zorina'
Summer flowering ı *Moderate fragrance*

HABIT Bush H/W 60cm/30cm (2ft/1ft) ı ZONES 4–11

'Anytime'

MINIATURE ı ORANGE PINK

This variety remains one of the best single-petalled Miniatures around, bearing huge clusters of semi-double, bright orange-pink flowers accented by a purplish eye – a characteristic it inherited from *Hulthemia persica* – throughout the season. The stamens are deep yellow. It makes a vigorous and dependable bush of medium height and spreading habit, with dark green, disease-resistant foliage.

'Angela Rippon'

'Anytime'

'Anytime' is an ideal plant to brighten any small area of the garden, performing freely even in semi-shaded places.

McGredy, New Zealand, 1973
'New Penny' × 'Elizabeth of Glamis'
Repeat flowering ⱼ *Moderate fragrance*

HABIT Bush H/W 60cm/60cm (2ft/2ft) ⱼ ZONES 5–11

'Arcanum'

MINIATURE ⱼ APRICOT BLEND

This is a beautiful rose, but one bred more for keen rose show exhibitors than the average rose-grower. The white to cream-colored flowers are attractively edged with deep apricot and sometimes pink. They are large and very high-centred, with thick petals that unfurl slowly. The blooms are borne mostly singly, on long stems, and while the foliage is larger than that of most Minis, it is in pleasing proportion to the size of the blooms. The plant is upright, bushy and quite tall, but has the major drawback of being susceptible to diseases, especially mildew. The large foliage is a real mildew magnet, and unless it is regularly sprayed with fungicide, you could find the disease spreading to other plants in your garden.

TUCkarc ⱼ Tucker, USA, 2000
Seedling × 'Kristin'
Repeat flowering ⱼ *Slight fragrance*

HABIT Bush H/W 60cm/45cm (2ft/18in) ⱼ ZONES 5–11

'Autumn Splendor'

'Arcanum'

'Baby Bloomer'

'Autumn Splendor'

MINI-FLORA ⱼ YELLOW BLEND

The full spectrum of fall/autumn colors is wonderfully reflected in each flower of this very attractive rose, making it quite an attention getter. The multi-petalled blooms have good exhibition form and stay fresh on the bush for a long time. The plant is tall and vigorous, with abundant deep dark green, disease-resistant foliage.

MICautumn ⱼ Williams, USA, 1999
Parentage unknown
Repeat flowering ⱼ *Slight fragrance*

HABIT Bush H/W 60cm/45cm (2ft/18in) ⱼ ZONES 5–10
🌹 Award of Excellence for Miniature Roses 1999

'Baby Bloomer'

MINIATURE ⱼ MEDIUM PINK

Producing an abundance of semi-double blooms of a soft pink blend all season long, mostly in attractive small clusters, this compact, low-growing variety is ideal for planting in a container, in front of your rose bed, or along borders or pathways. It is hardy and vigorous, with bright medium green, disease-resistant foliage. These qualities also make it a perfect landscaping variety, either to brighten an out-of-the-way spot or to use in a mass planting.

JACseboy ⱼ Zary, USA, 2007
Seedling × 'Boy Crazy'
Repeat flowering ⱼ *Light fragrance*

HABIT Bush H/W 45cm/30cm (18in/12in) ⱼ ZONES 5–11
🌹 Award of Excellence for Miniature Roses 2006

'Baby Boomer'

'Baby Grand'

'Baby Boomer'

MINIATURE ⱼ MEDIUM PINK

The American market has seen a veritable explosion of Miniatures of every color, form and habit since the 1990s. This award-winning variety is from the talented hands of Frank Benardella, the creator of many wonderful exhibition Miniatures. Naming varieties is an art form in itself, but this variety virtually named itself! The blooms are extremely prolific, with practically no rest period between cycles. They come mainly one to a stem, but occasionally in small clusters during the spring and the fall/autumn. The bush is exceptionally vigorous, growing to 1m (3ft) tall. The foliage is an attractive light green shade that nicely complements the pink blooms.

BENminn ⱼ Benardella, USA, 2003
'Ivory Beauty' × 'Kristin'
Repeat flowering ⱼ *Light fragrance*

HABIT Bush H/W 45cm/30cm (18in/12in) ⱼ ZONES 5–11
🌹 Award of Excellence for Miniature Roses 2003

'Baby Grand'

MINIATURE ⱼ MEDIUM PINK

This freely blooming variety produces small clusters of long-lasting, clear pink blooms throughout the season. The buds open to flat, quartered flowers very similar to many Old Garden Roses. The growth habit is bushy, compact and rounded, and the foliage dense and medium green. This is a plant that will thrive in your garden with very little care. It is also a great specimen for borders and walkways, or to plant in a small container to decorate your patio or deck.

POUlit ⱼ Poulsen Roser APS, Denmark, 1994
'Egeskov' × seedling
Repeat flowering ⱼ *Slight fragrance*

HABIT Bush H/W 30cm/25cm (12in/10in) ⱼ ZONES 5–11

'Baby Love'

'Blue Peter'

ABOVE 'Bees Knees'
RIGHT 'Behold'

The big, yellow/pink blend flowers have impeccable classical shape, similar to a classical Hybrid Tea, and hold their color for much longer than most yellow blooms. They are borne singly, on long stems. The plant is strong and vigorous, with an upright growth habit. The dull, dark green foliage has good resistance to mildew and other diseases.

JACkee ı Zary, USA, 1998
Seedling × 'Haute Pink'
Repeat flowering ı *Slight fragrance*

HABIT Bush H/W 45cm/25cm (18in/10in) ı ZONES 5–11

🌹 American Rose Society Members' Choice 2006

'Behold'

MINIATURE ı MEDIUM YELLOW

Finally, a great yellow Mini that has practically everything you could want in a Miniature rose. The double, bright yellow blooms, lighter on the reverse, are profuse, and are borne both singly and in small clusters all year long. The plant is vigorous and easy to grow, with a compact, round, bushy habit and an abundance of shiny, dark green foliage. 'Behold' is perfect for containers or borders or to brighten a corner in a small area, and looks truly stunning in a mass planting of 20-plus bushes.

SAVahold ı Saville, USA, 1996
('Rise 'n' Shine' × 'Sheri Ann') × ('Heideroslein' × 'Nozomi')
Repeat flowering ı *Light fragrance*

HABIT Bush H/W 45cm/30cm (18in/12in) ı ZONES 5–11

'Blue Peter'

MINIATURE ı MAUVE

'Azulabria', 'Bluenette'

'Blue Peter' is not really blue but lilac-purple. It is one of the smallest of the Miniatures,

and a real little charmer. It is not the first Miniature to claim to be blue: that was Ralph Moore's 'Mister Bluebird' of 1960, which for its presumptions has vanished from the catalogues. The flowers are semi-double, and the fragrance is only slight. The foliage is semi-glossy and light green.

RUlblun ı De Ruiter, The Netherlands, 1983
'Little Flirt' × seedling
Summer flowering ı *Slight fragrance*

HABIT Bush H/W 45cm/30cm (18in/12in) ı ZONES 5–11

'Brass Ring'

MINIATURE ı ORANGE BLEND

'Peek a Boo'

With this fine rose, Pat Dickson showed that he was just as good at breeding Miniatures as he was at breeding Hybrid Teas. 'Brass Ring' is of unusual breeding. It is a little large for the class and is usually listed as a 'Patio Rose'. The double blooms are copper-apricot, fading to rose-pink, and are borne in large clusters all along the arching branches – a charming sight indeed. The foliage is glossy and mid-green.

DICgrow ı Dickson, Northern Ireland, UK, 1983
'Memento' × 'Nozomi'
Summer flowering ı *Slight fragrance*

HABIT Bush H/W 45cm/30cm (18in/12in) ı ZONES 5–11

'Brass Ring'

'Baby Love'

MINIATURE ı DEEP YELLOW

You are sure to be captivated by the very small, five-petalled, deep-yellow flowers that this plant produces in profusion and almost continually throughout the year. It makes a small, vigorous, low-growing bush that is easy to maintain, with good resistance to fungal diseases. 'Baby Love' is an ideal plant for shaded areas, a small corner that needs brightening, or a small container on your patio or deck. The foliage is small, semi-glossy and medium green. To keep the flowers fresh for longer and prevent the color from fading, choose a location with at least 4–5 hours of sunshine.

SCRivluv ı Scrivens, England, 1992
'Sweet Magic' × seedling
Repeat flowering ı *Slight, licorice fragrance*

HABIT Bush H/W 60cm/30cm (2ft/1ft) ı ZONES 4–10

'Bees Knees'

MINIATURE ı YELLOW BLEND

This profuse bloomer has received much praise from gardeners and exhibitors alike.

'Butter Cream'

'Cachet'

'Cal Poly'

'Caliente'

'Candy Cane'

'Butter Cream'

MINI-FLORA | MEDIUM YELLOW

This excellent butter-yellow variety from the hands of successful amateur breeder Bob Martin has impeccable form and has proved itself a consistent winner at exhibitions. It flowers throughout the year, the blooms coming mainly one to a stem, but the color does tend to fade in strong sunlight. It forms a pleasing, well-rounded bush, with attractive, dark green foliage.

MARbutter | Martin, USA, 2004
'Anne Morrow Lindbergh' × 'Fairhope'
Repeat flowering | *Slight fragrance*

HABIT Bush H/W 60cm/45cm (2ft/18in) | ZONES 5–11

'Cachet'

MINI-FLORA | WHITE

This variety is one of the top exhibition Mini-Flora in the United States. The large, white blooms, borne both singly and in clusters, have lots of substance and keep their form and freshness for days. Like most roses in this color class, however, they are easily damaged by rain or overhead watering. The bush is vigorous, upright and free-blooming, but is prone to dropping its leaves during very hot weather.

TUCkach | Tucker, USA, 1997
Parentage unknown
Repeat flowering | *No fragrance*

HABIT Bush H/W 75cm/45cm (30in/18in) | ZONES 5–11

'Cal Poly'

MINIATURE | MEDIUM YELLOW

Long-lasting flowers of a butter-yellow color that does not fade even in the most intense heat are just one of the features of this very attractive variety. The double blooms are borne in small clusters and come fast and furious throughout the season. The plant is upright and bushy, and the foliage is semi-glossy and mid-green, with good disease resistance. Ralph Moore named it for California Polytechnic, the well-known university specializing in horticulture.

MORpoly | Moore, USA, 1991
('Little Darling' × 'Yellow Magic') × 'Gold Badge'
Repeat flowering | *Slight fragrance*

HABIT Bush H/W 30cm/25cm (12in/10in) | ZONES 5–11
Award of Excellence for Miniature Roses 1992

'Caliente'

MINIATURE | DARK RED

This outstanding, free-blooming variety comes from the hands of master amateur hybridizer Frank Benardella. The high-centred flowers, borne mostly singly, are of true Miniature size and almost look as though they are made of porcelain. They are long-lasting both on the bush and as cut flowers. The plant is low-growing and compact, with abundant disease-resistant, dark green foliage. Very easy to maintain, 'Caliente' makes an excellent container plant and is a good choice for borders or pathways.

BENdiez | Benardella, USA, 2006
'Ruby' × 'Timeless'
Repeat flowering | *Slight fragrance*

HABIT Bush H/W 60cm/30cm (2ft/1ft) | ZONES 5–10
Award of Excellence for Miniature Roses 2006

'Candy Cane'

CLIMBING MINIATURE | PINK BLEND

Although introduced in 1958, this very free-blooming variety is still popular in the United States. One of Ralph Moore's earlier successes, 'Candy Cane' bears huge, loose clusters of semi-double blooms, pink striped with white. Planted against a fence or a wall, it will present you with a beautiful tapestry of colors. The plant has good disease resistance and needs minimal care. Moore celebrated his 100th birthday in January 2007 – now that's longevity!

Moore, USA, 1958
Seedling × 'Zee'
Repeat flowering | *No fragrance*

HABIT Climbing H/W 1.8m/1.2m (6ft/4ft) | ZONES 5–11

'Chattooga'

MINIATURE | DEEP PINK

Tall and vigorous, with a spreading growth habit, 'Chattooga' needs plenty of room and is best planted toward the back of your rose bed. If you want to grow it in a container, you will need one with a capacity of at least

23 litres (5 gallons). The deep pink blooms are high-centred, and long-lasting both on the bush and as cut flowers. The flowers and the glossy foliage are both a little bigger than those of most Minis.

MICtooga ı Williams, USA, 2004
'Pierrine' × selected pollen
Repeat flowering ı *Light fragrance*

HABIT Bush H/W 45cm/25cm (18in/10in) ı ZONES 5–11

Award of Excellence for Miniature Roses 2005

'Chelsea Belle'

MINIATURE ı MEDIUM RED

A variety that needs very little care and yet performs magnificently all year, 'Chelsea Belle' bears very attractive double blooms of cherry-red with a white eye at the base of each petal and a silver reverse. The flowers have the classical Hybrid Tea form, and are borne on very long, straight stems – perfect for cutting. Even in hot climates the blooms come in small, attractive clusters. The plant has an

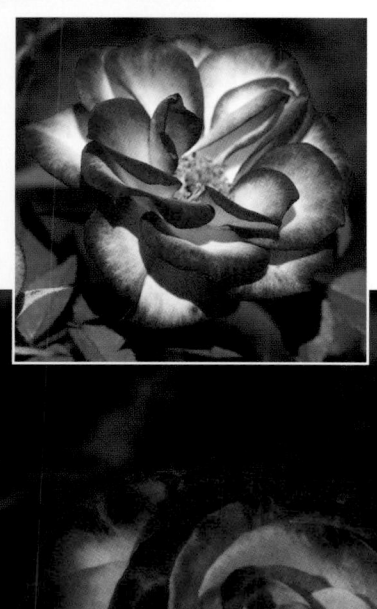

Top LEFT 'Chattooga'
Top RIGHT 'Chelsea Belle'
LEFT 'Child's Play'

upright growth habit and very dark green foliage. The hybridizers named it in memory of their favorite cocker spaniel, which was killed in an accident.

TALchelsea ı Taylor, USA, 1991
'Azure Sea' × 'Party Girl'
Repeat flowering ı *Light fragrance*

HABIT Bush H/W 60cm/30cm (2ft/1ft) ı ZONES 5–11

'Child's Play'

MINIATURE ı PINK BLEND

'Child's Play' is an outstanding Miniature in every category. The semi-double flowers, a delicate blend of porcelain-pink and white, are high-centred and sweetly fragrant. They are borne profusely throughout the season, singly and in clusters, and are long-lasting both on the bush and as cut flowers for a small bouquet. The plant is upright in habit and easy to grow, with good disease resistance.

SAVachild ı Saville, USA, 1991
('Yellow Jewel' × 'Tamango') × 'Party Girl'
Repeat flowering ı *Sweet fragrance*

HABIT Bush H/W 75cm/45m (30in/18in) ı ZONES 5–11

All-America Rose Selection 1993, Award of Excellence for Miniature Roses 1993

'Classic Sunblaze'

MINIATURE ı MEDIUM PINK

'Duc Meillandina', 'Duke Meillandina', 'Duke Sunblaze'

This variety was the first in the 'Sunblaze' series from the House of Meilland. The double flowers are a pure medium pink, and are usually borne in small clusters so profuse that they almost obscure the dark green foliage.

Especially long-lasting, they make outstanding cut flowers for the home – alas, with only a slight fragrance. The plant is compact in habit and easy to grow.

MEIpinjid ı Meilland, France, 1985
'Orange Meillandina' sport
Repeat flowering ı *Slight fragrance*

HABIT Bush H/W 45cm/25cm (18in/10in) ı ZONES 5–11

'Conundrum'

MINI-FLORA ı YELLOW BLEND

With its eye-catching, neon-like colors and outstanding classical Hybrid Tea form, this is a most attractive rose. The large, multi-petalled blooms unfurl slowly, making this variety popular with exhibitors. The plant is tall and vigorous, but the large, dark green foliage is very susceptible to mildew and rust. It is also prone to dieback during the summer season, but usually comes back strong once the weather cools off.

TUCkpuzzle ı Tucker, USA, 2002
'Cal Poly' × 'Kristin'
Repeat flowering ı *Light fragrance*

HABIT Bush H/W 75cm/45m (30in/18in) ı ZONES 5–11

'Cricket'

MINIATURE ı ORANGE BLEND

Raised by Jack Christensen, who raised some of the most spectacular Hybrid Tea roses in this book, 'Cricket' is a glowing little sun in brilliant orange and yellow, shining against very dark green foliage. The double, 25-petalled flowers are 3cm (1¼in) in diameter and give just a whiff of fragrance.

AROket ı Christensen, USA, 1978
'Anytime' × ('Zorina' × 'Dr A. J. Verhage')
Repeat flowering ı *Slight fragrance*

HABIT Bush H/W 45cm/25cm (18in/10in) ı ZONES 5–11

LEFT 'Conundrum'
BELOW 'Dancing Flame'

'Classic Sunblaze'

'Dee Bennett'

'Doris Morgan'

'Dr John Dickman'

'Cricket'

'Dancing Flame'

MINIATURE ı YELLOW BLEND

A real winner from the hands of its amateur creator, Robbie Tucker of Tennessee, this new variety is gradually taking over the rose show exhibition scene in both the United States and the United Kingdom. The double, yellow blend blooms have impeccable exhibition form and are long-lasting. They are borne mostly one to a stem, on nice straight stems. The bush is a prolific bloomer, with glossy, medium green foliage and good disease resistance.

TUCkflame ı Tucker, USA, 2001
Seedling × 'Kristin'
Repeat flowering ı *Apple fragrance*

HABIT Bush H/W 45cm/30cm (18in/12in) ı ZONES 5–11

'Dee Bennett'

MINIATURE ı ORANGE BLEND

This lovely rose was Harm Saville's tribute to the late Dee Bennett, the 'First Lady of Miniature Rose Hybridizing', who was born in Australia and was headquartered in the San

Diego area of Southern California. The double, exhibition form blooms, borne mostly singly, are a very attractive blend of orange and yellow, and are freely produced throughout the season. The plant is low-growing, round and compact in habit – perfect for a container or, indeed, to brighten any spot in the garden.

SAVadee ı Saville, USA, 1988
'Zorina' × ('Sheri Anne' × ['Yellow Jewel' × 'Tamango'])
Repeat flowering ı *Light fragrance*

HABIT Bush H/W 30cm/45cm (12in/18in) ı ZONES 5–11
❀ Award of Excellence for Miniature Roses 1989

'Doris Morgan'

MINIATURE ı DEEP PINK

With its high-centred blooms of an unusual deep neon-pink, this rose is increasingly gaining admirers. The double flowers are borne throughout the season, mostly singly and on long stems, but sometimes in small clusters. The plant is vigorous, prolific and quite tall, with a tendency to grow as wide as it is tall. It is a good choice for the middle of your garden or for a container, but you will need a container with a capacity of at least 23 litres (5 gallons).

BRImorgan ı Bridges, USA, 2003
'Jennifer' × select pollen
Repeat flowering ı *Slight fragrance*

HABIT Bush H/W 45cm/45cm (18in/18in) ı ZONES 5–11
❀ Award of Excellence for Miniature Roses 2003

'Dr John Dickman'

MINI-FLORA ı MAUVE

A small version of the Hybrid Tea 'Paradise', this is a beautiful rose, with deep lavender petals overlaid with red along the edges. The double flowers are high-centred, and are borne, mostly singly, on long, straight stems. The bush is vigorous, upright and tall, with hardly

any branching, and the foliage is greyish green, with good disease resistance.

BRImann ı Bridges, USA, 2001
'Purple Dawn' × select pollen
Repeat flowering ı *Slight fragrance*

HABIT Bush H/W 60cm/30m (2ft/1ft) ı ZONES 5–11

'Dresden Doll'

MINIATURE ı LIGHT PINK

'Dresden Doll' is perhaps the most charming of Ralph Moore's Miniature Moss Roses, and displays the best of old and modern characteristics. The small, soft pink flowers are perfect replicas of an old-fashioned, full-sized Moss Rose, loosely double and cupped in the old manner; and the buds are covered in scented moss. The plant's compact form, glossy foliage and perpetual flowering habit are very modern. The flowers are fragrant, too, although not quite as strongly so as an old Moss Rose.

Moore, USA, 1975
'Fairy Moss' × Moss seedling
Repeat flowering ı *Moderate fragrance*

HABIT Bush H/W 25cm/45cm (10in/18in) ı ZONES 5–11

'Dresden Doll'

'Dwarf Queen '82'

'Fairhope'

'Fancy Pants'

'Fashion Flame'

one stem — on a vigorous plant with matt, medium green foliage.

KINfancy । King, USA, 1986
'Baby Katie' × 'Rose Window'
Repeat flowering । *Slight, spicy fragrance*

HABIT Bush H/W 60cm/45m (2ft/18in) । ZONES 4–10

'Fashion Flame'

MINIATURE । ORANGE PINK

'Fashion Flame' is as lovely as any of Ralph Moore's creations. The small, double, exhibition form blooms are an unusual blend of coral-orange with a touch of lavender on the outer petals. They have 35 petals and are nicely fragrant. The foliage is large and coarse for a Miniature.

Moore, USA, 1977
'Little Darling' × 'Fire Princess'
Repeat flowering । *Slight fragrance*

HABIT Bush H/W 45cm/25cm (18in/10in) । ZONES 5–11

'Figurine'

MINIATURE । WHITE

The semi-double blooms are a very delicate light pink, not really white as registered, and have a porcelain-like quality. They are borne both singly and in clusters on very long stems, and are also long-lasting, making them excellent as cut flowers. The plant is upright, bushy and free-flowering, with very few prickles; the foliage is matt and dark green, with good resistance to black spot and mildew. 'Figurine' is an excellent variety for containers or beds, but it does have a tendency to spread, so give it some room.

BENfig । Benardella, USA, 1991
'Rise 'n' Shine' × 'Laguna'
Repeat flowering । *Slight fragrance*

HABIT Bush H/W 45cm/30cm (18in/12in) । ZONES 5–11

🌹 Award of Excellence for Miniature Roses 1992

'Dwarf Queen '82'

MINIATURE । DEEP PINK

'Zwergkönigin '82'

Apart from being deep pink instead of dark red, this variety is almost identical to Kordes's previous introduction 'Zwergkönig '78' ('Dwarf King '78'). The double flowers have excellent shape, and are borne on long stems on a compact, well-rounded bush. The foliage is small and medium green. The names 'Dwarf King' and 'Dwarf Queen' are not as unimaginative as they might seem — pick up your Grimm's Fairy Tales again and you will see.

KORwerk । Kordes, Germany, 1982
'Korkönig' × 'Sunday Times'
Repeat flowering । *Slight fragrance*

HABIT Bush H/W 25cm/20cm (10in/8in) । ZONES 5–11

'Fairhope'

MINIATURE । LIGHT YELLOW

Voted America's top exhibition Miniature rose by members of the American Rose Society,

'Fairhope' has dominated the rose show scene since it was introduced in 1998. The double, light yellow to cream blooms are magnificent, elegant and classically shaped, and are borne both singly and in clusters on long stems. The plant is upright and bushy, with dark green foliage, and blooms freely and consistently throughout the season. Not just easy to grow, this is a rose that is quite difficult to kill!

TALfairhope । Taylor, USA, 1998
'Azure Sea' × seedling
Repeat flowering । *Slight fragrance*

HABIT Bush H/W 60cm/30cm (2ft/1ft) । ZONES 5–11

'Fancy Pants'

MINIATURE । RED BLEND

The double, 40-petalled blooms are deep pink with a golden base and red-tinted petal edges, fading to deeper pink and sometimes russet as they age. They have magnificent exhibition form, and are borne both singly and in gigantic clusters — up to 30 blooms on

'Figurine'

TOP 'Foxy Lady'
LEFT 'Freegold'
CENTRE 'Glowing Amber'
RIGHT 'Good Morning America'

'Gizmo'

'Foxy Lady'

MINIATURE ı ORANGE PINK

This rather adult name, in a group where tradition has favored names reminiscent of childhood, was bestowed by Jack Christensen in 1980. The rose really is a beauty, blending salmon and cream in its long-pointed buds and double, 25-petalled blooms, which are 3cm (1¼in) in diameter. The bush is of dwarf habit, with small, neat foliage.

AROshrim ı Christensen, USA, 1980
'Ginger Snap' × 'Magic Carrousel'
Repeat flowering ı *Slight fragrance*
HABIT Bush H/W 45cm/30cm (18in/10in) ı ZONES 5–11

'Freegold'

MINIATURE ı DEEP YELLOW

'Free Gold', 'Penelope Keith'

This pleasing golden Miniature combines deep yellow with a shade that can only be described as old gold on the petal reverse. The small, double, 20-petalled blooms are perfect miniatures of exhibition-style Hybrid Tea Roses. The foliage is small, semi-glossy and light green.

MACfreego ı McGredy, New Zealand, 1983
'Seaspray' × 'Dorola'
Repeat flowering ı *Moderate fragrance*
HABIT Bush H/W 45cm/30cm (18in/10in) ı ZONES 5–11

'Gizmo'

MINIATURE ı ORANGE BLEND

This five-petalled rose is a real attention-getter when the flowers are fully open. The scarlet-orange petals have a very distinct white eye at the base, and the stamens are of a pronounced deep yellow. The flowers are borne in small clusters throughout the season on a vigorous, bushy, low-growing plant with semi-glossy, dark green foliage. 'Gizmo' is ideal for containers, and for half-shaded areas or areas that only get the morning sun.

WEKcatlart ı Carruth, USA, 1998
'Carrot Top' × 'Little Artist'
Repeat flowering ı *Slight, apple fragrance*
HABIT Bush H/W 60cm/60cm (2ft/2ft) ı ZONES 5–11
Rose Hills (California) Gold Medal and Golden Rose 2002

'Glowing Amber'

MINIATURE ı RED BLEND

A favorite both in the United States and the United Kingdom, this variety will quickly take centre stage in the garden thanks to its outstanding, neon-like colors. Long, pointed buds open to magnificent medium red blooms, double and high-centred, with a golden reverse. The flowers are borne both singly and in clusters on long stems, and they are long-lasting both on the bush and as cut flowers. The plant is upright, vigorous and prolific, but the lush dark green foliage can be susceptible to mildew. You can plant this variety in the ground or in a large container.

MANglow ı Mander, Canada, 1996
'June Laver' × 'Rubies 'n' Pearls'
Repeat flowering ı *No fragrance*
HABIT Bush H/W 60cm/30cm (2ft/1ft) ı ZONES 5–11

'Good Morning America'

MINIATURE ı MEDIUM YELLOW

Named for a popular morning television show in the United States, this variety is a favorite with home gardeners for its lovely yellow flowers and its free-blooming habit. Rose show exhibitors like it, too, but the very double blooms with their 45–50 petals can become top-heavy, resulting in crooked stems. It is a good garden performer with a tendency to spread, so give it plenty of room, whether in the ground or in a container. The foliage is lush, semi-glossy and dark green, with good disease resistance.

SAVagood ı Saville, USA, 1991
'Fantasia' × 'Rainbow's End'
Repeat flowering ı *Moderate, fruity fragrance*
HABIT Bush H/W 45cm/30cm (18in/10in) ı ZONES 5–11
Award of Excellence for Miniature Roses 1991

'Gourmet Popcorn'

'Gourmet Popcorn'

MINIATURE ı WHITE

This outstanding landscape rose is used extensively in both private and public gardens worldwide. The medium-sized, semi-double, pure white flowers are borne in extremely large clusters and produced almost continuously throughout the season. The plant is very vigorous and easy to maintain, with good disease resistance. It is also very adaptable, and can be grown in a container or a hanging basket or as a standard tree. When it is grown as a 45cm or 60cm (18in or 24in) patio tree, the canopy will easily mature and fill in within a season, and then start cascading down the sides.

WEOpop ı Desamero, USA, 1986
'Popcorn' sport
Repeat flowering ı *Light fragrance*
HABIT Bush H/W 75cm/45cm (30in/18in) ı ZONES 5–11

The Rose in Japan

PEOPLE IN THE WEST THINK OF JAPAN AS A LAND OF FLOWER-LOVERS. AND INDEED IT IS: THE IMAGE OF MADAME BUTTERFLY GATHERING CHERRY BLOSSOMS TO CELEBRATE HER LOVER'S RETURN IS ONE THAT STILL RINGS TRUE TODAY. EVEN THE RISING SUN OF JAPAN'S FLAG HAS BEEN INTERPRETED AS A CHRYSANTHEMUM, THE BEST-LOVED OF ALL JAPANESE FLOWERS AND THE EMBLEM CHOSEN FOR THE EMPEROR'S FAMILY SEAL.

The Japanese islands are abundantly rich in wild flowers: azaleas, peonies, the Japanese iris, wisteria, lilies, camellias, plum and cherry blossoms, and the chrysanthemum. Flowers are seen everywhere, displayed in what are possibly the world's most refined flower arrangements – even the samurai of old practised the art of Ikebana as a way of relaxing the body and focusing the mind – and featured in Japanese works of art of all kinds.

A different tradition

Several roses are native to Japan (among other parts of Asia), among them *R. multiflora*, *R. rugosa* and *R. wichurana*, all of which have given rise to beautiful garden roses in the West. At home,

however, they have been only mildly admired. True, there are fine old illustrated books on *bara* and *ibara*, as the rose is known in Japanese, but roses are scarcely ever to be seen in the great classical gardens of Japan, and they are not numbered among the noble flowers that scholars cultivated and wrote poems about.

The rose does not lend itself well to the traditional garden of Japan, which calls for evergreens and subtle seasonal changes within a tightly disciplined design. Its growth habit is too flimsy and wayward, and its flowers rather too eye-catching. It would seem, in fact, that the Japanese considered *bara* to be rather vulgar. It is perhaps telling that two of the earliest Japanese garden roses to reach the West, 'Seven Sisters' and the mildew-ridden 'Crimson Rambler', are said to have been found in the gardens of what are politely known as 'houses of joy'.

Japan had the refined China and Tea Roses from China for a thousand years before the West did, but it was not until the opening of Japan to Western influence with the Meiji Restoration that roses came into favor. Not that the new admiration for all things European and American extended to the well-upholstered Hybrid Perpetuals of the time; even with such traditional flowers as the peony and the camellia, the Japanese prefer more lightly built and graceful cultivars than the Chinese do.

The advent of the more elegant Hybrid Tea Roses helped the rose to find wider acceptance in Japan, but it was still a long way from challenging the traditional favorites when Japan's rejection of all things Western in the aftermath of the Second World War threatened to bring the rose into eclipse.

TOP OF PAGE In the West, artificial flowers are often made in imitation of the real thing, but in Japan they tend to be seen more as works of sculpture, and to be made out of such materials as ivory, tortoiseshell and glass. These stunning blooms, a triumph of the silversmith's art, were on display at a flower show in Osaka.

INSET TOP 'Saiun' (meaning 'Iridescent Cloud')

INSET ABOVE *Rosa rugosa* is widely known in the West as the 'Japanese Rose', but it grows wild in Korea and northern China as well, often within sight and spray of the sea. The name 'Ramanas Rose', sometimes still encountered in books, is a garbled version of the Japanese name.

LEFT The name of this rose, 'Tasogare', means 'in the twilight'. This variety bears prettily shaped, fragrant blooms in wide clusters on a spreading bush. It was raised by Moriji Kobayashi and introduced in 1977.

ABOVE 'Princess Aiko'
RIGHT 'Hatsukoi' (meaning 'First Love')

The triumph of 'Peace'

That that did not happen is, according to the late Seizo Suzuki, Japan's foremost rosarian, due to the introduction of Francis Meilland's wonderful 'Peace'. Here was a rose after the Japanese heart, its huge flowers wide and ruffled, its foliage handsome. If the peony was the king of flowers (as the Chinese held), then here, surely, was the queen.

The Japan Rose Society held its first national rose show in Tokyo in 1948, and interest in roses has grown ever since. The rose now ranks third in popularity in the flower shops, after the chrysanthemum and that other Westerner, the carnation; and if this trend continues, the rose may soon rival the chrysanthemum.

Japanese soils tend to be acid and the summers are hot and sweltering. Yet the Japanese grow magnificent roses; to go to one of the great flower shows, such as that at the Goodwill Dome in Tokyo or at Osaka, is to be overwhelmed by color and fragrance. All the latest roses from overseas can be seen on display, as well as the latest Japanese-bred roses. Starting in the 1960s, the late Seizo Suzuki, in cooperation with Keisei Nurseries, introduced a number of superb Hybrid Teas and Floribundas. These are relatively unknown outside Japan, with the exception of 'Olympic Torch' of 1966 and the 1998 AARS winner 'Mikado'. Suzuki is best remembered for the ever-blooming Shrub Rose with a fountain-like growth habit and bearing myriads of coral-pink flowers that he introduced under the name of 'Hanamigawa', meaning 'looking at cherry blossoms by the river'. In the West, it has the less evocative name of 'Ferdy'. 'Hanamigawa' built on a line of breeding initiated by Dr Toru Onodera, who created quite a stir back in 1968 with his 'Nozomi', a delightful creeping rose that gave rise to a new class called Ground Cover Roses.

Today, the elegant Hybrid Teas 'Saiun' and 'Hatsukoi' and the lovely pink Floribunda 'Princess Aiko' from Keisei are sterling examples of Japan's excellent breeding lines – which, it is to be hoped, may some day be exported for the rest of the world to enjoy.

From *R. multiflora* came, after nearly a hundred years, the modern Floribunda Roses, and from *R. wichurana* and *R. rugosa*, some of the finest climbers and Shrub Roses. Who knows what evolution of the rose Japan will sponsor next?

With thanks to Peter Okumoto for his research and assistance.

ABOVE Roses have not been a major motif in Japanese art, for all its preoccupation with flowers. Their modern-day popularity is reflected in much contemporary design, such as this superb silk intended for an *obi*, the sash worn around a kimono.

BELOW In a style of garden as disciplined as that of the Zen temple of Ryoaunji, in Kyoto, the rose, with its wayward growth and showy flowers, has no place.

'Green Ice'

'Green Ice'

MINIATURE I WHITE

Forget the fact that the flowers go green with age (a variable habit – sometimes they are quite green, at others only faintly so), this is one of the best white Miniatures there are, the small, double flowers flat and filled with petals like scaled-down Old Garden Roses. The plant is bushy, with glossy, leathery, bright green leaves.

Moore, USA, 1971
(R. wichurana × 'Floradora') × 'Jet Trail'
Repeat flowering I *Slight fragrance*
HABIT Bush (weeping) H/W 45cm/45cm (18in/18in) I ZONES 5–11

'Halo Rainbow'

'Halo Today'

'HALO' SERIES

Over the years, the legendary Ralph Moore, acclaimed as the 'Father of Modern Miniature Roses', has created a number of single and semi-double roses to which he attached the name 'Halo'. This halo effect, unique to his Miniatures, is due to the inner base of each petal being a quite different color from the rest of the flower. Apart from their color and being single or semi-double, all these varieties have virtually the same description. They are all low-growing, profuse bloomers, easy to grow and disease-resistant. To get the best from these roses, plant them where they will get no more than four hours of sun, preferably morning sun. With their few petals, the little flowers can wilt easily in strong sun, and the stamens may turn black.

'Halo Rainbow'

MINIATURE I PINK BLEND

Medium pink flowers with a creamy white halo. Single, five petals, about 5cm (2in) in diameter.

MORrainbow I Moore, USA, 1994
Seedling × 'Make Believe'
Repeat flowering I *No fragrance*
HABIT Bush H/W 30cm/25cm (12in/10in) I ZONES 5–11

'Halo Sunrise'

MINIATURE I YELLOW BLEND

Medium yellow flowers with a dark red halo. Single, 5–12 petals, 4cm (1½in) in diameter.

MORsunrise I Moore, USA, 1997
Parentage unknown
Repeat flowering I *No fragrance*
HABIT Bush H/W 30cm/25cm (12in/10in) I ZONES 4–10

LEFT 'Halo Sunrise'
BELOW 'Halo Sweetie'

'Halo Sweetie'

MINIATURE I PINK BLEND

Orange buds opening to peach-pink flowers with a lovely red halo. Single, five petals, 4cm (1½in) in diameter.

MORsweet I Moore, USA, 2002
Seedling × 'Halo Rainbow'
Repeat flowering I *Intense, damask fragrance*
HABIT Bush H/W 45cm/25cm (18in/10in) I ZONES 5–11

'Halo Today'

MINIATURE I ORANGE PINK

Orange-pink flowers with a very distinct pinkish lavender halo. Semi-double, 6–12 petals, 4cm (1½in) in diameter.

MORtoday I Moore, USA, 1994
('Anytime' × 'Gold Badge') × ('Anytime' × 'Lavender Jewel')
Repeat flowering I *No fragrance*
HABIT Bush H/W 45cm/25cm (18in/10in) I ZONES 5–11

'Harm Saville'

MINI-FLORA I DARK RED

Named after one of the 'giants' of Miniature rose hybridizing, this rose is a wonderful tribute to a man who left so many beautiful creations for future generations to enjoy. It is an excellent garden variety, producing prolific clusters of dark red blooms throughout the season. The plant is easy to maintain, being vigorous, upright and bushy, with good disease resistance.

WEKclauni I Carruth, USA, 2004
'Santa Claus' × 'Opening Night'
Repeat flowering I *Light fragrance*
HABIT Bush H/W 60cm/30cm (2ft/1ft) I ZONES 5–11

'Harm Saville'

'Hilde'

'Hula Girl'

'Irresistible'

'Holy Toledo'

'Incognito'

'Hilde'

MINIATURE ı RED BLEND

The beautiful, high-centred blooms are deep pink with an ivory reverse; during cooler weather the petals are covered by an attractive dark haze. 'Hilde' seems to be a slow starter, but once established it will continue to flourish and give you a plentiful supply of blooms – perfect for small bouquets. The bush is upright and has a tendency to spread. It is ideal as a low border, or plant it in a container with a capacity of at least 14 litres (3 gallons).

BENhile ı Benardella, USA, 1999
'Figurine' × 'Kristin'
Repeating flowering ı *Moderate fragrance*
HABIT Bush H/W 45cm/25cm (18in/10in) ı ZONES 5-11

'Holy Toledo'

MINIATURE ı APRICOT BLEND

'Holy Toledo' is one of the most widely admired of Miniatures for its wonderful color, brilliant apricot-orange with a yellow-orange reverse; the shape of its double, 28-petalled flowers;

its vigorous, bushy growth; and its polished, dark green foliage.

ARObri ı Christensen, USA, 1978
'Apricot Prince' × 'Magic Carrousel'
Repeat flowering ı *Slight fragrance*
HABIT Bush H/W 45cm/25cm (18in/10in) ı ZONES 4-10
🌹 Award of Excellence for Miniature Roses 1980

'Hula Girl'

MINIATURE ı ORANGE BLEND

The double, 45-petalled flowers are deep orange in bud but open to salmon-pink with a touch of yellow showing beneath. Tallish for the class, 'Hula Girl' has glossy, quilted foliage and a fine fruity fragrance.

Williams, USA, 1975
'Miss Hillcrest' × 'Mabel Dot'
Repeat flowering ı *Moderate, fruity fragrance*
HABIT Bush H/W 45cm/25cm (18in/10in) ı ZONES 5-11
🌹 Award of Excellence for Miniature Roses 1976

'Incognito'

MINIATURE ı MAUVE

Classified as mauve, this unusual variety has colors you will either love or hate. The long, pointed buds open to magnificent double, classically shaped blooms apparently inherited from one of its seed parents, 'Jean Kenneally'. In hot climates, they can go from scarlet to dull red to deep pink, with overlays of russet or even brown. The plant is tall and very prolific, and will give you masses of blooms throughout the season, singly and in clusters, to enjoy in the garden and as cut flowers for your home.

BRlincog ı Bridges, USA, 1995
'Jean Kenneally' × 'Twilight Trail'
Repeat flowering ı *Slight fragrance*
HABIT Bush H/W 45cm/25cm (18in/10in) ı ZONES 5-11

'Irresistible'

MINIATURE ı WHITE

One of Dee Bennett's best creations, 'Irresistible' has become a favorite worldwide in the years since it was introduced. Masses of impeccable white blooms with exceptional classical form are borne both singly and in clusters on a vigorous, tall-growing bush with lush, dark green foliage. The flower color can vary considerably with the weather conditions; in cooler weather, there may be green on the outside petals and a pink haze or even russet on the inner. This prolific bloomer is a plant every exhibitor should have in his or her arsenal. It is ideal for ground planting or for a large container.

TINresist ı Bennett, USA, 1989
'Tiki' × 'Brian Lee'
Repeat flowering ı *No fragrance*
HABIT Bush H/W 60cm/30cm (2ft/1ft) ı ZONES 4-11

'Janna'

MINIATURE ı PINK BLEND

Ralph Moore has often used the Floribunda 'Little Darling' in breeding his Miniatures, and 'Janna' has a double dose. The influence

'Janna'

'Jean Kenneally'

'Jeanne Lajoie'

'Ko's Yellow'

'Kaikoura'

'Jilly Jewel'

of 'Little Darling' shows in the finely shaped buds and the bicolored petals, pink with a cream reverse. The flowers are small and double; the foliage is leathery and olive-green. Miniatures like this are a great success with florists.

Moore, USA, 1970
'Little Darling' × ('Little Darling' × [R. wichurana × Miniature seedling])
Repeat flowering ı *Slight fragrance*

HABIT Bush H/W 30cm/20cm (12in/8in) ı ZONES 4–11

'Jean Kenneally'

MINIATURE ı APRICOT BLEND

Another winner from the creative hands of Australian-born Dee Bennett, 'Jean Kenneally' dominated the rose show scene in the United States, the United Kingdom and Australia during the 1980s and early 1990s, and has remained popular with exhibitors. The high-centred, apricot blooms are widely admired for their perfect form and long-lasting quality. The plant is tall and upright, and blooms profusely throughout the season. Its one drawback is that it is rather susceptible to diseases.

TINeally ı Bennett, USA, 1984
'Futura' × 'Party Girl'
Repeat flowering ı *Light fragrance*

HABIT Bush H/W 75cm/45cm (30in/18in) ı ZONES 4–10

🏵 Award of Excellence for Miniature Roses 1986

'Jeanne Lajoie'

CLIMBING MINIATURE ı MEDIUM PINK

This Climbing Miniature astonishes everyone who sees it. Tall growing, up to 1.8m (6ft), it has the ability to clothe itself with flowers, non-stop, from the ground up to the tip of each arching cane. The double blooms are medium pink with a darker reverse and nicely formed, and have a slight fragrance. This variety is best planted against a wall or a fence, but be sure to fan it out – even better, anchor it to the ground so that it self-roots and spreads.

Sima, USA, 1975
('Casa Blanca' × 'Independence') × 'Midget'
Repeat flowering ı *Slight fragrance*

HABIT Climbing H/W 1.8m/1.5m (6ft/5ft) ı ZONES 5–11

🏵 Award of Excellence for Miniature Roses 1977, American Rose Society Hall of Fame 2002

'Jilly Jewel'

MINIATURE ı PINK BLEND

The beautiful blooms of 'Jilly Jewel' are of a delicate pink blend and have classical, high-centred form. Produced in profusion throughout the season, they stay fresh-looking for a long time, both on the bush and as cut flowers. The plant is upright and bushy, with very attractive dark green foliage. It has a tendency to spread, so whether you are planting it in the ground or in a container, give it plenty of room. You really can't go wrong with this one.

BENmfig ı Benardella, USA, 2003
'Figurine' × 'Kristin'
Repeat flowering ı *Light fragrance*

HABIT Bush H/W 75cm/38cm (30in/15in) ı ZONES 5–11

'Kaikoura'

MINIATURE ı ORANGE BLEND

The name may sound Japanese, but it is in fact Maori, the name of a seaside village in the South Island of New Zealand. A popular exhibition rose in New Zealand, 'Kaikoura' is tall for a Miniature and bears abundant orange and red blooms throughout the season. The foliage is glossy and dark green.

MACwalla ı McGredy, New Zealand, 1978
'Anytime' × 'Matangi'
Repeat flowering ı *Slight fragrance*

HABIT Bush H/W 45cm/25cm (18in/10in) ı ZONES 5–11

'Ko's Yellow'

MINIATURE ı YELLOW BLEND

Sam McGredy named 'Ko's Yellow' in honor of Ko Schuurman, the wife of his colleague Frank Schuurman. It was she who first saw the potential of its classically formed, double, buff-yellow blooms and its bushy habit. The foliage is glossy and bright green. 'Ko's Yellow' was raised from an unusual breeding line.

MACkosyel ı McGredy, New Zealand, 1978
('New Penny' × 'Bambridge') × ('Border Flame' × 'Manx Queen')
Repeat flowering ı *Slight fragrance*

HABIT Bush H/W 45cm/25cm (18in/10in) ı ZONES 5–11

'Leading Lady'

MINI-FLORA | WHITE

This supremely elegant new variety, introduced in 2007, looks set to dominate the exhibition scene in the United States for some time to come. The long, tapered, light pink buds open gradually to magnificent white blooms that similarly take their time to unfurl. The flowers are large, high-centred and multi-petalled, and freely produced throughout the season, mostly singly but occasionally in clusters of 3–5. The plant is tall and vigorous, and needs plenty of space when planted in the ground. If you are growing it in a container, choose one with a capacity of at least 30 litres (7 gallons).

BENuno | Benardella, USA, 2007
Seedling × 'Timeless'
Repeat flowering | *Light fragrance*

HABIT Bush H/W 75cm/45cm (30in/18in) | ZONES 5–11

🌹 Award of Excellence for Miniature Roses 2007

'Lemon Delight'

MINIATURE | MEDIUM YELLOW

There is still no satisfactory full-sized, yellow Moss Rose, but there is one among the Miniatures – Ralph Moore's 'Lemon Delight'. A cross between two other Moore mossy Miniatures, it makes a compact, upright bush, with small, yellow blooms that open from long, mossy buds. The foliage is glossy and mid-green. A charmer, with a slight fragrance.

Moore, USA, 1978
'Fairy Moss' × 'Goldmoss'
Repeat flowering | *Slight fragrance*

HABIT Bush H/W 30cm/25cm (12in/10in) | ZONES 5–11

'Little Artist'

MINIATURE | RED BLEND

'Top Gear'

Introduced in 1978, 'Little Artist' was Sam McGredy's very first 'hand-painted' Miniature. The bush is compact, if a little tall by Miniature standards, and the semi-double flowers make quite a show with their bold splashes of red and white. The foliage is dark green.

MACmanly | McGredy, New Zealand, 1982
'Eyepaint' × 'Ko's Yellow'
Repeat flowering | *Slight fragrance*

HABIT Bush H/W 60cm/30cm (2ft/1ft) | ZONES 5–11

'Little Artist'

'Little Jackie'

MINIATURE | ORANGE BLEND

Every rosarian fell in love with this rose when it first came out, and it is still widely grown all over the world. The petals are the color of orange sherbet, with a buttery yellow reverse. The blooms are high-centred and unfurl slowly, and come on long stems that are ideal for cutting and exhibiting. The plant is a prolific bloomer, with an upright habit, and the small, semi-glossy, medium green foliage has good disease resistance.

SAVor | Saville, USA, 1982
('Prominent' × 'Sheri Anne') × 'Glenfiddich'
Repeat flowering | *Intense fragrance*

HABIT Bush H/W 45cm/25cm (18in/10in) | ZONES 5–11

🌹 Award of Excellence for Miniature Roses 1984, American Rose Society Hall of Fame 2003

'Luis Desamero'

MINIATURE | LIGHT YELLOW

Dee Bennett named this double, high-centred, pastel yellow rose for a very special rosarian friend who headed up the Award of Excellence Program and initiated the American Rose Society National Miniature Rose Show in the United States. The plant is tall-growing and blooms profusely throughout the season. The blooms can, however, fade in strong sunlight. In the years since its introduction, it has proved to be one of the top exhibition roses in the United States and the United Kingdom and, indeed, throughout the world.

TINluis | Bennett, USA, 1989
'Tiki' × 'Baby Katie'
Repeat flowering | *Fruity fragrance*

HABIT Bush H/W 75cm/45cm (30in/18in) | ZONES 5–11

'Leading Lady'

'Little Jackie'

'Luis Desamero'

'Lemon Delight'

'Magic Carrousel'

'Mary Marshall'

'Merlot'

'Magic Carrousel'

MINIATURE ı RED BLEND

MOORcar

One of Ralph Moore's greatest successes, 'Magic Carrousel' is admired for its reliable growth habit and the sheer prettiness of its shapely little double blooms, each of their white petals distinctly edged with cerise. Pick a bowl over several days and you will have a multicolored display. It makes a rather leggy bush, so prune it hard. The foliage is leathery and dark green, bronze-tinted when young.

MORousel ı Moore, USA, 1972
'Little Darling' × 'Westmont'
Repeat flowering ı *Slight fragrance*

HABIT Bush H/W 60cm/30cm (2ft/1ft) ı ZONES 4–11
🌹 American Rose Society Miniature Rose Hall of Fame 1999

'Mary Marshall'

MINIATURE ı ORANGE BLEND

Although introduced in 1970, Ralph Moore's 'Mary Marshall' still has a following. It is easy to grow, and its dainty, long-pointed buds open to long-lasting blooms of deep orange-pink with just a touch of coral. The foliage is small, semi-glossy and dark green.

Moore, USA, 1970
'Little Darling' × 'Fairy Princess'
Repeat flowering ı *Moderate fragrance*

HABIT Bush H/W 45cm/25cm (18in/10in) ı ZONES 5–11

'Memphis Music'

MINI-FLORA ı RED BLEND

The unique combination of dark red petals and randomly placed, bright yellow stripes and markings gives this variety great novelty value. It also has a good deal of charm on other counts. The blooms are very long-lasting, having exceptionally strong petals with a high starch content. Once the plant has established itself, the flowers are borne mostly one to a stem, with a form strikingly reminiscent of a Hybrid Tea. The bush has an upright growth habit with a tendency to spread, so give it plenty of room. It is, however, quite susceptible to diseases; keep a special lookout for mildew and rust.

WELmusic ı Wells, USA, 2007
'Memphis Magic' sport
Repeat flowering ı *Light fragrance*

HABIT Bush H/W 1m/60cm (3ft/2ft) ı ZONES 5–11

'Merlot'

MINIATURE ı RED BLEND

In 2001, Frank Benardella chose to name his new introductions after various varietal wines, adding new meaning to the term 'wine and roses' and perhaps providing a deeper insight into the secrets of breeding prize-winning roses! 'Merlot' is a prolific bloomer, covering itself throughout the season with small, medium

'Memphis Music'

'Miss Flippins'

red blooms with a white to silvery reverse. In hot climates the flowers are usually borne singly, and in cooler climates in clusters of up to five. They are very long-lasting, making them ideal for a small bouquet or even a boutonniere. The plant is of medium height, vigorous, upright and bushy, and covered all season with lush, dark green, disease-resistant foliage.

BENfebu ı Benardella, USA, 2001
'Figurine' × seedling
Repeat flowering ı *Light fragrance*

HABIT Bush H/W 60cm/30cm (2ft/1ft) ı ZONES 5–11
🌹 Award of Excellence for Miniature Roses 2002

'Miss Flippins'

MINIATURE ı MEDIUM RED

This variety has been acclaimed by rose exhibitors as the best red Miniature in the United States, and for good reason. The tall, vigorous plant produces exquisite, classically shaped, brilliant medium red blooms. They are borne singly or in big clusters, with strong, straight stems and shiny, dark green foliage. The plant is hardy, healthy-looking and very prolific, providing color throughout the season. It does tend to spread, so give it plenty of room. If a container is your only option, use a whisky barrel or a pot with a capacity of at least 30 litres (7 gallons). This plant's only drawback is its susceptibility to powdery mildew. As soon as you see the telltale signs on the bush, spray with an effective fungicide.

TUCkflip ı Tucker, USA, 1997
'Elizabeth Taylor' × 'Kristin'
Repeat flowering ı *No fragrance*

HABIT Bush H/W 60cm/30cm (2ft/1ft) ı ZONES 5–11

'Neon Cowboy'

MINIATURE ı RED BLEND

This eye-catching variety has single-petalled, scarlet blooms with a very distinct yellow eye. They are borne both singly and in small clusters, on quite short stems, and are freely produced throughout the season. Perfect for a small container, the plant has a low-growing, round and compact habit and glossy, dark green, disease-resistant foliage. To prevent the color from fading and make the flowers last longer, place it in a half-sun position. The name is inspired by the cowboy movie released in 2000, and is a playful reference to the breeder's personality.

WEKemilcho ı Carruth, USA, 2001
'Emily Louise' × ('Playboy' × 'Little Artist')
Repeat flowering ı *Slight fragrance*

HABIT Bush H/W 45cm/25cm (18in/10in) ı ZONES 5–11

'Neon Cowboy'

'New Beginning'

MINIATURE ı ORANGE BLEND

Aptly named, 'New Beginning' provides a constant, multicolored show of bright orange-red and yellow flowers. The plant is vigorous and disease-resistant, with a very symmetrical growth habit, and is one of the earliest roses to bloom in the spring. With its warm

'New Beginning'

color and continuous blooming, this is an excellent landscape rose, ideal for a low hedge or border.

SAVabeg ı Saville, USA, 1988
'Zorina' × seedling
Repeat flowering ı *Light fragrance*

HABIT Bush H/W 45cm/25cm (18in/10in) ı ZONES 5–1
🌹 All-America Rose Selection 1989

'Nozomi'

CLIMBING MINIATURE ı LIGHT PINK

'Heiderosslein Nozomi'

Although it is classified as a Climbing Miniature and will grow to 2.5m (8ft) tall if trained on a wall, 'Nozomi' is more popular as a ground cover. And a delightful specimen it is, sending out trailing shoots covered in sprays of single, blush-white flowers like apple blossom. Although it is not repeat blooming and has no fragrance, this unassuming rose is the most important rose yet raised in Japan.

'Nozomi'

Most of the new class of Ground Cover Roses have been bred from it, directly or indirectly. Breeder Dr Toru Onodera may describe himself as 'only an amateur rose-lover', but this 1968 creation assured him of a place in the history of the rose.

Onodera, Japan, 1968
'Fairy Princess' × 'Sweet Fairy'
Summer flowering ı *No fragrance*

HABIT Climber H/W 2.5m/1.2m (8ft/4ft) ı ZONES 4–11

'Old Glory'

MINIATURE ı MEDIUM RED

One of Frank Benardella's earlier creations — for which he borrowed the affectionate nickname for the United States flag — this bright red rose has remained popular in the United States. The large, double flowers age to blood-red and crimson. They are borne freely throughout the season, mostly singly but occasionally

'Old Glory'

in small clusters, on a vigorous plant that is easy to maintain. The foliage is semi-glossy and medium green.

BENday ꞏ Benardella, USA, 1988
'Rise 'n' Shine' × 'Harmonie'
Repeat flowering ꞏ *Very light fragrance*

HABIT Bush H/W 45cm/25cm (18in/10in) ꞏ ZONES 5–11

 Award of Excellence for Miniature Roses 1988

'Orange Honey'

MINIATURE ꞏ ORANGE BLEND

To see these orange and gold blooms at their dazzling best, grow this rose in light shade. The flowers are double and have a fruity fragrance. The bush is dwarf and spreading, and the foliage is matt green.

Moore, USA, 1979
'Rumba' × 'Over the Rainbow'
Repeat flowering ꞏ *Moderate, fruity fragrance*

HABIT Bush H/W 45cm/25cm (18in/10in) ꞏ ZONES 5–11

'Orange Sunblaze'

MINIATURE ꞏ ORANGE

'Orange Meillandina'

This is the first of the 'Sunblaze' or 'Meillandina' series that Meilland introduced in 1982 as the 'world's first indoor roses'. This claim has

'Orange Honey'

'Overnight Scentsation'

proved to be exaggerated, although the plants can be brought indoors for short periods while in bloom. The very double flowers are deep orange and slightly fragrant. The plant is upright and bushy, with small, matt foliage.

MEIjikatar ꞏ Meilland, France, 1982
'Parador' × ('Baby Bettina' × 'Mevrouw van Straaten van Nes')
Repeat flowering ꞏ *Slight fragrance*

HABIT Bush H/W 45cm/25cm (18in/10in) ꞏ ZONES 5–11

'Overnight Scentsation'

MINI-FLORA ꞏ MEDIUM PINK

This variety was the first rose to be taken into outer space, gaining a place on board the space shuttle in the late 1990s. It is better known for its heady perfume and its lovely garden display than for its form – the large, very double, pink blooms can sometimes fail to open properly in cooler climates. The plant is vigorous, bushy and prolific, with lush, medium green, disease-resistant foliage. If you are looking for fragrance in a rose, look no further. A small bouquet will fill an entire room with its scent.

SAVanight ꞏ Saville, USA, 1997
'Taxi' × 'Lavender Jade'
Repeat flowering ꞏ *Intense, damask fragrance*

HABIT Bush H/W 1m/60cm (3ft/2ft) ꞏ ZONES 5–11

'Oz Gold'

'Oz Gold'

MINIATURE ꞏ ORANGE BLEND

Introduced by Irishman turned New Zealander Sam McGredy, 'Oz Gold' is a brilliant, burnished, true golden yellow, with a touch of cerise on the outer petals. Each flower is perfectly formed in the Hybrid Tea style. The bush has a neat, low-growing habit, and the foliage is glossy and dark green.

McGredy, New Zealand, 1981
Seedling × seedling
Repeat flowering ꞏ *Slight fragrance*

HABIT Bush H/W 45cm/25cm (18in/10in) ꞏ ZONES 5–11

'Party Girl'

MINIATURE ꞏ YELLOW BLEND

While this rose has declined in popularity over the years, it has left a proud legacy. Many rose hybridizers who have used 'Party Girl' in their Miniature breeding programs have created prize-winning varieties. The apricot-yellow blooms are of exceptional quality, double and high-centred, and are borne singly and in small clusters throughout the year. The bush is upright and compact – ideal for a container or to provide color at the front of your rose bed. It was named in honor of Jan Shivers of the American Rose Society, whose penchant for party-going was well known in rose circles.

Saville, USA, 1979
'Rise 'n' Shine' × 'Sheri Anne'
Repeat flowering ꞏ *Moderate fragrance*

HABIT Bush H/W 60cm/45cm (2ft/18in) ꞏ ZONES 5–11

 Award of Excellence for Miniature Roses 1981, American Rose Society Hall of Fame 1999

'Orange Sunblaze'

'Party Girl'

'Petite Folie'

MINIATURE ı ORANGE BLEND

When this rose came out in 1968, no one knew quite what to make of it, as its leaves and flowers are Miniature, but the bush is Floribunda size. The small, double flowers are vermilion with a carmine reverse, and grow in trusses. The foliage is mid-green, bronze when young.

MEIherode ı Meilland, France, 1968
('Dany Robin' × 'Fire King') × ('CriCri' × 'Perla de Montserrat')
Repeat flowering ı *Slight, fruity fragrance*

HABIT Bush H/W 45cm/25cm (18in/10in) ı ZONES 4–10

'Petite Perfection'

MINIATURE ı RED BLEND

Living up to its name, 'Petite Perfection' bears blooms of outstanding color and exceptional

'Petite Perfection'

'Petite Folie'

quality. The ovoid buds open to double, exhibition form flowers of bright reddish yellow, with a deep yellow reverse. The flowers are borne both singly and in small clusters, and are long-lasting; they also retain their color extremely well as they age. The plant is vigorous, upright and bushy, and blooms profusely throughout the year—all in all, an excellent variety for a container or for the front of your rose bed.

JACrybi ı Walden, USA, 1999
Parentage unknown
Repeat flowering ı *Moderate fragrance*

HABIT Bush H/W 45cm/25cm (18in/10in) ı ZONES 5–11

'Pink Cameo'

CLIMBING MINIATURE ı MEDIUM PINK

'Climbing Pink Cameo'

Despite their charm, the Climbing Miniatures have never achieved wide popularity. Ralph Moore's 'Pink Cameo', introduced back in 1954, remains one of the very best. Try twining its 1.5m (5ft) long branches along a low fence; they will soon be adorned all season with petite, soft pink blooms. The foliage is coarse and mid-green.

Moore, USA, 1954
('Soeur Thérèse' × 'Skyrocket') × 'Zee'
Repeat flowering ı *Slight fragrance*

HABIT Climber H/W 1.5m/1.2m (5ft/4ft) ı ZONES 5–11

'Pink Cameo'

'Rainbow's End'

'Red Ace'

'Rainbow's End'

MINIATURE ı YELLOW BLEND

This is a truly beautiful rose in the classical Hybrid Tea mould. No garden should be without it. Among its many outstanding qualities, it is easy to grow and blooms almost continually. The double, 35-petalled flowers are deep yellow with red petal edges, ageing to red all over, and have excellent exhibition form. They are borne singly and in small clusters. The plant is upright, bushy and compact, with glossy, dark green, disease-resistant foliage. There is no better variety for the front of your rose bed or for a container.

SAValife ı Saville, USA, 1984
'Rise 'n' Shine' × 'Watercolor'
Repeat flowering ı *Slight fragrance*
HABIT Bush H/W 45cm/25cm (18in/10in) ı ZONES 5–11
Award of Excellence for Miniature Roses 1986

'Red Ace'

MINIATURE ı MEDIUM RED

There are two red Miniatures of this name – one, codenamed AmRUda, from De Ruiter of Holland, the other (shown here) produced by Harm Saville in 1980. Saville's 'Red Ace' is a shapely Hybrid Tea Rose in miniature, double in form and bright crimson in color. It makes a bushy, compact plant, graced by fine, glossy foliage. AmRUda is a much darker red.

Saville, USA, 1980
'Rise 'n' Shine' × 'Sheri Anne'
Repeat flowering ı *Slight fragrance*
HABIT Bush H/W 45cm/25cm (18in/10in) ı ZONES 5–11

'Rise 'n' Shine'

MINIATURE ı MEDIUM YELLOW

'Golden Meillandina', 'Golden Sunblaze'

It is not clear how this rose got the name 'Golden Meillandina', as it is not one of Meilland's but comes from California's Ralph Moore. Introduced in 1977, it is still, quite simply, the very best yellow Miniature there is. The rich yellow flowers are small and double, with 35 petals and excellent exhibition form. Like so many yellow roses, however, it is susceptible to black spot. The plant is bushy and upright, with fine, glossy foliage.

Moore, USA, 1977
'Little Darling' × 'Yellow Magic'
Repeat flowering ı *Moderate fragrance*
HABIT Bush H/W 45cm/25cm (18in/10in) ı ZONES 4–10
Award of Excellence for Miniature Roses 1978, American Rose Society Miniature Rose Hall of Fame 1999

RIGHT 'Rouletii'
TOP INSET 'Roller Coaster'
BOTTOM INSET 'Rise 'n' Shine'

'Roller Coaster'

MINIATURE | RED BLEND

'Minnie Mouse'

The semi-double flowers have 6–14 petals randomly striped in a dramatic mixture of red, creamy yellow and white – no two are identical. They are borne in small clusters against glossy, dark green foliage, creating the effect of a tapestry of colors. The plant has a tendency to send out new growth as strong canes, loaded with thorns, which arch, or 'weep', gracefully, making it ideal for containers or for a position where it can spill over a wall.

MACminmo | McGredy, New Zealand, 1987
('Anytime' × 'Eyepaint') × 'Stars 'n' Stripes'
Repeat flowering | Slight fragrance

HABIT Bush H/W 60cm/1m (2ft/3ft) | ZONES 5–10

'Rouletii'

MINIATURE (HYBRID CHINA) | MEDIUM PINK

Centifolia Minima, *R. rouletti*, *R. × centifolia minima*

Discovered growing in a pot on a windowsill in Switzerland, 'Rouletii' was introduced in 1922 by Henri Correvon. He named it after Roulet, the soldier who discovered it. The ancestor of the modern Miniatures, it is a pure-bred China Rose. It is rather like a scaled-down version of 'Old Blush', with double, soft rose-pink flowers and neat, pointed leaves. There is no scent. It blooms all year round, and should not be neglected in favor of its more up-to-date offspring.

Correvon, Switzerland, 1922
Parentage unknown
Repeat flowering | No fragrance

HABIT Bush H/W 45cm/25cm (18in/10in) | ZONES 4–11

'Roxie'

'Royal Salute'

'Roxie'

MIN-FLORA | ORANGE PINK

This lovely variety has large, orange-pink flowers and a growth habit that will appeal to many home gardeners. The blooms are borne both one to a stem and in small clusters. They do not have exhibition form, but they stay fresh for a long time, whether left on the bush or cut for a small bouquet. An excellent repeat bloomer, the bush is vigorous, medium and upright, with lots of glossy, dark green foliage. 'Roxie' would make a fine addition to any garden, especially if displayed in an attractive container on a patio or deck.

TUCkgrinnel | Tucker, USA, 2004
'Elsie Melton' × 'Kristin'
Repeat flowering | Slight fragrance

HABIT Bush H/W 1m/60cm (3ft/2ft) | ZONES 5–11

'Royal Salute'

MINIATURE | MEDIUM RED

'Rose Baby'

The birth of England's Prince William in June 1982 was saluted by two red roses: the full-sized 'Royal William' and this delightful Miniature from Sam McGredy. The bush is compact, the foliage glossy and dark, and the clusters of rosy red flowers so cheerful that all 'Royal Salute' needs is fragrance.

MACros | McGredy, New Zealand, 1982
'New Penny' × 'Marlena'
Repeat flowering | Slight to no fragrance

HABIT Bush H/W 45cm/25cm (18in/10in) | ZONES 5–11

'Salute'

MINIATURE | DARK RED

Dedicated to the men and women of the United States Armed Forces, this variety made its first appearance at the Fall 2003 American Rose Society National Convention in Washington D.C. It produces masses of small, dark red flowers, which come in little clusters. The bush is low-growing, with lots

'Salute'

'Scentsational'

of dark green foliage, and has good disease resistance. Easy to grow and maintain, it makes a good container or bedding plant.

SAVasalute | White, USA, 2003
('Vista' × 'Party Girl') × ('Party Girl' × 'Teddy Bear')
Repeat flowering | Light fragrance

HABIT Bush H/W 45cm/25cm (18in/10in) | ZONES 5–11
🏵 Award of Excellence for Miniature Roses 2004

'Scentsational'

MINIATURE | MAUVE

'Scentsational' was the first in a series of intensely fragrant Miniatures that Harm Saville created and introduced in the 1990s. The small, light mauve blooms are edged with pink and have a cream reverse. With excellent classical form, they are masterpieces in motion as the buds slowly unfurl to lovely, full-blown flowers with golden stamens and a stunning fragrance. The medium to tall plant has a tendency to spread, but it is a prolific bloomer with good disease resistance. Plant it in a container on your patio or deck and let the wonderful fragrance drift into your home.

SAVamor | Saville, USA, 1995
'Lavender Jade' × 'Silverado'
Repeat flowering | Intense fragrance

HABIT Bush H/W 45cm/25cm (18in/10in) | ZONES 5–11

'Snow Bride'

'Solar Flair'

'Starina'

'Stars 'n' Stripes'

'Snow Bride'

MINIATURE ι WHITE

'Snowbride'

Introduced back in 1982, this cream-colored beauty remains the best white Miniature around, and is hugely popular among exhibitors and home gardeners alike. High-centred and maintaining its form for days, it has dominated the white-flowered class at rose shows for many years and won countless gold certificates. Home gardeners love it first and foremost for its beauty, but also for the fact that it is very easy to grow and blooms almost continually. The plant is of medium height and bushy, with lush, semi-glossy, dark green foliage.

Jolly, USA, 1982
'Avandel' × 'Zinger'
Repeat flowering ι *Slight fragrance*

HABIT Bush H/W 45cm/25cm (18in/10in) ι ZONES 5–11

🏵 Award of Excellence for Miniature Roses 1982, American Rose Society Hall of Fame 2003

'Solar Flair'

MINI-FLORA ι YELLOW BLEND

This variety is one of Frank Benardella's loveliest creations. The impeccable yellow blooms

are edged with red, a feature that becomes more pronounced as they age. They have high-centred form and are borne mostly one to a stem, with occasional small clusters. The plant is upright and quite vigorous, with large, dark green foliage that can sometimes attract mildew. 'Solar Flair' would make a wonderful color accent in any rose garden, and would be perfect in a nice container to decorate an entranceway.

BENbaas ι Benardella, USA, 2004
'Antique Gold' × 'Brett's Rose'
Repeat flowering ι *Light fragrance*

HABIT Bush H/W 60cm/30cm (2ft/1ft) ι ZONES 5–11

'Starina'

MINIATURE ι ORANGE RED

The free-blooming 'Starina' continues to top the Miniature popularity polls with its perfectly shaped blooms of brilliant scarlet and its reliable, bushy growth. The foliage is dark and leathery. Its only fault is that the bushes are sometimes short-lived. It was a 1965 triumph for Marie-Louisette Meilland.

MEIgabi, MEIgali ι Meilland, France, 1965
('Dany Robin' × 'Fire King') × 'Perla de Montserrat'
Repeat flowering ι *Slight fragrance*

HABIT Bush H/W 45cm/25cm (18in/10in) ι ZONES 4–11

🏵 Japan Gold Medal 1968, Anerkannte Deutsche Rose (Germany) 1971, American Rose Society Miniature Rose Hall of Fame 1999

'Stars 'n' Stripes'

MINIATURE ι RED BLEND

Introduced by Ralph Moore in 1976 as his contribution to the United States Bicentennial, 'Stars 'n' Stripes' is the progenitor of many subsequent striped roses. It is a charmer in its own right, although some rosarians

have been heard to complain that it is somewhat shy of flowering. It is like a miniature version of *R. gallica versicolor*. The small flowers are striped in crimson and white, and sweetly scented. The foliage is mid-green and not very glossy.

Moore, USA, 1976
'Little Chief' × ('Little Darling' × 'Ferdinand Pichard')
Repeat flowering ι *Sweet fragrance*

HABIT Bush H/W 45cm/25cm (18in/10in) ι ZONES 5–11

'Starship'

MINI-FLORA ι YELLOW BLEND

Very similar in color and flower form to 'Solar Flair', this variety bears long-lasting yellow blooms edged with red, on long, straight stems. The dark green foliage is so large that it sometimes overwhelms the flowers, especially during hot weather, when the flowers shrink. It can also attract some diseases, especially mildew, but this is little price to pay if you are an avid exhibitor. Plant this tall variety in a large container or in the ground at the back of the garden.

BRIstar ι Bridges, USA, 2002
'Summer Sunset' × select pollen
Repeat flowering ι *No fragrance*

HABIT Bush H/W 1m/45cm (3ft/18in) ι ZONES 5–11

'Starship'

'Sun Sprinkles'

MINIATURE ı DEEP YELLOW

A special rose with exceptional attributes, 'Sun Sprinkles' is worthy of its awards. The blooms are a bright deep yellow, long-lasting and non-fading, and are produced very freely throughout the season. While the flowers may sometimes be of exhibition quality, this variety is mainly intended for garden display. The plant is upright, round and compact, with lush, dark green foliage and very good disease resistance.

JAChal ı Walden, USA, 1999
'Yellow Jacket' × seedling
Repeat flowering ı *Light, spicy fragrance*

HABIT Bush H/W 45cm/25cm (18in/10in) ı ZONES 4–10

🌹 All-America Rose Selection 2001, Award of Excellence for Miniature Roses 2001

'Sun Sprinkles'

'Sunspray'

'Sunspray'

MINIATURE ı DEEP YELLOW

This Miniature is one of the deepest and most brilliant of all yellow roses. At least it is so in the bud and the freshly opened flowers, with their distinctive, shell-shaped petals. Alas, they fade as they age and hang on the bush – the flip side, so to speak, of their exceptionally long life. Never mind: just snip the old flowers off, and the glossy-leafed bush will produce plenty more to take their place.

ARCasp ı Christensen, USA, 1981
'Gingersnap' × 'Magic Carrousel'
Repeat flowering ı *Slight, tea fragrance*

HABIT Bush H/W 45cm/25cm (18in/10in) ı ZONES 5–11

'Sweet Chariot'

MINIATURE ı MAUVE

This very desirable and profuse-blooming rose has small, lavender/purple blend flowers that come in gigantic clusters of up to 20. Its biggest asset, however, is its intense fragrance, which will fill the air all around it, especially if you plant it in a hanging basket. The flexible canes will then cascade over and down the sides, providing constant color and leaving a sweetly pungent aroma lingering in your backyard.

MORcari ı Moore, USA, 1984
'Little Chief' × 'Violette'
Repeat flowering ı *Intense, damask fragrance*

HABIT Bush (weeping) H/W 60cm/45cm (2ft/18in) ı ZONES 5–11

'Sweet Diana'

MINIATURE ı DEEP YELLOW

Low-growing and an excellent bloomer, 'Sweet Diana' produces long-lasting, non-fading flowers of deep yellow. They come singly and in small clusters, complemented

'Sweet Chariot'

by glossy, very dark green foliage. The bush is vigorous and easy to grow, with very good disease resistance – ideal for a container to provide color on your patio or deck. It was named by Harm Saville for one of his grand-daughters.

SAVadiana ı Saville, USA, 2001
'Cal Poly' × 'June Laver'
Repeat flowering ı *Light fragrance*

HABIT Bush H/W 45cm/25cm (18in/10in) ı ZONES 5–11

🌹 Award of Excellence for Miniature Roses 2002

'Teddy Bear'

MINIATURE ı RUSSET

The highly unusual color of this rose is guaranteed to provoke comment from visitors to your garden. It really is the same russet color as a child's teddy bear – a feature that makes it popular with flower arrangers. The urn-shaped buds open to russet, almost terracotta,

'Teddy Bear'

'Sweet Diana'

flowers with a lighter reverse, the petals gradually ageing to a mauve/pink combination. The 28-petalled blooms are sometimes classical in shape, but this variety is generally better suited to garden display than rose shows. Medium in height, upright and bushy, with semi-glossy, dark green foliage, it makes a good container variety.

SAVabear ı Saville, USA, 1989
'Sachet' × 'Rainbow's End'
Repeat flowering ı *Slight fragrance*

HABIT Bush H/W 30cm/25cm (12in/10in) ı ZONES 5–11

'Tidewater'

MINIFLORA ı WHITE

The long, pointed buds open to white, high-centred flowers blushed with pink on the petal edges. The flowers are borne singly, on long stems, and the matt, medium green foliage has good disease resistance. The bush is hardy and vigorous, with an upright growth habit, but it does have a tendency to spread unless controlled by judicious pruning. This is an excellent variety for beds or containers; it flowers freely throughout the year and will provide you with many delightfully fragrant cut flowers for the home.

BRItide ı Bridges, USA, 1991
'Jennifer' × seedling
Repeat flowering ı *Moderate fragrance*

HABIT Bush H/W 60cm/30cm (2ft/1ft) ı ZONES 5–11

'Tiffany Lynn'

MINIFLORA ı PINK BLEND

'Tiffany Lynn' is a very popular exhibition variety in the United States. The flowers are a delicate confection of color – light to medium pink along the edges, blending to white toward the centre. They are high-centred and very

'Tiffany Lynn'

'Tidewater'

long-lasting, and borne mostly singly on long, strong stems. The plant is upright, with a tendency to spread, and the large, semi-glossy foliage is quite susceptible to diseases, especially mildew. Delightful as it is, this variety requires quite a bit of maintenance, so it is more one for keenly competitive exhibitors than the average gardener.

Jolly, USA, 1985
('Tiki' × seedling) × 'Party Girl'
Repeat flowering ı *Light fragrance*

HABIT Bush H/W 1m/45cm (3ft/18in) ı ZONES 5–11

'Tom Thumb'

MINIATURE (MICRO) ı RED BLEND
'Peon'

'Rouletii' may have been the first of the modern Miniatures, but it was John de Vink's 'Peon', rechristened 'Tom Thumb' by Robert Pyle, that caught the public's fancy in 1936. It is still worth growing, even if its crimson flowers, with their white centres, look a trifle plain beside some of the more glamorous roses of more recent years. The very small foliage is leathery, semi-glossy and light green.

De Vink, The Netherlands, 1936
'Rouletii' × 'Gloria Mundi'
Repeat flowering ı *Slight fragrance*

HABIT Bush H/W 45cm/25cm (12in/8in) ı ZONES 5–11

'Valentine's Day'

CLIMBING MINI-FLORA ı DARK RED

The velvety red blooms – the classic color of love – are medium-sized and very double, and borne in clusters along spreading canes up to 1.8m (6ft) in length. The foliage is lush, very deep green and virtually impervious to diseases. A very hardy climber that

'Valentine's Day'

'Tom Thumb'

blooms quickly and repeatedly, this is a lovely variety to grow on a low fence or along a balcony, or to train up a trellis.

WEKamarav ı Carruth, USA, 2006
'Amalia' × 'Raven'
Repeat flowering ı *Slight fragrance*

HABIT Climber H/W 1.8m/1.8m (6ft/6ft) ı ZONES 5–11

'Wanaka'

MINIATURE ı ORANGE RED
'Longleat', 'Young Cale'

Sam McGredy considers 'Wanaka' to be his best Miniature, and it is certainly a beauty, the double, 40-petalled flowers holding their dazzling scarlet without fading. It is, indeed, so eye-catching that viewed from a little distance away it looks more like a geranium than a rose. The foliage is glossy and light green. It was named for an alpine town in the South Island of New Zealand.

MACinca ı McGredy, New Zealand, 1978
'Anytime' × 'Trumpeter'
Repeat flowering ı *Slight fragrance*

HABIT Bush H/W 45cm/30cm (18in/12in) ı ZONES 5–11

'Wee Man'

MINIATURE ı MEDIUM RED

'Silken Carpet', 'Tapis de Soie'

'Wee Man' is one of Sam McGredy's earlier Miniatures. The flowers are semi-double, with only 14 petals, and have little scent, but they are bright red and set off with golden stamens. They look their best planted in well-spaced clusters. The foliage is glossy and dark.

McGredy, New Zealand, 1974
'Little Flirt' × 'Marlena'
Repeat flowering ı *Slight fragrance*
HABIT Bush H/W 45cm/30cm (18in/10in) ı ZONES 4-10

'Work of Art'

CLIMBING MINIATURE ı ORANGE BLEND

This variety was named by Ralph Moore to capture the wonderful tapestry of colors it displays when in bloom. It is an excellent Climbing Miniature, with eye-catching flowers in a blend of orange and yellow. The flowers are double and classically shaped, and are borne both singly and in clusters on long stems. They are very long-lasting, and make excellent cut flowers. The plant is upright and vigorous, growing to 1.8m (6ft) tall, with lush, medium green, semi-glossy foliage. A profuse bloomer, it is very easy to maintain and has good disease resistance.

MORart ı Moore, USA 1989
Seedling × 'Gold Badge'
Repeat flowering ı *Slight fragrance*
HABIT Climbing H/W 1.8m/1m (6ft/3ft) ı ZONES 5-11

'X-Rated'

MINIATURE ı PINK BLEND

The hybridizer chose the name 'X-Rated' on the path to achieving her goal of covering all the letters of the alphabet in naming her roses. The flowers are cream-colored, with a blush of soft coral to pink on the petal edges. They are beautifully classical in shape, full-petalled and long-lasting, and are borne both singly and in clusters on long, straight stems – ideal both for exhibition and for cut flowers. The plant is vigorous, strong and healthy-looking, and produces a constant supply of blooms all year. It does have a tendency to spread, so whether you are planting it in the ground or in a container, give it plenty of room. The semi-glossy, medium green foliage can attract mildew, so be on the lookout.

TINx ı Bennett, USA, 1993
'Tiki' × 'Baby Katie'
Repeat flowering ı *Strong fragrance*
HABIT Bush 60cm/30cm (2ft/1ft) ı ZONES 4-10

'Y2K'

MINIATURE ı DEEP YELLOW

Probably the perfect yellow miniature for garden display, this variety loves all the sun it can get. The hotter it gets, the better it looks. The deep yellow flowers are non-fading, and as the temperature rises pink and coral tones emerge on the petals. The blooms are borne both singly and in clusters. They are produced in profusion throughout the season, and look magnificent against the plant's glossy, dark green foliage. Vigorous, easy to grow and highly disease-resistant, 'Y2K' will survive with minimal care. It is excellent for containers, walkways or borders, and looks its best in a mass planting. It was introduced in 1999 and named to capture the mania of the new millennium.

SAVyk ı Saville, USA, 1999
'Cal Poly' × 'New Zealand'
Repeat flowering ı *Slight, raspberry fragrance*
HABIT Bush H/W 45cm/25cm (18in/10in) ı ZONES 5-11

'X-Rated'

'Wanaka'

'Work of Art'

'Wee Man'

'Y2K'

The Cultivation of Roses

It is possible to buy books almost the size of this one devoted to giving detailed instructions on the right way to grow and prune roses. They may include a list of some of the author's favorite varieties and some nice photographs of them – but the sheer number of pages would be enough to give anyone the idea that the Queen of Flowers is temperamental and difficult to grow.

Not so! The rose may have won her ancient royal title – it was the Greeks who first bestowed it – by virtue of her sheer beauty and her fragrance, but her universal dominion is a tribute to her easy-going temperament. I have seen perfectly acceptable roses in tropical Singapore, almost on the Equator; some of the most beautiful I have ever seen and photographed were in the gardens of the Indian Rose Society in New Delhi; and I once met a gentleman from Latvia who regaled me with stories of how he succeeded in growing prize-winning roses in that country's harsh and icy climate. Beautiful roses can be grown just about everywhere people make gardens. The photographs in this book, which were taken in gardens all over the world, bear witness to that.

Still, if you could ask the rose where she is happiest – and thus easiest to grow – she would probably answer that as a child of the temperate zones her idea of heaven would be a temperate climate, where summers were warm but not sweltering and winters cool, or even cold, but not frigid. There she flourishes with little effort, and gardeners can choose their roses from the whole array the genus *Rosa* offers. Where the climate is more extreme, their choice is less free, but that is really no great hardship. Every rose is beautiful, and even the selection presented in this book is only a fraction of the more than 10 000 offered by nurseries around the world – and what gardener ever has the space and means to grow everything?

Which brings us to the first of nine rules of how to grow roses – one, indeed, that applies to gardening generally, no matter where you live:

Rule 1 • Choose varieties that flourish in your own climate

The maps on pages 450–451 give a broad-brush picture of the world's climates as seen from the rose-lover's point of view and allow us to make some preliminary selections.

In the tropics, heat and humidity favor bugs and fungus diseases at the expense of rosebushes, which usually go into shock during the hot season and flower most abundantly during the cool season. The star performers here are the Teas and Noisettes, which inherit their love of warm climates from their progenitor, the Burmese *R. gigantea*; but Modern Roses share that blood, too, and can be grown satisfactorily provided you choose your varieties for their strong resistance to disease and keep the spray gun handy. You would be well advised not to bother with the once-blooming Old Garden Roses, which need a period of winter chill to show their full beauty.

In arid and desert climates, heat and drought are the problems, but if water is available for irrigation, roses actually grow very well in those conditions. Keep them well mulched to keep the soil cool; and if you can arrange some shade in the hottest part of the day, they will thank you for it. But you will need to select varieties whose flowers can stand up to intense sunlight without scorching, fading or flopping open by breakfast time. Just which classes to choose from depends on whether you get winter frost in your area, and if so, how much.

Southern hemisphere gardeners do not need to worry about their roses being killed by frost, but frost can be limiting in the northern hemisphere. Where the temperature regularly falls below 0°F (−18°C), the Teas and Chinas and most Noisettes will need greenhouse cultivation, and even the modern bush roses will need protection from the cold in the form of loose soil and/or brushwood heaped over the bases of the plants. Let the temperature fall 15°F further (to −26°C), and only the most cold-tolerant roses (the Rugosas, some of the modern shrubs derived from them and from *R. pimpinellifolia*, and the toughest of the Wild Roses) will survive. (The map may suggest that the area of the world that gets as cold as that is much bigger than it is, but that is an illusion created by the distortions of Mercator's projection, which exaggerates distances the further you go from the Equator.)

Remember, however, that every rose in the catalogues is an individual with its own foibles and that even in climates that are ideal for roses a given variety that flourishes mightily in one garden may not do so well in a garden less than two hours' drive away where the microclimate is subtly different. As so often in gardening, local knowledge and experience are what count, and a trip to a nearby rose garden or a chat to the neighborhood rose enthusiast will quickly tell you which roses grow best in your area.

If a rose does prove unwilling to perform for you, then discard it – 'shovel prune it', in the neat American phrase. It won't have cost all that much, after all, and there are plenty of other candidates for its position. But (unless it was killed by frost in its first winter) do give it a decent chance to develop and become established, taking your cue from the judges at the trial grounds, who never assess a rose solely on its first year's performance.

While you are considering which roses you want to grow, turn your thoughts also to where you can best accommodate them, remembering the second rule of rose growing:

Rule 2 • Give roses plenty of sunshine

You do occasionally see a rosebush surviving in the shade, but roses must have at least half the day in sunshine to flourish. Nurserymen grow their plants out in fields open to the sun all day, and that is the ideal. It is one of the reasons why the traditional rose garden, with its beds cut out of the grass, evolved. It is not easy to back roses up against shrubbery and still ensure that they get enough sunshine. If you have the choice, morning sun is better than the hot sun of the afternoon. There are many rules in horticulture that can be fudged a bit, but this is not one of them. If a spot in your garden does not get

Potted tree roses on a balcony in Verona, Italy

The result is hardly pretty — just a few prickly sticks with some stringy roots attached — but it holds the promise of beauty to come, and it speaks much of the rose's inherent vitality that it can endure such drastic treatment and still come up smiling when it is planted.

In the United States, rosebushes are graded for quality, as Grades 1, 1½ and 2. Never content yourself with less than Grade 1, even if the price is higher. A runty bush in the nursery is likely to remain a runt forever.

Gardeners in other countries do not have the assistance of a widely used standard of quality, but a good-quality rosebush is still easy enough to recognize. Its branches will be sturdy, but the most important thing is that the roots be strong and copious. Feel the plastic package: if it seems to be mostly sawdust, choose another plant. It is usually the case that the biggest of the batch is the best buy, but remember that varieties vary in the thickness of their branches and how big they grow in their 'maiden' year in the nursery. The biggest here means the biggest available of that particular variety.

No reliable nurseryman, however — especially a rose specialist — would sell a second-grade plant, but a surprising number find their way into chain stores and supermarkets to tempt people who cannot resist a small price tag. When you remember that a rosebush is already two years old when you buy it, you will realize that roses are not really expensive.

Just as important, however, is how the plant has been handled after it was lifted. Check the branches again. They should be plump, and the bark between the thorns should be satin-smooth. (Whether it is green or brown depends on the variety.) If it is at all wrinkled or shrivelled-looking, then the plant has been allowed to dry out. Reject it, and if roses ordered by mail arrive in that condition, fire off a letter of complaint to the supplier at once. You can sometimes rehydrate them by completely burying them in wet soil for a week, but you are making a garden, not running a horticultural hospital.

Be wary of buying your roses at the local supermarket, or anywhere where the plants are kept indoors. The warmth can force them into wasting their energy on premature growth, which will only wither when the plant is taken out again into the cold of the garden. If you do decide to buy from such an outlet, ask the person in charge when the next batch is coming in and buy as soon as it arrives.

It has become common in recent years for garden centres to offer roses in containers during the flowering season, which allows people both to see what the rose they are buying looks like and to enjoy it immediately. The first thing to watch for here is that it has not had its roots crowded into too small a pot. Then look for vigorous growth, with no sign that the plant has been allowed to dry out at any stage, a catastrophe from which roses recover rather slowly. There will be no disease or bugs on the leaves, of course; nor will there be weeds in the pot. How many flowers it has open on shopping day is irrelevant.

Is it worth paying extra for certified virus-free plants? Yes, it is, especially with older varieties that have been showing their age — the improvement is remarkable. And no virus does its host any good, no matter how harmless it might appear. Virus-free roses are not common in the marketplace, however.

half a day's sun or more, don't waste your time planting roses there. Give it to plants that like and need shade. There are plenty of them to choose from — and while it may be heresy in some quarters to say it, they will be a welcome respite from roses, roses all the way.

Rule 3 • Roses like rich, rich soil

It used to be said that roses needed clay, but that is now known not to be true. Most rose-lovers nowadays agree that the fine, crumbly loam that suits most plants is the ideal (although if it is on the heavy side, the rose will not mind); but any fertile soil will do, except the sandiest (although even here the Rugosas will thrive, and lavish applications of organic matter will improve its texture) and the swampy. True, *R. nitida* and *R. palustris* will put up with wet feet, but few other roses will, so if your soil is poorly drained, it will be worth your while to lay agricultural drains or build up raised beds.

The debate over whether the soil should be acid or alkaline has been scientifically decided. It should be slightly acidic to allow all the necessary nutrients to be transferred most effectively to the plant. In practical terms, looking at roses all over the world for this book, it has struck me that the best always seemed to be growing in mildly acidic soil. Adding dolomite lime to rose beds to ensure mild acidity guarantees successful soil conditions.

Whatever your soil, prepare it generously. As one old rose-grower puts it, 'the rose prefers a rich diet to Cuisine Minceur'. Back in the days of Queen Victoria, the writers of rose books were fond of telling their readers that 'roses are gross feeders'. Not perhaps an image that flatters the Queen of Flowers, but it is true. The richer the soil the better, and while we may not be able to provide manure in the quantities advised when anyone who could afford a rose garden could afford to keep a horse or two, the prescription still holds. Before you plant, cultivate your rose beds deeply and incorporate as much old manure and compost — organic matter of any kind — as you can lay your hands on. Then leave it all to settle and mellow for several weeks before you plant. Remember, roses live for many years and you will not get the chance to do this preparation again. So do it generously.

Rule 4 • Start with the best plants you can buy

The rose is unusual among garden shrubs in two respects: first, it is almost always grafted, and second, it is traditionally sold bare-rooted — that is, dug up from the nursery field and presented to the customer with no soil around its roots. The nursery or garden centre will have either kept the uprooted plant 'heeled in' in a bed of loose soil or, more usually these days, put a handful or two of peat or half-rotted sawdust around its roots and bundled them up in plastic — both being courses of action designed to keep the plant from drying out. The branches are usually cut back fairly severely.

Hardiness zones

The idea of mapping a country by its lowest winter temperatures to assist farmers and gardeners in choosing what to plant has been around for quite a while, and it was in the United States that the first hardiness zone maps were devised, in the 1920s. These were superseded in 1960 by the first official hardiness zone map for the United States, produced by the Department of Agriculture and based on the lowest winter temperature recorded at its weather stations over the previous 10 years. The maps of America shown here are based on the revised version, which covers the whole of North America.

The zones are numbered from the coldest (zone 1) to the warmest (zone 11 and higher), each being 10°F (5.55°C) warmer than the next. Of course, the winter does not suddenly get that much warmer (or colder) as you cross the boundary from one zone to the next, but it is still accurate enough for most purposes to say that a plant is 'hardy to zone 6' or 'hardy to zone 4' or whatever, meaning that it will survive the winter in that zone but not colder winters.

Each entry in the book gives an estimate of the zones in which a particular rose can be expected to survive – but you may well find that it needs protection in winter in the coldest zone given and needs pampering in the warmest. As always, check with your local experts for guidance.

The concept of hardiness zones has been extended to the rest of the world, although it must be admitted that it does not translate all that well to Australia and South Africa, where the winters are rather shorter than they are in most parts of the northern hemisphere and heat and drought are just as significant as frost. It may raise a few eyebrows to find, for

instance, that Brisbane and Melbourne are both in Zone 9 – although that is perhaps not so important when we are talking roses as when we are considering tropical plants like mangoes or jacarandas. Again, local advice is invaluable.

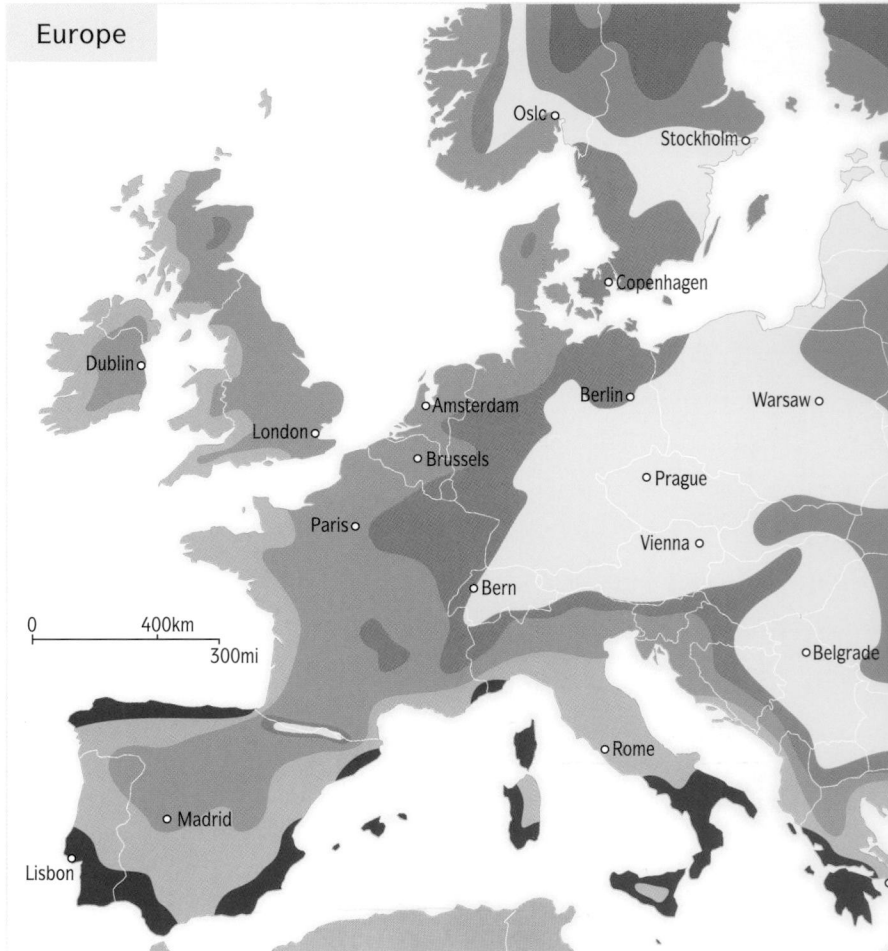

Europe

Average annual minimum temperature

Temperature (°F)	Zone color	Temperature (°C)
Below -50°F	1	-46°C and below
-50°F to -40°F	2	-46°C to -40°C
-40°F to -30°F	3	-40°C to -34.5°C
-30°F to -20°F	4	-34°C to -29°C
-20°F to -10°F	5	-29°C to -23°C
-10°F to 0°F	6	-23° to -18°C
0°F to 10°F	7	-18°C to -12°C
10°F to 20°F	8	-12°C to -7°C
20°F to 30°F	9	-7°C to -1°C
30°F to 40°F	10	-1°C to 4°C
40°F to 50°F	11	4°C to 10°C

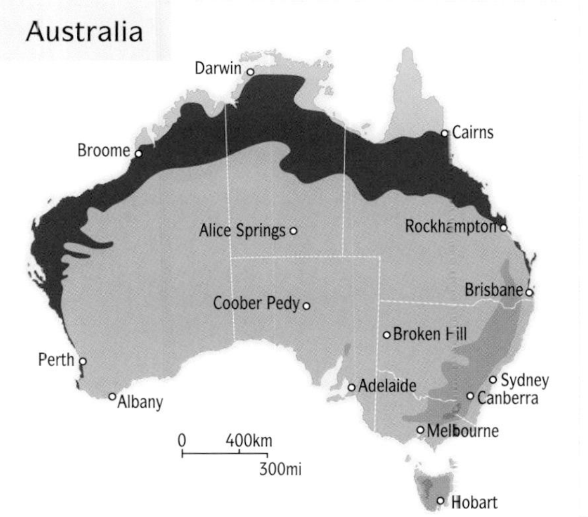

Australia

Darwin
Broome
Cairns
Alice Springs
Rockhampton
Coober Pedy
Brisbane
Perth
Broken Hill
Albany
Adelaide
Sydney
Canberra
Melbourne
Hobart

0   400km
300mi

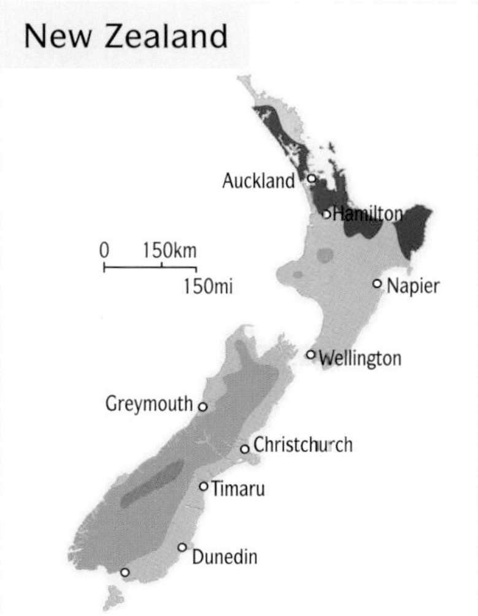

New Zealand

Auckland
Hamilton
0   150km
150mi
Napier
Wellington
Greymouth
Christchurch
Timaru
Dunedin

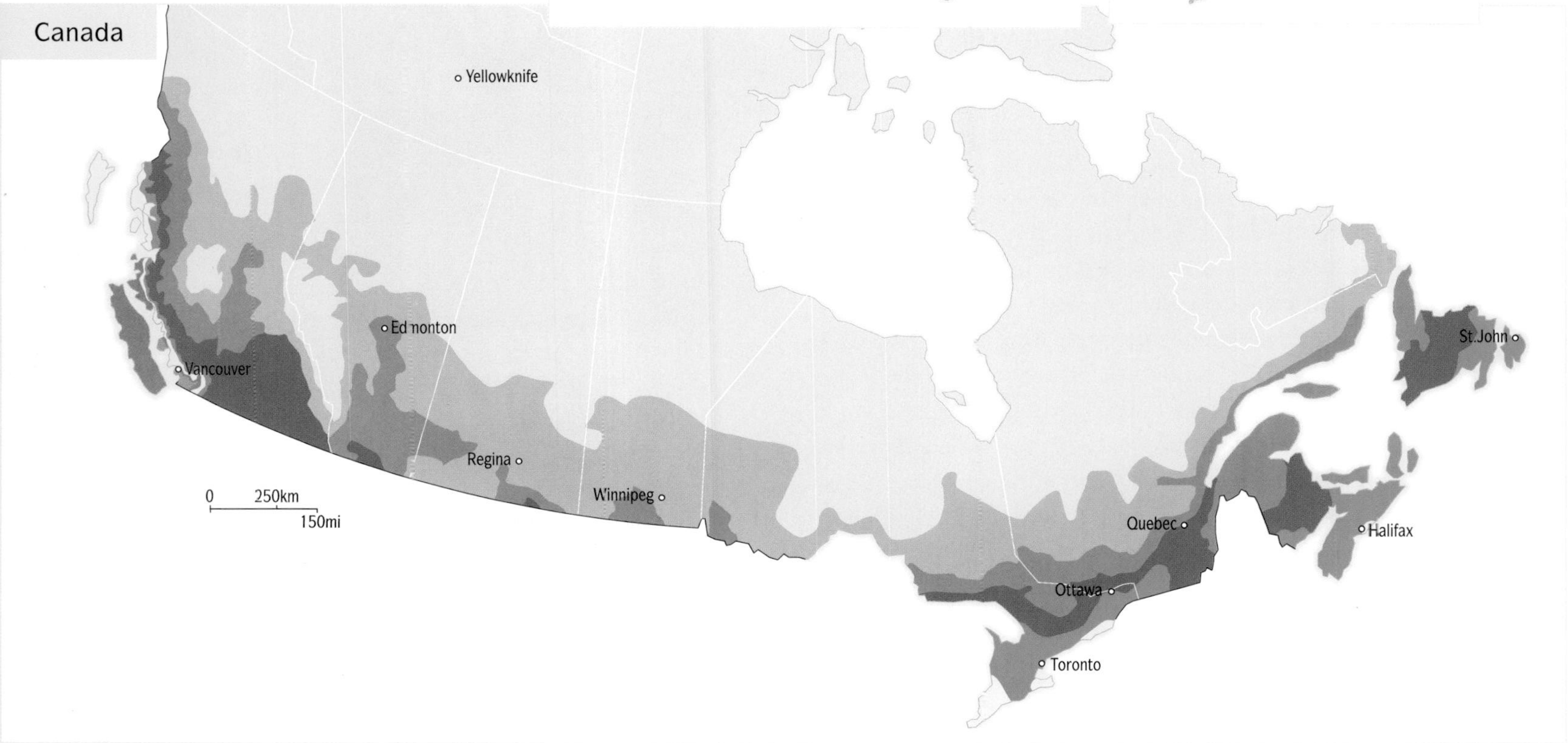

Canada

Yellowknife
Edmonton
Vancouver
St.John
Regina
Winnipeg
Quebec
Halifax
Ottawa
Toronto

0   250km
150mi

World hardiness zones

Roses grow well without protection.

Garden roses need protection against cold: many Wild Roses are hardy.

Too cold for all but the hardiest of Wild Roses.

Roses can be grown, but heat and humidity are likely to be a problem.

Roses can only be grown with irrigation in desert areas; most Wild Roses and many Old Garden Roses will dislike the summer heat.

Rule 5 • Plant with care

When you get your roses home, the ideal is to plant them at once, but if that is not possible they will come to no harm if left in their packaging for a few days – not in the warmth of the house, however, and not in the frost, either. Leaving them on a verandah or next to the window of an unheated garage will be fine. If they have arrived by mail, open the parcel at once so that the plants can breathe and so that you can check that everything is in order.

Planting is the most important thing you ever do to a rose. Do it well, and it is off to a good start. Do it carelessly, and it may be crippled for life.

Planting a bare-root rose is a trifle more complicated than just tipping an ordinary shrub out of its pot and placing it in a hole, but not much, and it takes less time to do it than to describe how it is done.

Don't rely on your eye to get the spacing right. In most climates you set bush roses about 1m (just over 3ft) apart – a bit further apart in warm climates, where roses grow very large, a bit closer in cold ones. Again, be guided by local custom. It is surprising how easily the eye can be confused once you have started digging holes, and then you find either that the plants have gone in too wide and they will not all fit, or that they are too close and you do not have enough. Either way you end up having to dig them all up and start over. A measuring stick is easier to use than a tape measure, and it can be easily improvised with a couple of pieces of masking tape around a rake handle. Mark the position of each plant with a short cane – the bamboo stakes used for house plants will be fine.

It is critical not to let the plants dry out. Take them to their planting site in a bucket of water – and if you have ordered more than one plant of each variety and these have been delivered in bundles, make sure you have extra labels handy.

The diagrams and their captions should make all clear, but this is the procedure. First, you make a hole wide enough to spread out the roots and deep enough so that the bud union will end up at soil level, more or less. In mild climates, whether the bud union sits right at soil level or a shade above does not matter much – it looks better if it is at soil level – but in seriously frosty climates it is desirable to bury it about 8cm (3in) deep to guard against the cold; if frost kills the union, then you have lost your rose even if the rootstock survives. Standard (tree) roses go in as deep as they were in the nursery: you will see the soil mark on the stem.

When to plant?

The best time for planting depends on your climate. It will be some time during the rose's dormant period. In a mild climate, where the ground does not actually freeze, you can plant from the late fall/autumn until early spring. In the southern hemisphere, this is from the end of May until the end of August; in the northern hemisphere, from the end of October until, say, mid-April.

Where winters are really hard, as in much of the United States north of the Mason-Dixon line, it is better to wait until the ground begins to warm up in spring rather than expect a bush with no new roots to endure months of freezing weather. However, trust the reputable growers. You can be sure that their plants will be shipped only at the appropriate planting time.

Roses bought growing in containers can be planted when you buy them, and the procedure is the same as planting any potted plant. Just remember to keep them watered.

Planting

Make a hole big enough to spread the roots right out; then arrange them over a mound of clean soil at the bottom. A stick laid over the top helps to ensure that the bud union (the junction of the rootstock and the branches) will end up where it should: at ground level or slightly below.

Half-fill the hole with soil (no fertilizer needed just yet), and add some water to settle everything in.

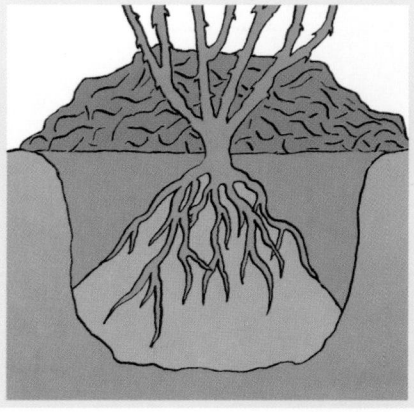

When the water has drained away, fill the hole to the top. Where winters are frigid, heaping mulch over the new bush will help to protect it.

In the spring, the mulch can be spread out and gently watered to expose the young shoots to light and air.

Then spread the roots out over a mound of soil at the bottom, fill up the hole a little over halfway with clean soil (no fertilizer at this stage; it may burn the delicate new roots), and tip in a bucket of water to settle it all in. There should, if your bed has been cultivated to a nicety, be no need to trample on the roots to firm them. When the water has drained away, fill the hole to the top with soil, and, if you like, heap some mulch up around the bush to be spread out later once the plant starts growing.

Heaping soil on the downhill side of bushes planted on slopes will help to hold water and control erosion. Ground Cover Roses would be the best choice on a slope as steep as this.

Wetting the foliage encourages black spot. One way of avoiding this is to lay a soaker hose upside down between the bushes. Mulch will effectively conceal it.

In dry climates, consider building a rampart of earth about 10cm (4in) high around the 'drip line' of each bush, to form a water-holding basin. It is a great water-saver, and the use of a trickle watering system also reduces water use.

A watering basin can be filled with mulch (rotted cow manure is ideal), which will not only save water but alleviate the crater-like effect of the basins.

Rule 6 • Keep your plants growing strongly

There is usually no need to water a young rosebush until it starts to grow in the spring. During the summer you should not allow roses to dry out, as drought does not encourage growth and flowering. Water deeply and infrequently (the roots go deep), but do try not to get the foliage wet any more than you have to, as wet leaves are an invitation to black spot. A soaker hose set upside down among the bushes, or a trickle irrigation system, can be most useful. So can

Roses in drought

For whatever reason, droughts seem to be occurring more frequently than they used to. When one strikes and you find yourself faced with restrictions on watering your garden, what do you do?

The answer, perhaps surprisingly, is *nothing*. By all means top up your mulch to conserve what water the soil still holds – before it dries out, not afterwards – and get rid of every weed that will rob the soil of that moisture; but otherwise do nothing. Do not water, do not fertilize, do not even remove the spent flowers. All these things are done to encourage new growth, and if there is insufficient moisture in the soil to support it, the plants may be irreparably damaged.

What we want is for our roses to simply stop growing and to husband their resources in the way their distant Mediterranean and Middle Eastern ancestors did when faced with the long, dry summers of those countries. They will look pretty miserable, to be sure; but when the rain returns, they will spring back to vigorous life. If the rains do not return until winter, they may not recover until the spring, and it will do the plants no harm if you skip pruning after a drought year except for removing any dead branches.

mulching the beds with any sort of organic matter that is available – compost, rotted manure, straw, composted shredded bark, even newspaper. Do not use sawdust, as it consumes nitrogen and can set like cement if it dries out. And beware of the chipped bark and woodchips sold as 'mulch' for landscapers. Very often these products have been treated with chemicals to discourage weeds, and they discourage roses just as effectively. They also consume nitrogen as they decay.

Mulch will also help to control weeds, which should never be allowed to flourish in rose beds. Not only do they make you, the gardener, look negligent, they rob the roses of water and nourishment, and by crowding the plants they create the sorts of conditions where rose pests and diseases can get started. Pull them out as soon as you see them appearing. Pull them by hand – don't ever be tempted to use weed-killers on rose beds, no matter how judiciously. Roses are very sensitive to them.

Rule 7 • Keep the soil fertile

As noted earlier, roses are greedy creatures, and even though you prepared the beds lavishly before you planted, you need to maintain them at a high level of fertility. That means regular fertilizing, and the time to do it is after each 'flush' of bloom, when the plant is gathering its forces for a new cycle of growth and flowering. But don't fertilize after the fall/autumn flush – you don't want the plants going into the winter loaded with tender young growth.

What kind of fertilizer you use is up to you. Some growers are content to give their plants a quick boost with chemical fertilizers, others say that they are the vegetable equivalent of steroids and force the plants to grow unnaturally. Certainly, chemicals do nothing to replenish the humus on which the health of the soil depends, whereas manure, blood and bone, rich compost and other organic fertilizers do. This is another reason for not using a 'landscaping' mulch. It is almost impossible to spread a bulky fertilizer like manure without first scraping up the woodchips, and then you have to replace them afterwards. With a 'soft' mulch, you can just put the fertilizer on top. Always water generously after fertilizing, to start washing the nutrients down to the roots.

Climbers an

How to perfect the atmosphere of a beautiful rose garden? The answer lies in a third dimension — and that third dimension is the powerful domain of climbers and ramblers. So many rose gardens use only two dimensions, width and depth, and neglect the added elegance given by height — and height is the domain of the climbers and ramblers. By lifting their flowers to eye level and above, they greatly enrich the garden.

Origins of climbers and ramblers

How do we define climbing roses, and what is the distinction between climbers and ramblers? Both types make long, limber shoots which the gardener can train to a support or trellis (they don't cling like ivy does, or twine like jasmine), but when we speak of climbers we mean those roses that have large flowers — at least Floribunda-size — and, for the most part, repeat their bloom, while ramblers bear small flowers in large and small clusters and very few of them repeat, although in their season their display can be simply gorgeous. They usually have slimmer, more flexible branches than the climbers proper.

The climbers fall into three main groups. The oldest are the Noisettes and Climbing Teas, which bloom almost perpetually but whose sensitivity to cold restricts them to gardens free of heavy frost. They remain firm favorites in the mild climates of the southern hemisphere, in the southern states of the United States, and in places like the south of France. Most are beautifully fragrant.

The climbing sports of Hybrid Teas and Floribundas have the same names (prefixed by 'Climbing') and bear the same flowers as the varieties from which they sported. Some repeat their bloom generously, others are decidedly stingy; most have rather stiff branches and flower best when their branches are trained horizontally along a fence or over a wall.

TOP 'Chaplin's Pink Climber'
ABOVE 'Crépuscule'

The modern Large Flowered Climbers are mostly of moderate growth habit and most are repeat blooming. They are of mixed origin, some deriving their climbing habit from 'New Dawn', the first cold-hardy repeat-blooming climber, others from R. × kordesii. With them we can group the taller Hybrid Musks, the tallest of David Austin's 'English Roses' and some of the ultra-hardy 'Canadian Explorer' series and their ilk.

The ramblers derive their habit of growth and their clustered flowers from several species, among them R. multiflora and R. sempervirens, but the largest and best-known group of ramblers is that derived from the Japanese Wild Rose R. wichurana, known as Wichurana Ramblers. They arrived on the scene in the late nineteenth century, and came mainly from French raisers like the Barbier brothers of Orléans, although American hybridists like New Jersey's W. A. Manda and Maryland's Walter Van Fleet also bred some notable varieties. They are known for their hardiness, lavish bloom and rich colors.

Using climbers and ramblers in the garden

The simplest way to use climbers and ramblers is to train them over a fence or wall — one that has been fitted with a trellis or wires to tie the branches to. You can tie all the shoots in to create a flat curtain of flowers, or allow some of the secondary shoots to arch gracefully out and create cascades of flowers, which looks very attractive on a high wall or a two-storey house. It depends on the effect you want, but match the rose to the space available — a vast grower like 'Mermaid', 'Lamarque' or 'Silver Moon' can swallow up all but the largest houses.

The usual rule of thumb when spacing climbing roses along a fence or wall of ordinary height — when the branches will be trained more or less horizontally — is to set them about 3m (10ft) apart, but the more moderate growers can be set 2m (6ft) apart, when the branches will interlock to create a tapestry of flowers. They will turn a wire or post-and-rail fence into a formidable barrier against invading wildlife, but if you are adorning a picket fence, the wider spacing is better. You don't want to hide the pickets entirely!

Roses of moderate growth that bloom well when their branches are trained vertically are often called pillar roses. The name describes their use — to adorn a verandah post or a free-standing pillar or tripod set out in the garden. If they are 3–4m (10–13ft) high, pillars of roses can make a spectacular focal point for a small garden. The flowers will be more prolific if you wind the branches around the support rather than let them grow straight up.

The ultimate way to display climbing roses is on a pergola, which can both frame the garden and provide a tunnel of scent and beauty as you walk under it. A pillar rose on each post or column, with stronger ones every third pillar to grow over the top — what could

Ramblers

be more glorious? But make the structure of generous size – not less than 2.5m (8ft) wide and tall or you will be forever dodging the prickles.

Or you could just plant a vigorous rambler or climber next to an unsightly outhouse or shed, or a decrepit old tree, and allow it to grow as it pleases until the eyesore vanishes in a great mound of roses . . .

ABOVE 'Alexandre Girault'
BELOW 'Climbing Iceberg'

Some moderate growers for walls and houses

'America': a prize-winning orange-pink climber

'Altissimo': a single, bright red climber with saucer-shaped petals and golden yellow stamens

'Climbing Lady Hillingdon': a Tea with buff-yellow flowers and rich fragrance

'Climbing Pinkie': sweet pink flowers in clusters and no thorns

'Dublin Bay': shapely, blood-red flowers

'Joseph's Coat' and 'Piñata': multi-colored flowers

'Madame Alfred Carrière': the hardiest of the Noisettes, with richly fragrant, white flowers

'Pierre de Ronsard': Old Garden Rose-style, soft pink blooms

'Fourth of July': red-and-white-striped blooms with an apple fragrance

'Guinée': almost-black flowers and rich fragrance

'Veilchenblau': a purple/mauve rambler with no thorns

'Zéphirine Drouhin': no thorns and vivid pink flowers with a wonderful fragrance

Some suggestions for pergolas or large walls and houses

'Climbing Iceberg': a classic white Floribunda, with large clusters of blooms

'Climbing Mademoiselle Cécile Brünner': grows to 6–10m (20–30ft) tall, with profuse sweet-smelling, light pink blooms

'Crépuscule': a peach to apricot Noisette that flowers all year in mild climates

'Dortmund': single, blazing red flowers in clusters

'Lamarque': scented, white flowers all year

'Mermaid': huge, single, creamy-yellow flowers and many thorns

'New Dawn': grows to 3.5–6m (12–20ft) tall, with light pink blooms in small clusters

R. banksiae lutea: evergreen, with little yellow flowers in profusion in spring

'Souvenir de Madame Léonie Viennot': a Tea with fragrant, azalea-pink flowers

'Veilchenblau': purple/mauve flowers and no thorns

Some suggestions for pillars

'Altissimo' (see above)

'Cornelia': Hybrid Musk with scented, warm pink flowers

'Long Tall Sally': single, white flowers

'Renae': soft pink flowers and no thorns

'Titian': vivid pink flowers

Many of the taller David Austin 'English Roses' make excellent pillar roses.

Disbudding

It is customary among exhibitors to thin the buds of Hybrid Teas to one per stem, so that the plant will concentrate its energy into that single perfect bloom. This is done by pinching off the side buds as soon as they are large enough to handle – but if you are content to enjoy your roses as they come, there is no need to do it. Similarly, do not bother thinning the shoots in the early spring in the hope of gaining fewer but gigantic flowers. Leave such tricks to the growers of exhibition chrysanthemums! Thinning the buds of Floribundas or the Old Garden Roses is unthinkable; their beauty lies largely in the profusion of their flowers.

Unless you are expecting hips, keep the spent flowers trimmed off to encourage the later ones, but do not take too much foliage. The same applies to cutting flowers for the house. It is advisable not to cut long-stemmed flowers at all from bushes in their first year, and even with established bushes try not to levy too many long-stalked blooms at any one time. How long is long? It depends on the variety: some offer longer stems than others, but always leave at least two leaves on each stem.

Rule 8 • Prune lightly

There is no subject that has rosarians arguing more than the 'right' way to prune – but the first thing to bear in mind is that it is not compulsory. Roses have been around for some 30 million years, so the fossil record tells us, and that was a long time before the invention of pruning shears. And you only have to come across an ancient rosebush that has grown to an enormous size and is smothered in flowers in some neglected old garden or cemetery to wonder why we bother!

Yet pruning does serve two purposes. It keeps the plants neat, and more importantly it keeps them young.

Pruning is nothing like as complicated as it sounds if you remember that its chief purpose is to keep the bushes young. A rose does not make a permanent framework of branches in the way a camellia or a hibiscus does but grows almost like an herbaceous plant. It constantly renews itself by sending up strong new shoots from the base to take the place of those of former years that have flowered themselves into feebleness. Eventually, old branches die; dead wood on a healthy rosebush is no cause for alarm.

So, take the job in three stages. First, remove dead wood entirely, followed by any branches that are evidently so old and infirm as to be unable to bear fine flowers any more, or else are just too small and skinny to do so. Then shorten the branches that you have decided to retain, cutting just above a growth bud. How much you shorten depends on climate; you prune harder in frosty areas and more lightly in mild ones.

Very hard pruning used to be the fashion, but is so no longer. The current recommendation is to shorten your retained branches by a third to a half. But in frosty climates you may be forced to go harder than that, as every bit of frost-damaged wood must be removed. Such wood may recover enough to produce a feeble flower or two, but then it will die. You recognize it by its pith – that of a sound branch is white, whereas if frost has struck it goes brown. Cut, bit by bit, until you come to white pith and then to a suitable bud.

Those are the principles. You can follow them pretty closely with the Hybrid Teas and Floribundas. Shrub Roses, old and new, are

Pruning

The first stage of pruning is to remove dead wood entirely; then prune any weak branches or those that cross over others and crowd out the centre of the bush.

Then shorten the branches you have elected to retain by a third to a half. Go gently in mild climates, harder in cold ones.

Cut just above a growth bud (found where a leaf has joined the stem), leaving no long stub to rot. Make sure your secateurs are sharp, and hold them so that the bruised bit of bark is on the part you cut off.

trimmed more lightly – if in doubt, just cut out the spent wood and see how the plant behaves. With climbers, don't shorten the current season's long canes that have not yet flowered except to remove any skinny ends, and cut back the short laterals that bore the flowers to two or three 'eyes'.

Many of the Wild Roses merely need tidying up – again, just cut out any dead and feeble wood. Ramblers are the simplest of all: few of them produce branches good for more than one flowering, so, as soon as the flowers are over, you cut the just-flowered branches right out to make way for the new ones. Simple, but labor-intensive, which is one reason why ramblers are less popular than they used to be.

The once-flowering Old Garden Roses can be pruned in winter like a bush rose, or, if you prefer, you can simply trim out the oldest, twiggiest branches just after flowering. The Miniatures can be treated with care, judging every cut, or you can just cut them down by half. It seems to make little difference to their performance. There is no need to fret about following the rules exactly – roses are not all that easy to kill!

Suckers from the understock should be removed as soon as you notice them. Rip them out, if feasible; but if they are too established for that, cut them as close to their origin as possible.

Ramblers are the simplest of all roses to prune. Immediately after they have bloomed, cut away all the branches that have just flowered, either to where a new shoot is arising or right to the ground. Simple, but a time-consuming and prickly job!

Repeat-blooming climbers, both large-flowered and cluster-flowered, are best pruned in winter. Remove old and worn-out wood, cutting either to a strong, young branch or right to the ground. Shorten the strong laterals that bore last year's flowers, and just take out the skinny tips of new canes.

But before you start, do make sure that your secateurs and pruning saws are really sharp – sharp enough to cut paper. Blunt tools will tear instead of cutting cleanly, and that will do far more harm to the plant than 'incorrect' pruning. Ask your local rose-grower to recommend someone who sharpens pruning shears; it is not an easy job. Or else buy an inexpensive new pair every year.

When you have finished pruning, snip off any old leaves remaining on the bushes, gather up all the debris and burn it, if possible, or take it to the tip or city rubbish dump. (It is likely to be harboring fungus spores and insect eggs, and is too prickly for the compost heap in any case.) Then give the bushes a post-pruning spray to clean up any bugs or fungus spores that may be hanging around and give the roses a clean start for the new season. This is well worth doing; you may find it is all the spraying you need. What to use? White oil (pest oil) at the 'winter strength' recommended for fruit trees is fine, and lime sulphur and chloride of lime are also traditional. Use only one; don't mix them either with each other or with anything else.

When to prune?

The traditional time to prune is when the plants are dormant and new growth is just around the corner. In mild climates, you can prune at any time during the winter, after the leaves have fallen but before new growth begins. In the southern hemisphere, this means from June to early August, with the optimum time being mid-July; in the northern hemisphere, from December to about the beginning of March. Where winters are severe – say, zone 6 and colder – the custom is to leave the task until early spring, when the risk of severe frost is past, as you don't want to encourage the plants to make new growth that might get killed off by a late frost. Even if the new growth is not killed such a frost may damage the developing flower buds and result in a crop of what are called 'blind shoots'. As always, follow local custom.

None of this prevents you from giving the bushes a tidy-up early in the winter, gently trimming back any long shoots that will wave about in winter gales – but that is not the same as pruning!

Winter protection

Readers in Britain and in the southern hemisphere can skip this section, but if you garden in the colder parts of North America or in central Europe – zone 6 or colder, more or less – you will need to consider protecting your roses against the cold of winter.

The best protection of all is continuous deep snow, but where that cannot be counted on the tradition is to mound soil up over the base of the bushes to a depth of at least 35cm (12in) and maybe put some branches, straw or similar on top to keep the rain off a bit. Obviously, you can't take that soil from the rose beds themselves, as that will expose the roots to the cold; it has to come from elsewhere, most likely the vegetable garden.

Some gardeners find that making a cage of wire netting around the bush and filling that with fallen leaves is sufficient; others swear by polystyrene 'rose cones' – but be guided by local practice. Climbers are awkward, as if their branches are killed, that means no flowers next season, and you may find yourself having to detach them from their supports, lay their branches on the ground and then cover them over. The same is true of standard (tree) roses, whose bud unions are too high to bury. The standard method here is to cut half the roots away, bend the stem over and then heap soil, or whatever materials you are using, up over the whole plant.

Whichever method you adopt, it is best to wait until a couple of hard frosts have pushed the bushes into dormancy but to act before the ground itself has frozen – and, of course, the whole show has to be removed as soon as the plants start growing in spring, when they can be pruned as usual.

It is all a lot of work, and nobody will think you lazy if you decide to forgo the Hybrid Teas, Floribundas and their ilk, almost all of which need protection in zone 5 and may need it in the colder parts of zone 6, and concentrate on those hardy varieties that will survive severe winters without protection. You will still have some beautiful roses to choose from.

Now – while the mass of thorny branches has been reduced and you can get at the beds without too much injury – is the time to get them ready for the upcoming season, pulling out any persistent weeds, forking in last year's mulch, and applying new mulch on top of a generous dressing of old manure.

Then you can sit back for a bit and admire the new leaves as they come in all their tones of red, bronze and mint-green, anticipating the flowers they presage.

Propagation

Most of us are content to expand our rose collection by buying plants, leaving the nurseryman to do the work of propagating them; but if you plan to go in for roses in a big way – or if you fall in love with an unlabelled or unprocurable rose in a friend's garden – it is nice to know that roses are quite easy to propagate.

The easiest way of all is by layering. You simply bend a branch down to the ground and bury a section of it. A couple of nicks will encourage new roots, and if you make your layer at some time shortly after mid-summer, you should be able to sever the new plant from its parent and transplant it the following winter. Naturally, the rose has to have branches limber enough to be bent to the ground, and this limits layering to climbers, ramblers, ground covers (some of which will, blackberry-like, layer themselves spontaneously) and the laxer shrub roses – bush roses are usually far too stiff.

Cuttings ('slips', as Grandma used to call them) are another easy method, and the diagrams show you how to take them. The traditional time is when you prune, but you can also take them in summer. In this case you need to cover them to keep the air moist around them. A greenhouse or cold frame is ideal, but you can put them in a pot and enclose the whole thing in a plastic bag the way you do with any summer cutting. Don't remove the top two leaves entirely – leave the stipules (the bracts at the base of the leaf). If these drop off after a week or so, all is going to plan; if they wither in place, the cutting is dying and you need to take fresh ones.

Always take more cuttings than you need. Not all roses strike equally easily, and not all cuttings grow into strong bushes. With most hybrid roses, a 50 per cent success rate is considered to be pretty good.

The nurseryman gets over the variability of plants grown from cuttings by grafting roses onto suitable understocks, which are chosen for the vigor of their roots. You and I can follow his example, as budding, the method of choice, is much the easiest of all forms of grafting. The diagrams make the procedure plain. Indeed, the hardest part may well be acquiring your understocks; nurserymen are often reluctant to sell them outside the trade.

The best way to obtain roots, therefore, is to buy a plant or two of a suitable variety and take cuttings from it yourself. One of the thornless clones of *R. multiflora* would be ideal, but 'Veilchenblau' and 'Gloire des Rosomanes' have their devotees, too. One nurseryman of my acquaintance suggests 'New Dawn', despite its prickliness, as it strikes very easily and makes splendid, strong roots. The cuttings are taken in the usual way – in summer, the fall/autumn or winter – except that you must excise all the 'eyes' except the top one (a razor blade will do it), or you will have a lifetime of unwanted suckers.

Plant your cuttings in a nursery bed about 50cm (20in) apart, and if they were rooted in the fall/autumn, they should be ready for budding the following summer. The best time is just after the first flowering, when the sap in the understock will be flowing strongly – encouraged by a watering a week or so before you plan to bud – and the buds mature. Follow the diagrams, using a razor blade if you do not have a special budding knife. Just as with cuttings, the bit of leaf stalk you use as a handle will tell you, by falling off, if the bud is going to take. If it withers in place, the bud has died.

Cuttings

The best cuttings come from a strong stem that has borne a good flower, preferably from the middle third of its length. Take cuttings either at pruning time or immediately after flowering. Clip off any leaves.

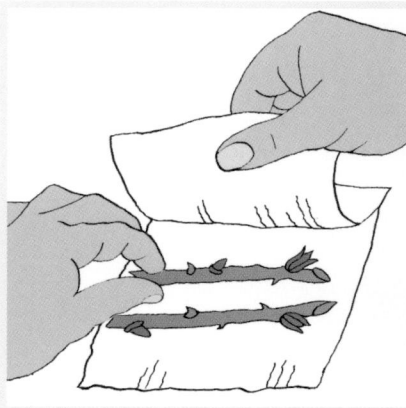

If you are not able to plant your cuttings immediately, roll them up in damp paper so that they do not dry out.

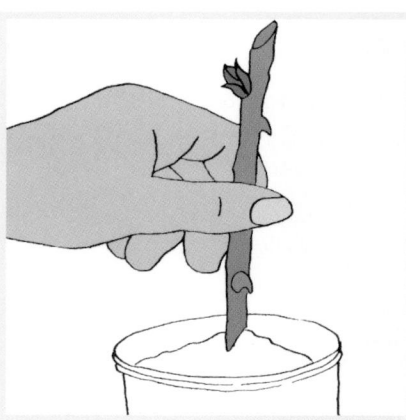

A dip in hormone rooting powder will increase your chances of success, but make sure it is fresh; it loses potency quite quickly.

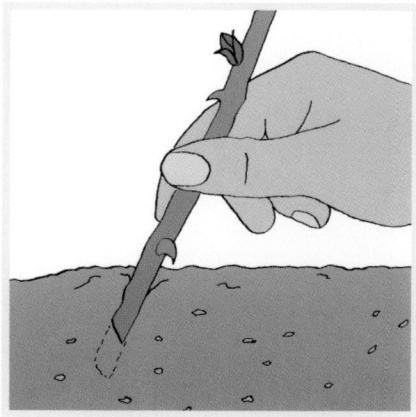

Traditionally, cuttings are inserted at an angle, but you can set them vertically if you prefer. They go in, into sandy soil, to half their length.

There will probably not be much further activity until winter, when you behead the stock entirely just above the bud. It will grow and flower that summer – in its first season the plant is called a 'maiden' – and the following winter the new plant will be ready for its permanent home.

Budding

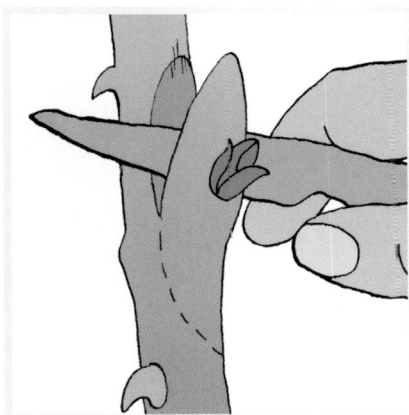

With a razor-sharp blade (the purpose-made budding knife is best) cut the bud from the stem, taking a shield-shaped piece of bark with it. The buds are ready when the thorns snap off easily and cleanly.

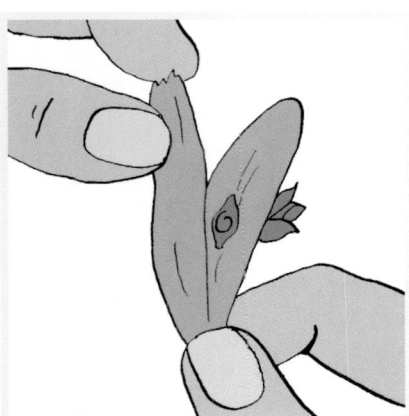

If there is a sliver of wood behind the bark, you can snap it out. If you cannot do so without taking the bud with it, leave it in.

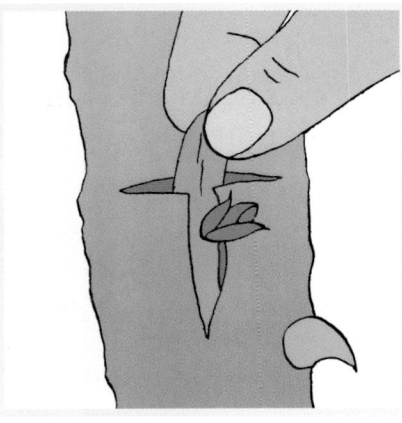

Make a T-shaped cut in the bark of the stock just above ground level and, using the back of the blade, lift back the flaps like a coat collar. If the bed has been well watered a day or two previously, this should be easy. Then just slip in the bud. Do not let it dry out while all this is going on. Hold it between your lips if need be.

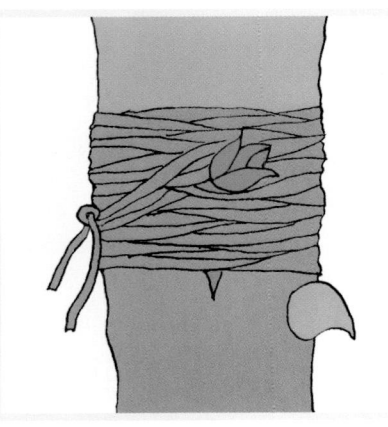

Tie the bud in place with raffia or budding tape. When the bud begins to swell, after three weeks or so, remove the tape. Raffia can be allowed to rot away over time. Come winter, the stock is cut away to just above the bud, which will take off and develop in spring.

Standards (tree roses) are made by budding onto exceptionally long rootstocks, setting two buds for symmetry, but I must confess to never having tried it. The very thought of trying to strike cuttings 1m (just over 3ft) long, even of so obliging a plant as *R. multiflora*, always defeated me.

Is it legal to propagate your own roses?

Not always. Almost all countries now provide that the creators of new varieties of roses (and other plants) enjoy copyright protection in their creations for a certain period of time, which varies from 17 years in the United States to 20 years in Australia (25 years for trees and grapes) and 23 years in New Zealand. The United States grants a 'plant patent', while other countries speak of 'plant variety rights' or suchlike, but the principle is the same. The variety can only be propagated by people who have been granted a licence by the raiser or the raiser's agent and who in return pay royalties.

Most countries allow amateur gardeners like you and me to propagate protected (patented, copyrighted) varieties for our own use, provided we do not sell the new plants, not even at a church fundraiser; although whether it would be ethical to buy two bushes and then propagate a big bed of a hundred is debatable. The United States, however, does not make that exception, and it is illegal there to propagate a patented variety unless you hold a licence to do so. Whether any home gardener has been prosecuted for propagating a few rosebushes I do not know, but it would usually be safe to propagate a rose that came out more than 20 years ago.

Rule 9 · Keep pests and diseases under control

Queens tend to have enemies; it is one of the problems of queenhood. The Queen of Flowers is no exception – the list of bugs waiting to pounce as soon as the gardener's back is turned seems longer than that for any other flower.

Happily, most are rare, and even the common pests and diseases are not nearly as bad as they sound; but even so, if the rose had no enemies, what joy there would be! It is all very well to say that there are remedies that can be sprayed on, but spraying is a chore, toxic chemicals are not good either for the environment or for us, and many gardeners are coming to feel that there is something immoral about putting the world at risk for a luxury crop like the rose. It is bad enough having to spray food crops.

Should you be one of them, you must begin with a firm resolve to grow only roses with an excellent reputation for disease resistance *in your area*. It is not just a matter of a rose's suitability for your climate; the bugs and fungi come in different strains (it is said that there are a dozen of the black spot fungus alone), and a rose may be resistant to one or even several of these but not to them all. If a rose does prove to be a disease magnet, then harden your heart and get rid of it, no matter how enchanting its flowers may be. Not only will it be a hospital case itself, it will be a source of infection for its neighbors. And resist the lure of 'non-toxic' or 'organic' sprays – never mind that Grandma may have used them back in the good old days. They are just as much of a chore to apply as any others, and as most are not as effective in any case as the products of the chemical factories, you could find yourself spraying more rather than less often.

Then be sure to follow the rules of rose-growing, particularly the one about sunshine. A rose that is growing vigorously can shake off its problems; one that is already struggling cannot. When we speak of 'disease resistance', we mean resistance to fungi, but a chemical-free garden is also a bird-friendly one, and birds will deal with most of the insects for you. You won't have an entirely bug-free garden, most likely, but many people who have thrown their spray guns away entirely find that they get no more bugs than they did when they sprayed every week.

If that all sounds a bit doubtful, you may wish to compromise by spraying only once a year, immediately after pruning, as advocated in the pruning section (page 457). The major pests and diseases are listed below in alphabetical order.

Aphids (alias greenfly) are the major insect pest, and they infest many other plants besides roses. They breed in enormous numbers on soft young shoots, sucking out enough sap to cripple them and, more insidiously, spreading viruses. So as soon as you see the advance guard, deal with them immediately. Squash them between your fingers or drown them with a squirt from the hose. Any insecticide, even the mildest, will wipe them out.

Fungi are more trouble, really, than insects, and most roses are liable to fungus attack at some time or other. Once fungi have taken hold, they are more difficult to get rid of, and the gardener has to do it alone – insects are preyed on by other insects like ladybugs and by birds, while fungi appear to have no natural enemies. The three most damaging fungi are rust, black spot and mildew, in that order (see the box opposite).

Katydids and other grasshoppers, caterpillars, and several pollen-eating beetles sometimes show an interest in rosebushes, but apart from the bronze Japanese beetle, cursed by American gardeners for its decimation of the flowers, they do little harm, and any the birds have not disposed of are easily dealt with by a squirt of insecticide. An American friend deals with her Japanese beetles by going out into the garden with a can of water with a little kerosene floated on top and shaking the beetles off the flowers into the can to drown. Not a sight for the squeamish, she says.

Nematodes live in the soil – especially in sandy soils in hot climates such as Florida – and eat the roots. A bad infestation can have devastating effects, but here control is simple. Order your roses budded on the nematode-resistant *R. fortuneana*, which, happily, flourishes mightily in sandy soils and warm climates. It has long been the favored understock in Western Australia.

The stems of standards (tree roses) can get sunburnt. One solution is to wrap them in tea-tree branches. Old sacking would be just as effective, if less pretty.

Beware of rose-sick soil

It sometimes happens that you want to replace a rose, or a bed of roses, with new ones. This is risky, as it usually happens that no matter how healthy and vigorous the old plants were, the new ones fail to make healthy new roots and grow properly. The soil has become 'rose sick'.

Plant pathologists prefer to speak of 'specific replant syndrome', but they still have not discovered the cause. It is said that this syndrome does not occur in America. It certainly does elsewhere, and the traditional prescription is to replace the soil of the entire bed with some that has not been used to grow roses for several years, or to replace at least a barrow-load from the site of each old plant – or to wait two years before replanting.

The first is hard work and the second is frustrating, but recent reports from Britain suggest that adding vast amounts of super-rich compost works; or you can modify the traditional technique by setting a big cardboard box in the bed, filling it with fresh soil, and planting your new rose in that. The box will rot in a year or so and the roots will grow through it; in the meantime it has isolated them from the rose-sick soil.

Scale insects live a sedentary life on the lowest parts of the bush, protecting themselves from their enemies by exuding a shield of wax, usually white but sometimes reddish. They are more damaging than they look, and should either be sprayed with white oil or swabbed with an old brush dripping with alcohol (denatured alcohol or methylated spirits), both of which will dissolve the wax and suffocate the insects.

Spider mites, aka red spider, congregate on the underside of the leaves and suck the sap out until the leaf is as dry as paper and falls off. They are very tiny, and you may need a magnifying glass to see them and the tiny webs they weave. They used not to be a serious problem with roses, but as their natural predators get killed off by insecticides (not being insects, the mites are immune), they are seen more often than they used to be. A special miticide is called for; and as they build up resistance very quickly, the latest should be used. They love dry-summer climates and hate water, so if you catch them early, a few drenchings with the hose will usually put paid to them. It is said that violets harbor them and should not be grown in rose beds.

Thrips are another of the insects that cause damage by their numbers. An individual one is so tiny as to be almost invisible, but if thrips congregate in their hundreds among the rose petals they will soon have them looking very bedraggled. Thrips are most likely to fly when a hot wind is blowing, and they prefer the paler-colored flowers. They usually vanish when the weather improves. If you must spray, then a systemic insecticide works best.

Black spot is the bane of rose-lovers in humid climates. Although there is no garden rose that is immune, there are many that have sufficient resistance to flourish with minimum attention from the spray gun.

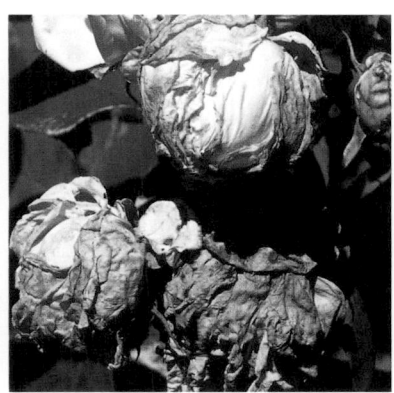

A bad case of thrips – these flowers of 'Michèle Meilland' are quite ruined.

The dark red roses are always said to be the most susceptible to mildew, and this bedraggled specimen of 'Deuil de Paul Fontaine' is a case in point.

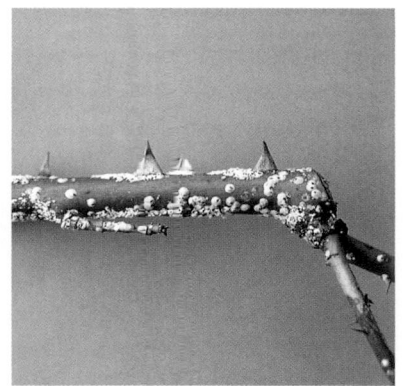

The white rose scale is a much more serious pest than it looks. It is often encountered on old and neglected bushes; removing it is the first step to restoring them to vigor.

Fungi

The three most important fungi are rust, black spot and mildew.

Rust is the most dangerous, and immediately you see it (it looks just as its name implies and usually starts on the underside of the lowest leaves), you should spray repeatedly with a copper-based fungicide as a matter of urgency. Otherwise the bush will soon be denuded of leaves and may even be killed. Fortunately, rust is not common and most Modern Roses are resistant to it. Again, if one proves not to be, get rid of it.

Black spot ranks next – once the telltale fringed black spots appear on a leaf, that leaf is doomed. The fungus can only take hold on damp leaves, which is why you are advised not to wet your bushes when watering, and why black spot is worst in warm, humid climates. The fairly new systemic fungicides have made controlling it easier, but if you live in a humid-summer climate it would be prudent to spray for prevention rather than cure, and that means once a fortnight during the whole growing season. Naturally, if you live in a black spot area, you will not give garden room to varieties known to be susceptible to the disease. Alas, they include very many of the yellows and yellow blends, which derive their color, glossy leaves and susceptibility from the Wild Rose *R. foetida*.

Mildew is a lesser evil than rust or black spot, but it can still be devastating. It usually strikes the young shoots and is worst in dry weather. As soon as you see it (when you have seen it once, you will recognize the distorted, unhappy look that precedes the grey mildew powder), spray it once or twice and give the bed a good watering. Keep up the spraying until the symptoms disappear and the new growth is clean – and be sure to keep the soil well watered in future.

The above applies to powdery mildew. Downy mildew is different, and its symptoms – dark mottling and shrivelling of the leaves – can be confused with black spot, especially as it is fairly rare. It is a problem in New Zealand and seems to be on the increase in the United States. The usual fungicides will control it.

Fortunately, you are unlikely to be troubled by rust, black spot and the mildews all at once, but you should still select your rose varieties for their resistance to whichever is the main problem in your area. Do that, and the post-pruning spray will most likely be all you need. If any fungus spore or insect can survive that, it is tough indeed!

Viruses

Viruses can survive anything, and the only way to deal with the two worst is to dig out and burn the affected bush or bushes as soon as the diagnosis is confirmed, to stop the disease from spreading. Fortunately, you will not suffer both at once – rose rosette virus is found only in the eastern United States, and rose wilt only in Australia.

Rosette is a relatively new phenomenon and is the result of bureaucratic bungling. In the 1940s it was fashionable to plant thickets of *R. multiflora* along highways in the eastern United States to act as living crash barriers. They were quite effective, but the species went feral and became a pest. Then someone came up with the idea that if the feral Multifloras were infected with rosette virus, they would all die off, solving the problem quickly and cheaply. Of course, they did not die off, and now the virus has not only spread to the native Wild Roses, it is beginning to appear on garden roses also. Its symptom is that it gives rise to what are called 'witches' brooms' on the infected plant – they look almost as though someone has grafted non-flowering Miniature Roses on its branches – and the whole plant slowly becomes stunted and dies. It is contagious, being spread by certain wingless mites.

Wilt is contagious, too, being spread by aphids. The name describes it: the young shoots wilt, turn black and die, and eventually the whole bush dies. It comes and goes: you can have a bad season and then not see it for years. It only occurs in Australia and perhaps in Italy – which is no consolation to those whose roses are afflicted by it; nor is the opinion of some plant pathologists that it is not a virus at all but the result of a fortuitous combination of growing conditions.

Mosaic virus, on the other hand, is universal, and is transmitted only by grafting: either grafting onto an infected rootstock ('Dr Huey' being the usual culprit) or using grafting buds that are already infected. You will recognize it by the way it makes yellowish scribbles or marbled patterns on the older leaves. The traditional consensus is that it does little harm, although it does no good either – it is known to adversely affect the ability of cuttings to strike and grafting buds to 'take' – and there is a campaign in the United States for the rose industry to take preventive action and adopt virus-treated propagating material. European nurseries prefer understocks grown from seedlings rather than cuttings, as rose viruses are not transmitted through the seed.

Designing a Rose Garden

'The garden for the rose, not the rose for the garden' was the slogan of that great Victorian writer on roses, the Reverend Dean Hole. Even now, many rose addicts (and this, surely, is the most addictive of all flowers!) would agree. For them, the design of a rose garden is simply a matter of accommodating and displaying as many of their favorite roses as possible. Lesser plants are relegated to positions too shady for the roses, or admitted with some reluctance to provide flowers outside the rose season.

While in an ordinary-sized suburban garden a purist (or obsessive) approach like this can easily lead to the garden becoming just a rose factory, it can lead to magnificence when carried out on a grand scale. Just take a look at the Roseraie de l'Haÿ or many another public rose garden. Such gardens tend to formality in their design, both because it is impossible to make a collection of rose beds cut out of a lawn, or linked by paved paths, look other than artificial, and because it is a way of bringing a measure of order and aesthetic unity to what can easily be seen as a shapeless jumble of bushes.

Few of us these days have the space or the money to make rose gardens in this manner, but there is much to learn from them. The first thing we can learn is the value of a simple green back-drop for roses. We may not have the space for stands of fine trees, but we can at least clad ugly walls, sheds or fences with creepers, and allow ground-covering plants to spill over paving and driveways. True, there are roses for these purposes, but most roses are too flimsy and shapeless in growth to form the framework of a garden; they are best used to fill in and decorate. The Rugosas are perhaps an exception. The second thing we can learn is the importance of allowing enough space for people to move among the roses. No one can admire roses if they have to duck and weave down a narrow pathway trying to avoid the thorny branches!

Not all of us will want to devote our gardens exclusively to roses; it may be our favorite flower, but we do not want to forgo the pleasure of the company of so many others. In that case we will espouse a different tradition, one best exemplified by such gardens as that of Claude Monet at Giverney, where roses grow in happy harmony with all sorts of other flowers. It is indeed an older tradition, for the formal, roses-only garden dates only from the time of the Empress Joséphine.

Before then, roses were grown mixed in with other plants – even the 'roseries' of the Middle Ages featured fragrant herbs and plants that we would now consign to the vegetable garden. Some would suggest that the rose should be banished there, too. Enjoy the flowers in vases, they say, but leave the scruffy, prickly bushes unvisited among the cabbages and beans. They have a point, but the rose's bad legs can be just as well camouflaged by ornamental plants as by capsicums. Blue flowers such as delphiniums and cam-panulas (and clematis to accompany climbing roses on walls) are indispen-sable, as the rose does not supply that color, but there is no need to confine yourself to them. Think, for instance, of dawn-pink irises with their flaring blooms and sword-like leaves setting off the roundness of a rose of similar hue such as 'Pink Chiffon'; of mahogany day lilies with the coral of 'Alexander' or 'Fragrant Cloud'; of regal lilies rising through the tumbling branches of 'Cardinal de Richelieu' in a blend of color and rich fragrance.

Just remember, when ordering and setting out your roses, to allow sufficient space for the other plants, so that the roses them-selves will not be overcrowded.

That is how I would design my rose garden, were I creating one now; and I would go further than that, not even thinking about roses until the permanent elements of the garden – space for sitting outside and for children to play; trees for shade; shrubs and climb-ers to mask unwanted views; paving, steps and paths – had all been allowed for. Only then would I fill in the spaces with roses and their companions. The garden would be satisfying without them; and when the time of roses arrived, it would be glorious indeed.

Roses consorting with foxgloves in a garden in Berkeley, California

Roses for special purposes

Some exceptionally fragrant roses

Ignore those who complain that roses have lost their fragrance. It is true that many of the Old Garden Roses are wonderfully fragrant, but there have always been scentless varieties as well, and among the Modern Roses there are many as richly scented as anyone could desire – and if you want a garden of scented roses there are many to choose from in this book. Here are 24 roses famous for their fragrance:

'Albertine'
'Buff Beauty'
'Communis' (aka 'Common Moss')
'Constance Spry'
'Crimson Glory'
'Double Delight'
'Evelyn'
'Fragrant Cloud'
'Francis Dubreuil'
'Kazanlik'
'Jaune Desprez'
'Just Joey'
'La France'
'Madame Isaac Pereire'
'Maiden's Blush'
'Maréchal Niel'
'Memorial Day Rose'
'Papa Meilland'
'Souvenir de la Malmaison'
'Sunsprite'
'Tiffany'
'Zéphirine Drouhin'
R. primula and the Sweet Brier Rose, *R. eglanteria*, are famous for their scented leaves.

Early-flowering roses

The first flowers of the season (like the first fruits) are always the most exciting; and while the rose season doesn't begin in earnest until spring has turned to summer, you can have roses earlier, almost from the time the daffodils begin to fade. Here are some that herald the season to come:

'Belle Portugaise'
'Golden Chersonese'
'Frühlingsmorgen'
'Madame Grégoire Staechelin'
'Maigold'
R. banksiae
R. hugonis
R. laevigata
R. sericea pteracantha
R. spinosissima altaica
R. stellata mirifica

Winter-flowering roses

In frosty climates, the only way to have roses in winter is to grow them under glass; but where frost is rare, many of the Teas, Chinas and Noisettes can be relied on to bloom through the winter – and indeed throughout the year. Give them a light trim and some fertilizer in the middle of the fall/autumn to encourage them to form a crop of flower buds before the cool weather sets in. Here are a dozen of the best:

'Crépuscule'
'Duchesse de Brabant'
'Général Galliéni'
'Lamarque'
'Lorraine Lee'
'Mutabilis'
'Nancy Hayward'
'Niphetos'
'Old Blush'
'Roulettii'
'Safrano'
'Souvenir de Madame Léonie Viennot'

Some roses without prickles

While we are all used to the idea that roses have thorns, there are times when we would rather not have them! It is not always realized that prickle-free roses exist; here are 15 roses with no prickles:

'Dupontii'
'Ghislaine de Féligonde'
'Madame Plantier'
'Madame Sancy de Parabère'
'Madame Legras de St Germain'
'Mrs John Laing'
'Pinkie, Climbing'
R. banksiae
R. blanda
R. multiflora (many forms)
'Reine des Violettes'
'Renae'
'Smooth Sailing' and the others of Harvey Davidson's 'smooth' Hybrid Teas
'Veilchenblau'
'Zéphirine Drouhin'

Some excellent roses for cutting

Any rose in the garden will live out its full life in water if you cut it in the cool of the day, re-cut its stem under water, and stand it in cool, deep water for a few hours before arranging it. Keep the arrangement in a cool place. The following last well and have reasonably long stems, and represent a range of colors:

'Blue Moon'
'Double Delight'
'Général Galliéni'
'Honey Dijon'
'Ingrid Bergman'
'Just Joey'
'Marilyn Monroe'
'Montezuma'
'New Day'
'Pascali'
'Pierre de Ronsard'
'Scentimental'
'Seduction' (aka 'Matilda')

Roses for hedges

The chief qualities needed in a hedging plant are that it be neat in growth, densely bushy from the ground up, and resistant to disease, so that it does not lose its foliage prematurely. The Hybrid Rugosas meet these requirements better than all other roses, but there are others almost as good. Here are some suggestions of different heights:

'Baronne Prévost'
'Cornelia'
'Gruss an Teplitz'
'Hermosa'
'Iceberg'
'Knockout'
'Lady Elsie May'
'Mutabilis'
'Nevada'
'Queen Elizabeth'
R. multiflora – the only rose that can be clipped to formal shapes
R. roxburghii
'Sally Holmes'

For a low, ultra-dense hedge, the old Scotch or Burnet roses are hard to beat.

A hedge of 'Iceberg' in London's Regents Park

Great Rose Gardens of the World

Rose gardens come in all shapes and sizes, from the elaborate geometrical designs of such great public rose gardens as those of Bagatelle, the Roseraie de l'Haÿ, Geneva, Monza, Werribee Park and the Botanic Garden in Adelaide to simple window boxes planted with some Miniature Roses or backyard patios dotted with container-grown Floribundas and Hybrid Teas. Whatever its scale, and whether its ambience is formal or informal, a rose garden breathes a message of tranquility and harmony. As we feast our senses on the sights and scents it offers us, we can hardly fail to relax and unwind, to take a break from our busy schedules and set aside our daily cares. For a real treat, in your own country or when travelling, visit one of the many wonderful gardens open to the public where you are invited to — literally and figuratively — stop and smell the roses. A selection of the world's best is presented here for your enjoyment.

A choice selection

Since 1994, the World Federation of Rose Societies (WFRS) has recognized the best public rose gardens throughout the world with the WFRS Award of Garden Excellence. To be eligible, the garden must be open to the public and demonstrate sustained performance in providing high-quality displays of roses; be educational, whereby the public's knowledge of and interest in roses are enhanced; assist in the preservation of the rose; and have a record of conducting international rose trials. To date the award has been bestowed on 29 gardens around the world. On these pages they are marked with an asterisk (*).

ABOVE An intimate corner of the Roseraie de l'Haÿ

INSET 'Roseraie de l'Haÿ', the splendid cultivar of *R. rugosa* raised by the garden's designer, M. Cochet, in 1902

La Roseraie de l'Haÿ, near Paris*

In creating his great garden at L'Haÿ-les-Roses outside Paris in 1893, retired department store magnate Jules Gravereaux sought to emulate the Empress Joséphine and collect every rose in the world. To a large extent he succeeded, and the Roseraie is one of the great museum gardens, preserving not only one of the world's greatest collections of the Old Garden Roses but a comprehensive selection of more recent varieties. Said to be the oldest existing roses-only garden in the world, it is a fine example of the formal gardens of its period, famous for its imaginative use of climbers and ramblers on pillars, arches and the great architectural trellis that forms its centrepiece. The roses are at their peak from May to July.

Le Parc de Bagatelle, Paris*

The Château de Bagatelle and its park date from the reign of Louis XV, but the rose garden, perhaps the most famous in the world, was not established until the first years of the twentieth century on the site of what was originally a small racecourse. Now the kiosk built by the Empress Eugénie overlooks a glorious display of roses of all types in beds edged with clipped box hedges and accented with tall pillars of climbing roses. In June each year all Paris eagerly awaits the verdict of the judges of the Concours on the new roses. Which beauties will be honored with gold medals, which will be passed over?

LEFT The Empress Eugénie's kiosk overlooks the rose garden at Bagatelle. The rose on the pillar is 'Mrs F. W. Flight'.

INSET Meilland's Hybrid Tea 'Jardins de Bagatelle' (1986)

Mottisfont Abbey, England

The Tudor mansion of Mottisfont in Hampshire passed to the ownership of the National Trust in 1957, but it was not until 1972 that the Trust decided to establish the British national collection of Old Roses in the walled gardens there. This was done under the guidance of the late Graham Stuart Thomas – Britain's, and perhaps the world's, foremost authority on these flowers – and displays his artistry in combining roses with a wide variety of perennial flowers. It is open all year, but the roses are at their peak in June.

Claude Monet's garden, Giverney

While it is not exclusively a rose garden, the garden created by the great Impressionist painter in Normandy is one of the most admired in the world, abounding with inspiration for the rose-lover who loves other flowers as well. It is open from April to October; the roses are at their best in June and July.

ABOVE The fountain, which forms the focal point of the First Garden at Mottisfont Abbey, is seen here through an arch adorned with 'Adélaide d'Orléans'. The pink rose overhanging the pool is 'Raubritter'.

RIGHT Climbing roses trained informally on pillars lend height to a wide border of cottage-garden flowers in Claude Monet's garden at Giverney.

Europa-Rosarium at Sangerhausen, Germany*

The Sangerhausen garden 60km (40 miles) north of Weimar was created in 1903 by the German Rose Society as a place to preserve the roses of the previous century, which were then falling from favor. The collection has been kept updated and is now the most comprehensive in the world, preserving many varieties that are extinct elsewhere and that are now being reintroduced to commerce. Long isolated behind the Iron Curtain, Sangerhausen and its roses are now freely accessible again to rose-lovers from all over the world. Open all year, it is at its best in June, July and September.

Vrijbroek Park, Belgium*

The Vrijbroekpark in Mechelin (Malines), near Antwerp, was originally laid out in the nineteenth century and bought by the city in 1922. It contains specialized gardens devoted to dahlias and to cannas, but it is especially famous for its three rose gardens – the original formal rosary; the one added in 1994, whose collection is arranged to display the history of the rose; and a third one, which displays the wild roses of Belgium. It hosts an annual competition for new roses and is at its best from June to September.

The Huntingdon Gardens, United States of America

The vast gardens created in San Marino, California, by the railway magnate Henry Huntingdon in the early years of the twentieth century are not devoted only to roses – they are also famous for their camellias and their extraordinary collection of succulent plants. Established in 1908, the rose garden boasts one of America's finest collections of roses of all types, arranged to show their history and development, and is in bloom from mid-April to November. Huntington's house is also open to the public and houses a fabulous collection of works of art and rare books.

ABOVE Modern Roses and perennials at Sangerhausen. The cherry-red Shrub Rose in the background is Kordes's 'Sangerhausen'.

INSET The memorial to Albert Hoffmann, who donated the land for the garden.

BELOW A marble goddess surveys the roses at the Huntingdon Gardens in San Marino, California.

Other rose gardens to visit

ASIA

China

The Botanical Garden, Beijing

India

The Centenary Rose Garden, Tamil Nadu*

The Indian Rose Society's gardens, New Delhi

Zakir Rose Gardens, Chandigarh

Israel

Wohl Rose Park, Jerusalem*

Japan

Bara Koen (the Rose Park), Fukayama*

Hana-no Miyako, Gifu

Jindai Botanic Garden, Tokyo

Utsubo Park, Osaka*

AUSTRALIA AND NEW ZEALAND

Australia

David Ruston's Garden, Renmark, South Australia

Parliament House Rose Gardens, Canberra

The Botanic Garden of Adelaide

The Royal Botanic Gardens, Melbourne and Sydney

New Zealand

Auckland Botanic Gardens

Dugal MacKenzie Garden, Palmerston North*

Nancy Steen Garden, Auckland

The Rogers' Garden, Hamilton*

EUROPE

Belgium

Château de Hex, Liège*

La Roseraie Environmentale, Chaumont-Gistoux

France

Delbard Gardens, Malicorne

Le Château de Droulon, Berry

Le Chemin de Rose, Angers

Le Parc de la Tête d'Or, Lyon*

Germany

Dornrosenschloss (Sleeping Beauty's Castle), Sababurg

Planten und Bloemen, Munich

Rosenneuheitengarten, Baden-Baden*

Italy

Il Roseto Carla Fineschi, Arezzo*

Il Roseto di Roma, Rome

Roseto Niso Fumigalli at Villa Reale, Monza

Spain

Rosaleda Ramon Ortiz, Madrid*

Roserar de Cervantes, Barcelona

Switzerland

Le Parc de la Grange, Geneva*

Schloss Heidig, Gelfingen

The Netherlands

The Historical Garden, Aalsmeer

Westbroek Park, The Hague

ISRAEL

Wohl Rose Park, Jerusalem*

NORTH AMERICA

Canada

Butchart Gardens, Saanich, BC

Montreal Botanic Gardens*

USA

Berkeley Rose Garden, Berkeley, California

Cranford Rose Garden, Brooklyn, New York

Inez Parker Memorial Rose Garden, San Diego, California*

San Jose Heritage Rose Garden, California

The American Rose Society, Shreveport, Louisiana*

Rose Hills Pageant of Roses, Whittier, California*

Washington Park, Portland, Oregon*

SOUTH AFRICA

Durbanville Rose Garden, Cape Town

Fresh Woods, Elgin*

King's Park, Bloemfontein

UNITED KINGDOM

Castle Howard, Yorkshire

City of Belfast International Rose Garden*

City of Glasgow International Rose Garden at Tollcross

Coughton Court, Warwickshire*

Duthie Park, Aberdeen

Queen Mary's Rose Garden, Regent's Park, London

Sissinghurst Castle, Kent

The Royal National Rose Society's Gardens of the Rose, St Alban's

Werribee Park, Australia

Opened in 1986, the Victoria State Rose Garden in the grounds of an historic mansion at Werribee Park, north of Melbourne, contains 5,500 roses of all types displayed in a formal design modelled on an heraldic Tudor rose. It is managed by Parks Victoria with support from the Victoria State Rose Garden Supporters. The roses are in bloom from October to April, but the property offers many other attractions and is well worth visiting at any time of year.

Aerial view of the rose garden at Werribee Park, Victoria

The World's Favorite

THE ANCIENT GREEKS SPOKE OF THE JUDGMENT OF PARIS — PARIS BEING THE MORTAL WHO WAS GIVEN THE TASK OF CHOOSING FROM AMONG THE RIVAL GODDESSES SHE WHO WAS THE FAIREST OF THE FAIR. ROSE-LOVERS MIGHT SIGH THAT HE HAD IT EASY! HE HAD TO CHOOSE FROM ONLY THREE CANDIDATES, WHEREAS EVERY YEAR THE MEMBERS OF THE PUBLIC ARE PRESENTED BY THE WORLD'S HYBRIDISTS WITH AS MANY AS A COUPLE OF HUNDRED NEW ROSES — ALL BEAUTIFUL AND ALL ACCOMPANIED BY ARDENT AND SOMETIMES SELF-INDULGENT (IF WELL-MEANING) SALES PITCHES — AND IT WAS RECOGNIZED A LONG TIME AGO THAT MORE OBJECTIVE INFORMATION WAS NEEDED.

As early as 1883, the National Rose Society of Great Britain (it wasn't 'Royal' then) had instituted the custom of awarding gold medals to what in its judges' opinion were the most worth-while new varieties presented by raisers at its shows each year. It might be argued — and was by many rosarians — that while a display of cut roses in vases may look sensational on the show bench, it does not indicate such important qualities as vigor of growth, freedom of flowering or resistance to disease. To assess those, it was desirable to compare the new varieties side by side while they were actually growing.

The development of trial grounds

It was the city of Paris that took the initiative some 20 years later and set up the first trial ground for new rose varieties in the Parc de Bagatelle. Here, hybridists were invited to submit their new creations for expert, impartial adjudication. The first awards were made in 1907, and the Concours de Bagatelle has been an annual event ever since; it has been cancelled only once, during wartime, in 1942.

There are now more than 30 trial grounds around the world (see below), and most have adopted a system of judging similar to that pioneered at Bagatelle. When the plants arrive from the hybridists, they are planted in the trial ground, where they will be grown for two years. They are identified only by number, all details of their

International rose trials

AFRICA
South Africa: Durbanville

ASIA
Japan: Gifu; Tokyo

AUSTRALIA and NEW ZEALAND
Adelaide, South Australia; Hamilton, New Zealand; Palmerston North, New Zealand

EUROPE
Austria: Baden bei Wien

Belgium: Kortrijk; Le Roeulx

Czech Republic: Hradec Králové

France: Bagatelle, Paris; Lyon (French-bred roses only); Nantes; Orléans; Saverne

Germany: Anerkannte Deutsche Rose (ADR); Baden-Baden

Italy: Genoa; Monza; Rome

Netherlands: The Hague

Republic of Ireland: Dublin

Spain: Barcelona; Madrid

Switzerland: Geneva

United Kingdom: Belfast; British Association of Rose Breeders (BARB); Glasgow; St Alban's (RNRS)

NORTH AMERICA
United States: AARS; Portland, Oregon; Rose Hills, California. The American Rose Society (ARS) also makes annual awards for Miniatures and for fragrance (although the fragrance award is not always awarded).

SOUTH AMERICA
Argentina: Buenos Aires
Chile: Santiago

Roses

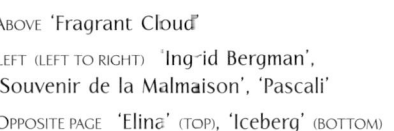

ABOVE 'Fragrant Cloud'
LEFT (LEFT TO RIGHT) 'Ingrid Bergman',
'Souvenir de la Malmaison', 'Pascali'
OPPOSITE PAGE 'Elina' (TOP), 'Iceberg' (BOTTOM)

raisers being kept secret until the awards are made. Generally, a local permanent panel of judges assesses them throughout the two-year test cycle, scoring them against such criteria as novelty, bud and flower form, color (on opening and on finishing), substance, growth habit, quantity of flowers, vigor/renewal, foliage, hardiness and disease/insect resistance. Fragrance may also be judged on a system graded from 1 (no detectable scent) up to 10 (very strong scent).

The final judging usually takes place on a date set to coincide with a peak bloom cycle – generally late spring or early summer or the fall/autumn. An invited international jury – made up of people such as rose-introducers and rose-breeders, representatives of city parks departments, landscape architects, and members of rose organizations at home and abroad – gives the final judgment.

Judgment day is often a gala occasion, with banquets and other festivities and the media in attendance. Prizes are awarded in the various classifications (large-flowered, cluster-flowered, climbers and so on), and there is usually a special award for fragrance and a top award for the highest-pointed variety, such as the 'Golden Rose of The Hague', the 'Rose Hills Golden Rose' (a Californian award) or the 'Gold Star of the South Pacific'. The prizewinners are usually then planted in the sponsor's parks or gardens so that members of the public can observe their attributes for themselves over the next few years.

Other major rose awards

A few of the major trials depart from this general model. The Royal National Rose Society, for instance, grows the candidate roses for three years at its trial ground at St Alban's and makes its awards entirely on the basis of its permanent judging committee's assessment of their all-season performance there. A rose first becomes eligible for award in its second year of trial (when most receive their awards) but remains eligible in its third year also, when the judges sometimes upgrade a particular rose's award – for example, from a certificate of merit to a gold medal.

All-America Rose Selections (a not-for-profit association of rose-growers and rose-introducers) judges roses on the basis of two years' performance in 21 trial gardens across the United States. Theirs is perhaps the world's most coveted award: it is said that nearly 40 per cent of roses sold in the United States are AARS winners.

The World Federation of Rose Societies (WFRS) has chosen to give accolades to roses in an entirely different way. Any rose, even one that has been in commerce for many years, may be nominated by the 37 member societies to be considered by the WFRS Triennial World Rose Convention for the title of 'World's Favorite Rose' and induction into the WFRS Hall of Fame. The first winner (it is said the vote was unanimous) was 'Peace', in 1976. At its Sydney conference in 1988, the WFRS established the Old Rose Hall of Fame, the first winner being 'Mademoiselle Cécile Brünner'.

WRFS 'World's Favorite Rose'

1976	'Peace' ('Gioia', 'Gloria Dei', 'Madame A. Meilland')
1979	'Queen Elizabeth'
1981	'Fragrant Cloud' ('Duftwolke', 'Nuage Parfumé')
1983	'Iceberg' ('Fée des Neiges', 'Schneewittcher')
1985	'Double Delight'
1988	'Papa Meilland'
1991	'Pascali' ('Blanche Pasca')
1994	'Just Joey'
1997	'New Dawn' ('Everblooming Dr W. Van Fleet')
2000	'Ingrid Bergman'
2003	'Bonica' ('Bonica '82', 'Demon')
2006	'Elina' ('Peaudouce') 'Pierre de Ronsard' ('Eden', 'Eden Rose')

WRFS Old Rose Hall of Fame

1988	'Mademoiselle Cécile Brünner'
1991	'Gloire de Dijon'
1994	'Old Blush'
1997	'Souvenir de la Malmaison'
2000	'Gruss an Teplitz'
2003	'Madame Alfred Carrière'
2006	'Madame Hardy'

Some Famous Rose-breeders

There have been many hundreds of dedicated rose-lovers, both amateur and professional, pursuing the quest for new and more beautiful roses. Some have their name attached to just one or two varieties; others have been more prolific – both in terms of roses and of sons and daughters who have carried on the work and the family name. The following are some of the best known, and almost all are represented in this book.

Austin, David A very influential contemporary English rose-breeder, whose 'English Roses' combine the grace and old-world flowers of the Old Garden Roses with the brighter colors and generous repeat flowering of the Moderns. He has recently been joined by his son, also named David.

Armstrong Nurseries A leading American firm since the 1940s, California-based and employee-owned. David Armstrong is himself responsible for some fine roses, such as 'Aquarius' and 'Kentucky Derby', but the firm has also introduced the creations of Herbert Swim, Jack Christensen and many other breeders.

Barbier et Cie A French firm founded in the early twentieth century and based near Orléans. It is responsible for some fine ramblers, of which 'Albéric Barbier' and 'Albertine' are the best known.

Barbier Frères' 'Albertine', 1921

Dee Bennett's 'Jean Kenneally', 1984

Beales, Peter A Norfolk nurseryman best known as an author and an authority on the Old Garden Roses, Beales has created few but excellent roses, such as 'Anna Pavlova' and 'James Mason'.

Benardella, Frank Often called 'the Picasso of Modern Miniatures', Benardella is an amateur from New Jersey. His sensational debut in 1985 with 'Black Jade' – still about as close to black as any rose has ever come – has been followed by the introduction of many other beauties, such as 'Jennifer', 'Leading Lady', 'Merlot' and 'Baby Boomer'.

Bennett, Dee Born in Australia, Cecilia Lucy Daphne Bennett (nee Panton, and 'Dee' to her friends and customers) emigrated to California as a war bride in 1948, but it was not until 1972 that (encouraged by Ralph Moore) she set up her backyard nursery, which she called 'Tiny Petals'. From it came a seemingly endless stream of superlative Miniatures, such as 'Jean Kenneally'. Her naming one of them 'X-Rated' raised some eyebrows, but she needed the name to help her complete her series of roses covering the entire alphabet!

Bennett, Henry Known as 'the father of the Hybrid Tea', this late-nineteenth-century cattle-farmer turned rose-breeder was one of the first people to raise roses exclusively according to the principles of controlled hybridization. 'Mrs John Laing' is probably his

Frank Benardella's 'Black Jade', 1985

best creation, but 'Lady Mary Fitzwilliam' is an important ancestor of Modern Roses.

Boerner, Eugene S. An American breeder, nicknamed 'Papa Floribunda' for the stream of superlative roses of that type he created as Director of Research for Jackson & Perkins from the mid-1940s until his death in 1966. His best Hybrid Teas are 'Diamond Jubilee' and 'First Prize'.

Brownell, Dr and Mrs Walter An American couple from Rhode Island, who from the 1920s to the late 1950s worked to develop 'sub-zero roses' for very cold climates. Their best-known rose today is 'Elegance'.

Buck, Dr Griffith J. A twentieth-century American rose-breeder and Professor of Horticulture at Iowa State University, for which he raised a long series of excellent roses combining grace and fragrance with ease of culture in the extreme climates of the American Mid-West.

Cant, Benjamin & Co. Britain's (and indeed the world's) oldest firm of rose-growers, founded in 1765. Ben Cant started to specialize in roses in 1853, although it was not until the late 1880s that he began to breed them, his most famous today being 'Mrs B. R. Cant'. His nephew Frank Cant also grew and bred roses, and the two firms were merged in 1967 under the name Cant's of Colchester. It is still run by Ben Cant's great-grandchildren, Martin, Angela and Roger Pawsey, the last being the creator of 'Just Joey'.

Carruth, Tom Texas-born and trained under Jackson & Perkins's Bill Warriner, Carruth is now Director of Research for Weeks's Roses in California. With a string of AARS winners to his credit, he specializes in unusual colors – striped roses like 'Scentimental' and 'Fourth of July' have been followed by mauves and purples like 'Blueberry Hill' and 'Neptune'. Well, he says, if Picasso could have a 'blue period', why can't he have one, too?

Christensen, Jack A contemporary American breeder, successor to Herbert Swim at Armstrong Nurseries and raiser of such beauties as 'Holy Toledo', 'Love Potion' and 'Voodoo'.

Clark, Alister An Australian amateur, active from about 1915 until the mid-1950s, whose creations remain very popular in his home country. The best known today are those derived from *R. gigantea*, like 'Lorraine Lee' and 'Nancy Hayward'.

Cochet-Cochet, P. C. M. A leading turn-of-the-century French rosarian, consultant to the Roseraie de l'Haÿ and creator of excellent *R. rugosa* hybrids, among them 'Roseraie de l'Haÿ' and 'Blanc Double de Coubert'.

Cocker, Alexander Founded in 1841, James Cocker & Sons of Aberdeen are one of Scotland's oldest rose-growers. (They hold the Queen's Royal Warrant.) While the firm had dabbled in rose-breeding in the 1890s, it was not until the 1960s that the founder's great-grandson Alec Cocker took it up again, making his debut with 'Alec's Red' in 1969. Working in close association with Jack Harkness, he followed up with such beauties as 'Morning Jewel', 'White Cockade' and 'Silver Jubilee'. He died in 1977, and his work is carried on by his widow, Anne, and their son Alex – and there is a sixth generation waiting in the wings!

Delbard, Georges A French raiser of both roses and fruit trees. He did not start breeding roses until the 1950s, and raised some in

Cants' 'Just Joey', 1972

collaboration with André Chabert. These joint creations are credited as being by Delbard-Chabert. Among his best known are 'Madame Georges Delbard' and 'Altissimo'. Now in the capable hands of his sons Arnaud and Henri, the Delbard firm maintains a magnificent display garden in the family's home town of Malicorne.

De Ruiter, Gijs A contemporary Dutch rose-breeder and a pioneer raiser of Miniatures in the 1950s, but best known today for Floribundas of the quality of 'Europeana'.

Dickson, Alexander, & Sons A Northern Irish family firm founded in 1836, sometimes known as Dickson's of Hawlmark. Since 1886, innumerable fine roses have come from the hands of Alex Dickson II ('George Dickson'); Alex III ('Shot Silk', 'Dame Edith Helen', 'Silver Lining'); and Alex III's son Patrick ('Red Devil', 'Disco Dancer', 'Elina'). The firm is currently headed by Patrick's son Colin, the fifth generation of the family to breed roses.

Dot, Pedro A Spanish raiser, celebrated for a long succession of brilliantly colored Hybrid Teas. He is even more celebrated for that paragon of Shrub Roses 'Nevada' and his pioneering work with Miniatures. He died in 1976, leaving his firm in the hands of his sons Simon and Marino.

Dubreuil, Francis A French tailor turned rose-grower and rose-breeder, best known today for 'Perle d'Or' and the dark red Tea named after himself – and for being the maternal grandfather of Francis Meilland, the raiser of 'Peace'.

Dupont, André Superintendent of the Empress Joséphine's rose garden and thought to be the first person to cross-fertilize roses artificially. He is commemorated in 'Dupontii'.

Fisher, Gladys A mid-twentieth-century American raiser, who specialized in roses of unusual colors. The mauve 'Sterling Silver' is her best-known rose.

Fryer, Garth An old British firm that has specialized in roses for nearly a century. Garth Fryer has made the firm famous with such excellent roses as 'Sunset Celebration' (aka 'Warm Wishes') and 'Day Breaker', both AARS winners.

Gaujard, Jean A mid-twentieth-century French raiser. He took over Pernet-Ducher's nursery on the master's death in 1924, and his best-known rose is 'Rose Gaujard', named for himself. His other creations are less well known outside France.

Geschwindt, Rudolph A late-nineteenth-century Hungarian raiser whose roses were marketed by Peter Lambert of Germany. His best-known rose today is 'Gruss an Teplitz' (1897).

Guillot, Père et Fils The still-flourishing Guillot firm was founded in Lyon by Jean-Baptiste (Guillot *père*) in 1829. 'Madame Bravy' (1848) is his best-known rose, but it is overshadowed by those of his son Jean-Baptiste-André (Guillot *fils*) – 'La France' (1867), 'Catherine Mermet' (1869) and the first Polyantha, 'Mignonette' (1880). His son Pierre bred roses also; and now his great-grandson Dominique Massad is carrying on the tradition.

Hardy, Alexandre Director of Paris's Jardins de Luxembourg from the 1820s until the late 1840s, who trained under Joséphine's gardeners at Malmaison. He used to give his new roses to friends rather than sell them commercially. 'Madame Hardy' keeps his name famous. 'Bon Silène', the delicious pear called 'Beurre Hardy', and that rare and botanically improbable hybrid × *Hulthemosa hardii* (whose portrait can be found on page 20), are also examples of his mastery.

Tom Carruth's 'Scentimental', 1997

Gareth Fryer's 'Day Breaker', 2003

Harkness, Jack The English firm of R. Harkness & Co. was founded in 1879, but it was not until 1962 that the late Jack Harkness took up hybridizing. Such roses as 'Escapade' and 'Alexander', and his development of the first hybrids of *Hulthemia persica* since Alexandre Hardy's, won him the reputation of being England's leading rose-breeder, a reputation upheld by his sons Philip and Robert.

Hill There were two American firms of this name, active in the first half of the twentieth century: E. G. Hill, famous for 'Columbia' and 'Madame Butterfly', and the Joseph Hill Company. Based in Richmond, Indiana, both were leading growers of cut-flower roses.

Horvath, Michael A late-nineteenth-century American raiser, remembered for his pioneering work with *R. wichurana*, although few of the roses he developed are still grown.

Howard, Fred A Californian raiser. His firm, Howard & Smith, were successful raisers of Hybrid Teas from just before World War I until the late 1950s. 'The Doctor' was once voted the most beautiful rose in America.

Jackson & Perkins America's largest firm of rose-growers. They have been in business since 1872, originally as growers of grapes and soft fruit, but the enormous success of 'Dorothy Perkins', raised by one of their staff, inspired them to switch to roses. This rose has been followed by an endless stream of beauties from the hands of J. H. Nicolas, Eugene Boerner, Bill Warriner and now Keith Zary, as well as from many of the leading European raisers.

Kordes, W., Söhne A German firm, founded in 1887. Its international reputation was made by Wilhelm Kordes II, possibly the greatest, and certainly the most imaginative,

of all rose-breeders, who gave the world 'Crimson Glory', 'Independence', 'Frühlings-morgen', 'Perfecta', 'Pinocchio', the Kordesii Climbers and many, many others. After his retirement in 1964 (he died in 1975), the firm was run by for many years by his son Reimer, creator of 'Sunsprite' (aka 'Friesia') and 'Colour Wonder' (aka 'Königin der Rosen'), and is now in the capable hands of Reimer's son Wilhelm and Thomas Proll.

Lacharme, François A leading French raiser of Hybrid Perpetuals, Bourbons and Noisettes in the mid-nineteenth century. 'Boule de Neige' and 'Souvenir du Docteur Jamain' are his best-known roses today.

Lambert, Peter A turn-of-the-century German hybridist, still celebrated for 'Frau Karl Druschki' and 'Gartendirektor Otto Linne', and for 'Trier', an ancestor of the Hybrid Musks. A founder of the German Rose Society, he was instrumental in the creation of the society's great museum garden at Sangerhausen.

Lammerts, Dr Walter An American (California-based) geneticist and plant breeder, responsible for introducing the Yunnan cultivars of *Camellia reticulata* to the West and for creating modern cultivars of *Leptospermum*. His roses are also of outstanding importance, and include 'Charlotte Armstrong' and 'Queen Elizabeth'.

Le Grice, Edward Burton A mid-twentieth-century English raiser whose systematic and careful breeding yielded a long series of Floribunda Roses of unusual distinction, including 'Dainty Maid', 'Allgold', 'Lilac Charm', 'News' and 'Victoriana', among many others. He died in 1977, and his firm is now run by his son Bill.

Laffay, Jean A leading French raiser from the early and mid-nineteenth century, who played an important part in the development of the Hybrid Perpetuals.

Leenders Brothers Inter-war Dutch raisers, notable for pink Hybrid Tea Roses of unusual refinement, the most important of which is 'Comtesse Vandal'.

Lens, Louis Belgium's leading twentieth-century rose-breeder. 'Pascali', one of his late creations (1963), is his masterpiece.

McGredy, Samuel, & Sons There have been no fewer than four Sam McGredys heading this old Northern Irish firm, founded in 1828 with nurseries at Portadown, near Belfast. Sam II started raising roses in about 1900,

among them 'The Queen Alexandra Rose'; Sam III followed in the 1920s and 1930s with roses such as 'Mrs Sam McGredy' and 'McGredy's Yellow'. His early death in 1934 led to a hiatus until the present Sam, Sam IV, reached his majority. He has followed 'Orangeade' (1959) with too many beautiful roses to mention. He moved his business to New Zealand in 1972. It is now called Sam McGredy Roses International. Sadly, his recent retirement has marked the end of the rose-breeding dynasty – although he still has enough seedlings in reserve to ensure the parade of McGredy roses isn't over yet.

Sam McGredy's 'Molly McGredy', 1969

Mallerin, Charles A Swiss railway engineer, the most celebrated of all amateur raisers of roses. Among his creations are 'Mrs Pierre S. Dupont' (1929), 'Virgo' (1947) and 'Spectacular' (aka 'Danse du Feu', 1954). He died in 1960.

Meilland, Francis A French hybridist, famous above all as the raiser of 'Peace', which he followed with many other roses nearly as remarkable. His father, Antoine Meilland ('Papa'), was a rose-grower who had served his apprenticeship under his father-in-law, Francis Dubreuil, and who had set up his own nursery near Lyon on his return from service in World War I. 'Peace' made the Meilland name world-famous and was followed by many, many others; but Francis died in 1958, at the young age of 46, leaving the firm in the hands his 18-year-old son, Alain (who is still in charge), and his widow, Marie-Louise, who became a notable rose-breeder herself. Now formally called Universal Rose Selections, Meilland has more roses in the WFRS Hall of Fame than any other breeder – 'Peace', 'Papa Meilland', 'Bonica' and 'Pierre de Ronsard'.

Moreau et Robert A mid-nineteenth-century French firm, famous for Moss Roses.

Moore, Ralph S. Moore is nicknamed 'the Father of Modern Miniatures', and it is fair to say that the wide popularity of the class is due more to him and his work than to anyone else. Nearly half of the Miniatures in this book have issued from his Sequoia Nurseries in California. One hundred years old at the time of writing, he is still going strong, still creating fine roses of all types, not just Miniatures. The grand old man of Rosedom, he has been notable for the generosity with which he has shared his knowledge with a new generation of American breeders.

Nabonnand, Clement, Gilbert and Pierre French brothers based on the Riviera in the late nineteenth century, who specialized in Teas. 'General Schablikine' is their best-known rose.

Noack, Werner A contemporary German raiser who has gained international attention for his 'Flower Carpet' series of Ground Cover Roses and the AARS-winning 'Lady Elsie May'.

Norman, Albert An English amateur breeder, a diamond-setter by trade, who won fame just after World War II with 'Ena Harkness' and 'Frensham'. He died in 1962.

Paul, William and George Nineteenth-century English growers, raisers and introducers of new roses from the late 1840s right up to the end of World War I. 'Paul's Scarlet Climber', 'Ophelia' and 'Mermaid' are their three best-known roses.

Pemberton, Reverend Joseph An English rosarian, sometime president of the (now Royal) National Rose Society, and creator in the years after World War I of the wonderful Hybrid Musks. On his death in 1926 his nursery passed to his gardener, J. A. Bentall, and his wife, Ann, raisers of 'Buff Beauty' and 'The Fairy'.

Pernet-Ducher, Joseph A French hybridist, dubbed 'the Wizard of Lyon' for his success in marrying *R. foetida* to the garden roses, thereby introducing shades of pure yellow, coral and flame. The strain, which began in 1900 with 'Soleil d'Or', was christened 'Pernetiana' in his honor. He had already made his mark with 'Madame Abel Chatenay', 'Madame Caroline Testout' and 'Mademoiselle Cécile Brünner'.

Poulsen A Danish firm, founded in 1878. Dines Poulsen raised several good roses in the first years of the twentieth century, but the famous Poulsen is his son Svend, virtual creator of the Floribunda Roses, with such varieties as 'Else Poulsen' and 'Kirsten Poulsen', both introduced in 1924. Under the direction, from the 1960s, of Svend's son Niels, and now of Niels's daughter Pernille and her husband, Mogens Olesen, the firm continues to raise splendid roses of all types. It is said that every five minutes a Poulsen rose is sold somewhere in the world.

Riethmuller, Frank An Australian amateur, who created many roses in his backyard in Sydney. Kordes introduced his roses in Germany, where 'Titian' enjoyed a long run of popularity.

Saville, F. Harmon An American amateur from Massachusetts, whose obsession with Miniature Roses first led him to experiment in breeding and then to turn professional in 1971. 'Rainbow's End' and 'Teddy Bear' are notable among his many fine creations. After his death, his firm, Nor'East Miniature Roses, passed to Wendy White and Bill DeVor of Greenheart Farms in California.

Schuurman, Frank A New Zealand raiser, a protégé of Sam McGredy. He specializes in Mini-Flora for the garden and the cut-flower trade.

Spek, Jan A mid-twentieth-century Dutch raiser, remembered for breeding superior understocks, for 'Golden Scepter' (aka 'Spek's Yellow') and for some very fine azaleas. Founded in 1890, his family firm continues to breed roses, chiefly greenhouse varieties.

Suzuki, Seizo Japan's foremost hybridist and long-time director of the Keisei Rose Research Institute. He created such outstanding roses as 'Olympic Torch', 'Mikado' and 'Ferdy'. He died in 2000.

Svejda, Felicitas A Canadian of Scandinavian descent, Dr Svejda worked for the Canadian government for 40 years on the development of roses hardy enough to withstand that country's severe winters. She retired in 1999.

Swim, Herbert C. An American raiser, associated for most of his career with Armstrong Nurseries but for a while working freelance in partnership with O. L. Weeks. He dominated American rose-breeding in the 1950s and 1960s. His own favorite among his many fine roses was 'Mister Lincoln'.

Tantau, Mathias, father and son German rose-breeders. Mathias Senior started the firm in 1906, but his son raised it to world fame with such roses as 'Super Star' (aka 'Tropicana'), 'Fragrant Cloud' and many

'Brigadoon', by Bill Warriner for Jackson & Perkins, 1992

more. In 1985 he handed the management of his firm over to Hans Jürgen Evers, whose father, Hein Evers, had worked for him for 50 years. Hans Jürgen's son Christian took over in 2000 and has already raised some notable roses, such as 'Cherry Parfait'.

Twomey, Jerry A retired American plant-breeder and seedsman, who turned his hand to roses in the late 1980s. 'Winning Colors' has been followed up with such beauties as 'Love and Peace'.

Van Fleet, Dr Walter An American doctor turned plant-breeder who during the inter-war years raised not only such fine climbing roses as 'Dr W. Van Fleet' but also strawberries and blight-resistant chestnuts for the United States Department of Agriculture.

Vibert, Jean-Pierre A French raiser whose career spanned the heyday of the Gallicas and their tribe and saw the rise of the Hybrid Perpetuals. Many of his roses are still held in high esteem.

Von Abrams, Gordon An American hybridist of the mid-twentieth century, who was associated with the firm of Peterson and Dearing. His use of unusual breeding lines produced such beauties as 'Pink Favorite', 'Memoriam' and 'Golden Slippers'.

Warriner, Bill The ex-Marine who took over at Jackson & Perkins on Gene Boerner's death and created many winners for them, including 'Pristine', 'Simplicity', 'Brigadoon' and 'America'. He died in 1991.

Welsh, Eric An Australian amateur from Gosford, New South Wales, specializing in Miniatures. His best-known rose internationally is 'Tracey Wickham'.

Zary, Keith Jackson & Perkins's hybridist since 1985 and raiser of such notable AARS winners as 'Gemini', 'Opening Night' and 'Tahitian Sunset'. Combining traditional breeding techniques with the latest technology, he raises between 300,000 and 400,000 seedlings a year.

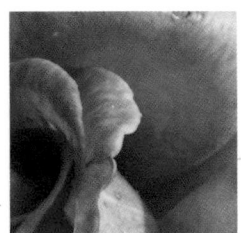

Glossary

Like most activities and pastimes, rose-growing has evolved its own special jargon, which is sometimes incomprehensible to the uninitiated. In this book, ordinary English is used as far as possible, but there are some rose terms that merit explanation.

Bicolor A rose with petals of two shades of colors: the upper surface of one color and the lower surface of another color. Often the two colors are sharply contrasting; for example, a rose maybe described as 'red with a yellow reverse'.

Blend A rose with two (or sometimes more) colors on each of its petals, but without the front/back contrast of a bicolor. 'Peace', blending yellow and pink, is the classic example.

Blue, blueing A red or pink rose that is said to 'blue' is one that tends to turn purplish with age. This is a fault, and is more likely to happen in cold weather or when the bloom is cut and brought indoors.

Briar Strictly speaking, this term refers to the Dog Rose (*R. canina*) and its relatives, including the Sweet Brier Rose (*R. eglanteria*) and the Austrian Briar (*R. foetida*). It is often used loosely to refer to any Wild Rose, especially one that is used as an understock. You sometimes hear it said that a rosebush has 'reverted to briar' when what has happened is that a careless gardener has allowed suckers from the stock to smother the cultivated variety that was budded on to it.

Bud For most of us, a bud is an immature flower that has not yet unfolded its petals, but rose-lovers often use the term to describe a rose until it is about half-open. The growth bud that forms in the axil of a leaf bud is also sometimes called a bud (or a 'bud-eye' or an 'eye').

Budding The form of grafting most often used for roses, where a bud-eye with a sliver of its bark is inserted beneath the bark of an understock.

Bush rose An ordinary rosebush, of more or less upright growth, which requires vigorous pruning each winter, as distinct from a climber or a Shrub Rose. The term encompasses the Hybrid Teas (large-flowered bush roses), the Floribundas (cluster-flowered bush roses) and the Miniatures. Strictly speaking, all roses are shrubs, but the term 'Shrub Rose' refers to a rose of more informal growth than a Hybrid Tea or a Floribunda and one suitable for including in a shrubbery.

Button eye A pretty effect sometimes seen in very double Old Garden Roses, where the central petals fold over and show their reverses, as in the photograph of 'Blanc de Vibert' on page 52.

Climbing rose, climber Strictly speaking, no rose climbs in the sense that a grape vine or a jasmine does. A climbing rose is one that makes shoots of considerable length, suitable for training over a fence or pergola, or into a shrub or tree, in the same way that one might use a true climbing plant. It will need tying in place to stay there.

Code name, international variety name The official name of a rose variety, which always incorporates the first three letters of the raiser's name (such as MEIsar or HARdincum), used worldwide for legal purposes such as grants of plant patents. The raiser or the raiser's agents are free to sell the rose to the public under any name thought suitable – these two are 'Papa Meilland' and 'Super Star' (aka 'Tropicana') – provided the code name also appears in the catalogue and on the label.

Cultivar This is botanists' jargon, short for 'cultivated variety', and means a variety of plant that has originated in gardens rather than in the wild. I have preferred the less pedantic term 'variety', while recognizing that most roses have in fact originated as garden plants, propagated as clones from outstanding individual plants.

Deadheading Removing the spent flowers to prevent the plant wasting energy on ripening unwanted hips.

Decorative All roses are decorative, but the term is officially used in show schedules to describe a Hybrid Tea that is too lightly built to be of use for exhibition.

Double A rose with more than its natural complement of petals, formed at the expense of stamens. For a rose to be described as 'fully double' it needs to have more than 30 petals (some of the Old Garden Roses can have up

'Remember Me'

to 80), with the stamens not prominent in the full-blown flower. A rose with 15–20 petals, opening to show its stamens, is described as 'semi-double'.

Exhibition rose A Hybrid Tea Rose with the potential to win prizes because it conforms to the exhibitor's ideal of a large rose 'with an abundance of petals, gracefully and symmetrically arranged around a well-formed centre'. Such a rose is described as having 'exhibition form'.

Grandiflora A term coined in America to describe a tall bush rose bearing well-formed, moderately sized blooms in small clusters. 'Queen Elizabeth' is the prototype. The rest of the world finds the class redundant and classifies such roses as Hybrid Teas or Floribundas as seems appropriate.

Ground cover A rose of prostrate habit, suitable for growing as ground cover (that is, to make a low mat of foliage and flowers and suppress weeds). It must be admitted that few roses do the job as well as such plants as the hypericums and the creeping junipers.

Hip The fruit of the rose, produced by any rose whose genes do not make it sterile. Modern Roses only ripen them into beauty in mild climates. The hips are quite a feature of some roses, such as *R. moyesii* and the Rugosas. Rose hips are edible, and can be made into jam, wine and syrup. They are one of the richest known natural sources of vitamin C. Sometimes 'hip' is archaically and pedantically spelt 'hep'.

Miniature A miniature camellia usually bears tiny flowers on a full-sized shrub, but a Miniature Rose is expected to be miniature in growth also, with everything – leaves, stems, flowers and all – reduced in perfect proportion on a bush that grows to about 35cm (14in) tall.

Once-blooming A rose that flowers only once a year (not only once in its life), in spring or summer according to the variety.

Own-root plant A plant growing on its own roots – that is, not grafted on those of an understock.

Patio Rose A relatively new and unofficial classification for Floribundas of short growth but with normal-sized flowers, suitable for decorating patios.

Pegging down A style of growing roses popular in Victorian days, where the long shoots of Hybrid Perpetuals and Bourbons were bent to the ground around the bush and fixed there with wooden pegs, so as to encourage blooms along their whole length. It can also be done with leggy Modern Roses such as 'Sally Holmes' and the taller 'English Roses'.

Pillar rose A climbing rose of moderate vigor, suitable for training up a pillar or verandah post, to make a column of bloom in season. It is an unofficial description rather than an officially recognized class, the vigor

A lovely example of a pillar rose

'Sally Holmes'

of any variety being partly dependent on how well it is grown.

Quartered A flower in which the petals are folded in segments, often four, as seen in the photograph of 'Baronne Prévost' on page 49. Such flowers were the very ideal of perfect form in the nineteenth century.

Prickles A botanist will tell you that a 'thorn' is an outgrowth from the wood, like those of a bougainvillea, and that roses do not have thorns, but 'prickles', which are developments of the bark. Be that as it may, the prickles of the rose are still sharp.

Rambler A climbing rose, usually bearing small flowers in bunches, with very long and flexible canes. 'Dorothy Perkins' is the classic example. Very few rambler roses are repeat flowering. They are often classed with the species that gave them birth, such as *R. multiflora*, *R. sempervirens* and *R. wichurana*.

Remontant, recurrent, repeat-blooming A rose does not grow and flower at the same time in the way that, for example, a hibiscus or a petunia does. It grows, makes flowers at the end of the shoots, and then repeats the process as many times as the warm weather allows. It 'rises again', as the French word 're-montant' suggests. I have normally preferred the less concise but easier English phrase 'repeat flowering', and have eschewed such exaggerations as 'continuous' and 'perpetual'.

Seedling In ordinary gardener's language, this means a baby plant, still in its nursery bed, but in rose parlance it means a new variety, raised from seed (of course), that has not yet been named and introduced to commerce. You will often see the phrase 'unnamed seedling' or just 'seedling' in rose parentages.

Shrub Rose A rose of more informal growth than a conventional Hybrid Tea or Floribunda. Not all Shrub Roses are of a large growth habit, however. *Rosa ecae*, for instance, is quite diminutive in stature.

Single A rose with the five petals of a Wild Rose; garden roses described as single, like 'Sparrieshoop' and 'Lilac Charm', are allowed a couple more.

Species In biology, a population of plants or animals that have similar characteristics and interbreed freely, such as *Homo sapiens*. Rosarians often use the term 'species' or 'Species Rose' to refer to any Wild Rose, and can find it confusing that two rather different roses (from their point of view) can be classed as belonging to the same species.

Sport A spontaneous change that leads a rose (or other plant) to produce a branch that is different from the rest of the bush and that, when propagated, retains the difference and thus gives rise to a new variety. 'Chicago Peace' is a sport from 'Peace', differing in the color of its flowers; 'Climbing Peace' differs in having a climbing habit.

Standard, tree rose A standard or tree rose is a rose budded on top of a long understock, so as to raise its branches aloft on a single stem, like a floral lollipop. The stem is usually about 1m (3ft) long; if less, the plant is called a half-standard; 'patio standards' have stems about 40cm (15in) tall. Weeping standards have longer stems still, with a climber or rambler budded on top in the hope that its branches and flowers will cascade to the ground.

Understock, rootstock Roses are one of the few common garden plants that are usually grafted, in their case by means of budding onto the root of a strong Wild Rose or cultivar (such as 'Dr Huey') – the root being called an understock. The junction is called the bud union, and any shoots that arise from below the bud union will be those of the rose that provided the roots. Such shoots are called suckers and should be removed as soon as discovered.

Watershoot The soft, watery shoots (also known as basal breaks or basal growths) that arise from the base of a rosebush and that form the foundation of the new wood for the future. Cherish them, and do not confuse them with suckers from the understock, which should be removed at once.

Bibliography

Many rosarians are avid collectors of books about roses, and fortunately publishers indulge them with an unending stream of titles catering to every taste and every special interest. Books, after all, are knowledge, and knowledge is the key to getting the maximum enjoyment from one's hobby, whatever it may be. Over the years I have accumulated a rose library of sorts, including many new titles and, as my circumstances have permitted, a number of the more expensive rare editions. Here is a selection of both old and new titles for your enjoyment.

Anderson, Frank J., *The Complete Book of 169 Redouté Roses,* Abbeville Press, New York, 1979.

Austin, David, *The Heritage of the Rose,* Antique Collectors' Club, London, 1988.

Beales, Peter et al., *Botanica's Roses: The Encyclopedia of Roses,* Random House, Australia, 1998.

Beales, Peter, *Classic Roses,* Henry Holt, New York, 1997.

Beales, Peter, *Passion for Roses,* Octopus, London, 2004.

Biswas, J. N., Choudhury, Bimai, and Chakraborti, K., *Wonderful Rose Gardens Around the World,* Bengal Rose Society, Calcutta, 2000.

Cairns, Tommy, *All About the Easiest Roses to Grow,* Meredith Books, Des Moines, Iowa, 2003.

Cairns, Tommy, *All About Roses,* Meredith Books, Des Moines, Iowa, 2007.

Cairns, Tommy, *Complete Guide to Roses,* Meredith Books, Des Moines, Iowa, 2006.

Cairns, Tommy (ed.), *Modern Roses 10,* American Rose Society, Shreveport, 1986.

Cairns, Tommy (ed.), *Modern Roses XI, The World Encyclopedia of Roses,* Academic Press, London, 2000.

Dorra, Mary Tonetti, *Beautiful American Rose Gardens,* Clarkson Potter, New York, 1999.

Eagle, Dawn and Barry, *Growing Miniature and Patio Roses in New Zealand,* David Bateman, Auckland, 1996.

Fagan, Gwen, *Roses at the Cape of Good Hope,* Breestradt Publikases, Cape Town, 1988.

Fitch, Charles Marden, *The Complete Book of Miniature Roses,* Hawthorn Books, New York, 1977.

Geldenhuys, Esther, *Roses: All You Need to Know About Roses in Southern Africa,* Struik Publishers, Cape Town, 1994.

Gibson, Michael, *Growing Roses,* Croom Helm, London, 1984.

Gibson, Michael, *The Rose Gardens of England,* Collins, London, 1984.

Griffiths, Trevor, *My World of Old Roses,* Whitcoulls, Christchurch, 1983.

Harkness, Jack, *Roses,* J. M. Dent & Sons, London, 1978.

Harkness, Jack, *The Makers of Heavenly Roses,* Souvenir Press, London, 1985.

Harkness, Peter, *The Photographic Encyclopedia of Roses,* Gallery Books, Surrey, England, 1991.

Harkness, Peter, *Roses, From the Archives of the Royal Horticultural Society,* Abrams, New York, 2005.

Hashmi, Mahmooda, *Indigenous and Wild Roses of Pakistan,* Pakistan National Rose Society, Islamabad, 2006.

Hayward, Margaret, *A New Zealand Guide to Miniature Roses,* Grantham House, New Zealand, 1988.

Hayward, Margaret, *Patio Roses,* Penguin, New Zealand, 1994.

Hessayon, D. G., *The Rose Expert,* pbi Publications, England, 2000.

Jekyll, Gertrude, and Morley, Edward, *Roses for English Gardens,* Country Life, London, 1901.

Joyaux, Francois, *La Rose de France: Rosa Gallica et Sa Descendance,* Imprimerie Nationale, France, 2000.

Krussmann, Gerd, *Roses,* Timber Press, Oregon, USA, 1981.

LeGrice, E. B., *Rose Growing Complete,* Faber and Faber, London, 1965.

Lord, Tony, *Designing with Roses,* Trafalgar Square, London, 2005.

Lloyd, David, and Beagent, Annie, *Spirit of The Rose,* Spirit of The Rose Ltd, England, 2004.

Martin, Clair G., *100 Old Roses for the American Garden,* Workman, New York, 1999.

Moody, Mary, and Harkness, Peter, *The Illustrated Encyclopedia of Roses,* Timber Press, Oregon, USA, 1992.

McCann, Sean, *Miniature Roses for Home and Garden,* Arco Publishing, New York, 1985.

McGredy, Sam, *Sam McGredy's Favorite Roses,* David Bateman, Auckland, 1997.

McGredy, Sam, *Look to the Rose,* David Bateman, Auckland, 1981.

Nottle, Trevor, *Growing Old-fashioned Roses in Australia and New Zealand,* Kangaroo Press, Sydney, 1983.

Pauwels, Ivo, *Louis Lens,* Brussels, 2003.

Phillips, Roger and Rix, Martin, *Roses,* Random House, New York, 1988.

Redouté, P. J., *Redouté's Roses,* facsimile of the plates of *Les Roses,* Wellfleet and the Natural History Museum, London, 1990.

Riston, Charles Quest, *Climbing Roses of the World,* Timber Press, Oregon, USA, 2003.

Rondeau, Anne-Sophie, *The Grand Rose Family,* Rustica Editions, Paris, 1998.

Swane, Valerie, *Growing Roses,* Kangaroo Press, Sydney, 1992.

Thomas, A. S., *Better Roses,* Angus & Robertson, Sydney, 1950.

Thomas, Graham Stuart, *The Old Shrub Roses,* J. M. Dent & Sons, London, 1957.

Thomas, Graham Stuart, *Shrub Roses of Today,* J. M. Dent & Sons, London, 1962.

Thomas, Graham Stuart, *Climbing Roses, Old and New,* Phoenix House, London, 1965.

Thomas, Graham Stuart, *A Garden of Roses, Watercolours by Alfred Parsons,* RA, Pavilion Books, London, 1987.

Young, James, *Classic Roses for Australian Gardens,* Cameron House, Australia, 2002.

Young, James, with Ruston, David, *The Joy of Roses,* 4cPublishers, Australia, 2004.

Stirling Macoboy's bibliography for the first edition also included the following:

Bassity, Matthew A. R., *The Magic World of Roses,* Hearthside Press, New York, 1966.

Beales, Peter, *Twentieth Century Roses,* Collins Harvill, London, 1988.

Coats, Peter, *Pleasures and Treasures: Roses,* Weidenfeld & Nicolson, London, 1962.

Cowles, Fleur, *The Flower Game,* Collins, London, 1983.

De Wolf, Gordon P. (ed.), *Taylor's Book of Roses,* Houghton Mifflin, Boston, 1986.

Dobson, Beverly R., and Schneider, Peter (ed.), *Combined Rose List* (annual: available from Box 677, Mantua, Ohio 44255, USA).

Edwards, Gordon, *Wild and Old Garden Roses,* Readers' Union, Newton Abbot, 1975.

Edwards, John Paul, and the editors of Sunset Magazine, *How to Grow Roses,* Lane Book Company, Menlo Park, 1960.

Fisher, John, *The Companion to Roses,* Viking, Harmondsworth, 1986.

Gault, S. Millar, and Synge, Patrick M., *Dictionary of Roses in Colour,* Ebury and Michael Joseph, London, 1971.

Genders, Roy, *The Rose: A Complete Handbook,* Hale, London, 1965.

Gordon, Jean, *The Pageant of the Rose,* Red Rose Publications, Woodstock, 1961.

Gore, Catherine Frances, *The Book of Roses, or The Rose Fancier's Manual,* London, 1838. Facsimile edition, Heyden, London and Philadelphia, 1978.

Griffiths, Trevor, *The Book of Old Roses,* Mermaid/Michael Joseph, London, 1983.

Haring, P. A. (ed.), *Modern Roses 9,* American Rose Society, Shreveport, 1986.

Keayes, Ethelyn Emery, *Old Roses,* Macmillan, New York, 1935.

McCann, Sean, *Miniature Roses,* David & Charles, London, 1985.

McFarland, J. Horace, *The Rose in America,* Macmillan, New York, 1923.

Malins, Peter, and Graff, M. M., *Peter Malins' Rose Book,* Dodd, Mead & Company, New York, 1979.

Mansfield, T. C., *Roses in Colour and Cultivation,* Collins, London, 1943.

Nisbett, Fred J., *Growing Better Roses,* Alfred A. Knopf, New York, 1974.

Pal, B. P., *The Rose in India, Indian Council of Agricultural Research,* Delhi (undated).

Park, Bertram, *Collins' Guide to Roses,* Collins, London, 1956.

Park, Bertram, *The World of Roses,* George S. Harrap, London, 1962.

Paul, William, *The Rose Garden,* Sherwood, Gilbert and Piper, London, 1848.

Ridge, Antonia, *For Love of a Rose,* Faber and Faber, London, 1963.

Ridge, Antonia, *The Man Who Painted Roses,* Faber and Faber, London, 1974.

Rose, Graham, and King, Peter, *The Love of Roses,* Quiller Press, London, 1990.

Rossi, B. V., *Roses: A Practical and Complete Guide for Amateur Rose Growers,* Robertson & Mullens, Melbourne (undated).

Shepherd, Roy E., *History of the Rose,* Macmillan, New York, 1954.

Steen, Nancy, *The Charm of Old Roses,* Herbert Jenkins, London, 1966.

Westrich, Josh, *Old Garden Roses,* Thames and Hudson, New York, 1988.

Young, Norman, *The Complete Rosarian,* St Martin's Press, New York, 1971.

Acknowledgments

It has been a great privilege to extend the life of this work, which was completed by Stirling Macoboy in 1993. The task of writing and updating a book of this size would be daunting indeed were it not for the willing support and cooperation of many rose aficionados and photographers, both domestic and international. Rose-growers are a dedicated minority with a passion to become rose evangelists and spread the word! I have singled out the following individuals for special mention, either for teaching me about roses – for which I am greatly indebted to them – or for providing photographs and images.

In North America
Syl Arena, Paseo Robles, California
Don and Paula Ballin, Highland Park, Illinois
Charold and Rich Baer, Portland, Oregon
Frank and June Benardella, Millstone Township, New Jersey
Tom Carruth, Weeks Roses, Upland, California
Luis Desamero, Studio City, California
Edmund Griffith, Jr, Mobile, Alabama
Ping Lim, Bailey Nurseries, St Paul, Minnesota
Ralph Moore, Sequoia Nursery, Visalia, California
Keith and Debbie Zary, Jackson & Perkins, Somis, California
Paul Zimmerman, Marily Young and Cliff Orent, Ashdown Roses, Campobello, South Carolina

In the United Kingdom
Peter Beales, Norfolk, England
Anne and Alex Cocker, Aberdeen, Scotland
Alice and Tony Bracegirdle, Ramsbottom, England
Ken and Anne Grapes, Norfolk, England
Michael and Gerta Roberts, Little Barney, Norfolk, England
Colin and Heather Horner, Stanstead, England

In Japan
Akira Ogawa, Japan Rose Society, Tokyo

In Italy
Helene Pizzi, Rome

In Australia
Margaret Macgregor, Melbourne
David Ruston, Renmark, South Australia
Ian Spriggs, Victoria

In New Zealand
Michael and Marion Brown, Christchurch
Dawn and Barry Eagle, Christchurch
Sam McGredy, Auckland
Lois Tabb, Christchurch

While the journey along the way to reaching this landmark has been a long one, I should not forget the very capable editorial assistance of Annette Carter and the publisher, Nola Mallon – both women committed to excellence and obviously rose-lovers!

My thanks also to Roger Mann for reading the manuscript and making many helpful suggestions. Thanks to you all for making this moment possible!

Tommy Cairns

Stirling Macoboy acknowledged his 'friends and rose-loving acquaintances' in the first edition as follows:

In North America
Shirley Beach, Victoria, British Columbia, Canada
Margaret Davis, OBE, Montecito, California
Maryanne Green, Santa Barbara, California
Jim Lichtman, Los Angeles, California
Al and Ginny Littau, New York, New York
Ross and Kathleen McWhae, Victoria, British Columbia, Canada
Professor Milton Meyer, Pasadena, California
Patricia Stemler Wiley, Watsonville, California
John Winston, Hollywood, California
David Wittry, Beverley Hills, California

In the United Kingdom
Penny Buckland, London
Bryan and Joanna Burley, Essex
Lucy Burley, London
David Garde, London
Diana Walsh, Hertfordshire

In New Zealand
Sam McGredy, Auckland
Nicole Roucheux, Auckland
Ion Scarrow
Merv Spurway, Christchurch

In South Africa
Nancy Gardiner, Pietermaritzburg
Keith Kirsten, Waterskloof
Una van der Spuy, Stellenbosch

In Australia
John Ballard, Canberra, Australian Capital Territory
Margo Balmain, Adelaide, South Australia
Rodney Beames, Adelaide, South Australia
Geoffrey Burnie, Sydney, New South Wales
Trish and Stephen Clifton, Vermont, Victoria
Brian Donges, Sydney, New South Wales
Walter Duncan, Watervale, South Australia
Eddie Graham, Milthorpe, New South Wales
Philip Grattan, Sydney, New South Wales
Pamela Jane Harrison, Camden, New South Wales
Roger Mann, Sydney, New South Wales
Dean Miller, Adelaide, South Australia
Rod Nelson, Sydney, New South Wales
Colin Olson, Coffs Harbour, New South Wales

Tony Rodd, Sydney, New South Wales
Ed Ramsay, Sydney, New South Wales
Deane Ross, Willunga, South Australia
David Ruston, Renmark, South Australia
Roy Rumsey, Sydney, New South Wales
Shirley Stackhouse, Sydney, New South Wales
Terry Williams, Bungonia, New South Wales

In Asia
Gloria Barreto, Hong Kong
Peter Okumoto, Kyoto, Japan

In Europe
Mme Rene-Paul Jeanneret, Paris, France
Arnaud de Vinzelles, Paris, France

Publisher's acknowledgments

Thanks are extended to all the following photographers and companies, who generously supplied photographs for this edition:

Andrew Ross, Ross Roses
Anthony Tesselaar International Pty Ltd
Syl Arena
The Art Archive, pages 12, 65, 88, 89, 130, 317, 354
Ashdown Roses Ltd
David Austin ® Roses
Rich Baer
Etienne Bouret 'Ami Roses'
Luis Desamero
Jon Dodson
Kent B. Krugh, www.woodlandrosegarden.com
Gary Matuschka, Treloar Roses
Colin Olson
Clifford Orent
Lorna Rose (Sydney)
Werribee Park, Parks Victoria
Wikimedia Commons
Marily A. Young

Illustrations: Shann Twelftree
Maps: Guy Holt Illustration & Design
Index: Alan Walker

Thanks also to Gabrielle Herro (Officelink), who provided valuable support in a number of areas; to Jacquelin Hochmuth for proofreading; and to Kim Lockwood for his assistance.

Captions for preliminary pages and introductions
page 1 'Sheila's Perfume'
pages 2–3 'Madame Zöetmans'
pages 4–5 *R. beggeriana*
pages 16–17 *R. rugosa rubra*
pages 38–39 'Queen of Bourbons'
pages 114–115 'Jude The Obscure'

3/4/10

Index

Numerals in **bold** denote main entry.
Numerals in *italics* denote photograph
or illustration.

Cataloging-in-Publication Data has been applied for and may be obtained from the Library of Congress.
   ISBN 10: 0-8109-9410-0
   ISBN 13: 978-0-8109-9410-2

Produced by Mallon Publishing, Melbourne 2007
Managing editor and copy editor Annette Carter
Design Pauline Deakin, Captured Concepts
   Lynn Twelftree Art & Design
Consultants Sarah Guest Roger Mann

Printed and bound in China
10 9 8 7 6 5 4 3 2 1

harry n. abrams, inc.
a subsidiary of La Martinière Groupe

115 West 18th Street
New York, NY 10011
www.hnabooks.com

we are zone 5   -20° - -10° average nremium   — zone 4 is colder
     almost 6 zone

Easy Elegance Roses   (2 locations near Burlington)

Black Magic 145
St. Patrick 377
Opening Night 319
Tiffany 391

Zone 5 (p450)
Zone 4 is Colder
Winter p457
Diseases 459-61

Black Magic 145
St. Patrick 377
Opening Night 319
Tiffany 391

Zone 5 (p450)
Zone 4 is Colder
Winter p457
Diseases 459-61